D0160735

Advances in Economics and Econometrics

This is the first of three volumes containing edited versions of papers and commentaries presented at invited symposium sessions of the Ninth World Congress of the Econometric Society, held in London in August 2005. The papers summarize and interpret key developments, and they discuss future directions for a wide variety of topics in economics and econometrics. The papers cover both theory and applications. Written by leading specialists in their fields, these volumes provide a unique survey of progress in the discipline.

Richard Blundell, CBE FBA, holds the David Ricardo Chair in Political Economy at University College London and is Research Director of the Institute for Fiscal Studies, London. He is also Director of the Economic and Social Research Council's Centre for the Microeconomic Analysis of Public Policy. Professor Blundell serves as President of the Econometric Society for 2006.

Whitney K. Newey is Professor of Economics at the Massachusetts Institute of Technology. A 2000–01 Fellow at the Center for Advanced Study in the Behavioral Sciences in Palo Alto, he is Associate Editor of *Econometrica* and the *Journal of Statistical Planning and Inference*, and he formerly served as Associate Editor of *Econometric Theory*.

Torsten Persson is Professor and Director of the Institute for International Economic Studies at Stockholm University and Centennial Professor of Economics at the London School of Economics. He was elected a Foreign Honorary Member of the American Academy of Arts and Sciences in 2001 and served as President of the European Economic Association in 2003.

Professors Blundell, Newey, and Persson are Fellows of the Econometric Society and served as Co-Chairs of the Program Committee of the Ninth World Congress of the Econometric Society, held in London in August 2005.

Econometric Society Monographs No. 41

Continued on page following the index

Advances in Economics and Econometrics

Theory and Applications, Ninth World Congress, Volume I

Edited by

Richard Blundell
University College London

Whitney K. Newey
Massachusetts Institute of Technology

Torsten Persson
Stockholm University

CAMBRIDGE
UNIVERSITY PRESS

CAMBRIDGE UNIVERSITY PRESS
Cambridge, New York, Melbourne, Madrid, Cape Town, Singapore, São Paulo

Cambridge University Press
32 Avenue of the Americas, New York, NY 10013-2473, USA

www.cambridge.org
Information on this title: www.cambridge.org/9780521871525

First published 2006

Printed in the United States of America

A catalog record for this publication is available from the British Library.

Library of Congress Cataloging in Publication Data
Advances in economics and econometrics : theory and applications, Ninth World
Congress / edited by Richard Blundell, Whitney K. Newey, Torsten Persson.
      p.   cm. – (Econometric Society monographs; no. 41)
    Edited versions of papers and a commentary presented at invited symposium sessions of
the ninth World Congress of the Econometric Society, held in London in 2005.
Includes bibliographical references and index.
        ISBN 0-521-87152-2 (hardback) – ISBN 0-521-69208-3 (pbk.)
        1. Econometrics – Congresses.   2. Economics – Congresses.   I. Blundell, Richard.
    II. Newey, Whitney K.   III. Persson, Torsten.   IV. Econometric Society.
    World Congress (9th : 2005 : London, England)   V. Title.   VI. Series.
    HB139 .A35   2005
    330–dc22   2006014485

ISBN-13   978-0-521-87152-5 hardback
ISBN-10   0-521-87152-2 hardback

ISBN-13   978-0-521-69208-3 paperback
ISBN-10   0-521-69208-3 paperback

Contents

Contributors

Daron Acemoglu
Massachusetts Institute of Technology

Dirk Bergemann
Yale University

Timothy Besley
London School of Economics

Matthew O. Jackson
California Institute of Technology

Philippe Jehiel
Paris-Jourdan Sciences Économiques (PSE)

Narayana R. Kocherlakota
Federal Reserve Bank of Minneapolis
and *University of Minnesota*

Per Krusell
Princeton University

David Martimort
University of Toulouse

Antonio Merlo
University of Pennsylvania

Benny Moldovanu
University of Bonn

Larry Samuelson
University of Wisconsin

Ilya Segal
Stanford University

Anthony A. Smith, Jr.
Yale University

Juuso Välimäki
Helsinki School of Economics

Introduction by the Editors

These volumes constitute the invited proceedings from the Ninth World Congress of the Econometric Society held on the campus of University College London on August 19–24, 2005.

As co-chairs of the Program Committee for the Congress, one of our most pleasant tasks was to select topics and authors for fifteen invited symposia – each organized around two papers. We chose topics for these invited papers that we thought were important, of current research interest, and where we could see a prospective long-run impact on the profession. All of the scholars that we first contacted agreed to contribute a paper. We encouraged them to write papers that would be of broad interest but would not necessarily be comprehensive literature surveys.

In the event, all symposia ran for two hours during which the authors presented their papers and an invited discussant made comments on both of them. This book collects revised versions of the thirty papers presented in the fifteen invited symposia, as well as some of the comments by the discussants.

In all but one day of the congress, three invited symposia were run in parallel: one in economic theory, one in an applied field, and one in econometrics. The three volumes making up the book are organized by the same principle.

Volume I contains the papers on economic theory, broadly defined. In Chapter 1, "The Economics of Social Networks," Matthew Jackson discusses a central field of sociological study, a major application of random graph theory, and an emerging area of study by economists, statistical physicists, and computer scientists. The chapter provides an illuminating perspective on these literatures, with a focus on formal models of social networks, especially those based on random graphs and those based on game-theoretic reasoning. Jackson highlights some of the strengths, weaknesses, and potential synergies between these two network modeling approaches.

Chapter 2, "Multi-Contracting Mechanism Design" by David Martimort, surveys the literature on common agency. Martimort describes the features that make common-agency games special, reviews the tools needed to describe equilibrium allocations under common agency, and uses a set of simple examples to illustrate such equilibrium allocations – under complete as well as asymmetric information – and their efficiency properties. The chapter concludes that common agency might perform quite well, especially in the presence of collusion or limited commitment.

Chapter 3, by Philippe Jehiel and Benny Moldovanu, is entitled "Allocative and Informational Externalities in Auctions and Related Mechanisms." Such externalities arise naturally in models embedding (multi-object) auctions in larger economic contexts, e.g., when bidders interact downstream once the auction has closed. In such settings, traditional auction formats need no longer be efficient and may give rise to multiple equilibria and strategic non-participation. Jehiel and Moldovanu discuss which allocations are possible and impossible to achieve under different approaches to implementation and in different information environments.

In Chapter 4, "The Economics of Relationships," Larry Samuelson discusses recent work in the theory of repeated games, which provides the tools for studying long-run relationships. He examines folk theorems for games with imperfect public and private monitoring and new techniques for studying equilibria when folk theorems are not helpful because players are not sufficiently patient or well informed. The chapter illustrates a number of recent applications that have moved the literature on repeated games from technical questions to findings of economic relevance. It concludes with a discussion of outstanding problems.

Following these chapters on game theory are two chapters on economic design. Chapter 5, "Information in Mechanism Design," written by Dirk Bergemann and Juuso Välimäki, examines endogeneity of private information and robustness to private information in mechanism design. The authors view information acquisition and robustness to private information as two distinct but related aspects of information management, which are important in many design settings. The chapter not only surveys the existing literature, but also points out directions for future work.

In Chapter 6, "Communication in Economic Mechanisms," Ilya Segal argues that full revelation of privately held information about preferences may often be impractical or undesirable. He then asks what minimal information must be elicited from agents to achieve the social goals of the mechanism designer. Segal relates this question to the work on communication complexity in computer science and dimensionality of message space in economics, where communication is measured in bits and real numbers, respectively. He outlines existing results on the topic, a substantial body of related work, and some extensions.

The next two chapters deal with macroeconomic theory. Chapter 7, by Naryana Kocherlakota, is entitled "Advances in Dynamic Optimal Taxation." It surveys the recent literature concerning the structure of optimal taxes in dynamic economies. As in the literature following Mirrlee's path-breaking work on optimal static taxation, there are no restrictions on the available policy instruments, and the optimal tax schedules are designed subject only to the private information held by private agents about skills and effort. Kocherlakota illustrates and explains the major results achieved so far and suggests where the literature may go next.

In Chapter 8, "Quantitative Macroeconomic Models with Heterogeneous Agents," Per Krusell and Tony Smith review recent work on dynamic stochastic macroeconomic models with individual heterogeneity in income, employment status, and wealth, to approximate empirical models in the applied consumption and labor literatures. They focus on the properties of such models – especially so-called approximate aggregation – and the computational methods for analyzing them. The chapter also presents a simple two-period setting that serves as a useful laboratory to examine the implications of the distribution of income in different economic settings.

The final section of the volume concerns political economy. In Chapter 9, "Modeling Inefficient Institutions," Daron Acemoglu asks why inefficient institutions emerge and persist, and he develops a simple framework to provide some answers to this question. He illustrates how a group may want to pursue inefficient policies to increase their income and directly or indirectly transfer resources from the rest of the society to themselves, and how the preferences over inefficient policies may translate into inefficient economic institutions. The chapter also provides a framework for the analysis of institutional change and institutional persistence.

While Acemoglu emphasizes the macro side of political economy, Chapter 10, "Whither Political Economy? Theories, Facts and Issues," by Antonio Merlo emphasizes the micro side. Merlo reviews current research on four of the fundamental institutions of a political economy: voters, politicians, parties, and governments. He identifies and discusses salient questions posed in the literature, presents some stylized models and examples, and summarizes the main theoretical findings. Moreover, the chapter describes available data, reviews relevant empirical evidence, and discusses challenges for empirical research in political economy.

Volume I ends with a discussion of Chapters 9 and 10, by Tim Besley.

Volume II contains papers on applied economics and applied econometrics, again broadly defined. For example, the first six chapters present a broad review and evaluation of developments in modern industrial economics. There is then an assessment of behavioral economics. This is followed by a detailed review of progress in dynamic labor economics. The volume rounds up with two insightful chapters on progress and new ideas in empirical development economics.

In Chapter 1 of Volume II, "Empirical Models of Auctions," Susan Athey and Phil Haile review some of the most innovative of the recent empirical applications and present three key insights that underlie much of the progress in the econometrics of auction models. The first is the usefulness of casting the identification problem as one of learning about latent distribution functions based on observation of certain order statistics. The second is the observation that equilibrium can be thought of as a state of mutual best responses. The third is the value of additional variation in the data beyond the realizations of bids.

Although observable variation in auction characteristics might initially seem to be minor nuisances to be dealt with, the authors argue that these kinds of variation often can be exploited to aid identification. Chapter 2, "Identification in Models of Oligopoly Entry" by Steve Berry and Elie Tamer reviews and extends a number of results on the identification of models that are used in the empirical literature. They present simple versions of both static and dynamic entry models. For simple static models, they show how natural shape restrictions can be used to identify competition effects. In the case of dynamic models, they examine existing results on the model with i.i.d. linear errors and then consider more realistic cases, such as when the distribution of fixed costs is unknown. Chapter 3, "Empirical Models of Imperfect Competition: A Discussion," by Liran Einav and Aviv Nevo discusses the first two chapters of this volume. Einav and Nevo note that in the empirical IO literature much progress has been made on identification and estimation of many different dimensions of firms' decisions. There are more flexible models of consumer demand and better methods to non-parametrically estimate bidder valuation in auctions, and significant progress has been made on estimating entry and dynamic games.

Chapter 4, "Recent Developments in the Economics of Price Discrimination" by Mark Armstrong, surveys the recent literature on price discrimination. The focus is on three aspects of pricing decisions: the information about customers available to firms; the instruments firms can use in the design of their tariffs; and the ability of firms to commit to their pricing plans. Armstrong notes that developments in marketing technology mean that firms often have access to more information about individual customers than was previously the case. The use of this information might be restricted by public policy toward customer privacy. Where it is not restricted, firms may be unable to commit to how they use the information. With monopoly supply, an increased ability to engage in price discrimination will boost profit unless the firm cannot commit to its pricing policy. Likewise, an enhanced ability to commit to prices will benefit a monopolist. With competition, the effects of price discrimination on profit, consumer surplus, and overall welfare depend on the kinds of information and/or tariff instruments available to firms. The paper shows that the ability to commit to prices may damage industry profit. Chapter 5, "Bounded Rationality in Industrial Organization" by Glenn Ellison, notes that three main approaches are found in the recent literature: rule-of thumb papers specify simple rules for behavior; explicit bounds papers consider agents who maximize payoffs net of cognitive costs; and the psychology and economics approach typically cites experimental evidence to motivate utility-like frameworks. Common to each recent literature is a focus on consumer irrationalities that firms might exploit. The paper then discusses several new topics that have been opened up by the consideration of bounded rationality and new perspectives that have been provided on traditional topics. Chapter 6, "Price Discrimination and Irrational Consumers: Discussion of Armstrong and Ellison" by Ken Hendricks, presents a review of these two chapters. In relation to the Armstrong paper he argues that one of the roles of theory is to classify the kinds of oligopoly markets where price discrimination is likely to occur, the form that it is likely to take, and the impact that it is likely to have on profits and welfare. He notes that the theme of firms exploiting consumers is also present in Ellison's chapter, which focuses primarily on irrational consumers. However, the main issues there are methodological, challenging the field to reexamine its traditional approach.

Chapters 7 to 9 turn to the field of behavioral economics. In Chapter 7, Colin Camerer shows how evidence from psychology and other disciplines has been used in behavioral economics to create models of limits on rationality, willpower, and self-interest and explores their implications in economic aggregates. The paper reviews the basic themes of behavioral economics: sensitivity of revealed preferences to descriptions of goods and procedures; generalizations of models of choice over risk, ambiguity, and time; fairness and reciprocity; non-Bayesian judgment; and stochastic equilibrium and learning. He argues that a central concern is what happens in equilibrium when agents are imperfect but heterogeneous. Camerer argues that neuroeconomics extends the psychological data use and suggests that it is likely to support rational choice theory in some cases, to buttress behavioral economics in some cases, and to suggest different constructs as well. In Chapter 8, "Incentives and Self-Control," Ted O'Donoghue and Matthew Rabin investigate the design of incentives for people subject to self-control problems in the form of a time-inconsistent taste for immediate gratification. They argue that because such present-biased people may not behave in their own long-run best interests, there is scope for firms, policymakers, friends and family, and the people themselves to create incentives for "better" behavior. They note that optimal incentive design, therefore, will attend to details that the conventional model would say are essentially irrelevant. The paper goes on to describe some general principles that have emerged in recent and ongoing research on incentives, highlighting the importance of heterogeneity among agents and providing for flexibility, and illustrating these principles with some simple examples. In his discussion presented in Chapter 9, Ariel Rubinstein argues that although there is no reason for economics to hide behind the traditional barriers, for behavioral economics to be a revolutionary program of research rather than a passing episode, it must become more open-minded and much more self-critical.

Turning to dynamic labor economics, in Chapter 10, "Dynamic Models for Policy Evaluation," Costas Meghir shows that the evaluation of interventions has become a commonly used policy tool, which is frequently adopted to improve the transparency and effectiveness of public policy. However, he argues that evaluation methods based on comparing treatment and control groups in small-scale trials are not capable of providing a complete picture of the likely effects of a policy and do not provide a framework that allows issues related to the design of the program to be addressed. Meghir shows how experimental data from field trials can be used to enhance the evaluation of interventions and illustrates the potential importance of allowing for longer-term incentive and general equilibrium effects. In Chapter 11, "Microeconometric Search-Matching Models and Matched Employer-Employee Data," Jean-Marc Robin suggests that the recent advent of matched employer-employee data has allowed significant progress in our understanding of individual labor earnings. He argues that viewing these empirical analyses through the lens of structural job search models can help clarify and unify some of its recurring findings. Among other things he shows how search frictions combined with a theoretically founded wage formation rule based on renegotiation by mutual consent can account for the widely documented dynamic persistence of individual wages. In his discussion of these two papers in Chapter 12, Joe Altonji argues that they provide useful analyses of developments in two important areas in labor economics and public finance. He examines the potential to utilize a continuum of models between a simple experimental or quasi-experimental analysis on the one hand and a dynamic structural model on the other, even in complicated dynamic settings where reduced form analysis is difficult. He also supplements the research agenda in search/matching models and the application using matched employer/ employee data.

Volume II concludes with two key papers on advances in development economics. Chapter 13, "Field Experiments in Development Economics" by Esther Duflo, observes that over the last decade, the long tradition in development economics of collecting original data to test specific hypotheses has merged with an expertise in setting up randomized field experiments. This in turn has resulted in an increasingly large number of studies where an original experiment has been set up to test economic theories and hypotheses. The paper extracts some substantive and methodological lessons from such studies in three domains: incentives, social learning, and time-inconsistent preferences. It makes the case that we need both to continue testing existing theories and to start thinking of how the theories may be adapted to make sense of the field experiment results, many of which are starting to challenge them. In Chapter 14, "Institutions and Development: A View from Below," Rohini Pande and Christopher Udry argue the case for greater exploitation of synergies between research on specific institutions based on micro-data and the big questions posed by the institutions and growth literature. They suggest two research programs based on micro-data that have significant potential. The first uses policy-induced variation in specific institutions within countries to understand how these institutions influence economic activity. The second exploits the fact that the incentives provided by a given institutional context often vary with individuals' economic and political status. The chapter analyzes the way variations in individual responses to the same institution can be used to both identify how institutions affect economic outcomes and to understand how institutional change arises in response to changing economic and demographic pressures.

Volume III contains papers on econometrics. The first five chapters are about identification and estimation when unobserved heterogeneity has nonlinear effects. This work is motivated by economic models where the common assumption of additive disturbances is not satisfied. The three chapters that follow concern weak instruments and empirical likelihood. These methods provide alternatives to classical instrumental variables inference, which can be important in applications. The next three chapters are about econometrics for financial markets. They summarize powerful approaches to analyzing the time series behavior of asset markets. The last two chapters return to the subject of unobserved heterogeneity, now in the context of nonlinear models for panel data. They consider bias correction methods for fixed effects estimation, a promising method of controlling for unobserved heterogeneity in panel data.

In Chapter 1 of Volume III, "Identification of Nonadditive Structural Functions," Andrew Chesher reviews recent work on identification of structural models with disturbances that are not additively separable. This chapter focuses on the case where there are no more disturbances than endogenous variables. In the one disturbance per equation case independence of the instrument and a conditional quantile of the disturbance can suffice for identification of the structural equation at a particular value of the disturbance. In the triangular model case, where the number of disturbances entering each equation is equal to the number of endogenous variables in that equation, local independence of instruments and disturbances suffices for identification of structural derivatives. Bounds are also given for the case with a discrete endogenous variable. In Chapter 2, "Nonadditive Models with Endogenous Regressors," Guido Imbens considers the case where the disturbance in the equation of interest can have any dimension. Identification and estimation with control functions is discussed, a control function being a variable that when conditioned on gives exogeneity. A control function for the triangular system is provided. Identification of certain policy effects is considered.

In Chapter 3, "Heterogeneity and Microeconometric Modeling," Martin Browning and Jesus Carro suggest that heterogeneity is more common in applications than usually allowed for, that how it is allowed for can often have large effects on results, and that it is difficult to allow for in a general way. They illustrate these suggestions with applied and theoretical examples. In particular, they consider a stationary first-order Markov chain model that allows for general heterogeneity, where they propose estimators and analyze their properties. Chapter 4, "Heterogenous Choice" by Rosa Matzkin, gives identification results for nonparametric choice models where disturbances enter nonlinearly. For models where choices are dependent variables, this paper describes very recent results on identification of demand models and discrete choice models that are important for understanding revealed preference with unobserved heterogeneity. For models where the choices are regressors, the paper gives control function and other identification results for structural effects. In Chapter 5, "Modeling Heterogeneity," Arthur Lewbel discusses the results from Chapters 3 and 4, showing that model interpretation depends critically on how the nonseparable disturbance enters.

Chapter 6, "Inference with Weak Instruments" by Donald Andrews and James Stock, reviews recent developments in methods for dealing with weak instruments (IVs) in IV regression models. The focus is more on tests (and confidence intervals derived from tests) than estimators. Power comparisons of the conditional likelihood ratio (CLR), Anderson-Rubin, and Lagrange multiplier tests are made. The paper also presents new testing results under "many weak IV asymptotics." Chapter 7, "Empirical Likelihood Methods in Econometrics: Theory and Practice" by Yuichi Kitamura, gives nonparametric maximum likelihood and generalized minimum contrast interpretations of the empirical likelihood estimator. This chapter presents an asymptotic optimality result for empirical likelihood under a large deviations optimality criterion. Monte Carlo results are given, illustrating substantial gains that can result. Also, the literature on higher-order properties of empirical likelihood is reviewed. Chapter 8, "Weak Instruments and Empirical Likelihood: A Discussion of Papers by D. W. K. Andrews and J. H. Stock and Yuichi Kitamura" by Richard Smith, considers inference for GMM with weak identification based on generalized empirical likelihood. It provides an asymptotic analysis for GMM that is a direct extension of the Andrews and Stock small sample analysis for IV. This chapter proposes a version of the CLR for GMM that is a precise analog to the IV case.

Chapter 9, "Estimating Continuous Time Models with Discretely Sampled Data" by Yacine Ait-Sahalia, starts with a familiar model and describes many of the most recent developments. It begins with identification and estimation of a univariate diffusion. This model is then progressively generalized to allow for different data generating processes (such as multivariate diffusions or jump processes), different observation schemes (such as incorporating market microstructure noise), and different sampling schemes (such as allowing for random time intervals). Chapter 10, "Variation, Jumps, and High Frequency Data in Financial Econometrics" by Neil Shephard and Ole Barndorff-Nielsen, describes the econometrics of realized volatility. This chapter focuses on quadratic variation and considers the detection of jumps. The impact of market frictions is considered. Chapter 11, "Discussion of Ait-Sahalia and Barndorff-Nielsen and Shephard" by Oliver Linton and Ilze Kalnina, considers an approach to allowing for market microstructure noise. It presents consistency results for estimation of quadratic variation in the presence of small measurement errors.

Chapter 12, "Understanding Bias in Nonlinear Panel Models: Some Recent Developments" by Manuel Arellano and Jinyong Hahn, describes and discusses the relationship among recently developed bias adjustments for nonlinear panel data models with fixed effects. These bias adjustments are used to reduce the bias order of fixed effect parameter and marginal effects as the number of time series observations grows with the number of cross-sectional observations. The paper shows that a wide variety of bias adjustments lead to similar results, including those based on profile likelihoods and those based on moment conditions. In Chapter 13, "Fixed and Random Effects in Nonlinear Panels: A Discussion of Arellano and Hahn" by Tiemen Woutersen, an alternative bias reduction approach is discussed. This approach, which predates many of the others, involves integrating the fixed effect over a prior distribution and produces bias reductions equivalent to the other methods.

We are grateful to Christina Lönnblad, Emma Hyman, and Emily Gallagher for assisting us in our work with putting the papers together into three volumes. We would also like to thank all the authors, not only for writing such excellent papers, but also for delivering in time for this book to appear less than a year after the Congress. Such prompt publication would, of course, not have possible without the keen support of our Cambridge University Press editor, Scott Parris.

London, Cambridge, and Stockholm, May 2006
Richard Blundell, Whitney Newey, and Torsten Persson

Advances in Economics and Econometrics

CHAPTER 1

The Economics of Social Networks
Matthew O. Jackson*

1 INTRODUCTION

Social networks are the fabric of many of our interactions. Such networks include the relationships among friends and relatives with whom we share information and favors on a regular basis, and reach as far as influencing decisions by many of the world's companies regarding with whom and how they conduct their business. The many regularities in network structure across applications make a scientific study of social networks a possibility. The deep and pervasive impact that networks have on behavior makes such a study a necessity.

The science of social networks was initiated by sociologists more than a century ago, and has grown to be a central field of sociological study over the past fifty years.[1] Over that same period, a mathematical literature on the structure of random graphs moved steadily along, with intermittent ties to the sociological literature.[2] While economists have occasionally showed interest in networks, an explosion of studies of networks using game-theoretic modeling techniques and economic perspectives has occurred over the last decade.[3]

* HSS 228-77, California Institute of Technology, Pasadena, California 91125, USA, jacksonm@hss.caltech.edu and http://www.hss.caltech.edu/~jacksonm/Jackson.html. I thank the Lee Center for Advanced Networking, The Guggenheim Foundation, and the Center for Advanced Studies in Behavioral Sciences for financial support. I am very grateful to collaborators on networks projects, who have helped me learn about social networks and the fascinating questions they present, and who are inexorably tied to the views I take herein. So I thank (in chronological order), Asher Wolinsky, Alison Watts, Bhaskar Dutta, Anne van den Nouweland, Toni Calvó-Armengol, Francis Bloch, Gary Charness, Alan Kirman, Jernej Copic, Brian Rogers, Dunia Lopez-Pintado, and Leeat Yariv. I also thank Yann Bramoullé, Toni Calvó-Armengol, Yannis Ioannides, Alan Kirman, Dunia Lopez-Pintado, Laurent Mathevet, Torsten Persson, Nicolas Quérou, Alessandro Vespignani, Stanley Wasserman, Duncan Watts, and Leeat Yariv for comments on an earlier draft. I am grateful to Tom Palfrey for an insightful discussion of the paper.

[1] See Freeman (2004) for some history of thought of the sociology literature.
[2] See Bollobás (2001) for a survey of the random graph literature.
[3] The books edited by Dutta and Jackson (2003) and Demange and Wooders (2004) contain surveys.

A recent awakening of an interest in social networks has also occurred in the computer science and statistical physics literatures, mainly over the past five or six years.[4] While these literatures are (slowly) becoming aware of each other, and on occasion drawing from one another, they are still largely distinct in their methods, interests, and approaches. My goal here is to provide some perspective on the research from these literatures, with a focus on the formal modeling of social networks, and to highlight some of the strengths, weaknesses, and potential synergies between the two main approaches.

Given the breadth of these combined literatures, and the fact that there are surveys covering the various literatures,[5] my aim here is not to try to give a comprehensive overview of the literatures, but rather to try to put some of the main contributions and techniques of formal modeling of social networks in context and to relate them to each other. I focus on two main threads of the literatures: the first is models of the formation of networks and the second is models of how social behavior and economic outcomes are influenced by network structure.

In order to provide some context, I start by giving some basic background on social networks and a very cursory look at a few things that have been learned from empirical studies. Next, I turn to discuss models of formation of networks. Here, I distinguish between two different approaches that have been taken. One has its roots in the random graph literature and models formation by specifying either some stochastic process or an algorithmic process through which the links in a network are formed. This literature has mainly deduced properties of large networks. The second approach is game theoretic and stems from the economics literature. It has mainly focused on models where the links are formed at the discretion of the nodes that derive benefits and face costs associated with various links and network configurations. These two approaches lead to complementary insights regarding networks, each of which is adapted to answering different sorts of questions. They also have different strengths and weaknesses that I highlight. Finally, I discuss models that take network structure as a given and study the influence that networks have on social and/or economic outcomes. This last area of study shows why the science of social networks is important for more than just an understanding of the networks themselves.

---

[4] See Newman (2003).

[5] The sociology literature is too vast for any article to adequately survey, but introductory texts, such as Wasserman and Faust (1994), as well as the recent history of thought book by Freeman (2004), are useful starting points. Concerning the economics literature, see Jackson (2003, 2004) for strategic modeling of networks; van den Nouweland (2004) for graphs and networks in cooperative game theory; Goyal (2004) for learning on networks; Ioannides and Datcher-Loury (2004) for networks in labor economics; Page and Kamat (2004) for farsighted formation of networks; and Bloch (2004) for networks in industrial organization. See Newman (2003, 2004) for surveys covering some of the recent statistical physics and part of the computer science literatures. There are also books that touch on some parts of the physics literature, such as Watts (1999) and Barabasi (2002). A text that bridges some of the modeling from the various literatures is by Jackson (2005).

2 SOME BACKGROUND ON NETWORKS

The systematic study of social networks by sociologists dates from the 1920s and 30s, took root in the 1960s, and has grown rapidly over the past four decades.[6] That literature includes many case studies from which has emerged a rich mosaic of characteristics that are shared by many social networks, as well as a taxonomy for measuring and describing social networks and a broad set of hypotheses and theories about network form and influence. Much of what I discuss in this section is either directly from that literature, or was influenced by it.

Just to get a feeling for one such case study, consider a network analyzed by Padgett and Ansell (1993). It is the network of marriages between the key families in Florence in the 1430s. Figure 1.1 provides the links between the key families in Florence at that time, where a link represents a marriage between members of the two linked families.[7]

As Padgett and Ansell (1993) explain, during this time period the Medici (with Cosimo de' Medici playing the key role) rose in power and largely consolidated control of the business and politics of Florence. Previously Florence had been ruled by an oligarchy of elite families. A key to understanding this, as Padgett and Ansell (1993) detail, can be seen in the network structure. To the extent that marriage relationships were keys to communicating information, business deals, and reaching political decisions, the Medici were much better positioned than other families, at least according to some measures of betweeness or centrality. Padgett and Ansell (1993) point out that, "Medician political control was produced by network disjunctures within the elite, which the Medici alone spanned." It should be emphasized that the Medici came to have such a special position in the network through careful planning. As Padgett and Ansell (1993) say (footnote 13), "The modern reader may need reminding that all of the elite marriages recorded here were arranged by patriarchs (or their equivalents) in the two families. Intraelite marriages were conceived of partially in political alliance terms." Thus, in order to understand how this network, and not some other network, came to arise it is important to have models of strategic network formation, a theme that I return to below.

2.1   Some Notation

Let $N = \{1, 2, \ldots, n\}$ denote a set of *nodes*, which represent the social agents that might be tied in a network of social relationships. In the example above, these are the Florentine families. In the next example these are individual people (researchers), and in other examples they might be firms, web pages, countries, etc.

A *network g* can be represented by an $n \times n$ matrix taking on values 0 or 1. The idea is that if $g_{ij} = 1$, then i is linked to j. In various applications, it might

---

[6] Again, see Freeman (2004) for some history of thought. Interestingly, while Freeman laments the disconnect between the traditional sociology literature and the emerging physics literature on networks, the gulf between the sociology and economics literatures seems to be equally large.

[7] The data here were originally collected by Kent (1978), but were first coded by Padgett and Ansell (1993) who discuss the network relationships in more detail.

Figure 1.1. 15th-Century Florentine Marriges (Padgett and Ansell (1993))

be that these links are undirected, as in the Florentine families example where marriage is a reciprocal relationship. In such settings $g_{ij} = g_{ji}$ by necessity. In other applications, such as an example where a link represents a citation of one research article by another, the network is naturally directed. In such cases, it is possible that $g_{ij} = 1 \neq 0 = g_{ji}$.[8]

For simplicity, I write ij to represent the *link* between i and j, and also write $ij \in g$ to indicate that i and j are linked under the network g. Shorthand notations for the network obtained by adding or deleting a link ij to or from an existing network g are $g + ij$ and $g - ij$, respectively.

For any network g and agent or node i, let $N_i(g)$ be the *neighborhood* of i in g, that is, the set of agents linked to i in the network g, so that $N_i(g) = \{j \mid ij \in g\}$.

The degree is the most basic characteristic of a node – it represents the number of links that each node has, and is thus simply the cardinality of $N_i(g)$. Generally, there tends to be a wide range of degrees across nodes within a network, and different applications will have very different distributions of degrees across nodes, a topic I return to below.

A *path* in a network $g \in G$ between agents i and j is a sequence of agents $i_1, \ldots, i_K$ such that $i_k i_{k+1} \in g$ for each $k \in \{1, \ldots, K-1\}$, with $i_1 = i$ and $i_K = j$. The *length* of such a path is $K - 1$, the number of links involved.[9]

---

[8] In some applications, the strength of a link or some other aspect of link may be important, or there may be different types of links that can be simultaneously held between nodes. For the purposes of this article, I stick with the basic model.

[9] In the case of directed networks, one can keep track of directed paths as well as undirected ones. I will be explicit when necessary, and otherwise assume that links are treated as if they are not directed.

A *component* of a network is a maximal connected subgraph. That is, g' is a component of g if: (a) g' is a subnetwork of g (so $ij \in g'$ only if $ij \in g$), (b) $ij \in g'$ and $k\ell \in g'$ implies that there is a path between i and k in g', and (c) $ij \in g'$ and $ik \in g$ implies $ik \in g'$. The network pictured in Figure 1.3 has two components, one consisting of the isolated node 25, and the other consisting of the graph between nodes 1 to 24.

The *distance* between two nodes i and j, denoted $d(i, j)$, is the minimum path length between i and j (and set to be infinite if no such path exists).

The *diameter* of a network g is defined as $\bar{d}(g) = \max_{i,j} d(i, j)$, the maximum distance between any two nodes. If a network is not connected (there are at least two nodes that have no path between them), then the diameter is infinite. As many social networks are not connected, the diameter is often reported for the largest component. For example, in Figure 1.1, the network is not connected as the Pucci are isolated, and the diameter of the largest component is 5 (the distance from the Pazzi to the Lambertes or the Pazzi to the Peruzzi).

Another characteristic of networks is referred to under a variety of names including cliquishness, transitivity, and *clustering*. While there are many variations, the basic idea is to measure how dense the network is on a very local level. Given a node, what fraction of that node's friends or neighbors are friends or neighbors of each other? In particular, if i has links to both j and k, are j and k linked to each other?[10] The percentage of times that the answer is "yes" with regard to a node i is i's clustering coefficient. One can then average across all nodes in the network. Thus the clustering for a node i is[11]

$$C_i(g) = \frac{\#\{jk \in g \mid k \neq j, \ j \in N_i(g), \ k \in N_i(g)\}}{\#\{jk \mid k \neq j, \ j \in N_i(g), \ k \in N_i(g)\}}.$$

In Figure 1.1, the clustering for the Medici is $1/15$, for the Bisteri $1/3$, and for the Guadagni 0. The average clustering coefficient is[12]

$$C^{avg}(g) = \sum_i \frac{C_i(g)}{n}.$$

Example 1 *Erdös Numbers and Co-authorship Networks Among Researchers*

---

[10] For a directed network, one can either treat links as if they are undirected, or else can look for cycles (when directed links ij and jk are present, one counts the percent of ki's).

[11] If the node i has fewer than two neighbors so that the denominator of $C_i(g)$ is 0, then one can adopt the convention of setting $C_i(g) = 1$. When averaging across i to determine average clustering, such a convention can make a difference and so it makes sense to ignore nodes that have fewer than two neighbors.

[12] Note that this weights the calculations by averaging across nodes rather than links. That is, a node that has just two neighbors is weighted the same as a node that has two hundred neighbors, even though the second node accounts for many more potential triangles in the network. An alternative measure simply examines the number of times the link ik is present over all combinations of pairs of links ij and ik in the network, and divides by the number of pairs of links present in the network. The difference between these two measures can be quite substantial.

Table 1.1. *Co-authorship networks*

	Biology	Economics	Math	Physics
Number of Nodes	1520521	81217	253339	52909
Avg. Degree	15.5	1.7	3.9	9.3
Avg. Path Length	4.9	9.5	7.6	6.2
Diameter	24	29	27	20
Clustering	.09	.16	.15	.45
% Size Largest Component	.92	.41	.82	.85

With some definitions in hand, let us turn to another example. These are networks that keep track of collaboration among researchers. Here a link represents the co-authorship of a paper during some time period covered by the study. The well-known and prolific mathematician Paul Erdös had many co-authors, and as a fun distraction many mathematicians (and economists for that matter) have found the shortest path(s) from themselves to Erdös. These networks are also of scientific interest themselves, as they tell us something about how research is conducted and how information and innovation might be disseminated. Such studies have now been conducted in various fields, including mathematics (Grossman and Ion (1995), de Castro and Grossman (1999)), biology and physics (Newman (2001, 2002)), and economics (Goyal, van der Leij and Moraga-González (2003)). Various statistics from these studies give us some impression of the network structure.[13]

Here we see that despite the noncomparabilities of the networks along many dimensions, average path length and diameters of each of the networks are very comparable. Moreover, these are of an order substantially smaller than the number of nodes in the network. This is an aspect of the "small-world" nature of social networks discussed below.

2.2   The Prevalence of Network Interactions

While the examples in the previous section give us an idea of the variety of networks that have been studied, it is also important for us to have an idea of what role networks might play in a society and how they might influence economic outcomes.

The most obvious and perhaps pervasive role of networks is as a conduit of information, and one of the most extensively documented roles for social networks in economics is that of contacts in labor markets.[14] The magnitude of use of social contacts as a method of matching workers and firms can be seen from various studies. One of the earliest studies, by Myers and Shultz (1951), was

---

[13] As these networks are not connected (there are many isolated authors), the figures for average path length and diameter are reported for the largest component.

[14] For a recent comprehensive overview of research on networks in labor markets see Ioannides and Loury (2004).

based on interviews with textile workers and found that 62 percent had found their first job through a social contact, in contrast with only 23 percent who applied by direct application, and the remaining 15 percent who found their job through an agency, ads, etc. A study by Rees and Shultz (1970) showed that these numbers were not peculiar to textile workers, but applied very broadly. For instance, the percentage of those interviewed who found their jobs through the use of social contacts as a function of their profession was: typist – 37.3 percent, accountant – 23.5 percent, material handler – 73.8 percent, janitor – 65.5 percent, and electrician – 57.4 percent. Moreover, the prevalent use of social contacts in finding jobs is robust across race and gender (see Corcoran, Datcher, and Duncan (1980)) and across country (see Pellizzari (2004)).

The role of social networks is not unique to labor markets, but it has been documented much more extensively. For example, networks and social interactions play a role in crime,[15] trade,[16] and social insurance,[17] as well as disease transmission, language and culture, and interactions of firms.

2.3   Some Basic Characteristics of Social Networks

Beyond the fact that social networks play a role in many interactions, we also know a great deal about some basic characteristics of social networks.

2.3.1   Small Worlds

One of the most influential studies of social networks was Stanley Milgram's (1967) ingenious "small-worlds" experiment. Milgram gave booklets with instructions to individuals in one place (Nebraska, in the original experiment). The objective was to get the booklet to a geographically distant individual (on the east coast), where the sender is given some information about the target (e.g., the person's name, occupation, and where they live). The key was that the subjects could only send the booklet to an acquaintance. The acquaintance could then forward the letter to another acquaintance, with the same objective of having the booklet eventually reach the target. The experiment collected information regarding the full chain that the booklets followed, including demographic information about each of the acquaintances along the route. One

---

[15] Reiss (1980, 1988) finds that two thirds of criminals commit crimes with others, and Glaeser, Sacerdote, and Scheinkman (1996) find that social interaction is important in determining criminal activity, especially with respect to petty crime, youth activity in crime, and in areas with less intact households.

[16] Uzzi (1996) finds that relation specific knowledge is critical in the garment industry and that social networks play a key role in that industry. Weisbuch, Kirman, and Herreiner (2000) study repeated interactions in the Marseille fish market and discuss the importance of the network structure.

[17] Fafchamps and Lund (2003) show that social networks are critical to the understanding of risk-sharing in rural Philippines, and De Weerdt (2002) provides similar analyses in Africa.

Table 1.2. *Comparisons across applications*

	WWW	Citations	Co-Author	Ham Radio	Prison	High School Romance
Number of Nodes	325729	396	81217	44	67	572
Randomness: r	0.5	.62	3.5	5.0	590	1000
Avg. Degree: m	4.5	5	1.7	3.5	2.7	.84
Avg. Clustering	.11	.07	.16	.06	.001	0

remarkable statistic was that roughly a quarter of the booklets reached their destination.[18] Of the chains that were successful, the maximum number of links that a booklet took was 12 and the median was 5! Given that these would generally not have taken the shortest routes from initial sender to target (as the senders are often not fully aware of the most efficient path to the target), these numbers were quite striking.

A simple back-of-the-envelope calculation gives some insight into this. If most individuals in the world have hundreds of acquaintances, then starting from a given individual, the network size (in terms of number of individuals reached) will expand by a factor on the order of a hundred raised to the power of the path length.[19] It will not take very long paths until the network is the size of the whole world's population.

2.3.2   "High" Clustering

While it is interesting that social networks exhibit small diameter and average path length, the same is also true of many other networks, including routing networks, power grids, and networks of neurons (e.g., see Watts (1999) and Newman (2003)). What tends to be a more distinguishing feature of social networks is their clustering (recall the definition above). Clustering is a simple but powerful concept that has roots tracing back to the work of Simmel (1908), who first explored triads (relationships between triples of individuals). Social networks tend to have significantly higher clustering coefficients than what would emerge if the links were generated by an independent random process. For example, Adamic (1999) finds a clustering coefficient of .11 for a portion of the www, which would compare with an expected clustering coefficient of .0002 for a (Bernoulli) randomly generated network with the same

---

[18] Given that twenty to thirty percent is a healthy response rate on a survey, and that having a booklet reach a destination required a chain of subjects to each respond, a twenty-five percent rate of reaching the target is impressive, especially in an unpaid experiment.

[19] This is clearly heuristic and a proper calculation is difficult, as one needs to account for overlap in neighborhoods, among other things. See Bollabás (2001) for some theorems bounding diameters in some classes of random graphs.

number of links. Figures for other networks are reported in Table 1.2 below, where we also see relatively high numbers compared to a benchmark random network. For example, if each link is formed with equal probability and link independently of each other, then the probability of two of node i's neighbors being connected to each other is simply the probability with which links are formed. In the first column of Table 1.2, this would be less than 5/325,000, as each node has an average of fewer than 5 links out of a potential number that is more than 325,000. The observed clustering of .11 is substantially higher.

2.3.3   Degree Distributions

Another easily identified property of a social network is its degree distribution. This gives some idea of the variation in the number of links across different nodes and provides us with some feeling for the shape of a network. Does it have "hub and spoke" like features where there are some very highly connected nodes and others with very few connections, or are connections more evenly distributed? Keeping track of the distribution of degrees in a network can be quite useful. For example, the degrees of the nodes in the Medici marriage network in Figure 1.1 are 0,1,1,1,1,2,3,3,3,3,3,3,4,4,6. From this we see that the Medici had more than twice the average degree (6 compared to 2.53) and twice the median degree.

One of the early studies documenting degree distributions was by Price (1965) who examined networks of citations among research articles. Price noticed that there were more highly connected and lowly connected nodes than what would be expected if links were selected independently and uniformly at random. Much of the recent interest in networks by statistical physicists was sparked by a similar study of Albert, Jeong and Barabasi (1999), which examined the structure of a portion of the www (in the Notre Dame domain). They also found a degree distribution that was distinctly different from what would have been generated by a random process of link formation where all links were equally likely. If links were formed uniformly at random with a link between any two nodes being formed independently of other links and with a probability p, then the degree distribution would approximate a binomial distribution, and would also be well-approximated by a Poisson distribution (see Section 3.1.1). Again, they found that the degree distribution had "fat tails," in that there were many more nodes with very high and very low degrees than would correspond to a binomial or Poisson distribution. In fact, they estimated that the distribution was approximately "scale-free" and followed a "power-law," where the relative frequency of nodes with a degree of k is proportional to $k^{-\gamma}$ for a parameter $\gamma > 1$.[20] The term "power law" clearly

---

[20] Such distributions date to Pareto (1896), after whom they are named, and have appeared in a wide variety of settings ranging from income distributions, and distribution of city

refers to the fact that the frequency can be expressed as the degree raised to a power. The term "scale-free" refers to the following property. Consider degree k and some other degree ck, for some scalar c. Their relative frequencies are $k^{-\gamma}/(ck^{-\gamma})$ or c^{γ}. Now consider some other degree k' and another degree ck'. Their relative frequencies are also c^{γ}. Thus, regardless of how we have rescaled things, relative frequencies depend only on relative sizes and not on the absolute scale.

An important caution to the literature is in order here. While it is clear that the degree distributions of many observed networks differ significantly from that of a purely random network; it is not clear that they are "scale-free." This is a point first made by Pennock et al. (2002).[21] A standard approach to outlining the degree distribution of many networks has been simply to plot the log(frequency) versus the log(degree) and see whether this "looks" linear. Of course, many things that are far from linear will appear linear on a log-log plot, as most of the data are squeezed into a small portion of the scale on a log-log plot; and such a distribution can be very difficult to distinguish from others, such as a lognormal distribution which can also appear quite linear. Simply fitting a line to the data on a log-log scale does not guarantee that the estimated coefficient means much of anything.

To get a better feeling for the shape of degree distributions, and whether most social networks exhibit features that are close to scale-free, it is possible to consider families of distributions and see which one best fits a given social network. We can do this with a family of degree distributions that have, at one extreme, networks whose links are generated uniformly at random, and at the other extreme, networks with scale-free distributions. Jackson and Rogers (2004) examine a family of degree distributions where the probability that a given node has degree k is given by $P(k) = c(k + rm)^{-(2+r)}$, where c is a constant (ensuring a sum to 1 across k's), m is the average degree, and r is a parameter which varies between 0 and ∞. More specifically, the model is one where new nodes are born over time and can attach to existing nodes either by choosing one uniformly at random or through a search process that makes the likelihood of meeting a given node proportional to the number of links the node already has. r represents the ratio of how many links are formed uniformly at random compared to how many are formed proportionally to the number of links existing nodes already have. As r approaches 0, the distribution converges to be scale-free, while as m tends to infinity the distribution converges to a negative exponential distribution, which corresponds to the degree distribution of a purely uniform and independent link formation process on a network that grows over time.

---

populations, to the usage of words in a language. For an informative overview, see Mitzenmacher (127).

[21] See Eeckhout (2004) for a similar point regarding Zipf's law as applied to city sizes, and also Ioannides (2004) for a similar point.

Using this model, we can back out the relative randomness in the formation process. Fits to a few networks[22] give us an idea of the variation across applications.[23]

Thus, we see a marked difference in the degree distributions, as well as clustering and average degree, across different social networks. As these characteristics are the more easily measured features of a social network, and carry a great deal of information about the shape of the network, they are quite useful. As we shall see below, it is also important to note how different the degree distributions are across different social networks, since we can relate the differences in structure to differences in resulting behavior on the networks.

There are many other features of social networks that have been explored but are beyond our scope here, as some of the basic features discussed previously already provide us with a good understanding of some of the models that I discuss below.

With a better feeling for social networks, let us now return to the two central issues: How networks are formed and how network structure affects the behavior of the individuals involved in the network. I turn to these in order.

3   MODELING NETWORK FORMATION

As mentioned in the introduction, the models of network formation have come primarily from two sources: the random graph literature (and the subsequent statistical physics literature) and the economics literature (building on game theoretic tools).

Let me emphasize from the outset how different these approaches have been. The random-graph-based literature builds networks either through a purely stochastic process where links appear at random according to some distribution,

---

[22] The www data are from an analysis of the links between web pages on the Notre Dame domain of the world wide web from Albert, Jeong, and Barabási (1999). The co-authorship data are from the above cited study by Goyal, van der Leij, and Moraga-González (2003). The citation network consists of the network of citations among all papers that have cited Milgram's (1967) paper or have the phrase "small worlds" in the title, and is from Garfield (http://garfield.library.upenn.edu/histcomp/index-small-world.html). The prison data record friendships among inmates in a study by MacRae (1960), the ham radio data record interactions between ham radio operators from Killworth and Bernard (1976), and the high school romance data collected romantic relationships between high school students over a period of a year and a half in a US high school and is from Bearman, Moody, and Stovel (2004). The number of nodes, average degree, and clustering numbers are as reported by the studies. The estimates on randomness are from Jackson and Rogers (2004). The fits on these estimated r's are high, with R^2's ranging between 93 and 99 percent.

[23] The clustering figure for the co-author data is actually for total clustering, as the average number is not available but is likely to be higher, given that the clustering is decreasing in degree. The clustering for the high school romance network is special because that network is mainly heterosexual in its relationships, so completed triads do not appear.

or else through some algorithm for building links. What this allows one to do, is show how observed networks at some given point in time might have resulted from some stochastic or mechanical process. Although this does not quite answer the *why* behind network formation, it does give us a great deal of insight into the *how*. That is, these sorts of models essentially match observed characteristics back to specific processes. Why one process operates in one setting, and another in a different setting is something essentially beyond the scope of the models.

The economic approach, in contrast, has tended to focus on equilibrium networks,[24] where links are formed at the discretion of self-interested agents who are or control the nodes. A big advantage of this approach is that it naturally incorporates the costs and benefits into the analysis, as the payoffs to agents are part of the model. This enables one to answer questions relating to whether or not the right networks form, in the sense of maximizing the total benefit to society. Such models also give us insight into the *why* behind network formation, as they trace network form to the incentives of the agents and the costs and benefits of different links. The main shortcoming of these models is that while they can tell us about tensions between incentives and efficiency, and trace incentives to primitives relating to costs and benefits, they generally stop short of giving predictions concerning things like which degree distribution should emerge. In a sense, they have not been as well suited for answering the *how* questions.

3.1   Random Models of Network Formation

3.1.1   *Erdös-Rényi (Bernoulli) Random Graphs*

The earliest and most extensively studied formal model of network formation is that of purely random graphs, with the canonical example being that of a pure Bernoulli process of link formation. That is, consider a set of nodes and then independently consider each possible link. With probability p have this link be part of the graph, and with probability $1 - p$ have that link be absent from the graph. This random graph formation process was explored in detail by Erdös and Rényi (1959, 1960, 1961) and has been studied extensively since then (see Bollobás (2001)).[25] There are a number of interesting properties that such Bernoulli networks have. These properties are generally established for large networks; that is, as the number of nodes tends to infinity.

---

[24] It has also provided some stochastic models of network formation, but mainly as a tool for selection among equilibrium networks. For example, see Jackson and Watts (2002a,b) and Goyal and Vega-Redondo (2005).

[25] Another closely related random graph model is one where all graphs with n nodes and exactly M edges are considered, and one is randomly selected (where equal probability is placed on each such graph). If $M = np$ and n is large, then many of the properties of the resulting graph are similar to those of the Bernoulli graph process.

Consider the degree distribution. The probability that any given node i has exactly k links is simply

$$\binom{n-1}{k} p^k (1-p)^{n-1-k}. \tag{1}$$

Even though links are formed independently, if we want to estimate the fraction of nodes in a network that will have a given degree, there will be some correlation across nodes. For instance, if $n = 2$, then it must be that both nodes have the same degree. As n becomes large, however, the correlation of degree between any two nodes vanishes, as the possible link between them is only one out of the $n-1$ that each might have. Thus, as n becomes large, the fraction of nodes that have k links will approach the expression in (1). For large n and small enough p (relative to n), this binomial expression is approximated by a Poisson distribution, so that the fraction of nodes that have k links is approximately

$$\frac{e^{-(n-1)p}((n-1)p)^k}{k!}. \tag{2}$$

This gives us a benchmark degree distribution for comparison.

Interestingly, the random graph generating process exhibits also a number of "phase" transitions as we vary the probability of forming links, p, relative to the number of nodes, n. When p is small relative to n, so that $p < 1/n$ (average degree is less than one), then the resulting graph consists of a number of disjoint and relatively small components, each of which has a tree-like structure. Once p is large enough relative to n, so that $p > 1/n$, then we see a "giant component" emerge. That is, almost surely the graph consists of one large component, which contains a nontrivial fraction of the nodes, and all other components are vanishingly small. To get some impression as to the size of the giant component, and why it emerges at the juncture where $p = 1/n$, let us do a simple (heuristic) calculation. Let q be the fraction of nodes in the giant component. The probability that a node i is not in the giant component is the probability that none of its neighbors are. If node i has degree k_i, then this probability is $(1-q)^{k_i}$. Given the approximation by a Poisson degree distribution, the fraction of nodes outside of the giant component would satisfy the equation

$$1 - q = \sum_k \frac{e^{-(n-1)p}((n-1)p)^k}{k!}(1-q)^k.$$

Since $\sum_k \frac{((n-1)p(1-q))^k}{k!} = e^{(n-1)p(1-q)}$, we end up with an approximation of

$$q = 1 - e^{-q(n-1)p}. \tag{3}$$

There is always a solution of $q = 0$ to this equation. In the case where the average degree is larger than 1 (i.e., $(n-1)p > 1$), and only then, there is also a solution for q that lies between 0 and 1. This corresponds to the phase transition I mentioned above. If average degree exceeds one, then there is a giant component which contains a non-trivial fraction of all nodes, and the size of the giant component is approximately described by the nonzero solution to (3). For instance, in Figure 1.3 the giant component contains $q = 24/25 = .96$ of the total nodes. Solving $q = 1 - e^{q(n-1)p}$ when $n - 1 = 24$ and $p = 1/6$ leads to an approximate q of .98.

Why we see just one giant component and all other components are of a much smaller order is fairly intuitive. In order to have two "large" components each having some nontrival fraction of n nodes, there would have to be no links between any node in one of the components and any node in the other. For large n, it becomes increasingly unlikely to have two large components but with absolutely no links between them. Thus, nontrivial components mesh into a giant component, and any other components must be of a much smaller order. Although not an entirely random network (see Table 1.2), we get an impression of this from the economics co-authorship network of Goyal, van der Leij, and Moraga-Gonzalez (2003): it has a total of 81217 nodes and a giant component of 33027 nodes, and yet the second largest component only consists of 30 nodes.

As we continue to increase p, we see another phase transition when p is proportional to $log(n)/n$. This is the threshold at which the network becomes "connected" so that all nodes are path-connected to one another. We again get some impression of why this is happening from our approximation of the size of the largest component in (3). When we plug in $p = log(n)/(n - 1)$ then q solves $q = 1 - n^{-q}$, which for large n gives q close to 1. The more formal analysis is quite involved and is detailed in Bollobás (2001). Once we hit the threshold at which the network becomes connected, we also see further changes in the diameter of the network as we continue to increase p relative to n. Below the threshold, the diameter of giant component is of the order of $log(n)$, then at the threshold of connectedness it hits $log(n)/loglog(n)$, and it continues to shrink as p increases.

One interesting characteristic of Bernoulli random graphs, is that for large n and p that is not too large, we see very little clustering. That is, if two links, say ij and jk, are both present and we ask with what probability ik is present, the answer is simply p. So, if p is relatively small, then so is clustering. In particular, if we examine large social networks, where p should be close to 0, then the clustering of a network goes to 0. Having p be close to 0 when n is large would be necessary if, for instance, there is some upper bound on the average degree. This is something we expect in many social networks as there is some bound on the number of links an individual can maintain. In fact, if p is small enough and n is large enough, it is not only that we expect low clustering, but in fact we do not expect any loops or cycles in the network; that is, with high probability all components of the network will be trees (see Bollobás (2001) for details).

While this is just a quick look at some of what is known about Bernoulli (Erdös-Rényi) random graphs, it gives us some feeling for some properties of purely random networks. This is useful since such Bernoulli random graphs provide a relatively good match for some aspects of some observed networks (e.g., the degree distributions of the prison friendships and high school romance networks reported in Table 1.2), and also because some of the types of phase transitions and features observed in these networks are also observed in other random network models.

Although the Bernoulli random graphs studied by Erdös and Rényi and others provide a useful benchmark model for social networks and fit in a few cases, their lack of clustering, among other things, means that they lack some basic features exhibited by many observed social networks. This has led researchers to explore other sorts of random network models. There are various generalizations of Bernoulli random graphs that have been useful in statistical analysis of observed networks. In particular, Frank and Strauss (1986) identified a class of random graphs that generalize Bernoulli random graphs, which they called "Markov graphs." Such random graph models were later introduced to the social networks literature by Wasserman and Pattison (1996) under the name of p* networks, and further studied and extended in various directions.[26] The basic idea is to allow for specific dependencies in a network, and these have proven to be useful in statistical estimation of some network properties, and in particular for dependencies in link formation.

3.1.2   Rewired Lattices and Clustering

Watts and Strogatz (1998) looked at a specific variation on a Bernoulli network, with the following issue in mind. They wanted to generate networks that exhibit both relatively low diameter and nondegenerate clustering. They developed a model that mixes purely random link formation with a lattice structure. The structure of their model is easy to understand. I discuss a particular example, and refer the reader to Watts (1999) for more detailed derivations and simulations of the model.

Suppose we start with a very structured network that exhibits a high degree of clustering. For instance, let us construct a large circle, but then connect a given node to the nearest four nodes rather than just its nearest two neighbors.

In such a network, each node's individual clustering coefficient will be $1/2$. To see this, consider some set of consecutive nodes 1, 2, 3, 4, 5, that are part of such a network for a large n. Consider node 3, which is connected to each of the other nodes. Out of all the pairs of 3's neighbors ($\{1, 2\}, \{1, 4\}, \{1, 5\}, \{2, 4\}, \{2, 5\}, \{4, 5\}$), we see that half of them are connected ($\{1, 2\}, \{2, 4\}, \{4, 5\}$).

Note, however, that the diameter of such a network is on the order of $n/4$, which is out of line with what we observed in Table 1.1 and Section 2.3.1, where the diameter was on the order of 20 for networks with hundreds of thousands of nodes. The main point of Watts and Strogatz (1998) is that by starting with such a highly clustered ring lattice, and then randomly rewiring enough (but not too many) links, we can end up with a network that has a much

---

[26] For instance, see Pattison and Wasserman (1999) for an extension to multiple interdependent networks on a common set of nodes.

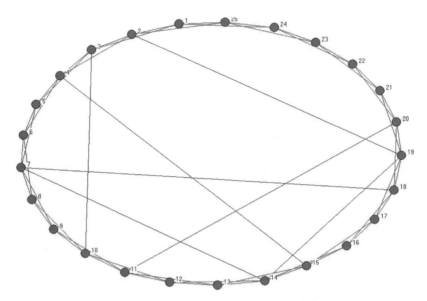

Figure 1.2. A Ring Lattice with Randomly Added Links

smaller diameter but still has substantial clustering. The rewiring can be done by randomly selecting some link ij and disconnecting it and then randomly connecting i to another node k chosen uniformly at random from those that i is not already connected to. Of course, eventually if too much rewiring is done, the clustering will vanish.[27] The interesting region is where enough rewiring has been done to substantially reduce (average and maximal) path length, but not so much that clustering vanishes. The key to this process is that the short cuts introduced by relatively few rewirings can dramatically decrease path lengths, and that this is a nonlinear relationship.

A slight variation of this original model proposed by Newman and Watts (1999) (see also Monasson (1999)) is easier to analyze in terms of its properties. That model starts with the same sort of ring lattice structure, but instead of rewiring links randomly, it simply adds links randomly. While precise diameter and path length numbers have still not been obtained for this model, we can easily derive upper bounds based on those for the corresponding random graphs, and in terms of diameter these bounds should not be too far off (at least when the corresponding random graph, ignoring the ring lattice, would be connected by itself). For instance if we introduce more than $log(n)/n$ random links, then we can expect a diameter of no more than $log(n)/loglog(n)$ (given what is known about Bernoulli random graphs).

While the rewiring of a ring lattice provides the high clustering and low path lengths that we observe in many social networks, the resulting degree

[27] That is, the network will take on the features of a random network, which has vanishing clustering as the number of nodes becomes large and the number of links per node is not growing too rapidly.

distributions are far from what is observed. In particular, in order to keep a reasonably high clustering coefficient in such a model, the initial ring lattice structure has to stay largely intact and has to represent a non-trivial fraction of an average node's links. This means that the resulting degree distribution has a great deal more regularity and less variance than what is generally observed.

3.1.3   Preferential Attachment and Scale-Free Degree Distributions

As mentioned above, in order to match the degree distributions that are observed in many social networks, one needs a process of link formation that differs from the pure Bernoulli (Erdös-Rényi) process, as observed distributions often exhibit fatter tails. The ideas behind generating distributions with "fat tails" date to Pareto (1896), for which the standard power distribution is named, and continued in Yule (1925) and were really crystallized and formalized by Simon (1955). The underlying principle is what is often referred to as a "rich-get-richer" structure, or essentially something akin to a lognormal growth system. If objects grow in size at a rate proportional to their current size, then we should expect "fat tails" in the distribution of sizes. In particular, Simon pointed out that in a system where objects are born at different times, and then grow lognormally once they are born, the resulting distribution of object size will follow a power-law or scale-free distribution.[28] This can be applied to distributions of wealth and city sizes, among many other things.[29]

Price (1965) first observed that some networks (in particular, citation networks) had degree distributions with special features. In a later seminal paper, Price (1976) adapted Simon's (1955) ideas to the setting of a growing (citation) network in order to generate scale-free degree distributions. The idea was that the number of citations that papers would gain over time were proportional to the number of citations they already had.[30] In the recent literature, such a process has been referred to by the name of "preferential attachment," as coined by Barabasi and Albert (2001), who developed a model similar to Price's (1976) model except that it is undirected, while Price's was directed.[31]

Let me briefly describe such a model, as it is useful in illustrating some of the techniques from that literature. Consider a system where a new node is born at each date. So let us index nodes by their date of birth $i \in \{0, 1, 2 \ldots, t, \ldots\}$. Upon birth (and only then), each new node forms m links with pre-existing

---

[28] Another explanation behind power laws is the idea of "HOT" (highly optimized tolerance) systems that underlies Carlson and Doyle (1999) and Fabrikant, Koutsoupias, and Papadimitriou (2002). That important idea addresses systems that are centrally optimized, rather than self-organizing.

[29] See Mitzenmacher (2004) for a nice overview.

[30] One can explain such a system via a simple process. If researchers randomly find a paper (which these days can be explained via a keyword search) and then search for additional papers via the references they find in the first paper, then the chance of being found is roughly proportional to the number of citations that a paper already has.

[31] See Newman (2003) (and also Mitzenmacher (2004)) for more discussion of the various naming of such processes and their development.

nodes.[32] The new node selects the nodes to link to in a random manner but with a probability that is proportional to the number of links that each given node already has. For example, if an existing node i has twice as many links as some other node j, then it is twice as likely to get a given link from the newborn node. So, roughly, the probability that any given existing node i gets a new link at time t is m times its degree relative to the overall degree of all existing nodes that time t, or $m \frac{k_i(t)}{\sum_{j=1}^{t} k_j(t)}$, where $k_i(t)$ is node i's degree at time t and $\sum_{j=1}^{t} k_j(t)$ is the normalization by the total degree of all nodes. As there are tm total links in the system at time t, $\sum_{j=1}^{t} k_j(t) = 2tm$. Thus, the probability that any given existing node i gets a new link in period t is $\frac{k_i(t)}{2t}$.

This results in a well-defined stochastic process (an infinite Markov chain). As the steady state distribution of a Markov process can be hard to solve for explicitly, the system is often approximated. For instance, if we approximate the random discrete time system by a continuous time system, where the degree of each node grows deterministically at the expected rate, then we can solve it explicitly. This is termed a "mean-field" approximation.

So, in this system, given that a node i is expected to gain roughly $\frac{k_i(t)}{2t}$ links in period t, the mean field approximation is to solve the system where

$$\frac{dk_i(t)}{dt} = \frac{k_i(t)}{2t}.$$

This differential equation with initial condition $k_i(i) = m$ leads to a solution of

$$k_i(t) = m \left(\frac{t}{i} \right)^{1/2}.$$

Thus, nodes are born over time and then grow. The system is now much simpler than the random system, in that the degrees of nodes can be ordered by their ages. The oldest nodes are the largest. To find out what the fraction of nodes is that exceeds some given level k at some time t, we just need to identify which node is at exactly level k at time t, and then we know that all nodes born before then are the nodes that are larger. Let $i_t(k)$ be the node which has degree k at time t, or such that $k_{i_t(k)}(t) = k$. From our above equation, we know that

$$\frac{i_t(k)}{t} = \left(\frac{m}{k} \right)^2.$$

The fraction of nodes that have degree smaller than k at time t are then the proportion born after node $i_t(k)$, or born after time $t \left(\frac{m}{k} \right)^2$. Thus, the distribution function is

$$F_t(k) = 1 - m^2 k^{-2}.$$

---

[32] There are some details to worry about in starting such a process. Early nodes may not end up being able to form m links. If we count early nodes as having m links, regardless of how many they actually formed, then the process is well defined.

This has a corresponding density or frequency of[33]

$$f(k) = 2m^2 k^{-3}.$$

Thus, we obtain a scale-free distribution with an exponent of -3.[34]

3.1.4   Hybrid Models

From the models we have discussed so far, we see that in each case there is some deficiency. The purely random graphs analyzed by Erdös and Rényi do not exhibit the clustering or degree distributions that match many observed networks. The rewired ring lattices of Watts and Strogatz (1998) do not exhibit degree distributions matching observed networks. Preferential attachment generates scale-free degree distributions that help account for the fat-tailed degree distributions observed in many applications. However, it turns out that preferential attachment generates networks that do not exhibit any clustering. Moreover, as we saw from Table 1.2, degree distributions differ substantially across applications and tend to lie somewhere between purely random and purely scale-free.

Thus, in order to match observed networks, we need several characteristics: relatively low diameter, nontrivial clustering, and a degree distribution that spans between purely random and scale-free networks. Recent models have made progress in generating networks that are closer to observed networks. Pennock et al. (2002), show that by use of a mixed model where some links are formed uniformly at random and others are formed via preferential attachment results in a degree distribution that spans between random and scale-free degree distributions. There are other models that are hybrids of random and preferential attachment (e.g., Kleinberg et al. (1999), Kumar et al. (2000), Dorogovtsev and Mendes (2001), and Cooper and Frieze (2003)). Interestingly, most of these ignore the fact that the resulting degree distributions are not scale-free, but instead try to show that the distribution is at least approximately scale-free for large degrees. Pennock et al. (2002) were the first to recognize the fact that many observed networks were not really scale-free, and thus that a hybrid model could better match observed degree distributions. Unfortunately, that model does not provide any clustering.

In order to generate clustering, and still have some sort of scale-free aspect to a degree distribution, Klemm and Eguíluz (2002, 2002b) have a variation of the preferential attachment model where nodes are declared either active or inactive. A new node enters as "active" and then some existing active node is randomly de-activated (with a probability inversely proportional to its degree).

---

[33] Note that the expression for F_t is in fact independent of t (which is an artifact of the continuous time mean-field approximation). Thus, the subscript is dropped from the expression.

[34] The specifics of the exponent -3 comes from the -2 in the distribution function, which is traced back to the fact that each link is shared by a new and old node. If these were in different proportions, the exponent would change. See Simon (1955) for more discussion of this, and Jackson and Rogers (2004) for an alternative model with additional variation in the exponent.

New nodes attach to each active node. Then with a probability μ, each of these links is rewired to a random node in the population chosen according to preferential attachment. This process thus has a fixed number of "active" nodes, and the fact that each entering node ends up connected to a proportion $1 - \mu$ of them, and that the list of active nodes only changes by one each period, results in significant clustering. The preferential attachment structure results in the scale-free distribution and small diameter. However, this sort of model only generates scale-free distributions.

Jackson and Rogers (2004) show that a hybrid model can result in all of the features of high clustering, small diameter, and a degree distribution that spans between purely random to scale-free. In that model, nodes are born over time and each node forms m links, just as in the preferential attachment model described above. However, instead of forming links randomly, the new nodes meet (and form links to) some existing nodes purely at random and then also meet some neighbors of these nodes.[35] Meeting neighbors introduces an element of preferential attachment, as the chance of meeting a node in that manner is proportional to how many neighbors it has. As the ratio of how many nodes are met at random compared to how many of their neighbors are met is varied, this process spans between one of completely random link formation to one of pure preferential attachment. However, it exhibits nontrivial clustering between these extremes, since new nodes will often form links both to an existing node and one of its neighbors, thus forming a completed triangle. Jackson and Rogers show that such a model can fit observed networks well on several dimensions at once (see Table 1.2).

3.2   Strategic Models of Network Formation

As I have provided extensive discussion of strategic models of network formation elsewhere (Jackson (2003, 2004)), here I will present a few examples to illustrate some key points about the literature on network formation that has emerged from economics and game theory.

There are two key aspects of an economic/game theoretic approach to modeling network formation:

(i) agents derive some utility from the network, and thus there is an overall societal welfare corresponding to any network that might arise, and

(ii) links are formed at the discretion of the agents who are (or control) the nodes, and resulting networks can be predicted through notions of equilibrium or possibly stochastic dynamic processes.

While economists are so used to looking at costs and benefits and using utility based models that (i) would be taken for granted, it is important to note that this perspective on network analysis is a key distinguishing feature from the

---

[35] See Vazquez (2003) for a related process which also exhibits clustering, where links are formed by first entering at a randomly selected node and then following a path emanating from the node.

"random" models discussed above. This is an important feature that allows one to assess the implications of various networks or formation processes to deduce whether "good" networks are emerging from society's perspective. Having utilities assigned to networks is, of course, also a prerequisite for an equilibrium analysis, (ii), which complements the "random" processes and provides different insights into network formation. Being able to evaluate the consequences of various network structures is necessary in order to move the study of social networks beyond a purely descriptive exercise, and having welfare measures and outcomes associated with different networks is essential in this regard. Also, when integrated with an equilibrium analysis we can analyze and understand the potential conflict that arises between the networks emerging through the choices of the parties involved and the networks that are best from a societal perspective.

Another important point to emphasize is that such a game theoretic perspective can help answer the questions as to *why* certain network features might appear. I will discuss this a bit more below with respect to contrasting views of "small-worlds" phenomena. I will also discuss the limitations of an economic/game theoretic approach, and the potential for hybrid approaches, which combine some randomness and heterogeneity with economic motivations for link formation.

3.2.1 An Economic Approach

Some of the first models bringing explicit utilities and choice to the formation of social links were in the context of modeling the tradeoffs between "strong" and "weak" ties in labor contact networks. These models were by Boorman (1975) and Montgomery (1991), and explored findings and hypotheses about different strengths of ties and their role in finding employment that were originally due to influential work by Granovetter (1974). Granovetter had observed that when individuals obtained jobs through their social contacts, while they sometimes did so through strong ties (people whom they knew well and interacted with on a frequent basis), they also quite often obtained jobs through weak ties (acquaintances whom they knew less well and/or interacted with relatively infrequently). This led Granovetter to coin the phrase "the strength of weak ties." Boorman's article and Montgomery's articles provided explicit models where costs and benefits could be assigned to strong and weak ties, and tradeoffs between them could be explored.

From a completely separate perspective, another use of utility functions in a network context emerged in the work of Myerson (1977). Myerson was originally interested in characterizing a cooperative game theoretic solution concept, the Shapley value, without directly imposing an additivity axiom. This led him to analyze a class of cooperative games[36] that were augmented with a graph

---

[36] For those not familiar with cooperative games, a standard formulation specifies a value or worth for every possible set of players. A solution, such as the Shapley Value, then predicts or suggests how the total value of the society as a whole (the "grand coalition"), should be split between its

structure. In particular, in these games the only coalitions that could produce value are those that are pathwise connected within the underlying graph. He thought of the graphs as indicating the possible cooperation or communication structures. So, starting with some given cooperative game and then augmenting it with such a graph, one ends up with a new cooperative game where the worth of any coalition is determined by how it is partitioned by the graph.[37] In that framework, a natural analog of the Shapley value (now termed "The Myerson Value") emerges and can be characterized with some simple axioms. Aumann and Myerson (1988) then recognized that different graph structures led to different allocations of value to the agents in the society, so they studied a specific extensive form game where links are considered one-by-one according to some exogenous order, and formed if both agents involved agree. While that game turns out to be hard to analyze even in three-person examples, it was an important precursor to the more recent economic literature on network formation.[38]

In contrast to the cooperative game setting, Jackson and Wolinsky (1996) explicitly considered networks, rather than coalitions, as the primitive. Thus rather than deducing utilities indirectly through a cooperative game on a graph, they posited that networks were the primitive structure and agents derived utilities based on the network structure in place. Once we have utility being derived from networks, we can take a game theoretic approach to modeling network formation by modeling the formation of links via the decisions of self-interested maximizing players.

As with any game theoretic setting, there are different approaches to modeling equilibrium. A standard equilibrium concept such as Nash equilibrium is not well suited to modeling network formation, as the consent of two players is generally needed to form a link or relationship.[39] For example, if we simply consider a game where each agent announces the links he wishes to form and we form links that are jointly announced, it is always a Nash equilibrium to have no links form. Each player announces an empty set of links since he or she (correctly) anticipates that all other players will do the same. There are various

---

members and how that depends on the values that are generated by all the possible subcoalitions. The reason that the information of the values of subcoalitions is important, is that it provides information about how much different players contribute to society as one can calculate, for instance, how much value would be lost if a given player were removed from the society or from some given subcoalition.

[37] For example, considering a coalition 1,2,3 and a graph that just has a link between 1 and 2, means that the coalition would generate value as if it were just 1,2 instead of 1,2,3 (normalizing isolated players to have value of 0).

[38] See Slikker and van den Nouweland (2001) for an overview of much of the cooperative game theoretic literature that has followed on communication and cooperation structures.

[39] There are some exceptions. In some purely directed settings, it is possible to form a link without the destination node's consent – such as forming a link to a web page or citing a paper. In such cases, the issue of mutual consent does not arise and a solution such as Nash equilibrium and its refinements can be used. See Jackson (2004) for more discussion and references on such equilibrium modeling issues.

ways around this, and a very simple one is to define a simple stability notion directly on networks. This was the approach followed by Jackson and Wolinsky (1996) who defined the following notion of pairwise stability. A network is pairwise stable if no player wants to sever a link and no two players both want to add a link.

More formally, let $u_i(g)$ denote the net utility that agent i receives under the network g, inclusive of all costs and benefits. A network g is *pairwise stable* if

(i) for all $ij \in g$, $u_i(g) \geq u_i(g - ij)$ and $u_j(g) \geq u_j(g - ij)$, and
(ii) for all $ij \notin g$, if $u_i(g + ij) > u_i(g)$ then $u_j(g + ij) < u_j(g)$.

The requirement that no player wishes to delete a link that he or she is involved in implies that a player has the discretion to unilaterally terminate his or her relationships. The second part of the definition can be stated in various ways. In order for a network to be pairwise stable, it is required that if some link is not in the network and one of the involved players would benefit from adding it, then it must be that the other player would suffer from the addition of the link. Another way to state this is that if we are at a network g where the creation of some link would benefit both players involved (with at least one of them strictly benefiting), then the network g is not stable, as it will be in the players' interests to add the link.

While pairwise stability is natural and quite easy to work with, there are limitations of the concept. For instance, it only considers deviations one link at a time by, at most, two players at a time. This is a current area of research (see Section 5), but nonetheless pairwise stability serves as a sensible starting point.

Given that we have well-defined payoffs to players as a function of the network, there are two obvious and standard notions of welfare that we can apply. The first is simply a utilitarian principle, which is to say the "best" network is the one which maximizes the total utility of the society. This notion was referred to as "strong efficiency" by Jackson and Wolinsky (1996), but I will refer to it simply as efficiency. Let $v(g) = \sum_i u_i(g)$ be the total value that accrues to society as a function of a network g. A network g is *efficient* relative to v if $v(g) \geq v(g')$ for all $g' \in G(N)$. It is clear that there will always exist at least one efficient network, given that there are only a finite set of networks.

The other natural notion of efficiency is that of Pareto efficiency. A network g is *Pareto efficient* relative to $(u_1, \ldots, u_n)$ if there does not exist any $g' \in G$ such that $u_i(g') \geq u_i(g)$ for all i with strict inequality for some i. To understand the relationship between the two definitions, note that if g is efficient relative to $v = \sum_i u_i$ then it is clearly Pareto efficient relative to $(u_1, \ldots, u_n)$. The converse is not true. What is true is that g is efficient relative to v if and only if Pareto is efficient relative to all $(\widehat{u}_1, \ldots, \widehat{u}_n)$ such that $\sum_i \widehat{u}_i = v$. Thus, efficiency is a stronger notion and is the more natural notion in situations where there is some freedom to reallocate value through transfers. Pareto efficiency is a less decisive notion, often admitting many networks, but it might be more reasonable in contexts where the payoff functions are fixed, and no transfers are possible.

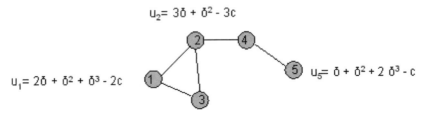

$u_2 = 3\delta + \delta^2 - 3c$

$u_1 = 2\delta + \delta^2 + \delta^3 - 2c$

$u_5 = \delta + \delta^2 + 2\,\delta^3 - c$

Figure 1.3. An Example of Payoffs in the (Symmetric) Connections Model

3.2.2   The Connections Model

A simple model of social connections from Jackson and Wolinsky (1996) is useful for illustrating the relationship between efficient and pairwise stable networks.

In the connections model links represent social relationships between players (nodes) – for instance friendships. These relationships offer benefits in terms of favors, information, etc., and also involve some costs. Moreover, players also benefit from indirect relationships. A "friend of a friend" also results in some indirect benefits, although of a lesser value than the direct benefits that come from a "friend." The same is true of "friends of a friend of a friend," and so forth. The benefit deteriorates in the "distance" of the relationship. This is represented by a factor δ_{ij} that lies between 0 and 1, which indicates the benefit from a direct relationship between i and j and is raised to higher powers for more distant relationships. For instance, in the network where player 1 is linked to 2, 2 is linked to 3, and 3 is linked to 4, player 1 gets a benefit of δ_{12} from the direct connection with player 2, an indirect benefit of $(\delta_{13})^2$ from the indirect connection with player 3, and an indirect benefit of $(\delta_{14})^3$ from the indirect connection with player 4. For $\delta_{ij} < 1$ this leads to a lower benefit from an indirect connection than a direct one. Players only pay costs, however, for maintaining their direct relationships.

We can write the net utility or payoff $u_i(g)$ that player i receives from a network g as

$$u_i(g) = \sum_{j \neq i: \ i \text{ and } j \text{ are path-connected in } g} (\delta_{ij})^{p_{ij}(g)} - \sum_{j \neq i: \ ij \in g} c_{ij},$$

where $p_{ij}(g)$ is the number of links in the shortest path between i and j and $c_{ij} > 0$ is the cost for player i of maintaining a link with j.

To see how this works, let us consider the special case, termed the "symmetric connections model," where the cost and benefit parameters are identical for all agents, so there exist $1 \geq \delta \geq 0$ and $c \geq 0$ such that $\delta_{ij} = \delta$ and $c_{ij} = c$ for all ij. Then, for instance, we can easily deduce utilities in the network pictured in Figure 1.6.

The highly stylized nature of the connections model allows us to begin to answer questions regarding which networks are efficient, or "best" from society's point of view, as well as which networks are likely to form when self-interested players choose their own links as modeled through pairwise stability.

The efficient networks are characterized as follows in the symmetric connections model:

(i) the complete network if $c < \delta - \delta^2$,
(ii) a star encompassing all nodes if $\delta - \delta^2 < c < \delta + \frac{(n-2)}{2}\delta^2$, and
(iii) the empty network if $\delta + \frac{(n-2)}{2}\delta^2 < c$.

The intuition behind this is very clear. If costs are very low, (i), it will be efficient to include all links in the network. In particular, if $c < \delta - \delta^2$, then adding a link between any two agents i and j will always increase total welfare. This follows because they are each getting at most δ^2 of value from any indirect connection between them, and since $\delta^2 < \delta - c$ the value of a direct connection between them increases their utilities (and might also increase the utilities of other agents). When the cost rises above this level, so that $c > \delta - \delta^2$ but c is not too high, it turns out that the unique efficient network structure is to have all players arranged in a "star" network. This can be seen from several observations, and a careful proof is not much more complicated. The first observation is that a star network involves the minimal number of links ($n - 1$) needed to connect all individuals. The second is that in a star network all nodes are within at most two links from one another. The third observation is that when $c > \delta - \delta^2$, then a path of length two between two nodes generates more utility than a path of length one. A star has the minimal number of links, and has all nodes at distances of two or less, and the most possible at a distance of two out of all networks that connect all individuals. It is also easy to check by direct calculations that if a small star generates positive total utility then a larger star generates more, and that a single star outperforms separate stars. Thus, if it is efficient to connect agents at all when $c > \delta - \delta^2$, then we should do it through a single star. The calculation in (iii) comes from checking whether or not the utility of a star including all nodes is positive.

Thus, in the connections model the set of efficient networks have a remarkably simple characterization: either costs are so low that it makes sense to add all links, or are so high that no links make sense, or costs are in a middle range and the unique efficient architecture is a star network.[40]

We can now compare the efficient networks with those that arise if agents form links in a self-interested manner. The pairwise stable networks are as follows.

(i) If $c < \delta - \delta^2$, then the complete network is the unique pairwise stable network.
(ii) If $\delta - \delta^2 < c < \delta$, then a star encompassing all nodes is pairwise stable, and there are also other pairwise stable networks.

---

[40] This characterization of efficient networks actually holds for a much broader set of environments, as long as utility depends on minimal distances between nodes and there is some sort of decay of value with distance and there are symmetries across agents, as shown by Bloch and Jackson (2003).

(iii) If $\delta < c < \delta + \frac{(n-2)}{2}\delta^2$, then all pairwise stable networks are inefficient, and are such that each agent has either no links or at least two links.

(iv) If $\delta + \frac{(n-2)}{2}\delta^2 < c$, then the empty network is the unique pairwise stable network.

In the case where costs are very low $c < \delta - \delta^2$, the direct benefit to the agents from adding or maintaining a link is positive, even if they are already indirectly connected. Thus, in that case the unique pairwise stable network will be the efficient or complete network. When costs are very high, then no links form and again we have an efficient outcome. The more interesting cases in the middle ranges of (ii) and (iii), so that the star is the efficient network, but is only sometimes pairwise stable and even then not uniquely so. It is easy to see why if $c > \delta$, then the efficient (star) network will not be pairwise stable. This follows since the center player gets only a marginal benefit of $\delta - c < 0$ from any of the links. This tells us that in this cost range there cannot exist any pairwise stable networks where there is some player who has just one link, as the other player involved in that link would benefit by severing it. For various values of $c > \delta$ there will exist nonempty pairwise stable networks, but they will not be star networks: as just argued, they must be such that each connected player has at least two links.

This simple model makes it obvious that there will be situations where individual incentives are not aligned with overall societal benefits. While this connections model is highly stylized, it still captures some basic insights about the payoffs from networked relationships and it shows that we can begin to understand the incentives that underlie network formation and see when resulting networks are efficient.

To get a broader feeling for the ideas of efficiency and stability, let us examine another simple example.

3.2.3   Networks Between Firms: An Industrial Organization Perspective

There are various ways in which firms form relationships that affect market outcomes. They can collaborate in research and development, they can merge, they can produce joint products and ventures, they can contract on specific supplier relationships, they can collude, etc. As the costs of production to various firms and resulting prices and quantities produced and demanded can all vary based on the different relationships between firms, this is a natural setting to apply network formation.[41]

Let us consider an example due to Goyal and Joshi (2003), which allows for easy characterizations of efficient and pairwise stable networks. When two firms form a link it lowers their respective costs of production. This is the only direct effect of a link. There are also indirect effects, as firms eventually

---

[41] See Bloch (2004) for a recent survey.

compete in the market. The cost structure, and thus the full network structure, affects how much each firm eventually sells on the market and the resulting profits.

In this model the marginal cost of production of firm i is given by $c_i(g) = a - bn_i(g)$, where $n_i(g) = |N_i(g)|$ is the number of neighbors that firm i has in the network g. (Set $a > (n-1)b > 0$ so that costs are always positive.) Thus, each additional alliance that a firm undertakes lowers its marginal cost of production by an amount b.

The eventual profits to firms can be considered under various assumptions about how they compete, with the two canonical ones being pure Cournot and pure Bertrand competition.[42]

Let us first consider Cournot competition, where the market demand is given by the inverse demand function with the price $p = \alpha - \sum_i q_i$, where $\alpha > 0$ is a given constant and q_i is the quantity of the good produced and offered for sale by firm i.

Under the assumption that α is large enough, it is easy to check that each firm's Cournot equilibrium profits are $(q_i(g))^2$, where[43]

$$q_i(g) = \frac{\alpha - a + nbn_i(g) - b\sum_{j\neq i} n_j(g)}{n+1}.$$

From this, as Goyal and Joshi point out, it is very easy to derive the pairwise stable networks. Note that the profits of a firm are increasing in $q_i(g)$. Note also that the network enters $q_i(g)$ in proportion to $nn_i(g) - \sum_{j\neq i} n_j(g)$. Thus, if links have a negligible cost, firm i gains with each link that it adds. If link costs are small enough, then the complete network is the unique pairwise stable network under Cournot competition.

In measuring efficiency here, one might also want to include consumer welfare as well as the payoffs to the firms. The consumer welfare (consumer surplus) is strictly increasing in the total quantity produced, so they would like to see the complete network formed. As it turns out, the firms' total profits are also increasing in the total number of links formed. Thus, the complete network is efficient whether or not the consumers are accounted for. While the full calculations take a few steps,[44] it is easy to compare the empty network to the complete

---

[42] For non-economists, Cournot competition refers to a situation where producers choose an amount to produce or a capacity and then the price that clears the market is determined by demand, while (pure) Bertrand competition refers to a situation where firms choose prices and then the lowest priced firm(s) produce to service the entire demand at that price. I will not try to describe these approaches to modeling oligopoly here, as they can be found in almost any "principles" textbook.

[43] A firm's profits are $(p - c_i(g))q_i$. The first order conditions lead to $\frac{\partial p}{\partial q_i}q_i + p - c_i(g) = 0$. Noting that $\frac{\partial p}{\partial q_i} = -1$, this implies that in equilibrium $q_i = p - c_i(g)$, and so profits are thus $(q_i)^2$. Solving $q_i = p - c_i(g) = \alpha - \sum_j q_j - c_i(g)$ simultaneously across i, gives the explicit expressions for the quantities. A sufficient condition for all quantities to be positive is that α is large, or that $\alpha - a - (n-1)(n-2)b > 0$.

[44] Consult Goyal and Joshi (2003, 2004).

network. If there are no links formed, then each firm's profits are $(\frac{\alpha-a}{n+1})^2$, while if all links form, then each firm's profits are $(\frac{\alpha-a+bn(n-1)-b(n-1)^2}{n+1})^2$. Clearly, the total profits are higher when all links form.

Next, let us consider the other textbook form of oligopoly: pure Bertrand competition where the firms charging the lowest price split the market. In this setting, if there are at least two firms who have the lowest cost level, then they will end up bidding their prices down to that cost and splitting the market, but making no profits as the price will equal their cost of production. In contrast, if there is one firm who has a lower cost than the other firms, then that firm will end up capturing the entire market at a price of the second lowest cost level.[45]

This makes it quite easy to deduce pairwise stable networks. If there is any positive cost to forming a link, then the only firms willing to form links must be earning a profit. However, the only time any firm earns a profit under pure Bertrand competition is when a single firm has a lower cost than all others, and then only that firm earns a positive profit. This means that at most one firm would ever be willing to bear the cost of a link. Thus, no links will form, and the unique pairwise stable network is the empty network.

Here, we see that the resulting network will not be efficient either from the firms' or the consumers' standpoints. From the industry profit standpoint, it would be better if some links were formed so that some firm earned positive profits (supposing small enough link costs), and in most cases the highest industry profits would actually involve a star network where the center firm would enjoy a very low cost and also see much higher costs and thus higher prices from its competitors. This would be the efficient network structure if link costs are small and only firms' profits are considered. From the consumers' perspective, it would be best to see a low price. When the consumers' welfare is also accounted for (and again, link costs are negligible), the efficient network would be one of what Goyal and Joshi (2003) call "interlocking stars." That is where there are two firms, i and j, that are each linked to every other firm, and firms other than i and j are only linked to i and j. This leads to the lowest price and no profits for the firms, but leads to a maximum of consumer surplus (as well as consumer surplus plus profits).

While the networks in these examples again turn out to be stark in their structure, we again see that there are some circumstances where incentives to form links are congruent with overall welfare, and other cases where they are not. In the connections model this depended on the link formation costs. In the above oligopoly models, it is the market structure that determines whether or not there is a tension between stability and efficiency.

---

[45] Working out equilibria in asymmetric Bertrand games has some subtle points if a continuum of prices is allowed. This occurs because the lowest cost firm would like to underbid the other firms by as small an amount as possible, which means that there are no pure strategy equilibria. However there are equilibria where the higher cost firms mix (with support in a small interval with its min at the second lowest cost), that will lead to the claimed outcome, as described by Blume (2003).

3.2.4   A General Tension between Stability and Efficiency

In situations where individual payoffs and welfare are determined by the entire structure of a network, there are naturally externalities present. The decision of some agents to form or sever links can have important consequences for other individuals who are not directly involved in those links but may be indirectly affected by them. In the connections model, a decision of the center agent in a star to maintain a link with some agent gives indirect benefits to all of the other agents. In the oligopoly model, the decision of one firm to link to another lowers both of their costs, which can be detrimental to the other firms.

Given that there are externalities present, it is expected that the networks that are stable do not correspond to those that are efficient. However, what is less expected, is that we cannot always correct this inefficiency by taxing and subsidizing agents for the links they form (even in a complete information setting). The fact that no "reasonable" set of transfers can help rectify the disparity between the equilibrium and the efficient networks is easily seen through the following simple example from Jackson and Wolinsky (1996). Consider the utilities pictured in the following figure. The utility of each agent in the complete network is 4. The utility of each connected agent in a linked pair is 6 (with the disconnected agent having utility 0). The efficient network is one with two links, where a total utility of 13 is generated, with the central agent getting a utility of 4.5 and the other two agents getting a utility of 4.25 each.

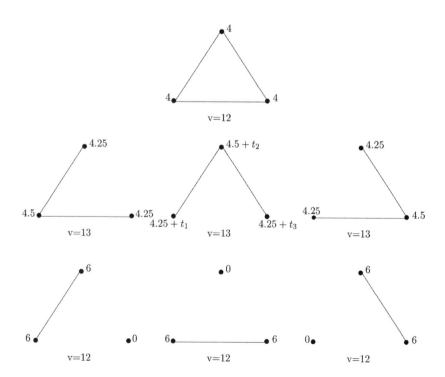

It is obvious in this example that in the absence of any transfers, the pairwise stable networks all fail to be efficient. The pairwise stable networks are only those involving a single link. In any other network some agent(s) have an incentive to sever a link (every agent has such an incentive in the complete network, and the center agent has an incentive to do so in each of the two link networks).

So, let us consider some possible transfers to try to support an efficient network as being pairwise stable. Given the symmetry of the example, it is enough to consider any of the two-link networks. Let us consider the middle one. We see that the payoffs with potential transfers are $4.25 + t_1, 4.5 + t_2$, and $4.25 + t_3$. In order to have the transfers be feasible, it must be that $t_1 + t_2 + t_3 \leq 0$. Given the complete symmetry between the first and third agents, let us set their transfers to be equal so that $t_1 = t_3$.

Given that we want to adjust the transfers so as to ensure that the middle two-link network is pairwise stable, we need to make sure that the first and third agents would not gain from adding the missing link. Thus, we need $t_1 = 0_3 \geq -.25$. However, in order to have the network be pairwise stable we also need the second agent, or center agent, to be willing to keep both of the links that are in place. As that agent gets a payoff of 6 if either link is deleted, it must be that $t_2 \geq 1.5$. However, now we have violated the feasibility condition as the total sum of transfers needs to be greater than one to ensure pairwise stability.[46]

There are ways around this, but they require treating agents unequally (e.g., setting t_1 and t_3 differently even though the agents are identical in the problem), or making transfers at some of the other networks in ways that violate some other conditions.[47] For instance, suppose that we set transfers so that we completely equalize utilities for all agents in each network. While this would require allocating utility to agents who may not even be connected to the network, it does provide all agents with incentives that coincide with the overall societal value.

3.2.5   Bargaining and Link Formation

Another important point is made by Currarini and Morelli (2000) who show that incorporating the allocation of utilities as part of the bargaining process that accompanies link formation can also lead to more efficient network formation.[48] They describe a specific extensive form game where players announce both the links they wish to form and the payoffs they demand. Players move in some

---

[46] This example extends for weaker notions of efficiency and a variety of notions of stability. See Jackson and Wolinsky (1996) to see extensions to other stability notions, and Jackson (2003) for details on weakening the efficiency criterion.

[47] See Dutta and Mutuswami (1997) for an analysis of ways to reallocate utility so that some efficient network is strongly stable for a wide variety of settings, when this equal treatment property is dropped.

[48] Mutuswami and Winter (2000) also discuss a similar network formation game and also show that such positive results hold in a broad range of settings, but under a slightly different formulation.

order. The basic idea is that players realize that they can maximize the payoff they can demand if they maximize the value of the overall network. In a setting where players move in turn, each one extracts a variation on their marginal contribution to the value of the efficient network (see Mutuswami and Winter (2002) for details). Although these results hinge on the structure of the link-formation-bargaining game, and in particular on its fixed ending point, which provides for the asymmetry in bargaining power across the agents (where, for instance, the last player to move is at a real disadvantage),[49] these results show that whether or not agents have the ability to bargain over their payoffs at the time of link formation can be important in determining the type of network that forms.

3.2.6   The Economics of Small Worlds

The results from the previous section illustrate some central lessons that have come from the game theoretic literature, namely that:

- equilibrium networks can differ from efficient networks,
- whether or not efficient and stable networks coincide is context-dependent,
- discrepancies between stability and efficiency can only sometimes be rectified through bargaining or transfers, and
- the networks that emerge in equilibrium, and the resulting allocation of costs and benefits, depend on various features of the formation process and equilibrium notion.

We also see that the game theoretic analysis has a very different flavor than the random graph models. In particular, the predicted equilibrium networks are often quite stark in their nature (stars, complete networks, interlinked stars, etc.). This is partly due to the fact that most of the models that have been solved have strong symmetries in the assumed payoff functions. Without any natural heterogeneity in the problem it is not surprising that very simple network structures emerge as predictions.

This does not mean that equilibrium models are only suited for deducing broad conclusions about tensions between incentives and efficiency, or other such questions. These models still have the possibility to provide lessons that are more descriptive in nature. For example, economic forces actually tell us a great deal about *why* we should expect to see "small worlds." That is, why should we see high clustering on a local level, and short average path length overall? Ideas related to this have been explored in a series of papers (Johnson

---

[49] See Bloch and Jackson (2003) for an analysis of endogenous transfers in settings that treat players more symmetrically (simultaneous move games). They relate the types of transfers that are needed to reach efficient networks to the types of network externalities that are present in the setting.

and Gilles (2000), Carayol and Roux (2003), Galeotti, Goyal, and Kamphorst (2004), Hojman and Szeidl (2004b), and Jackson and Rogers (2005)).

The basic ideas are as follows. Consider a situation where the cost of maintaining a relationship between two agents depends on their proximity. Proximity need not be geographic, but can refer to any sort of nearness according to some traits. It is relatively easier to form friendships when two people attend the same school, have the same profession, or have other things in common. Such low costs on a "local" level help explain why high clustering will be present in a network. The explanation for low average path length in a social network is (slightly) more subtle. Consider a network where costs are related to proximity. Suppose we end up with a network that exhibited small clusters of individuals who were tightly connected in small groups (those close to each other), and yet the average path length in the overall network was high, due to an absence of links across groups. We might imagine that forming a link that was not "local" in nature was fairly costly. However, with an absence of links across groups, by forming a link that was not "local" in nature one would gain substantial access to a number of agents. The fact that a single link can substantially shorten the distance to a large number of agents at once, is precisely what makes that link valuable. While one will not see as many links that are very costly, the large potential benefit that they bring will mean that they will be present and that overall distances in the network will have some upper bound.[50] These ideas are illustrated in the following figure.

This is a variation on the connections model called the "islands model" by Jackson and Rogers (2005). In that model, agents are located on separate islands (which might be geographic, professional, or relate to some other characteristics). There is a relatively low cost to linking to an agent on one's own island, $c > 0$, while the cost of linking to an agent on a different island is much higher, $C >> c$. The benefits accrue just as in the connections model. Even though the cost is much higher to linking across islands, we still see some links across islands, as if such links were not present, then the gain from linking would be quite substantial as adding one link would provide access to a large number of agents at path lengths of only one or two. In the figure above, it is easy to verify that the given network is pairwise stable when $c < .04, 1 < C < 4.5, \delta = .95$, and where the five agents who are completely connected to each other lie on the same island. While this example is suggestive, it is easy to see that these properties hold more broadly (e.g., see Jackson and Rogers (2005)).

This economic analysis of small worlds gives complementary insights to those of Watts and Strogatz (1998) discussed above, which gives more of an explanation of how it is possible to have both high clustering and short path

---

[50] This is reminiscent of Burt's (e.g., Burt (1992)) idea of structural holes. One will not see too many "structural holes," where the operational definition of a structural hole in this context would be that the addition of a link could substantially shorten distances among two otherwise disconnected or distantly connected groups of nodes.

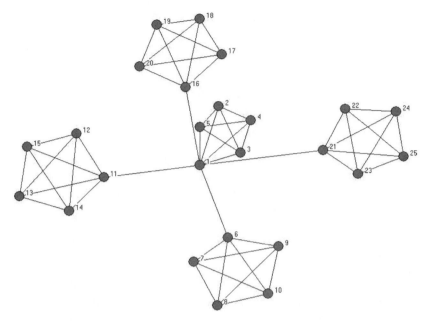

Figure 1.4. A Pairwise Stable Network in the Islands Model

length at the same time, whereas the above model gives more insight into why we should expect this to be what we see in most social networks. Also, a distinguishing feature between an economic modeling and a random modeling of these features concerns "shortcut" links (i.e., those which link distant parts of the network and if deleted would substantially alter the distance between the connected nodes). In a random model, while unlikely, shortcut links may occur in close proximity to each other. Under the economic approach, the cost of building a second shortcut link next to an existing one would outweigh the benefit.[51]

3.3   Discussion of Models of Network Formation

Let me now discuss some of the strengths and weaknesses of the two approaches to modeling network formation.

An unavoidable challenge in modeling networks is dealing with the complex combinatorial nature of the setting. The number of networks that can form is exponentially large in the number of nodes, which makes tractability a major issue. This has produced substantial hurdles for both the random and strategic approaches to network formation, and yet they have each made remarkable

---

[51] I thank Yann Bramoullé for pointing this out.

progress in advancing our understanding of what types of networks are likely to emerge.

The random graph-based models have a strength of producing specific networks, or distributions over possible networks, which exhibit significant heterogeneity that comes largely from chance and/or through birth dates. The models have provided some insight into how specific features of networks (e.g., fatter tails in the degree distribution) might be traced to certain aspects of a formation process (e.g., some form of preferential attachment). While these models are able to match increasingly long lists of features of observed networks, the processes end up being ad hoc, structured to match those features, and generally we need new processes each time we add a new feature. Another limitation is that the models are descriptions of processes, essentially algorithms, for generating networks. This has two implications. First, as discussed above, this helps answer the "how" of formation, but does not provide much insight as to the "why."[52] And second, a process does not provide us with methods to evaluate whether the emerging networks are good or bad, that is, whether the resulting networks are efficient.

These last weaknesses are the primary strengths of the game theoretic models. The game theoretic structure provides both a framework for evaluating networks and for understanding why (rather than how) certain networks are likely to emerge. This has resulted in some understanding of the relationship and tension between stable networks and efficient networks. The weakness of the game theoretic approach is that most of the explicit characterizations of equilibrium networks are often so stark that the predicted networks have overly simple structures. Thus, while such models can say something about whether the networks will end up being efficient or not, they have had a hard time predicting things like what sort of degree distribution the network might have. One can push the models to derive some general features, such as those of the "small-worlds" properties discussed in the last section, but deriving very clear pictures of emerging large social networks is still beyond the state of the art.

Interestingly, these two approaches are very complementary. This suggests that some combination of the two approaches might be very fruitful. Incorporating some random elements in terms of which links might be considered at a given time, and then some explicit payoffs and insight into why that link might or might not be added, should end up producing important new insights into the types of networks that we should expect to emerge in different settings, and the how and why behind them.[53]

---

[52] Another way to phrase this how versus why distinction is to distinguish between reduced form models versus structural models.

[53] There are some random dynamic models of network formation that are based on incentives to form links, such as Watts (2001), Jackson and Watts (2002a), Tercieux and Vannetelbosch (2004). However, those models use the random process to select from the set of pairwise stable networks, and are thus really more squarely in the game theoretic literature. While these might serve as a starting point, a truer hybrid would involve randomness that really limited the set of

4 BEHAVIOR ON NETWORKS

Let me now turn to the second main issue and discuss a few examples of models of networks that relate social network structure to behavior.

As with any scientific study one can be interested directly in the phenomenon itself, or one can be interested in its broader implications. That is, one might simply be interested in (social) networks, and understanding their character-istics, without any broader perspective. As networks are rich and complex by their very nature, they hold much intellectual interest. Nevertheless, we should also be interested in understanding how the networked patterns of social inter-actions are important in determining (human) behavior and social outcomes. It is this aspect that allows the science and modeling of networks to have relevance outside of itself.

Let me emphasize here that understanding how network structure impacts behavior and outcomes is also very important as a building block for the "eco-nomic approach" in the following sense. The discussion above takes as given that each player can be assigned a payoff as a function of a network. In many contexts those payoffs will be the result of some interaction. For instance, if agents are connected in a network and the network represents trading opportu-nities, then we must predict as a function of the endowments, preferences, and network structure which trades will be made at which prices and how that will determine agents' payoffs. Thus, from primitives and a network structure we can derive induced payoffs and understand how changes in network structure will change the overall efficiency or societal welfare, as well as individual in-centives to form or maintain links. We will see more of this below, and it is an essential part of modeling and understanding the impact of social networks.

There is one other aspect of understanding how network structure impacts behavior that also bears discussion. As different structures have different im-pacts on behavior, understanding them and having an associated cost/benefit or welfare analysis can lead to specific policy prescriptions. For instance, un-derstanding how the centrality of criminals affects their neighbors' criminal behavior has important implications for government policy (e.g., see Ballester, Calvo-Armengol, and Zenou (2003)). Understanding how social networks im-pact employment opportunities, social mobility, and human capital investments has implications for the subsidization of education (e.g., see Calvo-Armengol and Jackson (2003, 2004, 2005)).

4.1   Markets and Networks

There is a rich set of studies of markets and networks from an economics perspective (Kirman (1997), Ioannides (1997), Tesfatsion (1997), Weisbuch, Kirman, and Herreiner (2000), Kranton and Minehart (2001), Wang and

---

potential opportunities to form links in a much stronger way so that some potentially valuable links never even have the chance of being formed.

Watts (2002), Corominas-Bosch (2005), and Galeotti (2005)), as well as from the sociology literature (e.g., the exchange networks literature following Cook and Emerson (1978)). This is one of the most important and obvious applications of networks to economics as so many markets are not centralized but rather consist of a complex structure of bilateral trades and relationships.

A recent paper by Kakade et al. (2004) provides an example of a model that relates market outcomes to random graph-based network structures.[54] They examine a general equilibrium in a market, where the set of trades that can occur are governed by a social network. Their aim is to tie price dispersion to the statistical properties of the underlying network. This is done in the context of a simple buyer-seller model.[55] Buyers have cash endowments and a constant marginal value for a consumption good. Sellers have unit endowments of the consumption good (which they do not value) and desire cash. Buyers thus buy from the least expensive seller(s) with whom they are connected until they have exhausted their cash budget. Prices are seller-specific and determined to clear markets.[56] The full configuration of prices can be quite complex, but the basic intuition is that agents who have more connections should expect better prices, so the price that an agent pays or receives should be related to his or her degree and position in the network. The authors then examine a stochastic process for generating networks of links between buyers and sellers, which is similar to some discussed above (see Section 3.1.4) in that it is a combination of forming links completely at random and forming them in a manner based on preferential attachment. While the model is difficult to solve analytically, the authors do obtain some bounds in the extremes. For instance, they show that in the extreme where links are formed completely at random, and the probability of forming a link is high enough, then there is no price dispersion. In contrast, in the other extreme of pure preferential attachment there will generally be greater asymmetries in the degrees of nodes and there will be price dispersion. Through simulations, the authors then estimate the price dispersion that would result from observed trading patterns based on a United Nations data set of trade volumes.

Given the importance of understanding trade and market structure, this is still an area that deserves much more study. The model discussed above is specific both in its assumptions about transactions and the types of networks it considers, and yet this still proves to be difficult to handle analytically. Moreover, it seems

---

[54] Another important example is found in Kirman (1983) and Kirman, Oddou, and Weber (1986), who, in the context of core convergence in exchange economies, analyze the impact of limiting blocking coalitions to connected groups, where connection is defined relative to a Bernoulli random graph.

[55] See also Kakade, Kearns, and Ortiz (2004).

[56] This assumption embodies price-taking, which might be the weakest aspect of the model, given that much of the trading is done bilaterally. Corominas-Bosch (2004) presents an alternative buyer-seller formulation where prices are determined through an explicit bargaining game, and Kranton and Minehart (2001) provide a model where prices are determined through simultaneous auctions.

clear that the network structure underlying such trading relationships has a substantial strategic component to it, so the random graph models might not be ideal approximations of trading networks, although there is no empirical research to really work from on this question. Previous models based on strategic formation (e.g., Kranton and Minehart (2001) and Corominas-Bosch (2005)) are more tractable analytically, but only represent first-steps in modeling, as they fall short of including the heterogeneity needed (e.g., in endowments, preferences, and production technologies) to match most markets.

4.2   Labor Markets

As discussed in Section 2, it is well documented that networks of social contacts play an important role in employment. Recent work now brings network structures to the study of employment and wages over time. Calvó-Armengol and Jackson (2004) examine a model where agents only obtain information about jobs through a network of connections.[57] Jobs arrive exogenously to the network and agents occasionally lose a job according to some exogenous process. If an agent is already employed and hears about a job, then he or she passes the information on to his or her unemployed neighbors.[58] This passing of information to social ties means that agents' employment and wages over time will depend on their position in the social network, how many social ties they have, and how well employed those social ties are. They show that this results in correlation patterns in wages and employment of connected agents, and that these patterns depend on the network structure. Also, through simulations, they show that the correlation varies with the distance and location of agents in the network, as well as the structure of the network. They also show that the condition of an agent's social ties has an impact on their decision of whether to stay in the work force or drop out. This results in a contagion effect where if the neighbors of an agent drop out of the labor force, then that increases the likelihood that the agent will drop out, and so forth. This can lead to pockets of drop-outs and persistent unemployment, and among other things, can also help explain persistent differences in wages and drop-out rates across races.[59]

While these results show that incorporating social networks into models of labor markets is important for our understanding of employment and wage patterns, there is still much to be learned about how network structure matters. The empirical and theoretical work to date makes it clear that networks play a key role in labor markets. However, it would be very useful to have a richer

---

[57] See also Calvó-Armengol (2004) and Jackson and Lopez-Pintado (2005).

[58] See Calvó-Armengol and Jackson (2005) for a richer model where jobs are heterogeneous, the arrival rate may be state dependent, and job information may circulate indirectly through the network.

[59] Calvo-Armengol and Jackson (2005) study how investments in education based on social network status can also help us to understand the prevalence of social *immobility*, which has been found without exception in countries around the world.

understanding of how differences in the structures of agents' social networks impact their wage and employment over time, as well as how the network co-evolves with their career and job choices.

4.3   Learning and Networks

Another application of obvious importance in understanding how network structure impacts behavior is to understand how information propagates through a network, and in particular how people in a social network learn from one another. Taking a Bayesian perspective is a standard approach in economic modeling, and an obvious starting point. The model of Bala-Goyal (1998) builds from this perspective (see also Allen (1982) and Ellison and Fudenberg (1993, 1995)).

Bala and Goyal (1998) make a very simple but important point. Consider a series of agents connected in a social network who all face the same stationary, but random, environment. The network is fixed and time progresses in discrete dates where agents each choose one of a finite set of actions at each date. The payoffs to the actions are random and their distribution depends on an unknown state of nature. The agents are all faced with the same set of possible actions and the same unknown state of nature. They all have identical tastes and face the same uncertainty about the actions. Over time, each agent observes his or her neighbors' choices and outcomes. The main conclusion is that eventually the agents will converge to choosing the same action, based on the observation that over time players who observe each others' actions and payoffs should eventually come to choose the same action.[60] The intuition is as follows. We need only reason that any two neighbors earn the same long run utility, as this implies the same must be true network-wide. If one neighbor is doing better than another, then the neighbor with the poorer payoff will learn from observing the other agent, and eventually change behavior to obtain a similar payoff.[61] Note that the fact that all agents end up with the same long-run utility does not mean that all agents converge to choosing the "right" action. However, Bala and Goyal show that if the network is large enough, and there are enough agents who are optimistic about each possible action spread throughout the network, then the probability that the society will converge to the best overall action can be made arbitrarily close to 1. The idea is that there will be sufficiently many experiments by the optimistic agents so that the true payoff of each action will be learned and then the society will converge to the right action.

While the above lessons show the potential for the long-run conductance of information through a network, they do not give us much impression of what happens in the shorter run, which might often be quite relevant. Nor does the

---

[60] See Morris (2000) for another analysis of the spread and convergence of behavior through a network, but in a different context, where uncertainty regards strategic choices of others and players care about their neighbors' choices.

[61] Bala and Goyal work with a boundedly rational model. See Gale and Kariv (2003) for a Bayesian analysis. DeMarzo, Vayanos, and Zwiebel (2003) exaimine a different setting where beliefs are updated over time in a boundedly rational way, and where they need not converge across agents, as actions are only taken once and it is only information that is repeatedly passed.

analysis deal with worlds that are not stationary, or where actions are not taken repeatedly. Most critically, network structure does not enter the above discussion in any meaningful way. There are papers that have made more progress on understanding how network structure impacts beliefs. Gale and Kariv (2003) (see also Choi, Gale, and Kariv (2004) and Celen, Kariv, and Schotter (2004)) explore the interaction between network structure and beliefs under a variety of learning assumptions. Due to the complexity of some of the inference problems, they are able to provide a detailed understanding for long-run beliefs in small networks (e.g., three nodes) but leave open questions regarding more complex networks. DeMarzo, Vayanos, and Zwiebel (2003) are able to deal with more general network structures by assuming that agents follow a specific belief updating rule, where agents (erroneously) treat new iterations of information as independent of previous iterations. They document an intuitive relationship between the position of an agent in the network and their resulting impact on beliefs and opinions. These studies are important steps in developing a fuller understanding of how interaction structure affects information dissemination and belief formation.

4.4   Spread of Information, Viruses, Disease

Related to studies of learning through a network, which have focused on belief updating and action choice, there are also studies of the physical spread or transmission of infections and behavior that are transmitted directly or by chance, and not through some updating or optimization procedures. Examples include the spread of diseases, computer viruses, and also the spread of some types of behaviors, beliefs, and information. Standard models of such spreading come from the epidemiology literature, which has focused on the spread of contagious disease. One model that is useful to discuss a bit is the SIS model ("susceptible, infected, susceptible" model, see Bailey (1975)), which is a variation on the seminal model in the literature, the SIR model ("susceptible, infected, removed" (SIR) model, which dates to Kermack and McKendrick (1927)). Such models were originally based on random meetings of individuals. However, networked interactions were discussed as early as Rapoport (1953, 1953b), and eventually models that allow for network structure were studied by Anderson and May (1988) and Sattenspiel and Simon (1988). How infection rates depended on specific aspects of the network structure has more recently been studied by Kretschmar and Morris (1996), Pastor-Satorras and Vespignani (2000, 2001), Lopez-Pintado (2004), and Jackson and Rogers (2004), among others. In particular, these studies allow one to estimate infection rates based on degree distributions. I describe this setting in a bit more detail, as it offers one of the clearest understandings of how network structure can be related to outcomes, and the tools and methods used in such analyses look to be useful in other contexts.

Consider a network where a given healthy (also called "susceptible") node catches a disease in a given period with a probability $\nu k_i f_i$, where $\nu \in (0, 1)$ is a parameter describing a rate of transmission of infection in a given period, k_i is the (in-)degree of node i, and f_i is the fraction of i's neighbors who are infected.[62] Also suppose that any "infected" node recovers in a given period with a probability $\delta \in (0, 1)$. Thus, nodes are either susceptible or infected, and can alternate between these states depending on the state of their neighbors. This results in a Markov chain. We can then ask a series of questions. First, how high does the infection rate v have to be relative to the recovery rate δ in order to have the infection reach some non-zero steady state in the population? Second, can we estimate the long-run steady-state proportion of infected nodes? Third, can we relate the answer to these questions to the network structure?[63]

The heuristic (mean-field-based) approach that has been used in this literature to estimate infection patterns is as follows. Consider a large network whose degree distribution is described by P, where $P(k)$ is the proportion of nodes that have degree k. Moreover, let us make the (restrictive) assumption that there is no correlation in degree between linked nodes. Let $\rho(k)$ denote the steady-state infection rate of a node with degree k, and ρ be the average across nodes: $\rho = \sum_k \rho(k)P(k)$. The probability that a given link points to a node of degree k is $\frac{kP(k)}{<k>}$ (where $< k >$ is the average degree under P, $< k >= E_P[k]$). Note that this is different from the distribution of degrees across nodes, as nodes with higher degrees are proportionally more likely to be reached via any given link. Using this we estimate the probability that a given link points to an infected node in any given period in a steady state distribution under the mean-field hypothesis. This is represented by the parameter

$$\theta = \frac{\sum \rho(k)k P(k)}{< k >}. \tag{4}$$

To estimate the steady-state value of $\rho(k)$, we set the change in the proportion of nodes of degree k that are infected to 0. That is,

$$0 = \frac{d\rho(k)}{dt} = vk\theta(1 - \rho(k)) - \delta\rho(k).$$

Here, $vk\theta(1 - \rho(k))$ represents the number of healthy nodes that become infected, and $\delta\rho(k)$ represents the number of sick nodes that become healthy. These must be equal in a steady state.[64] Letting $\lambda = v/\delta$, we derive

$$\rho(k) = \frac{k\lambda\theta}{k\lambda\theta + 1}. \tag{5}$$

---

[62] This is obviously a fairly specific infection mechanism, but small infection rates offer a reasonable approximation of the probability of getting infected if infection rates are independent across neighbors (a questionable assumption if there is clustering). See Lopez-Pintado (2004) for the analysis of other infection mechanisms.

[63] See Jackson and Yariv (2005) for an analysis of such diffusion issues in a model where agents are faced with a choice of adopting a new behavior or technology and are best responding to their environment.

[64] The system here is clearly heuristic, as if we ran a Markov process on this system, all nodes would eventually converge to being susceptible and this is an absorbing state. To be careful, one needs to have some exogenous probability that the nodes become infected even when none of their neighbors are.

Equations 4 and 5 can the be solved simultaneously to derive the steady-state distributions.

It is easy to solve this when the network is completely regular so that all nodes have degree $< k >$. In that case, $\theta = \rho$ and (5) becomes

$$\rho = \frac{< k > \lambda \rho}{< k > \lambda \rho + 1}.$$

There is always a solution of $\rho = 0$, and then also another solution of $\rho = 1 - \frac{1}{\lambda < k >}$ which is greater than 0 only if $\lambda > \frac{1}{<k>}$. Thus, in order for infection to spread in the network, the relative infection/recovery rate has to exceed a threshold. This is another example of a phase transition, of which we saw examples earlier in the discussion of the properties of random graphs.

Pastor-Satorras and Vespignani (2000) solve this system in the case where the degree distribution is scale free (using $P(k) = 2 < k > k^{-3}$). They find an approximation of $\rho = 2e^{-1/<k>\lambda}$ (for small λ). Thus, they deduce that even with tiny values for λ, there will be some non-zero infection rate in a scale-free network. This contrasts with the fact that λ has to exceed a positive threshold in a regular network in order to reach a non-zero infection rate.

Lopez-Pintado (2004) uses the following approach to characterize situations where the solution for the steady state θ (and thus the steady-state infection rates $\rho(k)$ and ρ) will be non-zero.[65] Let

$$H(\theta) = \sum \frac{k P(k)}{< k >} \left(\frac{\lambda k \theta}{\lambda k \theta + 1} \right). \tag{6}$$

So fixed points of H correspond to steady-state distributions. Note that $H(0) = 0$, and that H is increasing and strictly concave in θ. Thus, in order for H to have another fixed point above $\theta = 0$, it must be that $H'(0) > 1$.[66] Let us check when this is true. Note that

$$H'(\theta) = \sum \frac{k P(k)}{< k >} \left(\frac{\lambda k}{(\lambda k \theta + 1)^2} \right).$$

That is, $H'(0) = \lambda E_P[k^2]/ < k >$. Thus, in order to have $\theta > 0$ (and thus a steady-state infection rate $\rho > 0$), we must have $\lambda > \frac{<k>}{<k^2>}$ (where $< k^2 >= E_P[k^2]$). In the regular network, this is the claimed threshold of $1/ < k >$, while in a scale-free network $< k^2 >$ is infinite and so the threshold is 0. For a Poisson degree distribution it falls somewhere between the two extremes.

The basic idea is that nodes with high degree can serve as a conduit for infection. Even very low infection rates can lead them to become infected as

[65] See also Pastor-Satorras and Vespignani (2001). Moreno, Pastor-Satorras, and Vespignani (2003) also allow for correlation among degrees in a family of distributions.

[66] Noting that H is continuous and increasing in θ, $H(0) = 0$, and $H(1) < 1$ (from equation (6), as this is the expectation of an expression that is always less than 1), it follows that there will be a fixed point above 0 whenever $H'(0) > 1$.

they have so many neighbors. They then can pass the infection on to a large number of nodes. The degree distribution then determines the relative makeup of the network in terms of nodes of different degrees. In a regular network, every node has the average degree. As we move to a Poisson distribution, we begin to see more of a spread in the distribution and some higher degree nodes and others of lesser degrees. This leads to a lower threshold at which infection can be sustained, as the higher degree nodes can begin to serve as the conduits as discussed above. As we continue to increase the spread in the degree distribution and move to a scale-free network, we have extremely high degree nodes, and very low degree nodes, and infections can be sustained at arbitrarily low net rates of contagion. Building on this methodology, Jackson and Rogers (2004) show one can completely order both the threshold rates of contagion needed to sustain an infection and the resulting infection rates in terms of the network's degree distribution, by ordering the distributions in the sense of second order stochastic dominance.[67] In terms of the thresholds for infection, it is clear from the above that as we change a network in the sense of second order stochastic dominance, then we increase $< k^2 >$ and so we decrease the threshold λ needed for an infection to be sustained ($\frac{<k>}{<k^2>}$).

What is a bit more subtle is that the behavior of the steady-state distributions as it relates to network structure exhibits very different features at low levels of λ than it does at high levels. See Jackson and Rogers (2004) for a detailed analysis, but the intuition can be expressed as follows. The change in infection rate due to a change in network structure (and in particular, a change in the degree distribution) comes from countervailing sources, as more extreme distributions have relatively more very high degree nodes and very low degree nodes. Very high degree nodes have high infection rates and serve as conduits for infection, thus putting upward pressure on average infection. Very low degree nodes have fewer neighbors to become infected by and thus tend to have lower infection rates than other nodes. As we make a mean-preserving spread in the degree distribution, the overall impact depends on how the (direct and indirect) increase in infection due to changing some nodes to have higher degree compares to the decrease in infection due to changing some nodes to have lower degree. When infection rates are already high, infection rates tend to increase less than linearly in the degree of a node (if simply due to the fact that they cannot increase above one). While if infection rates are low, then there is a more than offsetting increase in infection due to an increase of some nodes' degrees, as their increased degree not only increases their infection rates, but also leads to an increase in transmission.

Beyond the understanding of infection rates, the statistical characteristics of networks (e.g., comparing them in terms of stochastic dominance of degree distributions) can be used to deduce the impact that they have on behavior more generally (e.g., see Galeotti et al. (2005)).

---

[67] One can also order things in terms of first order stochastic dominance, but that relationship is quite obvious. If we simply increase the overall number of links then we will increase infection rates and decrease the threshold needed to sustain infection.

4.5   Public Goods

Another setting where we can see how network structure influences outcomes is the provision of local public goods.

For instance, consider a model analyzed by Bramoullé and Kranton (2005). Agents each choose an effort level $e_i \in [0, \infty)$. The agents are connected in a network, and they derive benefits not only from their own effort level but also from their neighbors – that is, the other agents to whom they are directly linked. For instance, think of agents each collecting information and then sharing that information with their direct neighbors. This includes a variety of applications, from consumers sharing information with their friends about products they have tried, to companies sharing information about production processes, to researchers sharing ideas and methods. For simplicity, the model only considers the benefits flowing to direct connections.

Agent i's utility in a network g when efforts $(e_1, \ldots, e_n)$ are exerted is

$$u_i(g, e) = b\left(e_i + \sum_{j \in N_i(g)} e_j\right) - ce_i,$$

where b is a continuously differentiable strictly concave function and $c > 0$ is a cost parameter.

Supposing that the solution $b'(e^*) = c$ is well defined and has $e^* > 0$, a great deal can be deduced about the structure of the equilibria. Given the payoff structure, it is clear that each neighborhood will have a total of at least e^* produced. Normalizing $e^* = 1$, this could happen in various ways. For instance, consider two agents connected to each other. Either one of them could exert effort 1 and the other 0, or they could each put in part of the effort. There is a sense in which the equilibria where some agents specialize and provide an effort of 1 and others provide an effort of 0 are more robust than the others.[68] Bramoullé and Kranton (2005) refer to these as specialized equilibria.

There is a complex structure to specialized equilibria, and there is a multiplicity of them. For instance, consider any maximal independent set of nodes.[69] Then have each node in the maximal independent set choose action e^* and all nodes outside of the set choose 0. As Bramoullé and Kranton point out, this is clearly an equilibrium, and moreover, all specialized equilibria must be of this form.

As this sort of public good model captures the substitutability of actions of neighbors that would apply to many settings, it provides a particularly interesting one for further study. The multiplicity of equilibria that Bramoullé

---

[68] See Bramoullé and Kranton (2005) for details. They examine a perturbation where each agent's actions can be perturbed by a small amount and then must have a best response process converge back to equilibrium.

[69] An independent set of nodes is a set such that no two nodes in the set are connected. A maximal independent set is an independent set which is not a strict subset of any other independent set. It is then easy to see that a maximal independent set is a set such that no two nodes inside the set are connected to each other and any node outside of the set is connected to at least one node inside the set.

and Kranton (2005) note, provides a hurdle in terms of making predictions about how network structure affects behavior, but there are well-defined ways in which some equilibria appear to be more natural or robust than others, and there is much that can be said about how behavior relates to structure in the context of large networks.[70]

4.6   Other Topics

There are many other areas that have been studied that relate network structure to outcomes, and ones that are of obvious social and economic relevance. For instance, Ballester, Calvo-Armengol, and Zenou (2004) examine how network structure influences criminal and other behavior in a model where there are local positive externalities (for instance learning or receiving help from friends that are also criminals) and global negative externalities (for instance overall competition). Within a class of such models they are able to completely characterize equilibrium outcomes and relate these to a measure of path-centrality in a network. This provides interesting new insights relating behavior to centrality in a network. Activity by players who are more central has more impact on other players' level of activity and leads to greater feedback effects.

There are also recent studies of risk-sharing on networks, which build on evidence from recent studies (e.g., Fafchamps and Lund (2003) and De Weerdt (2002)) that indicate that network structure plays a major role in determining how well risk is shared in rural societies. Theoretical studies have looked at two issues: how the network structure can be modified over time as an endogenous part of the risk-sharing (e.g., see Bloch, Genicot, and Ray (2005)), as well as how the network structure affects the equilibrium incentives (e.g., see Bramoullé and Kranton (2005b)).

There are also studies of play in games with complementarities in neighbors' actions, such as in the context of coordination games (e.g. Ellison (1993), Young (1998), Morris (2000), Jackson and Watts (2002b), Droste, Gilles, and Johnson (2000), Goyal and Vega-Redondo (2005), Feri (2003), Lopez-Pintado (2005)) as well as other structures with complementarities (e.g., Galeotti and Vega-Redondo (2005)). These studies have looked at both the change in play and co-evolution of the network itself. However, to date, most of the work has focused on very simple games (e.g., two-by-two coordination games), and there is much that is unknown beyond these special cases.

The wide variety of settings where network structure is an important determinant of behavior makes it clear that this is one of most wide open and important areas for further study.

5   WHITHER NOW?

As we have seen, there is much that we know about the structure and use of social networks, and a growing set of models to describe their emergence, roles,

---

[70] See Galeotti et al. (2005).

and importance in determining social outcomes. At the same time, as alluded to at many points in the discussion so far, there is much that we have yet to understand or model. Let me provide a partial list of some of what I see to be the most obvious and pressing issues for study.

- The above discussion of how network structure affects behavior illustrates that despite the difficult combinatorics faced in many applications, there is still much that we can deduce, at least by some approximation techniques. Given the wide variety of settings where social networks play a role, this continues to be a promising area and should also prove to be one of the main interfaces between theoretical and empirical work.

- One of the main points I made in the discussion of modeling of network formation is that there is a great potential to combine ideas from random graph models of network formation with those strategic formation models. These are largely complementary models and there look to be substantial gains in producing hybrids, both in terms of providing better fits of observed networks and leading to a better understanding of the tension between stability and efficiency.

- This also leads us to another aspect of network formation models that could be improved upon. Existing models generally deal with network formation at the link level. That is, either links are being randomly determined, or agents are deciding which links they would like to form. However, in many social settings, basic decisions are made that determine large sets of links all at once. For instance, the decision of which university to attend determines one's classmates and the decision of where to work determines one's colleagues, en masse. Models that deal with how such larger decisions impact social network structure are virtually nonexistent, and yet this is an essential part of what is often implied by the term "networking," as used in the vernacular regarding building social relationships.[71]

- There are also many facets of existing network formation models within the existing separate strands of random graph and game theoretic models that deserve further study.
  - With regards to models of strategic formation, there are questions of how to appropriately model equilibrium, given that the consent of parties might be needed to form links. Are social relationships considered one at a time, or many at once, and how does this depend on the setting? How coordinated are the decisions among groups of agents? To what extent are bargaining and/or transfers part of the process? Do agents take into account the impact their decisions will have on the further evolution of the network? These questions have

---

[71] See Ioannides and Soetevent (2005) for a first step in this direction. The rich literature on coalition formation (e.g., see the book by Demange and Wooders (2004) and references therein), could end up playing a role in these developments.

led to some recent research on the foundations of modeling strategic network formation,[72] of which a deeper understanding is needed.

- With regards to random networks, two things come to mind. First, there is great need for more detailed structural fitting of the models. For instance, as discussed above, "scale-free" networks are at best an idealization and benchmark and only some observed degree distributions exhibit such features, and even then only approximately and in one tail. Second, social networks exhibit much richer heterogeneity in the types of interactions and have correlation structures that are not adequately captured by existing models. In particular, things such as ethnicity, profession, and geography, produce neighborhood structures that are different from those predicted in existing models. Existing models have not really captured such features, and it is clear that such features should be very important in influencing opinion.[73]

• Another area that is crying out for attention, and just beginning to receive it, is the modeling of the strength of ties. The idea that social relationships are not 0-1 in their nature is quite clear, and was the center piece of one of the most influential social networks papers – Granovetter's (1973) article on the "strength of weak ties." Granovetter pointed out the importance of weaker social relationships (according to various measures of the level and/or frequency of interaction) in providing critical information. This work has produced volumes of empirical studies (e.g., see Granovetter (1995) and some of the references therein). Yet, until recently there were only a few models (Boorman (1975) and Montgomery (1991, 1992, 1994)) of how networks might form when both weak and strong ties are possible, and both of these models were specialized to the context of job contact networks. Recent interest in this subject has resulted in more general studies (e.g., Rogers (2005) and Bloch and Dutta (2005)) that investigate models where agents decide on how much effort or time to devote to their different relationships. A related issue is that relationships vary not only in their intensity, but also in their patterns over time. Interaction patterns tend to be sporadic. Understanding some of the timing of interactions, and more basically what is entailed in a relationship, might help shed better light on the differences between things such as strong and weak ties and how they differ across applications.

• The early models of how the allocation of total value or benefit among players depends on a network structure emerged from the cooperative game theory literature. The perspective that cooperative game theory

---

[72] See, for instance, Calvo-Armengol and Ilkilic (2004), Bloch and Jackson (2004), Tercieux and Vannetelbosch (2004), Ilkilic (2005), Slikker and van den Nouweland (2005), Chakrabarti (2005), and Dutta, Ghosal, and Ray (2005).

[73] See Watts, Dodds, and Newman (2002) for a model in this direction.

(even with graph-restricted games) gives to this problem is not always rich enough to address the issues that arise in a social network context (e.g., see Jackson (2005) for a discussion of this point). It is also clear, that the formation of social relationships often involves some bargaining. For instance, dowries are an obvious example. We have seen above how such bargaining can be instrumental in determining how efficient the resulting network structure is. Yet, the models that we have, both from a cooperative and a non-cooperative approach, are still far from giving us a full understanding of how value is shared among members of a social group, how this is determined by the network structure, and how this affects network formation.

- As the investigations in network analysis continue to multiply, so does the need for well-understood tools and methodology. For example, there are numerous measures of how "central" a node is in a network, ranging from simple comparisons of node degrees to detailed analyses of the eigenvalue structure of modified adjacency matrices. Such different measures are clearly identifying different facets of a node's role in a network. However, our current understanding of which (if any) existing measure is appropriate in which context comes almost entirely from seeing how measures operate on various examples and then judging which seems to be capturing what we are after.[74,75] Similarly, there are numerous other concepts in social network analysis that are associated with a variety of definitions and measures, and little to guide us in terms of understanding of the various properties that they possess. I am only aware of a few studies that examine the properties of different measures and definitions used in social network analysis,[76] while the extent of social network science clearly requires more.

- It is clear that the links that people maintain are different in nature. For example, they might relate to friends, relatives, co-workers, neighbors, or casual acquaintances. Each type of link might be active or useful under different circumstances, and might involve different costs

---

[74] See Borgatti (2003) for one study which tries to sort through some centrality measures.

[75] The same is true of identifying community structures in networks. A community structure is a partitioning of the nodes of a network into groups or "communities," with the idea that the nodes in the same community are somehow similar or equivalent according to some criterion. This can be useful in terms of simplifying a complex network into a simpler smaller network of relationships between communities. Many algorithms have been developed to identify community structures in networks, and yet most of what we know about the relative merits or deficiencies of various approaches and algorithms comes simply from examining whether they seem to give the "right" community structuring in various examples. An overview of some of this literature can be found in Newman (2004b) and a discussion of the importance of identifying the properties for identifying community structures can be found in Copic, Jackson, and Kirman (2005).

[76] For example, see van den Brink and Gilles (2000), Gomez et al. (2003), Monsuur and Storcken (2004), and Copic, Jackson, and Kirman (2005).

and benefits. Modeling the interaction between different overlapping network structures could potentially lead to new insights into things such as the dissemination of information throughout a population. For example, as Granovetter (1974) notes: "...much of the information about jobs that one receives through contact networks is a byproduct of other activities, and thus not appropriately costed out in a rational calculation of the costs and benefits of getting information."[77]

- As predictions from models continue to proliferate, experiments will provide an increasingly important testbed.[78] This is especially true of things like the dissemination of information, which can be very difficult to pinpoint outside of the controlled environment of a laboratory.
- The rich collection of case studies from the sociology literature is quite remarkable, partly because of the level of difficulty that researchers have historically faced in identifying network structures. This often involved interviews of subjects, or careful observation of some group over time, and limited both the scope and quality of the data that could be collected. Advances in both telephony and internet communication (including email), as well as computing technology, has recently made readily available large, detailed, and precise interaction patterns, which in some cases are less prone to measurement error and easier to work with. Moreover, such data sets give new dimensions to network structures as they have detailed time-stamps with which to study the dynamics of interaction. This greatly enhances the potential for empirical testing of increasingly complicated network models, and should also enrich the stable of questions for models to address.

References

[1] Adamic, L.A. (1999) "The Small World Web," *Proceedings of the ECDL* vol. 1696 of Lecture Notes in CS, 443–454.
[2] Albert, R., H. Jeong, and A. Barabási (1999) "Diameter of the World Wide Web," *Nature*, 401, 9 Sept., 130–131.
[3] Aizer, A. and J. Currie (2002) "Networks, Neighborhoods, and the Utilization of Publicly-Funded Prenatal Care in California," mimeo: UCLA.
[4] Anderson, R.M. and R.M. May (1988) Epidemiological parameters of HIV transmission," *Nature* 333:514–319.
[5] Aumann, R. and R. Myerson (1988) "Endogenous Formation of Links Between Players and Coalitions: An Application of the Shapley Value," In: Roth, A. (ed.) *The Shapley Value*, Cambridge University Press, 175–191.
[6] Bailey, N.T.J. (1975) *The Mathematical Theory of Infectious Diseases*, Griffin: London.

---

[77] I thank Yann Bramoullé for bringing this quote to my attention.

[78] Here I am referring to experiments with human subjects, although the term experiments is also used in some literatures to refer to simulations, often involving agent-based modeling techniques. These too are an increasingly relevant tool as technology now enables us to work with much richer models in simulations than we can handle analytically. See Kosfeld (2003) for some discussion and references.

[7] Bala, V. and S. Goyal (1998) "Learning from Neighbors," *Review of Economic Studies*, 65,595–621.

[8] Bala, V. and S. Goyal (2000a) "A Non-Cooperative Model of Network Formation," *Econometrica*, 68, pp 1181–1230.

[9] Ballester, C., A. Calvó-Armengol, and Y. Zenou (2003) "Who's Who in Networks: Wanted the Key Player," mimeo: Universitat Autonoma de Barcelona, IUI, GAINS, and CEPR.

[10] Barabási, A. (2002) *Linked*, Perseus Publishing: Cambridge, MA.

[11] Barabási A. and R. Albert (1999) "Emergence of Scaling in Random Networks," *Science*, 286: 509–512.

[12] Bearman, P., J. Moody, and K. Stovel (2004) "Chains of Affection: The Structure of Adolescent Romantic and Sexual Networks," manuscript, University of Chicago.

[13] Belleflamme, P. and F. Bloch (2002) "Market Sharing Agreements and Stable Collusive Networks," mimeo: University of London and GREQAM.

[14] Bianconi, G. and A.-L. Barabási (2001) "Competition and Multi-Scaling in Evolving Networks," *Europhys. Lett.* 54, 436–442.

[15] Bloch, F. and B. Dutta (2005) "Communication Networks with Endogenous Link Strength," mimeo: GREQAM.

[16] Bloch, F., G. Genicot, and D. Ray (2005) "Social Networks and Informal Insurance," mimeo: GREQAM, Georgetown University and NYU.

[17] Bloch, F. and M.O. Jackson (2003) "The Formation of Networks with Transfers among Players," forthcoming: *Journal of Economic Theory*, http://www.hss.caltech.edu/~jacksonm/nettransfer.pdf

[18] Bloch, F. and M.O. Jackson (2005) "Definitions of Equilibrium in Network Formation Games," http://www.hss.caltech.edu/~jacksonm/netequilibrium.pdf

[19] Bollobás, B. (2001) "Random Graphs: Second Edition," Cambridge University Press: Cambridge, UK.

[20] Boorman, S. (1975) "A Combinatorial Optimization Model for Transmission of Job Information through Contact Networks," *Bell Journal of Economics*, 6, 216–249.

[21] Bramoullé, Y. and R. Kranton (2005a) "A Network Model of Public Goods: Experimentation and Social Learning," mimeo: University of Toulouse and University of Maryland.

[22] Bramoullé, Y. and R. Kranton (2005b) "Risk-Sharing Networks," mimeo: University of Toulouse and University of Maryland.

[23] Brock, W. and S.N. Durlauf (2001) "Discrete Choice with Social Interactions," *Review of Economic Studies*, 68, 2, 235–260.

[24] Burt, R. (1992) *Structural Holes: The Social Structure of Competition,* Harvard University Press: Cambridge, MA.

[25] Callander, S. and C. Plott (2002) "Principles of Network Development and Evolution: An Experimental Study," mimeo: Caltech.

[26] Calvó-Armengol, A. (2004) "Job Contact Networks," *Journal of Economic Theory* 115, 191-206.

[27] Calvó-Armengol, A. and M.O. Jackson (2004) "The Effects of Social Networks on Employment and Inequality," *American Economic Review*, 94, 3, 426–454, June.

[28] Calvó-Armengol, A. and M.O. Jackson (2001) "Networks in Labor Markets: Wage and Employment Dynamics and Inequality," forthcoming: *Journal of Economic Theory*, http://www.hss.caltech.edu/~jacksonm/dyngen.pdf

[29] Calvó-Armengol, A. and M.O. Jackson (2005) "Like Father, Like Son: Labor Market Networks and Social Mobility," mimeo: Caltech and Universitat

Autònoma de Barcelona, http://www.hss.caltech.edu/~jacksonm/mobility.pdf, California Institute of Technology Working Paper #1242.

[30] Calvó-Armengol, A. and Y. Zenou (2004a) "Social Networks and Crime Decisions: The Role of Social Structure in Facilitating Delinquent Behavior," *International Economic Review*, 45, 935–954.

[31] Calvó-Armengol, A. and Y. Zenou (2004b) "Job Matching, Social Network and Word-of-Mouth Communication," *Journal of Urban Economics*, 57, 500–522.

[32] Carlson, J. and J. Doyle (1999), "Highly Optimized Tolerance: A Mechanism for Power Laws in Designed Systems," *Physical Review E*, 60(2), 1412–1427.

[33] Celen, B., S. Kariv, and A. Schotter (2004) "Learning in Networks: An Experimental Study," mimeo: Columbia, UC Berkeley, and NYU.

[34] Charness, G., M. Corominas-Bosch, and G.R. Frechette (2001) "Bargaining on Networks: An Experiment," forthcoming: *Journal of Economic Theory*.

[35] Charness, G. and M.O. Jackson (2004) "Group Play in Games and the Role of Consent in Network Formation," mimeo: University of California Santa Barbara and Caltech, http://www.hss.caltech.edu/~jacksonm/netgroup.pdf .

[36] Choi, S., D. Gale, and S. Kariv (2004) "Learning in Networks: An Experimental Study," mimeo: NYU and UC Berkeley.

[37] Cook, S. and M. Emerson (1978) "Power, Equity and Commitment in Exchange Networks," *American Sociological Review*, 43, 721–739.

[38] Copic, J., M.O. Jackson, and A. Kirman (2005) "Identifying Community Structures from Network Data," http://www.hss.caltech.edu/~jacksonm/netcommunity.pdf

[39] Corbae, D. and J. Duffy (2000) "Experiments with Network Economies," mimeo: University of Pittsburgh.

[40] Currarini, S. and M. Morelli (2000) "Network Formation with Sequential Demands," *Review of Economic Design*, 5, 229–250.

[41] De Weerdt, J. (2002) "Risk-Sharing and Endogenous Network Formation," mimeo: K.U. Leuven.

[42] Demange, G. (2004) "On Group Stability in Hierarchies and Networks," *Journal of Political Economy*, 112, 754–778.

[43] DeMarzo, P., D. Vayanos, and J. Zwiebel (2003) "Persuasion Bias, Social Influence, and Unidimensional Opinions," *Quarterly Journal of Economics*, 118(3), 909–968.

[44] Deroïan, F. (2003) "Farsighted Strategies in the Formation of a Communication Network," *Economics Letters*, 80, 343–349.

[45] Dorogovtsev, S.N. and J.F.F. Mendes (2001) "Scaling Properties of Scale-Free Evolving Networks: Continuous Approach," *Physical Review Letters*, 63.

[46] Droste, E., R.P. Gilles, and C. Johnson (2000) "Evolution of Conventions in Endogenous Social Networks," mimeo: Virginia Tech.

[47] Dutta, B., S. Ghosal, and D. Ray (2005) "Farsighted Network Formation," *Journal of Economic Theory*, 122, 143–164.

[48] Dutta, B. and M.O. Jackson (2000) "The Stability and Efficiency of Directed Communication Networks," *Review of Economic Design*, 5, 254–272.

[49] Dutta, B. and M.O. Jackson (2003) "On the Formation of Networks and Groups," in *Networks and Groups: Models of Strategic Formation*, edited by B. Dutta and M.O. Jackson, Springer-Verlag: Heidelberg.

[50] Dutta, B. and M.O. Jackson (2003b) editors: *Networks and Groups: Models of Strategic Formation*, Springer-Verlag: Heidelberg.

[51] Dutta, B. and S. Mutuswami (1997) "Stable Networks," *Journal of Economic Theory*, 76, 322–344.

[52] Dutta, B., A. van den Nouweland, and S. Tijs (1998) "Link Formation in Cooperative Situations," *International Journal of Game Theory*, 27, 245–256.

[53] Economides, N. (1996) "The Economics of Networks," *International Journal of Industrial Organization,* 16, 4, 673–699.

[54] Eeckhout, J. (2004) "Gibrat's Law for (All) Cities," *American Economic Review*, 94, 5, 1429–1451.

[55] Ellison, G. (1993) "Learning, Local Interaction, and Coordination," *Econometrica*, 61, 1047–1071.

[56] Ellison, G. and D. Fudenberg (1995) "Word-of-Mouth Communication and Social Learning," *The Quarterly Journal of Economics*, 110, 93–126.

[57] Erdös, P. and A. Rényi (1959) "On Random Graphs," *Publicationes Mathematical*, 6, 290–297.

[58] Erdös, P. and A. Rényi (1960) "On the Evolution of Random Graphs," *Publication of the Mathematical Institute of the Hungarian Academy of Sciences*, 5, 17–61.

[59] Erdös, P. and A. Rényi (1961) "On the Strength of Connectedness of a Random Graph," *Acta Math. Acad. Sci. Hungar.*, 12, 261–267.

[60] Fabrikant, A., E. Koutsoupias, and C. Papadimitriou (2002) "Heuristically Optimized Tradeoffs: A New Paradigm for Power Laws in the Internet," *Proceedings of the 29th International Colloquium on Automata, Languages, and Programming.*

[61] Fafchamps, M. and S. Lund (2003) "Risk-Sharing Networks in Rural Philippines," *Journal of Development Economics*, 71, 261–287.

[62] Falk, A. and M. Kosfeld (2003) "It's All About Connections: Evidence on Network Formation," mimeo: University of Zurich.

[63] Feri, F. (2003) "Network Formation with Endogenous Decay," Università Ca Foscari, Venezia.

[64] Fontaine, F. (2004) "Why Are Similar Workers Paid Differently? The Role of Social Networks," mimeo: Eurequa-CNRS.

[65] Frank, O. and D. Strauss (1986) "Markov Graphs," *Journal of the American Statistical Association*, 81, 832–842.

[66] Freeman, L.C. (2004) *The Development of Social Network Analysis: A Study in the Sociology of Science*, Empirical Press.

[67] Furusawa, T. and H. Konishi (2005) "Free Trade Networks," *Japanese Economic Review*, 56, 144–164.

[68] Gale, D. and S. Kariv (2003) "Bayesian Learning in Social Networks," *Games and Economic Behavior* 45(2), 329–346.

[69] Galeotti, A. (2005) "Consumers' Networks and Search Equilibria," mimeo: Caltech.

[70] Galeotti, A. and F. Vega-Redondo (2005) "Local Externalities and Complex Networks," mimeo: University of Essex.

[71] Galeotti, A., S. Goyal, M.O. Jackson, F. Vega-Redondo, and L. Yariv (2005) "Network Games," http://www.hss.caltech.edu/~jacksonm/netinfo-games.pdf

[72] Gilles, R.P. and S. Sarangi (2003) "The Role of Trust in Costly Network Formation," mimeo: Virginia Tech and Louisiana State University.

[73] Glaeser, E., B. Sacerdote, and J. Scheinkman (1996) "Crime and Social Interactions," *Quarterly Journal of Economics*, 111, 507–548.

[74] Goeree J.K., A. Riedl, and A. Ule (2003) "In Search of Stars: Network Formation among Heterogeneous Agents," mimeo: California Institute of Technology.

[75] Goyal, S. (2004) "Learning in Networks," in *Group Formation in Economics: Networks, Clubs, and Coalitions*, edited by G. Demange and M. Wooders, Cambridge University Press: Cambridge.

[76] Goyal, S. and S. Joshi (2000) "Networks of Collaboration in Oligopoly," forthcoming: *Games and Economic Behavior.*

[77] Goyal, S. and S. Joshi (2003) "Unequal Connections," mimeo: University of London and George Washington University.

[78] Goyal, S., M. van der Leij, and J.-L. Moraga-González (2003). "Economics: An Emerging Small World?," preprint: University of Essex.

[79] Goyal, S. and F. Vega-Redondo (2005) "Learning, Network Formation and Coordination," forthcoming: *Games and Economic Behavior*.

[80] Granovetter, M. (1973) "The Strength of Weak Ties," *American Journal of Sociology*, 78, 1360–1380.

[81] Granovetter, M. [1974](1995) *Getting a Job: A Study of Contacts and Careers*, 2nd edition, University of Chicago Press: Chicago.

[82] Grossman, J. W. (2000) "The Evolution of the Mathematical Research Collaboration Graph," *Proceedings of 33rd Southeastern Conference on Combinatorics* (Congressus Numerantium, 158, 2002, 201–212).

[83] Haller, H. and S. Sarangi (2005) "Nash Networks with Heterogeneous Links," *Mathematical Social Sciences*, 50, 181–201.

[84] Hojman, D. and A. Szeidl (2004) "Endogenous Networks, Social Games, and Evolution," forthcoming: *Games and Economic Behavior*.

[85] Ilkilic, R. (2004) "Pairwise Stability: Externalities and Existence," mimeo: Universitat Autonoma de Barcelona.

[86] Ioannides, Y.M. (1997) "Evolution of Trading Structures," in *The Economy as an Evolving Complex System II*, edited by B. Arthur S. Durlauf and D. Lane, Addison-Wesley, 129–167.

[87] Ioannides, Y.M. (2004) "Random Graphs and Social Networks: An Economics Perspective," mimeo: Tufts University.

[88] Ioannides, Y.M. and L. Datcher Loury (2004) "Job Information Networks, Neighborhood Effects and Inequality," *Journal of Economic Literature*, 42, 1056–1093.

[89] Jackson, M.O. (2003) "The Stability and Efficiency of Economic and Social Networks," in *Advances in Economic Design*, edited by S. Koray and M. Sertel, Springer-Verlag: Heidelberg, and reprinted in *Networks and Groups: Models of Strategic Formation*, edited by B. Dutta and M.O. Jackson, Springer-Verlag: Heidelberg.

[90] Jackson, M.O. (2004) "A Survey of Models of Network Formation: Stability and Efficiency," in *Group Formation in Economics; Networks, Clubs and Coalitions*, edited by Gabrielle Demange and Myrna Wooders, Cambridge University Press: Cambridge, U.K.

[91] Jackson, M.O. (2005a) "Allocation Rules for Network Games," *Games and Economic Behavior*, 51, 1, 128–154.

[92] Jackson, M.O. (2005b) "The Economics of Social Networks," Lecture prepared for the 9th World Congress of the Econometric Society, August 2005, forthcoming in the *Proceedings of the 9th World Congress of the Econometric Society*, edited by Richard Blundell, Whitney Newey, and Torsten Persson, Cambridge University Press, http://www.hss.caltech.edu/~jacksonm/netect.pdf

[93] Jackson, M.O. and B.W. Rogers (2004) "Search in the Formation of Large Networks: How Random Are Socially Generated Networks?," preprint: Caltech, http://www.hss.caltech.edu/~jacksonm/netpower.pdf

[94] Jackson, M.O. and B. Rogers (2005) "The Economics of Small Worlds," *Journal of the European Economic Association*, (Papers and Proceedings) 3(2–3): 617–627.

[95] Jackson, M.O. and A. van den Nouweland (2005) "Strongly Stable Networks," *Games and Economic Behavior*, 51: 420–444.

[96] Jackson, M.O. and A. Watts (2001) "The Existence of Pairwise Stable Networks," *Seoul Journal of Economics*, 14, 3, 299–321.

[97] Jackson, M.O. and A. Watts (2002a) "The Evolution of Social and Economic Networks," *Journal of Economic Theory*, 106, 2, 265–295.

[98] Jackson, M.O. and A. Watts (2002b) "On the Formation of Interaction Networks in Social Coordination Games," *Games and Economic Behavior*, 41, 2, 265–291.

[99] Jackson, M.O. and A. Wolinsky (1996) "A Strategic Model of Social and Economic Networks," *Journal of Economic Theory*, 71, 1, 44–74.

[100] Jackson, M.O. and L. Yariv (2005) "Diffusion in Social Networks," preprint: Caltech, http://www.hss.caltech.edu/~jacksonm/nettipping.pdf.

[101] Johnson, C. and R.P. Gilles (2000) "Spatial Social Networks," *Review of Economic Design*, 5, 273–300.

[102] Kakade, S.M., M. Kearns, and L.E. Ortiz (2004) "Graphical Economics," COLT.

[103] Kakade, S.M., M. Kearns, L.E. Ortiz, R. Pemantle, and S. Suri (2004) "Economic Properties of Social Networks," *Proceedings of Neural and Information Processing Systems* (NIPS), MIT Press.

[104] R. Kannan, L. Ray, and S. Sarangi (2005) "The Structure of Information Networks," forthcoming: *Economic Theory*.

[105] Kent, D. (1978) *The Rise of the Medici: Faction in Florence 1426–1434*, Oxford University Press: Oxford.

[106] Kirman, A.P. (1983) "Communication in Markets: A Suggested Approach," *Economics Letters*, 12, 1–5.

[107] Kirman, A. (1997) "The Economy as an Evolving Network," *Journal of Evolutionary Economics*, 7, 339–353.

[108] Kirman, A., C. Oddou, and S. Weber (1986) "Stochastic Communication and Coalition Formation," *Econometrica*, 54, 129–138.

[109] Kleinberg, J.M., S.R. Kumar, P. Raghavan, S. Rajagopalan, and A. Tomkins, (1999) "The Web as a Graph: Measurements, Models and Methods," in Proceedings of the International Conference on Combinatorics and Computing, *Lecture Notes in Computer Science*, 1627, 1–18.

[110] Klemm, K. and V.M. Eguíluz (2002a) "Growing Scale-Free Networks with Small World Behavior," *Physical Review E*, 65(3), 036123.

[111] Klemm, K. and V.M. Eguíluz (2002b) "Highly Clustered Scale-Free Networks," *Physical Review E*, 65(5), 057102.

[112] Kochen, M. (1989) *The Small World*, Albex: Norwood, NJ.

[113] Kosfeld, M. (2003) "Network Experiments," mimeo: University of Zurich.

[114] Kranton, R. and D. Minehart (2001) "A Theory of Buyer-Seller Networks," *American Economic Review*, 91 (3): 485–508.

[115] Krapivsky, P.L. and S. Redner (2002) "A Statistical Physics Perspective on Web Growth," *Computer Networks*, 39, 3, 261–276.

[116] Krishnan, P. and E. Sciubba (2005) "Links and Architecture in Village Networks," mimeo: University of Cambridge and Birkbeck College.

[117] Kumar, R., P. Raghavan, S. Rajagopalan, D. Sivakumar, A. Tomkins, and E. Upfal (2000) "Stochastic Models for the Web Graph," *FOCS 2000*.

[118] Lavezzi, A.M. and N. Meccheri (2005) "Social Networks in Labor Markets: The Effects of Symmetry, Randomness, and Exclusion on Output and Inequality," mimeo: University of Pisa.

[119] Lopez-Pintado, D. (2005) "Diffusion and Coordination in Random Networks," mimeo: Columbia University.

[120] Lopez-Pintado, D. (2004) "Contagion in Complex Networks," Universidad de Alicante.

[121] Lotka, A.J. (1926) "The Frequency Distribution of Scientific Productivity," *Journal of the Washington Academy of Sciences*, 16, 317–323.

[122] MacRae, J. (1960) "Direct Factor Analysis of Sociometric Data," *Sociometry*, 23, 360–371.

[123] Mauleon A., J. Sempere-Monerris, and V.J. Vannetelbosch (2005) "Networks of Manufacturers and Retailers," mimeo: CORE.

[124] McBride, M. (2003) "Imperfect Monitoring in Communication Networks," forthcoming: *Journal of Economic Theory*.

[125] Meléndez-Jiménez, M.A. (2004) "Network Formation and Coordination: Bargaining and the Division of Link Costs," mimeo: Universidad de Málaga.

[126] Milgram, S. (1967) "The Small-World Problem," *Psychology Today*, 2, 60–67.

[127] Mitzenmacher, M. (2004) "A Brief History of Generative Models for Power Law and Lognormal Distributions," manuscript: http://www.eecs.harvard.edu/~michaelm/ListByYear.html.

[128] Mobius, M.M. and T.S. Rosenblatt (2003) "Experimental Evidence on Trading Favors in Networks," mimeo: Harvard University.

[129] Monasson, R. (1999) "Diffusion, Localization and Dispersion Relations on 'Small-World' Lattices," *Eur. Phys. J. B* 12, 555–567.

[130] Monsuur, H. and T. Storcken (2002) "Centrality Orderings in Social Networks," in *Chapters in Game Theory: In Honor of Stef Tijs*, Theory and Decision Library Series C, vol. 31, Game Theory, Mathematical Programming and Operations Research, 157–181.

[131] Montgomery, J. (1991) "Social Networks and Labor Market Outcomes," *The American Economic Review*, 81, 1408–1418.

[132] Montgomery, J. (1992) "Job Search and Network Composition: Implications of the Strength-of-Weak-Ties Hypothesis," *American Sociological Review*, 57, 586–596.

[133] Montgomery, J. (1994) "Weak Ties, Employment, and Inequality: An Equilibrium Analysis," *American Journal of Sociology*, 99, 1212–1236.

[134] Moreno, Y., R. Pastor-Satorras, and A. Vespignani (2002) "Epidemic Outbreaks in Complex Heterogeneous Networks," *Eur. Phys. J. B*, 26, 521.

[135] Morris, S. (2000) "Contagion," *Review of Economic Studies*, 67: 57–78.

[136] Mutuswami, S. and E. Winter (2002) "Subscription Mechanisms for Network Formation," *Journal of Economic Theory*, 106, 242–264.

[137] Myers, C. and G.P. Shultz (1951) *The Dynamics of a Labor Market*, Prentice-Hall: NY.

[138] Myerson, R. (1977) "Graphs and Cooperation in Games," *Math. Operations Research*, 2, 225–229.

[139] Navarro, N. (2002) "Fair Allocation in Evolving Networks," mimeo: Universidad Carlos III de Madrid.

[140] Newman, M. (2003), "The Structure and Function of Complex Networks," *SIAM Review*, 45, 167–256.

[141] Newman, M. (2004a) "Coauthorship Networks and Patterns of Scientific Collaboration," *Proceedings of the National Academy of Sciences*, 101: 5200–5205.

[142] Newman, M.E.J. (2004b) "Detecting Community Structure in Networks," *Physical Review E* 69, 066133.

[143] Newman, M.E.J. and D. J. Watts (1999) "Renormalization Group Analysis of the Small-World Network Model," *Phys. Lett. A* 263, 341–346.

[144] Nieva, R. (2002) "An Extension of the Aumann-Myerson Solution for Reasonable Empty-Core Games," mimeo: Rochester Institute of Technology.

[145] Qin, C.-Z. (1996) "Endogenous Formation of Cooperation Structures," *Journal of Economic Theory*, 69, 218–226.

[146] Ochs, J. and I.-U. Park (2004) "Overcoming the Coordination Problem: Dynamic Formation of Networks," mimeo: University of Pittsburgh.

[147] Ozsoylev, H.N. (2003) "Knowing thy Neighbor: Rational Expectations and Social Interaction in Financial Markets," mimeo: University of Minnesota.

[148] Padgett, J.F. and C.K. Ansell (1993) "Robust Action and the Rise of the Medici, 1400–1434," *American Journal of Sociology*, 98: 1259–1319.

[149] Page, F. and S. Kamat (2004) "Farsighted Stability in Network formation," in *Group Formation in Economics: Networks, Clubs, and Coalitions*, edited by G. Demange and M. Wooders, Cambridge University Press: Cambridge.

[150] Page, F., M. Wooders, and S. Kamat (2005) "Networks and Farsighted Stability," *Journal of Economic Theory*, 120(2), 257–269.

[151] Pantz, K. and A. Ziegelmeyer (2003) "An Experimental Study of Network Formation," mimeo: Max Planck Institute.

[152] Pareto, V. (1896) "Cours d'Economie Politique." Droz, Geneva Switzerland.

[153] Pastor-Satorras, R. and A. Vespignani (2000) "Epidemic Spreading in Scale-Free Networks," *Physical Review Letters*, 86:14, 3200-3203.

[154] Pastor-Satorras, R. and A. Vespignani (2001) "Epidemic Dynamics and Endemic States in Complex Networks," *Phys. Rev. E* 63, 066117.

[155] Pattison, P.E. and S. Wasserman (1999) "Logit Models and Logistic Regressions for Social Networks: II Multivariate Relations," *British Journal of Mathematical and Statistical Psychology*, 52, 169–193.

[156] Pellizari, M. (2004) "Do Friends and Relatives Really Help in Getting a Job?" LSE CPE DP 623, March.

[157] Pennock, D.M., G.W. Flake, S. Lawrence, E.J. Glover, and C.L. Giles (2002) "Winners Don't Take All: Characterizing the Competition for Links on the Web," *PNAS*, 99:8, 5207–5211.

[158] Price, D.J.S. (1965) "Networks of Scientific Papers," *Science*, 149, 510–515.

[159] Price, D.J.S. (1976) "A General Theory of Bibliometric and Other Cumulative Advantage Processes," *J. Amer. Soc. Inform. Sci.* 27, 292–306.

[160] Rapoport A. (1963) "Mathematical Models of Social Interaction," in *Handbook of Mathematical Psychology*, edited by R.D. Luce, R.R. Bush, and E. Galanter, Wiley: New York, 2, 493–579.

[161] Rees, A. and G.P. Shultz (1970) *Workers in an Urban Labor Market*, University of Chicago Press: Chicago.

[162] Reiss, A.J. (1980) "Understanding Changes in Crime Rates," in *Indicators of Crime and Criminal Justice: Quantitative Studies*, Bureau of Justice Statistics, Washington, D.C.

[163] Reiss, A.J. (1988) "Co-Offending and Criminal Careers," in *Crime and Justice: A Review of Research, vol. 10*, edited by Tonry and Morris, University of Chicago Press: Chicago.

[164] Rogers, B.W. (2005) "A Strategic Theory of Interdependent Status," mimeo: Caltech.

[165] Simmel, G. (1908) "Sociology: Investigations on the Forms of Sociation," Duncker & Humblot: Berlin, Germany.

[166] Simon, H. (1955) "On a Class of Skew Distribution Functions," *Biometrika*, 42(3,4): 425–440.

[167] Skyrms, B. and R. Pemantle (2000) "A Dynamic Model of Social Network Formation," *Proceedings of the National Academy of Sciences*, 97, 9340–9346.

[168] Slikker, M. and A. van den Nouweland (2001) *Social and Economic Networks in Cooperative Game Theory*, Kluwer.

[169] Slikker, M., and A. van den Nouweland (2005) "Pair Stable Networks,"

[170] Tercieux, O. and V. Vannetelbosch (2004) "A Characterization of Stochastically Stable Networks," mimeo: Université catholique de Louvain.

[171] Tesfatsion, L. (1997) "A Trade Network Game with Endogenous Partner Selection," in *Computational Approaches to Economic Problems*, edited by H. Amman et al., Kluwer Academic Publishers, 249–269.

[172] Topa, G. (2001) "Social Interactions, Local Spillovers and Unemployment," *Review of Economic Studies*, 68, 261–296.

[173] Ule, A. and A. Riedl (2004) "Cooperation in Network Formation Games," mimeo: CREED.

[174] Uzzi, B. (1996) "The Sources and Consequences of Embeddedness for the Economic Performance of Organizations: The Network Effect," *American Sociological Review*, 61.

[175] van den Brink, R. and R.P. Gilles. (2000) "Measuring Domination in Directed Networks," *Social Networks*, 22: 141–157.

[176] van den Nouweland, A. (2004) "Static Networks and Coalition Formation," in *Group Formation in Economics: Networks, Clubs, and Coalitions*, edited by G. Demange and M. Wooders, Cambridge University Press: Cambridge.

[177] Vázquez, A. (2003) "Growing Network with Local Rules: Preferential Attachment, Clustering Hierarchy, and Degree Correlations," *Physical Review E*, 67(5), 056104.

[178] Wang, P. and A. Watts (2002) "Formation of Buyer-Seller Trade Networks in a Quality-Differentiated Product Market," mimeo: Penn State University and Southern Illinois University.

[179] Wasserman, S. and K. Faust (1994) *Social Network Analysis: Methods and Applications*, Cambridge University Press.

[180] Wasserman, S. and P. Pattison (1996) "Logit Models and Logistic Regressions for Social Networks: I. An Introduction to Markov Graphs and P*," *Psychometrika*, 61:401–425.

[181] Watts, A. (2001) "A Dynamic Model of Network Formation," *Games and Economic Behavior*, 34, 331–341.

[182] Watts, D.J. (1999) *Small Worlds: The Dynamics of Networks between Order and Randomness*, Princeton University Press.

[183] Watts, D.J. and S. Strogatz (1998), "Collective Dynamics of 'Small-World' Networks," *Nature,* 393, 440–442.

[184] Watts, D.J., P.S. Dodds, and M.E.J. Newman (2002) "Identity and Search in Social Networks," *Science* 296, 1302–1305.

[185] Weisbuch, G., A. Kirman, and D. Herreiner (2000) "Market Organization," *Economica*, 110, 411–436.

[186] Young, H.P. (1998) *Individual Strategy and Social Structure*, Princeton University Press: Princeton.

[187] Yule, G. (1925), "A Mathematical Theory of Evolution Based on the Conclusions of Dr. J. C. Willis," *F.R.S. Philosophical Transactions of the Royal Society of London (Series B)*, 213: 21–87.

[188] Zipf, G. (1949) *Human Behavior and the Principle of Least Effort*, Addison-Wesley: Cambridge, MA.

CHAPTER 2

Multi-Contracting Mechanism Design
David Martimort[1]

1 INTRODUCTION

Incentive Theory is by now a mature field that has deeply changed our view of organizations and markets over the last thirty years or so. In the conceptual framework proposed early on by Hurwicz (1972) and largely inspired by the planification literature, the whole economy is ruled by a *single (or complete) grand-contract*. Within this framework, decentralized information and strategic behavior by informed agents at the periphery of the organization can easily be handled by means of simple incentive constraints that fully describe the set of feasible allocations available under asymmetric information. Once equipped with the Revelation Principle,[2] modelers are able to describe the feasible set and assess the performance of an organization with a given objective function. The analysis can then proceed to determine the properties of the *optimal contract* chosen by a planner running this organization. Finally, one may also investigate the mechanisms that can be used to implement this outcome in practice.

This modelling framework is useful to understand how simple organizations and markets evolve in isolation from any external influence. Economists agree to recognize that a convenient set of modelling tools and theorems is now available to describe the simple contractual relationship between a buyer and a seller or between a regulator and regulated firms. We are also confident that the theory of auctions is a well-established body of literature which explains in detail one of the most basic resource allocation problems.

[1] I benefitted from many discussions on the topic of this lecture and on related issues with several coauthors, among which Antoine Faure-Grimaud, Marc Ivaldi, Fahad Khalil, and Humberto Moreira. Special thanks of course to Lars Stole, whose collaboration has shaped much of my views on multi-contracting mechanism design. Vianney Dequiedt, Denis Gromb, Jérôme Pouyet, Wilfried Sand-Zantman and Aggey Semenov kindly provided comments on an earlier version. I was lucky to discuss many of the ideas developed below with Jean-Jacques Laffont. Many thanks to Thomas Palfrey for his useful discussion at the 2005 World Congress of the Econometric Society and to Torsten Persson for his comments.
[2] Gibbard (1973), Green and Laffont (1977), Dasgupta, Hammond and Maskin (1978) and Myerson (1979).

Despite these successes, Incentive Theory has repeatedly been subject to criticisms coming from various horizons. The first line of criticism is external to the field and can be best summarized by the view held by some sociologists who argue that "[Incentive] Theory assumes that social life is [only] a series of contracts."[3] In my view, the discomfort of other social scientists towards Incentive Theory stems in part from the fact that it most often either focuses on the microeconomic bilateral relationship within a single principal-agent pair taken in isolation or, at the other extreme, it embraces the whole economy within a single grand-contract. By taking these two polar views, Incentive Theory fails to provide an intermediate perspective on the interactions between organizations and markets, which is the focus of organizational theorists in other fields of social sciences.

The second line of criticism is internal to economic theory. It comes from our skepticism towards the grand-contracting approach, which puts excessive emphasis on the *completeness* of the contract. Indeed, one of the most basic assumptions underlying the Revelation Principle is what Palfrey (1992) coined as the *control assumption*. This assumption stipulates that the planner can control all communications that agents of the organization can undertake. When such control is not feasible, the economy can no longer be ruled by a single mechanism but by complex interactions among multiple mechanism designers. In this context, contracts are necessarily *incomplete* in the sense that they cannot prevent an agent from contracting with other principals. Any departure from the outcome that could have been achieved under centralized contracting can then be associated to this incompleteness. The difference between the outcomes with and without centralized contracting gives us a measure of the corresponding transaction costs. Such analysis is a first step towards some comparative analysis showing how different contractual and organizational forms might reduce those transaction costs.

This survey covers a body of literature that has studied interactions among mechanism designers with an emphasis on common agency, a major example of multi-contracting. Under common agency, several principals contract with a common agent to influence his decision-making. This setting is relevant to discuss the organization of the firm as a nexus of contracts linking its management with various stakeholders be they shareholders, lenders, regulators, customers or suppliers. It also helps understanding the organization of the government as a collection of legislative committees, bureaus and regulatory agencies that do not necessarily cooperate. Section 2 provides more examples.

Ideally, a complete survey of multi-contracting should also cover hierarchical contracting, competition between hierarchies and collusion within organizations. Space constraints mean that I will only incidentally touch on these issues in passing. I will also focus on adverse selection and put aside moral hazard issues despite their importance. Nevertheless, common agency already

---

[3] From one of the leading organizational theorists, Perrow (1986).

offers a nice overview of some of the theoretical inquiries that the analysis of multi-contracting environments requires. Those inquiries can be classified as follows.

- On the positive side, one can take as given the existence of multi-contracting structures[4] and ask the following questions: What is the set of mechanisms available to competing principals? Which allocations are implementable as contract equilibria? How much welfare is lost when centralized contracting is absent? Do we get a measure of the transaction costs associated with multi-contracting?
- In a more normative perspective, and given that multi-contracting prevails both within and across organizations, one may look for some rationale behind those structures. Since centralized contracting internalizes the contractual externalities that arise under multi-contracting, the difficulty consists then in proving the latter's optimality or, at least, its good performances in specific contractual environments, which are necessarily constrained in some way to limit the benefits of centralized contracting.

Much of the research in the field has focused on the first issues. These efforts are covered in Sections 3 to 5 below. Much less effort has been devoted to the more normative issues which are addressed in Section 6. Section 7 briefly concludes and proposes alleys for further research.

2   EXAMPLES AND MODELLING ISSUES

I shall start by presenting a few examples of common agency models. In any such model, several principals P_i ($i \in \{1, \ldots, n\}$) want to influence a decision taken on their behalf by a common agent A. My goal here is to briefly highlight some of the basic issues arising in such modelling.

- **Example 1: Regulation.** Consider the regulation of a public utility by n distinct regulators (principals). For instance, one agency may be an economic regulator concerned by consumer surplus. Another one may be an environmental regulator controlling pollution. Regulators have specific objective functions given by

$$V_i = S_i(q) - t_i, \qquad i \in \{1, \ldots, n\}, \tag{1}$$

where q is the firm's output. This output may be multidimensional and of the form $q = (q_1, \ldots, q_n)$ where q_i might itself be an array of activities controlled

---

[4] For instance, competing regulatory agencies may receive their mandates at different points in time or from different governments and the allocation of powers between them is a consequence of either history or geography. Anti-trust policies may also preclude centralized contracting between competing retailers and their common manufacturer.

by regulator P_i. The surplus function $S_i(\cdot)$ is strictly concave in q, and captures the (algebraic) benefit of the firm's activity from regulator P_i's point of view. t_i is a regulatory transfer paid to the firm by P_i. The firm's profit can be written as:

$$U = \sum_{i=1}^{n} t_i - \theta C(q) \tag{2}$$

where $C(q)$ is a cost function, which is increasing and convex. The efficiency parameter θ is drawn from a cumulative distribution $F(\cdot)$ on the interval $\Theta = [\underline{\theta}, \bar{\theta}]$ with an atomless and everywhere positive density $f(\cdot)$. Depending on the informational environment under scrutiny, the parameter θ might either be private information for the firm or not. This information structure is common knowledge.

The reader familiar with the regulation literature will have recognized an extension of the framework developed by Baron and Myerson (1982). The only difference is the fragmented nature of regulatory control that is shared among several government units. I will be silent on the definition of social welfare underlying the regulators' objectives. Social welfare might be defined as the sum of these objectives if regulators have clear and separable objectives. However, regulatory agencies could also have overlapping missions.[5] In any case, it is useful to consider a hypothetical setting where all principals are merged into a single entity with the objective function $\sum_{i=1}^{n} V_i$.

Under complete information, efficiency requires to maximize the joint-payoff of the grand-coalition made of all principals and the agent. The first-best output $q^*(\theta)$ satisfies:

$$\sum_{i=1}^{n} S_i'(q^*(\theta)) = \theta C'(q^*(\theta)). \tag{3}$$

For future reference, it is also useful to describe the cooperative solution achieved *under asymmetric information* had all principals merged as one. The techniques to derive this second-best (or *interim efficient* in the sense of Holmström and Myerson (1983)) solution are by now standard.[6] The cooperative outcome $q^C(\theta)$ satisfies:

$$\sum_{i=1}^{n} S_i'(q^C(\theta)) = \left(\theta + \frac{F(\theta)}{f(\theta)}\right) C'(q^C(\theta)). \tag{4}$$

Under asymmetric information, the efficiency parameter θ is replaced by a virtual efficiency parameter $\theta + \frac{F(\theta)}{f(\theta)}$ that takes into account the fact that the agent's information rent is costly from the merged entity's viewpoint.

---

[5] An extreme case would be when social welfare maximization is replicated among the different agencies. Then, we have $S_1(\cdot) = \cdots = S_n(\cdot)$.

[6] See Laffont and Martimort (2002, Chapter 3).

- **Example 2: Lobbying.** Several lobbying groups (principals) want to influence a decision-maker (the common agent) who chooses the level of a public good or, more generally, a policy variable (a regulated price, an import tariff, or a number of permits). These principals non-cooperatively offer contributions to influence the agent's choice. Their objective functions are given by (1). The agent's utility function is again as in (2) where $C(q)$ should now be viewed as the opportunity cost of choosing a quantity q of public good.[7] Contrary to Example 1 where regulatory contracts are mandatory, the agent can now reject a subset of the contributions.

- **Example 3: Vertical Contracting.** Two competing retailers P_1 and P_2 (the principals) compete on a final market. They produce the final good with a one-to-one Leontieff technology using a common input produced by a manufacturer (the common agent). The agent's reservation payoff is, for simplicity, normalized to zero. The retailers' and manufacturer's profit functions are respectively given by:

$$V_i = P(q_i + q_{-i})q_i - t_i, \quad i = 1, 2, \quad \text{and} \quad U = t_1 + t_2 - \theta C(q_1 + q_2)$$

where the inverse demand function satisfies $P' < 0$ and $P'' \leq 0$, and the manufacturer's cost function is again increasing and strictly convex ($C' > 0, C'' > 0$). The manufacturer may either accept both offers, none or only one.

An efficient outcome maximizes now the profit of the vertically and horizontally integrated structure. The (symmetric) efficient production vector $q^*(\theta) = q_1^*(\theta) = q_2^*(\theta)$ is the monopoly outcome defined as:

$$2P'(2q^*(\theta))q^*(\theta) + P(2q^*(\theta)) = \theta C'(2q^*(\theta)). \tag{5}$$

A Few Issues: In all those examples, inefficient contractual outcomes may arise because of some underlying frictions in contracting. Those frictions may be due to arbitrary restrictions of the space of contracts. They may also stem from asymmetric information and the associated screening costs incurred by the principals in such contexts. A major difficulty of the common agency literature is precisely to understand the new frictions, if any, which are due to the principals' non-cooperative behavior. This analysis requires a careful study of the contracting possibilities available to the principals. Different contracting possibilities may either alleviate or exacerbate frictions depending on the context. When looking at those contracting possibilities, common agency introduces some new features that are not present under centralized contracting and that need to be carefully studied:

- Under centralized contracting, the agent has no other option than refusing the contract offered by the merged entity. This participation decision is most often modelled by introducing an exogenously given

---

[7] This may include the welfare of unorganized groups that are not active lobbyists.

reservation payoff for the agent. Under common agency, the agent may either be forced to accept all contracts at once or may be able to play some principals against others by threatening to accept only a subset of the offers he receives. We will talk about *intrinsic common agency* in the former case and *delegated common agency* in the latter.[8] Intrinsic common agency arises in Example 1. Delegated common agency occurs instead in Examples 2 and 3.

- Examples 1 and 3 also highlight another important feature of common agency. As we split control among different principals, we might also change the information available to those principals. In Example 1, an economic regulator may observe the firm's output whereas an environmental regulator has expertise to observe polluting emissions. In Example 2, retailer P_1 may not be able to observe and verify the amount of input sold by the manufacturer to retailer P_2. In the case of *public agency*, both principals may still be able to contract on the whole output vector $q = (q_1, q_2)$. Public agency always occurs in Example 2 but also in Example 3 if, for instance, both retailers can observe and verify the price at which the good is sold on the final market. Instead, in the case of *private agency*, output q_i is observed and verified only by P_i and the contract that this principal offers to the agent can only use this variable as a screening instrument. Still in Example 3, private agency occurs when retailers offer specific non-verifiable services which are included in the price package to their customers. As we move from public to private agencies, we limit the principals' contracting possibilities and may change the equilibrium sets of the common agency game.

Whether we have delegated/intrinsic, public/private or symmetric/asymmetric information offers a large panel of game forms that are all relevant in specific applications. Each of those games requires careful study. Nevertheless, I shall try to highlight below a few common themes of the literature.

Contract Spaces and Incompleteness: An important preliminary step is to define the contract spaces available to the principals. Before doing so, it is useful to think of an interesting class of contracts—nonlinear prices, which are often observed in practice, to see how they relate to the degree of incompleteness of the contracts:

- Under public agency, principals may offer nonlinear prices of the form $t_i(q)$ and let the agent choose the publicly observable output q. The only source of contractual incompleteness is the lack of centralized contracting.[9]

---

[8] Bernheim and Whinston (1986a) coined these expressions.

[9] Under delegated common agency, principals could also make discriminatory offers and link the agent's compensation to whether he accepts other principals' contracts or not.

• Under private agency, principals can only offer nonlinear prices, which link the agent's payment to the available observable, typically of the form $t_i(q_i)$. The agent still chooses the output $q = (q_1, q_2)$. Contracts are thus more incomplete. Not only do principals not cooperate in contracting, but they also contract on different variables.

Taxation and Revelation Principles: Under centralized contracting, the *Revelation Principle* characterizes the set of incentive-feasible allocations. This description in terms of direct and truthful mechanisms is quite tractable and amenable to a simple set of incentive constraints. Characterizing the set of implementable allocations is a crucial step of the analysis before proceeding to optimization once the organization's objective function has been defined. Unfortunately, for multi-contracting environments, the applicability of the Revelation Principle comes into question.

Under multi-contracting, one may be interested in analyzing the set $PBE(\Gamma_{\mathcal{M}_1 \times \ldots \times \mathcal{M}_n})$ of the perfect Bayesian equilibria of a common agency game $\Gamma_{\mathcal{M}_1 \times \ldots \times \mathcal{M}_n}$ obtained when each principal offers mechanisms using an arbitrary communication space $\mathcal{M}_i$ with the agent. A (trivial and somewhat abusive) version of the Revelation Principle would consist in replacing every communication space $\mathcal{M}_i$ by the set of types Θ so that any equilibrium σ^* in $PBE(\Gamma_{\mathcal{M}_1 \times \ldots \times \mathcal{M}_2})$ yields payoffs that can be replicated by an equilibrium $\tilde{\sigma}^*$ in $PBE(\Gamma_{\Theta^n})$ with truthtelling as a strategy profile for the agent in his relationship with each principal. This naive approach fails on three fronts:

• Principals may have used the agent as a pure correlating device when the communication spaces $\mathcal{M}_i$ are used. By restricting the agent to a truthful strategy vis-à-vis each principal, one may lose the possibility of correlating behavior. This difficulty can nevertheless be fixed by appending to the agent's type a public correlating device.
• Even when direct mechanisms are used, the agent may be mixing messages as part of the equilibrium behavior.[10]
• Equilibrium messages available with indirect mechanisms may play a significant role in preventing deviations. One can sustain equilibrium outcomes with indirect mechanisms, which would not survive with direct revelation mechanisms. Conversely, focusing on direct mechanisms may also introduce equilibria, which would not hold if deviations to a larger space of mechanisms were available to the principals. These difficulties are prevalent in economic applications as I will show below.

---

[10] The role of a mixed-strategy here is similar to what arises under centralized contracting and limited commitment. Peck (1996) provided some examples. In the context of competing hierarchies, Myerson (1982) already pointed out that truthful equilibria may not exist. He did not suggest analyzing mixed-strategy equilibria. He turned instead to develop the concept of *quasi-equilibria* which relaxes the truthtelling requirement.

These shortcomings mean that new tools are needed to characterize equilibrium outcomes. Two paths have been followed in the literature:

- The first path was suggested by McAfee (1993, footnote 7) and formally investigated by Epstein and Peters (1999).[11] It consists in redefining the agent's private information as the product of his own preference parameter times the so-called "*market information*," i.e., what the agent learns from observing other principals' offers. This process leads to an infinite regress since those offers can themselves depend on lower levels of "market information," etc. Epstein and Peters (1999) showed that the whole process converges. They defined a *universal type space* and correspondingly a *universal space of mechanisms* as limits of this infinite regress.
- The second path followed by Peters (2001, 2003), Martimort and Stole (2002) and Page and Monteiro (2003) is to give up the Revelation Principle even in its generalized form sketched above. Indeed, a Revelation Principle is only useful for modelling purposes as far as it allows a characterization of implementable allocations by means of simple incentive constraints. What really matters per se is not the kind of communication that a principal uses with his agent, but the set of options that this principal makes available to the agent. Alternatively, the agent could as well choose within this set of alternatives. This is the essence of the so-called "*Taxation Principle*."[12,13] Typically, in economic applications with quasi-linear payoff functions, the space of mechanisms allowing a full description of all pure-strategy equilibrium allocations is the space of nonlinear prices.[14]

Each of these alternative paths has its shortcomings.

First, the Revelation Principle for a universal type space has not been used so far in applications.[15] The beautiful structure of incentive constraints is lost when one cannot describe the agent's type by a true preference parameter. Moreover, "market information" may sometimes not add much. For instance, in a pure

---

[11] Although in settings where different principals may contract with different sets of agents.

[12] See Rochet (1985) for the Taxation Principle in the case of centralized contracting.

[13] Also called sometimes the "*Delegation Principle.*"

[14] A sketch of the argument is as follows. Consider for instance a private common agency game. A pure strategy equilibrium is an array of deterministic mechanisms where any such mechanism stipulates both a price and an action level as a function of the agent's message to each principal. Of course, one can easily prune strategies that are dominated to keep the resulting upper envelope of the price-activity pairs. This yields an array of nonlinear prices which form an equilibrium. See Martimort and Stole (2002).

[15] Calzolari and Pavan (2002) analyzed a dynamic common agency game with secret contracting and argued that market information can be summarized by the whole vector of past realized contractual choices that the agent may have made with other principals. This confirms that a standard (although somewhat generalized version) of the Revelation Principle applies in this context.

Nash equilibrium each principal must form beliefs over the others' strategies. Nothing on the offers of other principals is "unknown" when their preferences are common knowledge.[16] When principals are instead privately informed, the mere offer of their contracts reveals information to the agent. It is then quite natural for each principal to elicit what the agent has learned from others when contracting.[17]

Second, both approaches generally take as granted that an equilibrium exists. The question of existence has only been tackled recently by Page and Monteiro (2003) who showed that, under weak assumptions, there always exists a mixed-strategy equilibrium when principals offer nonlinear prices.

Let us summarize by highlighting one major theme of the existing literature:

Theme 1 *Direct revelation mechanisms generally do not suffice to describe the whole set of equilibrium allocations in a common agency game.[18] The standard version of the Revelation Principle fails.*

There economists seem to have lost one of their favorite tools. This pessimistic view is not totally correct. Indeed, the Revelation Principle is still useful to compute the payoff of a given principal at a best-response to any array of mechanisms (even indirect ones) offered by others. To illustrate, consider the case of a private agency with only two principals. Suppose that the agent has a quasi-linear utility function

$$U = t_1 + t_2 + v(q_1, q_2, \theta)$$

where q_i is the activity that the agent undertakes for principal P_i and θ is the adverse selection parameter distributed on some interval Θ.

From Peters (2001, 2003) and Martimort and Stole (2002), there is no loss of generality in looking for equilibria in nonlinear prices $\{t_i(q_i)\}_{i=1,2}$ as far as pure strategies are concerned. However, to compute P_i's best-response to the nonlinear price $t_{-i}(\cdot)$, one can first apply the Revelation Principle and use a direct revelation mechanism $\{t_i(\hat{\theta}), q_i(\hat{\theta})\}_{\hat{\theta} \in \Theta}$. This direct mechanism has to implement the same transfer-quantity pairs as the nonlinear price $t_i(q_i)$ offered at a best-response to $t_{-i}(q_{-i})$. In a second step, one can view the choice of q_{-i} within the options offered by P_{-i} as a non-verifiable variable from P_i's viewpoint since P_i cannot contract on it. The methodology of mixed models with adverse selection and moral hazard can then be successfully applied to

---

[16] This remark must of course be qualified. Indeed, in a mixed-strategy equilibrium where a principal randomizes over mechanisms, the realizations of this mixture may be observed by the agent before he makes his choices. This adds some dimension of private information that another principal may want to elicit by communicating with the agent.

[17] This is the route followed by Martimort and Moreira (2005). See Section 5 below.

[18] Direct revelation mechanisms might suffice when the agent's utility function is separable in the different activities he undertakes for the principals. For most common agency games of interest, this condition fails. See also Attar et al. (2005) on this issue.

derive best-responses.[19] Formally, the agent's indirect utility function *vis-à-vis* principal P_1 can be defined as

$$\hat{U}_1(q_1, \theta) = \max_{q_2 \in Q_2} t_2(q_2) + v(q_1, q_2, \theta) \tag{6}$$

where Q_2 is the range of $t_2(\cdot)$. This illustrates the role of q_2 as a moral hazard variable from P_1's viewpoint. In well-structured models, this indirect utility function inherits standard properties which make screening models tractable: monotonicity in θ, a (constant-sign) Spence-Mirrlees condition $\frac{\partial^2 \hat{U}_1}{\partial q_1 \partial \theta} > 0$ (or $\frac{\partial^2 \hat{U}}{\partial q_1 \partial \theta} < 0$), and concavity in q_1. Standard mechanism design techniques[20] can then be used to compute best-responses. Sections 3.1 and 4 offer examples.[21]

The approach consisting in using the standard Revelation Principle to compute best-responses was pursued by Martimort (1992, 1996a), Ivaldi and Martimort (1994), Martimort and Stole (2003a, 2003b), Mezzetti (1997), Biais, Martimort and Rochet (2000), Calzolari (2001), Laffont and Pouyet (2003), Diaw and Pouyet (2005) and Khalil, Martimort and Parigi (2004).[22]

3 EQUILIBRIA UNDER COMPLETE INFORMATION

Once equipped with the Revelation Principle, standard mechanism design characterizes the set of implementable allocations. Even though the Revelation Principle loses much of its bite in multi-contracting environments, characterizing equilibrium allocations that emerge as equilibria of common agency games remains crucial to understanding how far away those allocations might be from the frontier of incentive feasible allocations achievable under centralized contracting. Such an analysis provides insights on the transaction costs arising under multi-contracting. In this section, I first address this characterization issue in a private agency framework. This highlights two key features of those models:

---

[19] See Laffont and Martimort (2002, Chapter 7).

[20] See Laffont and Martimort (2002, Chapter 3).

[21] The last step consists in conveniently extending the nonlinear prices to validate the mere definition of the indirect utility function (6) and its use in computing the other principal's best-response. In practice, one might need to enlarge sufficiently the domain Q_2 where $t_2(\cdot)$ is defined, to be sure that a first order approach can always be used in computing the maximand of (6). This step was undertaken in Martimort (1992). When studying supply function equilibria, Klemperer and Meyer (1989) used a similar device. Stole (1991) gave conditions on utility functions such that those extensions might not always be needed.

[22] If one redefines the agent's action space so that the agent chooses in fact a nonlinear schedule and not an output, a version of the Revelation Principle might apply in well-structured environments as shown in Peters (2003). This author viewed nonlinear schedules as take-it-or-leave-it offers made by the principals to the agent. A more general mechanism would instead work as follows. First, the principal offers a set of nonlinear prices; second, the agent chooses one of these prices; and finally, the principal himself chooses a particular output. Some might argue that this approach gives too much freedom to the modeler in redefining the agent's action space.

the multiplicity of equilibria, and their systematic inefficiency. I then move on to public agency. Public agency restores efficiency. However, public agency also exacerbates the multiplicity problem. Refinements are needed to pin down an efficient equilibrium outcome.

3.1   Private Agency and Direct Externalities

Consider Example 3.[23] For simplicity, I now analyze a model with private and intrinsic agency[24] and assume that the manufacturer's cost parameter θ is common knowledge. Principals might now a priori offer the nonlinear prices $\{t_i(q_i)\}_{i=1,2}$ based only on the quantities they respectively buy from the agent.[25] As a benchmark, consider first the case where they use direct revelation mechanisms which, under complete information, leave a single option to the agent. These mechanisms can thus be identified with simple forcing contracts $\{(t_i, q_i)\}_{i=1,2}$.

Under intrinsic agency, the agent accepts both contracts when:

$$t_1 + t_2 - \theta C(q_1 + q_2) \geq 0. \tag{7}$$

At a best-response, each principal reduces his own payment to the agent up to the point where the participation constraint (7) binds. Inserting the corresponding value of the transfer t_i into P_i's objective function, it is easy to see that this principal wants to implement an output q_i, which maximizes the payoff of his bilateral coalition with the agent:

$$q_i \in \arg\max_{\tilde{q}_i} P(\tilde{q}_i + q_{-i})\tilde{q}_i + t_{-i} - \theta C(\tilde{q}_i + q_{-i}).$$

This *bilateral efficiency* requirement is key to any common agency game. We will encounter it under various forms in the sequel. The important issue is to understand how inefficiencies may arise when all contracts are bilaterally efficient.

The corresponding first order condition for bilateral efficiency characterizes the (unique) Nash equilibrium of this game. This is the "Cournot" outcome, $q_1(\theta) = q_2(\theta) = q^c(\theta)$ where $q^c(\theta)$ solves:

$$P'(2q^c(\theta))q^c(\theta) + P(2q^c(\theta)) = \theta C'(2q^c(\theta)). \tag{8}$$

Let us turn to the case where principals might now offer any nonlinear price defined over some larger domain Q_i. This expansion of the strategy space adds some flexibility to assess how a principal may react to unexpected changes in the agent's output. This flexibility generates new equilibrium outcomes.

---

[23] This vertical contracting model is drawn from Martimort and Stole (2003a).

[24] Intrinsic common agency may be justified when the agent wants to preserve some form of ex post competition between retailers or if the agent has made some specific investment that can be recovered only if both retailers use his product.

[25] Again, from Peters (2001, 2003) and Martimort and Stole (2002), this is the appropriate space of mechanisms to consider in this private agency context.

Nevertheless, bilateral efficiency still implies that P_i maximizes the payoff of the bilateral coalition he forms with the agent:

$$q_i \in \arg\max_{\tilde{q}_i} P(\tilde{q}_i + q^*_{-i}(\tilde{q}_i))\tilde{q}_i + t_{-i}(q^*_{-i}(\tilde{q}_i)) - \theta C(\tilde{q}_i + q^*_{-i}(\tilde{q}_i))$$

(9)

where $q^*_{-i}(\cdot)$ satisfies the first order condition:[26]

$$\frac{\partial t^*_{-i}}{\partial q_{-i}}(q^*_{-i}(\tilde{q}_i)) = \theta C'(\tilde{q}_i + q^*_{-i}(\tilde{q}_i)) \quad \text{for all } \tilde{q}_i \in Q_i.$$

(10)

Using the first order condition for (9) and equation (10), one can easily check that a symmetric equilibrium output q^e solves:

$$P'(2q^e)q^e\left(1 + \frac{\partial q^*_{-i}(q^e)}{\partial q_i}\right) + P(2q^e) = \theta C'(2q^e).$$

(11)

Any output between Cournot (corresponding to $\frac{\partial q^*_{-i}}{\partial q_i}(q^e) = 0$ or to simple forcing contracts) and Bertrand (corresponding to $\frac{\partial q^*_{-i}}{\partial q_i}(q^e) = -1$) can be sustained at equilibrium by specifying appropriate nonlinear prices for out of equilibrium outputs.[27] The intuition for these rather competitive outcomes is as follows. By offering a fairly flat schedule around the equilibrium point, a principal, say P_{-i}, makes the agent eager to produce more for himself if P_i reduces the amount he buys from the agent. P_i has no incentives to deviate since he fears that P_{-i} will flood the market following such deviation.

This example illustrates that out of equilibrium messages have a powerful *strategic value* in models with direct externalities between the principals. In our vertical contracting example, this strategic concern makes equilibrium outcomes more competitive than the Cournot outcome achieved with direct mechanisms.[28,29]

---

[26] This is sufficient provided that $t^*_{-i}(\cdot)$ is concave enough.

[27] Quadratic extensions of $t_i(q_i)$ for out of equilibrium transfer-output pairs suffice. Of course, the choice of those quadratic extensions should ensure the concavity of the agent's objective function. These second order conditions put constraints on the lower and upper bounds of the set of equilibrium outputs.

[28] Consider now that the two retailers are on two unrelated markets and enjoy monopoly power on each. P_1's profit does not depend on q_2 and vice versa. There is no longer any direct externality between principals. It is easy to check (see Martimort and Stole (2003a)) that the efficient outcome is sustained in equilibrium. It is achieved both with direct revelation mechanisms (forcing contracts) but also with more general nonlinear prices. This points at the crucial role that direct externalities play to create a strategic role to the extensions of the nonlinear prices of the equilibrium. This also illustrates one limit of Theme 1 since, in this case, the standard version of the Revelation Principle holds.

[29] Consider now the price competition version of the game. Contracts now depend on the final retail prices of the goods, i.e., they are of the form $t_i(p_i)$ ($i = 1, 2$). Goods are differentiated with respective demands $D_i(p_i, p_{-i})$. Profit functions for the retailers and the manufacturers are given by

$$V_i = p_i D_i(p_i, p_{-i}) - t_i, \quad i = 1, 2, \text{ and } U = t_1 + t_2 - \theta C(D_1(p_1, p_2) + D_2(p_1, p_2)).$$

Theme 2   *Out of equilibrium messages have a strategic value in models with direct externalities and private agency. Equilibrium outcomes may be inefficient even under complete information.*

Segal and Whinston (2003) and Martimort and Stole (2003a) characterized Nash outcomes under either intrinsic or delegated common agency and showed their multiplicity.[30] Segal and Whinston (2003) also compared common agency with the game where the agent makes offers.[31] Parlour and Rajan (2001) presented an interesting model of competition between lenders under complete information. That the common agent may default introduces an incentive constraint to induce repayment.[32] Principals interact through this constraint: the contract offered by a lender bestows a negative externality on others since the agent reneges on all contracts if he reneges at all. Multi-contracting can lead to non-competitive pricing if the agent's incentives to default are strong enough.

3.2   Public Agency

Public agency makes coordination between principals easier because they now contract on more variables than under private agency. The good side of expanding the contract space is thus that efficiency is restored. Its bad side is that the multiplicity problem is also exacerbated.

• **Coordination:** Staying with our vertical contracting example, consider the case of public agency. Both principals can now contract on the whole vector of outputs (q_1, q_2). Actually, contracts depending on the total output $q = q_1 + q_2$ sold on the final market suffice to highlight the coordination problem in this

---

Nonlinear prices help enforce equilibrium outcomes that are more collusive than the differentiated Bertrand outcome achieved with forcing contracts stipulating only a lump-sum payment and a retail price $\{(t_i, p_i)\}$ ($i = 1, 2$). The intuition is exactly the reverse of that in the quantity game.

[30] See also D'Aspremont and Dos Santos Ferreira (2005).

[31] The multiplicity of common agency equilibria is reminiscent of the multiplicity found in the vertical contracting literature where the agent makes secret offers to principals. The multiplicity arises there from the leeway in specifying beliefs on what contracts other principals receive when a given principal observes that the agent deviates. See O'Brien and Shaffer (1992), McAfee and Schwartz (1994) and Segal (1999) among others. With *passive beliefs*, each principal conjectures that others still receive the equilibrium contract following an unexpected deviation. Exactly as with direct mechanisms or forcing contracts in the common agency game, the Cournot outcome emerges. The vertical contracting literature has also investigated the case of *symmetric beliefs* such that, once the agent deviates vis-à-vis a principal, the latter thinks that others receive those alternative offers as well. Of course, in symmetric environments, such symmetric beliefs sustain the monopoly outcome, which cannot be replicated under common agency. Indeed, under common agency, subgame-perfection requires that the agent substitutes a little bit more of production of good i against a little bit less of production of good $-i$ so that a simultaneous output reduction never arises.

[32] To make it precise, this incentive constraint is not due to asymmetric information but stems from the impossibility to enforce repayments.

context. Relabelling transfers so that principals offer the agent contracts $s_i(q)$ specifying the shares of the grand-coalition's payoff they request respectively, payoffs can be written as:

$$V_i = s_i(q), \quad \text{for } i = 1, 2$$

and

$$U = q P(q) - \theta C(q) - s_1(q) - s_2(q).$$

Any output $\bar{q}$ giving a positive profit to the grand-coalition of the principals and the agent (i.e., such that $P(\bar{q})\bar{q} - \theta C(\bar{q}) \geq 0$) arises at equilibrium with simple forcing contracts. Suppose indeed that P_{-i} insists on a forcing contract of the kind

$$s_{-i}(q) = \begin{cases} \bar{s}_{-i} & \text{if } q = \bar{q} \\ +\infty & \text{if } q \neq \bar{q}, \end{cases}$$

for some pair $(\bar{q}, \bar{s}_{-i})$ and that no production takes place when principals insist on different outputs. Principal P_i's best response to such an offer by P_{-i} cannot influence total production since the agent either produces $\bar{q}$ or refuses contracting. Any non-negative payoff pair $(\bar{s}_1, \bar{s}_2)$ such that $P(\bar{q})\bar{q} - \theta C(\bar{q}) - \bar{s}_1 - \bar{s}_2 = 0$ is an equilibrium.

In sharp contrast with private agency, public agency only entails transaction costs when principals fail to coordinate. This point was already stressed by Bernheim and Whinston's (1986b) early investigation of delegated common agency games.[33]

Theme 3 *Under public agency and complete information, common agency games may be plagued with inefficient equilibria: a coordination problem.*

Altogether, Themes 2 and 3 show that extending the contracting spaces available to both principals, by moving from private to public agency, also enlarges the set of implementable outcomes. The comparison of the equilibrium sets with private and public agency also highlights how transaction costs change when the degree of contractual incompleteness increases as one moves from public to private agency.

• **"Truthfulness" as an Equilibrium Refinement:** As shown above, there nevertheless exists an equilibrium of the public agency game under complete information, which implements an efficient outcome. Our concerns should now be quite similar to those of the implementation literature. Can we find a class of strategies that ensures that efficiency is always reached at equilibrium? If yes, multi-contracting does not preclude efficiency, at least under complete information. This question has been addressed by Bernheim and Whinston

---

[33] See also the earlier contribution of Wilson (1979).

(1986b), albeit in the context of delegated common agency. Their insight can be best understood once one has in mind a standard result from Incentive Theory. Under complete information,[34] a principal can always delegate to his agent the choice of an optimal action from the point of view of their bilateral coalition by making this agent residual claimant. This is achieved with a "sell-out" contract of the form $t_i(q) = S_i(q) - k_i$, where $S_i(q)$ is P_i's benefit when action q is chosen and k_i is P_i's payoff from this delegation.

To understand more precisely the role of "sell-out" contracts, let us come back to Example 2 on lobbying under complete information. To compute P_i's best-response to an aggregate scheme offered by other principals $t_{-i}(\cdot)$, I proceed as under private agency. An output q is implemented at equilibrium by a nonlinear price $t_i(\cdot)$ when the transfer $t_i(q) = t_i$ is reduced up to the point where the agent's participation constraint is binding. Under delegated common agency, this participation constraint accounts for the fact that the agent may choose among the different contracts offered. It can be written as:

$$t_i + t_{-i}(q) - \theta C(q) = \max\left\{0, \max_{\{I \subset N-\{i\}, q\}} T_I(q) - \theta C(q)\right\}, \qquad (12)$$

where $T_I(q) = \sum_{i \in I} t_i(q)$ denotes the aggregate transfer offered by a set I of principals.[35] Given that transfer t_i, P_i wants to induce a production q, which maximizes $S_i(q) - t_i$. This amounts again to choosing an output q, which maximizes the bilateral payoff of the coalition he forms with the agent:[36]

$$q \in \arg \max_{\tilde{q}} S_i(\tilde{q}) + t_{-i}(\tilde{q}) - \theta C(\tilde{q}). \qquad (13)$$

Suppose that all other principals P_j for $j \neq i$ offer so-called *truthful* schedules, of the form $t_j(q) = \max\{0, S_j(q) - k_j\}$ for some constants k_j. These schedules correspond to the non-negative part of sell-out contracts. Assuming differentiability at the equilibrium point q, bilateral efficiency implies:

$$S_i'(q) + t_{-i}'(q) = \theta C'(q).$$

The agent's optimal output solves instead:

$$q \in \arg \max_{\tilde{q}} T_N(\tilde{q}) - \theta C(\tilde{q}).$$

---

[34] If the agent is risk-neutral; this is true more generally under ex ante contracting even when there is adverse selection or moral hazard. See Laffont and Martimort (2002, Chapters 2 and 4).

[35] The right-hand side of (12) takes into account that the agent has several options, either refusing all offers or taking only contracts from a coalition I, which would not include P_i. If (12) was not an equality, P_i could reduce his own contribution and still induce acceptance, a contradiction.

[36] From (12), it appears also that $t_i(q) \geq 0$ for the quantity q that P_i wants to induce. Given that all principals offer positive contributions, the agent accepts all contracts. Denoting then by q_{-i} the equilibrium output chosen by the agent to maximize the right-hand side of (12), we have $q_{-i} = \arg\max_{\{N-\{i\}, q\}} T_{N-\{i\}}(q) - \theta C(q)$. Then, from (13), we can show that $S_i(q) - t_i(q) \geq S_i(q_{-i})$. This condition can be interpreted as an individual rationality constraint for P_i. An immediate consequence is that, necessarily, $S_i(q) \geq S_i(q_{-i})$. By making a positive contribution, P_i shifts the agent's decision towards his own preferences.

Assuming concavity of this objective and that the maximum is achieved at an interior point, where contributions are positive yields the following first order condition:

$$T'_N(q) = t'_i(q) + t'_{-i}(q) = \theta C'(q). \tag{14}$$

Using the fact that principals P_j for $j \neq i$ offer truthful schedules yields:

$$t'_i(q) = S'_i(q). \tag{15}$$

At an equilibrium output q, the marginal contribution of a principal reflects his own marginal valuation. This condition can also be extended for any quantity that is not offered at equilibrium, as long as the corresponding contribution remains positive. This gives the expression of the truthful schedule offered by P_i:

$$t_i(q) = \max\{0, S_i(q) - k_i\} \quad \text{for some} \quad k_i. \tag{16}$$

Because each principal makes a contribution that reflects his own marginal valuation,[37] the equilibrium quantity is necessarily efficient for the grand-coalition made of all principals and the agent. As a refinement of the equilibrium set, *truthfulness* ensures efficiency.[38]

• **Consequences of "Truthfulness" for Equilibrium Payoffs:** Under delegated common agency, "truthfulness" has strong implications for the principals' equilibrium payoffs. Indeed, the agent's binding participation constraint (12) yields a set of inequality constraints that must be satisfied by any vector $(k_i)_{1 \leq i \leq n}$ of payoffs for the principals:

$$W_N - k_N = \max_{I \in N}\{0, W_I - k_I\} \tag{17}$$

where $W_I = \max_q\{S_I(q) - \theta C(q)\}$ is the aggregate surplus of a coalition I of principals. The fact that the schedule is truthful everywhere plays a key role to compute the right-hand side of (17) since, even when the agent chooses to contract only with a subset of principals, he continues to choose an efficient output from the point of view of the coalition he forms with these principals. Truthfulness affects the agent's reservation payoff, and thus feed-backs on the principals' payoffs.

Theme 4 *Truthful schedules solve the coordination problem but have strong implications on the principals' equilibrium payoffs in a delegated common agency game.*

---

[37] At least on its positive part.

[38] Our notion of efficiency concerns only the grand-coalition. This notion of efficiency should of course be distinguished from social welfare maximization. In a lobbying context, the definition of social welfare would also incorporate non-active interest groups.

The structure of payoffs in a delegated common agency game has been investigated by Laussel and Lebreton (2001) and Milgrom (2004).[39] This structure is deeply linked to the property of the characteristic function W_I. When $S_i' > 0$ for all i, principals have congruent preferences. The agent gets no rent under delegated common agency, and the existence of a vector $(k_i)_{1 \le i \le n}$ so that $W_N - k_N = 0 \ge W_I - k_I \ \forall I \subset N$ follows from the sub-additivity of W_I. When principals have more conflicting preferences, the agent may instead get a positive rent. Prat and Rustichini (2003) analyzed a multiprincipals-multiagents game when there is no externality across agents. Efficiency is strongly linked to the existence of a pure strategy equilibrium in the normal form game. They also generalized the link between the principals' payoffs under common agency and the characteristic function of some cooperative game. On this issue see also Perez-Castrillo (1994). Bergemann and Valimaki (2003) analyzed dynamic common agency games under complete information. They described payoffs for Markov-perfect truthful equilibria.

The public agency model above has been an important part of political economists' toolkit over the past ten years following Grossman and Helpman (1994, 2002). See also Helpman (1997), Rama and Tabellini (1998), Mitra (1999) and Helpman and Persson (2001) among many others. Dixit, Grossman and Helpman (1997) introduced redistributive concerns.

• **More on Refinements:** An important issue is to find a rationale for truthful menus since it might seem hard to justify that principals would offer a complete list of options without any concerns for copying with uncertainty or adverse selection. Following Bernheim and Whinston (1986b), one might select those equilibria because they are *coalition-proof*, i.e., immune to deviations by subsets of principals, which are themselves immune to deviations by subcoalitions, etc. Coalition-proof equilibrium payoffs can be implemented with truthful schedules in environments with quasi-linear utility functions.[40] Truthful menus can also cope with uncertainty on the agent's cost function. Laussel and Lebreton (1998) studied a public good context when contracts are offered by contributors ex ante, i.e., before the agent learns about his cost function.[41] Under ex ante contracting, incentive compatibility ensures that, for any realization of the underlying uncertainty, marginal contributions reflect the principals' preferences.[42]

---

[39] See also De Villemeur and Versaevel (2003).

[40] Although attractive, this approach has three weaknesses. First, it does not per se disqualify non-truthful strategies that would sustain the same payoffs. Second, in more complex environments, one can find common agency equilibria with truthful schedules that are not coalition-proof (see Konishi, Lebreton and Weber (1999)). Lastly, Kirchsteiger and Prat (2001) presented experimental evidence showing that principals may prefer using simpler "forcing contracts."

[41] The role of uncertainty in restricting equilibrium sets is already well known from the related literature on supply functions. See Klemperer and Meyer (1989).

[42] Equilibrium marginal contributions do not depend on the underlying distribution of types, something that can be puzzling. Another well-known problem with ex ante contracting is that transfers

4   EQUILIBRIA UNDER ADVERSE SELECTION

4.1   Private Agency with Indirect Externalities

Section 3.1 has shown how inefficiencies arise in models with private agency and direct externalities, even under complete information. To stress another source of inefficiency under multi-contracting, consider a case without direct externality but with private information on the agent's side. To fix ideas, let us modify slightly Example 1. Two regulators are interested in controlling two different activities of a regulated firm, say outputs q_1 and q_2. The regulators' and the firm's objective functions are

$$V_i = S_i(q_i) - t_i, \quad i = 1, 2, \quad \text{and} \quad U = t_1 + t_2 - \theta C(q_1, q_2),$$

where $S_i(\cdot)$ is now the strictly concave return of activity i and $C(\cdot)$ is strictly convex in $q = (q_1, q_2)$. There are no direct externalities between principals. The two activities are *complements* when $C_{12} < 0$, and *substitutes* when $C_{12} > 0$. The technological parameter θ is the firm's private information only.

I use now the methodology already reviewed in Section 2. Let us define the indirect cost function of the agent vis-à-vis P_1 as

$$\tilde{C}(q_1, \theta) = \min_{q_2 \in Q_2} \theta C(q_1, q_2) - t_2(q_2)$$

for a given nonlinear schedule $t_2(\cdot)$ (defined over some range Q_2) offered by P_2.

Let $q_2^*(q_1, \theta)$ denote the best choice of q_2 by the agent when his type is θ and he chooses an activity q_1 for P_1. Provided that the first order condition below is also sufficient, $q_2^*(q_1, \theta)$ is defined implicitly by:

$$t_2'(q_2^*(q_1, \theta)) = \theta C_2(q_1, q_2^*(q_1, \theta)).$$

Simple differentiation shows that raising the level of activity q_1 shifts also q_2 downwards (resp. upwards) when activities are substitutes (resp. complements) since $\frac{\partial q_2^*}{\partial q_1} < 0$ (resp. $\frac{\partial q_2^*}{\partial q_1} > 0$).

Consider the optimal output choice that P_1 wants to induce from an agent with such an indirect cost function $\tilde{C}(q_1, \theta)$. To compute P_1's best-response, we may restrict the analysis to direct revelation mechanisms $\{t_1(\hat{\theta}), q_1(\hat{\theta})\}_{\hat{\theta} \in \Theta}$ and, as suggested in Section 2, apply the Revelation Principle for a given nonlinear schedule $t_2(\cdot)$ offered by P_2. Pointwise optimization of P_1's objective yields:[43]

---

might no longer be positive for all realizations of the cost parameter. Ex post, the agent would prefer to renege on a contract if it turns out to stipulate a negative contribution. Martimort and Semenov (2005) studied that enforcement issue and how it leads to inefficient contracting outcomes in a lobbying context.

[43] Provided again that the solution $q_1(\theta)$ of (18) is monotonically decreasing to satisfy the second order condition.

$$S_1'(q_1(\theta)) = \tilde{C}_1(q_1(\theta), \theta) + \frac{F(\theta)}{f(\theta)} \tilde{C}_{1\theta}(q_1(\theta), \theta). \tag{18}$$

This is a condition for *bilateral incentive efficiency*. The contract between P_1 and the agent maximizes their coalitional payoff. However, costs are now replaced by *virtual costs* under adverse selection. Using the Envelope Theorem, (18) becomes:

$$S_1'(q_1(\theta)) = \left(\theta + \frac{F(\theta)}{f(\theta)}\right) C_1(q_1(\theta), q_2^*(q_1(\theta), \theta))$$
$$+ \frac{F(\theta)}{f(\theta)} C_2(q_1(\theta), q_2^*(q_1(\theta), \theta)) \frac{\partial q_2^*}{\partial q_1}. \tag{19}$$

Had the principals merged and offered cooperatively their contracts to the agent, the optimal output q_1 would instead satisfy:[44]

$$S_1'(q_1(\theta)) = \left(\theta + \frac{F(\theta)}{f(\theta)}\right) C_1(q_1(\theta), q_2(\theta)). \tag{20}$$

Under centralized contracting, the outcome is *interim efficient*. Comparing (19) and (20) highlights the new frictions involved under common agency. The common agency outcome departs from the cooperative solution by the new term $\frac{F(\theta)}{f(\theta)} C_2(q_1, q_2^*(q_1, \theta)) \frac{\partial q_2^*}{\partial q_1}$ on the right-hand side of (19).

When outputs are substitutes $\left(\frac{\partial q_2^*}{\partial q_1} < 0\right)$ distortions are smaller under common agency than under centralized contracting. Intuitively, each principal would prefer the other to think that the agent is of a lower type than what he really is. By inducing the agent to exert less activity for P_2, P_1 finds it less costly to decrease output q_1 for rent extraction purposes. The contractual externality between principals is positive. In equilibrium, output distortions are reduced compared with the cooperative solution.

When outputs are complements $\left(\frac{\partial q_2^*}{\partial q_1} > 0\right)$, the opposite holds. Each principal still prefers the other to think that the agent is of a lower type. However, this is now obtained by exacerbating output distortions compared with the cooperative outcome. The contractual externality is negative.

Theme 5 *With adverse selection and indirect externalities only, outputs are distorted in the intrinsic common agency game compared with the cooperative outcome. The direction of the distortion depends on whether the activities controlled by the principals are substitutes or complements in the agent's utility function.*

---

[44] A similar condition holds for $q_2(\theta)$.

To sharpen intuition, consider the case where $S_1(\cdot) = S_2(\cdot) = S(\cdot)$ and $C(\cdot)$ is symmetric in (q_1, q_2). Using (19), a symmetric equilibrium $q(\theta)$ satisfies the differential equation:[45]

$$S'(q(\theta)) = \left(\theta + \frac{F(\theta)}{f(\theta)}\right) C_1(q(\theta), q(\theta))$$
$$+ \frac{F(\theta)}{f(\theta)} \frac{\theta C_{12}(q(\theta), q(\theta)) C_2(q(\theta), q(\theta)) \dot{q}(\theta)}{C_2(q(\theta), q(\theta)) + \theta C_{12}(q(\theta), q(\theta)) \dot{q}(\theta)}. \qquad (21)$$

Two polar cases are worth studying:

• *Perfect complementarity:* We can write $C(q_1, q_2) = \hat{C}(\min(q_1, q_2))$ for some increasing and convex function $\hat{C}(\cdot)$. Since $C_{12}(q, q) = \infty$, in the limit (21) becomes

$$2S'(q(\theta)) = \left(\theta + 2\frac{F(\theta)}{f(\theta)}\right) \hat{C}'(q(\theta)). \qquad (22)$$

This is similar to the public agency case treated in Section 4.3 below.

• *Perfect substitutes:* Suppose now that $C(q_1, q_2) = \hat{C}(q_1 + q_2)$. Condition (21) becomes:

$$S'(q(\theta)) = \left(\theta + \frac{F(\theta)}{f(\theta)}\left(1 + \frac{\theta \hat{C}''(2q(\theta)) \dot{q}(\theta)}{\hat{C}'(2q(\theta)) + \theta \hat{C}''(2q(\theta)) \dot{q}(\theta)}\right)\right) \hat{C}'(2q(\theta)).$$
$$(23)$$

Given that competition between principals reduces distortions, an important issue is whether the first-best outcome $q^*(\theta)$ can be achieved at an equilibrium. (23) shows that this might not always be the case.[46]

Stole (1991) and Martimort (1992) analyzed equilibrium distortions under intrinsic and private common agency and asymmetric information. When symmetric principals control complementary activities, a multiplicity of equilibria exists and levels of activities in those equilibria can be ranked. Uniqueness arises with substitutes.[47] With quadratic utility functions and beta-distributions,

---

[45] The initial condition is $q(\underline{\theta}) = q^*(\underline{\theta})$ where the first-best outcome $q^*(\theta)$ satisfies $S'(q^*(\theta)) = \theta C_1(q^*(\theta), q^*(\theta))$. See Stole (1991) and Martimort (1992) for details.

[46] One has actually $\left(S''(q^*(\theta)) - 2\theta\hat{C}''(2q^*(\theta))\right) \dot{q}^*(\theta) = \hat{C}'(2q^*(\theta))$, and (23) holds only when $S'' = 0$. Even though both principals compete fiercely to attract the agent's services, the symmetric output is generally still below the first-best. Stole (1991) and Martimort (1992) gave examples, with perfect substitutes and quadratic cost functions, such that the equilibrium output is first-best.

[47] This multiplicity comes from the fact that the differential equation (21) is not Lipschitz at $\underline{\theta}$ and has a singularity. The behavior of the solutions and, in particular, its uniqueness depends on the local behavior at $\underline{\theta}$, which itself depends on whether the activities of the agent are complements or substitutes.

existence and characterization of an equilibrium with quadratic nonlinear contracts are obtained. Gal-Or (1991) and Martimort (1996a) used such characterizations to compare manufacturers-retailers structures under adverse selection. Manufacturers tend to choose a common retailer when they sell complement goods whereas exclusive dealing dominates otherwise. Mezzetti (1997) analyzed a model where two manufacturers sell differentiated products to a customer with an unknown preference parameter. Some types prefer to consume one good whereas others prefer the other. Although goods are substitutes, output distortions are exacerbated at equilibrium. This is due to the fact that principals have opposite rankings of the agent's type.

The private agency framework under adverse selection has also been used to study competing regulations in open economies (see Bond and Gresik (1996), Olsen and Osmudsen (2001, 2003), Calzolari (2001) and Laffont and Pouyet (2003)). A multinational firm may play national regulators one against the others to secure more information rent.

Biais, Martimort and Rochet (2000) analyzed competition among market-makers on financial markets. Investors have private information on their liquidity needs and on the value of an asset. Market-makers stand ready to provide liquidity according to nonlinear price-quantity schedules. There is a *common value* aspect in the model: the value of the asset for the market-makers is linked to the investors' signals. Because of this, ex post efficiency is not reached in the limit of a large number of market-makers although the limit equilibrium remains interim-efficient.

Biglaiser and Mezzetti (1993) analyzed a model where two principals compete for the exclusive services of an agent under both moral hazard and adverse selection. Principals are differentiated: one is relatively efficient at large output levels, the other is more efficient at low levels. In equilibrium, the most (resp. less) efficient agents deal with the high (resp. low) output principal. Principals compete fiercely for intermediate types.

Firms competing through nonlinear prices on oligopoly markets might want to choose which customers to target. To fully understand the welfare consequences of competitive screening, one must ask whether competition increases market coverage. Martimort and Stole (2003b) tackled this issue. Competition with delegated agency and substitutes leads to lower participation distortions relative to monopoly, whereas intrinsic agency or delegated agency with demand complements lead to greater distortions. On delegated versus intrinsic common agency games, see also Calzolari and Scarpa (1999). The literature on competition under nonlinear pricing is covered by Stole (2005).

4.2 Private Agency with Direct Externalities

The strategic role of nonlinear schemes was already stressed in Section 3.1. To justify the use of such schemes, one may want to introduce an adverse selection parameter in the agent's preferences so that principals use such schemes also for screening purposes. One may then ask how adverse selection affects the strategic value of contracts. Under adverse selection, the slope of a nonlinear price is now determined by incentive compatibility. This requirement is strong enough to significantly reduce the equilibrium set compared with complete information where the sole role of nonlinear prices is strategic. Moreover, the screening role of the contracts may call for lower levels of activities which might countervail their strategic role. Take for instance the case of two principals suffering from direct externalities as in Section 3.1. Whereas private agency under complete information induces high levels of outputs, adverse selection on the agent's cost may require decreasing those outputs, reducing thereby the strategic value of contracts.

Theme 6 *Under adverse selection and direct externalities, the strategic role of nonlinear prices might be reduced.*

Khalil, Martimort and Parigi (2004) analyzed interactions between financiers providing funds to an agent who has private information on his income. Two institutions are compared. Under public agency, lenders undertake monitoring activities that are publicly verifiable, and there is no direct externality between those principals. Under private agency, monitoring by either lender is private but still contractible with the agent. In both cases, each principal benefits from the other doing some monitoring since this may publicly reveal the agent's income. This introduces a direct externality between principals under private agency. The nature of the contractual externalities depends on the institution chosen. Under public agency, a lender wants to trick the other into believing that the agent has a lower income and does so by increasing monitoring. This reduces the loan repayment requested by the other and increases the share of income that can be kept by the first lender. There is excessive monitoring in equilibrium and equity-like contracts emerge. Under private agency, a given lender reduces his own contribution to the overall monitoring effort. Monitoring diminishes and may disappear at high income levels. Debt-like payments with flat repayments arise.

4.3   Public Agency

Under asymmetric information, the equilibrium nonlinear schedules no longer reflect the principals' marginal valuations contrary to what happens with "truthful" equilibria under complete information. This has important consequences both for efficiency and also for the distribution of principals' payoffs under delegated common agency.

I shall first use Example 1 on regulation and focus on the intrinsic common agency game. The n regulators offer non-cooperatively the nonlinear prices $\{t_i(q)\}_{1 \le i \le n}$ to the common agent whose type θ is private information. In the case of a linear cost function (i.e., $C(q) = q$), the agent's rent when taking all contracts is:

$$U(\theta) = \max_q \sum_{i=1}^{n} t_i(q) - \theta q.$$

Assuming concavity of the agent's objective, we have at any differentiability point $q(\theta)$:

$$\sum_{i=1}^{n} t_i'(q(\theta)) = \theta. \tag{24}$$

Proceeding as usual to compute P_i's best-response, we obtain:

$$q(\theta) \in \arg\max_{\tilde{q}} S_i(\tilde{q}) + t_{-i}(\tilde{q}) - \left(\theta + \frac{F(\theta)}{f(\theta)}\right)\tilde{q} \quad \forall i \in \{1, \ldots, n\}. \tag{25}$$

Again, the equilibrium quantity satisfies a *bilateral interim efficiency* condition. Assuming concavity of P_i's objective, the first order condition for (25) yields:[48]

$$S_i'(q(\theta)) + t_{-i}'(q(\theta)) = \theta + \frac{F(\theta)}{f(\theta)}, \quad \forall i \in \{1, \ldots, n\}. \tag{26}$$

From (24) and (26), P_i's marginal contribution at any equilibrium point satisfies

$$t_i'(q) = S_i'(q) - \frac{F(\theta(q))}{f(\theta(q))}, \tag{27}$$

where $\theta(q)$ is the inverse function of $q(\theta)$ defined in (28) below.[49]

Under adverse selection, each principal reduces the common agent's production to better extract his rent. Each principal bears the full cost of information revelation but only enjoys a part of its benefit. Marginal contributions are below their complete information values and the equilibrium output is reduced with respect to the cooperative outcome:

$$\sum_{i=1}^{n} S_i'(q(\theta)) = \theta + n\frac{F(\theta)}{f(\theta)}. \tag{28}$$

The distortion increases with the number of principals. As n increases, the outcome moves away from the interim efficiency frontier reached had they cooperated.

Theme 7   *Under adverse selection and public agency, although each contractual relationship is bilateral interim efficient, Nash equilibria are not interim efficient. Equilibrium contributions are not truthful.*

Laffont and Tirole (1993, Chapter 17) proposed an interesting application of public agency to a privatization problem. They analyzed a contractual

---

[48] This is the equilibrium condition provided a standard monotonicity condition holds.

[49] To ensure that $q(\cdot)$ is monotonically decreasing, we need to assume that $\frac{d}{d\theta}\left(\frac{F(\theta)}{f(\theta)}\right) > 0$.

equilibrium between a regulator and the regulated firm's equityholders who both control the firm's management. The cost of privatization is the excessive rent extraction under common agency.

Lebreton and Salani (2003) extended the lobbying model of Grossman and Helpman (1994) by introducing uncertainty on the weight that a decision-maker gives to social welfare in his objective function given that he values also the lobbyists' contributions. They characterized equilibria for a 0-1 decision. Martimort and Semenov (2005) analyzed a lobbying game with two lobbies having ideal points located in a one-dimensional policy space. Lobbies use monetary contributions to influence a political decision-maker who is privately informed about his ideal point.[50] The decision-maker is more likely to obtain some rent as the conflict of interests between the principals is exacerbated (i.e., the distance between their ideal points increases) and the shape of that rent depends both on the importance of ideological uncertainty and the degree of polarization between groups. The equilibrium policy is significantly shifted towards the agent's ideal point. An extreme form of "laissez-faire" equilibrium where the agent always chooses his ideal point and interest groups lose all influence might sometimes arise.

- **Impact of Adverse Selection on Payoffs under Delegated Agency:** The analysis of delegated common agency bears some similarity with that of intrinsic agency. One must nevertheless take care of the agent's type-dependent participation constraint:

$$U(\theta) = \max_q T_N(q) - \theta q \geq \max \left\{ 0, \max_{\{S \subset N-\{i\},q\}} T_S(q) - \theta q \right\} \forall \theta \in \Theta.$$

$$(29)$$

The delegated common agency game is solved in Martimort and Stole (2005a) when uncertainty on the cost parameter (i.e., $\bar{\theta} - \underline{\theta}$) is small enough, there are two principals and θ is uniformly distributed on Θ.[51] The set of principals' equilibrium payoffs can be characterized with simple inequalities, exactly as in the complete information model reviewed in Section 3.2. This characterization is nevertheless more complex since contributions' schedules are no longer truthful. Martimort and Stole (2005a) observed indeed that the right-hand side of (29) might depend on how schedules are extended for off the equilibrium outputs. Two cases are considered:

- *Natural equilibria* are such that the equilibrium schedules are obtained by integrating (27) and keeping only the positive part. For a uniform distribution,

---

[50] There is thus horizontal differentiation between different types instead of vertical differentiation as in Lebreton and Salaniè (2003).

[51] These assumptions ensure that the participation constraint (29) binds only for the least efficient type.

this yields

$$t_i(q) = \max \left\{ 0, \frac{1}{3}(2S_i(q) - S_{-i}(q) + \underline{\theta}q) - k_i \right\}$$

for some constant k_i and for any q both on and off the equilibrium.[52]
• *Simple equilibria* are such that

$$t_i'(q) = S_i'(q) - (\bar{\theta} - \underline{\theta}) \quad \text{for} \quad q \leq q(\bar{\theta}).$$

Marginal contributions are thus close to the truthful ones when $\bar{\theta} - \underline{\theta}$ is small enough. Otherwise, marginal contributions' schedules in both natural and simple equilibria are the same for any equilibrium output.

In the limit of a small uncertainty ($\bar{\theta} - \underline{\theta}$ converging to zero), the set of equilibrium payoffs achieved by the principals with natural and simple equilibria differ. Marginal contributions in natural equilibria keep track of the contractual externality that arises under adverse selection even when $\bar{\theta} - \underline{\theta}$ goes to zero. The value of bringing one principal in is thus lower with natural equilibria than with the truthful equilibria and that principal cannot ask for as much. The set of payoffs achieved as limits of natural equilibria is thus a strict subset of those achieved with truthful equilibria. Adverse selection becomes a selection device, albeit a crude one.[53] Instead, simple equilibrium payoffs converge towards the full set of truthful payoffs. This shows that one has to be cautious in justifying the use of nonlinear schedules under complete information by appealing to some underlying adverse selection environment. Whether the corresponding equilibrium payoffs converge towards those achieved with truthful equilibria of the complete information game or not depends on how equilibrium schedules are extended for off the equilibrium outputs even under adverse selection. To summarize, we have:

---

[52] Interestingly, marginal contributions in natural equilibria are unchanged when the cost parameter is drawn from a uniform distribution with a larger support.

[53] Adverse selection might sometimes be a powerful device. Take the following regulatory example (drawn from Martimort (1996b)). Two regulators offer subsidies t_i ($i = 1, 2$) to a regulated firm which produces one unit of a good at cost θ. The principals' benefits are respectively S_1 and S_2. Assume first that it is common knowledge that $\theta = \underline{\theta}$. Then, there exists a continuum of equilibria under intrinsic common agency. The principals' payoffs (V_1, V_2) are such that $V_1 + V_2 = S_1 + S_2 - \underline{\theta}$, $V_i \geq 0$, $i = 1, 2$. The firm gets zero rent. Assume now that θ is distributed on $\Theta = [\underline{\theta}, \bar{\theta}]$ according to some distribution function $F(\cdot)$. Because only one unit of the good can be produced, principals are restricted to offer simple transfers t_1 and t_2. The probability that those offers are accepted is $F(t_1 + t_2)$. Principal P_i's expected payoff is $(S_i - t_i)F(t_1 + t_2)$ whose maximum is achieved (assuming quasi-concavity of the objective which holds when the monotone hazard rate property $\frac{d}{d\theta}\left(\frac{F(\theta)}{f(\theta)}\right) > 0$ is satisfied) when $S_1 - t_1 = S_2 - t_2 = \frac{F(t_1+t_2)}{f(t_1+t_2)}$. When $\bar{\theta} - \underline{\theta}$ converges to zero, a unique equilibrium survives in the complete information game, which yields payoffs $V_1 = V_2 = \frac{S_1+S_2-\underline{\theta}}{2}$. This is the Nash-bargaining outcome had the principals decided to bargain over their respective shares of the cost of the public good.

Theme 8   *The set of equilibrium payoffs of a delegated common agency game under complete information may not be robust to the choice of the off the equilibrium extensions used under adverse selection.*

4.4   Sequential Common Agency

So far, I have focused on the case where competing principals make simultaneous offers. Let us now consider a sequential timing. To fix ideas, consider Example 1 on regulation. One may think of P_1 as being a Federal regulator acting as a Stackelberg leader whereas P_2 is a State regulator.

The sequential timing obliges one to think more deeply about the principals' incentives to participate in the game.[54] With sequential moves, the difficulty could be that P_1 offers transfers to the agent that are so low that inducing the agent's participation may become too costly for P_2. To avoid such issues, P_2 should have the right to shut down the firm. This might be captured by introducing a *no-veto constraint* stipulating that P_1 designs his own mechanism, taking into account that P_2 should not veto the firm's activity. As shown in the Appendix, the Stackelberg outcome is then defined as:[55]

$$\sum_{i=1}^{2} S_i'(q(\theta)) = \left(\theta + \frac{F(\theta)}{f(\theta)} \left(2 + \frac{d}{d\theta} \left(\frac{F(\theta)}{f(\theta)} \right) \right) \right) C'(q(\theta)). \tag{30}$$

Compared with (28) (taken in the case $n = 2$), output distortions are increased. To understand why that is, it is useful to think about the sequential revelation of information taking place under sequential common agency. For a given scheme $t_1(q)$ offered by P_1, P_2 wants to reduce the agent's output. Everything happens as if the output choice made by the implicit coalition he forms with A was made with virtual costs replacing true costs because of adverse selection. Since virtual costs increase faster than true costs, the incentives of that coalition for exaggerating costs are exacerbated. When he offers his own mechanism, P_1 anticipates this effect, which calls for more output distortion compared with the Nash outcome.[56]

Theme 9   *Under adverse selection and public agency, distortions are exacerbated with a sequential timing.*

---

[54] Implicit under simultaneous common agency is that principals obtain by contracting a payoff greater than their reservation values. This imposes some conditions on the way they can share contributions. Principals choose to participate because they earn more than by not contributing.

[55] This is the solution provided that it is weakly decreasing. Sufficient conditions for this are $\frac{d}{d\theta} \left(\frac{F(\theta)}{f(\theta)} \right) \geq 0$ and $\frac{d^2}{d\theta^2} \left(\frac{F(\theta)}{f(\theta)} \right) \geq 0$.

[56] The intuition given above implicitly refers to a direct revelation of information. In fact, there is no problem in using a sequential version of the standard Revelation Principle here. Although P_1 does not directly contract with P_2, he still anticipates the behavior of the coalition between P_2 and A exactly as if P_1 were contracting with P_2, who would then sub-contract with A. This analogy between sequential common agency games and hierarchical contracting is developed further in Section 6.1 below.

Baron (1985) was an early contribution on sequential common agency in a regulatory context where he analyzed the interaction between State and Federal regulators. Martimort (1996b) derived a formula similar to (30) in the case of a 0-1 project. Martimort (1999) developed the Stackelberg timing in the case where the agent's type can only take two values but production is continuous. Calzolari and Pavan (2005) and Kartasheva (2005) analyzed the strategic informational leakage that arises in sequential common agency games when the decision taken by the agent for one principal might be observed by followers before they offer themselves contracts. These models merge the difficulties of both the common agency and the limited commitment literatures.

5 INFORMED PRINCIPALS

The justifications for the use of menus have so far relied on adverse selection on the agent's side. In this section, I instead analyze the case where principals are privately informed. A principal may now use menus both to signal his type but also to learn about those of others. An important issue is thus to understand how the principals' information is aggregated. This is particularly relevant for Example 2 since lobbying groups do not only directly influence the agent but also want to convey information.

When principals are privately informed, the model combines the difficulties of both the informed principal and the common agency literatures. Two sets of issues should be addressed. The first one is related to the characterization of equilibria, with a focus on their multiplicity and the properties of output distortions. The second one is more normative. Are these equilibria interim efficient and, if yes, under which circumstances?

To fix ideas, consider two principals having the following preferences for a public good:

$$V_i = \beta_i q - t_i \quad \text{for} \quad i = 1, 2. \tag{31}$$

The preference parameters $(\beta_i)_{i \in \{1,2\}}$ are independently and identically distributed on $B = [\underline{\beta}, \bar{\beta}]$ according to the distribution $G(\cdot)$ (density $g(\cdot)$). This public good is produced by an agent who has no private information.

Martimort and Moreira (2005) looked for symmetric Bayesian equilibria where principals choose a nonlinear contribution within a menu $\{t(q, \hat{\beta})\}_{\hat{\beta} \in B}$.[57] The techniques used to compute these symmetric equilibria are reminiscent of those available to compute optimal strategies in first-price auctions. New difficulties stem from both the multiunit nature of bidding and the non-excludability of the public good.

---

[57] From Epstein and Peters (1999) we know that "market information" may matter in a common agency environment. One may wonder if the space of menus of nonlinear prices is not unnecessarily restricted. We will comment on this issue below.

In this Bayesian context, the principals' incentive compatibility constraints become:

$$\beta_i \in \arg\max_{\hat{\beta}_i} \mathop{E}_{\beta_{-i}} \left(\beta_i q(\hat{\beta}_i, \beta_{-i}) - t(q(\hat{\beta}_i, \beta_{-i}), \hat{\beta}_i) \right) \tag{32}$$

where the level of public good optimally chosen by the agent is given by

$$q(\hat{\beta}_1, \hat{\beta}_2) \in \arg\max_{q} \sum_{i=1}^{2} t(q, \hat{\beta}_i) - \theta C(q) \tag{33}$$

and the nonlinear contribution $\{t(q, \hat{\beta})\}_{\hat{\beta} \in B}$ satisfies the agent's participation constraint[58]

$$U(\theta, \hat{\beta}_1, \hat{\beta}_2) = \max_{q} \sum_{i=1}^{2} t(q, \hat{\beta}_i) - \theta C(q) \geq 0. \tag{34}$$

The contribution $t(q, \hat{\beta}_i)$ selected by P_i within the given menu is observed by the agent. When the equilibrium is fully separating, the agent is thus informed of the principals' types at the time of choosing how much to produce. This explains the form taken by his output choice (33) and his participation decision (34).

Martimort and Moreira (2005) showed that, provided one focuses on nondecreasing equilibrium allocations, the following *pointwise optimality* conditions characterize an interesting class of differentiable equilibria:

$$\beta_i + \frac{\partial t}{\partial q}(q(\beta_1, \beta_2), \beta_{-i}) - \theta C'(q(\beta_1, \beta_2))$$

$$= \frac{1 - G(\beta_{-i})}{g(\beta_{-i})} \frac{\partial^2 t}{\partial q \partial \beta_{-i}}(q(\beta_1, \beta_2), \beta_{-i}). \tag{35}$$

These conditions capture again the fact that contracts are *bilateral interim efficient*.

To better understand those conditions, consider an agent having an indirect utility function defined over (q, t_i) pairs as $t_i + t(q, \beta_{-i}) - \theta C(q)$ and suppose that this agent is privately informed on β_{-i}. Provided that the Spence-Mirrlees condition $\frac{\partial^2 t}{\partial q \partial \beta_{-i}} > 0$ holds, standard mechanism design techniques can be used to find the optimal contract that P_i (who is uninformed on the parameter β_{-i}) offers to such an agent. To compute this optimal contract, note that there is no loss of generality for P_i in using a direct revelation mechanism that induces the agent to reveal β_{-i}.[59] Moreover, in a private values environment with risk-neutrality, a given principal does not lose anything by revealing his type to the agent at the offer stage.[60] Everything happens as if the agent's endogenous information on P_{-i}'s type had to be screened by P_i.

---

[58] To simplify presentation, this constraint is written in the case of intrinsic common agency. Martimort and Moreira (2005) treated also the case of delegated common agency.

[59] Here we use the Revelation Principle to compute a best-response as in Section 2.

[60] See Maskin and Tirole (1990).

Instead of offering a direct revelation mechanism, P_i could as well have offered the nonlinear contribution $t(q, \beta_i)$ that is constructed from this direct revelation mechanism. Thus, there is no loss of generality in a priori restricting P_i to choose a best-response to the nonlinear price $t(q, \beta_{-i})$ selected by P_{-i} within the menu of nonlinear contributions $\{t(q, \hat{\beta})\}_{\hat{\beta} \in B}$. More complex mechanisms would not improve P_i's payoff when pointwise optimality holds. "Market information" à la Epstein and Peters (1999) has a nice and simple interpretation in our context: This is what has been learned by the agent from observing the other principal's offer.

Since the agent withdraws some costly information rent from learning β_{-i}, P_i designs a best-response, which induces less output in order to reduce this rent. Equilibrium outputs are downward distorted below the first-best, and each principal offers a contribution which is, at the margin, less than his own marginal valuation.[61] Note that P_i's incentives to reduce output depend on the cross-derivative $\frac{\partial^2 t}{\partial q \partial \beta_{-i}}$. Output distortions are greater at a best-response if the other principal offers himself a schedule which, at the margin, depends strongly on his type. This in turn makes P_i's marginal contribution steeper, which generates a multiplicity of equilibria.

Assuming that $G(\cdot)$ has a linear hazard rate, Martimort and Moreira (2005) show that there exist interim efficient equilibria with marginal contributions that are linear in types. Because the agent obtains some rent by endogenously learning private information, the equilibrium outcome can only be replicated by a centralized mechanism offered by an uninformed planner, if this planner gives a positive weight to the agent in his objective function. In the case of a 0-1 project, Laussel and Palfrey (2003) also obtained positive results on interim efficiency. The interim efficiency property of the common agency equilibria is surprising. Indeed, common agency differs from centralized contracting since the agent cannot commit and optimally reacts to earlier moves of the principals, whereas the uninformed mediator is endowed with such commitment under centralized contracting.

Theme 10 *Assume principals are privately informed, Bayesian-Nash equilibria are ex post inefficient, but they might sometimes be interim efficient.*

In the case of a 0-1 project, Menezes, Monteiro and Temini (2001) discussed the multiplicity and the ex post inefficiency of equilibria. Bond and Gresik (1997) studied the case where only one principal has private information and principals compete with piece-rate contracts. There exists then an open set of inefficient equilibria. Bond and Gresik (1998) analyzed competition between tax authorities for the revenue of a multinational firm when only one of these principals

---

[61] Note that this screening motive for downward distortions is somewhat different from the usual "free-riding" problem in centralized mechanisms à la Mailath and Postlewaite (1990). There, output is reduced by an uninformed mediator who offers a centralized mechanism to reduce the agents' incentives to underestimate their own marginal valuations.

knows the firm's cost parameter. Biglaiser and Mezzetti (2000) developed a model of privately informed principals competing for the services of an agent who is privately informed on his disutility of effort. Effort distortions are lower than with a single principal.

6   JUSTIFICATIONS OF COMMON AGENCY

One lesson in most of the previous sections is that transaction costs generally arise under multi-contracting. Equilibria most often fail to be (interim) efficient. This is somewhat puzzling given that multi-contracting prevails in organizations be they public (governments) or private (markets). A natural question is whether multi-contracting outcomes could also be achieved under centralized contracting provided that centralized contracting is subject to some extra constraints. In other words, I now investigate whether common agency performs well in *third-best environments*. Two different perspectives are taken. The first one (Section 6.1) draws a link between common agency and the literature on hierarchical contracting. I show that (sequential) common agency may sometimes implement the optimal centralized contracting outcome under the threat of collusion between agents. The second approach (Section 6.2) simply compares common agency and centralized contracting in specific third-best contexts plagued with contractual problems due to either collusion or limited commitment.

6.1   From Vertical Hierarchies to Common Agency

Consider a three-agent organization with a principal P, his privately informed agent A, and a supervisor S, who is only interested in his wage s_2.[62] The principal's, the supervisor's and the agent's utility functions are respectively:[63]

$$V_1 = S(q) - t_1 - s_2, \quad V_2 = s_2, \quad \text{and} \quad U = t_1 - \theta C(q).$$

The supervisor bridges the information gap between the principal and the agent by receiving a soft information signal $\sigma \in \{\sigma_1, \sigma_2\}$ (with respective probabilities p and $1 - p$) on the agent's type. This signal is observed by both S and A. Following the observation of σ_i, the agent's type is believed to be drawn from the cumulative distribution $F_i(\theta)$. The monotone hazard rate properties $\frac{d}{d\theta}\left(\frac{F_i(\theta)}{f_i(\theta)}\right) > 0$ $(i = 1, 2)$ hold as well as the following ranking between conditional hazard rates: $\frac{F_1(\theta)}{f_1(\theta)} \geq \frac{F_2(\theta)}{f_2(\theta)}$.

---

[62] Tirole (1986, 1992), Faure-Grimaud, Laffont and Martimort (2002, 2003), and Baliga and Sjöström (1998) (among others) present various models of hierarchical supervision.
[63] Outside opportunities are normalized at zero.

• **Benchmark:** Suppose that the principal learns directly σ_i. Second-best output distortions depend on the realized signal. The principal recommends an output $q^{SB}(\theta, \sigma_i)$ and leaves a rent $U^{SB}(\theta, \sigma_i)$ to the agent where:

$$S'(q^{SB}(\theta, \sigma_i)) = \left(\theta + \frac{F_i(\theta)}{f_i(\theta)}\right) C'(q^{SB}(\theta, \sigma_i))$$

and

$$U^{SB}(\theta, \sigma_i) = \int_{\theta}^{\bar{\theta}} C(q^{SB}(x, \sigma_i))dx. \tag{36}$$

Note that σ_1 (resp. σ_2) is good (resp. bad) news on the type distribution, and it is associated with large (resp. small) distortions.

• **Supervision:** Consider now a centralized organization where P offers to both S and A the wages $\{s_2(q, \hat{\sigma}_i), t_1(q, \hat{\sigma}_i)\}$, linking their compensations to the signal $\hat{\sigma}_i$ reported by the supervisor to the principal and to the output chosen by the agent.

A benevolent supervisor reports his signal to the principal (i.e., $\hat{\sigma}_i = \sigma_i$) and does not need to be paid for doing so. The solution is again described by (36). Because output distortions are greater following σ_1, the agent obtains more rent if σ_2 is reported to the principal. This creates a priori some scope for collusion between S and A.[64] My goal here is not to derive the whole class of collusion-proof incentive mechanisms. I shall first notice that an upper bound on what can be achieved by P is precisely given by (36) (i.e., the outcome in the absence of collusion) and then I shall show that sequential common agency achieves this outcome.

Suppose indeed that P only contracts with S who then contracts with A. With such delegation, the principal uses an explicit collusion between S and A on the equilibrium path. Assume that the supervisor has no veto rights and accepts contracting ex ante, i.e., before knowing signal σ and learning the agent's cost parameter. Consider then the simple *"sell-out"* contract: $\tilde{s}_2^i(q) = S(q) - k^*$ where k^* is a constant whose value will be determined below. This scheme does not depend of the supervisor's information. However, following acceptance of this mechanism, the supervisor uses his knowledge of σ_i to implement

---

[64] Suppose that the supervisor knows not only the realized signal σ_i but also the agent's cost parameter. There is then complete information between S and A. Because the signal affects neither the agent nor the supervisor's payoff and is soft, there is no way for the principal to learn about it. This is nothing else than the result that supervisory information is generally not valuable when it is soft and collusion between the supervisor and the agent takes place under complete information (see Tirole (1986) and Baliga (1999) on this topic). The optimal contract robust to collusion would pool over σ_i and implement an output $q^P(\theta)$ and a rent profile $U^P(\theta)$ independent of σ_i: $S'(q^P(\theta)) = \left(\theta + \frac{F(\theta)}{f(\theta)}\right) C'(q^P(\theta))$ and $U^P(\theta)) = \int_{\theta}^{\bar{\theta}} C'(q^P(x))dx$, where $F(\theta) = pF_1(\theta) + (1 - p)F_2(\theta)$ and $f(\theta) = pf_1(\theta) + (1 - p)f_2(\theta)$. This outcome can of course be implemented by contracting only with the agent.

the second-best outputs and rents $\{q^{SB}(\theta, \sigma_i), U^{SB}(\theta, \sigma_i)\}$ by offering a wage $y(q, \sigma_i)$ to the agent.[65,66]

Suppose now that P can only contract with A before S comes in and contracts himself with A. The setting is much like that of the sequential common agency game in Section 4.4, with the only differences being that S, who acts as a follower, has no veto rights and is privately informed about the type distribution. P can still achieve the second-best outcome by offering $\tilde{s}_2^i(q)$ to A and having S receive $s_2(q, \sigma_i) = \tilde{s}_2^i(q) - y(q, \sigma_i)$ from A. With this scheme the supervisor induces the second-best outputs and is just indifferent between participating or not. He brings nevertheless his expertise to the organization because outputs now depend on σ_i. Ultimately, this benefit accrues to the principal. Splitting contracting between the uninformed principal and the informed supervisor, but keeping a Stackelberg timing gives an implementation of the second-best, which is de facto collusion-proof.

Such organization nevertheless raises two issues. First, the supervisor suffers a loss from allowing the inefficient type to produce since he can only break even in expectation. If the supervisor had veto rights, he would shut down production of that type. Second, this organization does not give S enough incentives for gathering information.[67] The solution to both problems is to leave veto rights to S so that he gets an information rent related to his knowledge of supervisory information. This rent may then be large enough to induce information gathering. In that case, even though new distortions are associated to common agency, having two principals might still be useful.

Theme 11 *Sequential common agency may implement the centralized second-best outcome in a collusion-proof way if the informed principal acting as a follower has no veto rights. Otherwise, it implements a third-best outcome but might still be useful.*

This section has briefly touched on two important trends of the recent literature that are somewhat related, namely collusion in multi-agent organizations and hierarchical contracting. My purpose here is not to survey these topics but to give a bit of perspective to better understand what has been done above.

---

[65] Formally, we have $y(q, \sigma_i) = \theta^{SB}(q, \sigma_i)C(q) + U^{SB}(\theta^{SB}(q, \sigma_i), \sigma_i)$ where $\theta^{SB}(q, \sigma_i)$ is the inverse function of $q^{SB}(\theta, \sigma_i)$ defined on (36). The fee k^* is chosen by P to extract S's expected surplus

$$k^* = E_\sigma \left(\int_\Theta \left(S(q^{SB}(\theta, \sigma_i)) - \left(\theta + \frac{F_i(\theta)}{f_i(\theta)} \right) C(q^{SB}(\theta, \sigma_i)) \right) f_i(\theta)d\theta \right)$$

where $E_\sigma(\cdot)$ is the expectation operator with respect to σ.

[66] Although supervisory information is soft, it now becomes useful. The principal benefits from the fact that there is still asymmetric information on θ between S and A to delegate at no cost the control of the agent to the intermediate level.

[67] Suppose indeed that S must undertake a non-verifiable effort in gathering information prior to any contracting. If S has no veto rights, he is under the threat of the principal's opportunistic behavior. The principal offers a contract which indirectly does not reward the supervisor for information gathering. As a result, no information gathering takes place.

- **Collusion:** Laffont and Martimort (1997) modelled collusion under asymmetric information in multi-agent organizations. An uninformed third-party organizes a side-mechanism to facilitate collusion. This side-mechanism gives to the agents more than their reservation payoffs had they played non-cooperatively in the principal's grand-mechanism. It must also be incentive compatible because of asymmetric information within the coalition.[68] The optimal collusion-proof anonymous mechanism was derived in the case of two agents producing complementary inputs for the organization and having marginal costs that are independently distributed. Non-anonymous dominant strategy mechanisms may still achieve the second-best collusion-free outcome even under the threat of collusion. More generally, Laffont and Martimort (2000) showed that there exists a Bayesian mechanism that always implements the second-best outcome, even under the threat of collusion if types are not correlated. We also provided a Collusion-Proofness Principle under asymmetric information. Collusion-proof optimal contracts were then characterized even when types are correlated. Yardstick mechanisms, which are known to fully extract the agents' rents if types are correlated and agents do not collude,[69] are of little help with collusion. This is precisely when the principal benefits the most from the agents' competition because their incentives to collude are also the strongest.[70] In a hierarchical model of supervision, Faure-Grimaud, Laffont, and Martimort (2003) showed that delegating control of the agent to the supervisor may still be useful even if the latter is risk-averse. An equivalence exists between a centralized organization designed by the principal under the threat of collusion and a nexus of vertical contracts involving the principal and the supervisor on one side and the supervisor and the agent on the other. However, risk-aversion implies that delegation is costly.[71] As in our example above, supervisory information is useful even when it is soft and collusion is an issue.

---

[68] Quesada (2004) analyzed the case where an informed agent designs the mechanism for his colluding partner and argued that optimal mechanisms may be asymmetric in such contexts.

[69] See Crémer and McLean (1988).

[70] Considering the possibility of collusion also establishes some continuity between the contracting outcomes under independent and correlated information, something that is known not to hold under pure Bayesian-Nash behavior. Che and Kim (2005) pointed out that this continuity is lost when there are at least three agents and that a simple "sell-out" mechanism making the third-party residual claimant achieves the no-collusion outcome. Jeon (2005) obtained a similar result in the case of two agents only, but collusion is then hindered by the fact that agents are protected by limited liability. Dequiedt (2004) showed that collusion may be much more harmful to an organization if the collusive agreement takes place before acceptance of the grand-mechanism. Pavlov (2004) extended also the Laffont and Martimort (1997, 2000) framework to the case of a continuum of types and to the case where the third-party organizing the collusion may have redistributive concerns. He showed that simple mechanisms may sometimes fight collusion at no cost even if collusion can coordinate the agents' decisions to participate.

[71] For another model justifying delegation as an optimal response to collusion see Baliga and Sjostrom (1998). By using a different information structure, Celik (2004) demonstrated that a centralized organization may be preferred if it creates countervailing incentives within the coalition.

- **Vertical Hierarchies:** This implementation of the collusion-proof allocation through delegation brings us to the mechanism design approach of hierarchies.[72] In a model with two productive agents who are privately informed on their respective marginal costs, Melumad, Mookherjee and Reichelstein (1995) argued that delegation achieves the same outcome as a more centralized organization where the principal directly contracts with both agents.[73] This is no surprise in view of our previous discussion. Delegation relies explicitly on collusion on the equilibrium path, but we know that collusion does not harm the organization in the informational environment analyzed by these authors. Key to Melumad, Mookherjee and Reichelstein (1995) is the fact that the intermediate principal accepts contracts before learning information from lower levels of the hierarchies.[74] This contrasts with McAfee and Millan (1995) who instead analyzed hierarchical contracting when successive principals are protected by ex post participation constraints. Information rents add up along the hierarchy. A similar effect arises with the no-veto constraints in the model I sketched above.[75] Laffont and Martimort (1998) showed that delegation may dominate centralization when the latter suffers from collusion.

6.2   Collusion, Limited Commitment and Common Agency

Section 4.3 already showed that splitting the control of the agent among several principals under public agency leads to excessive rent extraction and to greater distortions compared with centralized contracting. Although those excessively low powered incentives may appear as a cost, compared with centralized contracting, they may be useful in contexts where high powered incentives create contractual hazards. I analyze two such environments of interests, both motivated by regulation, which offers an archetypical example to explain the separation between different governing bodies.

- **Collusion:** Consider Example 1 but now suppose that regulators are somewhat biased in favor of the regulated firm. The capture of the decision-maker by the

---

[72] See Mookherjee (2005) for a review.

[73] Baron and Besanko (1992) and Gilbert and Riordan (1995) also compared the decentralized organization with a consolidation where agents merge. The latter organization dominates under weak conditions. Baron and Besanko (1999) and Dequiedt and Martimort (2004) analyzed the agents' incentives to merge when it is costly (either because agents must get more utility than by remaining split apart in Baron and Besanko (1999) or because agents must incur a fixed cost to learn each other's types in Dequiedt and Martimort (2004)). Mookherjee and Tsugamari (2004) performed more general comparisons between the consolidated, the centralized, and the decentralized organizations depending on the degree of complementarity between the agents' inputs.

[74] See also Mookherjee and Reichelstein (2001) for a generalization to more complex organizations. An earlier vintage of that idea could be found in Crémer and Riordan (1987) who analyzed a model where only ex ante contracting is feasible.

[75] Faure-Grimaud and Martimort (2001) analyzed this no-veto constraint in a model with an uninformed and risk-averse intermediary.

regulated firm might be modelled in an ad hoc manner by assuming that each principal gives to the firm a positive weight α (but $\alpha < 1$[76]) in his objective function. With constant marginal cost, the equilibrium output now becomes:

$$\sum_{i=1}^{n} S_i'(q(\theta)) = \theta + n(1 - \alpha)\frac{F(\theta)}{f(\theta)}. \tag{37}$$

Two effects are at work simultaneously. On the one hand, having biased principals goes in the direction of giving too high-powered incentives to the firm. On the other hand, those distorted incentives are somewhat countered by the principals' non-cooperative behavior. From a social welfare viewpoint,[77] it may then be optimal to split tasks between biased regulators to come closer to the socially optimal distortion.[78]

In the model above, no explicit incentive scheme is used to correct the behavior of biased principals. Separation of powers is thus a substitute for these missing incentives. Along these lines, Laffont and Pouyet (2003) observed that regulation is subject to political risk and changes as different majorities alternate in office. However, when markets are opened and firms operate in several regulatory environments at the same time, regulatory competition induces very high-powered incentive schemes independently of the identity of national regulators. Market openness insulates the firm from national pressure.

From a theoretical viewpoint, it may be interesting to ask whether this separation of powers can be justified in a full-fledged model where the regulators' biases can be corrected by an incentive scheme. Doing so requires one to give up the common agency model and adopt a three-tier model of regulatory capture à la Laffont and Tirole (1993, Chapter 11). This model justifies the presence of the regulator as a way to bridge an informational gap between the privately informed regulated firm and the rest of society. It helps tracing out the consequences of the threat of capture on optimal regulation. A regulator has power because he learns some piece of information that is relevant for the firm. By not using this piece of information to improve welfare, the regulator may enjoy a share of the firm's information rent. Ensuring collusion-proofness comes at a cost for society. In response to the threat of capture, regulators should thus follow more bureaucratic rules, leaving little scope for discretion and implementing low-powered incentives for regulated firms. Laffont and Martimort (1999) asked whether separating powers between two regulators can reduce the cost of ensuring collusion-proofness and improve welfare. Two regulators may each learn one piece of information relevant to extract the firm's information rent.[79] It may turn out that both signals provide information rent to the firm; the

---

[76] This assumption ensures that the information rent of the firm is viewed as costly by each principal.

[77] The implicit definition of social welfare used here is: $W = \sum_{i=1}^{n} S_i(q) - \theta q - U$.

[78] A sufficient condition would be $n(1 - \alpha) < 1$.

[79] For instance, the firm's marginal cost parameter is the sum of two independent components, each of them being observed with some probability by a regulator.

collusive deal between a single regulator informed on both signals and the firm is thus quite efficient and the cost of ensuring collusion-proofness becomes quite large. With two regulators, the collusive deal between each of them and the firm takes place under asymmetric information on what the other has observed. This may induce each regulator to adopt a prudent behavior and reduce the bribes he requests from the firm. The cost of ensuring collusion-proofness decreases and welfare is improved under separation. Although the argument in Laffont and Martimort (1999) does not rely on whether the signals observed by the regulators are correlated or not, correlation reinforces the benefits of separation by instilling a dose of yardstick competition as in Laffont and Meleu (2001). Mishra and Anant (2004) built on Laffont and Martimort (1999) and studied the incentives of a regulatory body to extend its power towards other agencies' juridictions. Hiriart, Martimort and Pouyet (2005) analyzed the benefits of separating ex ante and ex post regulators in a sequential model.

• **Limited Commitment:** Let us think about a centralized contracting framework extended over two periods, but now assume that the principal has a limited ability to commit. Contracts can either be short term and cover only the current period, or long term but renegotiated as the principal learns new information from observing the agent's past performances.[80] With short-term contracting, information is only gradually revealed over time. An efficient agent is reluctant to reveal his type in the first period because he fears that the principal will use this information to extract his future rent. Because of this so-called ratchet effect, the usual trade-off between efficiency and rent extraction is hardened under non-commitment. One way to mitigate this effect is to offer high-powered incentives in the first period so that early revelation becomes more attractive to an efficient agent. Common agency offers another instrument to improve information revelation as shown by Olsen and Torsvick (1993). Under common agency, there is too much rent extraction in the second period of the relationship. This makes it less attractive for an efficient firm to hide its type in the first period. This reduces the likelihood of first-period pooling, and increases the scope for semi-separating allocations.

Although splitting regulatory powers among several principals improves information revelation, it also comes at a cost in the earlier periods of the relationships. Olsen and Torsvick (1995) analyzed the optimal number of principals that results from this trade-off.

Under centralized contracting, the benefits of renegotiating long-term contracts comes from the increased efficiency at the renegotiation stage. The cost stems from the fact that an efficient agent is unlikely to reveal his type in the

---

[80] For analysis of those two contractual settings, see respectively Laffont and Tirole (1993, Chapters 9 and 10) and the references therein.

first period to enjoy the greater rent that this second period renegotiated contract would bring. Renegotiation hardens again the rent-efficiency trade-off. Martimort (1999) stressed also the benefits of separation under renegotiation. Common agency[81] makes renegotiation less efficient and thus improves the collective ability to commit.

7 CONCLUDING REMARKS

Multi-contracting mechanism design offers a number of challenges for Incentive Theory. Those challenges certainly deserve further research both on the theory side and also in terms of the relevance for applications. Let me mention a few areas where progress would be welcome, going from the most theoretical ones to applications.

First, as discussed earlier, the characterization of incentive feasible allocations implemented as contract equilibria requires new tools that need to be better understood and studied in more general contexts than those highlighted in this paper. In particular, multiprincipal-multiagents games may raise new fascinating issues. The first issue concerns what kind of Revelation/Taxation Principle can be used in this context.[82] The second issue is related to the multiplicity problem. The mechanisms non-cooperatively offered by competing principals define a game played by agents and, following the implementation literature developed under centralized contracting,[83] one may be concerned with the multiplicity of equilibria of this game. Principals might disagree on the most preferred continuation equilibrium and there is no reason to give any of them the right to choose that continuation. In such contexts, principals might adopt prudent behavior and design mechanisms with an eye on the worst continuation equilibria that they may face.

Second, common agency games are generally plagued by a multiplicity of equilibria due to the lack of coordination among principals. As I suggested above, embedding these models in more complex informational environments might sometimes help selecting among those equilibria. The lack of robustness of some of the results to fine details of the information structure might then become troublesome if one wants to head towards a theory of robust contracting. More work should be devoted to the selection issue. In some contexts, and I think here mostly of applications for political science, convergence towards a particular equilibrium may follow learning procedures or may be a result of historical events, which should be explicitly modelled.

---

[81] Actually the model is one with sequential common agency.

[82] The role of menus in multiprincipal-multiagent games has been recently analyzed in Han (2004) who generalized Peters (2003) to the case of several agents. Yamashita (2005) extended also the Revelation Principle to those contexts by requiring that an agent reports not only his type but also which outcome is realized.

[83] See Moore (1992) and Palfrey (1992).

Third, the fact that equilibrium outcomes generally fail to be (interim) efficient, suggests that the transaction costs that arise in multi-contracting environments need to be better understood. One way to address this issue, which has been only briefly touched upon in this survey, consists in looking at those common agency games as implementation of more centralized mechanisms constrained in some way. The benefits of restoring a role for centralized mechanisms is twofold. First, it would eliminate the multiplicity problem due to coordination failures among principals. Second, it would allow one rely on optimization to characterize constrained-optimal mechanisms. In my view, this theoretical step is key to understanding the forces favoring multi-contracting practices.[84]

On a more applied stance, let me come back to some of the examples stressed in that survey to highlight a few possible avenues.

Models of regulation by multiple governing bodies should be adapted to better understand how agencies interact and compete to gain power. Most often, the missions of an agency are vaguely defined once it is enacted. As a result of this incompleteness, there is a continuous struggle among agencies and the set of contracting variables over which they respectively have control should be endogenized in some ways.

Still in the field of political science, models of influence by competing lobbies should be extended by adding private information either on the interest groups' or on the decision-maker's side. Taking into account the corresponding transaction costs may help to better understand various patterns of contributions and influence found in practice.[85]

A serious weakness of the common agency literature, when it applies to political science, is that existing models rely too much on monetary incentives. A typical example would be the relationship between heterogenous voters and politicians concerned with their reelection. More generally, more work should be devoted to understanding contractual externalities in environments where monetary incentives are not available.[86]

Finally, in the I.O. literature, a better understanding of manufacturers'/ retailers' structures certainly is required to develop models involving multiple principals and multiple agents interacting on the marketplace. Again, progress on those issues might be obtained by studying some specific examples.

All those extensions are still awaited to offer a more complete view of multi-contracting. This view is necessary if we want to reconcile Incentive Theory with the concerns of social scientists from other fields.

---

[84] One way of restoring some role for centralized contracting is suggested by Martimort and Stole (2005b) who showed that equilibria of a public common agency game under asymmetric information may be replicated as solutions of a collective problem.

[85] For some steps in this direction, see Martimort and Semenov (2005).

[86] I thank Thomas Palfrey for pointing this out to me in his discussion at the World Congress.

APPENDIX

• **Sequential Common Agency:** Given the nonlinear schedule $t_1(q)$ offered by P_1 to A, optimal contracting between P_2 and A leads us to choose an output which, according to (26), solves:

$$S_2'(q(\theta)) + t_1'(q(\theta)) = \left(\theta + \frac{F(\theta)}{f(\theta)}\right) C'(q(\theta)). \tag{38}$$

Define now P_2's payoff for each realization of θ as

$$V_2(\theta) = \max_q S_2(q) + t_1(q) - \left(\theta + \frac{F(\theta)}{f(\theta)}\right) C(q). \tag{39}$$

Using the Envelope Theorem, we get:

$$\dot{V}_2(\theta) = -\left(1 + \frac{d}{d\theta}\left(\frac{F(\theta)}{f(\theta)}\right)\right) C'(q(\theta)). \tag{40}$$

Using revealed preferences arguments and (39) yields the monotonicity condition

$$\dot{q}(\theta) \leq 0. \tag{41}$$

Because P_2 has veto rights, he could decide to shut down the production of an agent with type θ if the net benefit of having that type produce is negative. To avoid shut down, the following no-veto constraint must thus hold:

$$V_2(\theta) \geq 0. \tag{42}$$

Acting as a Stackelberg leader, P_1 anticipates this continuation of the contracting game and solves:

$$(\mathcal{P}_1^S) \quad : \quad \max_{\{q(\cdot), V_2(\cdot)\}} \int_\Theta \left(\sum_{i=1}^2 S_i(q(\theta)) - \left(\theta + \frac{F(\theta)}{f(\theta)}\right) C(q(\theta)) - V_2(\theta)\right) f(\theta) d\theta$$

subject to (40) to (42).

From (40) and the fact that (42) binds at $\bar{\theta}$ only, we get:

$$V_2(\theta) = \int_\theta^{\bar{\theta}} \left(1 + \frac{d}{dx}\left(\frac{F(x)}{f(x)}\right)\right) C'(q(x))dx. \tag{43}$$

Integrating by parts and inserting into the maximand above and optimizing pointwise leads to (30). This output schedule is decreasing if $\frac{d}{d\theta}\left(\frac{F(\theta)}{f(\theta)}\right) \geq 0$ and $\frac{d^2}{d\theta^2}\left(\frac{F(\theta)}{f(\theta)}\right) \geq 0$. $\quad$ Q.E.D.

References

Attar, A., D. Majumdar, G. Piaser and N. Porteiro (2005): "Common Agency Games with Separable Preferences," mimeo Core, Bruxelles.

Baliga, S. (1999): "Monitoring and Collusion with Soft Information," *Journal of Law, Economics and Organization*, 15, 434–440.

Baliga, S. and T. Sjosträm (1998): "Decentralization and Collusion," *Journal of Economic Theory*, 83, 196–232.

Baron, D. (1985): "Non-Cooperative Regulation of a Non-Localized Externality," *Rand Journal of Economics*, 16, 553–568.

Baron, D. and D. Besanko (1992): "Information, Control and Organizational Structure," *Journal of Economics and Management Strategy*, 1, 237–275.

——— (1999): "Informational Alliances," *Review of Economic Studies*, 66, 743–768.

Baron, D. and R. Myerson (1982): "Regulating a Monopolist with Unknown Costs," *Econometrica*, 50, 911–930.

Bergemann, D. and J. Välimäki (2003): "Dynamic Common Agency," *Journal of Economic Theory*, 111, 23–48.

Bernheim, D. and M. Whinston (1986a): "Common Agency," *Econometrica*, 54, 923–942.

——— (1986b): "Menu Auctions, Resource Allocations and Economic Influence," *Quarterly Journal of Economics*, 101, 1–31.

Biais, B., D. Martimort and J.C. Rochet (2000): "Competing Mechanisms in a Common Value Environment," *Econometrica*, 68, 799–837.

Biglaiser, G. and C. Mezzetti (1993): "Principals Competing for an Agent in the Presence of Adverse Selection and Moral Hazard," *Journal of Economic Theory*, 61, 302–330.

——— (2000): "Incentive Auctions and Information Revelation," *Rand Journal of Economics*, 31, 145–164.

Bond, E. and T. Gresik (1996): "Regulation of Multinational Firms with Two Active Governments: A Common Agency Approach," *Journal of Public Economics*, 59, 33–53.

——— (1997): "Competition between Asymmetrically Informed Principals," *Economic Theory*, 10, 227–240.

——— (1998): "Incentive Compatible Information Transfer Between Asymmetrically Informed Principals," mimeo University of Notre Dame.

Calzolari, G. (2001): "The Theory and Practice of Regulation with Multinational Enterprises," *Journal of Regulatory Economics*, 20, 191–211.

Calzolari, G. and A. Pavan (2002): "A Markovian Revelation Principle for Common Agency Games," mimeo Northwestern University.

——— (2005): "On the Optimality of Privacy in Sequential Contracting," *forthcoming Journal of Economic Theory*.

Calzolari, G. and C. Scarpa (1999): "Non-Intrinsic Common Agency," ENI-FEEM Nota di Lavoro 39.01.

Celik, G. (2004): "Mechanism Design with Collusive Supervision," mimeo UBC.

Che, Y.-K. and J. Kim (2005): "Robustly Collusion-Proof Implementation," mimeo University of Wisconsin.

Crémer, J. and R. McLean (1988): "Full Extraction of Surplus in Bayesian and Dominant Strategy Auctions," *Econometrica*, 56, 1247–1257.

Crémer, J. and M. Riordan (1987): "On Governing Multilateral Transactions with Bilateral Contracts," *Rand Journal of Economics*, 18, 436–451.

D'Aspremont, C. and R. Dos Santos Ferreira (2005): "Oligopolistic Competition as a Common Agency Game," mimeo CORE.

Dasgupta, P., P. Hammond and E. Maskin (1979): "The Implementation of Social Choice Rules," *Review of Economic Studies*, 46, 185–216.

De Villemeur, E. and B. Versaevel (2003): "From Private to Public Agency," *Journal of Economic Theory*, 111, 305–309.

Dequiedt, V. (2004): "Efficient Collusion in Optimal Auctions," mimeo INRA-GAEL Grenoble.

Dequiedt, V. and D. Martimort (2004): "Delegation and Consolidation: Direct Monitoring versus Arm's Length Contracting," *International Journal of Industrial Organization*, 22, 951–981.

Diaw, K. and J. Pouyet (2005): "Information, Competition, and (In)complete Discrimination," mimeo Ecole Polytechnique Paris.

Dixit, A., G. Grossman and E. Helpman (1997): "Common Agency and Coordination," *Journal of Political Economy*, 105, 752–769.

Epstein, L. and M. Peters (1999): "A Revelation Principle for Competing Mechanisms," *Journal of Economic Theory*, 88, 119–160.

Faure-Grimaud, A., J.-J. Laffont and D. Martimort (2002): "Risk-Averse Supervisors and the Efficiency of Collusion," *Contributions in Theoretical Economics*, Vol. 2, Issue 1, Article 5.

———— (2003): "Collusion, Delegation and Supervision with Soft Information," *Review of Economic Studies*, 70, 253–280.

Faure-Grimaud, A. and D. Martimort (2001): "The Agency Cost of Intermediated Contracting," *Economics Letters*, 71, 75–82.

Gal-Or, E. (1991): "A Common Agency with Incomplete Information," *Rand Journal of Economics*, 22, 274–286.

Gibbard, A. (1973): "Manipulation for Voting Schemes," *Econometrica*, 41, 617–631.

Gilbert, R. and M. Riordan (1995): "Regulating Complementary Products: A Comparative Institutional Analysis," *Rand Journal of Economics*, 26, 243–256.

Green, J. and J.-J. Laffont (1977): "Characterization of Satisfactory Mechanisms for the Revelation of Preferences for Public Goods," *Econometrica*, 45, 427–438.

Grossman, G. and E. Helpman (1994): "Protection for Sale," *American Economic Review*, 84, 833–850.

———— (2002): *Interest Groups and Trade Policy*, Princeton: Princeton University Press.

Han, S. (2004): "Menu Theorems for Bilateral Contracting," Micro Theory Working Papers, University Western Ontario.

Helpman, E. (1997): "Politics and Trade Policy," in *Advances in Economics and Econometrics: Theory and Applications*, ed. D. Kreps and K. Wallis. Cambridge: Cambridge University Press.

Helpman, E. and T. Persson (2001): "Lobbying and Legislative Bargaining," *Advances in Economic Analysis and Policy*, Vol. 1, Issue 1, Article 3. http://www.bepress.com/bejeap.

Hiriart, Y., D. Martimort and J. Pouyet (2005): "The Public Management of Environmental Risk: Separating Ex Ante and Ex Post Monitors," mimeo IDEI Toulouse.

Holmström, B. and R. Myerson (1983): "Efficient and Durable Decision Rules with Incomplete Information," *Econometrica*, 51, 1799–1819.

Hurwicz, L. (1972): "On Information Decentralized Systems," in *Decision and Organization (Volume in Honor of J. Marshack)*, ed. R. Radner and C. McGuire. Amsterdam: North Holland.

Ivaldi, M. and D. Martimort (1994): "Competition under Nonlinear Pricing," *Annales d'Economie et de Statistiques*, 34, 71–114.

Jeon, D.-S. (2005): "The Failure to Collude in the Presence of Asymmetric Information," mimeo Pompeu Fabra, Barcelona.

Kartasheva, A. (2005): "Optimal Design of Investment Promotion Policies," mimeo Georgia State University.

Khalil, F., D. Martimort and B. Parigi (2004): "Monitoring a Common Agent: Implications for Financial Contracting," forthcoming *Journal of Economic Theory*.

Kirchsteiger, G. and A. Prat (2001): "Inefficient Equilibria in Lobbying," *Journal of Public Economics*, 82, 349–375.

Klemperer, P. and M. Meyer (1989): "Supply Function Equilibria in Oligopoly under Uncertainty," *Econometrica*, 57, 1243–1277.

Konishi, H., M. Lebreton and S. Weber (1999): "On Coalition-Proof Nash Equilibria in Common Agency Games," *Journal of Economic Theory*, 85, 122–139.

Laffont, J.-J. and D. Martimort (1997): "Collusion under Asymmetric Information," *Econometrica*, 65, 875–912.

—————— (1998): "Collusion and Delegation," *Rand Journal of Economics*, 29, 280–305.

—————— (1999): "Separation of Regulators Against Collusive Behavior," *Rand Journal of Economics*, 107, 1089–1127.

—————— (2000): "Mechanism Design with Collusion and Correlation," *Econometrica*, 68, 309–342.

—————— (2002): *The Theory of Incentives: The Principal-Agent Model*, Princeton: Princeton University Press.

Laffont, J.-J. and M. Meleu (2001): "Separation of Powers and Economic Development," *Journal of Development Economics*, 64, 129–145.

Laffont, J.-J. and J. Pouyet (2003): "The Subsidiary Bias in Regulation," *Journal of Public Economics*, 88, 255–283.

Laffont, J.-J. and J. Tirole (1993): *A Theory of Incentives in Regulation and Procurement*, Cambridge: MIT Press.

Laussel, D. and M. Lebreton (1998): "Efficient Private Production of Public Goods under Common Agency," *Games and Economic Behavior*, 25, 194–218.

—————— (2001): "Conflict and Cooperation: The Structure of Equilibrium Payoffs in Common Agency," *Journal of Economic Theory*, 100, 93–128.

Laussel, D. and T. Palfrey (2003): "Efficient Equilibria in the Voluntary Contributions Mechanisms with Private Information," *Journal of Public Economic Theory*, 5, 449–478.

Lebreton, M. and F. Salanié (2003): "Lobbying under Political Uncertainty," *Journal of Public Economics*, 87, 2589–2610.

Mailath, G. and A. Postlewaite (1990): "Asymmetric Information Bargaining Problems with Many Agents," *Review of Economic Studies*, 57, 351–368.

Martimort, D. (1992): "Multi-Principaux avec Anti-Selection," *Annales d'Economie et de Statistiques*, 28, 1–38.

—————— (1996a): "Exclusive Dealing, Common Agency and Multiprincipal Incentive Theory," *Rand Journal of Economics*, 27, 1–31.

———— (1996b): "The Multiprincipal Nature of the Government," *European Economic Review*, 40, 673–685.

———— (1999): "Renegotiation Design with Multiple Regulators," *Journal of Economic Theory*, 88, 261–293.

Martimort, D. and H. Moreira (2005): "Common Agency with Informed Principals," mimeo IDEI Toulouse.

Martimort, D. and A. Semenov (2005): "How Does Ideological Uncertainty Affect Lobbying Competition: A Common Agency Perspective," mimeo IDEI Toulouse.

Martimort, D. and L. Stole (2002): "The Revelation and Delegation Principles in Common Agency Games," *Econometrica*, 70, 1659–1674.

———— (2003a): "Contractual Externalities and Common Agency Equilibria," *Advances in Theoretical Economics*, Vol. 3, Issue 1, Article 4. http://www.bepress.com/bejte.

———— (2003b): "Market Participation under Delegated and Intrinsic Common Agency Games," mimeo University of Chicago and IDEI Toulouse.

———— (2005a): "On the Robustness of Truthful Equilibria in Common Agency Games," mimeo IDEI and University of Chicago.

———— (2005b): "Common Agency Games with Common Screening Devices," in preparation.

Maskin, E. and J. Tirole (1990): "The Principal-Agent Relationship with an Informed Principal I: Private Values," *Econometrica*, 58, 379–410.

McAfee, P. (1993): "Mechanism Design by Competing Sellers," *Econometrica*, 61, 1281–1312.

McAfee, P. and J. McMillan, (1995), " Organizational Diseconomies of Scale," *Journal of Economics and Management Strategy*, 4, 399–426.

McAfee, P. and M. Schwartz (1994): "Opportunism in Multilateral Vertical Contracting: Non-Discrimination, Exclusivity and Uniformity," *American Economic Review*, 84, 210–230.

Melumad, N., D. Mookherjee and S. Reichelstein (1995): "Hierarchical Decentralization of Incentive Contracts," *Rand Journal of Economics*, 26, 654–672.

Menezes, F., P. Monteiro and A. Temini (2001): "Private Provision of Discrete Public Goods with Incomplete Information," *Journal of Mathematical Economics*, 35, 493–514.

Mezzetti, C. (1997): "Common Agency with Horizontally Differentiated Principals," *Rand Journal of Economics*, 28, 323–345.

Milgrom, P. (2004): *Putting Auction Theory to Work*, Cambridge: Cambridge University Press.

Mishra, A. and T. Anant (2004): "Activism, Separation of Powers and Development," mimeo University of Dundee.

Mitra, D. (1999): "Endogenous Lobby Formation and Endogenous Protection: A Long-Run Model of Trade Policy Formation," *American Economic Review*, 89, 1116–1134.

Mookherjee, D. (2005): "Delegation and Contractual Hierarchies: A Mechanism Design Approach," mimeo Boston University.

Mookherjee, D. and S. Reichelstein (2001): "Incentives and Coordination in Hierarchies," *Advances in Theoretical Economics*, Vol. 1, Issue 1, Article 4.

Mookherjee, D. and M. Tsumagari (2004): "The Organization of Supplier Networks: Effects of Mergers and Intermediation," *Econometrica*, 72, 1179–1220.

Moore, J. (1992): "Implementation in Environments with Complete Information," in *Advances in Economic Theory*, ed. J.-J. Laffont. Cambridge: Cambridge University Press.

Myerson, R. (1979): "Incentive Compatibility and the Bargaining Problem," *Econometrica*, 47, 61–73.

——— (1982): "Optimal Coordination Mechanisms in Generalized Principal-Agent Models," *Journal of Mathematical Economics*, 10, 67–81.

O'Brien, D. and G. Shaffer (1992), "Vertical Control with Bilateral Contracts," *Rand Journal of Economics*, 23, 299–308.

Olsen, T. and P. Osmudsen (2001): "Strategic Tax Competition: Implications of National Ownership," *Journal of Public Economics*, 27, 1–31.

——— (2003): "Spillovers and International Competition for Investments," *Journal of International Economics*, 59, 211–238.

Olsen, T. and G. Torsvick (1993): "The Ratchet Effect in Common Agency: Implications for Regulation and Privatization," *Journal of Law, Economics and Organization*, 9, 136–158.

——— (1995): "Intertemporal Common Agency and Organizational Design: How Much Decentralization," *European Economic Review*, 7, 1405–1428.

Page, F. and P. Monteiro (2003): "Three Principles of Competitive Nonlinear Pricing," *Journal of Mathematical Economics*, 39, 63–109.

Palfrey, T. (1992): "Implementation in Bayesian Equilibrium: The Multiple Equilibrium Problem in Mechanism Design," in *Advances in Economic Theory*, ed. J.-J. Laffont. Cambridge: Cambridge University Press.

Parlour, C. and U. Rajan, (2001): "Price Competition in Loan Markets," *American Economic Review*, 91, 1311–1328.

Pavlov, G. (2004): "Colluding on Participation Decisions," mimeo Northwestern University.

Peck, J. (1996): "Competing Mechanisms and the Revelation Principle," mimeo Ohio State University.

Perez-Castrillo, J. (1994): "Cooperative Outcomes through Non-Cooperative Games," *Games and Economic Behavior*, 7, 428–440.

Perrow, C. (1986): *Complex Organizations: A Critical Essay*, New York: McGraw Hill, 224.

Peters, M. (2001): "Common Agency and the Revelation Principle," *Econometrica*, 69, 1349–1372.

——— (2003): "Negotiation and Take-It-Or-Leave-It in Common Agency," *Journal of Economic Theory*, 111, 88–109.

Prat, A. and A. Rustichini (2003): "Games Played through Agents," *Econometrica*, 71, 989–1027.

Quesada, L. (2004): "Collusion as an Informed Principal Problem," mimeo University of Wisconsin-Madison.

Rama, M. and G. Tabellini (1998): "Lobbying by Capital and Labor Overtrade and Labor Market Policies," *European Economic Review*, 42, 1296–1316.

Rochet, J.-C. (1985): "The Taxation Principle and Multitime Hamilton-Jacobi Equations," *Journal of Mathematical Economics*, 14, 113–128.

Segal, I. (1999): "Contracting with Externalities," *Quarterly Journal of Economics*, 104, 337–388.

Segal, I. and M. Whinston (2003): "Robust Predictions for Bilateral Contracting with Externalities," *Econometrica*, 71, 757–792.

Stole, L. (1991): "Mechanism Design under Common Agency," mimeo Chicago University.

——— (2005): "Price Discrimination in Competitive Environments," in *Handbook of Industrial Organization*, ed. M. Armstrong and R. Porter. Amsterdam: North Holland.

Tirole, J. (1986): "Hierarchies and Bureaucracies: On the Role of Collusion in Organizations," *Journal of Law, Economics and Organization*, 2, 181–214.

——— (1992): "Collusion and the Theory of Organizations," in *Advances in Economic Theory: Proceedings of the Sixth World Congress of the Econometric Society*, ed. J.-J., Laffont. Cambridge: Cambridge University Press.

Wilson, R. (1979), "Auctions of Shares," *Quarterly Journal of Economics*, 93, 675–689.

Yamashita, T. (2005): "A Unified Approach to Mechanism Design," mimeo Stanford University.

CHAPTER 3

Allocative and Informational Externalities in Auctions and Related Mechanisms[*]

Philippe Jehiel and Benny Moldovanu

1 INTRODUCTION

General equilibrium analysis has identified several forms of externalities as obstacles on the road towards economic efficiency. The First Welfare Theorem fails in the presence of allocative externalities, i.e., when agents care about the physical consumption bundles of others. Akerlof's (1970) famous analysis demonstrated that the First Welfare Theorem may also fail in the presence of informational externalities, i.e., when agents care about the information held by others.

In contrast to general equilibrium analysis, auction theory is based on the premise of individual strategic behavior. This theory offers explicit models of price formation and allocative distribution that can be applied also to small markets. The belief that auctions yield competitive outcomes even if information dispersed is behind the practical appeal of auctions and behind their recent popularity.

Since Walrasian equilibria need not be efficient in the presence of various forms of externalities, it is of interest to understand what are the parallel consequences of external effects in auctions and other related mechanisms. This is the main purpose of the research summarized in the present paper.

Traditionally, the focus of auction theory has been on models that view auctions as isolated events. In practice, however, auctions are often part of larger transactions: For example, in privatization exercises such as license allocation schemes (see Jehiel and Moldovanu, 2003, and the surveys in Janssen, 2004), auctions shape the size and composition of future markets. Thus the auction typically affects the nature of the post-auction interaction among bidders. On the other hand, anticipated scenarios about future interaction influence bidding behavior: Already at the bidding stage agents need to care about who gets what, and about the information revealed to, or possessed by others, since these features will be reflected in the equilibrium of the post-auction interaction. Thus allocative and informational externalities naturally arise in models that embed

[*] Invited lecture at the World Congress of the Econometric Society, London, 2005.

auctions in larger economic contexts. This constitutes the main motivation for the present study.

In Section 2 we present a social choice model with a finite number of alternatives and transferable utilities that includes, as a special case, a general multi-object auction model where the alternatives are partitions of objects among agents. The model can incorporate allocative and informational externalities, as well as complementarities. We also sketch a typical application to license auctions.

In Section 3 we focus on the effects of allocative externalities. The induced endogeneity of valuations is the main driving force behind a wealth of new, specific phenomena. Traditional auction formats need not be efficient. They may create incentives for strategic non-participation and yield multiple equilibria with qualitatively different outcomes. We note that the presence of allocative externalities may also be responsible for the emptiness of the core, thereby suggesting that allocative externalities may be an important source of (coalitional) instability. We discuss the use of optimal threats in revenue maximization, and the conflicts that arise among various designers' goals, such as welfare maximization and revenue maximization. In particular, flexible auction formats need not be preferable as they may allow bidders to achieve more concentrated market structures.

Furthermore, we observe that in environments with limited commitment abilities, resale markets ensure that, in the long run, the welfare performance is unaffected by the initial allocation of property rights if agents are patient enough. But the final outcome induced by the resale markets need not be efficient, thereby suggesting that a desirable initial allocation, coupled with restrictions on the resale markets, may be preferable. The section ends with a brief survey of applications.

In Section 4 the emphasis is on informational externalities and on several impossibility results in such frameworks. In order to consistently and generally model the preferences of bidders, private signals must be vectors rather than scalars. This feature distinguishes our framework from most auction models for a single object (that were the traditional domain of much of auction theory).[1] Analyzing incentive constraints with multidimensional signals is technically complex, but indispensable. For the general social choice model developed in Section 2 we characterize Bayes-Nash incentive compatible mechanisms under the assumption that signals are independent. A key requirement is that equilibrium utility (as a function of type) is a convex potential. Simple corollaries include general payoff and revenue equivalence theorems.

We next proceed to show that, in the presence of informational externalities, Bayes-Nash implementation of the welfare-maximizing choice function is impossible in generic settings with multidimensional signals. Thus,

---

[1] For one-object auction models that allow for several informational dimensions (e.g., on a private value component and common value component), see, among others, Maskin (1992), Pesendorfer and Swinkels (1998), Compte and Jehiel (2002a), and Jackson (2003).

welfare-maximizing multi-object auctions do not exist, unless the allocation problem is separable across objects (e.g., there are neither allocative externalities nor complementarities) or signals are one-dimensional. This is in sharp contrast with the case of private values (no informational externalities) in which the celebrated Vickrey-Clarke-Groves mechanism ensures that welfare-maximizing choice rules can be implemented in dominant strategy whatever the dimensionality of the private information held by agents (and whether or not there are allocative externalities).

We next explore which social choice rules can be robustly implemented in the presence of informational externalities, where robust implementation refers to implementation via mechanisms that do not finely depend on the beliefs of the agents or designer. In contexts with informational externalities, robust implementation is associated with *ex-post implementation*, which is the analog of implementation in dominant strategy in the private values setup. It turns out that no social choice rule that makes use of the private information can be ex post implemented, as soon as two agents have at least two dimensions of private information. We contrast this impossibility result with the characterization of dominant-strategy implementable social choice rules for private values setups obtained by Roberts (1979). We also identify non-generic settings where ex post implementation and ex post welfare-maximization are possible. Section 5 concludes the chapter.

We wish to emphasize here that the present paper is not meant to be a survey of auction theory and mechanism design: There is a wealth of interesting and relevant issues that will not be addressed here. Interested readers can consult, for example, Klemperer (1999) or Milgrom (2004).

2   A GENERAL MULTI-OBJECT AUCTION MODEL

We start with a general social choice model with $N + 1$ agents, indexed by $i = 0, 1, 2, \ldots N$ and K social alternatives, indexed by $k = 1, 2, \ldots K$. Each agent gets a private signal about the state of the world $\theta^i \in \Theta^i \subseteq \Re^m$. We denote $\theta = (\theta^0, \theta^1, \ldots \theta^N)$, $\Theta = \times_{i=0}^N \Theta^i$, $\theta^{-i} = (\theta^0, \ldots, \theta^{i-1}, \theta^{i+1}, \ldots, \theta^N)$ and so on.

Agents have quasi-linear utility functions that depend on the chosen alternative, on private signals, and on monetary payments: If alternative k is chosen, and if agent i obtains a monetary transfer t^i, then her utility[2] is given by $u^i(k, \theta, t^i) = v_k^i(\theta^0, \theta^1, \ldots \theta^N) + t^i$ where v_k^i may, a priori, be any function of $(\theta^0, \theta^1, \ldots \theta^N)$.

The special case of auctions is included as follows: A set of M objects (possibly heterogenous) is allocated among a seller (who will be called agent zero) and N potential buyers. Here a social alternative is a partition of the

---

[2] More generally, agent i's utility may depend also on monetary transfers made to other players. These are situations with "financial externalities." We do not include them in our present analysis. The reader interested in the effect of such externalities on auctions should consult Dasgupta and Tsui (2004), Ettinger (2002) and Goeree et al. (2004).

goods among the agents: $P = (P_0, P_1, \ldots P_N)$, where P_i represents the bundle allocated to agent i. Let $\mathcal{P}$ denote the set of all partitions.

For each partition P, agent i obtains a signal θ_P^i that influences values for that partition. Thus $\theta^i = (\theta_P^i)_{P \in \mathcal{P}}$, and we write $v_P^i(\theta) = v_P^i(\theta_P^0, \ldots, \theta_P^N)$. This specification includes a large variety of auction/mechanism design models studied in the literature. Here are a few prominent examples:

1) For any partitions P and P' such that $P_i = P_i'$ assume that $\theta_P^i = \theta_{P'}^i \equiv \theta_{P_i}^i$, and $v_P^i(\theta) = v_{P'}^i(\theta) \equiv v_{P_i}^i(\theta_{P_i}^i)$. This is a "pure private values" model where agent i only cares about the bundle allocated to her in each partition and the signal pertaining to that bundle. There are neither allocative nor informational externalities.

2) For any θ and θ' such that $\theta_P^i = \theta_P'^i$, assume that $v_P^i(\theta) = v_P^i(\theta') \equiv v_P^i(\theta_P^i)$. This is a model where agent i only cares about his own signal about the partition (i.e., there are no informational externalities), but i may care about the entire partition of objects (i.e., there are allocative externalities).

3) For any partitions P and P' such that $P_i = P_i'$ assume that $v_P^i(\theta) = v_{P'}^i(\theta)$. It follows that θ^j can be re-parameterized as $\theta^j = (\theta_X^j)_{X \in 2^M}$ where X is a subset of the M objects, and $v_P^i(\theta)$ can be re-written as $v_{P_i}^i(\theta_{P_i}^0, \ldots, \theta_{P_i}^N)$. This is a model where agent i only cares about the bundle allocated to him in each partition (i.e., there are no allocative externalities), but i does care about the information about that bundle available to other agents (i.e., there are informational externalities).

4) $v_P^i(\theta)$ depends in a general way on the entire partition P and on the entire profile of signals θ. This is the most general model that admits both allocative and informational externalities.

5) Assume that there are no allocative externalities. If $v_{P_i \cup P_i'}^i(\cdot) > (<) v_{P_i}^i(\cdot) + v_{P_i'}^i(\cdot)$ for some bundles of object P_i, P_i', then this is a model that exhibits complementarities (substitutabilities).

A Typical Application

In industrial organization contexts, allocative externalities often arise because bidders care about the ensuing market structure, which is affected by the auction's outcome. Informational externalities arise because private information on the cost structure typically affects the competitors' profits. Finally, information is naturally multi-dimensional because there are various aspects to the cost structure and different objects for sale.

As an illustration, consider the recent European process of allocating UMTS licenses to telecom firms (for further details, see Klemperer, 2002 and Jehiel and Moldovanu, 2003). The allocation proceeded via a sequence of national auctions and beauty contests. We focus below only on the basic features that parallel those in the model sketched above:

1) The auctioned objects were licenses to operate a third-generation mobile telephony network in a certain country. The licenses differed in a multitude of dimensions such as the size and distribution of the population, spectrum capacity, duration, required investment size, and deployment speed, etc. Private information was multi-dimensional since many types of licenses were sold, and since the bidding firms had heterogenous assessments about technical network requirements, present and future regulatory frameworks, future demand characteristics, future operation costs, etc.

2) The value of a bundle of licenses for a given firm is calculated by the expected revenue in the future market from holding that bundle, minus the required infrastructure and operation costs. The expected profit crucially depends on the number of licenses (or competitors) within one country, on their identity (e.g., small local firms or large supranational ones), on the license holdings of competitors in other countries (that determine what integrated services they can offer), and so on. Thus, a major feature was the presence of allocative externalities.

3) In any reasonable oligopoly scenario, competitors' cost parameters[3] affect one's own profit. Since competitors were likely to have some information about their operation method, future technological development and future demand, the auctions also involved informational externalities.

3   ALLOCATIVE EXTERNALITIES

In this section we review design issues that are related to the presence of allocative externalities. In order to abstract from other effects, we first assume that there is complete information, and we come back later to the additional phenomena due to asymmetric information.

We illustrate a number of insights through the following situation appearing in Industrial Organization models: There are N potentially active firms in the market. An innovation protected by a patent is auctioned among the firms. The acquiring firm is able to produce at a lower cost, but the magnitude of the cost reduction may depend on the identity of the acquiring firm. Let v_i^i denote the change in profit of firm i if i acquires the innovation; v_i^i is referred to as i's valuation. Let v_i^j denote the change of profit of firm j when firm i acquires the innovation. This change of profit is caused by the modified oligopolistic competition after the innovation is introduced (which is typically less favorable for j). We refer to v_i^j as the *externality* exerted by i on j. This specification fits into the general model presented above by noting that, in the case of one single object, the partition P can be simply described by the firm i who acquires the innovation.

3.1   Endogenous Valuations

Assume that the innovation is auctioned using a second-price sealed-bid auction.[4] That is, each firm i submits a bid b_i, and the firm with highest bid wins the auction and pays the second highest bid. Ties are resolved as usual.

In the traditional setup without externalities, it is a (weakly) dominant strategy for firms to bid their values for the auctioned object (see Vickrey, 1961). Here, the mere notion of value is not well defined. Indeed, how much i is willing

---

[3] This is just an example; information about demand parameters is another.
[4] The same insights apply to all other standard formats.

to pay in order to win very much depends on her expectation about who is going to win if she does not. For example, if i expects j to win her net value of winning (compared to the loss scenario) is $v_i^i - v_j^i$. Similarly, if i expects k to win her value is $v_i^i - v_k^i$. These two values need not coincide, and thus it is impossible to say how much i values the innovation independently of her expectations over alternative market scenarios. Of course, expectations must be consistent with equilibrium play. The observation that valuations depend here on expectations translates into the possibility of multiple equilibria with quite different outcomes:

Example 1 *(Jehiel and Moldovanu, 1996) Let $N = 3$, and let $v_i^i = v$ for all i. Let the externality terms be: $v_1^2 = v_2^1 = -\alpha$, $v_1^3 = v_2^3 = -\gamma$, and $v_3^1 = v_3^2 = -\beta$ where $\alpha > \gamma > \beta > 0$.*

It is readily verified that, in one equilibrium, firms 1 and 2 compete with each other (since they are very afraid of each other). The resulting outcome is that either firm 1 or 2 wins the auction and pays $v + \alpha$. In another equilibrium, 1 and 3 are in competition. The resulting outcome is that 3 wins the auction (because 3 is more afraid of 1 than 1 is afraid of 3, e.g., $\gamma > \beta$) and pays $v + \beta$ – a much lower price than in the previous equilibrium. Firm 2 is not willing to outbid 3 because 2 is not that afraid of 3.

3.2   Strategic Non-Participation

In auctions without externalities, not participating in the auction is equivalent to participating and making an irrelevant bid.[5] In the presence of externalities, this is no longer the case. By staying out, a bidder may induce an outcome that turns out to be more favorable to her than the outcome that would have arisen if she had participated (see Jehiel and Moldovanu, 1996). We illustrate it through the following example:

Example 2 *(Hoppe, Jehiel and Moldovanu, 2005) Let $N = 3$. Firms 1, 2 are incumbents, while firm 3 is a potential entrant. The incumbents do not value the object (innovation, license, etc.) per se: $v_1^1 = v_2^2 = 0$. Moreover, $v_1^2 = v_2^1 = 0$. The entrant has value $v_3^3 = v$, and it creates an externality $v_3^1 = v_3^2 = -\alpha$ on incumbents. We assume that $v < \alpha$.*

If all firms participate, there are, essentially, three continuation equilibria: two in pure, and one in mixed strategies. In a pure strategy equilibrium, one of the incumbents, say firm 1, wins and pays v. In this equilibrium firm 2 bids zero since there is no point winning: That outcome is equivalent to the outcome when she lets 1 win. In the mixed strategy equilibrium, firms 1 and 2 mix between a bid of zero (say), and a bid slightly above v, and the entrant sometimes wins.

---

[5] Participation costs are assumed to be null.

The strategic interaction between incumbents resembles a war of attrition: Each incumbent is willing to deter entry but prefers that the other one pay the price of entry deterrence. Assume then that one of the above bidding equilibria is played. At least one incumbent, say 1, wins at price v with positive probability. But, 1 would be strictly better off by not participating in the auction. In that case, the auction is among bidders 2 and 3, and 2 wins because $\alpha > v$. Clearly, firm 1 benefits from such a deviation. Thus, in any equilibrium, at least one of the firms will choose not to participate with positive probability.[6]

In Hoppe, Jehiel and Moldovanu (2005), we build on Example 2 to show that increasing the number of objects may change the nature of the interaction between the incumbents. When two objects are auctioned, the two incumbents have an easy way to collude within the auction: each buys one object at price v, thereby deterring entry. If allowing two entries is also an equilibrium, the two-object auction now resembles a coordination game between the two incumbents, rather than a war of attrition (as in the one-object auction). This is somewhat reminiscent of the finding that, in multi-object auctions, collusion may mean sharing the items for sale (see Wilson 1979). But, the channel through which this occurs here is specific to the presence of allocative externalities.

3.3   Participation Decisions and Optimal Mechanisms

Above we considered standard auction formats. We wish now to analyze how the auction designer can exploit the bidders' participation decisions in order to increase her revenue. The key observation is that, by augmenting the auction design by appropriate threats, the designer is also able to extract payments from bidders who do not win. This subsection summarizes insights from Jehiel, Moldovanu and Stacchetti (1996) (see also Kamien, Oren and Tauman 1992 for an early analysis of a setting where non-acquirers make payments to the auctioneer).

Assume that all externalities are negative, i.e., $v_i^j \leq 0$ for all $i, j \neq i$. If firm i stays out, the worst scenario for firm i would be that the winner is firm $j(i)$ where $j(i) \in \arg\min_j v_j^i$. We let $\underline{v}^i = \min_{j \neq i} v_j^i$, and augment the mechanism by the specification that if agent i does not participate, the winner is firm $j(i)$. In line with the mechanism design literature we assume first that the designer has the commitment power to implement such threats.

If firm i refuses to participate, it will get a minimal payoff. In equilibrium,[7] all firms participate, and the outcome is chosen so as to maximize welfare. This is so because the designer can internalize social welfare by asking every firm

---

[6] The argument assumes that the set of participants is public information. One way to avoid strategic non-participation is to keep the set of bidders secret. But, such policies may have other drawbacks (see Compte and Jehiel, 2002b, and DasVarma, 2002).

[7] There could, a priori, be equilibria where several firms decide not to participate. But, by suitably defining what the mechanism does when several firms do not participate, one can guarantee that participation is a weakly dominant strategy (see Jehiel et al. 1996).

i to pay the difference between i's payoff in the welfare maximizing outcome and $\underline{v}^i$.

Proposition 3 *The outcome of the revenue maximizing mechanism also maximizes welfare for the agents. The extracted revenue is*

$$R = -\sum_i \underline{v}^i + \max\left\{0, \max_i \sum_j v_i^j\right\}.$$

The above argument can be viewed as an expression of the celebrated Coase theorem.[8] Observe that, in the presence of allocative externalities, as soon as there are at least three bidders, welfare is usually not maximized by standard auctions.

To illustrate Proposition 3, consider Example 2 again. Given that $v < \alpha$, the outcome that maximizes welfare (among agents) is that the object is sold to either incumbent (or, equivalently, that the seller keeps the object). The threat to either incumbent is that, if either of them refuses to participate, the object is sold to the entrant. The entrant is not threatened. Each incumbent is willing to pay α to avoid entry, and the revenue to the designer is 2α.[9]

More generally, if the designer also cares about consumers' surplus and not only about revenue, then total welfare will be maximized in equilibrium, and the payoff of the designer will be given by

$$W = -\sum_i \underline{v}^i + \max\left\{0, \max_i(\sum_j v_i^j + CS_i)\right\}$$

where CS_i is the change in consumers' surplus resulting from a sale to firm i.

3.4 Credibility and Resale

In the above application, the designer can commit to personalized and fine-tuned threats. What happens if commitment power is limited? In Jehiel and Moldovanu (1999) we consider[10] a model where firms can sell and further resell the object before a (sufficiently far away) deadline T, at which time the current owner of the good must use it. We assume that agents are unable to commit to actions at future stages (in particular, they are unable to commit not to resell, or to sell to a specific agent if some pre-specified event occurs). At each stage, the current owner makes an offer to a set of agents. The offer may

---

[8] This holds despite the fact that the participation constraints are endogenous, unlike those in Coase's original analysis. The point is that reservation values can be set independently of the chosen outcome.

[9] If we restrict attention to mechanisms where only the winner can make payments, the revenue falls down to α.

[10] See also Brocas (2003) for a study of an auction with negative externalities where the seller has no credible threats.

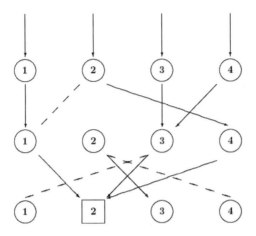

include a sale in exchange for payments. If an approached agent refuses the deal, one period of time elapses, and the owner makes a new offer. The main finding of Jehiel and Moldovanu (1999) is:

Proposition 4 *The identity of the initial owner does not affect the identity of the agent who consumes at date T. The consumer at date T need not maximize total welfare unless all agents have veto power over all transactions.*

The following example illustrates the result:

Example 5 *Let $N = 4$, and let $T \geq 2$. The values are: $v_1^1 = 6.5$, $v_2^2 = 10.1$, $v_3^3 = 9$, $v_4^4 = 7$; $v_1^2 = v_1^3 = v_1^4 = 0$; $v_2^1 = v_2^3 = -1$, $v_2^4 = -2$; $v_3^1 = -2$, $v_3^2 = 0$, $v_3^4 = -1$; $v_4^1 = v_4^2 = 0$, $v_4^3 = -1$.*

The welfare maximizing firm is 1. But, no matter who the initial owner is, the object will be consumed by firm 2 at stage T. At stage $T - 1$, firm 1 sells to 2 without extracting any payment from 3 and 4 because these prefer that 1 is the final owner rather than 2. Firm 2 sells to 3 while extracting $v_3^4 - v_2^4 = 1$ from 4. Firm 3 sells to 2 while extracting $v_2^1 - v_3^1 = 1$ from 1. Firm 4 sells to 2 without extra payments from 1 and 3. At stage $T - 2$, firms 1 and 3 do not sell. Firm 2 sells to 4 while extracting $v_2^1 - v_3^1 = 1$ from firm 1. Firm 4 sells to 3 without extra payment from firms 1 and 2. At stage $T - 3$ and any earlier stages, no matter who is the current owner, the innovation ends up in the hands of firm 2 at stage T.

A main feature of the above equilibrium is that, at some stages, firms that oppose the deal are simply excluded from the agreement. Veto power (i.e., the consent of all agents is needed for a change of ownership) restores efficiency.

If resale cannot be forbidden, the above result suggests that it is welfare irrelevant how the initial property rights are assigned: Eventually the same final physical outcome results. But, it is erroneous to conclude that mechanism design is irrelevant. Indeed, since the final outcome need not be efficient, it may be a good idea to try to allocate the object efficiently in the first place, and then control the resale market to some extent.[11]

There are several limitations to the above model: 1) The result relies on the existence of a deadline;[12] 2) There is only one object for sale; 3) Only the current owner is able to make proposals. Gomes and Jehiel (2005) were able to generalize the main result without these assumptions. They also show that efficiency must occur in the long run if the efficient allocation of goods is such that no group of agents can force a move to another allocation that hurts i without her consent.

3.5   Core and Externalities

We make now a brief detour to remind the reader that, from the viewpoint of coalitional deviations, the presence of allocative externalities is a source of instability. The following result is a corollary of Proposition 6 in Jehiel and Moldovanu (1996).

Proposition 6 *Suppose that welfare is maximized by letting firm i^* buy the object. If there exists a subset T of buyers, $i^* \notin T$, and a buyer $i \in T$ such that*[13] $\sum_{j \in T \cup \{i^*\}} v_{i^*}^j < \sum_{j \in T \cup \{i^*\}} v_i^j$ *then the core of the associated market with externalities is empty.*[14]

The intuition for the above Proposition is as follows: Stability against coalitional deviations requires welfare maximization, so that in any core outcome the object is sold to i^*. Buyers $j \neq i^*$ can always refuse to make any payment, and buyers $j \neq i$ are thus assured to get at least $\sum_{j \neq i^*} v_{i^*}^j$ collectively. Buyer j cannot get strictly more than $v_{i^*}^j$ as otherwise the coalition of the seller and firm i^* could do better by just ignoring j. Thus, j must get exactly $v_{i^*}^j$. Thus, if the above condition holds, the coalition of the seller and buyers in $T \cup \{i^*\}$ can

---

[11] An extreme option is to forbid resales, as was done in the case of spectrum license auctions.

[12] Chien (2004) analyzes the same model with an infinite horizon and focuses on the resulting differences.

[13] When the condition holds, the welfare maximizing state i^* is not *negative externality-free* (see Gomes and Jehiel 2005) since the coalition of the seller and buyers in T can allocate the object to i, hurting agents outside $T \cup \{i^*\}$. Spoliation is the key reason for the inexistence of a stable outcome.

[14] With externalities, the core notion depends on assumptions about reactions to coalitional deviations by agents in the complement. Our result holds for the most permissive definition, the α-core, where the complement is assumed to choose the worst course of action from the point of view of the deviators. Any core is empty if the α-core is.

improve on the candidate core allocation by re-allocating the object to i rather than i^*. It follows that the core must be empty.

3.6   The Conflict between Welfare and Revenue

In this subsection, we briefly consider an auction where the number of auctioned objects is endogenously determined by the bidders' behavior, and where externalities are created by the effects on downstream payoffs.[15]

Consider spectrum auction. Conventional wisdom suggests that disaggregating spectrum, say, into small capacity blocks, and letting the bidders aggregate the blocks to form licenses of whatever capacity they need is a good idea. After all, the designer is not usually knowledgeable about how much the firms value the licenses, or about how valuable extra capacity is. But, this argument ignores the possibility that the auction's flexibility may be used by firms to induce concentrated market structures.

Example 7   *There are four identical blocks for sale, and let $N = 5$. A bidder needs at least one block (small license), and bidders may buy up to two blocks (large license). Each bidder i submits a schedule $b_i = (b_i(1), b_i(2))$ where $b_i(m)$ is the bid for m blocks, $m = 1, 2$. Blocks are allocated and payments are made according to a uniform price auction. For any partition P of the four blocks in which firm i receives m blocks, and a total of n firms get at least one block, define $v_P^i = \pi(m, n)$.*

If $\pi(2, 2) - \pi(1, 3) > \pi(1, 3)$, the auction outcome is a duopoly because the extra profit gained by switching from a small license in a triopoly to a large license in a duopoly is larger than the profit with a small license in triopoly. That is, two firms buy two blocks each, the equilibrium price for a block is $\pi(1, 3)$, and a winner pays $2\pi(1, 3)$. In contrast, a less flexible format could, for example, mandate that three licenses (two small, one big) are sold. The assessment of the two formats depends, basically, on the partial derivatives of π. If the derivative with respect to capacity is larger (presumably it is positive), the flexible format is likely to be preferable. If, however, the derivative with respect to the size of the market (presumably negative) is larger, then the less flexible format is likely to be preferable because of the increased consumer surplus in a less concentrated market.

Sometimes it is also argued that welfare maximization for bidders and revenue go hand in hand in auctions.[16] But again this view ignores that "value," and hence "revenue" may be driven by the desire to squeeze consumers' surplus.

---

[15] This is inspired by the German UMTS license auction that took place in 2001. The treatment follows Jehiel and Moldovanu (2003).

[16] There are many caveats to this claim even without allocative externalities. For example, revenue maximization requires the use of reserve prices, or handicaps in asymmetric contexts, or quantity discounts in multi-object auctions.

Since the value of a monopoly position is larger than the combined values of oligopolists, it is intuitive that an auction for monopoly (which is a form of bundling) will yield more revenue than an auction that creates several winners that compete against each other (at an extreme such an auction yields no revenue at all if firms expect a "Bertrand" type of interaction). But welfare, including consumer surplus, will be small under monopoly. Thus, revenue and efficiency may be quite unrelated to each other if there are allocative externalities (see also Janssen and Moldovanu, 2004).

3.7   Private Information

Private information on allocative externality terms can yield *private value* models without informational externalities if i knows the externality terms v_j^i caused to her, or it can yield *interdependent value* models if i has private information on the externality terms v_i^j she causes to others (of course, mixtures are also possible).

Jehiel and Moldovanu (2000) analyze a sealed-bid second-price auction with entry fees and reserve prices in a model where bidders have one dimensional private information that influences both their valuations and the externality terms. Specifically, in a two bidder model $\theta^i = v_i^i$ is private information, and v_j^i is a function of both θ^i and θ^j, i.e., $v_j^i(\theta^i, \theta^j)$. This model captures situations where each firm has private information about the reduction on marginal cost induced by an innovation, and where the cost structure is public information before the market interaction.

This model displays both private and interdependent value components: When i compares the alternative where he wins to the one where the seller keeps the object, his net value is θ^i. When i compares the alternative where he wins with the one where the other bidder wins, his net value is $\theta^i - v_j^i(\theta^i, \theta^j)$, which depends both on i and j's private information. Only the second comparison is relevant if there is no reserve price, and then the analysis is analogous to the one in Milgrom and Weber's (1982) framework: In a symmetric two-bidder setting, i.e., $v_j^i(x, y) \equiv v_i^j(x, y) = e(x, y)$, where the function $x \to x - e(x, x)$ is increasing, type θ^i bids[17] $b(\theta^i) = \theta^i - e(\theta^i, \theta^i)$.

The auction with a reserve price R is more interesting. For the sake of illustration, assume that the externality function is given by a constant $-e$, where $e \geq 0$, and consider R inside the support of valuations.[18] The equilibrium is such that bidders with valuation below R bid below R (say zero), and bidders with valuations above R bid above $R + e$. Thus, there is no relevant bid between R and $R + e$.[19] The reason for this discontinuity is as follows: When the marginal type $v_i^i = R$ considers whether to make a relevant bid or not, the

---

[17] With more than two bidders with asymmetries, the features mentioned in the above subsections (multiplicity of equilibria, strategic non-participation, etc.) occur also here.

[18] We also assume that the valuations are identically and independently distributed.

[19] A similar discontinuity may arise in the affiliated model of Milgrom and Weber (1982).

benchmark is that the seller keeps the object. As soon as a bidder makes a relevant bid, the effect of marginally decreasing the bid is now that the other bidder sometimes wins. Thus, in the relevant bid area the bid function must be $\theta^i + e$.

Another interesting observation is that the seller's optimal reserve price may be below the seller's valuation, a situation that never occurs without externalities.[20] The reason is that selling more often frightens bidders when there are negative externalities, and therefore they bid higher in order to win.

In the case of positive externalities, the equilibrium bidding function still has two distinct parts. But consistently combining the two parts requires now that a positive measure of valuations θ^i bids R.[21] Moreover, with positive externalities, entry fees and reserve prices need not lead to equivalent revenues.

Moldovanu and Sela (2003) study a patent auction where the post-auction interaction is à la Bertrand. There, the analog of the function $\theta^i - v^i_j(\theta^i, \theta^j)$ is decreasing, and pooling occurs even with negative externalities. Goeree (2000), Das Varma (2003) and Molnar and Virag (2004) study a variant of the above model where the cost structure is not made public after the auction. In this case, the winning bid has the extra feature of conveying some information about the cost structure of the winning bidder, and there is an extra signaling motive appearing in the bidding strategy.

We now briefly consider revenue-maximizing auctions. There are two difficulties linked to the presence of allocative externalities: 1) Information is typically multi-dimensional; 2) Participation constraints are typically determined by the mechanism itself and are type-dependent.

Jehiel, Moldovanu and Stacchetti (1999) consider a symmetric, private values setup with multi-dimensional private information and negative externalities: Bidder i knows her valuation v^i_i and the externalities v^i_j caused to her. For example, the unique symmetric equilibrium of a second-price auction among N bidders is given by $b(v^i_i, v^i_{-i}) = v^i_i - \frac{1}{N-1} \sum v^i_j$. Thus, the equilibrium bids are set at valuation minus average externality.

As in the complete information case (see Subsection 3.3), the optimal auction will include some threat in case a bidder does not participate. But, in this private value model, there is no way to fine-tune the threat for i by using information revealed by others. It turns out that it is enough to care about the participation constraint of the type whose valuation is smallest and whose externalities are closest to zero. The threat (taking the form of a fixed allocation rule in case i does not participate) can be designed so that the participation constraints of all other types of bidder i are automatically satisfied as soon as i's incentive constraints are satisfied. Thus, even though participation constraints are a priori type-dependent, the fact that they are endogenously

---

[20] The optimal reserve price also depends on the number of bidders.

[21] Pooling also appears in the resale auctions studied by Haile (2000). The possibility of resale translates into a "reduced form" positive externality.

determined by the mechanism (through the choice of threats) allows us to avoid some of the complications inherent to exogenous type-dependent participation constraints.[22]

Jehiel, Moldovanu and Stacchetti (1999) show that a second-price auction with an appropriately defined entry fee is the revenue-maximizing mechanism in a class of mechanisms where the object is always sold, and where agents are constrained to make one-dimensional bids. They also characterize the equilibrium of the second price auction with reserve prices and show that it is never optimal to set a small reserve price. Thus, either there should be no reserve price or the reserve price should be such that the object is not sold with a significant probability. This result cannot arise in a one-dimensional setting with a smooth, strictly positive density function, and it should also be contrasted with the finding in multi-dimensional monopoly problems where there is no competition among consumers. There, it is always optimal to exclude some set of consumers no matter what the support of consumers' valuations is (see Armstrong, 1996). By contrast, in the auction setup, it may be revenue-enhancing for the seller to always sell the good.

Jehiel, Moldovanu and Stacchetti (1996) construct the revenue-maximizing auction in a setting where bidder i knows her valuation v_i^i and the negative externality $v_i^j \leq 0$ she exerts on other bidders j. This is a model with interdependent values (or informational externalities). If i does not participate, the auctioneer optimally decides to sell the good to the agent $j(i) = \arg\min_j \widetilde{v}_j^i$ where $\widetilde{v}_j^i$ is agent j's report in a direct mechanism.

Figueroa and Skreta (2004) generalize the analysis of optimal mechanisms to multi-object settings with externalities but assume that agents have one-dimensional signals.[23]

Das Varma (2002) builds on the model of Jehiel, Moldovanu and Stacchetti (1999), and he observes that the ascending English auction may sometimes generate more revenue than sealed-bid auctions. This happens because bidders have incentives to stay longer in the auction in cases where their worst enemy also stays in the auction. The insight is particularly interesting in light of the revenue equivalence theorem in auctions (see subsection 4.1 below). Even in a symmetric, independent, private values context with risk neutral bidders, the ascending and the sealed-bid auctions need not be revenue-equivalent if there are allocative externalities.

Caillaud and Jehiel (1998) examine the possibility of collusion in the presence of negative externalities among agents when private information bears on valuations. They show that information sharing among the ring members need not be efficient even if side-payments are allowed, which is in sharp contrast with the finding in externality-free auction setups (see, for example, Graham and Marshall, 1986).

---

[22] See Jullien (2000) for an analysis of such constraints in one-dimensional principal-agent setting.
[23] See also Caillaud and Jehiel (1998) and Brocas (2003).

3.8   Applications

Auction models with allocative externalities offer an unified framework for all situations where competing firms or agents buy important inputs that affect the nature of downstream interaction. Some effects of externalities on bidding behavior have been previously identified in the literature on the "persistence of monopoly" (see, for example, the classic paper by Gilbert and Newbery, 1982, and also Krishna, 1993 and Rodriguez, 2002) and in the literature on patent licensing (see the classic contributions of Katz and Shapiro 1986, and Kamien and Tauman, 1986). Similar effects appear in the auctions of capacity studied by McAfee (1998). Roughly speaking, the general framework presented here extends "the persistence of monopoly" approach beyond monopoly/duopoly market structures, and it extends the literature on patent licensing by allowing for asymmetries between agents and by considering allocation mechanisms that go beyond standard auctions.

Inderst and Wey (2004) analyze large auction-like deals (such as privatizations, mergers and takeovers) that change the nature of an industry by affecting the number and the identity of the operating firms. It is an immediate consequence of the theory of auctions with negative externalities that a takeover premium must be observed in horizontal mergers where each firm is negatively affected if the target is acquired by another competitor.

Perez-Castrillo and Wettstein (2002) and Waehrer (2003) study the properties of bidding games and other mechanisms for allocating public goods or bads, such as siting of hazardous facilities.

Maeda (2003) and Burguet and Sempere (2005) analyze trading models for the emission of noxious gases. Using some insights developed for resale markets with externalities (see Jehiel and Moldovanu, 1999), Burguet and Sempere emphasize both the inadequacy of bilateral trading mechanisms for internalizing all existing externalities and the need for multilateral schemes. A related point is made by Bagwell, Mavroidis and Staiger (2004) who propose an innovative auction of retaliation rights for dispute settlements within the World Trade Organization.

4   INFORMATIONAL EXTERNALITIES

In this section we focus on the role of informational externalities. The theoretical interest in such settings is not new. The classic contributions of Wilson (1969) and Milgrom and Weber (1981), and the large literature following them analyzed one-object auctions with symmetric bidders. In contrast, the focus of the more recent literature is on multi-object auctions and on the effects of asymmetries (see Maskin, 1992) on welfare-maximization.

The section will be divided in several parts. In Subsection 4.1 we develop general insights about incentive compatibility and payoff equivalence with multi-dimensional signals. In Subsection 4.2 we inquire whether the celebrated

Vickrey-Clarke-Groves analysis can be extended to settings with informational externalities. In Subsection 4.3 we ask which social choice functions (not necessarily welfare-maximizing) can be implemented independently of the distributions of signals (i.e., in an ex-post equilibrium).

4.1 Incentive Compatibility and Payoff Equivalence

Recall the social choice framework described in Section 2. Agents have quasi-linear utility functions that depend on the chosen alternative k, on private signals $\theta = (\theta^0, \theta^1, \ldots, \theta^N)$, and on a monetary payment $t^i : u^i(k, \theta, t^i) = v_k^i(\theta) + t^i$.

The revelation principle asserts that, for any Bayes-Nash equilibrium of any given mechanism, one can construct an equivalent equilibrium of a direct revelation mechanism where all agents truthfully report their private information. Thus, for the characterization results, we focus below on truth-telling equilibria in direct revelation mechanisms.

Denote by $v^i(\theta)$ the vector $(v_k^i(\theta))_{k \in K}$, and let $\Delta^{|K|-1}$ denote the simplex of probability distributions over the finite set of alternatives. A *direct revelation mechanism* is given by a pair (Ψ, t) where $\Psi : \Theta = \times_{i=0}^N \Theta^i \to \Delta^{|K|-1}$ is the *allocation rule*, and $t : \Theta \to \Re^{N+1}$ is the *payment rule*.

We assume below that types are independent. Given a mechanism (Ψ, t), define $\bar{v}^i(\tau^i, \theta^i) = E_{\theta^{-i}}[\Psi(\tau^i, \theta^{-i}) \cdot v^i(\theta)]$ and $\bar{t}^i(\tau^i) = E_{\theta^{-i}}[t^i(\tau^i, \theta^{-i})]$. Then $U^i(\tau^i, \theta^i) = \bar{v}^i(\tau^i, \theta^i) + \bar{t}^i(\tau^i)$ represents agent i's expected utility when all other agents report truthfully and when i has true type θ^i but reports type τ^i.

A mechanism (Ψ, t) is *incentive compatible* if:

$$\forall i, \theta^i, \quad V^i(\theta^i) \equiv U^i(\theta^i, \theta^i) = \sup_{\tau^i \in \Theta^i} U^i(\tau^i, \theta^i). \tag{1}$$

The function $V^i(\theta^i)$ represents agent i's expected utility in a truthful Bayes-Nash equilibrium. There are several versions of characterization results in the literature. The one below is due to Krishna and Maenner (2001):[24]

Theorem 8 *Assume that for each i the type set Θ^i is convex and that $u_i(k, \theta^{-i}, \cdot, t^i)$ is a convex function of θ^i. Then, in any incentive compatible mechanism (Ψ, t), the expected equilibrium utility function $V^i(\theta^i)$ is convex and is determined by the allocation rule Ψ up to an additive constant. For any $\theta^i, \tau^i \in \Theta^i$, and for any smooth path γ joining θ^i to τ^i in Θ^i, it holds that $V^i(\theta^i) = V^i(\tau^i) + \int q^i \cdot d\gamma$ where q^i is a subgradient[25] of V^i at θ^i.*

---

[24] Although these authors give an independent proof, it was pointed out to us by Ennio Stacchetti that the integral formula below follows from a known result in convex analysis. See Theorem 2.3.4. in Hiriart-Urruty and Lemarechal C. (2001). For another result that substitutes convexity of the utility function with a differentiability requirement see Milgrom and Segal (2002).

[25] Consider a convex function $F : C \to \Re$ where $C \subset \Re^d$. A vector $x^* \in \Re^d$ is a *subgradient* of F at $x \in C$ if for all $y \in C$ it holds: $F(y) \geq x^* \cdot (y - x)$. Whenever F is differentiable (a.e.) the subgradient is unique and coincides with the usual gradient.

The main complication added by the presence of multi-dimensional signals is the requirement that q^i, which is fully determined by Ψ, be a (sub)gradient of a convex function V^i. Whereas this requirement reduces to a standard monotonicity condition in the one-dimensional case, it involves both a monotonicity condition and a differential condition on the cross derivatives of q^i (yielding the path independence condition) if signals are multi-dimensional. These consequences of multi-dimensional constraints in the context of auctions have been first pointed out by Jehiel, Moldovanu, and Stacchetti (1996, 1999).[26]

To get some geometric intuition about the added complexity, consider the following example:

Example 9 *There are two objects, A and B, and one bidder. The bidder obtains a two-dimensional private signal (v_A, v_B) about the values of the two goods. The bundle is worth $v_A + v_B$.*

Any deterministic, incentive compatible mechanism divides the two-dimensional set of types into areas of constant allocation. The gradient of the equilibrium utility is given here by the probabilities with which the bidder gets the objects. Thus, the vector q is either $(0, 0)$, $(0, 1)$, $(1, 0)$ or $(1, 1)$. Convexity of V (or, equivalently, monotonicity of q) implies that, as we increase valuations, q is only allowed to "jump" from $(0, 0)$ to either $(0, 1)$, $(1, 0)$ or $(1, 1)$, and from $(0, 1)$, $(1, 0)$ to $(1, 1)$. This is similar to the insight obtained in one-dimensional models. But, there is an additional twist here: If a jump occurs, the integral of q will not depend on the path of integration (i.e., the vector field q is conservative) if and only if "the jump vector" is perpendicular to the boundary between the areas where each alternative is chosen. For example, the boundary between areas where the buyer either gets both objects or none must have a slope of $45°$ (since the jump is $(1, 1) - (0, 0) = (1, 1)$), while the boundaries between areas where the buyer gets either one object or two are either horizontal, or vertical lines. While here these observations could be derived from the Taxation Principle of monopolistic screening, the analog conditions become very involved in auctions where there are several interacting agents. The requirement of conservativeness on the vector field q yields partial differential equations that determine boundaries, which need not be straight lines (for these insights and an application, see Jehiel, Moldovanu and Stacchetti, 1999).

An important corollary of Theorem 8 is the so-called payoff and revenue equivalence result. Consider two incentive compatible mechanisms (Ψ, t) and (Ψ, s) that implement the same allocation rule Ψ, and thus yield the same expressions for $\bar{v}^i$ and q^i. Choose an arbitrary type $\widetilde{\theta}^i$, and let $V^i_t(\widetilde{\theta}^i)$ and $V_s(\widetilde{\theta}^i)$ denote the expected equilibrium utility in the truth-telling equilibria of (Ψ, t) and (Ψ, s), respectively. Payoff and revenue equivalence follow immediately

[26] Analogous results appeared earlier in the monopolistic screening literature (see Rochet, 1985).

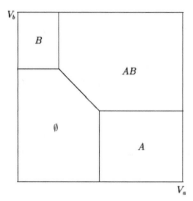

from the above theorem by noting that:

$$\forall i, \theta^i, \ \bar{t}^i(\theta^i) = V_t^i(\widetilde{\theta}^i) - \bar{v}^i(\theta^i, \theta^i) + \int q^i \cdot d\gamma$$

$$\forall i, \theta^i, \ \bar{s}^i(\theta^i) = V_s^i(\widetilde{\theta}^i) - \bar{v}^i(\theta^i, \theta^i) + \int q^i \cdot d\gamma.$$

The above equations yield together:

$$\forall i, \theta^i, \ \bar{t}^i(\theta^i) - \bar{s}^i(\theta^i) = V_t^i(\widetilde{\theta}^i) - V_s^i(\widetilde{\theta}^i) = const.$$

In other words, expected transfers in the two mechanisms are, up to a constant, the same. Analogous payoff equivalence results for dominant-strategy or ex post implementation can be proved along similar lines, but these no longer require that the distribution of signals be independent across agents. Moreover, they deliver equivalence up to a constant of actual transfers rather than expected transfers (see, for example, Chung and Ely, 2001).

4.2   Welfare Maximization

In this subsection we ask whether the welfare-maximizing rule can be Bayes-Nash implemented. Our main results (Theorems 10 and 11) assert that this is generically impossible when agents have multi-dimensional private information.

Let us first briefly review the classic insight of Vickrey (1961), Clarke (1971), and Groves (1973) for private values auction, where each agent i cares only about his own private signal but may care about the entire partition of objects (thus allocative externalities are permitted).

For the auction application, we assume that $v_P^i(\theta) \equiv v_P^i(\theta^i)$. For any profile of signals θ, define $P^*(\theta) \in \arg\max_{P \in \mathcal{P}} \sum_j v_P^j(\theta^j)$ to be a welfare-maximizing allocation rule.[27] Let P_{-i} be a partition of objects where agent i is allocated

---

[27] If the argmax is not unique, any selection will do.

the empty set, and let $\mathcal{P}_{-i}$ denote the set of such partitions. For any profile θ^{-i} define $P^*_{-i}(\theta^{-i}) = \arg\max_{P_{-i} \in \mathcal{P}_{-i}} \sum_{j \neq i} v^j_{P_{-i}}(\theta^j)$ to be the welfare-maximizing partition of objects in the absence of i.

The VCG mechanism is the direct revelation mechanism where, for each reported profile of signals θ, the designer implements partition $P^*(\theta) = \arg\max_{P \in \mathcal{P}} \sum_j v^j_P(\theta^j)$, and makes a transfer to i given by $t^i(\theta^{-i}) = \sum_{j \neq i} v^j_{P^*(\theta)}(\theta^j) - \sum_{j \neq i} v^j_{P^*_{-i}(\theta^{-i})}(\theta^j)$.

Truth-telling is a dominant strategy for each player whatever the dimensionality of θ^i, and whatever the form of v^i because the transfers ensure that each agent's objective is aligned with the welfare criterion. Except in degenerate cases, agents in a VCG mechanism have strictly positive interim incentives to report truthfully because of the uncertainty (still to be resolved at the time of the reporting) about the chosen alternative.

To simply state our impossibility results for frameworks with informational externalities, we consider a linear specification of preferences, and we assume that the designer has no private information. We let $v^i_k(\theta^1, \ldots, \theta^N) = \sum_{j=1}^N a^j_{ki} \theta^j_{ki}$, and assume that $a^i_{ki} \geq 0$ for all k, i. The signal θ^i of agent i is drawn from a space $\Theta^i \subseteq \mathbb{R}^{K \times N}$ according to a continuous density $f_i(\theta^i) > 0$, independently of other agents' signals θ^{-i}.

Consider a direct revelation mechanism (DRM) (Ψ, t) where $\Psi_k(\tau^1, \ldots \tau^N)$ is the probability that alternative k is chosen given the report profile $\tau = (\tau^1, \ldots \tau^N)$, and $t^i(\tau^1, \ldots \tau^N)$ is the transfer received by agent i given the report profile τ.

Using the methodology developed for Theorem 8, let $V^i(\theta^i)$ be agent i's expected utility in a truth-telling equilibrium of a direct revelation mechanism:

$$V^i(\theta^i) = U^i(\theta^i, \theta^i) = \sup_{\tau^i} U^i(\tau^i, \theta^i)$$

where

$$U^i(\tau^i, \theta^i) = \sum_k \left\{ a^i_{ki} q^i_k(\tau^i) \theta^i_{ki} + \sum_{j \neq i} a^j_{ki} \int_{\Theta^{-i}} \Psi_k(\tau^i, \theta^{-i}) f_{-i}(\theta^{-i}) d\theta^{-i} \right\}$$
$$+ \bar{t}^i(\tau^i)$$
$$q^i_k(\tau^i) = \int_{\Theta^{-i}} \Psi_k(\tau^i, \theta^{-i}) f_{-i}(\theta^{-i}) d\theta^{-i}.$$

The function $q^i_k(\tau^i)$ is agent i's equilibrium interim expected probability that alternative k is chosen conditional on i's report τ^i.

Recall that V^i is convex, and hence twice continuously differentiable almost everywhere. At such point of differentiability, we obtain by the Envelope

Theorem that:

$$\frac{\partial V^i}{\partial \theta^i_{ki}}(\theta^i) = a^i_{ki} q^i_k(\theta^i)$$

$$\frac{\partial V^i}{\partial \theta^i_{kj}}(\theta^i) = 0 \text{ for } j \neq i.$$

By Schwarz's Theorem, the cross derivatives of V^i at θ^i must be equal. This implies for all $k, k', i, j \neq i$:

$$a^i_{ki} \frac{\partial q^i_k(\theta^i)}{\partial \theta^i_{k'i}} = a^i_{k'i} \frac{\partial q^i_{k'}(\theta^i)}{\partial \theta^i_{ki}} \tag{2}$$

$$a^i_{ki} \frac{\partial q^i_k(\theta^i)}{\partial \theta^i_{k'j}} = 0. \tag{3}$$

Consider now a welfare-maximizing allocation rule: $\Psi_{k^*}(\theta^1, \ldots, \theta^N) = 0$ if $k^* \notin \arg\max_k \sum_{i=1}^{N} v^i_k(\theta^1, \ldots, \theta^N)$. For such rules we can directly compute the induced interim expected probabilities that each alternative is chosen. The impossibility result is obtained by showing that these functions cannot generically satisfy (2) and (3).

Theorem 10 *(Jehiel and Moldovanu 2001) Let (Ψ, t) be a welfare-maximizing DRM and assume that the following conditions are satisfied. (1) There exist i, j, k such that $i \neq j$, $a^i_{ki} \neq 0$ and $a^i_{kj} \neq 0$. (2) There exists an open set of θ^i such that, depending on the realization of θ^{-i}, the welfare-maximizing alternative is either k or k'. Then (Ψ, t) cannot be incentive compatible.*

Proof. Conditions 1 and 2 ensure that, for an open set of signals θ^i, the interim expected probabilities (that each alternative is chosen) induced by any value maximizing DRM must satisfy $\partial q^i_k(\theta^i)/\partial \theta^i_{kj} \neq 0$. This is incompatible with (3).

For the proof we have only used identities (3). This is enough because the signal θ^i of agent i has dimension $N \times K$, which, in particular, is larger than the dimension of the alternatives K. The above result is not too surprising as it seems impossible to elicit information that has more dimensions than the number of alternatives the agent cares about. Maskin (1992) provided an early example with this flavor, but he used the stronger ex-post equilibrium concept.

It is important to understand what happens to the impossibility result if the dimension of the signals is no larger than K, the number of payoff-relevant alternatives, i.e., when the simple insight obtained above does not necessarily hold. Consider the same setting as above, except that agent i receives a

K-dimensional signal[28] $\theta^i = (\theta^i_k)$ and $v^i_k(\theta^1, \ldots, \theta^N) = \sum_{j=1}^N a^j_{ki} \theta^j_k$. Identities (2) become now:

$$\forall i, k, k' \neq k, \quad a^i_{ki} \frac{\partial q^i_k(\theta^i)}{\partial \theta^i_{k'}} = a^i_{k'i} \frac{\partial q^i_{k'}(\theta^i)}{\partial \theta^i_k}. \tag{4}$$

Theorem 11 *(Jehiel and Moldovanu 2001) Let* (Ψ, t) *be a welfare-maximizing DRM and assume that the following conditions are satisfied: (1) There exist i, k and k' such that $a^i_{k'i} \neq 0$. (2) There exists an open set of θ^i such that, depending on the realization of θ^{-i}, the welfare-maximizing alternative is either k or k'. Then, if (Ψ, t) is Bayes-Nash incentive compatible, it must be the case that:*

$$\frac{a^i_{ki}}{a^i_{k'i}} = \frac{\sum_{j=1}^N a^i_{kj}}{\sum_{j=1}^N a^i_{k'j}}. \tag{5}$$

Proof. The result follows from the observation that a welfare-maximizing DRM must satisfy

$$\sum_{j=1}^N a^i_{kj} \frac{\partial q^i_k(\theta^i)}{\partial \theta^i_{k'}} = \sum_{j=1}^N a^i_{k'j} \frac{\partial q^i_{k'}(\theta^i)}{\partial \theta^i_k}. \tag{6}$$

To see this, consider a setting where all agents' preferences coincide with total welfare. If a DRM chooses the welfare-maximizing alternative (without any transfer), every agent has obviously an incentive to report truthfully. Thus, conditions (4) must be satisfied for such preferences, yielding (6). In other words, condition (6) must hold for the interim expected probabilities generated by any mechanism that chooses the welfare-maximizing alternative! But, the incentive constraints (with respect to the original preferences) imply conditions (4). Combining (4) and (6) we get (5).

Since the above formulation is relatively abstract, it is helpful to consider a simple auction example:

Example 12 *There are two objects A and B, and two bidders $i = 1, 2$. Each bidder i receives a signal[29] $\theta^i = (\theta^i_A, \theta^i_B)$. Bidder i's valuations (which depend only on i's bundle) are given by: $v^i_X(\theta) = \theta^i_X + a^{-i}_{Xi}\theta^{-i}_X$, $X = A, B$; $v^i_{AB}(\theta) = v^i_A(\theta) + v^i_B(\theta) + s^i_{AB}$. We refer to s^i_{AB} as i's synergy term and assume that these terms are common knowledge.*

Consider a direct truthful mechanism with associated interim expected probabilities $q^i_P(\theta^i)$, where the partition $P = P_{ij}$, denotes the allocation where object

---

[28] That is, from the viewpoint of the above more general model, we assume that $\theta^j_{ik} = \theta^j_k$.

[29] Note that every bidder receives a signal of lower dimension than the the number of partitions, or even than the number of bundles he cares about.

A is allocated to agent i and object B to agent j (thus P_{ii} denotes the allocation where i gets both objects, and so on). At points of twice continuous differentiability (a.e.), we obtain by the Envelope Theorem that:

$$\frac{\partial V^i}{\partial \theta_A^i}(\theta^i) = q_{P_{ii}}^i(\theta^i) + q_{P_{ij}}^i(\theta^i); \quad \frac{\partial V^i}{\partial \theta_B^i}(\theta^i) = q_{P_{ii}}^i(\theta^i) + q_{P_{ji}}^i(\theta^i)$$

$$\frac{\partial}{\partial \theta_B^i}[q_{P_{ii}}^i(\theta^i) + q_{P_{ij}}^i(\theta^i)] = \frac{\partial}{\partial \theta_A^i}[q_{P_{ii}}^i(\theta^i) + q_{P_{ji}}^i(\theta^i)]. \tag{7}$$

Consider now the welfare-maximizing allocation rule, and let $\widetilde{q}_P^i(\theta^i)$ denote the expected probability that the partition P is chosen conditional on i's signal θ^i. Since such an allocation can be implemented whenever agents' preferences coincide with total welfare, $\widetilde{q}$ must satisfy:

$$\frac{\partial}{\partial \theta_B^i}[\widetilde{q}_{P_{ii}}^i + \widetilde{q}_{P_{ij}}^i + a_{Aj}^i \widetilde{q}_{P_{ji}}^i + a_{Aj}^i \widetilde{q}_{P_{jj}}^i](\theta^i)$$

$$= \frac{\partial}{\partial \theta_A^i}[\widetilde{q}_{P_{ii}}^i + \widetilde{q}_{P_{ji}}^i + a_{Bj}^i \widetilde{q}_{P_{ij}}^i + a_{Bj}^i \widetilde{q}_{P_{jj}}^i](\theta^i). \tag{8}$$

Unless $a_{Aj}^i = a_{Bj}^i = 0$ (i.e., unless there are no informational externalities), equations (7) and (8) are not compatible. To see that, assume for concreteness that the partition P_{jj} is never welfare-maximizing (because s_{AB}^j is negative with a large absolute value), and assume that $a_{Bj}^i = 0$ while $a_{Aj}^i > 0$. Then $\widetilde{q}_{P_{jj}}^i = 0$, and it is readily verified that (7) and (8) are incompatible because $\frac{\partial}{\partial \theta_B^i}\widetilde{q}_{P_{ji}}^i \neq 0$ whenever[30] $\frac{\partial}{\partial \theta_B^i}[\widetilde{q}_{P_{ii}}^i + \widetilde{q}_{P_{ij}}^i + a_{Aj}^i \widetilde{q}_{P_{ji}}^i] = \frac{\partial}{\partial \theta_A^i}[\widetilde{q}_{P_{ii}}^i + \widetilde{q}_{P_{ji}}^i]$.

In some non-generic cases, the welfare-maximizing allocation rule can be implemented even when there are informational externalities. This is, for example, the case when $s_{AB}^i = 0$, $i = 1, 2$ and when $a_{Xi}^{-i} < 1$, $X = A, B, i = 1, 2$. Given the separability of the problems in this case, the efficient allocation takes the form:

$$q_{P_{ii}}^i(\theta^i) = q_A^i(\theta_A^i)q_B^i(\theta_B^i); \quad q_{P_{ij}}^i(\theta^i) = q_A^i(\theta_A^i)[1 - q_B^i(\theta_B^i)]$$

$$q_{P_{ji}}^i(\theta^i) = [1 - q_A^i(\theta_A^i)]q_B^i(\theta_B^i); \quad q_{P_{jj}}^i(\theta^i) = [1 - q_A^i(\theta_A^i)][1 - q_B^i(\theta_B^i)]$$

where $q_X^i(\theta_X^i)$ denotes the interim expected probability that good X is allocated to i conditional on θ_X^i. Conditions (7) and (8) are always met for such separable allocation functions, no matter what a_{Xj}^i are,[31] and the welfare-maximizing rule can be implemented using separate, one-dimensional second-price auctions.

---

[30] For example, if the synergy term s_{AB}^i is non-positive, and if partition P_{ji} is sometimes welfare maximizing, one gets $\frac{\partial}{\partial \theta_B^i}\widetilde{q}_{P_{ji}}^i > 0$.

[31] The requirement that $a_{Xj}^i < 1$ is derived from the standard one-dimensional incentive compatibility condition that an agent with a higher signal should receive the good with a higher probability.

To sum up, welfare-maximizing is impossible in auctions with interdependent values and multidimensional signals[32] except in cases where the allocation problem can be divided in separate one-object, one-dimensional auctions. Such a separation is usually impossible if there are complementarities/substitutabilities and/or allocative externalities.[33]

4.2.1   Possibility Results and Applications

One-Dimensional Signals.   For a two-bidder, one-object auction with interdependent values Maskin (1992) has shown that welfare maximization can be achieved if both bidders have a one-dimensional signal and if a single crossing condition holds. This observation has been extended to other one-dimensional settings. Krishna (2003) derives conditions (stronger than single-crossing) ensuring the efficiency of the English ascending auction even if there are more bidders. Kirchkamp and Moldovanu (2004) experimentally compare the performance of the English and second-price sealed-bid auctions with interdependent valuations: As predicted by theory, the English auction is superior from an efficiency point of view. Dasgupta and Maskin (2000), Perry and Reny (2002) and Ausubel (2004) present welfare-maximizing bidding schemes for multi-object auctions where agents have one-dimensional signals.

Within the above described linear model, we provide now a condition ensuring that welfare maximization can be obtained when each agent i receives a one-dimensional signal $\theta^i \in \Re$, and i's value of alternative k is given by $v_k^i(\theta^1, \ldots, \theta^N) = \sum_{j=1}^{N} a_{ki}^j \theta^j$.

Theorem 13   *(Jehiel and Moldovanu 2001) Suppose that for all i, k, k', $a_{ki}^i / a_{k'i}^i > 1 \Rightarrow (\sum_{j=1}^{N} a_{kj}^i) / \sum_{j=1}^{N} a_{k'j}^i > 1$. Then there exists a welfare-maximizing, Bayesian incentive compatible mechanism.*

The set of parameters for which welfare maximization can be achieved is now an open set, and it has positive measure. The fundamental difference is due to the incentive constraints that now reduce to a simple monotonicity condition (without the complex integrability requirement). The relevant mechanism for the above result follows the Vickrey-Clarke-Groves logic by completely dampening the influence of one's own signal on one's own transfer.

Gresik (1991), Fieseler, Kittsteiner and Moldovanu (2003), Kittsteiner (2003), Jehiel and Pauzner (2004), Ornelas and Tuner (2004) and Brusco,

---

[32] This result applies to the the the design of private industries. If firms hold multi-dimensional private information (say on fixed and marginal cost), then it is impossible to induce a welfare maximizing market structure even if there are no costs to public funds. This is illustrated in Jehiel and Moldovanu (2004), and contrasts the analysis of Dana and Spier (1994), Auriol and Laffont (1992), and McGuire and Riordan (1995).

[33] Jehiel, Moldovanu and Stacchetti (1996) contains an early impossibility result in a one-object auction with allocative externalities, interdependent values and multi-dimensional signals.

Lopomo, and Wiswanathan (2004) analyze properties of trading models with interdependent values and one-dimensional signals in a variety of settings that combine features of the classical models due to Akerlof (1970), Myerson and Satterthwaite (1983) and Cramton, Gibbons and Klemperer (1987). For example, Fieseler et al. (2003) show that negative (positive) informational externalities make it easier (harder) to construct welfare-maximizing, budget balanced and individual-rational mechanisms than in analogous cases with private values. Jehiel and Pauzner (2005) show that extreme ownership structures may dominate mixed ownerships in partnership dissolution setups with interdependent values and one-sided private information.

Hain and Mitra (2004) and Kittsteiner and Moldovanu (2005) analyze scheduling and queueing problems, respectively, where agents have private information about processing times. This naturally yields a model with informational externalities since waiting costs depend on information available to others. Gruener and Kiel (2004) focus on collective decisions with interdependent values in the absence of monetary transfers. Finally, Bergemann and Valimaki (2002) focus on the incentives for information acquision with interdependent values.

Correlated Signals. Our impossibility results (Theorems 10 and 11) assumed that the signals are independently distributed across agents. If the signals held by various agents are correlated, it is possible to design subtle transfer devices whereby the belief held by agent i on the signal of agent j is elicited for free (see Crémer and McLean 1988, Theorem 2). When j's belief about i's signal completely determines the signal held by i[34], a welfare-maximizing allocation can be (approximately) implemented, using the logarithmic scoring rule used in Johnson et al. (1990) and Johnson et al. (2003). It is important to note that considering the class of efficient ex-post implementable mechanisms (as in Crémer and McLean 1985, 1988, Theorem 1) is not useful here,[35] since there are no such mechanisms in frameworks with informational externalities and multi-dimensional signals.

To illustrate Johnson et al.'s idea, suppose that agent j believes that i's signal is distributed according to the density $\beta(\theta^i)$, and that agent j is asked to report her belief to a designer who observes the realization of θ^i (in equilibrium this will be reported by i). Suppose further that (up to a constant) agent j receives $\ln \widetilde{\beta}(\theta^i)$ conditional on θ^i, where $\widetilde{\beta}$ is the report made by j about β.[36] Agent j will optimally choose to report her true belief because $\int \beta(\theta^i) \ln \widetilde{\beta}(\theta^i) d\theta^i \leq \int \beta(\theta^i) \ln \beta(\theta^i) d\theta^i \Leftrightarrow \int \beta(\theta^i) \ln \frac{\widetilde{\beta}(\theta^i)}{\beta(\theta^i)} d\theta^i \leq 1$ and because $\int \beta(\theta^i) \ln \frac{\widetilde{\beta}(\theta^i)}{\beta(\theta^i)} d\theta^i \leq \ln(\int \beta(\theta^i) \frac{\widetilde{\beta}(\theta^i)}{\beta(\theta^i)} d\theta^i) = 0$ by the concavity of the logarithm, and by $\int \widetilde{\beta}(\theta^i) d\theta^i = 1$.

---

[34] In two recent papers, Neeman (2004) and Heifetz and Neeman (2005) challenge the view that, generically, there is a one-to one mapping from j's belief onto i's type in the correlated case.

[35] McLean and Postelwaite (2004) use this approach, but only for situations where agents are informationally small.

[36] We assume (for now) that the report made by j is not used to implement a social alternative.

The welfare-maximizing allocation can now be (approximately) implemented whenever there is a one-to-one mapping from j's belief onto i's signal: By having a transfer that puts a sufficiently large weight on $\ln \tilde{\beta}(\theta^i)$, agent j will have the right incentive to report her true belief on i's signal (the belief being isomorphic to her type). This result does not rely on the form of the preferences, and it is solely driven by the fact that different types correspond to different beliefs and that beliefs can be elicited for free when there is no restriction on the size of the transfers. Arbitrarily large transfers (via the weight on $\ln \tilde{\beta}(\theta^i)$) are required whenever distributions of types are almost independent across agents. If bounds on transfers are imposed (because, say, of limited liability constraints) our impossibility result persists whenever the distribution of signals is not too far from the independent case.

Conditioning on Extra Information. Mezzetti (2004) considers a different informational environment. After the social alternative has been chosen, and before monetary payments have been concluded, the agents observe their payoff from the chosen alternative.[37] Thus, agents receive information in addition to their initial signals. Mezzetti observes that an efficient mechanism can be implemented in two stages: In stage 1, agents report their signals; based on the reports, the value-maximizing alternative is implemented. In stage 2, transfers are implemented according to a VCG mechanism based on reports about the observed payoffs in the alternative chosen at stage 1. Mezzetti's insight is valuable, but the proposed mechanism suffers from a number of serious drawbacks. First, at stage 2, agents are completely indifferent about their announcement, since it only serves to compute the transfers received by others. This is in sharp contrast with the agents' strictly positive incentive (due to the unresolved uncertainty about the chosen alternative) to report their true types in the VCG mechanism in the private values case. Second, in many applications, a significant amount of time may elapse before the payoff attached to a chosen alternative is revealed to an agent. Then, allowing for transfers that are contingent on information that becomes available in a distant future seems impractical.[38]

4.3   Ex-post Implementation without Welfare Maximization

Bayesian mechanism design has been criticized on the ground that both the designer and the agents need a lot of information about the distribution of

---

[37] Hansen (1985) is an early paper on auction with contingent payments in settings where additional information becomes available.

[38] This pertains also to the lemons market. Mezzetti's philosophy suggests that there is no problem for a buyer and a seller to agree on price after the buyer observes quality (say after one year of driving a used car). In our opinion, such mechanisms are fragile due to the noisy and subjective assessments of quality, moral hazard, verifiability, etc.

the private signals in order to choose their best course of action.[39] *Robust implementation* seeks for a stronger notion of implementation where the agents and the designer do not need such precise information. In private value contexts this leads to *dominant strategy implementation*, whereas the analogous concept for settings with informational externalities is *ex-post implementation*:[40] Agents should find it optimal to report their true signals even after learning the signals received by others. Such a notion is necessary for robustness since, in particular, implementation should be possible for the degenerate belief that other agents' signals are given by a specific realization. It is also sufficient in quasi-linear environments since ex-post implementation requires that, whatever their beliefs about others' types, agents find it optimal to report their true types whenever other agents are expected to report truthfully. These ideas have been recently formalized by Bergemann and Morris (2005).[41]

An immediate corollary of the main result in Subsection 4.2 is that, generically, the welfare-maximizing allocation cannot be robustly implemented if there are multi-dimensional signals and informational externalities. (If it were, welfare-maximizing Bayes-Nash implementation would be possible for any prior, including the independent case; but this was shown to be false!)

It turns out that, for generic valuation functions, no deterministic social rule that makes use of the agents' reports can be ex-post implemented. To formally state this result, consider choice functions $\psi : S \to K$ with the property that there are transfers functions $t^i : S \to \mathbb{R}$, such that truth-telling is an *ex-post equilibrium* in the incomplete information game that is induced by the direct revelation mechanism $\left(\psi, \left(t^i \right)_{i \in N} \right)$, i.e.,

$$v^i_{\psi(\theta)} (\theta) + t^i (\theta) \geq v^i_{\psi \left(\widetilde{\theta}^i, \theta^{-i} \right)} (\theta) + t^i \left(\widetilde{\theta}^i, \theta^{-i} \right) \qquad (9)$$

for all $\theta^i, \widetilde{\theta}^i \in \Theta^i$ and $\theta^{-i} \in \Theta^{-i}$. Such a choice rule ψ is said to be *ex-post implementable*. We call a choice function ψ *trivial* if it is constant on the interior Θ of the type space.

By requiring optimality of i's truth-telling for every realization of other agents' types θ^{-i}, inequality (9) treats θ^{-i} as if it were known to agent i. Her incentive constraint is thus equivalent to a monopolistic screening problem for every θ^{-i}. Thus, the designer can post personalized prices $p^i_k \left(\theta^{-i} \right)$ for the various alternatives, and let the individuals choose among them. In equilibrium all agents must agree on a most favorable alternative.

---

[39] This is sometimes referred to as *Wilson's critique*.

[40] This notion corresponds to the *uniform equilibrium* first defined by d'Aspremont and Gerard Varet (1979), and to *uniform incentive compatibility* as defined by Holmstrom and Myerson (1983). The term *ex-post equilibrium* is due to Cremer and McLean (1985).

[41] See also Dasgupta, Hammond, and Maskin (1979) and Ledyard (1978) for early, related arguments in private value frameworks.

Lemma 14 (Ex-Post Taxation Principle) *A choice function ψ is ex-post implementable, if and only if for all $i \in \mathcal{N}$, $k \in \mathcal{K}$ and $s^{-i} \in S^{-i}$, there are transfers $\left(p_k^i \left(\theta^{-i} \right) \right)_k \in (\mathbb{R} \cup \{\infty\})^N \setminus (\infty, \dots, \infty)$ such that:*

$$\psi(\theta) \in \arg\max_{k \in \mathcal{K}} \left\{ v_k^i(\theta) - p_k^i \left(\theta^{-i} \right) \right\}. \tag{10}$$

The difficulty of finding an ex-post implementable rule is that (10) should be simultaneously satisfied for all agents i.

To illustrate our impossibility result, we now reduce the problem by assuming that there are only two agents, $i = 1, 2$ and two alternatives k, l. Because agents' incentives are only responsive to differences in payoffs, it is convenient to focus on *relative* valuations[42] μ^i and *relative* prices δ^i :

$$\mu^i(\theta) = v_k^i(\theta) - v_l^i(\theta); \ \delta^i \left(\theta^{-i} \right) = p_k^i \left(\theta^{-i} \right) - p_l^i \left(\theta^{-i} \right).$$

Assuming, that relative prices δ are continuous, the taxation principle implies that at a signal θ, such that agent i is indifferent between the two alternatives, agent j should also be indifferent (since they agree on the preferred alternative). That is,

$$\mu^i(\theta) - \delta^i \left(\theta^{-i} \right) = 0 \Leftrightarrow \mu^j(\theta) - \delta^j \left(\theta^{-j} \right) = 0. \tag{11}$$

Assuming further that relative prices δ are differentiable, condition (11) implies that the gradients of agents' payoff functions must be parallel on the *indifference set* (i.e., the set of signal profile where agents are indifferent between the two alternatives). That is,

$$\begin{pmatrix} \nabla_{\theta^i} \mu^i(\theta) \\ \nabla_{\theta^{-i}} \mu^i(\theta) - \nabla_{\theta^{-i}} \delta^i \left(\theta^{-i} \right) \end{pmatrix} \text{ and } \begin{pmatrix} \nabla_{\theta^i} \mu^{-i}(\theta) - \nabla_{\theta^i} \delta^{-i} \left(\theta^i \right) \\ \nabla_{\theta^{-i}} \mu^{-i}(\theta) \end{pmatrix} \tag{12}$$

are parallel on the indifference set. For differentiable relative price functions, this implies the following proposition.

Proposition 15 *(Jehiel et al. 2005) Let (ψ, t) be a non-trivial ex-post incentive compatible mechanism. If the relative transfers δ^i are differentiable for all $i \in \{1, 2\}$ then, there exists an indifference signal profile $\widehat{\theta}$, and a vector y (with the dimensionality of θ^i) such that $\nabla_{\theta^i} \mu^i(\theta)$ and $(\nabla_{\theta^i} \mu^{-i}(\theta) - y)$ are parallel for every indifference signal profile $\theta = (\widehat{\theta}^i, \theta^{-i})$.*

Jehiel et al. (2005) extend the above intuition to the case where the relative price function is neither differentiable, nor continuous. This yields:

---

[42] For technical simplicity, we assume that relative valuations satisfy the mild requirement $\nabla_{\theta^i} \mu^i(\theta) \neq 0$ for all $\theta \in \Theta$.

Theorem 16 *(Jehiel et al. 2005) Assume that the dimension of the signal θ^i is at least two for each agent $i = 1, 2$. Then, for generic preferences,[43] only trivial social choice rules are ex-post implementable.*

As an illustration, consider a setting with bilinear valuations and two-dimensional signals $\theta^i = (\theta^i_k, \theta^i_l) \in [0, 1]^2$.

Example 17 *Define valuations v by:*

$$v^i_k(\theta) = a^i_k \theta^i_k + b^i_k \theta^i_k \theta^{-i}_k = \theta^i_k \left(a^i_k + b^i_k \theta^{-i}_k \right)$$
$$v^i_l(\theta) = a^i_l \theta^i_l + b^i_l \theta^i_l \theta^{-i}_l = \theta^i_l \left(a^i_l + b^i_l \theta^{-i}_l \right)$$

where $a^i_k, b^i_k, a^i_l, b^i_l \neq 0$. Thus, $\mu^i(\theta) = a^i_k \theta^i_k - a^i_l \theta^i_l + b^i_k \theta^i_k \theta^{-i}_k - b^i_l \theta^i_l \theta^{-i}_l$.

For a vector $y = (y_k, y_l)^T$ we have

$$\nabla_{\theta^i} \mu^i(\theta) = \begin{pmatrix} a^i_k + b^i_k \theta^{-i}_k \\ -a^i_l - b^i_l \theta^{-i}_l \end{pmatrix}; \ (\nabla_{\theta^i} \mu^{-i}(\theta) - y) = \begin{pmatrix} b^{-i}_k \theta^{-i}_k - y_k \\ -b^{-i}_l \theta^{-i}_l - y_l \end{pmatrix}.$$

It is readily verified that $b^1_l b^2_k - b^1_k b^2_l = 0$ is necessary for such vectors to remain parallel when we vary θ^{-i}_k and θ^{-i}_l. It follows from Proposition 15 that a non-trivial choice function ψ is implementable only if $b^1_l b^2_k - b^1_k b^2_l = 0$. The above condition is obviously non-generic. The set of parameters where it is satisfied has zero Lebesgue-measure in the 8-dimensional space of coefficients that parameterize the bi-linear valuations in this example.

The impossibility result of Theorem 16 should be contrasted with an elegant result due to Roberts (1979). Roberts requires that each agent i get a one-dimensional signal for each social alternative.[44] Applied to auctions, this means $\theta^i = (\theta^i_P)_{P \in \mathcal{P}}$, where $\theta^i_P \in \Re$, and $v^i_P(\theta) \equiv v^i_P(\theta^i_P)$. He also assumes that 1) There are at least 3 relevant partitions, and 2) For any $x \in \Re^{|\mathcal{P}|}$ there exists $\theta^i = (\theta^i_P)_{P \in \mathcal{P}} \in \Theta^i$ such that $\{v^i_P(\theta^i_P)\}_{P \in \mathcal{P}} = x$. With these assumptions, Roberts shows that a deterministic social choice function Ψ is dominant-strategy implementable only if there is a set of real weights $\{\alpha_i\}_{i=1,2,...N}$, not all equal to zero, and a set of real weights $\{\lambda_P\}_{P \in \mathcal{P}}$ such that $P^\lambda(\theta) = \arg \max_{P \in \mathcal{P}} [\sum_j \alpha^j v^j_P(\theta^j_P) + \lambda_P]$.

Thus, dominant strategy implementable social choice functions must maximize a weighted average of the agents' values, augmented by a partition-specific weight. Jehiel et al. (2004) call these functions *affine maximizers*. The "rich preference space" condition 2 above[45] implies that agents must care about the

---

[43] The result holds both for topological and measure-theoretic notions of genericity.

[44] This last assumption can be relaxed. See Jehiel et al. (2004).

[45] Bickchandani et al. (2004), Gui et al. (2004) and Lavi et al. (2004) characterize dominant-strategy implementability on restricted domains where condition 2 need not hold.

entire partition of goods. Thus, there must be allocative externalities for Roberts' characterization to hold.

4.3.1   Possibility Results

We now review several situations that allow for non-trivial ex-post implementation. In all cases, the geometric condition of Proposition 15 is less restrictive.

1) Theorem 16 heavily relies on the impossibility of simultaneously satisfying the incentive constraints of several agents. If there is only one strategic agent, non-trivial ex-post implementation is possible.[46]

2) If all agents have a one-dimensional signal,[47] or if only one agent has a multi-dimensional signal then non-trivial ex-post implementation is possible for some open set of preferences (see Jehiel et al. 2005).

3) Consider preferences $v_k^i(\theta)$ that are additively separable, i.e., $v_k^i(\theta) = f_k^i(\theta^i) + h_k^i(\theta^{-i})$. It is readily verified by the standard VCG analysis that $\arg\max_k \sum_i f_k^i(\theta^i)$ can be ex-post implemented. Under some technical conditions, only such affine maximizers can be implemented (see Jehiel, Meyer-ter-Vehn and Moldovanu 2004). This is the counterpart to Roberts' (1979) result in the private values case.

4) Another non-generic but interesting class is studied by Bikchandani (2004). He considers a one-object auction without allocative externalities and observes that by not selling the object for a sufficiently large subset of signals, a non-trivial (yet very inefficient) choice rule can be ex-post implemented.

5   CONCLUSION

We have studied the effects of allocative and informational externalities in auctions and related mechanisms. Because values become endogenous, standard auctions cease to be welfare maximizing in the presence of allocative externalities, and they give rise to a wealth of new phenomena. But the traditional Vickrey-Clarke-Groves mechanisms achieve welfare maximization in such frameworks, as long as there are no informational externalities. Informational externalities can be satisfactorily dealt with only in settings where signals are one-dimensional (and where a single-crossing property holds). For example, an English ascending auction is welfare maximizing in one-object symmetric settings, and generalized Vickrey-Clarke-Groves mechanisms are welfare maximizing even in asymmetric settings as long as signals are scalars. The situation drastically changes when information is multi-dimensional (as required by general multi-object applications): VCG mechanisms have

---

[46] This should be contrasted with the impossibility of efficient Nash-Bayes implementation, which holds as soon as at least one agent has multi-dimensional private information.

[47] In this case, the geometric condition merely requires that some scalars (rather than vectors) are multiples of each other.

no analogues, and robust implementation does not allow the use of private information.

We have tried to show that externalities naturally arising in many applications have a significant effect on the outcome of auctions and other mechanisms. From an empirical viewpoint, it is now time to investigate the role (magnitude and effect on bidding strategies) of allocative externalities in auctions – this could parallel the exciting recent work on common value auctions (see Athey and Haile, 2005).

From a theoretical viewpoint, the above analysis leaves open a number of important questions. In particular, since informational externalities make it impossible to implement the welfare-maximizing allocation, what does the second-best allocation look like in such contexts? Since ex-post implementation is generally impossible with informational externalities, what is a good way to achieve robust implementation?

References

Akerlof, G. (1970): "The Market for Lemons: Quality Uncertainty and the Market Mechanism," *Quarterly Journal of Economics* **89**, 488–500.

Armstrong, M. (1996): "Multiproduct Nonlinear Pricing," *Econometrica* **64**, 51–76.

d'Aspremont, C. and L.A. Gérard-Varet (1979): "Incentives and Incomplete Information," *Journal of Public Economics* **11**, 25–45.

Athey, S. and P. Haile (2005): "Empirical Models of Auctions," this volume.

Auriol, E. and J-J. Laffont (1992): "Regulation by Duopoly," *Journal of Economics and Management Strategy* **1**, 507–533.

Ausubel, L. (2004): "An Efficient Ascending-Bid Auction for Multiple Objects," *American Economic Review* **94**, 1452–1475.

Ausubel, L. and P. Milgrom (2002): "Ascending Auctions with Package Bidding," *Frontiers of Theoretical Economics* **1**, 1–42.

Bagwell, K., P. Mavroidis and R. Staiger (2004): "The Case for Auctioning Countermeasures in the WTO," discussion paper, Columbia University.

Bergemann, D. and S. Morris (2005): "Robust Mechanism Design," *Econometrica* **73**, 1521–1534.

Bergemann, D. and J. Välimäki (2002): "Information Acquisition and Efficient Mechanism Design," *Econometrica* **70**, 1007–10035.

Bikhchandani, S. (2004): "The Limits of Ex Post Implementation Revisited," mimeo, UCLA.

Bikchchandani, S., S. Chatterji and A. Sen (2004): "Incentive Compatibility in Multi-Unit Auctions," discussion paper, UCLA.

Brocas, I. (2003): "Endogenous Entry in Auctions with Negative Externalities," *Theory and Decision* **54**, 125–149.

Brusco, S., G. Lopomo and S. Wiswanathan (2004): "Merger Mechanisms," mimeo, SUNY, Stony Brook.

Burguet, F. and J. Sempere (2005): "Trade Permits for Greenhouse Emissions," discussion paper, UAB, Barcelona.

Caillaud, B. and P. Jehiel (1998): "Collusion in Auction with Externalities," *Rand Journal of Economics* **29**, 680–702.

Chung, K.-S. and J. Ely (2001): "Ex-post Incentive Compatible Mechanism Design," discussion paper, Northwestern University.

Clarke, E. (1971): "Multipart Pricing of Public Goods," *Public Choice* **8**, 19–33.

Coase, R. H. (1960): "The Problem of Social Cost," *Journal of Law and Economics* **3**, 1–44.

Compte, O. and P. Jehiel (2002a): "On the Value of Competition in Procurement Auctions," *Econometrica* **70**, 343–355.

Compte, O. and P. Jehiel (2002b): "Information Acquisition in Auctions: Sealed-Bid or Dynamic?" mimeo, PSE and UCL.

Cramton, P., R. Gibbons and P. Klemperer (1987): "Dissolving a Partnership Efficiently," *Econometrica* **55**, 615–632.

Cremer, J. and R. McLean (1985): "Optimal Selling Strategies under Uncertainty for a Discriminating Monopolist when Demands are Interdependent," *Econometrica* **53**, 345–362.

Cremer, J. and R. McLean (1988): "Full Extraction of the Surplus in Bayesian and Dominant Strategy Auctions," *Econometrica* **56**, 1247–1257.

Dana, J. and K. Spier (1994): "Designing a Private Industry: Government Auctions with Endogenous Market Structure," *Journal of Public Economics* **53**, 127–147.

Dasgupta, P., P. Hammond and E. Maskin (1979): "The Implementation of Social Choice Rules: Some General Results on Incentive Compatibility," *Review of Economic Studies* **46**, 185–216.

Dasgupta, P. and E. Maskin (2000): "Efficient Auctions," *Quarterly Journal of Economics* **115**, 341–388.

Das Varma, G. (2002): "Standard Auctions with Identity Dependent Externalities," *Rand Journal of Economics* **33**, 689–708.

Das Varma, G. (2002): "Who Else is Bidding? The Pareto Optimality of Disclosing Bidder Identities," *Review of Economic Design* **7**, 155–171.

Das Varma, G. (2003): "Bidding for a Process of Innovation under Alternative Modes of Competition," *International Journal of Industrial Organization* **21**, 15–37.

Fieseler, K., T. Kittsteiner and B. Moldovanu (2003): "Partnerships, Lemons and Efficient Trade," *Journal of Economic Theory* **113**, 223–234.

Figueroa, N. and V. Skreta (2004): "Optimal Auction Design for Multiple Objects with Externalities," mimeo, University of Minnesota.

Gilbert, R. and D. Newbery (1982): "Preemptive Patenting and the Persistence of Monopoly," *American Economic Review* **72**, 514–526.

Goeree, J. (2003): "Bidding for the Future: Signaling in Auctions with an Aftermarket," *Journal of Economic Theory* **108**, 345–364.

Gomes, A. and P. Jehiel (2005): "Dynamic Processes of Social and Economic Interactions: On the Persistence of Inefficiencies," *Journal of Political Economy* **113**, 626–667.

Graham, D. and R. Marshall (1987): "Collusive Bidder Behvaior at Single-Object Second-Price and English Auctions," *Journal of Political Economy* **95**, 1217–1239.

Green J., J.J. Laffont (1979): "Incentives in Public Decision Making," North Holland.

Gresik, T.A. (1991): "Ex-Ante Inceive Efficient Trading Mechanisms without the Private Valuations Restriction," *Journal of Economic Theory* **55**, 41–63.

Gruener, H.P. and A. Kiel (2004): "Collective Decisions with Interdependent Valuations," *European Economic Review* **48**, 1147–1168.

Gui, H., R. Mueller and R. Vohra (2004): "Dominant Strategy Mechanisms with Multidimensional Types," discussion paper, Northwestern University.

Groves T. (1973): "Incentives in Teams," *Econometrica* **41**, 617–631.

Hain, R. and M. Mitra (2004): "Simple Sequencing Problems with Interdependent Costs," *Games and Economic Behavior* **48**, 271–291.

Hansen R. (1985): "Auctions with Contingent Payments," *American Economic Review* **75**, 862–865.

Heifetz, A. and Z. Neeman (2004): "On the Generic (Im)possibility of Full Surplus Extraction in Mechanism Design," mimeo, Boston University.

Hiriart-Urruty, J.P. and Lemarechal C. (2001): *Fundamentals of Convex Analysis*, Heidelberg: Springer–Verlag .

Holmström B. (1979): "Groves, Schemes on Restricted Domains," *Econometrica* **47**, 1137–1144.

Holmström B. and R. Myerson (1983): "Efficient and Durable Decisions Rules with Incomplete Information," *Econometrica* **51**, 1799–1819.

Hoppe, H., P. Jehiel and B. Moldovanu (2005): "License Auctions and Market Structure," forthcoming, *Journal of Economics and Management Science*.

Inderst, R. and C. Wey (2004): "The Incentives for Takeovers in Oligopoly," *International Journal of Industrial Organization* **22**, 1067–1089.

Jackson, M. (2003): "Efficiency and Information Aggregation in Auctions with Costly Information," *Review of Economic Design* **8**, 121–141.

Janssen, M. (2004): *Auctioning Public Assets*, Cambridge: Cambridge University Press.

Janssen, M. and B. Moldovanu (2004): "Allocation Mechanisms and Post-Allocation Interaction," in *Auctioning Public Assets*, M. Janssen (ed.), Cambridge: Cambridge University Press.

Jehiel, P., M. Meyer-ter-Vehn and B. Moldovanu (2004b): "Potential and Implementation," discussion paper, University of Bonn.

Jehiel, P., M. Meyer-ter-Vehn, B. Moldovanu and W. Zame (2005): "The Limits of Ex-post Implementation," discussion paper, University of Bonn.

Jehiel, P. and B. Moldovanu (1996): "Strategic Non-participation," *Rand Journal of Economics* **27**, 84–98.

Jehiel, P. and B. Moldovanu (1999): "Resale Markets and the Assignment of Property Rights," *Review of Economic Studies* **66**, 971–991.

Jehiel, P. and B. Moldovanu (2000): "Auctions with Downstream Interaction among Buyers," *Rand Journal of Economics* **31**, 768–791.

Jehiel, P. and B. Moldovanu (2001): "Efficient Design with Interdependent Valuations," *Econometrica* **69**, 1237–1259.

Jehiel, P. and B. Moldovanu (2003): "An Economic Perspective on Auctions," *Economic Policy* **36**, 271–308.

Jehiel, P. and B. Moldovanu (2004): "The Design of an Efficient Private Industry," *Journal of the European Economic Association* **2**(2–3), 516–525.

Jehiel, P., B. Moldovanu and E. Stacchetti (1996): "How (not) to Sell Nuclear Weapons," *American Economic Review* **86**, 814–829.

Jehiel, P., B. Moldovanu and E. Stacchetti (1999): "Multidimensional Mechanism Design for Auctions with Externalities," *Journal of Economic Theory* **85**, 814–829.

Jehiel, P. and A. Pauzner (2005): "Partnership Dissolution with Interdependent Values," forthcoming, *Rand Journal of Economics.*

Johnson, S., J.W. Pratt and R. Zeckhauser (1990): "Efficiency Despite Mutually Payoff-Relevant Private Information: The Finite Case," *Econometrica* **58**, 873–900.

Johnson, S., N. Miller, J.W. Pratt and R. Zeckhauser (2003): "Efficiency Design with Multidimensional, Continuous Types, and Interdependent Valuations," mimeo, Kennedy School, Harvard University.

Jullien, B. (2000): "Participation Constraints in Adverse Selection Models," *Journal of Economic Theory* **93**, 1–47.

Kamien, M., S. Oren and Y. Tauman (1992): "Optimal Licensing of Cost-Reducing Innovations," *Journal of Mathematical Economics* **21**, 483–509.

Kamien, M. and Y. Tauman (1986): "Fees versus Royalties and the Private Value of a Patent," *Quarterly Journal of Economics* **101**, 471–492.

Katz, M. and C. Shapiro (1986): "How to License Intangible Property," *Quarterly Journal of Economics* **101**, 567–590.

Kirchkamp, O. and B. Moldovanu (2004): "An Experimental Study of Auctions with Interdependent Valuations," *Games and Economic Behavior* **48**, 54–85.

Kittsteiner, T. (2003): "Partnerships and the Double Auction with Interdependent Valuations," *Games and Economic Behavior* **44**, 54–76.

Kittsteiner, T. and B. Moldovanu (2005): "Priority Auctions and Queue Disciplines that Depend on Processing Time," *Management Science* **51**, 236–248.

Klemperer, P. (2001): "How (Not) to Run Auctions: The European 3G Telecom Auctions," *European Economic Review* **46**, 829–845.

Klemperer, P. (1999): "Auction Theory: A Guide to the Literature," *Journal of Economic Surveys* **13**, 227–286.

Krishna, K. (1993): "Auctions with Endogenous Valuations: The Persistence of Monopoly Revisited," *American Economic Review* **83**, 147–160.

Krishna, V. (2003): "Asymmetric English Auctions," *Journal of Economic Theory* **112**, 261–288.

Krishna, V. and E. Maenner (2001): "Convex Potentials with an Application to Mechanism Design," *Econometrica* **69**, 1113–1119.

Laffont, J.-J. and E. Maskin (1982): "The Theory of Incentives: an Overview" in *Advances in Economic Theory*, edited by W. Hildenbrand, Cambridge University Press 31–94.

Laffont, J.-J. and D. Martimort (1997): "Collusion under Asymmetric Information," *Econometrica* **65**, 875–912.

Lavi, R., A. Muálem and N. Nisan (2004): "Towards a Characterization of Truthful Combinatorial Auctions," discussion paper, Hebrew University, Jerusalem.

Ledyard, J. (1978): "Incentive Compatibility and Incomplete Information," *Journal of Economic Theory* **18**, 171–189.

Maeda, A. (2003): "The Emergence of Market Power in Emission Rights Markets: The Role of Initial Permit Distribution," *Journal of Regulatory Economics* **24**, 293–314.

Maskin, E. (1992): "Auctions and Privatization," in *Privatization: Symposium in Honor of Herbert Giersch*, edited by H. Siebert, 115–136. Tuebingen/ J. C.B. Mohr.

Maskin, E. (2001): "Auctions and Efficiency," in *Advances in Economics and Econometrics*, Vol. 1, M. Dewatripont et al. (eds.), Econometric Society Monographs, Cambridge University Press.

McAfee, P. (1998): "Four Issues in Market Design," *Revista Analisis Economico* **13**, 7–24.

McGuire, T. and M. Riordan (1995): "Incomplete Information and Optimal Market Structure: Public Purchases from Private Providers," *Journal of Public Economics* **56**, 125–141.

McLean, R. and A. Postlewaite (2004): "Informational Size and Efficient Auctions," *Review of Economic Studies* **71**, 809–827.

Mezzetti, C. (2004): "Mechanism Design with Interdependent Valuations: Efficiency," *Econometrica* **72**, 1617–1626.

Milgrom, P. (2004): *Putting Auction Theory to Work*, Cambridge: Cambridge University Press.

Milgrom, P. and I. Segal (2002): "Envelope Theorems for Arbitrary Choice Sets," *Econometrica* **70**, 583–601.

Milgrom, P. and R. Weber (1982): "A Theory of Auctions and Competitive Bidding," *Econometrica* **50**, 1089–1122.

Moldovanu, B. and A. Sela (2003): "Licensing Bertrand Competitors," *International Journal of Industrial Organization* **21**, 1–13.

Molnar, J. and G. Virag (2004): "Revenue Maximizing Auctions with Externalities and Signaling," working paper, University of Rochester.

Monderer D. and L. Shapley (1996): "Potential Games," *Games and Economic Behavior* **14**, 124–143.

Muller, R. and R. Vohra (2003): "On Dominant Strategy Mechanisms," discussion paper, Northwestern University.

Myerson R. and M. Satterthwaite (1983): "Efficient Mechanisms for Bilateral Trading," *Journal of Economic Theory* **28**, 265–281.

Neeman, Z. (2004): "The Relevance of Private Information in Mechanism Design," *Journal of Economic Theory* **117**, 55–77.

Ornelas, E. and J. Turner (2004): "Efficient Dissolution of Partnership and the Structure of Control," mimeo, University of Georgia.

Perez-Castrillo, D. and D. Wettstein (2002): "Choosing Wisely: A Multibidding Approach," *American Econmic Review* **92**, 1577–1587.

Perry, M. and P. Reny (2002): "An Efficient Auction," *Econometrica* **70**, 1199–1213.

Pesendorfer, W. and J. Swinkels (1998): "Efficiency and Information Aggregation in Auctions," *American Economic Review* **90**, 381–411.

Riley, J. and W. Samuelson (1981): "Optimal Auctions," *American Economic Review* **71**, 381–392.

Roberts, K. (1979): "The Characterization of Implementable Choice Rules" in *Aggregation and Revelation of Preferences*, edited by J.J. Laffont, North Holland.

Rochet, J. C. (1985): "The Taxation Principle and Multitime Hamilton Jacobi Equations," *Journal of Mathematical Economics* **14**, 113–128.

Rodriguez, E.G. (2002): "Auctions of Licences and Market Structure," *Economic Theory* **19**, 283–309.

Vickrey, W. (1961): "Counterspeculation, Auctions and Competetive Sealed Tenders," *Journal of Finance* **16**, 8–37.

Wilson, R. (1979): "Auctions of Shares," *Quarterly Journal of Economics* **93**, 675–689.

Wilson, R. (1969): "Competitive Bidding with Asymmetric Information" *Management Science* **13**, 816–820.

Waehrer, K. (2003): "Hazardous Facility Siting when Cost Information Is Private," *Journal of Public Economic Theory* **5**, 605–622.

CHAPTER 4

The Economics of Relationships[1]

Larry Samuelson

1   INTRODUCTION

1.1   Relationships: Two Illustrations

Each year, about $60 billion dollars worth of diamond jewelry is sold world-wide. Over the course of its journey from mine to warbrobe, a diamond typically passes through numerous intermediaries in search of just the right buyer. Because diamonds are easy to conceal, difficult to distinguish, portable and valuable, there are many opportunities to cheat on diamond deals. One would accordingly expect them to be handled with the utmost care. To the contrary, virtually no care at all is taken:[2]

> Once gems leave the vault-like workshops, they do so in folded sheets of tissue paper, in the pockets of messengers, dealers and traders. They are not logged in and out . . . or marked to prevent substitution. They are protected from embezzling only by the character of those who transport. . . . On that slender record, gems worth thousands of dollars traverse the street and are distributed among buyers from Bombay to Buenos Aries, Pawtucket and Dubuque.

In Puccini's opera *Gianni Schicchi*, the deceased Buoso Donati has left his estate to a monastery, much to the consternation of his family.[3] Before others learn of the death, Donati's relatives hire the actor Gianni Schicchi, who is to

[1] This paper was prepared for presentation at the 2005 World Congress of the Econometric Society in London. I thank Bo Chen, Georg Nöldeke, George Mailath, Torsten Persson, and Colin Rowat for comments. I am grateful to George Mailath for a long collaboration that culminated in Mailath and Samuelson (2006), from which this paper draws heavily and to which the reader is frequently referred for elaboration. I thank the National Science Foundation (SES-0241506) for financial support.
[2] This account of diamond transactions is taken from Richman (2005) (the sales figure from page 10 (footnote 29) and the quotation from page 14 (noting that it is originally from an article by Roger Starr, "The Real Treasure of 47th Street," in the *New York Times* (March 26, 1984, Section A, p. 18)).
[3] The use of *Gianni Schicchi* to illustrate the incentives in an isolated interaction is due to Hamermesh (2004, p. 164).

impersonate Buoso Donati, write a new will leaving the fortune to the family, and then feign death. Anxious that Schicchi do nothing to expose the plot, the family explains that there are severe penalties for tampering with a will and that any misstep puts Schicchi at risk. All goes well until the time arrives for Schicchi to write the new will, at which point he instructs that the entire estate be left to the great actor, Gianni Schicchi. The relatives watch in horror, afraid to object lest they end up paying the penalties with which they had threatened Schicchi.

The outcomes in these situations are strikingly different. Those involved in the diamond trade face constant opportunities to return one less diamond than they received, with the recipient unable to prove they had been shortchanged, but refrain from doing so. Gianni Schicchi sees a chance to steal a fortune and grabs the money. The diamond handlers are involved in a relationship. They know they will deal with one another again and that opportunistic behavior could have adverse future consequences, even if currently unexposed. Gianni Schicchi was not involved in a relationship with the family of Buoso Donati. Nothing came into play beyond the current interaction, which he turned to his advantage.

Throughout our daily lives, we similarly react to incentives created by relationships (or their absence).

1.2   What Is a Relationship?

A relationship is an interaction featuring

- (i) agents who are tied together with identified partners over a number of periods,
- (ii) incentives that potentially spill across periods, and
- (iii) future behavior that depends on current actions (in order to create current incentives) not through contracts but through the provision of appropriate future incentives.

Alternative terms for such interactions include "relational contract" and "relational incentive contract" (e.g., Baker, Gibbons, and Murphy (2002), Levin (2003)).

The need for relationships arises out of information, incentive, property right, or contracting problems that push us away from competitive markets (Debreu (1959)) or contracting (Coase (1960)) as means for effectively allocating resources. In the diamond market, for example, the formal remedies for reneging on a deal are ineffective: "The truth is that if someone owes you money, there's no real way to get it from him if he doesn't want to pay you."[4] The legal difficulties that prevented Buoso Donati's family from writing a contract with Gianni Schicchi recur in a variety of relationships, perhaps most notably those governed by antitrust legislation.

---

[4] Richman (2005, p. 18), reporting a personal interview with a diamond dealer.

In the face of such incentive problems, it can make a great deal of difference to Alice whether she anticipates dealing with Bob once or whether she has a continuing relationship with Bob.[5] Forming a relationship potentially allows the two of them to create more effective current incentives by appropriately configuring their future interactions.[6]

Work on "relationship-specific investments"[7] has focused on the inefficiencies that can arise when two trading partners are locked together but cannot write complete contracts. We thus have the first characteristic of a relationship, but the remaining two aspects, repeated interactions with incentives that potentially spill over from one interaction to the next, are missing. A repeated relationship-specific-investment problem would bring us into the realm of relationships. Similarly, though the distinctions become murkier, a *repeated* alternating-offers bargaining problem would constitute a relationship, while a single such interaction would not.

Much of this paper will be concerned with the standard tool for examining relationships, the theory of repeated games. The focus on "relationships" in motivating this inquiry reflects a belief that much of the challenge and much of the recent work is concerned not simply with developing the technical tools of repeated games, but with using those tools to say something about the economics of relationships.

1.3   Why Study Relationships?

Economics is often (perhaps somewhat narrowly) defined as the study of resource allocation. Within this study, attention is typically focused on the role of prices and markets. We touch here on a few points of entry into the large literature, much of it from outside economics, describing how relationships provide an alternative mechanism that also plays an important role in allocating resources.

Greif and his coauthors (Greif (1997, 2005), Greif, Milgrom, and Weingast (1994)) highlight the role of appropriate institutions in making possible the trade upon which modern economies are built. In some cases, these institutions provided the foundations for markets and contracts. In other cases, they "thickened" the information flows, allowing relationships to come to the fore.[8]

---

[5] Alice is interested in whether she will trade again with Bob rather than someone else not because they trade different goods, but because they are characterized by different past behavior and information.

[6] The mere fact that current exchanges might have implications for the future does not suffice to create a relationship. People constantly trade claims on future resources, often in the form of money or savings or via a variety of other contracts, but the contractural nature of these claims prompts us to stop short of calling them a relationship.

[7] See Malcomson (1997) and Schmitz (2002) for surveys of the large literature.

[8] Similarly, Richman (2005) attributes the preponderance of Jewish merchants in the diamond trade to the resulting ability to strengthen information flows so that relationships can be effective.

Relationships continue to play an important role in our contemporary economy. Macauley (1963) (an early and often-echoed classic) argues that business-to-business relations typically rely on the prospect of future interactions rather than contracts or legal recourse to shape deals and to mediate disputes. Ellickson (1991) suggests that such a reliance on relationships is pervasive. Putnam's (2000) concerns about deteriorating social capital sound very much like a lament that our relationships are deteriorating.

Evolutionary psychology (e.g., Cosmides and Tooby (1992a,b)) suggests that our evolutionary past may have equipped us with a fundamental ability to sustain relationships. The argument here is that monitoring relationships was at one point so crucial to our evolutionary success that our brains have developed specialized resources for doing so.

The common theme is that understanding relationships can help us understand how our economy allocates resources and help us design our economy to better allocate resources.

1.4 An Example

An example will help put relationships into context. Consider an economy with two goods, x and y, and an even number N of agents with utility functions $u(x, y) = \ln(1 + x) + \ln(1 + y)$. In each period $t = 0, 1, \ldots$, each agent is endowed with one unit of good y. Each agent is also endowed with either zero or two units of good x in each period, with each endowment being equally likely and with precisely half of the agents receiving each endowment. An agent maximizes the (expected value of) the normalized (by $1 - \delta$) discounted sum of payoffs, given by $(1 - \delta) \sum_{t=0}^{\infty} \delta^t u(a^t)$, where a^t is the agent's period-t consumption bundle.

In the absence of trade, we have the autarkic equilibrium in which the consumption bundles $(0, 1)$ and $(2, 1)$ are equally likely in each period. Expected utility is given by

$$\frac{1}{2}[\ln 1 + \ln 2] + \frac{1}{2}[\ln 3 + \ln 2] = \frac{1}{2} \ln 12 \approx 1.24.$$

At the other end of the spectrum, we have an economy with complete markets. A state ω in this economy now identifies, in every period, which agents are endowed with two units of good x. Trades can be made contingent on the state. The symmetric efficient allocation is the unique competitive equilibrium allocation of the economy, in which each agent consumes one unit of x and one unit of y in each period, removing all individual uncertainty from the outcome, for a utility of:

$$\frac{1}{2}[\ln 2 + \ln 2] + \frac{1}{2}[\ln 2 + \ln 2] = \frac{1}{2} \ln 16 \approx 1.39.$$

Now suppose that in each period t, no trade can occur involving a commodity dated in some subsequent period (the contracting difficulty that potentially gives rise to relationships). We then have a countable number of separate markets, one for each period, each of which must clear independently. Each such market again has a unique competitive equilibrium in which goods x and y trade on a one-to-one basis. An agent endowed with no units of good x consumes half a unit of each good, while an agent endowed with two units of good x consumes three-halves of each good. Expected utility is

$$\frac{1}{2}\left[\ln\left(\frac{3}{2}\right) + \ln\left(\frac{3}{2}\right)\right] + \frac{1}{2}\left[\ln\left(\frac{5}{2}\right) + \ln\left(\frac{5}{2}\right)\right] = \ln\left(\frac{15}{4}\right) \approx 1.32.$$

Can the agents do better, given their inability to contract? Suppose that in each period, agents are randomly (and independently across periods) sorted into pairs, fortuitously arranged so that one agent has two units of x and the other has none (an assumption to which we return). Let each agent who finds himself endowed with two units of good x give one unit to his x-less partner in that period, as long as no agent has yet failed to deliver on this implicit promise. Should any agent ever fail to make this transfer, the autarkic equilibrium appears in each subsequent period. The resulting outcome duplicates that of the complete-markets outcome. Moreover, this behavior is an equilibrium if the agents can make the required observations and are sufficiently patient.[9]

This arrangement brings us two-thirds of the way to a relationship. The incentives for current behavior involve the dependence of future behavior on current outcomes, and this dependence is enforced not by contractural arrangements but by future incentives. However, the agents are still anonymous – there is no need for agents to be tied together in relationships.

It is important for this arrangement that every agent observe every aspect of the history of play, so that any missed transfer triggers a switch to the autarkic equilibrium. Suppose instead that the agents can observe only whether a transfer is made *in their pair*. At first glance, it appears as if this information limitation is devastating. An agent who consumes her two units of good x rather than sharing with her hapless partner is on to a new partner before any retribution can be extracted. However, suppose that an agent follows the practice of making a transfer whenever endowed with two units of good x, unless a previous opponent failed to deliver on such a transfer, in which case the current agent makes no transfer. A defection thus sets off a contagion of defections that eventually returns to haunt the original transgressor, even when encountering partners for the first time. If the population is not too large and the players are sufficiently patient, then we have an equilibrium duplicating the complete-markets outcome.[10]

---

[9] The incentive constraint for an agent to carry on with the prescribed behavior, rather than pocketing his two units of good x when so endowed (at the cost of subsequent autarky), is given by $(1 - \delta)\ln 6 + \delta\frac{1}{2}\ln 12 \leq \frac{1}{2}\ln 16$, or $\delta \geq 0.74$.

[10] See Ahn and Suominen (2001), Ellison (1994), Kandori (1992), Harrington, Jr. (1995), and Okuno-Fujiwara and Postlewaite (1995).

If the population is too large, then the previous scheme will be unable to support risk sharing. As an alternative, suppose the agents can arrange to meet the *same* opponent in every period. Suppose now, even more fortuitously (and more deserving of future commentary), that only one agent in a pair is endowed with two units of x in each period, with that agent's identity randomly drawn each period. Let the equilibrium call for the agent with two units of good x to offer one unit to the agent with none, as long as such behavior has prevailed in the past, and to retain his endowment otherwise. The incentive constraint for this to be an equilibrium is that

$$(1 - \delta) \ln 6 + \delta \frac{1}{2} \ln 12 \leq \frac{1}{2} \ln 16,$$

which we can solve for $\delta \geq 0.74$ (cf. footnote 9), regardless of population size. The agents are exploiting their relationships to achieve the complete-markets outcome. A relationship concentrates the flow of information across periods, with each agent entering the current period knowing the history of his opponent's play, allowing more effective incentives to be created.

Could we generate the information flow required to sustain incentives without sorting agents into relationships, while stopping short of assuming that all information is publicly available? Money can convey information (Kocherlakota (1998), Kocherlakota and Wallace (1998)). Suppose we introduce money into the economy by endowing the agents with certificates. An agent endowed with no x could exchange a certificate for a unit of the good, while agents called upon to relinquish a unit of x could exchange it for a certificate, confident that the latter will elicit the required reciprocation when needed. An agent need no longer worry whether future partners can observe that he has contributed when endowed with x, instead showing the resulting certificate when the need arises.

Unfortunately, there will inevitably be some agents who encounter extraordinarily long strings of bad luck, in the form of zero endowments of good x, and others who run into similar strings of good luck. Eventually, the former will run out of certificates, while the latter will have accumulated so many that they prefer to buy more than one unit of good x in a period. We may then be able to achieve some risk sharing, but cannot do so perfectly.

An analogous problem arises in relationships, buried beneath the assumption that only one of the agents in a relationship is endowed with x at a time. We have no reason to expect such coordination. Instead, there will inevitably be periods in which neither agent is endowed with x, as well as periods when both are. In these cases, the relationship is stuck. One could respond by creating larger relationships, matching pools of people in each period instead of just two. Presumably, however, the information flows required to make the relationship work deteriorate as the group grows larger. Otherwise, we would simply mass the entire economy into a single relationship.

If forced to rely exclusively on either relationships or money, we thus face a tradeoff. The relationships must remain small, in order to capture their informational advantages, but at the cost of unavoidable idiosyncracy in endowments within a period. Money is vulnerable to idiosyncratic draws across periods. Relationships thus have a useful role to play, but are not a panacea for inadequate formal arrangements.[11] At the same time, designing appropriate relationships may yield great gains.

1.5   Preview

The following sections organize recent developments in the study of reputations into five areas:

1. **Payoffs for patient players.** The basic tool for modeling relationships is the theory of repeated games. The primary results here are folk theorems, characterizing the set of equilibrium payoffs for the limiting case of (arbitrarily) patient players. Section 2 describes recent work.

2. **Characterizing payoffs.** It may not be easy to determine whether a folk theorem holds, and we may be interested in situations in which the folk theorems do not apply, perhaps because players are not sufficiently patient or the information flows are not sufficiently rich. Section 3 describes methods for characterizing the set of equilibrium payoffs in a repeated game.

3. **Characterizing behavior.** Much of the initial work in repeated games studied the set of equilibrium payoffs. Attention has increasingly turned to the study of the behavior behind these payoffs. This work bridges the gap between the theory of repeated games and the economics of relationships. Section 4 presents examples.

4. **Reputations.** The concept of a reputation is a familiar one. We readily speak of people having reputations for being diligent or trustworthy, or of institutions as having reputations for providing high quality or being free of corruption. Section 5 considers reputations.

5. **Modeling relationships.** Perhaps the most important remaining questions concern how we are to interpret and use models of a relationship. When are relationships effective? Which of the many equilibria should we expect to see in a relationship? Why should we expect the people involved to come to an equilibrium at all? Section 6 considers some of these questions.

2   PAYOFFS FOR PATIENT PLAYERS

We begin with the best-known results in repeated games, the folk theorems. It is helpful to illustrate these results with a familiar example, the prisoners' dilemma, illustrated in Figure 4.1. Suppose the prisoners' dilemma is (infinitely) repeated, played in each of periods $0, 1, \ldots$. The two players share a common discount factor δ and maximize the discounted sum of their average payoffs.

---

[11] As David Levine noted in his discussion, there are many desperately poor countries who have lots of relationships.

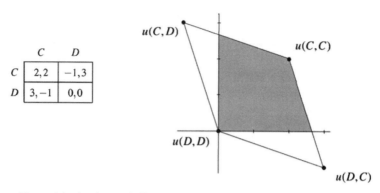

	C	D
C	2,2	−1,3
D	3,−1	0,0

Figure 4.1. A prisoners' dilemma stage game, the set of feasible payoffs (the polygon and its interior), and the set of folk-theorem outcomes (the shaded area) for the infinitely repeated prisoners' dilemma.

2.1   Perfect Monitoring

There is a subgame perfect equilibrium of this repeated game in which both players defect at every opportunity. However, there are many other equilibria if the players are patient and can perfectly monitor each others' actions. With Aumann and Shapley (1976), Friedman (1971), and Rubinstein (1977, 1979), as predecessors, and subsequently pursued by Abreu, Dutta, and Smith (1994) and Wen (1994), the basic folk theorem for subgame perfect equilibria in discounted repeated games is due to Fudenberg and Maskin (1986).[12] In general, let A be a finite set of pure strategy profiles for a stage game. Let $\underline{v}_i = \min_{\alpha_{-i} \in \mathscr{A}_{-i}} \max_{\alpha_i \in \mathscr{A}_i} u_i(\alpha_i, \alpha_{-i})$ identify the *minmax* value for player i (where $\mathscr{A}_i$ and $\mathscr{A}_{-i}$ are the sets of mixed strategies for player i and the remaining players). This is the smallest payoff to which the other players can constrain player i, if they are determined to reduce his payoff. Let $\mathscr{F}^\dagger$ be the convex hull of the payoff profiles produced by the action profiles in A. This is the set of feasible payoffs.

Proposition 1 (The Perfect-Monitoring Folk Theorem) *Suppose $\mathscr{F}^\dagger$ has nonempty interior. Then for every $v \in \text{int}\,\mathscr{F}^\dagger$ with the property that $v_i > \tilde{v} > \underline{v}_i$ for some $\tilde{v} \in \mathscr{F}^\dagger$ and for all i, there exists $\underline{\delta} < 1$ such that for all $\delta \in (\underline{\delta}, 1)$, there exists a subgame perfect equilibrium of the perfect-monitoring repeated game with value v.*

Intuitively, this result indicates that every feasible, individually rational payoff can be obtained in the repeated game, as long as the players are sufficiently patient. Figure 4.1 illustrates this result for the case of the prisoners' dilemma.

---

[12] The statement here is taken from Mailath and Samuelson (2006, Proposition 3.8.1).

2.2   Imperfect Public Monitoring

An important ingredient in the folk theorem for perfect-monitoring games is that the players can observe each others' behavior.[13] For example, this allows them to punish defection in the prisoners' dilemma.

We might expect the players to have quite good information about others' play, but perhaps not perfect information. If so, we are interested in games of *imperfect* monitoring. Green and Porter (1984) and Porter (1983) popularized games of imperfect *public* monitoring, meaning that the agents observe noisy signals of play, but all agents observe the same signals.

We first illustrate with the prisoners' dilemma of Figure 4.1. We assume that in each period, players observe (only) either signal $\underline{y}$ or signal $\bar{y}$, generated according to a probability distribution that depends upon the action profile a taken in that period according to:

$$\Pr\{\bar{y} \mid a\} = \begin{cases} p, & \text{if } a = CC, \\ q, & \text{if } a = DC \text{ or } CD \\ r, & \text{if } a = DD, \end{cases} \tag{1}$$

where $0 < r < q < p < 1$. For example, we might interpret the prisoners' dilemma as a partnership game whose random outcome is either a success ($\bar{y}$) or failure ($\underline{y}$).[14]

Let us first examine the counterpart of the grim trigger strategy for this game of imperfect monitoring. Players initially cooperate, and do so as long as the signal $\bar{y}$ is received, but switch to permanent defection once $\underline{y}$ is received. For these strategies to constitute an equilibrium, it is again necessary and sufficient that an agent be willing to cooperate when called upon to do so, or

$$(1 - \delta)2 + \delta p V \geq (1 - \delta)3 + \delta q V, \tag{2}$$

where V is the expected value of playing the game, given that no one has yet defected. The calculation recognizes that with probability p (if the agent cooperates) or q (if the agent defects), the signal $\bar{y}$ appears and the game enters the next period with expected payoff V, while with the complementary probability, signal $\underline{y}$ appears and subsequent defection brings a zero payoff. We can solve $V = (1 - \delta)2 + \delta p V$ for V and then insert in (2) to calculate that the proposed strategies are an equilibrium if $\delta(3p - 2q) \geq 1$. Hence, we have an equilibrium if the players are sufficiently patient and the signals are sufficiently informative, in the sense that p must be large enough relative to q. However, the equilibrium payoff of $V = 2(1 - \delta)/(1 - \delta p)$ falls short of 2, the payoff produced by grim trigger in the perfect-monitoring game.

---

[13] We encountered the importance of good information about previous actions in Section 1.4.

[14] Can't player 1 figure out what 2 has chosen by looking at payoffs? The standard interpretation is that player i's payoffs are determined as a function of i's actions and the public signal, so that the payoffs given in Figure 4.1 are the expected ex ante payoffs as a function of the agents' actions. The players thus face a prisoners' dilemma, while realized payoffs reveal no information beyond the signal.

Perhaps we have simply chosen our strategy poorly. The punishment of permanent defection seems particularly ill-advised in this setting, knowing that a point will certainly arise at which the signal $\underline{y}$ triggers the punishment. We can indeed do better with more carefully designed strategies featuring temporary punishments. However, no equilibrium gives payoffs $(2, 2)$, no matter how patient the players.

This limitation reflects a basic property of equilibria in games of imperfect monitoring: punishments happen. The only way to create incentives for the players to do anything that is not myopically optimal is to ensure that some signals bring lucrative continuation play and others bring bleak continuation play. But if this is to be the case, unlucky signal realizations will sometimes bring punishments, even though no one has done anything to warrant such a response.[15] Our only hope for preserving efficiency in the face of regular punishments is to ensure that only some players or perhaps only one player is punished at a time, with the others being rewarded. Unfortunately, the symmetry of the signal technology in the prisoners' dilemma characterized by (1) or in the oligopoly games examined by Green and Porter (1984) and Porter (1983) precludes such individualized punishments, dooming the players to inefficiency.

Against this background, Fudenberg, Levine, and Maskin (1994) produced a startling result, identifying conditions under which individualized punishments can be constructed that allow a folk theorem for games of imperfect public monitoring. Understanding that the terms "pairwise full rank" and "individual full rank" are yet undefined, we have (cf. Mailath and Samuelson (2006, Proposition 9.2.1)):

Proposition 2 (The Public-Monitoring Folk Theorem) *Suppose $\mathscr{F}^{\dagger}$ has nonempty interior, and all the pure action profiles yielding the extreme points of $\mathscr{F}^{\dagger}$ have pairwise full rank for all pairs of players. If the vector of minmax payoffs $\underline{v} = (\underline{v}_1, \ldots, \underline{v}_n)$ is Pareto inefficient and the profile $\hat{\alpha}^i$ that minmaxes player i has individual full rank for all i, then for all $v \in \mathrm{int}\,\mathscr{F}^{\dagger}$ with $v_i > \underline{v}_i$ for all i, there exists $\underline{\delta} < 1$ such that for all $\delta \in (\underline{\delta}, 1)$, v is a (sequential) equilibrium payoff.*

There are two keys to this result. First, we need the set of feasible payoffs to have an interior. This ensures that, in response to a signal that is relatively likely when player i deviates, we can adjust continuation payoffs to be worse for i but better for the other players. Second, we need the signals to be sufficiently informative to give us information not only about whether a deviation has occurred, but also about who has deviated. This is reflected in the "individual full rank" and "pairwise full rank" conditions in the theorem. We leave the statement and discussion of these conditions to Fudenberg, Levine, and Maskin

---

[15] Why would anyone participate in such an equilibrium? It is not clear that players can choose their equilibrium, but it is worth noting that this equilibrium can bring higher expected payoffs than an equilibrium in which no one is ever punished.

(1994), where they first appeared, or Mailath and Samuelson (2006, Chapter 9). Intuitively, they ensure that a deviation from equilibrium play by each player i has a distinctive effect on the public signals, so that there exists a signal that is "relatively likely when player i deviates." For example, the prisoners' dilemma with which we introduced imperfect monitoring in this section *fails* these conditions. Given action profile CC, the signals respond to deviations (i.e., $\underline{y}$ is more likely if someone played D), but respond identically regardless of who deviated.

2.3   Private Monitoring

Just as players may not always have precise information about previous play, so may they often not have precisely the same information. We are then in the realm of *private* monitoring.

2.3.1   Belief-Based Equilibria

We begin with the prisoners' dilemma of Figure 4.1. Suppose that if player 1 cooperates, player 2 observes signal $\bar{y}_2$ with probability ε and signal $\underline{y}_2$ with probability $1 - \varepsilon$. The probabilities are reversed if 1 defects. Let player 1 observe the analogously and independently distributed signals $\bar{y}_1$ and $\underline{y}_1$.

When ε is very small, the two players almost certainly observe each others' actions. How much difference could it make that they don't have exactly the same information? Consider a strategy profile in which the agents play CC in the first period, and in which signal $\underline{y}_i$ causes agent i to switch to a punishment phase beginning with D. Suppose that each player adopts such a strategy, and that player 1 dutifully chooses C in the first period but unluckily draws signal $\underline{y}_1$. Player 1 can then reason, "Player 2 has certainly chosen her equilibrium action of C (since that is how the equilibrium hypothesis asks me to reason), and has almost certainly observed $\bar{y}_2$ (since I played C, and there is not much noise in the signals), and hence is prepared to continue with cooperation next period. If I choose D, I make it very likely that she sees $\underline{y}_2$ and switches to her punishment phase. If I choose C again, then there is a good chance we can avoid the punishment phase altogether, at least for a while." As a result, player 1 will not enter the punishment phase, precluding the optimality of the strategy profile. Even the tiniest amount of privateness disrupts the proposed equilibrium.[16]

On the strength of this reasoning, initial expectations were that equilibria in repeated games presented very little prospect for effectively using intertemporal incentives. This in turn raises the fear that repeated games of public or perfect monitoring might be a hopelessly special case. These expectations were displaced by a surprising result.

---

[16] See Bagwell (1995) for a precursor of this argument.

Say that private monitoring is ε-*perfect* if, for each player i and each action profile a, there is a signal that player i receives with probability at least $1 - \varepsilon$ when action profile a is played. Working with a class of prisoners' dilemma including the case of Figure 4.1, Sekiguchi (1997) showed the following:

Proposition 3 *For all $\eta > 0$, there exists $\bar{\varepsilon} > 0$ and $\underline{\delta} < 1$ such that for all $\delta \in (\underline{\delta}, 1)$, if the private monitoring is at least $\bar{\varepsilon}$-perfect, then there is a sequential equilibrium in which each player i's average payoffs are within at least η of $u_i(C, C)$.*

It is not surprising that the monitoring technology is required to be sufficiently informative (ε small), for much the same reason that we need the players to be patient. Otherwise, we have no hope of creating intertemporal incentives. The surprise here is the ability to achieve efficiency with private signals.

We can provide an indication of the basic technique involved in the equilibrium construction. Suppose that each player mixes in period 1, placing probability $1 - \xi$ on C and probability ξ on D. Suppose further that ξ is large relative to ε, the measure of noise in the private monitoring. Let player i continue with action C in the second period if i happened to choose C in the first period and observed signal $\bar{y}_i$, and otherwise let i switch to action D. Now consider again our previously problematic case, that in which 1 played C and observed signal $\underline{y}_1$. Player 1 can now reason, "I've seen signal $\underline{y}_1$. Either player 2 chose C and I happened to see the unlikely signal $\underline{y}_1$, or 2 chose D and I received the (then relatively more likely) signal $\underline{y}_1$. Because ε is small relative to ξ, the latter is more likely. Hence, 2 will likely enter the punishment phase next period, and so should I."

There are many details to be taken care of in converting this intuition into an equilibrium. We must ensure that 1 indeed finds it a best response to enter the punishment, given that 1 thinks 2 is likely but not certain to do so. We must make sure that we have the indifference conditions required for mixing in the first period. Finally, this mixing itself introduces some inefficiency. Fortunately, this cost can be made small as ε becomes small, opening the door to an efficiency result.

Mailath and Morris (2002, 2005) pursue the study of belief-based equilibria, examining games in which the monitoring is almost public (i.e., the players almost certainly receive the same signal) but not necessarily almost perfect (i.e., significant noise can persist in the relationship between signals and actions). They show that strict equilibria in games of public monitoring induce corresponding equilibria in nearby games of almost-public monitoring if the equilibrium strategies exhibit bounded recall (and establish mild conditions under which it is not the case for strategies of unbounded recall). The intuition is that the links between past and future play characteristic of equilibria in public monitoring games are preserved by belief-based strategies in private monitoring games only if players have sufficiently precise beliefs about their opponents' signals. This is the case for bounded recall strategies, where only recent signals are relevant for behavior and the noise induced by private monitoring does not compound endlessly.

2.3.2   Belief-Free Equilibria

The equilibrium constructed by Sekiguchi (1997) is a *belief-based* equilibrium in the sense that each player keeps track of beliefs about the signals the other player has observed. We describe here a more recent but all the more surprising development, *belief-free* equilibria, introduced by Piccione (2002), simplified and extended by Ely and Välimäki (2002), and characterized by Ely, Hörner, and Olszewski (2005).

We continue with our prisoners' dilemma example, allowing arbitrary private monitoring technologies. We consider an equilibrium in which each player i's strategy is built from four mixtures, that we refer to as $\alpha^{C\bar{y}_i}, \alpha^{C\underline{y}_i}, \alpha^{D\bar{y}_i}, \alpha^{D\underline{y}_i}$. In each period, player i chooses C with probability $\alpha^{C\bar{y}_i}$ if i chose C and saw $\bar{y}_i$ in the previous period (choosing D with complementary probability); chooses C with probability $\alpha^{C\underline{y}_i}$ if he chose C and saw $\underline{y}_i$; and so on. It is then useful to think of player i's strategy as consisting of four states, one corresponding to each of the mixtures i might choose, and as player i being in one of these states in each period, depending upon his experience in the previous period.

The potential difficulty in showing that these strategies are an equilibrium is that each time player i is called upon to mix, i must be indifferent between the actions C and D. The payoffs to these actions depend upon what player j is doing, again raising the potentially very difficult problem of player i having to keep track of beliefs about what player j has observed and hence is playing. The surprising result is that this is unnecessary. One can choose the various mixtures so that player i is indifferent between C and D no matter what state player j is in, and hence no matter what i believes about player j. Hence, i can dispense with the need to keep track of beliefs at all, prompting the name "belief-free" equilibrium.

One's first thought is that the conditions required to support such indifference must be hopelessly special, often failing and allowing very little control over the payoffs they produce when they are satisfied. To the contrary, it turns out that there are many such equilibria. Indeed, we have a partial folk theorem. In our prisoners' dilemma example, such strategies allow any payoff profile v with $v_i \in (0, 2)$ to be achieved as an equilibrium outcome if the players are sufficiently patient and the monitoring sufficiently close to perfect.[17]

Ely, Hörner, and Olszewski (2005) provide a general characterization of the set of belief-free payoffs in games with patient players. They find that the prisoners' dilemma is rather special, in that belief-free equilibria do not immediately yield a general folk theorem. However, belief-free behavior can serve as

---

[17] More complicated strategies allow equilibria to be constructed in which one player receives a payoff larger than 2.

a point of departure for constructing folk theorems. Matsushima (2004) uses review strategies, familiar from Radner's (1985) work on repeated principal-agent problems, to extend the belief-free folk theorem for the prisoners' dilemma with almost perfect private monitoring to cases in which the monitoring is quite noisy. Hörner and Olszewski (2005) prove a general folk theorem for almost-perfect private monitoring using profiles that exploit the essential features of belief-free equilibria:

Proposition 4 *Suppose $\mathscr{F}^{\dagger}$ has nonempty interior. Then for every $v \in \text{int}\,\mathscr{F}^{\dagger}$ with $v_i > \underline{v}_i$ for all i, there exists $\underline{\delta} < 1$ and $\bar{\varepsilon}$ such that all $\delta \in (\underline{\delta}, 1)$, if the private monitoring is at least $\bar{\varepsilon}$-perfect, then there is a subgame perfect equilibrium of the repeated game with value v.*

This provides the strongest and most complete results for private-monitoring games. However, interest in repeated games centers around the ability to create incentives by using the history of play to coordinate on a continuation equilibrium. In the belief-free equilibria of private-monitoring games, this sense of using histories to coordinate continuation play is lost – instead of coordinating future play with player j, player i gives no thought to what j might do.[18] It remains to be seen whether belief-free equilibria will become the standard tool for working with such games.

2.4   Interpreting the Folk Theorem

The folk theorem asserts that "anything can be an equilibrium," in the sense that the only payoffs for which equilibrium behavior in a repeated game cannot account are either infeasible or offer some player less than his minmax payoff. This result is sometimes viewed as an indictment of the repeated games literature, implying that game theory has no empirical content.

An argument that repeated games have too many multiple equilibria is unconvincing on four counts. First, the game-theoretic study of long-run relationships deepens our understanding of the incentives for opportunistic behavior and the institutional responses that might discourage such behavior, even without unique equilibria. For example, repeated games help us understand why efficiency might require the ability to punish some players while rewarding others (cf. Section 2.2) or why we might see nonstationary behavior in stationary settings (Section 4.1).

Second, we are often interested in cases in which the conditions for the folk theorem fail (cf. Section 4.2). The players may be insufficiently patient or the monitoring technology may be insufficiently informative. The techniques

---

[18] In addition, it is not clear whether such belief-free equilibria can be purified (Harsanyi (1973)), possibly foreclosing one of the most popular interpretations of the mixtures that play a pervasive role in such equilibria.

developed for working with repeated games allow us to characterize equilibrium payoffs when the folk theorem holds *and* when it fails.

Third, the folk theorem places bounds on payoffs but says nothing about *behavior*. As repeated games find application in economics, interest increasingly focuses on its behavioral implications. For example, we may want to know not just whether the firms in a market can use their repeated interactions to support collusion, but what behavioral evidence this collusion might leave if they do.

Finally, there is a classical view of game theory in which constructing one's model consists of specifying the game, at which point the calculation of an equilibrium is part of the analysis of the model. If one takes this view and is interested in the theory as a tool of economic analysis, then a natural response to the great multitude of equilibria is to look for some other tool. However, an alternative view treats both the construction of the model and the selection of an equilibrium as part of the modeling exercise. Equilibrium behavior that might be quite plausible in some contexts may be uninteresting in others. We would then be concerned if the game did *not* exhibit multiple equilibria, and hence the flexibility to be applied to the wide variety of contexts that can be modeled as repeated games. We can lament the multiplicity of the folk theorem only if we had hoped to have the model do the work that properly falls to the modeler. We return to this issue in Section 6.2.

3   CHARACTERIZING PAYOFFS

Section 2 describes progress in understanding the set of equilibrium payoffs for arbitrarily patient players with a sufficiently informative monitoring structure, culminating in the folk theorems. Suppose, however, we were interested in agents who are not perfectly patient, or in games in which the monitoring structure is not sufficiently informative as to allow a folk theorem. Can we characterize the set of payoffs?

Less is known about these questions. For example, we do not have a complete understanding of how the set of equilibrium payoffs for the prisoners' dilemma varies in the discount factor.[19]

3.1   Self-Generation

The point of departure for characterizing equilibrium payoffs is given by Abreu, Pearce, and Stacchetti's (1986, 1990) characterization of equilibrium payoffs as self-generating sets. We illustrate with pure strategies in games of perfect monitoring (see Mailath and Samuelson (2006, Chapters 2 and 7) for a presentation of the general case).

---

[19] Stahl (1991) provides a complete characterization for the case in which players can use a public random variable to correlate their actions. Mailath, Obara, and Sekiguchi (2002) illustrate the complexities that can arise when they cannot do so.

We say that a pure action profile $a^* \in A$ is *enforceable* on the set of payoff *profiles* $\mathcal{W}$ if there exists some specification of continuation payoffs $\gamma : A \to \mathcal{W}$ such that, for each player i and action $a_i \in A_i$,

$$(1 - \delta)u_i(a^*) + \delta\gamma_i(a^*) \geq (1 - \delta)u_i(a_i, a_{-i}^*) + \delta\gamma_i(a_i, a_{-i}^*).$$

A payoff $v \in \mathscr{F}^\dagger$ is *pure-action decomposable on* $\mathcal{W}$ if there exists an action profile a^* enforceable on $\mathcal{W}$ such that $v_i = (1 - \delta)u_i(a^*) + \delta\gamma_i(a^*)$, where γ is a function that enforces a^*.

In other words, an action profile is enforceable if we can arrange continuation payoffs as a function of the current actions, so as to make it a best response for each agent to play their part of the action profile in the current period. A payoff is decomposable if it can be produced by an enforceable action profile.

The next step is to notice that subgame perfection requires every agent to choose a best response at every opportunity. This suggests that we should be interested in the case where the set of continuation payoff profiles is the set of subgame-perfect equilibrium payoffs. Letting $\mathscr{E}$ be the set of subgame-perfect equilibrium payoff profiles, Abreu, Pearce, and Stacchetti's (1990) show:

Proposition 5 *If the payoff profile v is pure-action decomposable on $\mathscr{E}$, then v is a subgame-perfect equilibrium payoff. Any set of payoff profiles $\mathcal{W}$ with the property that every payoff in $\mathcal{W}$ can be pure-action decomposed on $\mathcal{W}$ is a set of subgame-perfect equilibrium payoffs. The set $\mathscr{E}$ of pure subgame-perfect equilibrium payoffs is the largest such set.*

The first statement simply repeats that subgame-perfect equilibria couples choices that are currently optimal with equilibrium continuation payoffs. The second statement gives us a method for identifying subgame-perfect equilibrium payoffs as "self-generating" sets of payoffs. The third identifies the set of subgame-perfect equilibrium payoffs as the largest such set. These results generalize to mixed strategies and to public monitoring.

To illustrate, let us again consider the prisoners' dilemma of Figure 4.1. We ask when there exists a subgame-perfect equilibrium in which both players cooperate in every period. In light of Proposition 5, this is equivalent to identifying the discount factors for which there is a self-generating set of payoff profiles $\mathcal{W}$ containing $(2, 2)$. If such a set $\mathcal{W}$ is to exist, then the action profile CC must be enforceable on $\mathcal{W}$, or,

$$(1 - \delta)2 + \delta\gamma_1(CC) \geq (1 - \delta)3 + \delta\gamma_1(DC)$$

and

$$(1 - \delta)2 + \delta\gamma_2(CC) \geq (1 - \delta)3 + \delta\gamma_2(CD),$$

for $\gamma(CC)$, $\gamma(DC)$, and $\gamma(CD)$ in $\mathcal{W}$. These inequalities are least restrictive when $\gamma_1(DC) = \gamma_2(CD) = 0$. In addition, the singleton set of payoff profiles $\{(0, 0)\}$ is itself self-generating (since there are no incentive issues in asking players to defect, and hence a future of defection suffices to make defection optimal in the first period). We thus sacrifice no generality by assuming the self-generating set contains $(0, 0)$, and can then set $\gamma_1(DC) = \gamma_2(CD) = 0$. Similarly, the pair of inequalities is least restrictive when $\gamma_i(CC) = 2$ for $i = 1, 2$. We can thus take $\mathcal{W}$ to be the set $\{(0, 0), (2, 2)\}$. Inserting the continuation values in the incentive constraints and simplifying, the conditions for decomposability hold when $\delta \geq \frac{1}{3}$. This inequality is thus necessary for the existence of a subgame-perfect equilibrium giving payoff $(2, 2)$, and is also sufficient, since it implies that the set $\{(0, 0), (2, 2)\}$ is self-generating.

3.2   Bounding Payoffs

The techniques for identifying sets of equilibria described in Section 3.1 allow the calculation of equilibrium payoffs to be reduced to what looks like a dynamic programming problem. There is just one hitch – the crucial constraint in calculating equilibrium payoffs is that continuation payoffs come from the set $\mathcal{E}$, the set of equilibrium payoffs that one is trying to calculate.

Remarkably, Fudenberg and Levine (1994) and Fudenberg, Levine, and Maskin (1994), with a refinement by Kandori and Matsushima (1998) and with Matsushima (1989) as a precursor, eliminate this self-reference, leading to what is now the standard tool for identifying equilibria.

We illustrate with the prisoners' dilemma of Figure 4.1, with the (imperfect) monitoring technology given by (1). Suppose we are interested in the equilibrium that maximizes the weighted sum $\lambda_1 v_1 + \lambda_2 v_2$ of the players' payoffs, for any values λ_1 and λ_2 that are not both zero (and that may be negative), and suppose that we knew that this equilibrium began with the play of CC. Then the resulting equilibrium payoff profile v^* must be decomposable, meaning that there must exist a function γ, associating equilibrium payoff profiles with signals, that allows us to characterize v^* as

$$\lambda_1 v_1^* + \lambda_2 v_2^* = \max_{v, \gamma} \lambda_1 v_1 + \lambda_2 v_2$$

$$\text{subject to} \quad v_i = (1 - \delta)2 + \delta[p\gamma_i(\bar{y}) + (1 - p)\gamma_i(\underline{y})], \quad i = 1, 2$$

$$v_i \geq (1 - \delta)3 + \delta[q\gamma_i(\bar{y}) + (1 - q)\gamma_i(\underline{y})], \quad i = 1, 2$$

$$\gamma(\cdot) \in \mathcal{E}.$$

The first equation ensures that we are maximizing the sum of the players' payoffs, the second that we hit the desired payoff, the third imposes the incentive constraints, and the fourth ensures that continuation payoffs are equilibrium payoffs. Now notice that the set of payoffs $H = \{\gamma : \lambda_1 \gamma_1 + \lambda_2 \gamma_2 \leq \lambda_1 v_1^* + \lambda_2 v_1^*\}$ must contain $\mathcal{E}$, the set of subgame-perfect equilibrium payoffs, since by construction no equilibrium gives a weighted sum of payoffs higher than $\lambda_1 v_1^* + \lambda_2 v_1^*$ and H contains any payoff profile with a lower sum. Let us then replace the final constraint in our characterization of v^* with the less demanding $\lambda_1 \gamma_1(\cdot) + \lambda_2 \gamma_2(\cdot) \leq \lambda_1 v_1^* + \lambda_2 v_2^*$, and then redefine the variables to let $\tilde{\gamma}_i = \frac{\delta}{1-\delta}[\gamma_i - v_i]$, to obtain:

$$\lambda_1 v_1^* + \lambda_2 v_2^* \leq \max_{v, \tilde{\gamma}} \lambda_1 v_1 + \lambda_2 v_2$$

$$\text{subject to} \quad v_i = 2 + [p\tilde{\gamma}_i(\bar{y}) + (1-p)\tilde{\gamma}_i(\underline{y})], \quad i = 1, 2$$

$$v_i \geq 3 + [q\tilde{\gamma}_i(\bar{y}) + (1-q)\tilde{\gamma}_i(\underline{y})], \quad i = 1, 2$$

$$\lambda_1 \tilde{\gamma}_1(\cdot) + \lambda_2 \tilde{\gamma}_2(\cdot) \leq 0.$$

In the course of making these transformations, we have replaced a characterization of v^* with an upper bound on v^* (since we allowed a larger set of continuation payoffs). In return, we have very conveniently eliminated the set of equilibrium payoffs from the problem, getting us around having to speculate about the object we hope to calculate, and eliminated the discount factor.

We have assumed that the equilibrium maximizing the weighted sum of the players' payoffs begins with the play of CC. This need not be the case. For example, if $\lambda_1 = \lambda_2 = -1$ (so that our maximization is actually minimizing payoffs), then the solution is an equilibrium in which both players defect in every period. But whatever weighted sum we are maximizing, the equilibrium must begin with *something*, and so we can represent v^* as

$$\lambda_1 v_1^* + \lambda_2 v_2^* \leq \max_{\alpha, v, \tilde{\gamma}} \lambda_1 v_1 + \lambda_2 v_2 \tag{3}$$

$$\text{subject to} \quad v_i = \big\{ u_i(\alpha) + [\text{prob}(\bar{y} \mid \alpha)\tilde{\gamma}_i(\bar{y})$$

$$+ \text{prob}(\underline{y} \mid \alpha)\tilde{\gamma}_i(\underline{y})] \big\} \tag{4}$$

$$v_i \geq u_i(\alpha_i', \alpha_{-i}) + [\text{prob}(\bar{y} \mid (\alpha_i', \alpha_{-i}))\tilde{\gamma}_i(\bar{y}) \tag{5}$$

$$+ \text{prob}(\underline{y} \mid (\alpha_i', \alpha_{-i}))\tilde{\gamma}_i(\underline{y})]$$

$$\lambda_1 \tilde{\gamma}_1(\cdot) + \lambda_2 \tilde{\gamma}_2(\cdot) \leq 0. \tag{6}$$

This gives us a straightforward problem we can solve for bounds on equilibrium payoffs. For example, we can show that, no matter what the discount factor, the symmetric equilibrium payoff in the prisoners' dilemma, based on Figure 4.1 and the noisy monitoring technology (1), is inefficient:[20] It suffices to show that in any equilibrium beginning with CC, the sum of the two players' payoffs is bounded away from 4.[21] Setting $\lambda_1 = \lambda_2 = 1$, the incentive constraint given by (4)–(6) (taking α to be CC) implies

$$\tilde{\gamma}_i(\bar{y}) \geq \tilde{\gamma}_i(\underline{y}) + \frac{1}{p-q}.$$

[20] Hence, it is not simply that we chose our strategies unwisely in Section 2.2, but that we are doomed to inefficiency. This is consistent with our observation at the end of Section 2.2, that this game and monitoring technology fail the sufficient conditions of Proposition 2.

[21] This leaves open the possibility that mixed equilibria may allow symmetric payoffs that are arbitrarily close to efficient, but a similar argument excludes this possibility as well.

Hence, we must have (inserting this result in (4) and recalling from (6) that $\tilde{\gamma}_1 + \tilde{\gamma}_2 \leq 0$)

$$v_1^* + v_2^* \leq 4 + p(\tilde{\gamma}_1(\bar{y}) + \tilde{\gamma}_2(\bar{y})) + (1 - p)(\tilde{\gamma}_1(\underline{y}) + \tilde{\gamma}_2(\underline{y}))$$
$$= 4 + (\tilde{\gamma}_1(\bar{y}) + \tilde{\gamma}_2(\bar{y})) - (1 - p)(\tilde{\gamma}_1(\bar{y}) + \tilde{\gamma}_2(\bar{y})$$
$$-\tilde{\gamma}_1(\underline{y}) - \tilde{\gamma}_2(\underline{y})) \leq 4 - 2\frac{1 - p}{p - q}.$$

We are thus bounded away from efficiency by an amount that approaches zero as the monitoring approaches perfection, i.e., as $p \rightarrow 1$.

We can go further. For any pair of weights $(\lambda_1, \lambda_2) \equiv \lambda$, let $\alpha(\lambda)$ be the action profile that solves (3)–(6). Then the set of equilibrium values must be contained in the set

$$H^*(\lambda) = \{\gamma : \lambda_1\gamma_1 + \lambda_2\gamma_2 \leq \lambda_1 v_1(\alpha(\lambda)) + \lambda_2 v_1(\alpha(\lambda))\},$$

since this is the set containing the set of subgame-perfect equilibrium payoffs that got us started on the simplification of the characterization. This must hold for every λ. Hence, the set of subgame-perfect equilibria must be contained in the intersection $\cap_\lambda H^*(\lambda)$ of the sets $H^*(\lambda)$, for every nonzero $\lambda \in \mathbb{R}^2$. This provides a tool for bounding the set of subgame-perfect equilibrium payoffs, regardless of the discount factor, whose usefulness we've seen in examining the public-monitoring prisoners' dilemma. Fudenberg and Levine's (1994) result is:

Proposition 6   *If $\cap_\lambda H^*(\lambda)$ has a nonempty interior, then the set of equilibrium payoffs converges to $\cap_\lambda H^*(\lambda)$ as $\delta \rightarrow 1$.*

This is a straightforward recipe for characterizing the set of equilibrium payoffs for patient players.

4   CHARACTERIZING BEHAVIOR

Theoretical models based on repeated games have been used to examine a variety of economic relationships. This section provides two examples.

4.1   Adverse Selection

We first examine a problem of repeated adverse selection.[22] This exercise illustrates the behavioral insights that can emerge from studying a relationship as well as the pitfalls that can arise in interpreting equilibrium behavior.

There are two firms, denoted 1 and 2. In each period of the repeated game, Nature first independently draws, for each firm, a constant marginal cost equal

---

[22] We work with a simplified version of a model from Athey and Bagwell (2001) and Athey, Bagwell, and Sanchirico (2004).

to either $\underline{\theta}$ or $\bar{\theta} > \underline{\theta}$, with the two values being equally likely. The firms then simultaneously choose prices, drawn from $\mathbb{R}_+$. There is a unit mass of consumers, each potentially buying a single unit of the good, with a reservation price of $r > \bar{\theta}$. A consumer purchases from the firm setting the lower price if it does not exceed r. Consumers are indifferent between the two firms if the latter set identical prices, in which case we specify consumer decisions as part of the equilibrium. A firm from whom the consumers all purchase at price p, with cost θ, earns payoff $p - \theta$.

The stage game has a unique symmetric Nash equilibrium. A firm whose cost level is $\bar{\theta}$ sets price $\bar{\theta}$ and earns a zero expected profit. A low-cost firm chooses a price according to a distribution $F(p)$ with support on $[\frac{\underline{\theta}+\bar{\theta}}{2}, \bar{\theta}]$.[23] The expected payoff to each firm from this equilibrium is given by $\frac{1}{4}[\bar{\theta} - \underline{\theta}]$. If r is much larger than $\bar{\theta}$, the firms are falling far short of the monopoly profit. An upper bound on the payoffs in a symmetric-payoff equilibrium arises if both firms set price r, but with high-cost firms selling output only if both firms are high cost, for an expected payoff to each firm of

$$\frac{1}{8}(r - \bar{\theta}) + \frac{3}{8}(r - \underline{\theta}) \equiv v^*.$$

The repeated game is one of imperfect public monitoring, in the sense that, given a strategy that attaches different prices to different cost levels, the stage-game outcome reveals only one of these prices. We are interested in an equilibrium of the repeated game that maximizes the firms' payoffs, subject to the constraint that they receive the same payoff.

Proposition 7 *For any $\eta > 0$, there exists a $\underline{\delta} < 1$ such that for all $\delta \in (\underline{\delta}, 1)$, there exists a pure-strategy perfect equilibrium with payoff at least $v^* - \eta$ for each player.*

We present an equilibrium with the desired property. Our candidate strategies for the firms specify that a high-cost firm choose price r and a low-cost firm price $r - \varepsilon$ for some small $\varepsilon > 0$, after any history featuring no other prices, and that any history featuring any other price prompt a switch to the stage-game Nash equilibrium. We also specify that if an out-of-equilibrium price has ever been set, consumers thereafter split equally between the two firms whenever the latter set identical prices.

To describe the behavior of consumers in response to equilibrium prices, define three market share "regimes," B (balanced), I and II, each specifying how consumers behave when either the firms both set price r or both set

---

[23] It is straightforward that prices above $\bar{\theta}$ are vulnerable to being undercut by one's rival and hence will not appear in equilibrium, so high-cost firms must set price $\bar{\theta}$. The lower bound p on the support of the low-cost firm's price distribution must make the firm indifferent between selling with probability 1 at that price and selling with probability $\frac{1}{2}$ at price $\bar{\theta}$, or $p - \underline{\theta} = \frac{1}{2}(\bar{\theta} - \underline{\theta})$, giving $p = \frac{\underline{\theta}+\bar{\theta}}{2}$.

State	Prices			
	$r-\varepsilon, r-\varepsilon$	$r-\varepsilon, r$	$r, r-\varepsilon$	r, r
B	split	1	2	split
I	1	1	2	1
II	2	1	2	2

Figure 4.2. Market share regimes B, I, and II.

price $r - \varepsilon$. These regimes are shown in Figure 4.2, where "split" indicates that the market is to be split equally, and otherwise the indicated firm takes the entire market. Play begins in regime B, which treats the firms identically and splits the market whenever they set the same price. Regime I rewards firm 1 and Regime II rewards firm 2. The regime shifts to I whenever firm 1 sets price r and firm 2 sets price $r - \varepsilon$, and shifts to II whenever firm 2 sets price r and firm 1 sets price $r - \varepsilon$. Hence, a firm is rewarded for choosing price r (while the opponent chooses price $r - \varepsilon$) by a presumption that the firm subsequently receives the lion's share of the market if the two firms set equal prices.

The prescribed actions always allocate the entire market to the low-cost producer, ensuring that the proposed equilibrium outcome is efficient. The three market share regimes differ in how the market is to be allocated when the two firms have the same cost level. The payoffs thus shift along a frontier passing through the equilibrium payoff profile, with a slope of -1. Transitions between states thus correspond to transfers from one agent to the other. As we have noted in Section 2.2, these are precisely the types of punishments we should expect if we are to achieve efficient outcomes under imperfect monitoring.

It is straightforward that expected payoffs from this strategy profile approach v^* for each firm (as we make ε small and the firms patient), and that if firms are sufficiently patient, neither will ever prefer to abandon equilibrium play, triggering permanent play of the stage-game Nash equilibrium, by setting a price other than r or $r - \varepsilon$. Another straightforward calculation completes the argument, verifying that each firm always prefers to "identify its cost level truthfully," in the sense that it prefers to make the appropriate choice from the set $\{r - \varepsilon, r\}$, given the history of play and its realized cost.

Two features of this equilibrium are noteworthy. First, the incentive for firm 1 to set a high price when drawing cost $\bar{\theta}$ is that a low price is punished by a shift to regime II. The distinguishing feature of regime II is that indifferent consumers purchase from firm 2. Firms thus set high prices because consumers punish them for low prices. How crazy can a model be in which firms collude because their customers punish them for not doing so?

Upon reflection, perhaps not so crazy – we actually see such arrangements. Firms routinely advertise that they will "never knowingly be undersold" and that they will "meet any competitor's price," schemes that appear to be popular with consumers. These pricing policies are commonly interpreted as devices to facilitate collusion by making it less profitable to undercut a collusive price. Consumers who march into store 1 to demand the lower price they found at store 2 are in fact punishing store 2 for its low price (rather than store 1 for its high price), in the process potentially allowing the firms to collude.

More generally, we return to Section 2.4's point that we cannot evaluate an equilibrium within the confines of the model. Instead, we must select an equilibrium as part of constructing the model of the strategic interaction in question. Depending upon the nature of this interaction, consumers may well behave in such a way as to support collusion on the part of the firm. This behavior may appear counterintuitive in the stark confines of the model, while being perfectly natural in its actual context.

Second, the firms are ex ante symmetric in our model, and we have focused attention on maximizing their payoffs given that they earn the same expected payoffs. It is then natural to suspect that the resulting equilibrium would feature symmetric and stationary outcomes – that along the equilibrium path, we would see the same (symmetric) outcome in each period. Instead, we find an equilibrium that makes important use of nonstationarity and asymmetry along the equilibrium path.[24] This is not simply an artifact of the particular equilibrium we have examined (nor an artifact of this game, being instead a common phenomenon). Efficiency requires that the firms sometimes set price r and sometimes price $r - \varepsilon$ for small ε, all without a high-cost firm having an incentive to sweep up all the consumers by setting price $r - \varepsilon$. This can be done only if future payoffs following the equilibrium prices r and $r - \varepsilon$ differ, giving rise to nonstationary equilibrium outcomes. If these in turn are to create effective incentives without inefficiency, they must be asymmetric.

4.2   Consumption Dynamics

Our second example illustrates the insights that can be obtained in models where the folk theorem fails. We are motivated by the observation that individual consumption is commonly observed to be positively correlated with current and lagged values of individual income. People consume more when they earn more, and people consume more when they have earned more in the past. If a risk averse agent's income varies, there are gains to be had from smoothing the resulting consumption stream by insuring against the income fluctuations. Why aren't consumption fluctuations perfectly insured?

This section works with a model in which agents are subject to perfectly observed income shocks.[25] However, the agents are unable to commit to insurance contracts. In particular, in each period, and after observing the current state, each agent is free to abandon the current insurance contract. This is the

---

[24] The asymmetry is not simply ex post, in the sense that firms with different cost realizations are treated differently, but ex ante, in the sense that the firms fare differently conditioned on cost realizations, depending upon the history of play.

[25] We draw here on a model of Kocherlakota (1996), discussed by Ljungqvist and Sargent (2004, Chapters 19–20). See also Koeppl (2003), Ligon, Thomas, and Worrall (2002), Thomas and Worrall (1988).

contracting imperfection that brings relationships into the picture.

The stage game features two consumers, 1 and 2. There is a single consumption good. A random draw first determines the players' endowments of the consumption good to be given by one of three possibilities (with player 1's endowment of the consumption good listed first in each bundle):

	Endowment	Probability
Endowment $e(1)$	$(\bar{y}, \underline{y})$	$\frac{1}{3}$
Endowment $e(m)$	$(\frac{1}{2}, \frac{1}{2})$	$\frac{1}{3}$
Endowment $e(2)$	$(\underline{y}, \bar{y})$	$\frac{1}{3}$,

where $\bar{y} \in (\frac{1}{2}, 1]$ and $\underline{y} = 1 - \bar{y}$. After observing the endowment, players 1 and 2 simultaneously transfer nonnegative quantities of the consumption good to one another, and then consume the resulting net quantities evaluated according to the utility function $u(\cdot)$. The function u is strictly increasing and strictly concave.

This stage game has a unique Nash equilibrium outcome in which no transfers are made, with a payoff denoted by $\underline{v}$ for each player. Because the consumers are risk averse, this outcome is inefficient.

Suppose now that the consumers are infinitely lived, playing the game in each period $t = 0, 1, \ldots$. The endowment draws are independent across periods. If the discount factor is high enough, then there exists a full-insurance equilibrium in which each player's consumption in each period is independent of the endowment and the history of play. The transfers required to achieve such consumption are enforced by a switch to the stage-game Nash equilibrium (i.e., to mutual minmaxing) should they fail to be made.

Suppose that δ falls short of the value for which full insurance is possible, so that the folk theorem fails, but is large enough that some nontrivial equilibria exist. We will examine the efficient, symmetric-payoff equilibrium for this case. We can construct a first candidate for such an equilibrium by assuming that whenever endowment $e(i)$ is received, agent i transfers ε to agent j. Any failure to do so triggers permanent play of the stage-game Nash equilibrium. We choose ϵ as large as possible, namely to satisfy

$$(1 - \delta)u(\bar{y} - \varepsilon) + \delta\frac{1}{3}\left(u(\bar{y} - \varepsilon) + u\left(\frac{1}{2}\right) + u(\underline{y} + \varepsilon)\right)$$
$$= (1 - \delta)u(\bar{y}) + \delta\underline{v}.$$

This is the incentive constraint that an agent having drawn a high endowment be willing to transfer ε and continue with equilibrium play rather than pocketing the relatively favorable endowment and switching to the stage-game Nash equilibrium (for value $\underline{v}$). Given our assumption that the discount factor is large enough to support more than the autarky equilibrium, but too small to support full insurance, this equation is solved by some $\varepsilon \in (0, \bar{y} - \frac{1}{2})$. This equilibrium leaves consumption untouched in endowment $e(m)$, while smoothing consumption in endowments $e(1)$ and $e(2)$.

	h	ℓ
H	2,3	0,2
L	3,0	1,1

Figure 4.3. The product choice game.

This equilibrium provides some insurance, but we can provide more. Let us separate ex ante histories into two categories, category 1 and category 2. A history is in category i if agent i is the most recent one to have drawn a high endowment (and no one has failed to make a prescribed transfer). Now fix $\zeta > 0$, and let the strategy profile prescribe consumption $(\frac{1}{2} + \zeta, \frac{1}{2} - \zeta)$ whenever the agents find themselves facing endowment $e(m)$ after a category 1 history and consumption $(\frac{1}{2} - \zeta, \frac{1}{2} + \zeta)$ when facing endowment $e(m)$ after a category 2 history. In essence, we are using consumption in endowment $e(m)$ to reward the last agent who has had a large endowment and transferred part of it to the other agent.

These strategies introduce risk in endowment $e(m)$, but with a second-order effect on total expected payoffs (when ζ is small). However, because we now allocate endowment $e(m)$ consumption in order to reward the last agent to make a transfer, this adjustment gives a first-order increase in the expected continuation payoff to agent i after a history in category i. This relaxes the incentive constraints facing agents when drawing endowments $e(1)$ and $e(2)$ (imposed by switching to the stage-game Nash equilibrium after any deviation from prescribed play). We can thus couple the increase in ζ with an increase in ε, thereby allowing more insurance in endowments $e(1)$ and $e(2)$. Intuitively, we are now spreading risk across time as well as states within a period, exchanging a relatively large transfer from a high-endowment agent for a relatively lucrative continuation payoff. In terms of consumption dynamics, agents with high endowments in their history are more likely to have high current consumption. The assumptions that behavior is efficient but the discount factor is lower than required by the folk theorem thus lead to a model of consumption dynamics.

5 REPUTATIONS

It is common to speak of people, firms, governments, and other institutions as having reputations. The idea of a reputation typically carries some connotation of foregoing an opportunity for short-terms gains, in return for rewards arising from links between current actions and future expectations about behavior.

We illustrate reputation results in the context of the "product choice" game shown in Figure 4.3. We think of player 1 as a firm who can produce high quality (H) or low quality (L). Player 2 is a consumer who simultaneously purchases either a high-cost product from the firm (h) or a low-cost product (ℓ).

The consumer prefers to buy the expensive product if the firm is providing high quality, and the low-cost product otherwise. For example, a patient may prefer heart surgery from a competent physician but a folk remedy from a quack. The firm finds high quality expensive and so always earns a higher payoff from low quality, but prefers that the consumer choose the high-cost option. The stage game has a unique Nash equilibrium in which $L\ell$ is played, for payoffs (1, 1).

There are two approaches to thinking about reputations. The "equilibrium interpretation" approach selects an equilibrium of the repeated game and then interprets various of its features in reputation terms. For example, when the players are sufficiently patient, there is an equilibrium in the repeated product-choice game in which Hh is played in every period, with any deviations from such play prompting a switch to (permanent) play of the stage-game equilibrium $L\ell$. We might then refer to the firm as maintaining a reputation for high quality along the equilibrium path, and any deviation as having destroyed this reputation. However, there is no necessary link between past behavior and expectations about future behavior in such models. For example, there remains an equilibrium in which $L\ell$ is played in every period, and it remains an equilibrium to continue with such behavior even if player 1 desperately tries to build a reputation by playing H in the first thousand periods. The idea of a reputation is helpful in keeping track of the behavior in the selected equilibrium but adds nothing formal to the analysis.

The "adverse selection" approach to reputations, considered here, rests upon the introduction of incomplete information concerning players' characteristics. For example, suppose there is some small probability that player 1 in the product choice game is a commitment type who always plays H, otherwise being the normal type specified by the stage game. This incomplete information is a mechanism for creating a necessary link between past play and expected future behavior. In particular, there is no longer an equilibrium of the repeated product-choice game in which the normal type of player 1 and player 2 invariably choose $L\ell$. Given such a candidate equilibrium, the normal type would choose H in the first period, leading player 2 to conclude she was facing the commitment type and hence leading to subsequent play of Hh. Results in the adverse selection approach consist of statements about the set of equilibria rather than statements about a particular equilibrium.

5.1   Short-Run Opponents

Our examination of the adverse selection approach to reputations begins with a setting in which player 1 is a long-run player, who appears in every period of the infinitely repeated game. The role of player 2 is filled by a succession of short-run players, each of whom participates in the market for only a single period. For example, a new customer may come to the firm every period. As a result, each player 2 chooses a myopic best response to player 1's behavior.

Suppose first that actions are perfectly monitored.[26] There are two possible types of player 1, a "normal" type whose payoffs are given by Figure 4.3 and a "Stackelberg" type who always plays H. The game begins with a draw of player 1's type, revealed only to player 1, and perhaps attaching very high probability to player 1 being normal. In general, let

$$v_1^* = \max_{a_1} \min_{\alpha_2 \in B(a_1)} u_1(a_1, \alpha_2),$$

where $B(a_1)$ is the set of player 2 myopic best replies to a_1. This is player 1's pure Stackelberg payoff, identifying the payoff player 1 could earn in the stage game if 1 could publicly choose an action before 2 chooses, with 2 then choosing a best response. Let a_1^* denote the accompanying pure "Stackelberg" action. In the product choice game, this payoff is 2, secured by choosing action H. Let μ be the prior probability attached to the Stackelberg type. We have:

Proposition 8 *For any $\mu > 0$ and $\varepsilon > 0$, there exists a $\underline{\delta} < 1$ such that for any $\delta \in (\underline{\delta}, 1)$, the payoff to the normal type of player 1 in any Nash equilibrium of the repeated game is at least $v_1^* - \varepsilon$.*

To see what lies behind this result, fix an equilibrium of the game and consider player 1's options. One possibility is to play a_1^* in every period. The key step to the reputation result describes the consequences of such play:

Lemma 1 *For any $\eta > 0$, there is a number $n(\eta)$ such that if the normal type of player 1 chooses a_1^* in every period, the number of periods in which player 2 can attach probability less than $1 - \eta$ to player 1 choosing a_1^* is less than $n(\eta)$.*

Thus, if player 2 observes ever-longer strings of action a_1^*, then eventually player 2 must come to expect action a_1^* to be played with high probability. In particular, suppose we reach a period t in which player 1 has hitherto played the Stackelberg action and player 2's current expectation is that the Stackelberg action need *not* appear. This can only happen if equilibrium play attaches some probability to the event that player 1 is the normal type and will not play the Stackelberg action. But then Bayes' rule ensures that observing the Stackelberg action in period t results in a posterior that must put increased weight on the Stackelberg type. As a result, the probability that player 2 attaches to seeing action a_1^* cannot long remain small, with player 2 eventually believing either that she is almost certainly facing the Stackelberg type or facing a normal type who plays like the Stackelberg type. Either way, player 2 must expect to see the Stackelberg action.

---

[26] The basic result (Proposition 8 below) is from Fudenberg and Levine (1989). Celentani and Pesendorfer (1996) present an analogous result for dynamic games. Fudenberg and Levine (1992) extend the argument to imperfect monitoring.

This characterization of beliefs allows us to establish the lower bound on player 1's equilibrium payoffs. Let the normal type of player 1 choose a_1^* in every period. After some finite number of periods, player 2 must believe that a_1^* is sufficiently likely as to play a best response, giving player 1 the payoff v_1^*. Player 1 may earn lower payoffs in the early periods before 2 expects a_1^*, but these early periods are insignificant if player 1 is sufficiently patient. This ensures a repeated-game payoff arbitrarily close to v_1^* for a patient player 1.

With some additional technical complication, a similar result applies to games of imperfect monitoring (cf. Fudenberg and Levine (1992)), or to games of perfect or imperfect monitoring in which the Stackelberg type may play a *mixed* action.[27] We illustrate with the product choice game. Player 1 would like player 2 to choose h. It suffices for this that player 1 be (known to be) committed to H, but there is a sense in which this is more of an investment in high quality than is required. It would suffice for 2 to find h a best response that player 1 choose H with probability just over $\frac{1}{2}$. The reputation argument ensures that, if the commitment type of player 1 chooses such a mixture, under either perfect or imperfect monitoring the (patient, normal) player 1 must receive a payoff in any equilibrium of the repeated game that is arbitrarily close to that from being known to be committed to such a mixture, in this case $\frac{5}{2}$.

This is all the more remarkable in light of the fact that, in the case of perfect monitoring and no uncertainty about player 1's type, player 1's payoff in the product choice game is bounded above by 2, while under imperfect monitoring, player 1's payoff is bounded strictly below 2. The adverse-selection-based reputation thus not only pushes player 1 to the top of the set of equilibrium payoffs, but expands the set itself.

This discussion may leave the impression that reputation arguments depend critically upon having just the right commitment type in the model, and perhaps on having only that type, or having that type be sufficiently likely. None of these is the case. The arguments extend to the case in which player 1 may be one of an infinite number of possible types, which may not include the Stackelberg type. The bound on player 1's payoff is given by allowing him to "choose" from the set of possible types the one to whose behavior it would be most profitable to commit, regardless of the how likely are the various types. The arguments further extend to cases with (sufficiently small) uncertainty about player 2's type.

Cripps, Mailath, and Samuelson (2004b) establish conditions under which player 1 will eventually spend his reputation. Under fairly general conditions, player 2 must eventually learn player 1's type, with play converging to an equilibrium of the complete-information game defined by player 1's type.[28] In the product-choice game, for example, reputation effects may constrain player

---

[27] Because player 2 observes only the realized actions of player 1 and not the underlying mixture, perfectly monitored opponents who play mixed actions present inference problems similar to those of imperfectly monitored opponents.

[28] Jackson and Kalai (1999) examine another sense in which reputations are temporary in finitely repeated games.

1's ex ante payoff to be very close to $\frac{5}{2}$, but his continuation payoff is eventually less than 2.

To build intuition for this result, suppose that player 1 may be either a normal or Stackelberg type, and that we have a candidate equilibrium in which player 2 does not learn player 1's type. Then player 2 must expect Stackelberg-type behavior from both types of player 1. Otherwise, she would eventually get enough information, even under imperfect monitoring, to sort out which type of player she faced. Player 2, being a short-run player, will then play a best response to the Stackelberg type. But then the normal type of player 1 has an incentive to deviate from the Stackelberg behavior, potentially contradicting player 2's belief that player 1 will exhibit Stackelberg behavior.[29]

This is a limiting result, describing beliefs and behavior in the possibly very distant future. While the short-run properties of equilibria are interesting, we believe that the long-run equilibrium properties are also relevant in many situations. For example, an analyst may not know the age of the relationship to which the model is to be applied – we sometimes observe strategic interactions from a well-defined beginning, but we also often encounter ongoing interactions whose beginnings are difficult to identify. Long-run equilibrium properties may be an important guide to behavior in the latter cases. Alternatively, one might take the view of a social planner who is concerned with the continuation payoffs of the long-run player and with the fate of all short-run players, even those in the distant future. Our analysis also suggests that the short-run players may have definite preferences as to where they appear in the queue of short-run players. Finally, interest often centers on the *steady states* of models with incomplete information, again directing attention to long-run properties.

We view these results as suggesting that a model of *long-run* reputations should incorporate some mechanism by which the uncertainty about types is continually replenished. For example, Holmström (1999), Cole, Dow, and English (1995), Mailath and Samuelson (2001), and Phelan (2005) assume that the type of the long-run player is governed by a stochastic process rather than being determined once and for all at the beginning of the game. In such a situation, reputations can indeed have long-run implications. We return to this in Section 5.3.

5.2   Two Long-Run Players

Section 5.1 examined a model in which player 1, the reputation builder, faced short-run opponents. In many reputation settings, such as a firm facing a

---

[29] Three assumptions are embedded here. First, the structure of the game and signals is such that player 1 knows player 2's belief, and hence knows there is a profitable deviation. Cripps, Mailath, and Samuelson (2004a) relax this assumption. Second, the normal player 1 does not find Stackelberg behavior a best response to player 2's (best response to Stackelberg) behavior. Third, the monitoring is imperfect, and hence the normal player 1's deviation cannot prompt too draconian a punishment.

succession of consumers, this seems quite natural. Suppose now that both players are long-run players, with (possibly different) discount factors δ_1 and δ_2. We assume that player 1 may be a normal player or may be another, perhaps Stackelberg, type.

Consider the product choice game. We can again proceed by arguing that if player 2 always observes action H, player 2 must eventually believe the continued play of H is quite likely. This suffices to ensure a *short-run* player 2 plays h, the second important piece in the argument. However, the same is not necessarily the case for a long-run player 2. In particular, 2's expectation that H will very likely be played in the future is consistent with 2 attaching probability to player 1 being a normal type whose strategy calls for action H, a Stackelberg type committed to H, and (recalling that reputation results are consistent with a variety of types for player 1) also a "punishment" type who plays H until the first time 2 plays h, after which the punishment type plays L. The latter type is of no concern to a short-run player 2, but if a long-run player 2 thinks this latter type sufficiently likely (a belief that continued observations of H will do nothing to dispel), 2 will play ℓ. We thus cannot simply transfer the previous argument to the case of two long-run players without imposing some additional structure on the problem.[30]

Conflicting Interests.   We begin with a result from Schmidt (1993). Let v_1^* and a_1^* again be the (pure action) Stackelberg payoff and action for player 1. We say that the stage game has *conflicting interests* if $\max_{\alpha_2 \in \mathscr{A}_2} u_2(a_1^*, \alpha_2) = \min_{\alpha_1 \in \mathscr{A}_1} \max_{\alpha_2 \in \mathscr{A}_2} u_2(\alpha_1, \alpha_2)$. Hence, player 2's best response to player 1's Stackelberg action minmaxes player 2.

Proposition 9 *Let the stage game have conflicting interests. Then for any $\delta_2 < 1$ and $\varepsilon > 0$, there exists a $\underline{\delta}_1 < 1$ such that for all $\delta_1 \in (\underline{\delta}_1, 1)$, the expected payoff of the normal type of player 1 is at least $v_1^* - \varepsilon$.*

As expected, the basic tool in the argument is to note that when facing a steady stream of a_1^*, player 2 must eventually come to expect the Stackelberg action. The argument that a long-run player 2 will then play a best response to a_1^* exploits the fact that this best response minmaxes player 2 (given conflicting interests), which in turn must be better than 2's payoff from any other response. We then note that there are no punishments worse for player 2 than being minmaxed, and hence nothing that can induce player 2 to consistently *not* play a best response to a_1^*. This allows a sufficiently patient player 1 to be assured a payoff close to the Stackelberg payoff.

This argument requires an asymmetry in discount factors. Fixing player 2's discount factor allows us to impose a bound on the number of times 2 can fail

---

[30] The simplicity of the product choice game requires that we work with a punishment type whose behavior may appear counterintuitive or contrived. However, there is in general no obvious way of avoiding this difficulty by restricting attention to a set of "plausible" commitment types.

	Enter	Out
A	2,2	5,0
F	−1,−1	5,0

	L	R
T	0,0	3,1
B	1,3	0,0

Figure 4.4. Chain-store (left) and battle of the sexes game.

to play a best response to a_1^*. We then let player 1's discount factor approach 1, to ensure that these periods have an insignificant effect on 1's payoff.

What sorts of games exhibit conflicting interests? The prisoners' dilemma does, but the reputation result is of no interest here, since player 1's Stackelberg type always defects and the result ensures player 1 a payoff of at least 0. The product choice game does not exhibit conflicting interests. The chain-store game (Figure 4.4) satisfies conflicting interests, and the result implies that player 1 (the incumbent) can earn a payoff arbitrarily close to that to be had from being committed to fighting entry.

Can we expand the result beyond games of conflicting interests? Cripps, Schmidt, and Thomas (1996) show that in the absence of conflicting interests, a sufficiently patient player 1 can be assured a payoff arbitrarily close to that which arises if player 1 commits to an action and player 2 chooses the response that is worst for player 1, conditional on 2 earning at least her minmax payoff. In the battle of the sexes game, shown in Figure 4.4 (and which does not have conflicting interests), the minmax utilities for the two players are $(\frac{3}{4}, \frac{3}{4})$. Suppose that with positive probability player 1 is thought to be the Stackelberg type who always plays T. The set of responses to T in which player 2 receives at least her minmax utility is the set of actions that place at least probability $\frac{3}{4}$ on R, ensuring player 1 a payoff of $\frac{9}{4}$. Hence, fixing δ_2, a very patient normal player 1 must receive a payoff very close to $\frac{9}{4}$.[31]

Imperfect Monitoring. Celentani, Fudenberg, Levine, and Pesendorfer (1996) show that reputations can be more effective in games of imperfect monitoring. As we have seen, the difficulty in establishing a reputation when facing a long-run player 2 is that consistently playing like the commitment type will lead player 2 to expect such behavior on the equilibrium path, but imposes few restrictions on what 2 can believe about play off the equilibrium path. Celentani, Fudenberg, Levine, and Pesendorfer (1996) note that the sharp distinction between being on and off the equilibrium path disappears in games of imperfect monitoring. Player 2 should then have ample opportunity to become well acquainted with all of player 1's behavior, including any punishment possibilities. They exploit this insight to show that, without requiring conflicting interests, for any player 2 discount factor δ_2 and $\varepsilon > 0$, there is a $\underline{\delta}_1$ such that

[31] In the product choice game, ℓ ensures 2 her minmax payoff and is always the worst action for player 1. The reputation result thus places a lower bound on 1's payoff that is no higher than can be earned when 2 always chooses ℓ.

for all $\delta_1 \in (\underline{\delta}_1, 1)$, the normal type of player 1 earns at least $v_1^* - \varepsilon$ in every Nash equilibrium of the repeated game. Indeed, by allowing more sophisticated commitment types, they show that player 1 can be assured a payoff arbitrarily close to the largest stage-game payoff consistent with individual rationality for player 2.

Commitment Types who Punish.   Evans and Thomas (1997) (see also Evans and Thomas (2001)) take an alternative approach to player 2's concerns about out-of-equilibrium punishments. Suppose we have a commitment type who punishes player 2 for *not* playing a best response to the Stackelberg action. In the product choice game, for example, suppose that a commitment type plays L once, the first time player 2 fails to choose h; plays L twice, the next time; and so on. Eventually, player 2 faces arbitrarily long punishments for not playing h. Now let the normal player 1 mimic this behavior. For familiar reasons, player 2 must come to expect such play, and must choose a best response, ensuring a patient (normal) player 1 a payoff close to 2 in the product choice game. In general, by choosing the commitment type carefully, we again have the result that player 1 can be assured a payoff arbitrarily close to the largest stage-game payoff consistent with individual rationality for player 2. This is once more a strong result, one that does not require imperfect monitoring. The argument does require somewhat more active commitment types than those appearing in many reputation results. No longer does it suffice for a commitment type to simply play the action for which player 1 would like to develop a reputation, such as H in the product choice game. Instead, the commitment type must play an active role in "teaching" player 2 to play a best response to this action.

Reputations with Long-Run Opponents.   The message that emerges from these results is that reputations can be effective against long-run opponents, but that the conditions for reputation building become more stringent than required for short-run opponents. Once again, the arguments do not require that *only* the right commitment types be present, or that the various commitment types appear in the right proportions, or that uncertainty be limited to only one player. However, if the results are to apply to a general class of games (beyond conflicting interests), then we must have either imperfect monitoring or relatively sophisticated commitment types. One of the missing elements in the study of reputations is a theory of commitment types that would provide some guidance as to what sort of uncertainty about types captures the intuitive links between current behavior and future expectations that lie at the heart of a reputation.

Cripps, Mailath, and Samuelson (2004a) extend the "temporary reputations" result of Cripps, Mailath, and Samuelson (2004b) to games with two long-run players, showing that the ex ante and asymptotic implications of reputation models can be quite different. We again see that an assessment of reputation results must depend upon the setting for which the model is intended.

Symmetric Long-Run Players.   What if both are long-run players and equally patient, or $\delta_1 = \delta_2 < 1$? Notice first that some asymmetry must be involved

	L	R
T	2, 1	0, 0
B	0, 0	−1, 2

	L	R
T	2, 0	0, −1
B	1, 0	0, 1

Figure 4.5. Strictly dominant action game (left) and game of strictly conflicting interests (right).

in a reputation argument. The essence of a reputation result is a lower bound on the reputation builder's payoff, with particular emphasis on the cases in which this lower bound is close to a suitably defined "Stackelberg" payoff. Both players cannot earn nearly their Stackelberg payoff in the battle of the sexes (Figure 4.4), for example, since payoffs near (3, 3) are not feasible. We can then hope only for sufficient conditions for one player to develop such a reputation. But then we have no hope for such conditions in a perfectly symmetric game.

In moving from a short-run player 2 through a long-run but less patient player 2 to two long-run and equally patient players, we have wrung all of the asymmetry out of the players' discounting. We must accordingly look for asymmetries in the structure of the game. Two results are available.[32]

Suppose first that player 1's pure Stackelberg action is a strictly dominant action for the normal type in the stage game, and that player 2's best response to this action produces the highest stage-game payoff available to player 1, as in Figure 4.5. Such a game is said to be a *strictly dominant action game*. Notice that conflicting interests are not required. Chan (2000) shows that if such a game is perturbed to add a single possible commitment type for player 1, in the form of a type who always plays the Stackelberg action, then the normal player 1 receives the Stackelberg payoff v_1^* in any sequential equilibrium.

Second, a game of *strictly conflicting interests* is a game of conflicting interests in which (*i*) the combination of player 1's Stackelberg action and any of player 2's best responses yields the highest stage-game payoff possible for player 1 and the minmax payoff v_2 to player 2, and (*ii*) every other action profile giving player 1 this maximum payoff also minmaxes player 2. Figure 4.5 presents an example (with Stackelberg action T). Cripps, Dekel, and Pesendorfer (2004) show that for sufficiently patient players, player 1's equilibrium payoff in such a game must be arbitrarily close to the Stackelberg payoff.

5.3   An Alternative Reputation Model

This section presents an alternative reputation model, based on Mailath and Samuelson (2001) and Mailath and Samuelson (2006, Chapter 18). Our motivation for this analysis is threefold.

---

[32] Cripps and Thomas (1997) and Celentani, Fudenberg, Levine, and Pesendorfer (1996) present examples showing that incomplete information can be remarkably ineffective in bounding equilibrium payoffs when players are equally patient.

First, existing models do not readily capture the full spectrum of issues encompassed in the popular use of the word "reputation." We would like a model in which reputations have the properties of assets – things of value that require costly investments to build and maintain, that can be enhanced or allowed to deteriorate, that gradually run down if neglected, and that can be bought and sold.

The repeated games of adverse selection that form the heart of existing work on reputations may well have equilibria capturing many of these features. The argument that player 2 must eventually come to expect the Stackelberg action if player 1 invariably plays it is suggestive of a reputation-building phase, while we have also identified conditions under which reputations are optimally depleted. However, these models do not provide the explicit links between the structure of the interaction and equilibrium behavior that would be especially useful in studying reputations.

Second, reputations in standard models are built by mimicking behavior to which one would like to commit. We refer to these as "pooling" reputations, since the payoff bounds arise out of pooling one's actions with those of the commitment type. In contrast, this section focuses on "separating" reputations, in which players strive to distinguish themselves from types for whom they would like not to be mistaken. Consumers may approach the market not in terms of finding a firm who necessarily provides good service, but with avoiding the one who is incapable of doing so. The normal firm may then find that there are effectively no Stackelberg types with whom to pool, but that providing good service is essential in distinguishing himself from inept types.

Third, many equilibria in repeated games require what often appears to be an implausible degree of coordination among the players. We will work in this section with models deliberately designed to limit such coordination.

5.3.1   The Model

The model is based on a variant of the product choice game (cf. Figure 4.3). Player 1, a long-run firm, can choose either high quality (H) or low quality (L) in each period. Low quality is costless, while high quality imposes a cost of $c > 0$. We assume throughout that c is sufficiently small as to make high quality the Stackelberg action for the firm.

We interpret player 2 as a continuum of consumers. Each consumer recognizes that their actions have a negligible effect on the market outcome and hence no effect on future play, and thus behaves myopically. In each period, each consumer buys one unit of the good from the firm. The good generates two possible utility levels for the consumer, which we take to be 0 and 1. The realized utility is random and depends upon the quality chosen by the firm, with a good outcome (utility 1) appearing with probability ρ_H if the firm chose high quality and ρ_L if the firm chose low quality, where $0 < \rho_L < \rho_H < 1$. Each consumer pays a price equal to the expected utility of the good.

The various player 2s receive idiosyncratic signals: If the firm chooses high quality, then each consumer receives a good utility with probability ρ_H, and precisely ρ_H of the consumers receive good utilities. This idiosyncracy in signals disrupts the coordination that typically plays a central role in creating intertemporal incentives. Suppose we attempted to construct an equilibrium in which player 1 always chooses H, deterred from choosing L by the fact that bad outcomes trigger punishments. A consumer who has just received a bad outcome has no way of knowing whether this is simply an unlucky draw from the firm's choice of high effort or whether it is a signal that the firm chose low effort. By itself, this inference problem is not particularly problematic. In a standard public-monitoring game, bad signals trigger punishments even though players know they are *not* an indication of deviation (in equilibrium) (Section 2.2). However, for this behavior to be consistent with equilibrium, it is important that there be coordination in the punishment, not only among the small anonymous players but also with player 1. This is possible because an agent receiving a bad signal knows that everyone else also received a bad signal. The idiosyncratic signals disrupt these inferences. As a result, the current repeated game has a unique pure-strategy equilibrium in which the firm always exerts low effort. Something must be done if there is to be an equilibrium in which player 1 chooses H.

We now add incomplete information about player 1's type. There are two types of firm, *normal* and *inept*. An inept firm can only choose low effort. Notice that the extra type of player 1 is not a Stackelberg type, but a type with whom player 1 would like not to be confused. Reputation concerns in this model will arise out of player 1's efforts to separate from a bad type rather than pool with a good type.

Consider a candidate equilibrium in which the normal player 1 always chooses H. When there is uncertainty about player 1's type, each short-run player's signals provide information about player 1. Given the proposed behavior, the more likely is the firm to be normal, the more likely is high effort and hence the higher the price paid by the consumer. It then seems as if we should have an equilibrium in which the firm optimally exerts high effort because doing so increases the consumer posterior that the firm is normal and hence leads to higher future prices. Unfortunately, this behavior contains the seeds of its own destruction. Eventually, the consumers' posteriors will come arbitrarily close to attaching probability one to the firm's being normal. At this point, further experience has virtually no effect on consumer posteriors and hence on prices. But then the firm has an irresistible incentive to deviate to low effort, unraveling the putative equilibrium. Increased patience might allow this unraveling to be postponed, but it cannot be avoided. Hence, even with the possibility that the firm is inept, there is a unique pure-strategy equilibrium in which the firm always exerts low effort. In essence, a firm attempting to build a reputation does too good a job of it. Consumers eventually become so certain the firm is normal that the incentives to invest further in consumers' beliefs disappear.

To obtain an equilibrium with consistent high effort, consumers' posteriors about the firm must be bounded away from certainty. For example, the consumers may have bounded memory, using only some finite number of their most recent observations in drawing inferences about the firm's type. Overwhelming evidence that the firm is normal could then never be amassed.

We adopt a different approach here, assuming that in every period there is probability $\lambda \in (0, 1)$ that the firm is replaced by a new firm whose type is randomly drawn from a prior distribution over types. Consumers understand the possibility of such replacements but cannot observe them. Intuitively, the possibility of changing types plays a role whenever one's response to a disappointing experience with a firm known for good outcomes is not simply "I've been unlucky" but also "I wonder if something has changed?" This again ensures that consumers can never be too certain about the firm, and hence that the firm always faces incentives to choose high effort.[33]

In introducing the prospect that a firm's characteristics or even identity are constantly subject to revision, we place an upper bound on the effective discount factors, no matter how patient the firm happens to be. As a result, appealing to the limit as the discount factor gets arbitrarily close to one is no longer an effective way to create incentives. However, if the cost of effort c is sufficiently small, then we have a "high effort" equilibrium in which the normal firm always chooses high effort.

Proposition 10 *There exists $\bar{c} > 0$ such that a high effort equilibrium exists for all $0 \leq c < \bar{c}$.*

We thus have the seemingly paradoxical result that it can be good news for the firm to have consumers constantly fearing that the firm might "go bad." If replacements continually introduce the possibility that the firm has turned bad, then the firm can never do "too good" a job of convincing consumers it is normal. But then the incentive for the firm to continually reinforce consumer beliefs induces the firm to consistently choose high quality. This opens the door to a model of reputations.

Ely, Fudenberg, and Levine (2002) and Ely and Välimäki (2002) present an alternative model in which a reputation builder's attempts to separate himself from a bad type has strikingly counterproductive effects, consigning the reputation building to his lowest possible payoff. The "bad reputation" games of Ely, Fudenberg, and Levine (2002) and Ely and Välimäki (2002) feature a richer set of actions for the firm, in which the action that most effectively distinguishes the normal player from his inept counterpart is bad for consumers (unlike the action H in the current model). In addition, consumers in the bad reputation model have the option of not purchasing from the firm, shutting

---

[33] See Holmström (1999) for an early application of this idea and Hörner (2002) for an alternative approach.

off the information flow that is essential to building a reputation. As a result, the circumstances in which player 1 is most anxious to separate from the inept type are precisely those in which he cannot do so because consumers anticipate an unfavorable action from the firm and hence refrain from purchasing, unleashing an unraveling that precludes any chance of building a reputation.

6   MODELING RELATIONSHIPS

Many technical questions remain open in the study of relationships – results to be generalized, assumptions to be relaxed, proofs to be refined, and necessary and sufficient conditions to be pushed closer together. However, the more challenging questions involve how we apply and interpret these techniques.

6.1   Designing Relationships

If relationships are important in allocating resources, then the theory of relationships should provide guidance as to how we might design relationships to do so more effectively. It is now taken for granted that economists can offer useful advice on how to design markets or contracts. What do we have to say about relationships?

This section offers one elementary example, taken from Andreoni and Samuelson (2005) (see Baker, Gibbons, and Murphy (2002) for an alternative approach). We begin with the observation that experiments with the prisoners' dilemma consistently find considerable heterogeneity in behavior. Some agents always defect while others cooperate, even in the one-shot prisoners' dilemma (though with the incidence of cooperation falling over the course of a finitely repeated prisoners' dilemma). Moving beyond the experimental laboratory and the prisoners' dilemma, we note that people often act "cooperatively" – they donate to charity, they vote, they provide public goods, they come to the aid of those in need – in circumstances under which many economic models would suggest that they not do so.

How do we explain such behavior? One possibility is to posit that we are observing people in relationships and that their cooperative behavior is part of an equilibrium of the corresponding repeated game. This is the analogue of the equilibrium interpretation approach to reputations (cf. Section 5). We pursue here an alternative model that is again centered around relationships but is more closely related to the adverse selection approach to reputations.

In constructing this model, we pursue Section 5.3's suggestion that a reputation model should identify links between the structure of an interaction and equilibrium behavior. We need a rich enough implementation of the prisoners' dilemma to make this possible, though also parsimonious enough to be tractable. We accordingly consider two-period games whose stage games are

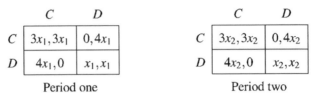

	C	D
C	$3x_1, 3x_1$	$0, 4x_1$
D	$4x_1, 0$	x_1, x_1

Period one

	C	D
C	$3x_2, 3x_2$	$0, 4x_2$
D	$4x_2, 0$	x_2, x_2

Period two

Figure 4.6. *Stage games for the twice-played prisoners' dilemma, where* $x_1, x_2 \geq 0$.

the prisoners' dilemmas shown in Figure 4.6. Let $\lambda = \frac{x_2}{x_1+x_2}$. We consider a class of such two-period prisoners' dilemma games in which $x_1 + x_2$ is fixed, but λ ranges from zero to one. Hence, the total payoffs at stake over the two periods of the relationship are help fixed, but their distribution across the periods varies. When $\lambda = 0$, all of the payoffs are concentrated in the first of the two prisoners' dilemmas. As λ increases, the second period becomes relatively more important, with $\lambda = \frac{1}{2}$ corresponding to equal payoffs in the two periods and $\lambda = 1$ corresponding to all payoffs being concentrated in the second period.

Without something further, these games are a variation on a finitely repeated prisoners' dilemma with complete information, in which persistent defection is the only equilibrium outcome. We now introduce an element of adverse selection in the model, beginning with the assumption that some people have preferences that lead them to sometimes prefer cooperation in the prisoners' dilemma. We study a model in which (*i*) players prefer that their opponents cooperate in the prisoners' dilemma, (*ii*) players sometimes prefer to cooperate themselves, (*iii*) players are more likely to prefer cooperation when their opponent is more likely to cooperate, and (*iv*) players differ in the strength of this taste for cooperation. For some players, the taste for cooperation will be sufficiently weak that defection will be a dominant strategy in the stage game, making them the counterpart of the normal types in familiar reputation models. Others will sometimes or perhaps always prefer to cooperate.[34] The game begins with each players' type (i.e., preferences) independently drawn from a distribution over the set of such preferences. We thus have a two-stage game of incomplete information.

As in the reputation models of Section 5, players' actions now balance immediate payoff effects with information revelation and the attendant implications for future payoffs. We are especially interested in how an appropriately designed relationship can leverage such preferences to enhance the extent of cooperation (i.e., in links between the structure of the interaction and equilibrium behavior). The obvious structural feature to investigate is the distribution of payoffs across the two periods, parameterized by λ. The argument will provide an indication of why it might be effective to have a relationship "start

---

[34] We can view this model as an extension of Kreps and Wilson (1982) and Milgrom and Roberts (1982), involving a continuum of types.

small," beginning with relatively small stakes and building up to more important interactions.[35]

With the help of some additional (primarily technical) structure, Andreoni and Samuelson (2005) isolate an equilibrium of the game with (among others) two features on which we focus here:

- The incidence of first-period cooperation increases as λ does.
- Certain outcomes of the game become more likely, and others less likely, as λ grows. For example, when λ is small, an outcome of mutual cooperation in the first period should be followed by mutual cooperation in the second. However, as λ increases above a threshold, the incidence of mutual cooperation followed by one defection (denoted by CC, DC) increases, and the incidence of mutual cooperation followed by mutual defection (CC, DD) becomes positive but has an ambiguous comparative static in λ.

Cooperation in the first period, by enhancing an opponent's estimate of one's unobserved taste for cooperation, leads to more opponent cooperation in the second period. Holding other things equal, this enhances the value of first-period cooperation. More importantly, second-period cooperation is more valuable the higher is λ. As a result, higher values of λ induce agents to cooperate more in the first period as an investment in second-period cooperation, as well as inducing a number of more specific behavioral shifts, including those described in the second point above.

These behavioral patterns give rise to conflicting effects on payoffs. As λ increases, we trade off increased first-period cooperation for decreased first-period payoffs, as payoffs are shifted to the second period. The combined effects suggest that the expected monetary payoff from the two-period game initially increases in λ, achieves an interior maximum at a value of $\lambda > \frac{1}{2}$, and then decreases.

Andreoni and Samuelson (2005) report the results of an experimental investigation of the model. Figures 4.7 and 4.8 report partial results from this experiment, corresponding to the two equilibrium features highlighted above. Figure 4.7 shows that the incidence of cooperation indeed increases as λ increases, shifting the stakes to the second period. Figure 4.8 provides results for the incidence of outcomes CC, DC and CC, DD as a function of λ. Both figures report expected patterns of play. In addition, the total payoffs from the experimental interaction are maximized when the second-period stakes are one-and-a-half to two times as large as those of the first period.

Results such as these suggest that our theoretical models may be helpful in designing relationships to more effectively allocate resources. This is one of the more exciting possibilities for future work in the economics of relationships.

---

[35] Models in which relationships optimally start small are examined by Diamond (1989) and Watson (1999, 2002).

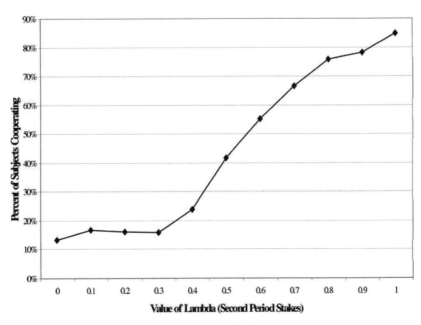

Figure 4.7. Percentage of experimental subjects cooperating in the first period of the two-period prisoners' dilemma, as a function of λ.

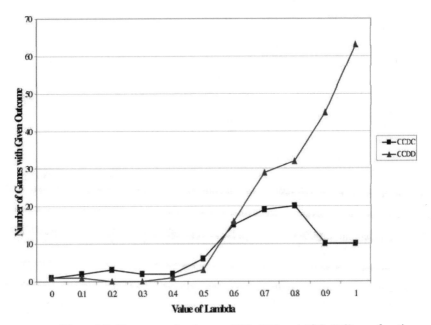

Figure 4.8. Frequency of outcomes (CC, DD) and (CC, DC) as a function of λ.

6.2   Equilibrium

Repeated games have many equilibria. Which ones should command our attention when studying relationships? Behind this simple question lurks a collection of more difficult ones, culminating in questions about how we interpret an equilibrium and even how we interpret a repeated game.

6.2.1   Efficiency

It is common to be especially interested in equilibria that are efficient in the repeated game. The reasoning appears to proceed as follows. "An equilibrium of the repeated game involving nontrivial intertemporal incentives requires coordination on the part of the players. Something must lie behind this coordination, perhaps some explicit process in which the players could communicate and agree on an equilibrium. But given this chance to select an equilibrium, it seems as if the players would certainly choose an efficient one." Alternatively, an equilibrium with nontrivial intertemporal incentives is often viewed as something that requires the players' active participation, while simply repeating the Nash equilibrium of the stage game in each period is viewed as something more passive. But why would the players actively strive for anything less than efficiency? This view implicitly appears when we speak of firms as "colluding" when setting prices above those of the stage-game Nash equilibrium, with no such word required for repetition of the stage-game equilibrium, and suggests that any equilibrium of interest featuring nontrivial intertemporal incentives should be efficient.

These arguments lead to two puzzles. First, if there is some process that directs attention to efficient equilibria, why does it occur just once at the beginning of the game? Why doesn't the same process come into play every time a new period appears with a new continuation equilibrium? Pursuing this question leads to the idea of a renegotiation-proof equilibrium, in which the players are assumed to never settle for an inferior continuation equilibrium. A body of work has grown around this idea.[36] Interestingly, there is also a large body of research in economics centered on the premise that economic systems do *not* always yield efficient outcomes, explaining events such as bank failures (Diamond and Dybvig (1983)), discrimination (Coate and Loury (1993)) or economic depressions (Cooper and John (1988)) in terms of coordination on an inefficient equilibrium. One cannot help but be struck by these contrasting views of efficiency.

---

[36] One might first think of rejecting an equilibrium σ if, after any history of play, it prescribes continuation play that is strictly dominated by some other equilibrium σ'. However, it is then natural to limit the set of possible blocking equilibria σ' to those that are not similarly blocked, building a self-reference into the definition that can lead to all sorts of difficulties. Some useful examples of the literature include Abreu, Pearce, and Stacchetti (1993), Asheim (1991), Baliga and Evans (2000), Benoit and Krishna (1993), Bernheim and Ray (1989), Evans and Maskin (1989), Farrell and Maskin (1989), and Wen (1996).

Second, it is not clear what to make of the view that an equilibrium with nontrivial intertemporal incentives somehow involves more active coordination than does the repetition of a stage-game Nash equilibrium. In all but the simplest of games, the assertion that *any* equilibrium is played involves a belief that the players can somehow coordinate their behavior. Even in games with unique Nash equilibria, it is not clear that we can obviously expect equilibrium play: Simply asserting the players are rational, and that this rationality is common knowledge does not suffice for equilibrium play. The standard story in game theory is now an evolutionary one: that either the players' own history or a collective history that they share with others brings them to equilibrium.[37] We can apply similar ideas to repeated games, but there appears to be no reason to believe that equilibria with nontrivial intertemporal incentives will be treated differently than those without, nor that the outcome will be efficient. People live lives full of intertemporal tradeoffs. Why should we expect the default position to be that they ignore these tradeoffs in a repeated game, other than for the fact that stage games came first in the development of game theory?

What can we conclude? Our theory of relationships needs a more carefully considered account of what we are doing when we select an equilibrium, addressing both the question of which equilibrium might be selected and why we might expect an equilibrium at all. Returning to a recurring theme, this equilibrium selection is properly viewed as part of the modeling process. We need methods for dealing with this part of the modeling that will move us beyond our current "I know it when I see it."

6.2.2   *Punishments*

The question of how players coordinate on an equilibrium reappears when thinking about the role of punishments in creating incentives. It is common to assume that deviations from equilibrium play trigger the subsequent play of a stage-game Nash equilibrium. There are often more severe punishments available, and the use of such punishments could make a difference.[38] Why work with Nash reversion?

In some applications, nothing is lost by focusing on Nash reversion. In the prisoners' dilemma and the product choice game, the (unique) stage-game Nash equilibrium gives each player the minimum payoff consistent with individual rationality, ensuring that there are no more severe punishments. In other cases,

---

[37] Kalai and Lehrer (1993) provide one perspective on this process, while the large bodies of work on learning (Fudenberg and Levine (1998)) and evolutionary games (Samuelson (1997), Weibull (1995)) provide others.

[38] For example, these more severe punishments can allow a particular outcome to be supported as equilibrium behavior for a broader range of discount factors, or can expand the set of equilibrium payoffs, including efficient equilibrium payoffs, in the limiting case as the discount factor approaches one.

Nash reversion is adopted as an analytical convenience. It frees us from having to worry about incentives off the equilibrium path. As long as one ensures that the results do not depend upon the restrictions inherent in this analytical convenience, the restriction raises no difficulties. However, the preference for Nash reversion is sometimes fueled by the view that it may be reasonable to think of players as coordinating on repeated-game equilibria that bring them high payoffs, but absurd to think of them as actively coordinating on low payoffs.

The foundations of this last view are less apparent. The industrial organization literature contains no lack of models and stories about price wars – coordinated punishments looking very much like the combination of a temporary penalty coupled with a return to higher payoffs that characterizes the work of Abreu (1986) or Fudenberg and Maskin (1986). In this setting, actively coordinated punishments look quite reasonable. It is not clear that a price war requires more coordination or is less "natural" than Nash reversion. Again, we return to the need for better insight into how we view the equilibria of the repeated games with which we work.

6.2.3   Markov Equilibrium

It is common, especially in applications, to restrict attention to Markov equilibria. A typical characterization of Markov equilibrium is that it restricts attention to only "payoff relevant" information about the history of play. The motivation is that the players in the game should find some types of information more salient than others, and the term payoff relevance is designed both to identify the salient information and provide the motivation for its being salient.

Markov equilibria are also sometimes motivated as being simple, an argument somewhat in tension with the observation that a precise specification of "payoff relevant" (see Maskin and Tirole (2001)) is neither obvious nor simple. A second source of tension arises out of the fact that, in repeated games (i.e., games involving precisely the same stage game in every period, as opposed to dynamic games, where the stage game evolves over the course of play), Markov equilibria must feature a stage-game Nash equilibrium in each period. This clashes with the view that equilibria featuring nontrivial intertemporal incentives, perhaps allowing cooperation in the prisoners' dilemma, are often of interest in such games.

The first step on the road to Markov equilibrium seems straightforward enough. The players in a repeated game, as in any other game, are surrounded by all sorts of information. Their histories of play already contain a wealth of information. If we take seriously that the model is a tool for examining real strategic interactions, then we must recognize that the environment in which the interaction takes place contains another wealth of information that we have excluded from the model. It also seems quite plausible that the players cannot make use of all of the available information, so that some criterion for which information is to be salient must play a role.

	L	C	R
T	4,4	0,5	0,5
M	5,0	3,3	0,0
B	5,0	0,0	1,1

Figure 4.9. Stage game.

To go further, observe that we conventionally do *not* restrict players to conditioning their behavior only on information that is contained in the model. To focus on this point, put repeated games aside and consider a one-shot interaction in which two firms must both decide whether to enter a market that is large enough to hold just one of them. The game is symmetric, with nothing to distinguish the two players. A theory of equilibrium selection that strictly confines itself to information contained within the game must respect this symmetry, choosing the game's unique symmetric equilibrium, in which each firm mixes between entering the market and staying out (e.g., Harsanyi and Selten (1988)). However, many analysts would choose an asymmetric pure-strategy equilibrium in which one firm enters and the other does not, when working with the game. The interpretation of the asymmetry in the equilibrium would be that it reflects some asymmetry present in the actual interaction – one firm got there first, or was larger, or had lower costs – that can show up in the model only in the form of an equilibrium selection that is not grounded in any information contained in the model. Returning to the point that the construction of the game and the selection of an equilibrium jointly comprise our model of the strategic interaction, there is no reason to expect the equilibrium to respect informational criteria that can be defined only in terms of the game.

Now let us move closer to repeated games by considering the stage game shown in Figure 4.9. Suppose this game is played once. There are two pure Nash equilibria, (M, C) and (B, R). Though some might have a preference for the efficient equilibrium, it would be common to admit either as equilibrium candidates, with the relevant one depending upon details of the context in which the game is played. The way the game has been played in the past might be cited as a particularly relevant detail.

Now suppose that the game is played twice, with the players maximizing the sum of their payoffs over the two interactions. An application of Maskin and Tirole's (2001) payoff relevance concludes that nothing about first-period play is payoff relevant, and hence that second-period play must be independent of the first-period history. This precludes the efficient equilibrium in which (T, L) is played in the first period followed by (M, C) (with first-period deviations prompting play of (B, R)). But if either (M, C) or (B, R) are considered reasonable equilibria when the game is played once, with the choice between the two resting upon environmental details not captured by the game, why cannot first-period play serve the same function when reaching the second period of the repeated game?

This suggests that in the course of thinking about equilibria in repeated games, we need an account of which aspects of their history *and* their environment the players come to think of as relevant and which they ignore. One of the difficulties here is that which information is relevant is itself likely to be an equilibrium phenomenon, raising the specter of an infinite regress. One possibility is an evolutionary approach. Some very limited beginnings along these lines, in one-shot games, are taken by Binmore and Samuelson (2000, 2005).

6.2.4   Complexity

One cannot work with repeated games without coming to the view that some strategies and some equilibria are more complex than others. In addition, it seems quite compelling that simple strategies should have their attractions. Identifying precisely what one means by simple is somewhat more challenging.

An early formulation of complexity in repeated games captured the idea that strategies should not contain contingencies that are never used (Abreu and Rubinstein (1988), Rubinstein (1986)). The literature that grew out of these beginnings took the view that the complexity of a strategy was properly assessed within the confines of the game in which the strategy is played. For example, an argument about complexity might proceed as follows: "Consider the strategy grim trigger in the prisoners' dilemma. It includes the specification that the player defect in response to previous defection. In equilibrium this capability is never used. Hence, the strategy can be simplified by deleting this capability with no effect on how the game is played, and players who are concerned about complexity should surely do so. Once the ability to punish has been deleted, however, we no longer have an equilibrium." Complexity considerations thus suggest that this cooperation in the repeated prisoners' dilemma is suspect.

There are several ways of responding to this point while keeping the analysis within the confines of a single game.[39] However, let us return to an observation made in Section 1.3, that an ability to monitor interactions and punish transgressions may be part of our evolutionary heritage (Cosmides and Tooby (1992a,b)). If evolution has equipped us with a propensity to monitor and punish,

---

[39] For example, we can ensure that all possibilities are on the equilibrium path, and hence that the equilibrium is not threatened by "free" simplifications by working with imperfect public monitoring. Alternatively, we could look for a strategy that cooperates almost all of the time, but incorporates defections into its equilibrium play that could provide tools for punishing that are not completely redundant and hence are not candidates for deletion.

then perhaps we should not remain within the confines of the game when assessing complexity. Instead, we might think of players as having a "punishment" phase in their thinking, flexible enough that it can be applied whenever needed, and that survives precisely because it is sometimes needed (perhaps in games where the discount factors and incentives are such that punishment is the only possible equilibrium outcome). If so, then attaching a punishment capability to a strategy should not be viewed as making the strategy more complex. This in turn suggests that viewing the repeated play of a stage-game Nash equilibria as being particularly simple may be misleading. Cooperating in the prisoners' dilemma, with deviations punished, may be effectively just as simple as always defecting.

6.2.5   Modeling Games

How do we pull these ideas together? One clear theme is that we need to think of the structure of the repeated game and the accompanying equilibrium as jointly determined as part of the model of the strategic interaction. Second, in constructing this model, we must ask ourselves how the agents themselves model the interaction. What information do they view as relevant, and what relevant information do they ignore? Do they view it in isolation, or as part of a larger interaction? Do they view it as repeated, or do they ignore the prospect of the future? For the same reasons that economists work with models to examine a reality that is too complicated to study in full detail, so should we expect the players in the game to rely on models. There is then no reason to expect their view of "payoff relevant" or "simple" or "requiring coordination," or even of the boundary of the model, to match ours.

We thus need a theory of relationships that begins with a model of how the agents perceive their environment. For example, Jehiel (2005) examines a model in which agents fail to distinguish histories that a conventional analysis would necessarily identify as distinct, including histories of different lengths. The agents thus effectively play a different extensive form than that posited by the modeler. Samuelson (2001) examines a model in which evolution determines such features as whether agents treat distinct games differently or as being identical.

The difficulty is that the modeling choices embedded in such an analysis inevitably seem arbitrary, while often themselves being an equilibrium phenomenon that simply pushes the problems back one step. Returning to a point raised in each of the preceding two subsections, my inclination is to think that an evolutionary approach provides the best hope for making progress in the face of such obstacles. The result would not be another exercise in evolutionary game theory, with the players' behavior adjusting shaped by an adaptive process, but would be a study of how the actual process of evolution has shaped the way people analyze their strategic interactions. Such an approach faces great challenges but also promises great rewards in our understanding of relationships.

References

ABREU, D. (1986): "Extremal Equilibria of Oligopolistic Supergames," *Journal of Economic Theory*, 39(1), 191–225.

ABREU, D., P. DUTTA, AND L. SMITH (1994): "The Folk Theorem for Repeated Games: A NEU Condition," *Econometrica*, 62(4), 939–948.

ABREU, D., D. PEARCE, AND E. STACCHETTI (1986): "Optimal Cartel Equilibria with Imperfect Monitoring," *Journal of Economic Theory*, 39, 251–269.

——— (1990): "Toward a Theory of Discounted Repeated Games with Imperfect Monitoring," *Econometrica*, 58, 1041–1064.

——— (1993): "Renegotiation and Symmetry in Repeated Games," *Journal of Economic Theory*, 60(2), 217–240.

ABREU, D., AND A. RUBINSTEIN (1988): "The Structure of Nash Equilibrium in Repeated Games with Finite Automata," *Econometrica*, 56(6), 1259–1281.

AHN, I., AND M. SUOMINEN (2001): "Word-of-Mouth Communication and Community Enforcement," *International Economic Review*, 42(2), 399–415.

ANDREONI, J., AND L. SAMUELSON (2005): "Building Rational Cooperation," *Journal of Economic Theory*, Forthcoming.

ASHEIM, G. (1991): "Extending Renegotiation-Proofness to Infinite Games," *Games and Economic Behaivor*, 3(3), 278–294.

ATHEY, S., AND K. BAGWELL (2001): "Optimal Collusion with Private Information," *RAND Journal of Economics*, 32(3), 428–465.

ATHEY, S., K. BAGWELL, AND C. SANCHIRICO (2004): "Collusion and Price Rigidity," *Review of Economic Studies*, 71(2), 317–349.

AUMANN, R. J., AND L. S. SHAPLEY (1976): "Long-Term Competition – A Game Theoretic Analysis," reprinted in *Essays in Game Theory in Honor of Michael Maschler*, ed. by N. Megiddo (1994), pp. 1–15. Springer-Verlag, New York.

BAGWELL, K. (1995): "Commitment and Observability in Games," *Games and Economic Behavior*, 8(2), 271–280.

BAKER, G., R. GIBBONS, AND K. J. MURPHY (2002): "Relational Contracts and the Theory of the Firm," *Quarterly Journal of Economics*, 117(1), 39–84.

BALIGA, S., AND R. EVANS (2000): "Renegotiation in Repeated Games with Side-Payments," *Games and Economic Behavior*, 33(2), 159–175.

BENOIT, J., AND V. KRISHNA (1993): "Renegotiation in Finitely Repeated Games," *Econometrica*, 61(2), 303–323.

BERNHEIM, B. D., AND D. RAY (1989): "Collective Dynamic Consistency in Repeated Games," *Games and Economic Behavior*, 1(4), 295–326.

BINMORE, K., AND L. SAMUELSON (2000): "Evolution and Mixed Strategies," *Games and Economic Behavior*, 34, 200–226.

——— (2005): "The Evolution of Focal Points," *Games and Economic Behavior*, Forthcoming.

CELENTANI, M., D. FUDENBERG, D. K. LEVINE, AND W. PESENDORFER (1996): "Maintaining a Reputation against a Long-Lived Opponent," *Econometrica*, 64(3), 691–704.

CELENTANI, M., AND W. PESENDORFER (1996): "Reputation in Dynamic Games," *Journal of Economic Theory*, 70(1), 109–132.

CHAN, J. (2000): "On the Non-Existence of Reputation Effects in Two-Person Infinitely-Repeated Games," Johns Hopkins University.

COASE, R. (1960): "The Problem of Social Cost," *Journal of Law and Economics*, 2, 1–40.

COATE, S., AND G. C. LOURY (1993): "Will Affirmative-Action Policies Eliminate Negative Stereotypes?," *American Economic Review*, 83(5), 1220–1240.

COLE, H. L., J. DOW, AND W. B. ENGLISH (1995): "Default, Settlement, and Signalling: Lending Resumption in a Reputational Model of Sovereign Debt," *International Economic Review*, 36(2), 365–385.

COOPER, R., AND A. JOHN (1988): "Coordinating Coordination Failures in Keynesian Models," *Quarterly Journal of Economics*, 103(3), 441–463.

COSMIDES, L., AND J. TOOBY (1992a): "Cognitive Adaptations for Social Exchange," in *The Adapted Mind*, ed. by J. H. Barkow, L. Cosmides, and J. Tooby, 163–228. Oxford University Press, Oxford.

——— (1992b): "The Psychological Foundations of Culture," in *The Adapted Mind*, ed. by J. H. Barkow, L. Cosmides, and J. Tooby, 19–136. Oxford University Press, Oxford.

CRIPPS, M. W., E. DEKEL, AND W. PESENDORFER (2004): "Reputation with Equal Discounting in Repeated Games with Strictly Conflicting Interests," *Journal of Economic Theory*, 121(2), 259–272.

CRIPPS, M. W., G. MAILATH, AND L. SAMUELSON (2004a): "Disappearing Private Reputations," Washington University in St. Louis, University of Pennsylvania, and University of Wisconsin.

——— (2004b): "Imperfect Monitoring and Impermanent Reputations," *Econometrica*, 72(2), 407–432.

CRIPPS, M. W., K. M. SCHMIDT, AND J. P. THOMAS (1996): "Reputation in Perturbed Repeated Games," *Journal of Economic Theory*, 69(2), 387–410.

CRIPPS, M. W., AND J. P. THOMAS (1997): "Reputation and Perfection in Repeated Common Interest Games," *Games and Economic Behavior*, 18(2), 141–158.

DEBREU, G. (1959): *Theory of Value*. Yale University Press, New Haven.

DIAMOND, D. W. (1989): "Reputation Acquisition in Debt Markets," *Journal of Political Economy*, 97(4), 828–862.

DIAMOND, D. W., AND P. H. DYBVIG (1983): "Bank Runs, Deposit Insurance and Liquidity," *Journal of Political Economy*, 91(3), 401–419.

ELLICKSON, R. C. (1991): *Order without Law: How Neighbors Settle Disputes*. Harvard University Press, Cambridge, Massachusetts.

ELLISON, G. (1994): "Cooperation in the Prisoner's Dilemma with Anonymous Random Matching," *Review of Economic Studies*, 61, 567–588.

ELY, J. C., D. FUDENBERG, AND D. K. LEVINE (2002): "When is Reputation Bad?," Northwestern University, Harvard, and University of California at Los Angeles.

ELY, J. C., J. HÖRNER, AND W. OLSZEWSKI (2005): "Belief-Free Equilibria in Repeated Games," *Econometrica*, 73(2), 377–416.

ELY, J. C., AND J. VÄLIMÄKI (2002): "A Robust Folk Theorem for the Prisoner's Dilemma," *Journal of Economic Theory*, 102(1), 84–105.

EVANS, R., AND E. MASKIN (1989): "Efficient Renegotiation-Proof Equilibria in Repeated Games," *Games and Economic Behavior*, 1(4), 361–369.

EVANS, R., AND J. P. THOMAS (1997): "Reputation and Experimentation in Repeated Games with Two Long-Run Players," *Econometrica*, 65(5), 1153–1173.

——— (2001): "Cooperation and Punishment," *Econometrica*, 69(4), 1061–1075.

FARRELL, J., AND E. MASKIN (1989): "Renegotiation in Repeated Games," *Games and Economic Behavior*, 1(4), 327–360.

FRIEDMAN, J. W. (1971): "A Noncooperative Equilibrium for Supergames," *Review of Economic Studies*, 38(1), 1–12.

FUDENBERG, D., AND D. K. LEVINE (1989): "Reputation and Equilibrium Selection in Games with a Patient Player," *Econometrica*, 57(4), 759–778.

——— (1992): "Maintaining a Reputation when Strategies are Imperfectly Observed," *Review of Economic Studies*, 59(3), 561–579.

——— (1994): "Efficiency and Observability with Long-Run and Short-Run Players," *Journal of Economic Theory*, 62(1), 103–135.

——— (1998): *Theory of Learning in Games*. MIT Press, Cambridge.

FUDENBERG, D., D. K. LEVINE, AND E. MASKIN (1994): "The Folk Theorem with Imperfect Public Information," *Econometrica*, 62(5), 997–1031.

FUDENBERG, D., AND E. MASKIN (1986): "The Folk Theorem in Repeated Games with Discounting or with Incomplete Information," *Econometrica*, 54(3), 533–554.

GREEN, E. J., AND R. H. PORTER (1984): "Noncooperative Collusion Under Imperfect Price Information," *Econometrica*, 52, 87–100.

GREIF, A. (1997): "Microtheory and Recent Developments in the Study of Economic Institutions through Economic History," in *Advances in Economics and Econometrics: Theory and Applications, Seventh World Congress*, ed. by D. M. Kreps and K. F. Wallis, 79–113. Cambridge University Press, Cambridge.

——— (2005): *Institutions and the Path to the Modern Economy: Lessons from Medieval Trade*. Cambridge University Press, Cambridge.

GREIF, A., P. MILGROM, AND B. R. WEINGAST (1994): "Coordination, Commitment, and Enforcement: The Case of the Merchant Guild," *Journal of Political Economy*, 102(4), 745–776.

HAMERMESH, D. S. (2004): *Economics is Everywhere*. McGraw Hill/Irwin, New York.

HARRINGTON, JR., J. E. (1995): "Cooperation in a One-Shot Prisoners' Dilemma," *Games and Economic Behavior*, 8(2), 364–377.

HARSANYI, J. C. (1973): "Games with Randomly Distributed Payoffs: A New Rationale for Mixed–Strategy Equilibrium Points," *International Journal of Game Theory*, 2, 1–23.

HARSANYI, J. C., AND R. SELTEN (1988): *A General Theory of Equilibrium Selection in Games*. MIT Press, Cambridge, Massachusetts.

HOLMSTRÖM, B. (1999): "Managerial Incentive Problems: A Dynamic Perspective," *Review of Economic Studies*, 66(1), 169–182.

HÖRNER, J. (2002): "Reputation and Competition," *American Economic Review*, 92(3), 644–663.

HÖRNER, J., AND W. OLSZEWSKI (2005): "The Folk Theorem for Games with Private Almost-Perfect Monitoring," Northwestern University.

JACKSON, M. O., AND E. KALAI (1999): "Reputation versus Social Learning," *Journal of Economic Theory*, 88(1), 40–59.

JEHIEL, P. (2005): "Limited Foresight May Force Cooperation," *Review of Economic Studies*, 123(2), 81–104.

KALAI, E., AND E. LEHRER (1993): "Rational Learning Leads to Nash Equilibria," *Econometrica*, 61, 1019–1046.

KANDORI, M. (1992): "Social Norms and Community Enforcement," *Review of Economic Studies*, 59(1), 63–80.

KANDORI, M., AND H. MATSUSHIMA (1998): "Private Observation, Communication and Collusion," *Econometrica*, 66(3), 627–652.

KOCHERLAKOTA, N. R. (1996): "Implications of Efficient Risk Sharing without Commitment," *Review of Economic Studies*, 63(3), 595–609.

——— (1998): "Money Is Memory," *Journal of Economic Theory*, 81(2), 232–251.

KOCHERLAKOTA, N. R., AND N. WALLACE (1998): "Incomplete Record-Keeping and Optimal Payment Arrangements," *Journal of Economic Theory*, 81(2), 272–289.

KOEPPL, T. V. (2003): "Differentiability of the Efficient Frontier when Commitment to Risk Sharing is Limited," European Central Bank.

KREPS, D. M., AND R. J. WILSON (1982): "Reputation and Imperfect Information," *Journal of Economic Theory*, 27(2), 253–279.

LEVIN, J. (2003): "Relational Incentive Contracts," *American Economic Review*, 93(3), 835–857.

LIGON, E., J. P. THOMAS, AND T. WORRALL (2002): "Informal Insurance Arrangements with Limited Commitment: Theory and Evidence from Village Economies," *Review of Economic Studies*, 69(1), 209–244.

LJUNGQVIST, L., AND T. J. SARGENT (2004): *Recursive Macroeconomic Theory*. MIT Press, Cambridge, Massachusetts, second ed.

MACAULEY, S. (1963): "Non-Contractual Relations in Business: A Preliminary Study," *American Sociological Review*, 28, 55–67.

MAILATH, G. J., AND S. MORRIS (2002): "Repeated Games with Almost-Public Monitoring," *Journal of Economic Theory*, 102(1), 189–228.

——— (2005): "Coodination Failure in a Repeated Game with Almost Public Monitoring," University of Pennsylvania and Yale University.

MAILATH, G. J., I. OBARA, AND T. SEKIGUCHI (2002): "The Maximum Efficient Equilibrium Payoff in the Repeated Prisoners' Dilemma," *Games and Economic Behavior*, 40(1), 99–122.

MAILATH, G. J., AND L. SAMUELSON (2001): "Who Wants a Good Reputation?," *Review of Economic Studies*, 68, 425–442.

——— (2006): *Repeated Games and Reputations: Long-Run Relationships*. Oxford University Press, Oxford.

MALCOMSON, J. M. (1997): "Contracts, Hold-Up and Labor Markets," *Journal of Economic Literature*, 35(4), 1916–1957–136.

MASKIN, E., AND J. TIROLE (2001): "Markov Perfect Equilibrium: I. Observable Actions," *Journal of Economic Theory*, 100(2), 191–219.

MATSUSHIMA, H. (1989): "Efficiency in Repeated Games with Imperfect Monitoring," *Journal of Economic Theory*, 48(2), 428–442.

——— (2004): "Repeated Games with Private Monitoring: Two Players," *Econometrica*, 72(3), 823–852.

MILGROM, P. R., AND J. ROBERTS (1982): "Predation, Reputation and Entry Deterrence," *Journal of Economic Theory*, 27(2), 280–312.

OKUNO-FUJIWARA, M., AND A. POSTLEWAITE (1995): "Social Norms in Random Matching Games," *Games and Economic Behavior*, 9(1), 79–109.

PHELAN, C. (2005): "Public Trust and Government Betrayal," *Journal of Economic Theory*, Forthcoming.

PICCIONE, M. (2002): "The Repeated Prisoner's Dilemma with Imperfect Private Monitoring," *Journal of Economic Theory*, 102, 70–83.

PORTER, R. H. (1983): "Optimal Cartel Trigger Price Strategies," *Journal of Economic Theory*, 29(2), 313–338.

PUTNAM, R. D. (2000): *Bowling Alone*. Simon and Schuster, New York.

RADNER, R. (1985): "Repeated Principal-Agent Problems with Discounting," *Econometrica*, 53(5), 1173–1198.

RICHMAN, B. D. (2005): "How Communities Create Economic Advantage: Jewish Diamond Merchants in New York," Duke Law School Legal Studies research paper series, Number 65; Harvard Law School Law and Economics research paper series, Number 384.

RUBINSTEIN, A. (1977): "Equilibrium in Supergames," Master's thesis, Hebrew Univeristy of Jerusalem, reprinted in *Essays in Game Theory in Honor of Michael Maschler*, ed. by N. Megiddo (1994), 17–28, Springer-Verlag, New York.

——— (1979): "Equilibrium in Supergames with the Overtaking Criterion," *Journal of Economic Theory*, 21(1), 1–9.

——— (1986): "Finite Automata Play the Repeated Prisoners' Dilemma," *Journal of Economic Theory*, 39(1), 83–96.

SAMUELSON, L. (1997): *Evolutionary Games and Equilibrium Selection*. MIT Press, Cambridge.

——— (2001): "Analogies, Adaptation, and Anomalies," *Journal of Economic Theory*, 97, 320–366.

SCHMIDT, K. M. (1993): "Reputation and Equilibrium Characterization in Repeated Games of Conflicting Interests," *Econometrica*, 61(2), 325–351.

SCHMITZ, P. W. (2002): "Simple Contracts, Renegotiation under Asymmetric Information, and the Hold-Up Problem," *European Economic Review*, 46(1), 169–188.

SEKIGUCHI, T. (1997): "Efficiency in Repeated Prisoner's Dilemma with Private Monitoring," *Journal of Economic Theory*, 76(2), 345–361.

STAHL, D. O. (1991): "The Graph of the Prisoners' Dilemma Supergame Payoffs as a Function of the Discount Factor," *Games and Economic Behavior*, 3(3), 368–384.

THOMAS, J.J. AND T. WORRALL (1988): "Self-Enforcing Wage Contracts," *Review of Economic Studies*, 55(4), 541–553.

WATSON, J. (1999): "Starting Small and Renegotiation," *Journal of Economic Theory*, 85(1), 52–90.

——— (2002): "Starting Small and Commitment," *Games and Economic Behavior*, 38(1), 176–199.

WEIBULL, J. W. (1995): *Evolutionary Game Theory*. MIT Press, Cambridge.

WEN, Q. (1994): "The "Folk Theorem" for Repeated Games with Complete Information," *Econometrica*, 62(4), 949–954.

——— (1996): "On Renegotiation-Proof Equilibria in Finitely Repeated Games," *Games and Economic Behavior*, 13(2), 286–300.

CHAPTER 5

Information in Mechanism Design

Dirk Bergemann[*] and Juuso Välimäki[†]

1 INTRODUCTION

The mechanism design literature of the last thirty years has been a big success on a number of different levels. A beautiful theoretical literature has shown how a wide range of institutional design questions can be formally posed as mechanism design problems with a common structure. We can understand institutions as solutions to well-defined maximization problems subject to incentive constraints. Elegant characterizations of optimal mechanisms have been obtained. Market design has become more important in many economic arenas both because of new insights from theory and developments in information technology. A very successful econometric literature has tested auction theory in practice.

The basic issue in mechanism design is how to truthfully elicit private and decentralized information in order to achieve some private or social objective. The task of the principal is then to design a game of incomplete information in which the agents have indeed an incentive to reveal the information. The optimal design depends on the common prior, which the principal and the agents share about the types of the agents. Unfortunately, the general theory, the applications and the empirical work have rather different natural starting points. The theoretical analysis begins with a given common prior, often over a small set of types, and then analyzes the optimal mechanism with respect to this prior. Yet, the fine details of the specified environment incorporated in the common prior are rarely available to the designer in practice.

In this survey, we shall pursue two distinct but closely related arguments. The first part of this survey is centered on the issue of endogenous information structures in mechanism design. In traditional mechanism design literature, the set of possible types for the participants in the design problem is exogenously given. This may be a reasonable approximation in situations such as determining

[*] Department of Economics, Yale University, 28 Hillhouse Avenue, New Haven, CT 06511, dirk.bergemann@yale.edu.
[†] Department of Economics, Helsinki School of Economics and University of Southampton, 00100 Helsinki, Finland, valimaki@hkkk.fi.

Pareto efficient allocations in an exchange economy where individual preferences are private information. It is equally clear that for many applications it is not reasonable to assume that the relevant information is independent of the mechanism chosen.

To illustrate the point concretely, consider decision making in committees. If committee members have to invest privately in order to have useful information, then it is clear that their willingness to invest in such information depends on the choice of the decision making process. If additional information has little impact on the eventual decision, there is no point to acquiring it. As a second, slightly different application, where the participants' information depends on the mechanism chosen, consider the optimal design of auctions. The auctioneer may have control over pieces of evidence that determine the bidders' valuation for the object on sale. Whether it is in the auctioneer's best interest to disclose this information depends on the properties of the auction to follow.

We view information acquisition and information disclosure as two different aspects of an information management problem that we believe is important in many mechanism design settings. In our view, in many examples of great practical interest, it is not accurate to view the distribution of types as independent from the choice of the mechanism. At the most abstract level, we may think about mechanisms as institutions that coordinate societies on particular collective choices. As long as the relevant information is produced within the economies, it should be clear that this production is guided by economic incentives. Hence a good mechanism ought to provide incentives for efficient collective choices given the information collected, but at the same time a good mechanism should also provide the participants with good incentives for producing the relevant information.

We review the existing literature on information acquisition and disclosure in a number of applications. It is our intention to show that by adding an information acquisition stage a number of features arise across the spectrum of applications. Two aspects deserve mention here. With information acquisition, the extensive form, and in particular the timing, becomes more important than in standard mechanisms. Second, randomizations play a role in settings that can be analyzed using pure strategies in the basic model.

In the second part of this survey, we analyze mechanism design when the principal and the agents have little common knowledge and the type space is large. The starting point here is the influential formulation of the robustness question due to Robert Wilson. Wilson emphasized that academic mechanism designers were tempted to assume too much common knowledge among the players and suggested that more robust conclusions would arise if researchers were able to relax those assumptions. Practitioners have often been led to argue in favor of using simpler but apparently sub-optimal mechanisms. It is argued that the optimal mechanisms are not "robust" – that is they are too sensitive to fine details of the specified environment. In response to these concerns, attractive and influential results have been obtained by imposing (in a somewhat ad hoc way) stronger solution concepts and simpler mechanisms motivated by robustness considerations. A natural theoretical question to ask is whether it is possible to explicitly model robustness in such a way that stronger solution concepts and simpler mechanisms arise endogenously. To the extent that the agents have or can get access to private information about their own valuation, the valuations of other agents, or the beliefs of the others, the designer is led to adopt a robust mechanism. Consequently, in this survey we shall study mechanism design when we relax both the *small* and the *given* type space assumptions.

The remainder of this survey is organized as follows. Section 2 provides the basic model and notation for the survey. Section 3 is meant to emphasize the perspective of this survey. We shall first discuss the role of information acquisition in generalized Vickrey-Groves-Clark mechanisms and then talk about the role of strategic information in first price auctions. In Section 4 we survey the role of information management in mechanism design. Section 5 frames the concern for robust mechanism by emphasizing the importance of strategic uncertainty. We discuss recent results on robust mechanisms and show how classic auction results are modified by the introduction of large type spaces expressing strategic uncertainty. Section 6 concludes the survey and discusses a number of open and noteworthy research issues.

2   SETUP

2.1   Payoff Environment

We consider a finite set of agents, indexed by $i \in \mathcal{I} = \{1, \dots, I\}$. The agents have to make a collective choice y from a set Y of possible outcomes. The *payoff type* of agent i is $\theta_i \in \Theta_i$. We write $\theta \in \Theta = \Theta_1 \times \cdots \times \Theta_I$. Each agent has utility function $u_i : Y \times \Theta \to \mathbb{R}$. An important special case is the *quasi-linear environment*, where the set of outcomes Y has the product structure $Y = Y_0 \times Y_1 \times \cdots \times Y_I$, where $Y_1 = Y_2 = \cdots = Y_I = \mathbb{R}$, and a utility function:

$$u_i(y, \theta) = u_i(y_0, y_1, \dots, y_I, \theta) \triangleq v_i(y_0, \theta) + y_i,$$

which is linear in y_i for every agent i.

The collective choice problem is represented by a social choice correspondence $F : \Theta \to 2^Y \backslash \emptyset$, a social choice function is given by $f : \Theta \to Y$. If the true payoff type profile is θ, the planner would like the outcome to be an element of $F(\theta)$, or $f(\theta)$. This environment is fixed and informally understood to be common knowledge. We allow for interdependent types – one agent's payoff from a given outcome depends on other agents' payoff types. The model is said to be a *private value model* if for all θ, θ':

$$\theta_i = \theta_i' \implies u_i(y, \theta) = u_i(y, \theta'). \tag{1}$$

If condition (1) is violated, then the model displays *interdependent values*.

The payoff type profile is understood to contain all information that is relevant to whether the planner achieves her objective or not. It incorporates many classic problems such as the efficient allocation of an object, the efficient provision of a public good, and arriving at a decision in a committee.

Much of the recent work on interdependent values has used the solution concept of ex post rather than Bayesian equilibrium. The analysis of ex post equilibrium is considerably more tractable because incentive compatible transfers can often be derived with ease and single crossing conditions generating incentive compatibility are easy to identify.[1]

Definition 1 *A direct mechanism* $f : \Theta \to Y$ *is ex post incentive compatible if, for all i and* $\theta \in \Theta$,

$$u_i \left(f \left(\theta \right), \theta \right) \geq u_i \left(f \left(\theta_i', \theta_{-i} \right), \theta \right), \text{ for all } \theta_i' \in \Theta_i.$$

The notion of ex post incentive compatibility requires agent i to prefer truthtelling at θ if all the other agents also report truthfully. In contrast, the notion of dominant strategy implementation requires agent i to prefer truthtelling for all possible reports by the other agents, truthtelling or not.

Definition 2 *A direct mechanism* $f : \Theta \to Y$ *is incentive compatible in dominant strategies if, for all i and* $\theta \in \Theta$,

$$u_i \left(f \left(\theta_i, \theta_{-i}' \right), \theta \right) \geq u_i \left(f \left(\theta' \right), \theta \right), \text{ for all } \theta' \in \Theta.$$

If there are private values (i.e., each $u_i (y, \theta)$ depends on θ only through θ_i), then ex post incentive compatibility is equivalent to dominant strategies incentive compatibility.

2.2   Information Acquisition

In problems of choice under uncertainty, the starting point of the analysis is often the situation where an agent holds a prior probability distribution on the states of the world $\omega \in \Omega$ and must decide on an optimal action $y \in Y$. One way to model information acquisition is then to assume that the agent has access to a statistical experiment that yields additional information on ω. Each outcome in the experiment results in a posterior belief on Ω. Since the posterior belief represents the payoff relevant information of the agent, we denote (in accordance with the previous subsection) the set of probability distributions on Ω by Θ with a generic element $\theta \in \Theta$.

For the purposes of the current survey, it is easiest to formulate the information acquisition decision of the agent as a choice amongst a set of distributions

---

[1]   Ex post incentive compatibility was discussed as "uniform incentive compatibility" by Holmstrom and Myerson (1983). Ex post equilibrium is increasingly studied in game theory (see Kalai (2004)) and is often used in mechanism design as a more robust solution concept (Cremer and McLean (1985)). A recent literature on interdependent value environments has obtained positive and negative results using this solution concept: Dasgupta and Maskin (2000), Bergemann and Välimäki (2002), Perry and Reny (2002), Jehiel and Moldovanu (2001), Jehiel, Moldovanu, Meyer-ter-Vehn, and Zame (2005), and Bikhchandani (2005).

on Θ. We index the experiments by $\alpha \in A$ and hence an experiment results in a distribution $F^\alpha (\theta)$ on Θ. We also write the utility function of the agent directly in terms of the posterior and the chosen action $u (y, \theta)$. Under suitable regularity conditions, there is an optimal action $y (\theta)$ for each θ. If we denote the cost of observing experiment α by $c (\alpha)$, the information acquisition problem can be written concisely as follows:

$$\max_{\alpha \in A} \left\{ \int_\Theta u (y (\theta), \theta) \, d F^\alpha (\theta) - c (\alpha) \right\}.$$

To see a concrete example that fits the framework above, consider the case where $\omega \in \{0, 1\}$. Then we may identify Θ with $[0, 1]$ where $\theta = \Pr\{\omega = 1\}$. Let θ_0 indicate the prior distribution of the agent and consider the following family of experiments:

$$F^\alpha (\theta) = \begin{cases} (1 - \theta_0) \alpha & \text{for} & \theta < \theta_0, \\ 1 - \theta_0 \alpha & \text{for} & \theta_0 \leq \theta < 1, \\ 1 & \text{for} & \theta = 1. \end{cases}$$

Here α is the probability of observing a perfectly informative signal on ω. It is easy to generate richer examples of this structure.

When considering the mechanism design problem, all relevant information for the mechanism is contained in the vector of posteriors $(\theta_1, \ldots, \theta_I)$. It is thus possible to consider the posteriors directly as the inputs that the mechanism designer elicits from the participants in the mechanism. The choice of individual experiment α_i determines the appropriate distribution for the posteriors θ_i. Since these posteriors are in general multi-dimensional (and quite often infinite dimensional), it is clear that unless further assumptions on the payoff structures are made, the task of designing mechanisms in such settings is very complicated. We shall consider throughout the case where the ex ante investment in information is covert. As a result, the mechanism cannot be written as directly depending on α_i.

3   MOTIVATING EXAMPLES

3.1   Information Acquisition in Generalized VCG auctions

Our first example examines the role of information acquisition in a single unit auction with interdependent values. More specifically, we are interested in the possibility of inducing the bidders to gather information in a socially efficient manner.

The auction has two bidders, each of whom has statistically independent private information on a different binary aspect $\omega_i \in \{\underline{\omega}_i, \overline{\omega}_i\} = \{0, 1\}$ of the good. We denote by θ_i bidder i's probability assessment on the event $\{\omega_i = \overline{\omega}_i\}$.

We assume that player i's payoff from obtaining the object at price y_i takes the following linear form:

$$u_i(\theta) = \alpha\theta_i + \beta\theta_j - y_i, \tag{2}$$

where we assume that $\alpha > 0$. If $\beta = 0$, we are in the private values case. When $\alpha = \beta$, we have a model with pure common values.

Denote the allocation of the object in the auction by $y_0 \in \{1, 2\}$. Efficiency requires that

$$y_0(\theta_i, \theta_j) = i \quad \text{if} \quad (\alpha - \beta)(\theta_i - \theta_j) > 0.$$

Hence a necessary condition for incentive compatibility of the efficient allocation is that $\alpha \geq \beta$. Under this condition it is easy to verify that the direct mechanism consisting of

$$y_i(\theta_i, \theta_j) = \begin{cases} (\alpha + \beta)\theta_j & \text{if} \quad \theta_i \geq \theta_j, \\ 0 & \text{if} \quad \theta_i < \theta_j, \end{cases}$$

and

$$y_0(\theta_i, \theta_j) = i \quad \text{if } \theta_i \geq \theta_j,$$

is ex post incentive compatible. This mechanism is called the generalized *Vickrey-Clarke-Groves (VCG)* mechanism and its analysis in the interdependent values case is due to Maskin (1992) and Dasgupta and Maskin (2000).

With statistical independence of types, the revenue equivalence theorem implies that the expected payoffs of the two bidders in all efficient mechanisms coincide with the payoffs in the generalized VCG mechanism. As we are focusing here on socially efficient information acquisition, it is natural to ask whether an individual bidder's incentives to acquire additional information coincide with those of a utilitarian social planner.

Our main finding in Bergemann and Välimäki (2002) implies that when $\beta < 0$, the generalized VCG auction gives too low incentives for information acquisition to the individual bidders. If $\beta > 0$, the agents have an incentive to engage in excessive information acquisition.

To see the intuition for this result, notice that the generalized VCG mechanism allocates the object to i only if $\theta_i \geq \theta_j$. For $\theta_i \geq \theta_j$,

$$u_i(\theta_i, \theta_j) - u_i(\theta_j, \theta_j) = \max\{u_i(\theta_i, \theta_j), u_j(\theta_i, \theta_j)\} - u_i(\theta_j, \theta_j),$$

and hence the gains from higher θ_i are the same for bidder i and for the social planner. Bidder i's payoff is zero in the generalized VCG mechanism for all $\theta_i < \theta_j$. If $\beta > 0$ then the utilitarian planner's payoff is increasing also for $\theta_i < \theta_j$. Hence the payoff to bidder i has a sharper kink at θ_j than the planner's utility function. As a result, bidder i is locally more risk loving than the planner and hence she has stronger incentives to acquire information. It should be noted that when $\beta = 0$, bidder i's payoff equals the planner's payoff as a function of θ_i

(up to a constant) and as a result, private incentives for information acquisition coincide with the planner's incentives in a private value environment.

This example shows how efficient use of information is often incompatible with efficient acquisition of information. It is clear that a second-best mechanism would sacrifice some of the allocational efficiency relative to the generalized VCG mechanism in order to achieve better alignment of private and social incentives in the information acquisition stage. Full exploration of this trade-off remains an open question at this time.

3.2   Strategic Information in First-Price Auctions

Our second example demonstrates the importance of modeling information about other players' types. In a setting with independent private value we consider a first-price auction among two bidders for a single object. For simplicity, we consider a discrete space of values and bids. The valuations are given for each i by:

$$\theta_i \in \Theta_i = \{1, \ 2, \ 3\},$$

and the feasible bids for each i are given by:

$$b_i \in B_i = \{1/2, \ 1, \ 3/2, \ 2, \ 5/2, \ 3\}.$$

The valuations are distributed uniformly and independently according to a common prior $p\left(\theta_i, \theta_j\right)$:

$$
\begin{array}{cccc}
 & t_j^1 \ t_j^2 \ t_j^3 & \\
t_i^1 & \frac{1}{9} \ \frac{1}{9} \ \frac{1}{9} & \theta_i^1 \\
t_i^2 & \frac{1}{9} \ \frac{1}{9} \ \frac{1}{9} & \theta_i^2 \\
t_i^3 & \frac{1}{9} \ \frac{1}{9} \ \frac{1}{9} & \theta_i^3 \\
 & \theta_j^1 \ \theta_j^2 \ \theta_j^3 &
\end{array}
\tag{3}
$$

The private information of bidder i, her type t_i, consists of her true valuation, θ_i (payoff relevant type), and her belief about the valuations of the other bidders, the posterior distribution, $p\left(\theta_j | \theta_i\right)$. In the standard model of auctions, each payoff type θ_i is associated with exactly one belief type, and hence the additional notation of a type t_i may appear at first glance redundant.

We wish to consider a richer environment in which each bidder receives some additional private information about her competitor. To keep matters simple, let us suppose that every bidder with a high valuation, i.e., $\theta_i = 3$, obtains some additional information. This additional information, represented by two distinct types, t_i' and t_i'', refines her view about the strength of her competitor as follows:

$$
\begin{array}{cccc}
\theta_j^1 \ \theta_j^2 \ \theta_j^3 & \Pr\left(t_i | \theta_i = 3\right) & \\
p\left(\theta_j | t_i'\right) \ \frac{3}{6} \ \frac{2}{6} \ \frac{1}{6} & \frac{2}{3} & \leftarrow \text{"weak" competitor} \\
p\left(\theta_j | t_i''\right) \ 0 \ \frac{2}{6} \ \frac{4}{6} & \frac{1}{3} & \leftarrow \text{"strong" competitor}
\end{array}
$$

The last column in the above matrix represents the likelihood that a bidder with a high valuation receives either one of the two possible pieces of information, t_i' or t_i''. The posterior beliefs, $p\left(\theta_j \mid t_i\right)$ over the valuations θ_j of bidder j differ across the two types, t_i' or t_i'', indicating that bidder j is a weak or strong competitor, respectively. We also observe that the aggregate distribution over valuations θ_j given θ_i has not changed. The common prior on the new type space is now:

$$
\begin{array}{c|cccc|c}
 & t_j^1 & t_j^2 & t_j^3 & t_j^4 & \\
\hline
t_i^1 & \frac{1}{9} & \frac{1}{9} & \frac{1}{9} & 0 & \theta_i^1 \\
t_i^2 & \frac{1}{9} & \frac{1}{9} & \frac{2}{27} & \frac{1}{27} & \theta_i^2 \\
t_i^3 & \frac{1}{9} & \frac{2}{27} & \frac{1}{27} & 0 & \theta_i^3 \\
t_i^4 & 0 & \frac{1}{27} & 0 & \frac{2}{27} & \theta_i^3 \\
\hline
 & \theta_j^1 & \theta_j^2 & \theta_j^3 & \theta_j^3 &
\end{array}
\tag{4}
$$

Observe that the distributions over valuations θ are identically, uniformly, and independently distributed in both type spaces. Yet, as we consider how the new information affects bidding in the first-price auction, we observe a few important differences. In the small type space, the unique equilibrium bidding strategy $b_i^*(t_i)$ is given by:

$$
b_i^*(t_i) = \frac{1}{2}\theta_i(t_i),
$$

which is also the bidding strategy in the continuous version of the model. However, in the larger type space the bidding strategy changes as the bidders use their additional information to modify their bidding strategy. The unique equilibrium bidding strategy $b_i^{**}(t_i)$ is indeed given by:

$$
b_i^{**}(t_i) = \frac{1}{2}\theta_i(t_i), \quad \text{for } t_i = t_i^1, t_i^2
$$

but

$$
b_i^{**}\left(t_i^3\right) = 1 \neq \frac{3}{2} = b_i^*\left(t_i^4\right), \quad \text{for } t_i = t_i^3, t_i^4.
$$

The introduction of strategic uncertainty and more private information for the bidders has then a number of important implications for the equilibrium. First, even though the distribution of valuations remains identical across the two type spaces, the larger type space leads to lower bids and lower revenues for the auctioneer. Types t_i^3 and t_i^4 share the same payoff type, $\theta_i = 3$, but have different private information about their competitors and hence different equilibrium bids. In a second-price auction, the bidding strategy would remain identical across the type spaces, and hence the revenues would stay constant as well. We also find that in the larger type space the first-price auction does not lead to an efficient allocation. The bids of types t_i^2 and t_i^3 are identical even though $\theta_i\left(t_i^2\right) < \theta_i\left(t_i^3\right)$. In Section 5, we show more generally that type spaces richer than the standard payoff type space lead to a failure of the revenue equivalence theorem, do not permit a revenue ranking between first and second-price auction, and lead to a failure of efficiency in the first-price auction.

4 INFORMATION MANAGEMENT

4.1   Information Acquisition in Committees

We start our survey of recent contributions to the literature on information acquisition with the problem of optimal committee design when information is costly to acquire. Most papers in this area assume that the committee members have common objectives and also that monetary transfers are not used. As a result, it is probably easiest to see what additional insights costly information acquisition brings into the model in this context.

For concreteness, we phrase our discussion of the model in terms of a jury problem. The celebrated Condorcet Jury Theorem (see e.g., Black (1958)) states in its traditional form that decision making in juries under majority rule outperforms decision making by any single individual and as the number of participating voters increases, the probability of the correct social decision converges to one. The underlying idea is that in majority decisions the information of several jury members is aggregated and therefore such decisions are superior to those arrived at by any individual jury member.

The jury chooses between two alternatives: $y_0 \in \{0, 1\}$ where 0 stands for acquitting and 1 stands for convicting the defendant. At the trial there is uncertainty regarding the possible guilt of the defendant. We model this by a binary state $\omega \in \{0, 1\}$ where 0 stands for innocence and 1 indicates guilt and for simplicity we assume that the prior probability satisfies: $\Pr\{\omega = 1\} = \frac{1}{2}$. All jury members are assumed to have the same payoff functions $u(y_0, \omega)$ satisfying:

$$u(0, 0) = u(1, 1) = 0, \ u(0, 1) = -d_0, \quad \text{and} \quad u(1, 0) = -d_1.$$

In other words, convicting guilty and acquitting innocent defendants is costless. The costs of wrongful conviction is $d_1 > 0$ and the cost of wrongful acquittal is $d_0 > 0$.

At the trial, jury members are presented with evidence on the guilt of the defendant. This is modeled through signal s_i observed by juror i. We assume that the signals are binary, i.e., $s_i \in \{0, 1\}$ and correlated with truth in the sense that $\Pr\{s_i = 0 \,|\, \omega = 0\} = p > \frac{1}{2}$ and $\Pr\{s_i = 1 \,|\, \omega = 1\} = q > \frac{1}{2}$. Furthermore, we assume that signals are independent across jurors conditional on the state ω. Decisions in the jury are reached by majority voting. The vote of juror i is denoted by $v_i : S_i \to [0, 1]$, where $v_i(s_i)$ is understood to be the probability of voting to convict after observing signal s_i. The jury decision is given by:

$$y_0 : \{0, 1\}^I \to [0, 1],$$

where $y_0(v)$ gives the probability of convicting given vote profile v.

The logic behind the Condorcet Jury Theorem runs as follows. If the jury members vote based on their private signal, then the vote counts provide a better signal of ω than the individual s_i. The problem with this argument is, as pointed out by Austen-Smith and Banks (1996), that in general it is not in the interest of an individual juror to vote in accordance with their private signal. When the voting stage is seen as a Bayesian game, sincere voting, i.e. $v_i(0) = 0$, $v_i(1) = 1$ for all i is not a Bayesian equilibrium of the game. The reason for this is that at the moment of casting their votes, each jury member must condition her beliefs about the innocence of the defendant on the event that her own vote is pivotal. In a majority rule vote, this implies that the other jury members' votes are equally split. If $p > q$, equal split together with sincere voting implies that $\omega = 1$ is much more likely than $\omega = 0$ and as a result, the individual juror has an incentive to discard her own information. Feddersen and Pesendorfer (1998) compare the expected equilibrium payoff from different voting rules ranging from simple majority to unanimity as a function of the cost parameters d_0 and d_1. By concentrating on symmetric equilibria where the individual jurors' strategies are responsive to private signals, they show that a wide range of rules can be optimal.

To see how costly information acquisition changes the situation, Persico (2004) considers a simple modification to the jury problem above. The signal of each jury member is observed only with cost $c > 0$. This cost is assumed to be private and as a result, a discrepancy between social and private incentives for acquiring information arises.[2] While Feddersen and Pesendorfer (1998) obtain the result that the expected payoff from jury decisions increases with the number of members of the jury, Persico (2004) concludes that optimal jury size is bounded even if the private costs of information acquisition are not accounted for in the social welfare calculation. The reason for the difference in the results depends on the fact that information acquisition by the jurors brings in an element of moral hazard into the decision making process. In order for the jurors to be willing to pay for information, their probability of being pivotal must remain non-negligible. This is only possible in juries of bounded size. Perhaps more interestingly, Persico (2004) finds that the optimal voting rule is independent of d_0 and d_1 and instead depends on the statistical nature of evidence, i.e., on p and q. For the special case where $p = q$, he shows that for small c, the optimal supermajority in the jury decisions converges to p.

A second remarkable property of jury design under costly information acquisition is that the voting rule is efficient given the information acquired by the jury members. In the setting of Persico (2004), this property arises partially from the fact that the analysis focuses on pure strategy equilibria. Under this restriction, any sub-optimal decision rule would imply that some agents do not acquire information. Mukhopadhaya (2003) concentrates on the symmetric mixed strategy equilibrium and shows that for a fixed voting rule, increasing the

---

[2] In the literature on jury decisions, the role of monetary transfers has been ignored. This seems to be a reasonable approximation to most committee decision making processes that are observed in the real world. In addition, Persico (2004) shows that with monetary transfers the problem of inducing efficient information acquisition can be trivially solved.

jury size may decrease the accuracy of decisions when information acquisition is costly.

Gershkov and Szentes (2004) consider the optimal method of inducing information acquisition and eliciting it truthfully from homogenous committee members subject to the requirement that the decisions must be ex post efficient. In other words, they require that given the information collected in the committee, the decision must agree with the optimal one. They show that the optimal method of gathering information is to approach the committee members sequentially but withholding the previous record of both who has been approached and what information has been transmitted. It is also interesting to note that their optimal mechanism features randomized decisions on whether to collect additional information.

In a similar problem, Smorodinsky and Tennenholtz (2005) show that a sequential mechanism is also optimal in a class of mechanisms that arrive at the correct social decision with probability 1. In this paper, there is no trade-off between costs of information acquisition and the accuracy of the decision.

Gerardi and Yariv (2005) remove the restriction on ex post efficiency of the mechanism. They show that the optimal decision rule is not generally of the type considered in Persico (2004), but rather that it may involve randomizations and ex post inefficient decisions.

The issue of signal accuracy is addressed in Li (2001). In that paper, all jury members invest in information that is useful for determining the guilt of the defendant. In contrast to the other papers surveyed here, Li assumes that the signals are publicly observable. As a result his model is very close to traditional free-riding models of informational externalities. He shows that in order to provide good incentives for information acquisition, it may be optimal to distort the rule mapping signals to decisions. Martinelli (2006) considers a voting model in which the citizens have identical preferences but have a continuous choice regarding the precision of their private information. As the number of participating citizens increases, each individual agent decreases the precision of her private information, but with $c'(0) = c''(0) = 0$ at zero precision, in the limit the simple majority rule leads to the election of the best candidate with probability one.

Finally, Cai (2003) considers the optimal size of a committee under a fixed decision rule in a committee when the members have heterogenous payoff functions. If individual committee members have preferences different from those of the designer of the committee, they have an incentive to distort their reports to the designer. The main observation of the paper is that preference diversity may increase the individual members' incentives for acquiring information. As a result, the optimal size of committees may be higher under preference diversity as the free rider problems are alleviated.

To summarize, the papers reviewed in this section demonstrate in a simple setting how mechanism design problems must be modified in order to take into account the costs of getting informed. When jury members have the same objectives, but bear the cost of information acquisition privately, free riding becomes an issue in models where information acquisition decisions are not observable. If it is possible to commit to decision rules at the start of the game, free riding can be fought to some extent by an appropriate choice of the decision rule. Sometimes this may involve taking decisions that are sub-optimal in light of the collected information. Even when restricted to ex post optimal decision rules, the design of an appropriate extensive form for eliciting information from the jury members provides insights into the general problem.

4.2   Information in Principal-Agent Models

Throughout this paper, we assume that information acquisition is covert, in other words, the principal does not see whether the agent has acquired additional information or not. It is easy to see in the single agent setting that information acquisition adds an element of moral hazard on top of the original adverse selection model. Consider for instance the model where a principal sells an indivisible object to an initially uninformed agent. At cost c, the agent can learn privately her valuation for the object. It is clear that timing plays a crucial role in the analysis of this model. If the principal offers contracts after information acquisition, the model reduces to an adverse selection model conditional on the equilibrium level of information acquisition. If the contract is offered prior to information acquisition, we are in the traditional moral hazard world where the principal extracts all surplus from the agent. Finally, if contract offers and information acquisition decisions are simultaneous, information acquisition decisions are often in mixed strategies and the principal tries to screen the informed buyers from the uninformed.

The role of information acquisition in a principal-agent setting has been investigated in a series of papers by Cremer and Khalil (1992), Cremer, Khalil, and Rochet (1998a), and Cremer, Khalil, and Rochet (1998b). In Cremer and Khalil (1992), the basic problem is a standard adverse selection problem of regulating a monopolist with unknown cost as in Baron and Myerson (1982). The new element is that the agent does not know her type at the moment the contract is offered. She can learn her type, say her marginal cost, either before or after signing the contract. A cost c must be paid to acquire information prior to signing the contract, whereas after signing the contract the type is revealed at zero cost. Information acquisition is therefore socially inefficient. The private benefit for the agent, however, is that she may be able to reject contract offers that would not be profitable given her marginal cost. Cremer and Khalil (1992) show that the ability of the agent to acquire information decreases the downward distortion at the production stage. The optimal contract raises the expected value of the contract, type by type, so that the agent will have no incentive to acquire the information in equilibrium.

The distinction between costly pre-contract and free post-contract information is also central in a recent study by Matthews and Persico (2005) on the excess refund puzzle. They consider the optimal price and refund policy of sellers when the potential buyers can either engage in costly research to assess the value of the object or wait until delivery and inspection of the object. As the return of the object is costly, the optimal selling policy has to find a balance between returns and sales. Similar to Cremer and Khalil (1992), they show that it might be optimal for the seller to offer a refund policy sufficiently generous so as to prevent the buyer in equilibrium to acquire information. The distortion in the refund policy relative to the socially optimal policy leads to an excess in refunds.

In Cremer, Khalil, and Rochet (1998a), the setting is modified by assuming that all information about the cost structure has to be acquired at some fixed cost c. Again, the impact of information acquisition affects both the production schedule and the rent to the agent. For a sufficiently small c, the optimal contract is the standard Baron-Myerson contract. As the cost of information acquisition increases, the value of the contract decreases for the principal. The optimal contract reduces the distortion for low cost types, and increases it for high cost types. This is the most efficient way to increase the rent for the agent so that she has an incentive to acquire the information. At higher c, it is optimal to leave a rent to the uninformed agent. As the principal cannot receive the entire surplus, the production level is below the ex ante efficient level. As information is costly, it may not be optimal to acquire information even from a social point of view. An open issue is then whether the design of the contract by the principal will lead the agent to take a socially efficient decision regarding information acquisition or whether it will introduce a systematic distortion in the decision of the agent.

Finally, in Cremer, Khalil, and Rochet (1998b), the decision by the agent to get informed is taken covertly before the contract is offered. This reversal in the timing of the decision introduces strategic uncertainty for the principal as the agent may randomize over information acquisition. The resulting equilibrium is one in which the principal offers a menu of contracts, one of which is chosen by the informed and the other is chosen by the uninformed agent. The two contracts display partial pooling, in a sense that for low marginal cost of production, informed and uninformed will produce the same quantity. For intermediate and high production cost, the informed agent will see more downward distortions, and relative to standard Baron-Myerson type contracts, the production will be higher (lower) for medium- (high-) cost types. The change in the production schedule is enacted so as to efficiently generate surplus for the informed agent and give him incentives to acquire information.[3]

4.3   Information Acquisition in Auctions

Within the field of mechanism design, auction theory has seen the largest number of contributions in the last decade. Surprisingly few of those papers have

---

[3] A literature on *delegated expertise* that started with Demski and Sappington (1987) considers information acquisition in the moral hazard model. A recent contribution by Malcolmson (2004) reflects the state of this literature. Starting with Aghion and Tirole (1997), this model has investigated the role of information acquisition in the optimal design of organizations from an incomplete contract point of view.

focused explicitly on costly information acquisition. This is somewhat puzzling given the close connections between auctions and price formation processes in competitive markets. Milgrom (1981) explores the issue of information acquisition in a model similar to the one presented in the motivating example. His main concern is on determining whether the model can be used in providing foundations for the fully revealing rational expectations equilibrium. The connections to the rational expectations equilibrium have been since worked on extensively, but the issue of information acquisition has received considerably less attention. In our view, the questions relating to socially optimal information acquisition remain open for a large class of auctions models.[4]

Early contributions to the literature compared the revenue generation across different auction formats, most notably between first- and second-price auctions. Matthews (1977) and Matthews (1984) obtained the result that the two formats lead to the same expected revenue in a special case of an affiliated model. This result is also later found in a sequence of papers on the independent private information case. These include Hausch and Li (1991), Tan (1992), and Stegeman (1996). The most direct way of seeing why private values settings lead to the same revenue rankings for different auction formats is to observe that by the revenue equivalence theorem, they are equivalent to the Vickrey auction. Hence the ex ante incentives for investing in information (or even to make more general investments) must be the same. Rogerson (1992) makes this point in a more general mechanism design setting than the current auctions model.

If the auction designer has a utilitarian welfare objective, it is again easy to see that the agents have the correct incentives to acquire information in a socially optimal manner. In the Vickrey auction, individual payoffs, when viewed as functions of own payoff type only, coincide with the sum of payoffs to all players (up to the addition of a constant). As a result, individual incentives coincide with those of the planner.

Information acquisition in auctions has also been modeled as an auction with costly entry. Johnson (1979), French and McCormick (1984), McAfee and McMillan (1987), and Levin and Smith (1994) formulate entry as a model in which potential bidders do not possess private information until they incur an entry cost. Upon incurring the cost, they acquire a private signal about the value of the object.

In a more general model of affiliated values, Persico (2000) shows that the incentives for information acquisition are, in general, different across different auction formats. In particular, he shows that the marginal incentives for acquiring additional information are higher for first-price auctions than for second-price auctions. This may overturn the general superiority of second-price auctions as demonstrated in Milgrom and Weber (1982). In a model with affiliated values, additional information allows more accurate predictions of other players' bids. As the transfers in a first-price auction depend on own bids,

---

[4] A notable exception is Jackson (2003) who shows that in an auction setting with a large number of bidders and costly information acquisition information aggregation may fail and not lead to the efficient allocation.

it is important to obtain such information in order to be able to shade own bids optimally.

In Bergemann and Välimäki (2002), we consider the possibility of maintaining the utilitarian optimal allocation in a model of interdependent but statistically independent valuations. Each bidder i acquires information on ω_i and this information is independent across the bidders. As explained above, we can view the information acquisition decision as a choice of distributions over the posterior beliefs θ_i on Ω_i. Bidder i has an expected payoff

$$u_i(\theta) = u_i(\theta_1, \ldots, \theta_I) = \int_\Omega \widetilde{u}_i(\omega_1, \ldots, \omega_I)\, d\theta_1(\omega_1) \ldots d\theta_I(\omega_I),$$

where we recall that $d\theta_i(\omega_i)$ is the conditional distribution over ω_i given the realization of signal or posterior θ_i. The utilitarian planner would like to allocate the object to bidder i such that

$$u_i(\theta) \geq u_j(\theta) \text{ for all } j \in \{1, \ldots, I\}.$$

As explained in the motivating example, this can be done using the generalized VCG mechanism when the utility functions satisfy the single crossing property:

$$\frac{\partial u_i(\theta)}{\partial \theta_i} \geq \frac{\partial u_j(\theta)}{\partial \theta_i} \text{ for all } i, j \in \{1, \ldots, I\}.$$

We assume that ω_i and s_i satisfy monotone likelihood ratio property for all α_i. Furthermore, we assume that the experiments are indexed in such a manner that $\alpha > \alpha'$ implies that experiment α is better in the sense of Lehman's order of effectiveness than α'. For this ordering, it makes sense to assume that $c(\alpha)$ is strictly increasing in α. Our main finding in Bergemann and Välimäki (2002) is that if $\widetilde{u}_j(\omega_i, \omega_{-i})$ is decreasing in ω_i for all $j \neq i$, then the VCG auction gives too low incentives for information acquisition to the individual bidders. If $\widetilde{u}_j(\omega_i, \omega_{-i})$ is increasing in ω_i for all $j \neq i$, then the individual agents have an incentive to engage in excessive information acquisition.

It should be pointed out that this result does not guarantee that all the equilibria of the information acquisition game between the individual bidders feature excessive information acquisition in the case where $\widetilde{u}_i(\omega)$ is increasing in ω_j. It is simply a local comparison of individual and social incentives for information acquisition. As such, it shows that the utilitarian optimum is not achievable, but it does not tell us definitively whether equilibrium information acquisition is excessive or not. In any case, it is clear that the best mechanisms must trade off losses at the information acquisition stage and losses at the allocation stage. In Bergemann, Shi, and Valimaki (2005), we verify that in a model with binary information acquisition decisions equilibria of the information acquisition game feature excessive information acquisition when $\widetilde{u}_i(\omega)$ is increasing in ω_j.

4.4   Dynamic Auctions

Section 4.3 dealt with static mechanisms where the information acquisition decision is taken prior to executing the mechanism. In dynamic auctions such as the ascending price auction, information about the valuations of the opponents is disclosed as the mechanism is run. As a result, the timing of information acquisition becomes a key consideration for the bidders in such auctions. One of the main insights of the papers reviewed in this section is that the dynamic auction formats may make it easier to arrive at socially optimal decisions, and they may also generate higher revenues to the seller than their static counterparts.

Compte and Jehiel (2000) compare the performance of a second-price sealed bid auction and an ascending price auction in the presence of information acquisition. They consider a private value environment in which all but one agent are privately informed about the value, but the final bidder has to pay a cost to acquire and assess her valuation for the object. The ascending auction then provides the uninformed bidder with an option to acquire information should the chances of winning as expressed by bidding and drop-out behavior of the competitor be reasonably good. They show that the ascending price auction generates a higher expected welfare than the sealed bid auction. If the number of bidders is sufficiently large, then the ascending price auction also increases the expected revenue for the seller. Compte and Jehiel (2004) use the fact that the ascending price auction offers the uninformed bidder an option value to show that if some additional information is likely to arrive in the future, then the uninformed bidder will stay in the auction even when the price has reached her expected valuation. Rezende (2005) offers a dynamic auction model in which the private information of each bidder is characterized by her initial and unbiased estimate of the value of the object and a private cost to learn the true value of the object. In an ascending price auction, each bidder observes the current price level (but not the drop-out behavior of the competing bidders) and decides if and when to acquire the additional information. It is shown that this sequential auction format is guaranteed to generate larger revenues relative to the sealed bid auction provided the number of bidders is sufficiently large. A recent paper by Cremer, Spiegel, and Zheng (2003) shows how the seller can extract the entire surplus from buyers when information is costly to acquire.[5]

The cost of acquiring information motivates the analysis of indicative bidding in Ye (2005). Commonly, the sale of assets or entire companies is conducted through a two-stage auction process. In the first stage, a large group of bidders is invited to make indicative, but non-binding offers, and in the second stage a subset of the first stage bidders is invited to make final bids for the object of sale. Ye (2005) derives the optimal auction in the presence of information or due diligence costs between the first and second stage bids.

---

[5] A complementary literature in theoretical computer science investigates mechanism design when it is costly to elicit the preference profile, see e.g., Parkes (2004). This literature emphasizes the role of proxy bidding and the use of indirect mechanisms.

4.5   Information Disclosure in Auctions

Up to this point our discussion of auctions has focused on the case where bidder i can obtain an additional signal s_i on ω_i. In the previous section, we allowed for the possibility of learning about other bidders' valuations during the auction. In some circumstances it is natural to consider also the case where other players may provide additional information to a bidder. In this section we concentrate on the case where the auctioneer has access to signals that she may reveal to the bidders. Examples of such information disclosures include allowing the bidders to inspect the object prior to the auction and providing an independent evaluation of the authenticity of a painting, etc.

While the focus in the previous sections was on the case where information is costly to acquire, a natural starting point for this section is the case where information is free. The reason for this difference is that in contrast to the previous setting, it may now be in the best interest of the auctioneer not to provide the bidders with full information even when there is no charge associated with this information release. Once the form of optimal information release has been determined, we can address the question of optimal information production by the auctioneer.

Since the discovery of the 'linkage principle' in Milgrom and Weber (1982), a lot of attention has been devoted to the question of information disclosure by an informed auctioneer. As shown by Milgrom and Weber in an affiliated values model, it is revenue enhancing for the auctioneer to disclose information publicly to the participants in a wide range of auction formats.

In the last few years, the issue of information disclosure in auctions has received a lot of attention. If the affiliated values model is asymmetric in the sense that the public information affects the bidders' valuations in a differential manner, Ganuza (2004) shows that linkage principle may fail and it may be optimal for the auctioneer to reveal her private information partially. Furthermore, Perry and Reny (1999) and Foucault and Lovo (2003) show that linkage principle does not necessarily hold in auctions with multi-dimensional signals. With independent information, Board (2005) shows that releasing information is in general revenue decreasing for second-price auctions when there are only two bidders.[6]

Starting with Mares and Harstad (2003), more general ways of communicating information to the bidders have been considered. Mares and Harstad assume that the auctioneer can commit to revealing the information to only one of the bidders. They give examples where this type of proprietary disclosure of information dominates public disclosure in terms of generating higher revenues. They also show that it may be particularly useful for the

---

[6] Ivanov (2005) considers information disclosure in the model of strategic information transmission of Crawford and Sobel (1982). As in Bergemann and Pesendorfer (2001), the principal controls the information structure, but only the agent can observe the realization of the signal. In consequence, the optimal information structure is again coarse, yet improves the ex ante welfare of the principal.

seller to release the proprietary information to bidders that are initially disadvantaged.

Information disclosure has also been studied in models with private information. For such models, the effects behind the original linkage principle are absent and the incentives for disclosing information must have a different origin. Bergemann and Pesendorfer (2001) study a model where an auctioneer chooses the form of a signal s_i to show to each bidder i. More specifically, the auctioneer chooses a general information structure S_i of Ω_i and bidder i observes signal $s_i \in S_i$ associated with a conditional probability $p(\omega_i | s_i)$. The auctioneer does not know the signal realization, but calculates its distribution from her prior distribution on Ω_i. Once bidders have their information, an optimal auction in the sense of Myerson (1981) is run. The main result of the paper is that it is in general optimal for the auctioneer to provide each bidder with a coarse partition, which reveals information only partially, and, if feasible assign asymmetric partitions. This is easily seen in a two-bidder example where $\omega_i \in \{1, 3\}$ and the prior on Ω_1 is independent of the prior on Ω_2 and $\Pr\{\omega_i = 1\} = \frac{1}{2}$ for $i \in \{1, 2\}$. By choosing $S_1 = \{\{1\}, \{3\}\}$ and $S_2 = \{\{1, 3\}\}$ and running the auction where bidder i wins if $s_1 = \{3\}$ and pays 3 and bidder 2 wins if $s_1 = \{1\}$ and pays 2. The expected revenue from this auction is $\frac{5}{2}$, which is more than the optimal revenue of 2 when no information is released or $\frac{9}{4}$ when all information is released.

In Eso and Szentes (2004), a different approach to information disclosure is adopted. Rather than giving the information for free to the potential bidders, the auctioneer sells additional information to possibly privately informed bidders. The starting point for this paper is that bidders may have some initial private information relating to their valuation for the object. In addition to this, the auctioneer possesses information that determines the total valuation. To model this, let v_i be a random variable representing the private information of bidder i and let s_i denote the signal controlled (but not observed) by the seller. The main result of the paper shows that when s_i is independent of v_i, the seller can obtain the same revenue as she could if s_i were observable to her. The mechanism that allows for this is one where the bidders pay for the right to participate in an auction whose payment and allocation rules are determined by the initial bids. Furthermore, the paper shows that it is optimal to disclose s_i to bidder i (at a cost). For the case where v_i is degenerate, the result is reminiscent of the results on optimal entry fees to auctions. The key difference to the model in Bergemann and Pesendorfer (2001) is that here the participation decision of the bidders takes place prior to observing s_i and hence the individual rationality constraints for the bidders differ across the two papers.

Cremer, Spiegel, and Zheng (2004) consider a sequentially optimal auction in which the seller incurs a cost to disclose the information to each individual bidder. They show that the optimal sequencing is similar to a symmetric information search problem after replacing true by virtual utilities. Shavell (1994) combines the study of information acquisition and disclosure in a simple auction setting. The study is motivated by a series of legal cases highlighting the tension between information acquisition and disclosure (see Kronman (1978) for the legal analysis of this joint problem). A seller owns a single good, which she offers to competing buyers. The buyers value the object identically but are uncertain about its true value. The seller can generate information about the true value of the object, but her cost of doing so is private information. The analysis distinguishes between two cases: when information has no social value and when it has social value. In the first case, the object has the same value to all buyers who value it higher than the seller, whereas in the second case, the optimal use for (or investment in) the object by the buyer will depend on its value. In the case of pure common values, it is socially wasteful to generate information. Yet, with voluntary disclosure, sellers with a low cost of producing information generate the information and disclose the value if it is above a critical value v^* and are silent if the true value is below v^*. The typical unraveling result fails as sellers with a high cost do not produce information. In consequence, the buyer interprets silence as resulting either from ignorance or from low quality. As ignorance is a possibility, an informed seller may be able to extract a value higher than v, conditional on $v < v^*$. This provides cover for the informed type and the incentive to generate information. On the other hand, if information disclosure is mandatory, the seller follows the efficient policy and always acquires information at the socially optimal rate, and therefore acquires no information in the case of pure common values.

The issue of disclosure is of course also relevant in principal-agent models. Lewis and Sappington (1994) consider an optimal monopoly pricing model with incomplete information. The seller can choose how much information, which improves their estimate about their taste for the products, to disclose to the buyers. They show that typically the optimal release of information is either not to release any information or to release the maximal amount of information. In Lewis and Sappington (1994), the informative signal is private information to the buyer and not observable by the seller. Johnson and Myatt (2006) model advertising as the disclosure of information and analyze the optimal level of advertising in the context of an optimal monopoly pricing problem. Ottaviani and Prat (2001) show in an affiliated value model of monopoly pricing and public disclosure of the signal, that the principal is always better off by committing to disclose any affiliated signal publicly. This result is an extension of the linkage principle from auction models to monopoly pricing models.

4.6   Information and Privacy

A more implicit source of information acquisition arises in repeated interactions with private information. Consider the relationship of a customer with one or more suppliers. If her willingness to pay for the current transaction provides some information regarding her future purchases, then the optimal selling policy today may be affected by considerations about the future value of the relationship. A series of recent papers analyzes these issues, partly motivated by discussion about the role of privacy in electronic retailing. Acquisti and Varian

(2005) suggest a two period model in which a single customer purchases repeatedly from a single seller and analyze the optimal pricing policy of the seller. With forward looking buyers and perfectly correlated willingness to pay across the two periods the optimal pricing policy is a sequence of static prices, reminiscent of the analysis of the ratchet effect (see Freixas, Guesnerie, and Tirole (1985)). However, if the buyer displays some myopia, then dynamic pricing, taking into account past purchase decision, is optimal even under full commitment. Taylor (2002) also considers a two period model but with different suppliers in every period. The customer's willingness to pay is positively, but not perfectly correlated, and the initial supplier can sell the transaction information to future suppliers. The paper considers two different regimes regarding the transmission of information, an anonymity and a recognition regime. In line with the ratchet effect, it is shown that forward looking buyers prefer the anonymity regime, but with some myopia, the customer recognition regime and the resulting dynamic pricing may be preferred by customers and sellers. Calzolari and Pavan (2005) consider a two period model in which a single customer interacts sequentially with two different sellers. The buyer's willingness to pay for the two goods is perfectly correlated. The focus of the paper is on the optimal disclosure policy of the firms, in particular whether the first firm should be allowed to sell the transaction information to the second firm. Calzolari and Pavan (2005) show that if the goods are complements then the optimal disclosure policy is to provide full information. If the goods are substitutes, then the optimal information policy is non-disclosure.

In an earlier paper, Rothkopf, Teisberg, and Kahn (1991) argued that the advantage of privacy protection conferred by the English auction is one reason why the Vickrey auction is adopted less frequently in practice than might have been expected from its multitude of theoretical advantages. If the true valuation of the winning bidder is revealed in the bidding process, this may open the door for opportunistic behavior by the seller or by third parties. If bidders have such a fear, it may no longer be in their best interest to bid their valuation in the Vickrey auction. In the English auction, only the valuation of the losing bidders can be inferred. As the winning bidders maintain (at least partially) their private information, there is less reason to distort bidding behavior.

5 ROBUSTNESS

In the first part of the survey, we emphasized the role of endogenous information for the design and the performance of mechanisms. In the second part of the survey, we report when and how mechanisms can achieve their objective even if the planner has little information about the agents' beliefs about each other. As we have seen in the second motivating example, acquiring information about other bidders naturally gives rise to type spaces where the players' own payoffs do not give a sufficient description of the strategic environment, but where one must account for higher order beliefs as well. The main task here is to identify which properties of the mechanism guarantee that the mechanism is robust to strategic uncertainty and hence large type spaces.

The discussion of robustness is an old theme in the mechanism design literature. Hurwicz (1972) discussed the need for "nonparametric" mechanisms (independent of parameters of the model). Wilson (1985) states that a desirable property of a trading rule is that it "does not rely on features of the agents' common knowledge, such as their probability assessments." Dasgupta and Maskin (2000) "seek auction rules that are independent of the details – such as functional forms or distribution of signals – of any particular application and that work well in a broad range of circumstances."

5.1   Wilson Doctrine

> Game theory has a great advantage in explicitly analyzing the consequences of trading rules that presumably are really common knowledge; it is deficient to the extent it assumes other features to be common knowledge, such as one player's probability assessment about another's preferences or information.

> I foresee the progress of game theory as depending on successive reductions in the base of common knowledge required to conduct useful analyses of practical problems. Only by repeated weakening of common knowledge assumptions will the theory approximate reality. Robert Wilson (1987)

Our starting point is the influential formulation of robustness due to Robert Wilson. Wilson emphasized that academic mechanism designers were tempted to assume too much common knowledge information among the players, and suggested that more robust conclusions would arise as researchers were able to relax those common knowledge assumptions. He suggested that the problem is that we make too many implicit common knowledge assumptions in our description of the planner's problem. A possible modeling strategy therefore is to first make *explicit* the *implicit common knowledge* assumptions and then weaken them. The approach to modeling incomplete information introduced by Harsanyi (1967–68) and formalized by Mertens and Zamir (1985) is ideally suited to this task. Harsanyi argued that by allowing an agent's type to include her beliefs about the strategic environment, her beliefs about other agents' beliefs, and so on, any environment of incomplete information could be captured by a type space. With this sufficiently large type space, the universal type space, it is true that there is common knowledge among the agents of each agent's set of possible types and each type's beliefs over the types of other agents.

However, as a practical matter, applied economic analysis tends to assume much smaller type spaces than the universal type space, and yet *maintains* the assumption that there is common knowledge among the agents of each agent's type space and each type's beliefs over the types of other agents. An important early paper by Neeman (2004) showed how rich type spaces can be used to relax implicit common knowledge assumptions in a mechanism design context. In particular, he considered a model of surplus extraction as Cremer and McLean (1985) and showed how rich type spaces may lead to a failure of the surplus extraction result. Heifetz and Neeman (2006) strengthen this insight and show that generic priors do not permit full surplus extraction. We shall shortly see further instances in which the small type space assumption imposes very substantive restrictions.

5.2   Robust Mechanism Design

In order to accommodate a planner who knows little about the agents' beliefs about other agents' types, a recent literature has looked at mechanisms that implement the social choice correspondence in *ex post equilibrium*. Bergemann and Morris (2005c) consider a situation where each player has one of a set of possible payoff types, and the social planner seeks to implement a social choice objective mapping payoff type profiles to sets of acceptable outcomes. They are interested in partial implementation – i.e., whether truthtelling in the direct mechanism is consistent with the social choice correspondence. The usual approach to this would be to assume a commonly known prior on the payoff types. Partial implementability is then equivalent to Bayesian incentive compatibility in the direct mechanism. Bergemann and Morris (2005c) ask instead when it is possible to implement the social choice correspondence in equilibrium, whatever the players' beliefs and higher order beliefs about other players' types.

Holding fixed the payoff environment, one can construct many type spaces where an agent's type specifies both her payoff type and her belief about other agents' types, as we illustrated in the introductory example. Crucially, there may be many types of an agent with the same payoff type. Intuitively, the larger the type space, the harder it is to implement the social choice objective, as there are more incentive constraints to be satisfied, and so the more "robust" the resulting mechanism is. The smallest type space is the *payoff type space* where the possible types of each agent are equal to the set of payoff types and a common knowledge prior over this type space is assumed. This is the canonical type space in the mechanism design literature. The largest type space is the union of all possible type spaces that could have arisen from the payoff environment. This is in many circumstances equivalent to working with a *universal type space* in the sense of Mertens and Zamir (1985).[7] There are many type spaces in between the payoff type space and the universal type space that are also of interest. While maintaining that the above payoff environment is common knowledge, one would like to allow the agents to have all possible beliefs and higher order beliefs about their types. A flexible framework for modeling such

---

[7] Yet, Bergemann and Morris (2001) and Battigalli and Siniscalchi (2003b) emphasize that type spaces may allow for more correlation than is captured in the belief hierarchies of types as in Mertens and Zamir (1985). More precisely, identifying types that have identical hierarchies may lead to a loss of information. Dekel, Fudenberg, and Morris (2005) and Ely and Peski (2006) propose interim rationalizability as a solution concept under which all type spaces that have the same hierarchies of beliefs also have the same interim rationalizable outcomes.

beliefs and higher order beliefs are "type spaces."A type space is a collection

$$\mathcal{T} = \left(T_i, \widehat{\theta}_i, \widehat{\pi}_i\right)_{i=1}^I.$$

Agent i's *type* is $t_i \in T_i$. The type of agent i must include a description of her payoff type. Thus there is a function

$$\widehat{\theta}_i : T_i \to \Delta\left(\Theta_i\right),$$

with $\widehat{\theta}_i(t_i)$ being the probability distribution of agent i's *payoff type* when her type is t_i. In particular, agent i might be uncertain about her own payoff type. A type of agent i must also include a description of her beliefs about the types of the other agents. Write $\Delta(Z)$ for the space of probability measures on the Borel field of a measurable space Z. The belief of type t_i of agent i is a function

$$\widehat{\pi}_i : T_i \to \Delta\left(T_{-i}\right),$$

with $\widehat{\pi}_i[t_i]$ being agent i's *beliefs* when her type is t_i. Thus $\widehat{\pi}_i(E)[t_i]$ is the probability that type t_i of agent i assigns to other agents' types, t_{-i}, being an element of a measurable set $E \subseteq T_{-i}$.

A type space $\mathcal{T}$ is a *payoff type space* if each $T_i = \Theta_i$ and each $\widehat{\theta}_i$ is the identity map. Type space $\mathcal{T}$ is *finite* if each T_i is finite. Finite type space $\mathcal{T}$ has *full support* if $\widehat{\pi}_i(t_i)[t_{-i}] > 0$ for all i and t. Finite type space $\mathcal{T}$ satisfies the *common prior assumption* (with prior p) if there exists $p \in \Delta(\mathcal{T})$ such that

$$\sum_{t_{-i} \in T_{-i}} p(t_i, t_{-i}) > 0 \text{ for all } i \text{ and } t_i$$

and

$$\widehat{\pi}_i(t_{-i})[t_i] = \frac{p(t_i, t_{-i})}{\sum_{t'_{-i} \in T_{-i}} p\left(t_i, t'_{-i}\right)}.$$

Definition 3   *A direct mechanism $f : T \to Y$ is interim incentive compatible on type space $\mathcal{T}$ if*

$$\int_{t_{-i} \in T_{-i}} u_i \left(f(t_i, t_{-i}), \widehat{\theta}(t_i, t_{-i})\right) d\widehat{\pi}_i(t_i)$$

$$\geq \int_{t_{-i} \in T_{-i}} u_i \left(f\left(t'_i, t_{-i}\right), \widehat{\theta}(t_i, t_{-i})\right) d\widehat{\pi}_i(t_i)$$

for all i, $t \in T$ and $t'_i \in T_i$.

The notion of interim incentive compatibility is often referred to as Bayesian incentive compatibility. We use the former terminology as there need not be a common prior on the type space. It should be emphasized that a direct mechanism f can prescribe varying allocations for a given payoff profile θ as different types, t and t', may have an identical payoff profile $\theta = \widehat{\theta}(t) = \widehat{\theta}(t')$. By inspection of the ex post incentive constraints in Definition 1, ex post incentive compatibility is sufficient for interim incentive compatibility, but is it necessary?

Bergemann and Morris (2005c) show that interim incentive compatibility on all common prior payoff type spaces is equivalent to ex post incentive compatibility in separable environments. An environment is called *separable* if the outcome space has a common component and a private value component for each agent. Each agent cares only about the common component and her own private component. The social choice correspondence picks a unique element from the common component and has a product structure over all components. In separable environments, interim implementation on all common prior payoff type spaces implies ex post implementation. Whenever the social choice correspondence is a function, the environment has a separable representation since the private value components can be made degenerate. A second leading example of a separable environment is the problem of choosing an allocation when arbitrary transfers are allowed and agents have quasi-linear utility. If the allocation choice is a function but the planner does not care about the level and distribution of transfers, then the environment is separable.

This result provides a strong foundation for using ex post equilibrium as a solution concept in separable environments. Since ex post implementation implies interim implementation on all type spaces (with or without the common prior or the payoff type restrictions), it also shows the equivalence between ex post implementation and interim implementation on all type spaces. To the extent that the mechanisms required for ex post implementation are simpler than the mechanisms required for Bayesian implementation, these results contribute to the literature on detail free implementation and the "Wilson doctrine."

For separable environments, the restriction to payoff type spaces is not important. But interestingly, outside of separable environments the restriction matters. Bergemann and Morris (2005c) report a simple example of a two agent quasi-linear environment where the balanced budget requirement holds: Transfers must add up to zero. In this example, ex post implementation and interim implementation on all type spaces are both impossible, but interim implementation on all common prior payoff type spaces is possible. The quasi-linear environments with budget balance is a leading example of an economic nonseparable environment. With two agents, there is an equivalence between ex post implementation and interim implementation on all type spaces. With at most two payoff types for each agent, there is the stronger equivalence between ex post implementation and interim implementation on all payoff type spaces. But with three or more agents with three or more types, equivalence between ex post implementation and interim implementation on all type spaces breaks down.

For other approaches to formalizing robust mechanism design, see Chung and Ely (2003), Duggan and Roberts (1997), Eliaz (2002), Hagerty and Rogerson (1987), and Lopomo (1998, 2000), and Auriol and Gary-Bobo (2005).

Chung and Ely (2004) consider the optimal auction with private values in large type spaces. They show that a dominant strategy mechanism may achieve a higher payoff than any Bayesian equilibrium mechanism, provided that the type space is large. The intuition is that for any given mechanism there may exist a type space that exposes weaknesses in the incentive constraints and leads to an inferior expected revenue result in comparison to a dominant strategy mechanism in which the agents are only asked to report their payoff type, but not to report any belief type.

5.3   Robust Implementation

The revelation principle only establishes that the direct mechanism has *an* equilibrium that achieves the social choice function. In general, there may be other equilibria that deliver undesirable outcomes. In the spirit of the "Wilson doctrine," it is then natural to look for implementation results that are *robust* to different assumptions about what players do or do not know about other agents' types. While the possibility of multiple equilibria seems relevant for practical mechanism design problems, the theoretical literature has not resulted in many practical insights (with a few recent exceptions such as Ausubel and Milgrom (2005) and Yokoo, Sakurai, and Matsubara (2004)).

In light of the earlier results on robust incentive compatibility, it is natural to ask whether implementation in Bayesian equilibrium for all possible higher order beliefs is equivalent to ex post implementation in the payoff type space. Bergemann and Morris (2005a) investigate the conditions required for ex post implementation, i.e., they ask whether it is the case that all ex post equilibria deliver outcomes in the social choice correspondence. The task for the designer, who does not know the agents' types, is to choose a mechanism such that in *every* equilibrium of the mechanism, agents' play of the game results in the outcome specified by the social choice objective at every type profile.

The complete information implementation literature (see Maskin (1999)) makes the assumption of common knowledge of preferences, the Bayesian implementation literature (see Postlewaite and Schmeidler (1986), Palfrey and Srivastava (1989), and Jackson (1991)) makes the assumption that there is common knowledge of a prior on a fixed set of types. This assumption is unlikely to be valid for practical market designers, and it imposes a substantive constraint when viewed as a restriction on all possible beliefs and higher order beliefs. Bergemann and Morris (2005b) show that robust implementation is a more stringent requirement than ex post implementation. While the incentive compatibility constraints for this problem are the same as for the ex post implementation problem,[8] the resulting "robust monotonicity" condition (equivalent to Bayesian monotonicity on all type spaces) is strictly stronger than ex post monotonicity (and Maskin monotonicity). The resulting robust monotonicity

---

[8] This follows from results in Bergemann and Morris (2005c).

notions provide full implementation counterparts to the robust mechanism design (i.e., partial implementation) questions discussed earlier. In particular, they show that interim implementation on all type spaces is possible if and only if it is possible to implement the social choice function using an iterative deletion procedure. The observation about iterative deletion illustrates a general point well known from the literature on epistemic foundations of game theory (e.g., Brandenburger and Dekel (1987), Battigalli and Siniscalchi (2003b)): Equilibrium solution concepts only have bite if we make strong assumptions about type spaces, i.e., we assume small type spaces where the common prior assumption holds.

By exploiting the equivalence between robust and iterative implementation, Bergemann and Morris (2005b) obtain necessary and sufficient conditions for robust implementation in general environments. The necessity argument is conceptually novel, exploiting the iterative characterization. The necessary conditions for robust implementation are ex post incentive compatibility of the social choice function and a condition – *robust monotonicity* – that is equivalent to requiring interim monotonicity on every type space. The robust monotonicity condition is very strong and implies both Maskin monotonicity and ex post monotonicity conditions (but is strictly weaker than dominant strategies). As an added benefit, the robust implementation analysis removes the frequent gap between pure and mixed strategy implementation in the literature. The iterative characterization comes with the additional benefit that tight implementation results can be proved via a fixed point of a contraction mapping.

An important paper of Chung and Ely (2001) analyzes the single (and multi-unit) auction with interdependent valuations with dominance solvability (elimination of weakly rather than strictly dominated actions). In a linear and symmetric setting, they reported sufficient conditions for direct implementation that coincide with the ones derived in Bergemann and Morris (2005b). In the environment with linear aggregation, under strict incentive compatibility, the basic insight extends from the single unit auction model to general allocations models, with elimination of strictly dominated actions only (thus Chung and Ely (2001) require deletion of weakly dominated strategies only because incentive constraints are weak). By comparing the conditions for ex post and robust implementation, it becomes apparent that robust implementation typically imposes additional constraints on the allocation problem.

5.4   Local Robustness

The approach of robustness in the above literature requires that a mechanism could be implemented for all possible types spaces. This robustness criterion is therefore clearly very demanding and it is plausible to investigate weaker local robustness criteria. In addition, the approach above requires that the allocation problem can be defined independent of the beliefs of the designer and the agents. Yet there are cases such as revenue maximizing mechanism (e.g., optimal pricing and optimal auction), that depend on the beliefs of the designer.

Bergemann and Schlag (2005) investigate a robust version of the classic problem of optimal monopoly pricing with incomplete information. The robust version of the problem is distinct in two aspects. First, instead of a given true distribution of valuations, the seller only knows that the true distribution is in a neighborhood of a given model distribution. The enlargement of the set of possible priors represents model misspecification. Second, the objective function of the seller is formulated as a regret minimization rather than a revenue maximization problem. The regret is the difference between the actual valuation of the buyer for the object and the actual revenue obtained by the seller. The regret of the seller can be positive for two reasons: (i) the buyer has a low valuation relative to the price and hence does not purchase the object, or (ii) she has a high valuation relative to the price and hence the seller could have obtained a higher revenue. For a given neighborhood of possible distributions, they then characterize the pricing policy that minimizes maximal regret. They describe how the robust policies depend on the model distribution and the size of the risk as represented by the size of the neighborhood.

Segal (2003) also considers optimal pricing with unknown demand. In his model, the seller does not know the distribution from which the buyers' valuations are drawn. However, she knows that the valuation of each buyer represents an independent draw from the same distribution. He then suggests an optimal pricing mechanism in which the seller offers individualized prices. The price of individual i however only depends on the information she received from all customers but i. By making the price independent of the report of agent i, the equilibrium strategy of each bidder is an ex post equilibrium strategy. Similarly, Baliga and Vohra (2003) consider trading models when buyers and sellers do not know the distribution of valuations. They consider dynamic and adaptive mechanism with and without intermediaries. They show that as the number of traders becomes large, the adaptive mechanism achieves the same expected revenue as if the seller were to know the true distribution of the demand. Goldberg, Hartline, and Wright (2001) consider a similar problem, but in contrast do not even make the i.i.d. assumption about the valuations of the customers. Without any Bayesian information, they derive the optimal selling mechanism under the competitive ratio. In other words, they maximize the worst case revenue relative to the optimal revenue, which could be obtained if the seller were to know the true valuations of the buyers. The worst case analysis and the notion of competitiveness is central in many optimal design problems analyzed in computer science (see the recent survey to online design problems by Borodin and El-Yaniv (1998)). In auction theory, Neeman (2003) analyzes the competitiveness of the second-price auction. A recent article by Prasad (2003) presents negative result, and in particular shows that the standard optimal pricing policy of the monopolist is not robust to small model misspecifications.

5.5   Rationalizability and Robustness

An alternative approach of allowing richer beliefs and strategic uncertainty into standard mechanism design is to relax the solution concept from equilibrium to rationalizability, an approach pursued by Battigalli and Siniscalchi (2003a) and Dekel and Wolinsky (2003). Battigalli and Siniscalchi (2003a) consider the standard private value auction with a continuum of valuations and bids. They show that any positive bid up to some level above the Nash equilibrium is rationalizable. In contrast, Dekel and Wolinsky (2003) consider a setup with a finite number of valuations and bids, but allow for some degree of affiliation. They show that as the number of bidders increases, the set of rationalizable bids converges to the bid closest to the true valuation. Similarly Cho (2005) considers the first price auction in a model with affiliated values, and analyzes rationalizable strategies after imposing the additional restriction that all feasible bidding strategies have to be monotone. He shows that the winning bid in the set of rationalizable bidding strategies converges to the competitive equilibrium price as the number of bidder increases. Cho (2004) extends the rationalizability analysis to large uniform and double price auctions.

5.6   Strategic Uncertainty in Auction Theory

We finally discuss how rich type spaces and strategic uncertainty modify and change central results in auction theory. Fang and Morris (2005) illustrate the role of large type spaces for the revenue equivalence theorem. They analyze a model of independent private values with two bidders. However, each bidder receives a two-dimensional signal, the first element is her private valuation (the valuation type) and the second element is a noisy signal about the valuation of her competitor (the information type). The addition of the second signal enriches the strategic information of each bidder but obviously reduces common knowledge among bidders and auctioneer. The model is thus a natural generalization of the discrete type framework offered in the motivating example. In this simple setting, they compare first and second price auctions and conclude that the revenue equivalence theorem fails and that no definite revenue ranking exists with multidimensional signals, even though the setting remains a private value model. Naturally, the additional strategic information does not change the bidding strategy in the second price auction, but affects the bidding strategy in the first price auction. The additional information can have two distinct effects on the bidding strategy. Suppose that bidder 1 receives a signal that bidder 2 is likely to have a similar valuation. Relative to her bidding strategy without the strategic information, she now has essentially two choices. She can either increase her bid to improve her chances of winning, or she can lower her bid, and focus on winning against lower valuation types of her opponent. The optimal response to the strategic information will depend on the informativeness of the signal and may go either way. In consequence, bidding may become more fierce or more subdued, leaving the revenue ranking open to go in either direction. The multi-dimensional private value model is closely related to the affiliated value model of Wilson (1977) and Milgrom and Weber (1982). Yet, in Fang and Morris (2005), the belief of bidder 1 about bidder 2 depends directly on the value type of bidder 2 rather than the value type of bidder 1 as in the affiliated value model.

Kim and Che (2004) analyze the role of strategic information in a similar setting. In an independent private value setting with I bidders, a subset of bidders observe the valuation of each agent in its subset but no additional information about the agents in the complementary set. They also find that the revenue equivalence theorem fails and establish that a second price auction generates a higher expected value than the first price auction. Andreoni, Che, and Kim (2005) pursue an experimental study of this setup and largely confirm the theoretical predictions. Ye (2004) considers an auction with entry. Each bidder has to incur a cost before learning her own valuation. Yet, in contrast to earlier work, each bidder will also receive some noisy information about the value of the competing bidders. If the information potentially available to the bidders after entry is sufficiently rich, then he shows that the Vickrey auction is the only optimal sealed bid auction. Finally a recent paper by Feinberg and Skrypacz (2005) pursues the logic of multi-dimensional types, in particular the separation between payoff types and belief types in the context of bargaining under incomplete information.

6 CONCLUSION

In this survey we emphasized the role of information for mechanism design. First, we discussed an emerging literature on the role of endogenous information for the design and the efficiency of the relevant mechanism. Second, we argued that in the presence of endogenous information, the robustness of the mechanism of the type space becomes a natural desideratum. We then discussed some recent approaches to robust mechanism design and implementation.

During our discussion of the recent contributions, we have indicated that many questions remain wide open, and in fact the current research poses and creates many new questions. We end this survey by collecting a few of them.

As we consider the role of information acquisition, it is natural to consider dynamic mechanisms, particularly those in which information is acquired sequentially. Recent work by Compte and Jehiel (2000) showed that the ascending price auction, improves upon the static second price auction by allowing for contingent information acquisition. Yet in the ascending price auction, information arrives in a particular way. The estimated expected value of the competing bidder is increasing over time. It is then natural to ask whether a descending price auction might sometimes be more favorable for information acquisition than an ascending price auction. The advantage of a descending price auction is that bidders receive over time information that their bids are more likely to be competitive, otherwise the clock would have been stopped by a competitor. Interestingly, Klemperer (2002) suggests a sequential combination of English and Dutch auction to enhance entry and deter collusion. A combination of English and Dutch auction could also be optimal to generate information and hence competition among the bidders. As many bidding processes are inherently dynamical in nature, we believe that there are further theoretical as well as practical reasons to investigate information acquisition in dynamic settings. Bidding in a takeover contest and negotiating the terms for a business proposal are obvious examples. The dynamic nature of the bidding process here reflects the actual fact finding about the proposed outcomes and in addition determines the strategic positions based on the information currently at hand.

We saw that the ex post efficient mechanisms may lead to excessive information acquisition in typical auction settings. We can then ask how the ex post efficient mechanism should be modified to achieve a second best solution. There are two natural modifications. The slope of the probability that an agent gets the object could be reduced until information acquisition in equilibrium coincides with the social equilibrium. With a completely randomized decision to allocate the object, the agent will not have any incentives to acquire information. Thus if we change the probability from efficient to completely inefficient, we eventually correct the incentives to acquire information. For the given interim probability distribution, we can then identify the allocation that leads to the lowest loss in terms of efficiency.

In the area of robustness, much of the recent work focused on testing the robustness of a social choice function or mechanism, which can be identified independent of the beliefs of the agents and the designer; the problem of finding an efficient allocation is a classical example. In many relevant design problems, the beliefs of the designer and the agents enter into the determination of the mechanism, the leading example here is seller maximizing revenue from an optimal auction. Formulating the robust mechanism design problem for this class of problems becomes conceptually more difficult. In order to maximize revenue, the designer must be endowed with some beliefs over the agents' types. To formalize a notion of robustness, one ought to consider a set of possible beliefs.

Bergemann and Morris (2005d) suggest one possible way to proceed by maintaining the assumption that the principal is certain about the true distribution over payoff types, but allow the principal to be uncertain about agents' beliefs and higher order beliefs about other agents' types. For a given prior distribution over payoff types, they try to find (i) the optimal mechanism for a given type space, and (ii) the worst case type space which minimizes the revenue of the designer. Even though the distribution over payoff types is kept constant at a given prior, the strategic uncertainty severely limits the designer to extract the surplus. They show that in many instances, the revenue of the auctioneer can be reduced to the level which could be obtained in the ex post equilibrium of the game.

We discussed in some detail the role of large type spaces for implementation. If the agents possess large amounts of private information relative to the designer, then their ability to coordinate actions ought to increase and hence the equilibrium multiplicity problem may become severe. If the agents succeed in coordinating their actions on equilibrium play, which is undesirable from the principal's point of view, then the issue of multiplicity is essentially an issue of collusion among the agents. It is thus conceivable that a common framework and characterization techniques to understand robustness, equilibrium multiplicity, and collusion in the context of mechanism design might emerge as one result of this research on large type spaces.

ACKNOWLEDGMENTS

This study was partially supported by the National Science Foundation Grants CNS 0428422 and SES 0518929 and Yrjö Jahnsson's Foundation. We would like to thank Xianwen Shi and Rahul Deb for excellent research assistance. Bergemann would like to acknowledge joint research with Stephen Morris in the area of this survey. We would like to thank our discussant, Roger Myerson, and the co-editor, Torsten Persson for their insightful comments and editorial advice. We thank Sven DeVries, Dino Gerardi, and Michael Riordan for helpful conversations.

References

ACQUISTI, A., AND H. VARIAN (2005): "Conditioning Prices on Purchase History," *Marketing Science*, 24, 367–381.

AGHION, P., AND J. TIROLE (1997): "Formal and Real Authority in Organizations," *Journal of Political Economy*, 1–29.

ANDREONI, J., Y.-K. CHE, AND J. KIM (2005): "Asymmetric Information About Rivals' Types in Standard Auctions: An Experiment," Discussion paper, University of Wisconsin and University of Southern California.

AURIOL, E., AND R. GARY-BOBO (2005): "On Robust Constitution Design," Discussion paper, University of Poulouse and University of Paris 1.

AUSTEN-SMITH, D., AND J. BANKS (1996): "Information Aggregation, Rationality, and the Condorcet Jury Theorem," *American Political Science Review*, 90, 34–45.

AUSUBEL, L. M., AND P. MILGROM (2005): "The Lovely But Lonely Vickrey Auction," in *Combinatorial Auctions*, ed. by P. Cramton, R. Steinberg, and Y. Shoham.

BALIGA, S., AND R. VOHRA (2003): "Market Research and Market Design," *Advances in Theoretical Economics*, 3.

BARON, D., AND R. MYERSON (1982): "Regulating a Monopolist with Unknown Costs," *Econometrica*, 50, 911–930.

BATTIGALLI, P., AND M. SINISCALCHI (2003a): "Rationalizable Bidding in First Price Auctions," *Games and Economic Behavior*, 45, 38–72.

——— (2003b): "Rationalization and Incomplete Information," *Advances in Theoretical Economics*, 3, Article 3.

BERGEMANN, D., AND S. MORRIS (2001): "Robust Mechanism Design," Cowles Foundation, Yale University.

——— (2005a): "Ex Post Implementation," Discussion Paper 1502, Cowles Foundation for Research in Economics, Yale University.

——— (2005b): "Robust Implementation: The Role of Large Type Spaces," Discussion Paper 1519, Cowles Foundation, Yale University.

——— (2005c): "Robust Mechanism Design," *Econometrica*, 73, 1771–1813.

——— (2005d): "Robust Revenue Maximization," Discussion Paper, Yale University and Princeton University.

BERGEMANN, D., AND W. PESENDORFER (2001): "Information Structures in Optimal Auctions," Cowles Foundation Discussion Paper 1323, Yale University.

BERGEMANN, D., AND K. SCHLAG (2005): "Robust Monopoly Pricing: The Case of Regret," Discussion Paper 1527, Yale University and European University Institute.

BERGEMANN, D., X. SHI, AND J. VÄLIMÄKI (2005): "Information Acquisition in Large Markets," Discussion Paper, Yale University and University of Helsinki.

BERGEMANN, D., AND J. VÄLIMÄKI (2002): "Information Acquisition and Efficient Mechanism Design," Econometrica, 70, 1007–1033.

BIKHCHANDANI, S. (2005): "The Limits of Ex Post Implementation Revisited," Discussion Paper, University of California at Los Angeles.

BLACK, D. (1958): The Theory of Committees and Elections. Cambridge University Press, Cambridge.

BOARD, S. (2005): "Revealing Information in Auctions: The Efficiency Effect," Discussion Paper, University of Toronto.

BORODIN, A., AND R. EL-YANIV (1998): Online Computation and Competitive Analysis. Cambridge University Press, Cambridge.

BRANDENBURGER, A., AND E. DEKEL (1987): "Rationalizability and Correlated Equilibria," Econometrica, 55, 1391–1402.

CAI, H. (2003): "Optimal Committee Design with Heterogeneous Preferences," Discussion Paper, UCLA.

CALZOLARI, G., AND A. PAVAN (2005): "On the Optimality of Privacy in Sequential Contracting," Journal of Economic Theory.

CHO, I. (2004): "Rationalizability and Monotonicity in Large Uniform Price and Double Auctions," Discussion Paper, University of Illinois at Urbana-Champaign.

——— (2005): "Monotonicity and Rationalizability in Large First Price Auction," Review of Economic Studies, forthcoming.

CHUNG, K.-S., AND J. ELY (2003): "Implementation with Near-Complete Information," Econometrica, 71, 857–871.

CHUNG, K.-S., AND J. C. ELY (2001): "Efficient and Dominance Solvable Auctions with Interdependent Valuations," Discussion Paper, Northwestern University.

——— (2004): "Foundations of Dominant Strategy Mechanisms," Discussion Paper, Northwestern University.

COMPTE, O., AND P. JEHIEL (2000): "On the Virtues of the Ascending Price Auction: New Insights in the Private Value Setting," Discussion Paper, CERAS-ENPC.

——— (2004): "The Wait and See Option in Ascending Auctions," Journal of the European Economic Association, 2, 494–503.

CRAWFORD, V., AND J. SOBEL (1982): "Strategic Information Transmission," Econometrica, 50, 1431–1452.

CREMER, J., AND F. KHALIL (1992): "Gathering Information Before Signing a Contract," American Economic Review, 82, 566–578.

CREMER, J., F. KHALIL, AND J.-C. ROCHET (1998a): "Contracts and Productive Information Gathering," Games and Economic Behavior, 25, 174–193.

——— (1998b): "Strategic Information Gathering Before a Contract is Offered," Journal of Economic Theory, 81, 163–200.

CREMER, J., AND R. MCLEAN (1985): "Optimal Selling Strategies Under Uncertainty for a Discriminating Monopolist When Demands Are Interdependent," Econometrica, 53, 345–361.

CREMER, J., Y. SPIEGEL, AND C. ZHENG (2003): "Optimal Selling Mechanisms with Costly Information Aquisition," Discussion Paper, Northwestern University.

———(2004): "Optimal Search Auctions," Discussion Paper, Northwestern University.

DASGUPTA, P., AND E. MASKIN (2000): "Efficient Auctions," *Quarterly Journal of Economics*, 115, 341–388.

DEKEL, E., D. FUDENBERG, AND S. MORRIS (2005): "Interim Rationalizability," Discussion Paper, Tel-Aviv University, Harvard University, and Yale University.

DEKEL, E., AND A. WOLINSKY (2003): "Rationalizable Outcomes of Large Independent Private-Value First Price Discrete Auctions," *Games and Economic Behavior*, 43, 175–188.

DEMSKI, J., AND D. SAPPINGTON (1987): "Delegated Expertise," *Journal of Accounting Research*, 25, 288–310.

DUGGAN, J., AND J. ROBERTS (1997): "Robust Implementation," Mimeo, University of Rochester.

ELIAZ, K. (2002): "Fault Tolerant Implementation," *Review of Economic Studies*, 69, 589–610.

ELY, J. C., AND M. PESKI (2006): "Hierarchies of Belief and Interim Rationalizability," *Theoretical Economics*, 1.

ESO, P., AND B. SZENTES (2004): "Optimal Information Disclosure in Auctions and the Handicap Auction," Discussion Paper, Northwestern University and University of Chicago.

FANG, H., AND S. MORRIS (2005): "Multidimensional Private Value Auctions," *Journal of Economic Theory*, forthcoming.

FEDDERSEN, T., AND W. PESENDORFER (1998): "Convicting the Innocent: The Inferiority of Unanimous Jury Verdicts under Strategic Voting," *American Political Science Review*, 92, 23–35.

FEINBERG, Y., AND A. SKRYPACZ (2005): "Uncertainty About Uncertainty and Delay in Bargaining," *Econometrica*, 73, 69–91.

FOUCAULT, T., AND S. LOVO (2003): "Linkage Principle, Multi-Dimensional Signals and Blind Auctions," Discussion Paper, HEC School of Management.

FREIXAS, X., R. GUESNERIE, AND J. TIROLE (1985): "Planning under Incomplete Information and the Ratchet Effect," *Review of Economic Studies*, 52, 173–191.

FRENCH, K., AND R. MCCORMICK (1984): "Selaed Bids, Sunk Costs, and the Process of Competition," *Journal of Business*, 57, 417–441.

GANUZA, J.-J. (2004): "Ignorance Promotes Competition: An Auction Model of Endogeneous Private Valuation," *RAND Journal of Economics*, 35.

GERARDI, D., AND L. YARIV (2005): "Information Acquisition in Committees," *Games and Economic Behavior*, forthcoming.

GERSHKOV, A., AND B. SZENTES (2004): "Optimal Voting Scheme with Costly Information Aquisition," Discussion Paper, University of Chicago.

GOLDBERG, A., J. HARTLINE, AND A. WRIGHT (2001): "Competitive Auctions and Digital Goods," in *12th Annual ACM-SIAM Symposium on Discrete Algorithms*, pp. 735–744, Washington, D.C. ACM-SIAM.

HAGERTY, K., AND W. ROGERSON (1987): "Robust Trading Mechanisms," *Journal of Economic Theory*, 42, 94–107.

HARSANYI, J. (1967–68): "Games with Incomplete Information Played by 'Bayesian' Players," *Management Science*, 14, 159–189, 320–334, 485–502.

HAUSCH, D., AND L. LI (1991): "Private Values Auctions with Endogenous Information: Revenue Equivalence and Non-Equivalence," University of Wisconsin-Madison.

HEIFETZ, A., AND Z. NEEMAN (2006): "On the Generic (Im)Possibility of Full Surplus Extraction in Mechanism Design," *Econometrica*.

HOLMSTRÖM, B., AND R. MYERSON (1983): "Efficient and Durable Decision Rules with Incomplete Information," *Econometrica*, 51, 1799–1819.

HURWICZ, L. (1972): "On Informationally Decentralized Systems," in *Decisions and Organizations*, ed. by C. McGuire, and R. Radner, 297–336. North-Holland, Amsterdam.

IVANOV, M. (2005): "Optimal Strategic Communication: Can a Less Informed Expert Be More Informative," Discussion Paper, Pennsylvania State University.

JACKSON, M. (1991): "Bayesian Implementation," *Econometrica*, 59, 461–477.

——— (2003): "Efficiency and Information Aggregation in Auctions with Costly Information," *Review of Economic Design*, 8, 121–41.

JEHIEL, P., AND B. MOLDOVANU (2001): "Efficient Design with Interdependent Valuations," *Econometrica*, 69, 1237–1259.

JEHIEL, P., B. MOLDOVANU, M. MEYER-TER-VEHN, AND B. ZAME (2005): "The Limits of Ex Post Implementation," Discussion Paper, ENPC and University of Bonn.

JOHNSON, J., AND D. MYATT (2006): "On the Simple Economics of Advertising, Marketing, and Product Design," *American Economic Review*, forthcoming.

JOHNSON, R. (1979): "Auction Markets, Bid Preparation Costs and Entrance Fees," *Land Economics*, 55, 313–318.

KALAI, E. (2004): "Large Robust Games," *Econometrica*, 72, 1631–1666.

KIM, J., AND Y.-K. CHE (2004): "Asymmetric Information About Rivals' Types in Standard Auctions," *Games and Economic Behavior*, 46, 383–397.

KLEMPERER, P. (2002): "What Really Matters in Auction Design," *Journal of Economic Perspectives*, 16, 169–189.

KRONMAN, A. (1978): "Mistake, Disclosure, Information and the Law of Contracts," *Journal of Legal Studies*, 7, 1–34.

LEVIN, D., AND J. SMITH (1994): "Equilibrium in Auctions with Entry," *American Economic Review*, 84, 585–599.

LEWIS, T., AND D. SAPPINGTON (1994): "Supplying Information to Facilitate Price Discrimination," *International Economic Review*, 35, 309–327.

LI, H. (2001): "Theory of Conservatism," *Journal of Political Economy*, 109, 617–636.

LOPOMO, G. (1998): "The English Auction Is Optimal Among Simple Sequential Auctions," *Journal of Economic Theory*, 82, 144–166.

——— (2000): "Optimality and Robustness of the English Auction," *Games and Economic Behavior*, 36, 219–240.

MALCOLMSON, J. (2004): "Principal and Expert Agent," Discussion Paper 193, Oxford University.

MARES, V., AND R. HARSTAD (2003): "Private Information Revelation in Common Value Auctions," *Journal of Economic Theory*, 109, 264–282.

MARTINELLI, C. (2006): "Would Rational Voters Acquire Costly Information?," *Journal of Economic Theory*, forthcoming.

MASKIN, E. (1992): "Auctions and Privatization," in *Privatization: Symposium in Honor of Herbert Giersch*, ed. by H. Siebert, 115–136. J.C.B. Mohr, Tuebingen.

——— (1999): "Nash Equilibrium and Welfare Optimality," *Review of Economic Studies*, 66, 23–38.

MATTHEWS, S. (1977): "Information Acqusition in Competitive Bidding Process," California Institute of Technology.

———— (1984): "Information Acquisition in Discriminatory Auctions," in *Bayesian Models in Economic Theory*, ed. by M. Boyer and R. Kihlstrom, 181–207. North-Holland, Amsterdam.

MATTHEWS, S. A., AND N. PERSICO (2005): "Information Aquisition and the Excess Refund Puzzle," Discussion Paper, University of Pennsylvania.

MCAFEE, P., AND J. MCMILLAN (1987): "Auctions with Entry," *Economic Letters*, 23, 343–347.

MERTENS, J., AND S. ZAMIR (1985): "Formalization of Bayesian Analysis for Games with Incomplete Information," *International Journal of Game Theory*, 14, 1–29.

MILGROM, P. (1981): "Good News and Bad News: Representation Theorems and Applications," *Bell Journal of Economics*, 12, 380–391.

MILGROM, P., AND R. WEBER (1982): "A Theory of Auctions and Competitive Bidding," *Econometrica*, 50, 1089–1122.

MUKHOPADHAYA, K. (2003): "Jury Size and the Free Rider Problem," *Journal of Law, Economics and Organization*, 19, 24–44.

MYERSON, R. (1981): "Optimal Auction Design," *Mathematics of Operations Research*, 6, 58–73.

NEEMAN, Z. (2003): "The Effectiveness of English Auctions," *Games and Economic Behavior*, 43, 214–238.

———— (2004): "The Relevance of Private Information in Mechanism Design," *Journal of Economic Theory*, 117, 55–77.

OTTAVIANI, M., AND A. PRAT (2001): "The Value of Public Information in Monopoly," *Econometrica*, 69, 1673–1683.

PALFREY, T., AND S. SRIVASTAVA (1989): "Mechanism Design with Incomplete Information: A Solution to the Implementation Problem," *Journal of Political Economy*, 97, 668–691.

PARKES, D. (2004): "Auction Design with Costly Preference Elicitation," *Annals of Mathematics and Artificial Intelligence*, 1–38.

PERRY, M., AND P. RENY (2002): "An Ex Post Efficient Auction," *Econometrica*, 70, 1199–1212.

PERRY, M., AND P. J. RENY (1999): "On the Failure of the Linkage Principle in Multi-Unit Auctions," *Econometrica*, 67, 895–900.

PERSICO, N. (2000): "Information Acquisition in Auctions," *Econometrica*, 68, 135–148.

———— (2004): "Committee Design with Endogenous Information," *The Review of Economic Studies*, 71(1), 165–94.

POSTLEWAITE, A., AND D. SCHMEIDLER (1986): "Implementation in Differential Information Economies," *Journal of Economic Theory*, 39, 14–33.

PRASAD, K. (2003): "Non-Robustness of some Economic Models," *Topics in Theoretical Economics*, 3, 1–7.

REZENDE, L. (2005): "Mid-Auction Information Acquisition," Discussion Paper, University of Illinois.

ROGERSON, W. (1992): "Contractual Solutions to the Hold-Up Problem," *Review of Economic Studies*, 59, 777–793.

ROTHKOPF, M., T. TEISBERG, AND E. KAHN (1991): "Why Are Vickrey Auctions Rare," *Journal of Political Economy*, 98, 94–109.

SEGAL, I. (2003): "Optimal Pricing Mechanism with Unknown Demand," *American Economic Review*, 93, 509–529.

SHAVELL, S. (1994): "Acquisition and Disclosure of Information Prior to Sale," *RAND Journal of Economics*, 25, 20–36.

SMORODINSKY, R., AND M. TENNENHOLTZ (2005): "Overcoming Free Riding in Multi-Party Computations – The Anonymous Case," Discussion Paper, Technion.

STEGEMAN, M. (1996): "Participation Costs and Efficient Auctions," *Journal of Economic Theory*, 71, 228–259.

TAN, G. (1992): "Entry and R and D in Procurement Contracting," *Journal of Economic Theory*, 58, 41–60.

TAYLOR, C. (2002): "Private Demands and Demands for Privacy: Dynamic Pricing and the Market for Customer Information," *RAND Journal of Economics*, forthcoming.

WILSON, R. (1977): "A Bidding Model of Perfect Competition," *Review of Economic Studies*, 44, 511–518.

——— (1985): "Incentive Efficiency of Double Auctions," *Econometrica*, 53, 1101–16.

YE, L. (2004): "Optimal Auctions with Endogenous Entry," *Contributions to Theoretical Economics*, 4, 1–27.

——— (2005): "Indicative Bidding and a Theory of Two-Stage Auctions," Discussion Paper, Ohio State University.

YOKOO, M., Y. SAKURAI, AND S. MATSUBARA (2004): "The Effect of False-Name Bids in Combinatorial Auctions: New Fraud in Internet Auctions," *Games and Economic Behavior*, 46, 174–188.

CHAPTER 6

Communication in Economic Mechanisms*
Ilya Segal

1 INTRODUCTION

This chapter considers the problem of finding allocations that satisfy certain social goals when economic agents have private information regarding their preferences. This problem has been discussed since at least the early 20th-century debate on alternative economic mechanisms, but it has received renewed attention recently in the literature on "market design," which proposes mechanisms to solve various allocation problems of practical importance. For example, the "two-sided matching problem" arises in allocating workers across firms, students across schools, or medical interns across medical schools (Roth and Sotomayor (1990)). The "combinatorial auction problem" arises in allocating bundles of indivisible items among bidders (Cramton et al. (2006)). Both agents' preferences and social goals in these problems differ substantially from those in the classical economies studied earlier. In particular, agents' preferences often exhibit nonconvexities and indivisibilities, and the social goals may include exact or approximate efficiency, voluntary participation, stability to group deviations, and even some notions of fairness.

A major theme in the "market design" literature is that the choice of mechanism is not determined by incentives alone. Indeed, if incentive compatibility were the only concern, it could be verified with a direct revelation mechanism. However, full revelation of agents' preferences is often impractical or undesirable, for several reasons: First, sometimes full revelation requires a prohibitive amount of communication – e.g., a bidder in a combinatorial auction would have to announce his valuations for all possible bundles of objects, whose

* This chapter was prepared for the 9th World Congress of the Econometric Society, London, August 19–24, 2005. I gratefully acknowledge financial support of the National Science Foundation (grants SES 0214500, 0427770). I also thank my discussant, Roger Myerson, and the participants of too many seminars and conference presentations where some of the research surveyed in the chapter was presented. In particular, I am grateful to Susan Athey, Jonathan Levin, Eric Maskin, Paul Milgrom, Andy Postlewaite, Thomas Sjostrom, and James Jordan for discussions related to this topic. Last but not least, I am indebted to my coauthors Noam Nisan and Ronald Fadel for helping clarify my understanding of the topics discussed in this chapter.

number is exponential in the number of objects. Second, agents may have to incur "evaluation costs" to learn their own preferences. Finally, the more information is revealed, the more deviations exploiting the revealed information become available to agents or the designer, as noted in the literature on communication and mechanisms without perfect commitment (e.g., Myerson (1991, Section 6) and Salanie (1997, Section 6)). For all these reasons, the "market design" literature has examined a variety of mechanisms that aim to achieve the desired goals without fully revealing agents' preferences. For example, in the many proposed "iterative" combinatorial auction designs, bidders submit and modify their bids for various bundles over time. This raises the question: What is the minimal information that must be elicited from the agents in order to achieve the goals? Note that the question arises even if agents are willing to communicate sincerely.

An early discussion of the communication problem can be found in Hayek's (1945) critique of socialist planning. Hayek called attention to the "problem of the utilization of knowledge that is not given to anyone in its totality," when "practically every individual ... possesses unique information of which beneficial use might be made." He argued that "we cannot expect that this problem will be solved by first communicating all this knowledge to a central board, which, after integrating all knowledge, issues its orders." Instead, "the ultimate decisions must be left to the people who are familiar with the ... particular circumstances of time and place." At the same time, the decisions must be guided by prices, which summarize the information needed "to co-ordinate the separate actions of different people." While Hayek did not discuss allocation mechanisms other than the price mechanism and central planning (full revelation), he noted that "nobody has yet succeeded in designing an alternative system" that would fully utilize individual knowledge.

While Hayek's ideas inspired economists to study the workings of price mechanisms, their place among all other conceivable allocation mechanisms and their domain of applicability have remained unclear. For example, consider the best-known results about price mechanisms – the Fundamental Welfare Theorems. The First Welfare Theorem says that announcing supporting prices is *sufficient* to verify the Pareto efficiency of an allocation, but not that it is *necessary*. The Second Welfare Theorem says only that supporting prices can be constructed for a given Pareto efficient allocation once all the information about the economy is available. However, once all the information is available, an efficient allocation can be computed and imposed directly, without using prices.[1] The theorems have nothing to say about possible efficient non-price mechanisms in an economy with distributed knowledge of preferences.

A major advance in understanding the role of prices was made by the literature on the "informational efficiency" of Walrasian equilibria, spurred by

---

[1] There are many computational optimization techniques that do not compute supporting dual variables – e.g., the ellipsoid method or the simplex method for linear programming (Karloff 1991).

Hurwicz (1977) and Mount and Reiter (1974). In contrast to the Fundamental Welfare Theorems, the literature followed Hayek in modeling allocation mechanisms in an economy with *decentralized knowledge of preferences*. (Similar techniques were independently developed in the computer science literature on "communication complexity," which considered discrete communication problems – see Kushilevitz and Nisan (1997)). The literature considered the problem of verifying Pareto efficiency in economies with convex preferences, and showed that the Walrasian equilibrium verifies an efficient allocation using the minimal number of real variables among all continuous verification mechanisms. However, the recent "market design" problems have different preference domain (e.g., with nonconvexities and indivisibilities, Walrasian equilibria or continuous mechanisms may not exist), different social goals (e.g., coalitional stability or approximate efficiency), and different relevant communication costs (e.g., the number of bits, or the cost of evaluating preferences).

It turns out that the necessity of price revelation can be demonstrated in a general social choice setting that covers most recent "market design" problems. This is shown in Segal (2005), who characterizes the class of social choice problems (defined by preference domains and social goals) for which any communication mechanism must reveal supporting "prices" (which in general take the form of abstract subsets of alternatives offered to the agents). The class turns out to include a number of important economic problems. Segal (2005) also suggests an algorithm for deriving the form of budget sets that need to be used to verify the solution of a given problem with minimal information revelation. These results have implications for the communication costs of various social choice problems, measured in bits, real numbers, evaluation costs, or in other ways. In particular, the results are used to see which problems can be solved in a practical way and which problems cannot, and what role prices must have in mechanisms that solve them.

The objective of this chapter is to survey the results described above, a substantial body of related work, and some potential extensions. We begin in Section 2 with a very simple example in which the concepts of communication and minimally informative messages are defined, and the necessity of price revelation is demonstrated. Section 3 extends these ideas to a large class of social choice problems. In Section 4 we apply the general analysis to several social choice problems, including classical convex economies, combinatorial auctions and two-sided matching. In each of these applications, we derive the space of budget equilibria corresponding to minimally informative messages, and use this space to identify the communication cost. Section 5 discusses and relates several alternative measures of communication cost, such as the number of real variables versus bits transmitted, communication cost of individual agents rather than in the aggregate, the number of preference evaluations performed by agents, and some notions of privacy preservation. Section 6 discusses some further issues, such as comparison between the costs of communication and verification, probabilistic (average-case) social goals, the additional communication cost of incentivizing agents, and the role of prices when agents' utilities are interdependent. Many of the questions raised in Section 6 are still open and require further investigation.

2   A SIMPLE EXAMPLE

We illustrate the main ideas with a very simple example: One object is to be allocated between two agents with valuations v_1, v_2. Each agent's valuation is his privately observed *type*, and the the valuation pair (v_1, v_2) is called the *state*. Suppose that we know a priori that the valuations lie in the set $\{0, 1, 2, 3\}$. The goal is to find an "optimal" allocation, which for now we define as efficiency – giving the object to the agent with the higher valuation (when the valuations coincide, both allocations are optimal). What communication is needed to find an optimal allocation?

To begin with, we measure the communication cost as the number of bits needed to encode the agents' messages, as in the "communication complexity" literature (Kushilevitz and Nisan 1997).[2] While in this simple example the communication cost proves to be trivial, the ideas developed in this section will prove useful in much more complex settings.

2.1   Communication Protocols

An obvious way to find an optimal outcome is by asking agents to reveal their private information:

Protocol 1 (Full Revelation): The agents announce their valuations v_1, v_2 (encoded in bits). Since each agent needs $\log_2 4 = 2$ bits to encode his valuation, in total 4 bits are sent. The object is allocated to agent 1 if $v_1 > v_2$ and to agent 2 otherwise.

Can we find an optimal allocation with less communication? The answer is yes, by letting agents make announcements sequentially and condition their announcements on the past announcements. Thus, we define sequential communication as follows:

Definition 1 *A communication protocol is (i) an extensive-form game form in which all moves are binary, (ii) agents' strategies in this game (each agents' strategy contingent on his private type as well as history), and (iii) an assignment of allocations to the terminal nodes of the game.*

We assume that agents obey the prescribed strategies – e.g., agents could well be computers who follow their programs. (The problem of providing incentives

---

[2] Thus, agents are forced to communicate using only binary messages (bits). If instead they could communicate using a k-letter alphabet, a letter from the alphabet could be encoded using $\log_2 k$ bits, so the communication length would only be reduced by the constant factor $\log_2 k$. Thus, the choice of the alphabet is relatively unimportant in large problems.

not to deviate is discussed in Subsection 6.2 below.) We want the protocol to implement in every state an optimal allocation for this state. Consider the following example:

Protocol 2 (One-sided Revelation): Agent 1 announces his valuation v_1 (encoded in 2 bits), then agent 2 announces an allocation of the object (1 bit). Thus, 3 bits are sent in total. Agent 2's strategy is to allocate the object to agent 1 if $v_1 > v_2$ and to himself otherwise.

In Protocols 1 and 2, the number of bits sent is the same in any state (v_1, v_2). In other protocols, the amount of communication may differ across states:

Protocol 3 (English Auction): The protocol starts with a price $p = 0$, and then agents send messages in sequence:

1. Agent 2 says "stop" or "raise." If he says "stop," allocate the object to agent 1, otherwise set $p = 1$ and continue.
2. Agent 1 says "stop" or "raise." If he says "stop," allocate the object to agent 2, otherwise set $p = 2$ and continue.
3. Agent 2 says "stop" or "raise." If he says "stop," allocate the object to agent 1, otherwise allocate the object to agent 2.

Each agent's strategy is to say "raise" when his valuation exceeds the current price p and say "stop" otherwise. Given these strategies, the protocol always implements an optimal allocation. Depending on the agents' valuations, the protocol may stop after the agents send 1, 2, or 3 bits.

We now focus on the simplest measure of the communication cost, known as "worst-case" communication complexity – the largest number of bits sent across all states.[3] Can we find a protocol with a lower communication cost than the protocols above?

Protocol 4 (Bisection): Agent 1 says "low" if $v_1 \in \{0, 1\}$ or "high" if $v_1 \in \{2, 3\}$ (1 bit). Then agent 2 announces an allocation (1 bit). Agent 2's strategy is as follows: If agent 1 said "low," agent 2 allocates the object to agent 1 if $v_2 = 0$ and to himself otherwise. If agent 1 said "high," agent 2 allocates the object to himself if $v_2 = 3$ and to agent 1 otherwise. This protocol finds an optimal allocation using 2 bits.

---

[3] Alternatively, given a probability distribution over valuation pairs (v_1, v_2), we could consider "average-case" communication complexity as the *expected* number of bits sent in the protocol (this is also known as "distributional" complexity). In Protocol 3, this expected number could be close to 1 if the valuations are very likely to be low. This is related to Shannon's (1948) information measure, which allows coding more frequent messages with shorter strings of bits. We consider average-case communication complexity in Subsection 6.3 below.

Table 6.1. *State Space*

		v_2			
		0	1	2	3
v_1	0	1, 2	2	2	2
	1	1	1, 2	2	2
	2	1	1	1, 2	2
	3	1	1	1	1, 2

Can we find an optimal allocation using fewer than 2 bits in the worst case? In general, how can we find the communication complexity of a given *problem*, defined as the *minimal* communication complexity of a protocol solving this problem? To tackle this question, it is convenient to represent communication geometrically in the state space. In our example, the state space is described by a matrix, where in each state (cell) we put the set of optimal allocations (Table 6.1).

Each node of a communication game tree corresponds to an "event" – a subset of the state space in which the node is reached. Note that since agent 1's message at any of his decision nodes depends only on his own type, it slices the corresponding event into sub-events horizontally; similarly, agent 2's messages slice events vertically. Thus, by induction on the depth of the node we can see that the event corresponding to any node must be a product set. In computer science, such events are called "rectangles," although they need not be geometric (i.e., contiguous) rectangles.

Now consider the rectangles corresponding to the terminal nodes of a protocol. Note that such rectangles must partition the state space (since in each state, exactly one terminal node is reached). Also, if the protocol finds an optimal allocation, then for each rectangle corresponding to a terminal node there must exist a single allocation that is optimal on the whole rectangle, and which could be assigned to the node. In computer science, rectangles with this property are called "monochromatic." Thus, the terminal nodes of the protocol must partition the state space into monochromatic rectangles. The partitions generated by Protocols 1–4 are shown in Table 6.2.

The worst-case communication complexity W of a protocol is the maximal depth of the corresponding binary tree. Since the number T of terminal nodes in such a tree is at most 2^W, we must have $W \geq \log_2 T$. Thus, the worst-case communication complexity of finding an optimal allocation can be bounded below by bounding below the size of any partition of the state space into monochromatic rectangles.[4]

---

[4] The bound in general will not be tight, for two reasons: First, some partitions of the state space cannot arise in any communication protocol (Kushilevitz and Nisan 1997, Figure 2.1). Second, the inequality $W \geq \log_2 T$ is tight only in balanced trees (such as Protocols 1, 2, and 4) and strict in unbalanced trees (such as Protocol 3).

Table 6.2. *Communication Partitions*

Protocol 1

		v_2			
		0	1	2	3
v_1	0	2	2	2	2
	1	1	2	2	2
	2	1	1	2	2
	3	1	1	1	2

Protocol 2

		v_2			
		0	1	2	3
v_1	0	2	2	2	2
	1	1	2	2	2
	2	1	1	2	2
	3	1	1	1	2

Protocol 3

		v_2			
		0	1	2	3
v_1	0	1	2	2	2
	1	1	2	2	2
	2	1	1	1	2
	3	1	1	1	2

Protocol 4

		v_2			
		0	1	2	3
v_1	0	1	2	2	2
	1	1	1	1	2
	2	1	1	1	2
	3	1	1	1	2

2.2   Verification Protocols

Since characterizing all communication protocols has proven to be very hard, a lot of attention has been put into providing lower bounds on communication complexity. As discussed before, such a bound can be obtained by finding the minimal size of a partition of the state space into monochromatic rectangles. We can further simplify the problem by allowing the rectangles to overlap, i.e., allow *coverings* rather than partitions of the state space.

A covering of the state space into monochromatic rectangles can be interpreted as a *verification protocol* (also called "nondeterministic communication" in computer science – see Kushilevitz and Nisan (1997, Chapter 2)). To understand verification, imagine an omniscient oracle who knows the agents' valuations and consequently the optimal allocation(s), but needs to prove to an ignorant outsider that an allocation x is indeed optimal. The oracle does this by publicly announcing a message $m \in M$. Each agent i either accepts or rejects the message, doing this on the basis of his own type. (Thus, the set of states on which the message is accepted is a rectangle.) The acceptance of message m by all agents must *verify* to the outsider that allocation x is optimal. (Thus, the rectangle is monochromatic.) The (worst-case) complexity of a verification protocol with message space M is the minimum number of bits needed to encode a message, which is $\log_2 M$.[5]

---

[5] Such communication is called "nondeterministic" in computer science because the oracle "guesses" an acceptable message (and there may be more than one such message in a given state). In contrast, the communication protocols defined in the previous subsection are called "deterministic."

While verification protocols are patently unrealistic, their examination proves useful for the following reasons:

1. Any communication protocol can be verified by the oracle sending all the messages instead of the agents, and having each agent accept the message sequence if and only if all the messages sent in his stead are consistent with his strategy given his type. The oracle's message space M is thus identified with the set of the protocol's terminal nodes (message sequences). Therefore, verification is a generalization of communication, and so communication cost is bounded below by verification cost.

2. A famous economic example of verification is Walrasian equilibrium. The role of the oracle is played by the "Walrasian auctioneer," who announces the equilibrium prices and allocation. Each agent accepts the announcement if and only if his announced allocation constitutes his optimal choice from the budget set delineated by the announced prices. We will describe a natural extension of such price-based verification mechanisms to general social choice problems in Section 3.

3. A verification protocol may be viewed as the steady state of an iterative communication protocol. At each stage of the iteration, a message $m \in M$ is announced, and each agent reports a direction in which the message should be adjusted to become "more acceptable" to him. Examples of such iterative processes include "tatonnement" processes for finding Walrasian equilibria, "deferred acceptance algorithms" for finding stable matchings, and ascending-bid auctions for finding efficient combinatorial allocations. In some settings, the iterative processes converge very quickly, though in general this cannot be guaranteed (see Subsection 6.1 below).

2.3 Minimally Informative Messages and Prices

In order to verify optimality using the smallest number of bits, we need to find a minimal covering of the state space with monochromatic rectangles. For this purpose, we want to use larger rectangles, corresponding to messages that reveal less information about the agents' types. Formally, we define the following partial "informativeness" order on messages:

Definition 2 *Message m is* less informative *than (or* verified by*) message $\tilde{m}$ if m is accepted on a larger set of states (rectangle) than $\tilde{m}$. Also, m is a* minimally informative message verifying (the optimality of) allocation x *if any less informative message verifying x is as informative as m.*

Graphically, a minimally informative message m verifying x corresponds to a maximal rectangle contained in the set of states in which x is optimal. Typically, a given allocation may be verified by many minimally informative

Table 6.3. *Minimally Informative Message*

		v_2			
		0	1	2	3
	0	2	2	2	2
v_1	1		2	2	2
	2			2	2
	3				2

messages, which are not comparable in the informativeness order. For example, with two agents, one minimally informative rectangle could be tall and narrow (revealing little information about agent 1 and much about agent 2), while another short and wide (revealing much about agent 1 and little about agent 2).

It can be seen that for any message m verifying x there exists a less informative message m' that is a minimally informative message verifying x.[6] Thus, starting with any verification protocol, we can replace every message with a minimally informative message verifying the same allocation, and obtain a verification protocol with the same number of messages that uses only minimally informative messages. (Furthermore, this replacement may allow us to discard some of the messages while still covering the state space with the remaining rectangles.)

We proceed to characterize the minimally informative messages in our simple example. The states in which allocating the object to agent 2 are optimal are marked with "2" in Table 6.3. The minimally informative messages verifying the optimality of allocating the object to agent 2 correspond to the largest rectangles that fit into this set, i.e., that do not extend below the diagonal. These are exactly the geometric rectangles with one corner on the diagonal and another in the top-right state $(v_1, v_2) = (0, 3)$.

Note that any minimally informative message verifying allocation 2 can be described as a "price equilibrium": The oracle names a price $p \in \{0, 1, 2, 3\}$ and the allocation of the object to agent 2, and each agent accepts if and only if the allocation is optimal to him given the price. That is, agent 2 accepts if and only if he is willing to buy at price p (i.e., $v_2 \geq p$), and agent 1 accepts if and only if he is willing *not* to buy at price p (i.e., $v_1 \leq p$). (The rectangle depicted in Table 6.3 corresponds to $p = 1$.) Thus, *the minimally informative messages verifying allocation to agent 2 are characterized as price equilibrium messages for prices $p \in \{0, 1, 2, 3\}$.* Symmetrically, the same is true for minimally informative messages verifying allocation to agent 1. This implies that any communication protocol that finds an optimal allocation must reveal enough information to construct a supporting price equilibrium.

---

[6] This observation is trivial when the state space is finite. For general state spaces, this is shown in Segal (2005, Lemma 2).

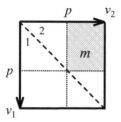

Figure 6.1.

This observation implies a lower bound on the communication cost: Since each price $p \in \{0, 1, 2, 3\}$ has to be used in the diagonal state $(v_1, v_2) = (p, p)$ (regardless of which of the two optimal allocations is verified in this state), we need to use at least 4 messages. Thus, the worst-case communication cost is at least $\log_2 4 = 2$ bits. This lower bound is achieved by Protocol 4.[7]

Suppose now that the agents' valuations instead lie in the [0,1] interval. The minimally informative messages verifying an allocation again correspond to price equilibria (see Figure 6.1), but now any price $p \in [0, 1]$ is a unique equilibrium price in the diagonal state $(v_1, v_2) = p$, and so any verification protocol must use an infinite number of messages. Formally, we will allow infinite protocols with infinite message spaces, and measure their "dimensionality" – i.e., how many real numbers are announced by the agents or the oracle (see Subsection 5.1 below for technical details). Intuitively, the message space in the example must have at least the same dimensionality as the diagonal – i.e., be at least one-dimensional. This lower bound is tight: Just like in Protocol 2, we can find an optimal allocation with agent 1 revealing his valuation with one real number, and then agent 2 reporting an optimal allocation with 1 bit.

2.4   Other Social Goals

The result on the necessity price revelation can be extended to social goals other than efficiency:

Example 1 (Approximate efficiency): Take $\varepsilon > 0$, and say that allocating the object to agent i is "optimal" if and only if $v_i \geq v_{-i} - \varepsilon$. Minimally informative messages verifying that allocation to agent 2 is optimal are described by the geometric rectangles with one corner on the line $v_2 = v_1 - \varepsilon$ and another in the top-right corner of the state space (see Figure 6.2). Such messages can be interpreted as price equilibria in which the agents face different prices p_1, p_2

---

[7] A set of states with the property that no two elements of the set can share a message is called a "fooling set" in computer science, and "a set with the uniqueness property" in the economic literature on communication. The size of such a set bounds below the size of the message space. The novelty here is that the fooling set (in our example, the diagonal) is not chosen *ad hoc* but characterized as the set of states with a unique supporting price. This characterization can be extended to a large class of social choice problems.

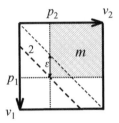

Figure 6.2.

for the object such that $p_2 = p_1 - \varepsilon$. This observation can again be used to bound below the communication cost. Note that two diagonal states with coordinates further apart than ε cannot share a price equilibrium (regardless of which allocation it supports). With continuous valuations in $[0,1]$, we can find $1/\varepsilon$ such distinct diagonal points, hence we need to use at least $1/\varepsilon$ distinct messages, and the communication cost is at least $\log_2(1/\varepsilon)$ bits. This lower bound is almost achieved by letting agent 1 announce his valuation rounded off to a multiple of ε, and agent 2 then report an optimal allocation.[8]

Note also that there exist social goals that *cannot* be verified with a price equilibrium:

Example 2 (Minimize efficiency): An allocation is "optimal" if it allocates the object to the agent with the *lower* valuation. No price equilibrium with prices p_1, p_2 supporting allocation of the object to agent 2 can verify that the allocation is optimal: If it is ever an equilibrium, it will remain an equilibrium in state $(v_1, v_2) = (0, 3)$, in which the object must go to agent 1.

Example 3 (Egalitarian efficiency): In addition to allocating the object efficiently, we must also determine a payment between the agents to equalize their utilities – i.e., if agent i is "wins" the object, he must pay $v_i/2$ to the "loser." This payment cannot be verified with a price equilibrium: Any price equilibrium would remain an equilibrium when the winner's value goes up, but egalitarian efficiency requires that the winner's payment to the loser must increase.

The examples suggest that price equilibria can only be used to verify social goals that are somehow "congruent" with private preferences (such as efficiency or approximate efficiency), but not those opposing or orthogonal to private preferences (such as minimization of efficiency or equalization of utilities).

Finally, note the difference between whether (a) price equilibria *can* be used to verify a social goal, and (b) the *minimally informative messages* verifying

---

[8] Compare this to the earlier finding that *exact* efficiency with continuous valuations would require one-dimensional continuous communication. The relationship between continuous communication and discrete approximation is discussed in more detail in Subsection 5.1 below.

the social goal are price equilibria. (a) means that in any state, for any optimal allocation x in the state there exists a price equilibrium that verifies the optimality of x. E.g. the efficiency of an allocation in state (v_1, v_2) can always be verified with a price equilibrium, say, setting price $p = (v_1 + v_2)/2$. This is similar to the traditional Fundamental Welfare Theorems (although the example fails the usual convexity assumptions of the theorem). In the previous subsection, we have also shown that (b) holds for the goal of efficiency. Yet, for social goals other than efficiency, (a) does not imply (b):

Example 4: Suppose there are three possible allocations and a single agent. (We could add a second agent with a constant utility over the allocations.) A state is described by the agent's valuations (v_1, v_2, v_3) for the three allocations. An allocation is defined as "optimal" if the agent's utility from it is at least as high as from *at least one* of the other two allocations. Any optimal allocation in any state can be verified with a price equilibrium, e.g., with prices $(p_1, p_2, p_3) = (v_1, v_2, v_3)$ for the three allocations. However, consider a message in which the agent verifies that allocation 1 is optimal. This is a minimally informative message verifying allocation 1, but it is not equivalent to a price equilibrium: It does not reveal any prices at which the agent prefers allocation 1 to allocation 2 or to allocation 3, since it does not bound above either $v_2 - v_1$ or $v_3 - v_1$ (it only reveals that *one* of the differences is nonpositive, but does not reveal which one).

3   GENERAL SOCIAL CHOICE PROBLEMS

3.1   Setup

We now extend the observations made in Section 2 to general social choice problems. Let N be a finite set of agents, and X be a set of social alternatives. (With a slight abuse of notation, the same letter will denote a set and its cardinality when this causes no confusion.) Let $\mathcal{P}$ denote the set of all preference relations over set X that are rational (i.e., complete and transitive). Each agent i's preference relation is assumed to be his privately observed *type*, and the set of his possible types is denoted by $\mathcal{R}_i \subset \mathcal{P}$. A *state* is a preference profile $R = (R_1, \ldots, R_N) \in \mathcal{R}_1 \times \ldots \times \mathcal{R}_N \equiv \mathcal{R}$, where $\mathcal{R}$ is the *state space*, also known as *preference domain*. The goal of communication is to implement a *choice rule*, which is a correspondence $F : \mathcal{R} \twoheadrightarrow X$. For every state $R \in \mathcal{R}$, the set $F(R) \subset X$ describes the *optimal* alternatives in this state.

We focus on the verification problem described in Section 2: An omniscient oracle knows the agents' valuations and consequently the optimal allocation(s), but he needs to prove to an ignorant outsider that an allocation x is indeed optimal. He does this by publicly announcing a message $m \in M$. Each agent i either accepts or rejects the message, doing this on the basis of his own type. The acceptance of message m by all agents must verify to the outsider that allocation x is optimal.

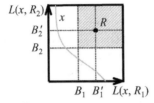

Figure 6.3.

We can define two notions of verification:

Definition 3 *A verification protocol* verifies *choice rule F if* $\forall R \in \mathcal{R}$ $\exists x$ $\in F(R)$ $\exists m \in M$ *that is acceptable in state R and verifies x. The protocol* fully *verifies* choice rule *F if* $\forall R$ $\forall x \in F(R)$ $\exists m \in M$ *that is acceptable in* state R and verifies x.

Thus, simple verification requires only *one* optimal alternative to be verifiable in each state, while full verification requires *all* optimal alternatives to be verifiable. We are ultimately interested in simple verification (communication is not required to find more than one optimal alternative), but full verification will prove a useful intermediate concept.

3.2   Verification with Budget Equilibria

We extend the notion of a "price equilibrium" to this general social choice setting, in which we may not even have any divisible goods in which prices could be measured. Thus, we consider abstract budget sets, which are general subsets of the space of alternatives (and which may or may not be delineated by prices). A *budget equilibrium message* consists of a proposed alternative $x \in X$ and a *budget set* $B_i \subset X$ for each agent i. Each agent $i \in N$ accepts message $(B_1, \ldots, B_N, x)$ if and only if there is no alternative in his budget set B_i that he strictly prefers to the proposed alternative x. $(B_1, \ldots, B_N, x)$ is a *budget equilibrium in state* $R \in \mathcal{R}$ if it is accepted by all agents in this state.[9] It is convenient to define $L(x, R) = \{y \in X : xRy\}$ – the *lower contour set* of preference relation R_i at alternative x. Then the budget equilibrium condition can be written as $B_i \subset L(x, R_i)$ for all agents i.

To represent a budget equilibrium message graphically, it is convenient to "order" the agents' preferences by the ranking of alternative x, i.e., by the set inclusion order on $L(x, R_i)$ (see Figure 6.3). Since in general this is not a

---

[9] A number of related concepts have been suggested, including "social equilibrium" (Debreu 1952), "social situations" (Greenberg 1990), "effectivity functions" (Moulin and Peleg 1982), "effectivity forms" (Miyagawa 2002), "opportunity equilibrium" (Ju 2001), and "interactive choice sets" (Serrano and Volij 2000). However, all these papers have motivated the concept by incentives, rather than deriving it from communication among sincere agents.

complete order, a one-dimensional axis can only represent a "slice" of an agent's type space. (The setting studied in Section 2 was a special case in which each agent's type in fact *was* one-dimensional – ordered by his willingness to pay for the object.) Yet, however imprecise, Figure 6.3 allows us to develop some useful intuitions. A budget equilibrium message (B_1, B_2, x) is the set of states in which $B_i \subset L(x, R_i)$ for $i = 1, 2$, and in the figure it is represented with a geometric rectangle with one corner at (B_1, B_2) and another in the right-hand corner of the state space (where $L(x, R_1) = L(x, R_2) = X$).

Figure 6.3 also makes it clear that increasing budget sets makes a budget equilibrium more informative: Budget equilibrium (B', x) is more informative than budget equilibrium (B, x) whenever $B_i \subset B_i'$ for all agents i. Graphically, the rectangle corresponding to (B', x) is then included in the rectangle corresponding to (B', x).

We can now define a *budget protocol* as a verification protocol in which the oracle's message space M is a collection of budget equilibria, such that each equilibrium $(B_1, \ldots, B_N, x)$ from M verifies the equilibrium alternative x. Which choice rules can be verified with a budget protocol? Traditional Fundamental Welfare Theorems say that in a convex exchange economy, an allocation is Pareto efficient if and only if it can be verified with a Walrasian equilibrium (which is a kind of budget equilibrium). The theorems have been extended to some "non-classical" social choice problems, for which different kinds of budget equilibria have been proposed.[10] We extend these results to general social choice rules, by characterizing choice rules F that are fully verified with a budget protocol.

According to the definition of full verification, we want to check that for any alternative $x \in X$, in each state $R \in \mathcal{R}$ in which x is optimal there exists a budget equilibrium (B, x) verifying x. To check this, it suffices to check the largest budget sets supporting x in state R, i.e., $B_i' = L(x, R_i)$ for each i (see Figure 6.3). That this budget equilibrium (B', x) verifies x means that x must remain optimal in any state R' "above" R, i.e., in which $L(x, R_i) = B_i' \subset L(x, R_i')$ for each i. This property of choice rule is formally known as follows:

Definition 4 (Maskin (1999)) *Choice rule F is* monotonic *if $\forall R \in \mathcal{R}$, $\forall x \in F(R)$, and $\forall R' \in \mathcal{R}$ such that $L(x, R_i) \subset L(x, R_i')$ $\forall i \in N$, we have $x \in F(R')$.*

Theorem 1 *A choice rule F is fully verified by a budget protocol if and only if it is monotonic.*[11]

---

[10] Including the Pareto rule in public-good economies (Milleron 1972) and general economies with numeraire (Mas-Colell 1980; Bikhchandani and Mamer 1997; Bikhchandani and Ostroy 2002), and stable many-to-one matching problems with and without transfers (Kelso and Crawford 1982; Hatfield and Milgrom 2005).

[11] This implies that F is *verified* by a budget protocol if and only if has a nonempty-valued monotonic subcorrespondence.

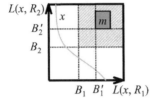

Figure 6.4.

Results equivalent to Theorem 1 are stated in Williams (1986, Theorem 2), Miyagawa's (2002, Theorem 1), Ju (2001), and Greenberg (1990, Theorem 10.1.2). The present formulation and the idea of the proof are from Segal (2005).

The deficiency of Theorem 1 is that, just like the traditional Fundamental Welfare Theorems, it does not rule out that choice rule F could be verified with a non-budget protocol that might reveal less information and have lower communication costs than any budget protocol verifying F. To rule this out, we would like to require the following stronger property:

Definition 5   *Choice rule F satisfies the* Budget Equilibrium Revelation Property *(BERP) if for any message verifying the optimality of an alternative $x \in X$ there exists a less informative budget equilibrium (B, x) that verifies the optimality of x.*

BERP is illustrated in Figure 6.4. When applied to a message m that fully reveals a state R (i.e., corresponds to a single point $\{R\}$ in Figure 6.4), BERP says that for any $x \in F(R)$ we can construct a budget equilibrium (B, x) in state R that verifies x. Thus, BERP implies that F is fully verified with a budget protocol, and so by Theorem 1 that F is monotonic. However, BERP is stronger, since it requires a budget equilibrium verifying x to be constructed without knowing the exact state, upon observing *any message* verifying x. Note that BERP ensures that any minimally informative message verifying an alternative in F must be equivalent to a budget equilibrium message.

Contrary to the impression created by Figure 6.4, not all monotonic choice rules satisfy BERP. Figure 6.4 is misleading when feasible contour sets $L(x, R_i)$ cannot be ordered, in which case there do exist monotonic choice rules that do not satisfy BERP (see Example 4 in Section 2). Yet, the figure can be still used to develop intuition for which rules do satisfy BERP. To check whether a message $m = m_1 \times m_2$ verifies some budget equilibrium (B_1, B_2, x) that verifies x, it again suffices to check the largest budget sets that support x in all states from m, which are $B_i' = \cap_{R_i \in m_i} L(x, R_i)$ for each i (see Figure 6.4). Thus, it suffices to check that this equilibrium verifies x, i.e., that x is optimal in any state R' in which $B_i' \subset L(x, R_i') \; \forall i \in N$. Formally, this property can be defined as follows

Definition 6 *Choice rule* F *is* Intersection-Monotonic (IM) *if* $\forall m = m_1 \times \ldots \times m_N \subset \mathcal{R}$, $\quad \forall x \in \cap_{R \in m} F(R)$, *and* $\quad \forall R' \in \mathcal{R}$ *such that* $\cap_{R \in m} L(x, R_i) \subset L(x, R_i') \; \forall i \in N$, *we have* $x \in F(R')$.

Theorem 2 *Choice rule* F *satisfies the Budget Equilibrium Revelation Property if and only if it is Intersection-Monotonic.*

Intersection monotonicity is fairly easy to verify: just as with monotonicity, it suffices to check changes in one agent i's preferences holding all other agents' preferences fixed (i.e., letting $m_j = \left\{ R_j' \right\}$ for $j \neq i$) – the full property would then follow by iterating over agents. Thus, Theorem 2 offers a simple way to check whether a given choice rule satisfies BERP, i.e., whether its verification requires revelation of supporting budget sets.

3.3 Examples of Intersection-Monotonic Rules

Segal (2005) shows that a number of important choice rules are intersection-monotonic on the universal preference domain $\mathcal{P}^N$ (and therefore on any smaller domain), including:

- Weak Pareto efficiency.[12]
- A notion of approximate Pareto efficiency (e.g., with quasilinear utilities, approximating the maximal achievable total surplus within ε).
- The weak core.
- Stable matching.
- The envy-free rule (requiring that no agent envies another agent's allocation).

More generally, the class of IM rules includes any rule from the following class:

Definition 7 *Choice rule* F *is a* Coalitionally Unblocked (CU) *choice rule if for some blocking correspondence* $\beta : X \times 2^N \twoheadrightarrow X$,

$$F(R) = \{x \in X : \beta(x, S) \subset \cup_{i \in S} L(x, R_i) \; \forall S \subset N\} \; \forall R \in \mathcal{R}.$$

In words, for each coalition $S \subset N$ and each candidate alternative $x \in X$, the blocking correspondence defines a "blocking set" $\beta(x, S) \subset X$. An alternative $x \in X$ is optimal in state R if and only if no coalition $S \subset N$ can find a strict Pareto improvement over x in its blocking set $\beta(x, S)$.[13] It is easy to see that

---

[12] The strong Pareto rule is not even monotonic, let alone IM. Note, however, that the weak and strong Pareto criteria coincide for preferences that are strictly monotonic and nonsatiated in some divisible economic good.

[13] CU choice rules have also been known as "respecting group rights," with $y \in \beta(x, S)$ interpreted as the "one-way right" of coalition S to block alternative x with alternative y (Hammond 1997, Section 5). The "rights" literature, initiated by Sen (1970), is concerned with the problem that

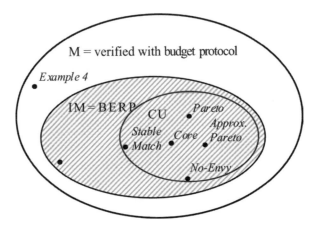

Figure 6.5.

all the above examples of choice rules are CU rules, for different specifications of the blocking correspondence. Segal (2005) shows that any CU choice rule is IM. There do exist IM rules that are not CU, but their economic significance is unclear. A Venn diagram for choice rules summarizing the above results is drawn in Figure 6.5.

3.4   The Budget-Shrinking Algorithm

Now we look for minimally informative messages verifying a given choice rule, which under BERP must be equivalent to budget equilibria. We propose an algorithm to construct such budget equilibria for any given IM choice rule. Thus, for any given social choice problem, the algorithm constructs and characterizes the budget equilibria that verify the problem with minimal revelation of information. For simplicity, we restrict attention to IM choice rules that are extendable to the universal preference domain $\mathcal{R} = \mathcal{P}^N$. (In particular, note that any CU choice rule is extendable to $\mathcal{P}^N$ using the same blocking correspondence.)

The proposed algorithm obtains a minimally informative message verifying a given alternative x by starting with any message verifying x and stretching the corresponding rectangle sequentially agent-by-agent.[14] For an IM choice rule, we can focus on budget equilibrium messages, and their stretching corresponds to shrinking the agents' budget sets. As illustrated in Figure 6.6, we can start

---

individual and group rights may be incompatible with each other on the universal preference domain, i.e., that "group rights-respecting" choice rules may be empty-valued. In the applications considered in Section 4 below, the preference domains and coalitional rights will be defined to ensure nonempty-valuedness.

[14] The algorithm is independently proposed by Segal (2005) and Hurwicz and Reiter (2006, who call it the "rectangle method"). However, Segal's (2005) application of the algorithm to the special case of intersection-monotonic choice rules allows us to focus on budget equilibrium messages, and stretch them by shrinking the agents' budget sets.

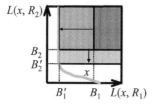

Figure 6.6.

with a budget equilibrium (B_1, B_2, x) verifying alternative x, and "stretch" the rectangle in the direction of agent 1 as much as possible, while still verifying x. This stretching, illustrated with the horizontal arrow, corresponds to "shrinking" agent 1's budget set from B_1 to B_1'. Next, "stretch" the rectangle described by budget equilibrium (B_1', B_2, x) in the direction of agent 2. This stretching, represented with the vertical arrow, corresponds to "shrinking" agent 2's budget set from B_2 to B_2'. This yields a budget equilibrium message (B_1', B_2', x) that can no longer be stretched, i.e., corresponds to a minimally informative verifying message. (The same procedure works with any number of agents: sequential agent-by-agent stretching yields a minimally informative verifying message.)

Note that the resulting equilibrium (B_1', B_2', x) can be described by the "boundary" state $R \in \mathcal{P}^N$ in which the agents' lower contour sets at x coincide with B_1', B_2', and x is on the verge of becoming non-optimal. Formally, the boundary states R for alternative x and the corresponding minimally informative budget equilibria are characterized by the condition

$$B_i = L(x, R_i) = \bigcap_{R_i' \in \mathcal{R}_i : x \in F(R_i', R_{-i})} L(x, R_i') \quad \forall i \in N. \qquad (*)$$

In words, each agent i's budget set is his smallest lower contour set for which x is still optimal, holding other agents' preferences fixed.

When the preference domain $\mathcal{R}$ is a strict subset of $\mathcal{P}^N$, we face the following complications:

- There typically exist many budget equilibria that are equally informative to (*) but have even smaller budget sets. For example, in exchange economies in which preferences are known to be monotone in consumption, a Walrasian budget equilibrium, in which the budget sets are half-spaces, is equivalent to the budget equilibrium in which the half-spaces are replaced with their boundary hyperplanes (i.e., waste is not allowed). The budget equilibria characterized by (*) have the largest budget sets among those that are equally informative, and it proves convenient to focus on them (if only because they are guaranteed to exist). Thus, in shrinking agent i's budget set, we only shrink it to the intersection of the feasible lower contour sets in $\mathcal{R}_i$ for which x is still optimal, and not any further, even when such shrinking might yield an equally informative message.

- Since not all subsets of X may serve as lower contour sets, the "boundary states" characterized by (*) are not guaranteed to be in $\mathcal{R}$. However, it is still true that (*) with $R \in \mathcal{P}^N$ characterizes (up to equivalence) the minimally informative verifying budget equilibria.

If a boundary state R satisfying (*) *does* fall in the preference domain $\mathcal{R}$, then we can see that $(L(x, R_1), \ldots, L(x, R_N), x)$ is a unique (up to equivalence) budget equilibrium verifying x in state R. Such an equilibrium cannot be discarded if we want to verify alternative x in state R with a budget protocol. This observation will prove useful for bounding below the size of the message space, and thus the communication cost. (A simple example of this occurred in Section 2, in which the boundary states were those on the diagonal.) A complication arises when there are many optimal alternatives in state R: since we do not require *full* verification, we do not have to verify any given $x \in F(R)$. In such situations, we resort to additional application-specific tricks to bound below the number of budget equilibria needed for verification.

4   SOME APPLICATIONS

4.1   Pareto Efficiency in Convex Economies

In a *smooth convex exchange economy*, the alternatives represent the consumption of L divisible goods by the N agents, hence $X = \mathbb{R}_+^{NL}$. Each agent i's preference domain consists of convex preferences described by differentiable utility functions of his own consumption $x_i \in \mathbb{R}_+^L$ with a nonnegative nonzero gradient everywhere. The feasible set consists of allocations of a given positive aggregate endowment $\bar{x} \in \mathbb{R}_{++}^L$: $\bar{X} = \{x \in X : \sum_i x_i = \bar{x}\}$.[15] The goal is to verify an allocation that is Pareto efficient within $\bar{X}$.

We use the budget-shrinking algorithm described in Subsection 3.4 to derive minimally informative messages verifying the Pareto efficiency of an allocation $x \in \bar{X}$ with $x \gg 0$.[16] The derivation can be illustrated in the standard Edgeworth box depicted in Figure 6.7. Start with a state R in which x is Pareto efficient, which means that agent 1's indifference curve passing through x is below agent 2's indifference curve passing through x. Note that given smoothness, the two curves must be tangent at x; let p denote the agents' common marginal rate of substitution at x. Now we shrink agent 1's lower contour set as much as possible, while preserving the Pareto efficiency of x and keeping agent 1's preferences convex. This shrinking is illustrated with the left-down arrows in the figure. The furthest we can shrink agent 1's lower contour set is to that of linear preferences – a hyperspace with gradient p. This yields a Walrasian budget set for agent 1 described by the commodity price vector p.

---

[15] We consider a space X of alternatives that is larger than the feasible set $\bar{X}$, to allow budget sets to include infeasible allocations, as the Walrasian budget sets do.

[16] We restrict attention to $x \gg 0$ to avoid the problem of non-existence of supporting Walrasian prices (see, e.g., Mas-Colell et al. (1995, Figure 16.D.2)).

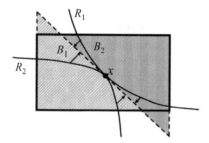

Figure 6.7.

Next, we shrink agent 2's lower contour set as illustrated with the right-up arrows, yielding for him a Walrasian budget set with the same commodity price vector p. Thus the budget-shrinking algorithm yields a Walrasian equilibrium. Furthermore, any Walrasian equilibrium is invariant to budget shrinking – i.e., satisfies (*). A formalization of this argument yields

Proposition 1 *A message is a minimally informative message verifying the Pareto efficiency of allocation $x \in \bar{X}$ with $x \gg 0$ in a smooth convex exchange economy[17] if and only if it is equivalent to a* Walrasian equilibrium *supporting x, i.e., a budget equilibrium (B, x) with*

$$B_i = \{y \in X : p \cdot y_i \le p \cdot x_i\} \ \forall i \in N \tag{1}$$

for some commodity price vector $p \in \mathbb{R}_+^L$ such that $\|p\| = 1$. Any such equilibrium is a unique Walrasian equilibrium supporting allocation x in any state in which it is an equilibrium.

The proposition implies that the minimal message space required for verifying any interior Pareto efficient allocation in any convex economy is the space of Walrasian equilibria. We now discuss the implications of this finding for the verification cost measured as the dimension of the message space. (We keep the arguments informal; see Subsection 5.1 for how the dimension could be formally defined.) Informally, since a feasible allocation $x \in \bar{X}$ is described with $(N - 1)L$ real variables, and a normalized price vector p is described with $L - 1$ real variables, the space of Walrasian equilibria has dimension $(L - 1) + (N - 1)L = NL - 1$. This compares favorably to full revelation of agents' utility functions, which would require an infinite-dimensional message space.

If we don't want *full* verification, and only need to verify *one* efficient allocation in each state, we can further reduce the dimension of the state space. In fact, it is possible to verify Pareto efficiency without any communication – e.g., by always giving all the endowment to agent 1. We rule out

---

[17] If non-smooth preferences are allowed, Walrasian equilibria remain minimally informative messages verifying Pareto efficiency, but other such messages emerge – see Segal (2005) for details.

such corner allocations, focusing on "non-dictatorial" Pareto efficiency. Note that the nondictatorial Pareto rule can be verified by fixing an "endowment allocation" $\omega \in \bar{X}$ with $\omega \gg 0$ and announcing a Walrasian equilibrium (B, x) such that $\omega \in B_i$ for all i, which exists in any convex economy (Mas-Colell et al. 1995, Section 17.BB). Since such equilibria satisfy the additional "budget constraints" $\sum_l p_l \omega_{il} = \sum_l p_i x_{il}$ for all i, they can be communicated using $(L - 1) + (N - 1)(L - 1) = N(L - 1)$ real numbers.

In fact, it is impossible to verify nondictatorial Pareto efficiency using fewer than $N(L - 1)$ real numbers. This can be shown using a "fooling set" consisting of the *Cobb-Douglas economies*, in which each agent i's utility function takes the form $u_i(x_i) = \prod_l x_{il}^{\alpha_{il}}$ with a positive parameter vector $\alpha \in \mathbb{R}_{++}^L$, with the normalization $\sum_l \alpha_{il} = 1$. Note that all nondictatorial Pareto efficient allocations in a Cobb-Douglas economy are interior, and the first-order equilibrium conditions imply that no two distinct Cobb-Douglas economies share an interior Walrasian equilibrium. Therefore, verification requires using a subspace of Walrasian equilibria whose dimension is at least that of Cobb-Douglas economies, which is $N(L - 1)$:

Corollary 1 *The verification cost of nondictatorial Pareto efficiency in the convex exchange economy is exactly $N(L - 1)$ real numbers, and it is achieved by the Walrasian equilibrium protocol with a fixed endowment.*

Corollary 1 was first established in the "informational efficiency" literature (Hurwicz 1977; Mount and Reiter 1974) for verification protocols satisfying a continuity property. Here it has been derived in a different way – from the purely set-theoretic characterization of minimally informative messages as Walrasian equilibria (Proposition 1). Unlike the old approach, the set-theoretic approach does not require any topological restrictions on communication or any scalar measure of the communication cost, and easily extends to other social choice problems, including those considered in the "market design" literature.[18]

4.2   Efficiency in Quasilinear Economies

In *economies with numeraire*, the space of alternatives take the form $X = K \times \mathbb{R}^N$, where K is a finite set of *(non-monetary) allocations*, and $\mathbb{R}^N$ describes the *transfers* of numeraire (money) to the agents. The feasible set takes the form $\bar{X} = \{(k, t) \in X : \sum_i t_i = 0\}$, i.e., requires a balanced budget.

For simplicity, we let each agent i's preference domain $\mathcal{R}_i$ consist of preferences R_i over $(k, t) \in X$ that are quasilinear in his consumption of numeraire,

---

[18] The analysis also extends to convex economies with public goods. For such economies, the budget-shrinking algorithm yields *Lindahl equilibria*, i.e., budget equilibria described by linear anonymous prices for the private goods and linear personalized "Lindahl" prices for the public goods. This can in turn be used to derive the dimensionality of the message space needed to verify Pareto efficiency (which was first obtained by Sato (1981)).

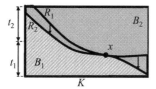

Figure 6.8.

i.e., described by a utility function of the form $u_i(k) + t_i$.[19] Pareto efficiency is then equivalent to requiring that the non-monetary allocation $k \in K$ maximize the total surplus $\sum_i u_i(k)$, regardless of the allocation of numeraire. (The example in Section 2 was a special case with two non-monetary allocations, in which surplus-maximization required giving the object to the agent with the higher valuation.)

We use the budget-shrinking algorithm of Subsection 3.4 to derive minimally informative messages verifying Pareto efficiency. We illustrate this algorithm in an Edgeworth box depicted in Figure 6.8, in which the vertical dimension represents allocations of numeraire between the agents, and the horizontal dimension represents the non-monetary allocations $k \in K$ (arranged in no particular order). Start with a state R in which x is Pareto efficient, which means that the indifference curve of agent 1 passing through x is above the indifference curve of agent 2 passing through x. Shrink the lower contour set of agent 1 as much as possible, while preserving the Pareto efficiency of x (as illustrated with the downward arrows in the figure). The furthest we can shrink it is until agent 2's indifference curve (unlike in the previous subsection, there is no convexity restriction to hold us back). Once this shrinking is completed, agent 2's lower contour set cannot be shrunk without violating the Pareto efficiency of x. The obtained budget sets for the two agents can be delineated by general nonlinear and personalized prices $p_i(k)$ ($i = 1, 2$, $k \in K$), specifying the cost of allocation k to agent i in terms of numeraire. The fact that the two budget sets' boundaries coincide means that the sum of the prices, $p_1(k) + p_2(k)$, must be the same for all allocations $k \in K$. The budget equilibria described in this way are the only budget equilibria that are invariant to the budget-shrinking procedure, i.e., satisfy (*). The argument extends to any number of agents, yielding the following result:

Proposition 2 *A message is a minimally informative message verifying the Pareto efficiency of allocation $(k, t) \in \bar{X}$ in a quasilinear economy if and only*

---

[19] In fact, the analysis of this subsection holds on the larger preference domain where each agent i's preferences are (i) independent of other agents' transfers t_{-i}, (ii) continuous and nondecreasing in his own transfer t_i, and (iii) allow compensation (i.e., for any $x \in X$ and any $k \in K$ there exists $t \in \mathbb{R}$ such that $(k, t) R_i x$). This follows from the observation that any lower contour set of a preference relation satisfying (i)–(iii) is also a lower contour set of some quasilinear preference relation.

if it is equivalent to a valuation equilibrium *supporting* (k, t), *i.e., a budget equilibrium* $(B, (k, t))$ *in which*

$$B_i = \left\{ \left(k', t' \right) \in X : p_i \left(k' \right) + t_i' \leq p_i \left(k \right) + t_i \right\} \ \forall i \in N \tag{2}$$

for some price vector $p \in \mathbb{R}^{NK}$ *satisfying*

$$\sum_i p_i \left(k' \right) = \sum_i p_i \left(k \right) \text{ for all } k' \in K. \tag{3}$$

Any such equilibrium is a unique valuation equilibrium supporting allocation (k, t) *in the state given by the agents' utility functions* $u_i = p_i$ *for each i.*

Valuation equilibria were introduced by Mas-Colell (1980) and studied by Bikhchandani and Mamer (1997) and Bikhchandani and Ostroy (2002). These papers have extended classical welfare theorems to such equilibria: An allocation is Pareto efficient if and only if it is supported by a valuation equilibrium. The contribution of Proposition 2 lies in showing that valuation equilibria constitute *minimally informative* verification of Pareto efficiency in an economy with numeraire.

Proposition 2 implies that the minimal message space required for verifying any efficient allocation in an economy with numeraire is the space of valuation equilibria. Normalizing the prices (e.g., so that $\sum_k p_i (k) = 0$ for each agent i) we can describe a price vector satisfying (3) using $(N - 1)(K - 1)$ real numbers.

If we don't require *full* verification, we only need to verify *one* efficient allocation in each state, and so need not use all valuation equilibria. However, it turns out that *all* the possible normalized valuation prices $p \in \mathbb{R}^{NK}$ satisfying (3) still must be used. Indeed, while in the "boundary" state given by utility functions $(u_1, \ldots, u_N) = \left(p_1, \ldots, p_N \right)$ all allocations are efficient by (3), by the second part of Proposition 2, the agents' budget sets must be described by the same prices p no matter which allocation the equilibrium supports. Therefore, verifying Pareto efficiency with quasilinear preferences requires the announcement of an $(N - 1)(K - 1)$–dimensional price vector.

This lower bound on the communication cost is in fact achieved by the communication protocol in which the first $N - 1$ agents announce their normalized utility functions, and then the last agent chooses a surplus-maximizing allocation. To summarize:

Corollary 2 *The continuous verification cost Pareto efficiency in a quasilinear economy is* $(N - 1)(K - 1)$ *real numbers, and it is achieved with a communication protocol.*

A large number of problems with more restricted quasilinear preferences has been considered, and we describe two of them below.

4.2.1 Combinatorial Allocation

In this problem, a set L of objects is to be allocated among the agents, and so the allocation set can be written as $K = N^L$. The preference domain consists of those quasilinear preferences in which each agent i's utility depends only on his own consumption bundle $k^{-1}(i)$ and is nondecreasing in this bundle (in the set inclusion order). For the particular case of $N = 2$, the budget-shrinking algorithm yields valuation equilibria in which each agent i's price $p_i(k)$ is nondecreasing in his bundle $k^{-1}(i)$, and we can normalize prices so that $p_i(k) = 0$ when $k^{-1}(i) = \varnothing$.[20] In the state $(u_1, u_2) = (p_1, p_2)$, all allocations are efficient by (3), but the normalized price vector in any valuation equilibrium must coincide with p. Thus, the communication cost is bounded below by the dimensionality of this price space, which is $2^L - 1$. This lower bound is achieved with a communication protocol in which agent 1 announces his utility function and agent 2 chooses an efficient allocation. To summarize:

Corollary 3 *The continuous verification cost of efficient combinatorial allocation of L objects between two agents is $2^L - 1$, and it is achieved with a communication protocol.*

Corollary 3 was obtained by Nisan and Segal (2004). A number of other results have been obtained on the potential communication savings in combinatorial allocation problems when agents' utility functions are a priori restricted to lie in certain classes, such as those complement-free utilities, submodular utilities, utilities with substitute objects, utilities with homogeneous objects, etc. For some of these results, see Nisan and Segal (2004), Dobzinski et al. (2005), and Babaioff and Blumrosen (2005).

4.2.2 Binary Utilities

Suppose that agents' utilities are known to be $u_i(k) \in \{0, 1\}$ for all $k \in K$. Then the budget-shrinking algorithm yields valuation equilibria described by prices $p_i(k) \in \{0, 1\}$ for all i, k, and we can normalize prices so that $p_i \neq (1, \ldots, 1)$ for each agent i (since this price would be equivalent to $p_i = (0, \ldots, 0)$). In the state $(u_1, \ldots, u_N) = (p_1, \ldots, p_N)$, all allocations are efficient by (3), but the normalized price vector in any valuation equilibrium must coincide with p. Thus, the communication cost measured in bits is bounded below by the binary logarithm of size of this price space. The number of possible price vectors in $\{0, 1\}$ satisfying $\sum_i p_i(k) = r$ for a given integer r is $\binom{N}{r}^K$, since for each allocation we allocate r "1's" among N agents' utilities. For simplicity taking $r = N/2$ (with N even) and using Stirling's formula yields the lower bound.

---

[20] Application of the budget-shrinking algorithm to the case of $N > 2$ agents appears more complicated, and we have not attempted it.

Corollary 4 *The communication cost of efficiency with binary utilities is asymptotically at least NK bits as $N \to \infty$.*

Thus, as the number of agents grows, the cost is asymptotically the same as that for full revelation of utilities.

This setting can be interpreted as "approval voting," interpreting $u_i(k) = 1$ as agent i's "approval" of allocation k, with the goal being to find an allocation approved by most agents. Conitzer and Sandholm (2005) derive the above result with a different proof.[21]

4.3   Approximate Efficiency in Quasilinear Economies

When finding an exactly efficient allocation is prohibitively costly, we may want to allow approximate efficiency. Consider again quasilinear economies, fix $\varepsilon > 0$, and say that an allocation is ε-*efficient* if it maximizes the total surplus within ε (regardless of the transfers).[22] Note that the goal of ε-efficiency can be described as a CU choice rule (see Subsection 3.3), by requiring the grand coalition to pay a tax ε in numeraire for blocking a candidate allocation (and not allowing any smaller coalition to block). Then an allocation is unblocked if and only if it is ε-efficient. Thus, the defined choice rule is IM, and therefore satisfies the Budget Equilibrium Revelation Property.

To characterize the minimally informative budget equilibria verifying ε-efficiency, we again use the budget-shrinking algorithm. Note that in the Edgeworth box depicted in Figure 6.8, an allocation x is ε-efficient if and only if agent 1's indifference curve passing through x does not fall below agent 2's indifference curve passing through x by more than ε. Shrinking agent 1's lower contour set yields a "budget line" that is ε below agent 2's indifference curve at all off-equilibrium allocations. After that, agent 2's lower contour set cannot be shrunk. Thus, the sum of the prices delineating the agent's budget sets must be higher by ε for any off-equilibrium allocation than for the equilibrium allocation. (Intuitively, agents should be "penalized" for deviations to off-equilibrium allocations.) Formally, we have:

Proposition 3 *A message is a minimally informative message verifying ε-efficiency of allocation $x = (k, t) \in \bar{X}$ in a quasilinear economy if and only if it is equivalent to an ε-valuation equilibrium supporting x, i.e., a budget equilibrium (B, x) with budget sets described by (2) for some price vector*

---

[21] Conitzer and Sandholm (2005) also characterize the communication costs of several other common voting rules. Some of these rules, such as approval voting and the majority rule, are interesection-monotonic, and so their results can be alternatively derived by characterizing supporting budget sets. Others are not even monotonic, and the results are proven using different "fooling sets."

[22] This is a "worst-case" notion of approximation. Average-case approximation is discussed in Subsection 6.3 below.

$p \in \mathbb{R}^{NK}$ *satisfying*

$$\sum_i p_i\left(k'\right) = \sum_i p_i\left(k\right) + \varepsilon \text{ for all } k' \in K \setminus \{k\}. \tag{4}$$

Any such equilibrium is a unique ε-valuation equilibrium in the state given by the agents' utility functions $u_i = p_i$ for all i.

Observe that if agents' utility functions are bounded, then any approximation $\varepsilon > 0$ can be achieved with finite communication in which agents announce their utilities rounded off to multiples of ε/N. Thus, arbitrarily close approximation can be achieved with discrete communication, and so the communication cost of approximation should be measured in bits. In Subsection 5.1 below we discuss how this cost relates to the cost of exact efficiency measured in real numbers.

Now we focus on the setting of "binary utilities" described in the previous subsection. In this setting, the agents' utilities are in $\{0, 1\}$, and the budget-shrinking algorithm yields prices in $\{0, 1\}$. Note that approximation within $\varepsilon = N - 1$ can be achieved with a "dictatorial" protocol in which one agent announces an allocation that maximizes his utility. Approximation within $\varepsilon < N - 1$ requires finding an allocation that gives utility 1 to at least two agents. The communication complexity of this can be bounded below by counting how many "diagonal" states, i.e., states with total surplus 1 for all allocations, can be "covered" with a given ε-valuation equilibrium, and dividing by the total number of diagonal states. This gives a lower bound on the number of price equilibria that need to be used, yielding (see Segal 2005):

Corollary 5 *With binary utilities, the communication cost of achieving a better approximation of efficiency than letting one agent choose an allocation is at least $(K - 1)\log_2\left(1 + 1/\left(N - 1\right)\right)$ bits.*

Interpreting the problem as "approval voting," this means that the cost of finding even an alternative that is approved by more than one voter is proportional to the number of alternatives. The result can also be applied to the combinatorial allocation problem, by constructing a "large" subset K of allocations such that the agents can have arbitrary utilities for allocations from K, and that all allocations that are better than dictatorial allocations lie in K. Nisan and Segal (2004) construct such a set K whose size is exponential in the number of objects. Corollary 5 then implies that any improvement upon giving all objects to one agent requires exponential communication.

4.4   Stable Many-to-One Matching

Now we consider the problem of stable many-to-one matching, which is studied in Roth and Sotomayor (1990), henceforth RS. In the problem, the set N of agents is partitioned into the set F of firms and the set W of workers. A

Figure 6.9.

matching between firms and workers is a binary relation $x \subset F \times W$. With a slight abuse of notation, we let $x(i)$ denote the set of agent i's matching partners in matching x. We restrict the space of alternatives to include only *many-to-one* matchings, in which a worker cannot match with more than one firm: $X = \{x \subset F \times W : |x(w)| \leq 1 \, \forall w \in W\}$. We examine matching problems without externalities, i.e., those in which each agent i's preferences depend only on the set $x(i)$ of his matching partners.

A coalition S can deviate from a candidate match $x \in X$ by (i) breaking any matches and (ii) creating new matches between its members; formally, it can deviate to any match $y \in X$ such that $y \setminus (S \times S) \subset x \setminus (S \times S)$.[23] This describes a CU choice rule as defined in Subsection 3.3 above, which is therefore intersection-monotonic, hence satisfying the Budget Equilibrium Revelation Property. We proceed to characterize the minimally informative budget equilibria verifying stability.

Intuitively, since a worker's preferences depend only on his employer, his budget set can be described in terms of the available employers. On the other hand, a firm has preferences over *groups* of workers, and so its budget sets can be described in terms of such available groups. Describing such a combinatorial budget set for a firm would require exponential communication (2^W bits).

Fortunately, it turns out that *minimally informative* budget equilibria verifying stability don't use combinatorial budget sets for firms. To see this, note that a budget equilibrium verifies stability if and only if each firm f's budget set includes any group consisting of some workers who do not have f in their budget sets and some of those currently employed by f. Indeed, this ensures that no deviation can make firm f and all of its new hires strictly better off. In the minimally informative budget equilibria, characterized by (*), firms must have minimal budget sets necessary for verification, which means that each firm f's budget set must include *exactly* the groups consisting of some of f's current employees and some of those workers who do not have f in their budget set. Thus, the firms' budget sets are implied by the workers' budget sets, and they can be described by listing *individual* workers that are available to the firm. In such an equilibrium, each potential off-equilibrium match is allocated to either the firm's or the worker's budget set but not both. (Such an equilibrium is illustrated in Figure 6.9, in which the equilibrium matching is described with

---

[23] We might also ban a coalition from breaking matches between outsiders, but this is irrelevant when externalities in preferences are ruled out.

dashed vertical lines, firm's budget sets are described with downward arrows and workers' budget sets are described with upward arrows.) Formally, the argument yields:

Proposition 4 *A message is a minimally informative message verifying the stability of a many-to-one matching x if and only if it is equivalent to a* match-partitional equilibrium *supporting x, i.e., a budget equilibrium (B, x) satisfying*

$$B_f = \{y \in X : y(f) \subset \omega(f)\} \; \forall f \in F,$$
$$B_w = \{y \in X : y(w) \subset \phi(w)\} \; \forall w \in W,$$

for some $\phi, \omega \subset F \times W$ such that $\phi \cap \omega = x$ and $\phi \cup \omega = F \times W$. Furthermore, any such equilibrium is a unique match-partitional equilibrium supporting matching x in any state $R \in \mathcal{R}$ in which $L(x, R_i) = B_i$ for all $i \in N$.

The finding that combinatorial budget sets for firms need not be used brings about an exponential reduction in the communication cost. Indeed, the workers' budget sets are described by a relation $\phi \subset F \times W$, which is communicated with at most FW bits, the equilibrium matching x is communicated with $W \log_2(F + 1)$ bits, and the firms' budget sets ω are implied by the conditions $\phi \cap \omega = x$ and $\phi \cup \omega = F \times W$. Thus, the cost of verifying a stable matching is $O(FW)$ as $F, W \to \infty$. This is exponentially smaller than that of full revelation of a firm's preference rankings over subsets of workers, which asymptotically takes $\log_2(2^W!) \sim W \cdot 2^W$ bits as $W \to \infty$ (using Stirling's formula).

If we are not required to *fully* verify stability, we only need to verify *one* stable matching in each state, and need not use all match-partitional equilibria. However, we can show that "almost" all such equilibria need to be used. This is true even if the preference domain is restricted to include only preferences that are strict and *one-to-one*, i.e., each firm prefers being unmatched to matching with more than one worker, and so we can restrict attention to matchings x in which $|x(i)| \le 1$ for all $i \in N$. With such preferences, Segal (2005, Lemma 5) shows that the uniqueness of a stable matching in state R can be ensured by adding one matched firm-worker pair, and completing other agents' preferences in a way consistent with R. Therefore, using the second part of Proposition 4, for any match-partitional budget equilibrium (B, x) on the first $F - 1$ firms and $W - 1$ workers, we can construct a state R in which the unique stable matching coincides with x and the unique supporting match-partitional budget sets coincide with B for the first $F - 1$ firms and $W - 1$ workers. Thus, we can bound below the communication cost of stability by that of describing a budget equilibrium with $F - 1$ firms and $W - 1$ workers. Since any worker's budget set may include any of the firms in addition to its current employer (if in fact he is employed), we have the following lower bound.

Corollary 6 *The verification cost of stable matching between W workers and F firms with strict one-to-one preferences is at least $(F - 2)(W - 1)$ bits. The communication cost of finding a stable many-to-one matching between W workers and F firms on any preference domain that includes strict one-to-one preferences and guarantees the existence of a stable matching is asymptotically at least FW as $F, W \to \infty$.*

Corollary 6 generalizes quadratic lower bounds obtained by Gusfield and Irving (1989) for finding a stable one-to-one matching with $F = W$ using particular querying languages. Specifically, they only allow queries of the form "which partner has rank r in your preference ranking" (their Theorem 1.5.1) or "what rank partner i has in your preference ranking" (their Theorem 1.5.2). The corollary establishes that allowing general communication does not reduce the communication cost.

The communication cost of actually of *finding* a stable matching may in principle be substantially higher than that of verification. However, when firms' preferences are restricted to be strict and substitutable (RS Definition 6.2), a stable matching exists and can be found using only slightly more communication. This can be done with a Gale-Shapley "deferred acceptance algorithm" (RS Theorems 6.7, 6.8), which takes at most $3FW$ steps, at each of which a match is proposed, accepted, or rejected. Since a match is described with at most $\log_2 (FW)$ bits, we have a deterministic protocol that communicates at most $3FW \log_2 (FW)$ bits. This only slightly exceeds the verification cost, and is still exponentially less than full revelation of firms' preferences over combinations of workers.[24]

5 DIFFERENT MEASURES OF COMMUNICATION COST

5.1   Continuous versus Discrete Communication

Here we discuss in greater detail the definition of continuous communication cost and its relation to the discrete communication cost measured in bits. In a continuous communication protocol, agents should be able to send real-valued elementary messages, but we also want to allow finite-valued messages (say, to communicate discrete allocations), without counting the latter toward the communication cost. Thus, the worst-case cost of continuous communication is defined as the maximum number of real-valued elementary messages sent in the course of the protocol. In a verification problem, we can identify the

---

[24] Indeed, it would take $\log_2 (2^W)! \sim 2^W \cdot W$ bits to describe a strict preference rankings groups of workers when W is large (using Stirling's formula). Even if a firm's preference relation is known to be strict and substitutable, the number of bits needed to describe such a relation is still exponential in W, as shown by Echenique (2005, Corollary 5).

communication cost with the dimension of the oracle's message space M, i.e., the number of real numbers needed to encode the oracle's message. For this purpose, we must have a topology on M.

A well-known problem in continuous communication is the possibility of "smuggling" multidimensional information in a one-dimensional message space with a one-to-one encoding. Traditionally, dimension smuggling has been ruled out by imposing a continuity restriction on the communication protocol (Abelson 1980; Luo and Tsitsiklis 1991; Mount and Reiter 1974; Walker 1977). For example, Mount and Reiter (1974) and Walker (1977) require the "message correspondence" from states into messages to have a continuous selection in any neighborhood. This requirement rules out *a priori* some important communication protocols, e.g., those in which agents announce discrete allocations.[25]

A different way to rule out "smuggling" is proposed by Nisan and Segal (2004). They note that when many dimensions are "smuggled" into a one-dimensional message, a small error in the message would yield a huge error in its "meaning," i.e., the set of states it represents. Thus, smuggling can be avoided by using a metric on messages that is not arbitrary but based on their meaning. Specifically, the distance between messages m and m' can be defined as the Hausdorff distance between the corresponding rectangles in the state space $\mathcal{R}$.[26] The communication cost is then defined as a metric dimension of the message space M.[27] In contrast to the traditional approach, this approach does not rule out any protocols, and in particular allows protocols that mix continuous and discrete messages.

Another advantage of the Nisan-Segal definition is that it implies a relation between continuous communication and discrete approximation:

Proposition 5 *(Nisan-Segal 2004) A protocol verifying a certain social goal with a message space whose box-counting dimension is d can be discretized into a protocol verifying approximation of the goal within ε using asymptotically $d \log \varepsilon^{-1}$ bits as $\varepsilon \to 0$.*

Intuitively, the oracle can communicate a message rounded-off within ε using roughly $d \log \varepsilon^{-1}$ bits, and the round-off yields a small distortion in the

---

[25] For example, consider the setting of Section 2 in which an object is allocated between two agents with valuations in [0,1]. The protocol in which agent 1 announces his valuation with 1 real number and then agent 2 reports an optimal allocation with 1 bit is discontinuous on the diagonal, where the optimal allocation switches. Insisting on continuity would require a two-dimensional message space (as in full revelation), which we believe overstates the communication cost in that example.

[26] This distance is based on an underlying metric on the state space $\mathcal{R}$ of preference relation profiles. In turn, the latter can be derived from a given metric on X along the lines suggested by Debreu (1983).

[27] There are different notions of metric dimension – e.g., the Hausdorff dimension, the box-counting dimension, and the packing index (Edgar 1990), but in all economic examples considered they yield the same answers.

meaning of the message. This means that the discretized protocol yields an allocation that is optimal for some state that is not too far from the true state, and therefore approximates an optimal allocation. Thus, metric dimension d of the message space is indicative of the communication complexity of achieving a "fast" approximation of efficiency, in which each additional bit reduces the error by the same factor $(e^{1/d})$.[28]

On the other hand, it turns out a somewhat slower but still practical approximation is sometimes achieved with much less communication than that implied by the continuous cost of exact optimality. A dramatic example of this obtains in Calsamiglia's (1997) model of allocating a homogeneous divisible good between two agents in a quasilinear economy. In this model, exact surplus-maximization requires infinite-dimensional communication (which can be shown by adapting Corollary 2 to an infinite set of allocations K), but Nisan and Segal (2004) demonstrate a protocol that approximates the maximal surplus within ε using $O\left(\varepsilon^{-1}\right)$ bits. This approximation is still considered "fast" (polynomial) in computer science. In cases like this, the continuous measure of communication cost used in the economic literature seriously overstates the "hardness" of the problem.

5.2   Individual Communication Cost and Distributed Communication

We can reduce the communication costs of individual agents by not having them observe all the communication, i.e., by creating non-trivial information sets in the communication protocol. Also, the allocation need not be broadcast to all agents: instead, we could require that each agent i at the end of communication announce the component x_i of the alternative that he is concerned about. (Formally, we write the space of alternatives as $X = X_1 \times \ldots \times X_N$, so that each agent i's preferences depend only on component x_i of $x = (x_1, \ldots, x_N) \in X$.)[29] The individual communication cost of an agent can be defined as the number of elementary messages (bits or real numbers) that he must observe and send. This model of "distributed communication" better captures Hayek's idea of decentralization.[30] When the number of agents is large, distributed communication could allow a substantial savings in agents' individual communication costs.

Similarly to the aggregate communication cost, individual communication costs can be bounded below by considering a distributed version of the

---

[28] Related observations are made by Hurwicz and Marschak (2003a,b).

[29] Instead of requiring that agent i announce x_i we could require that he only *learn* x_i: If describing x_i is relatively "cheap," as it is in most applications, then requiring that agent i announce x_i would not increase his communication burden substantially.

[30] An intermediate model, in which publicly broadcast messages are followed by agents privately choosing their allocations, has been considered in economics under the name "parametric communication" (Calsamiglia 1987).

verification problem: The oracle has a message space M_i for each agent i, and he announces a "distributed message" $(m_1, \ldots, m_N) \in M \subset M_1 \times \ldots \times M_N$, where M is interpreted as the set of "legal" messages. Each agent i observes only his own message m_i, and accepts or rejects it based on his own type. Each agent i also has a function $h : M_i \to X_i$ that gives his allocation as a function of his message. Message $(m_1, \ldots, m_N) \in M$ *verifies* the choice rule if whenever each agent i accepts his message m_i, the resulting alternative $(h_1(m_1), \ldots, h(m_N))$ is optimal. The oracle should be able to verify an optimal alternative in each state. The communication cost of agent i is identified with the size of his message space M_i. Note that any distributed communication protocol can be converted into this distributed verification by letting M_i consist of agent i's information sets over the terminal nodes of the communication protocol. Thus, distributed verification offers a lower bound on distributed communication.

We say that choice rule F satisfies the *Distributed Budget Equilibrium Revelation Property (DBERP)* if for any distributed protocol verifying the choice rule there exists a function $b_i : M_i \to 2^{X_i}$ such that for any distributed message $(m_1, \ldots, m_N) \in M$, each agent i can construct his budget set $b_i(m_i) \subset X_i$ on the basis of his own message m_i so that budget equilibrium $(b_1(m_1), \ldots, b_N(m_N), h_1(m_1), \ldots, h_N(m_N))$ verifies allocation $(h_1(m_1), \ldots, h_N(m_N))$. The difference from BERP is that each agent should be able to construct his budget set on the basis of the communication *he observes*. Still, the same argument as that behind Theorem 2 shows that DBERP holds for any intersection-monotonic choice rule: Letting m_i represent the set of agent i's types for which he accepts the message, he can construct his budget set $b_i(m_i) = \cap_{R_i \in m_i} L(h_i(m_i), R_i)$, and by intersection monotonicity the resulting budget equilibrium $(b_1(m_1), \ldots, b_N(m_N), h_1(m_1), \ldots, h_N(m_N))$ verifies allocation $(h_1(m_1), \ldots, h_N(m_N))$. Thus, for IM choice rules, any distributed communication must reveal to each agent his own budget set, in addition to his own allocation. The necessity of observing one's own budget set can be used to bound below the size of the agent's message space, and therefore his individual communication cost. The "hard" cases for distributed communication are the ones in which individual communication cost grows with the number of agents, e.g., as it does in the matching problem.

The distributed communication model outlined above still requires a "center" to maintain the consistency of communication observed by different agents. In a verification protocol, the "center" must verify that $(m_1, \ldots, m_M) \in M$. In a communication protocol, the "center" could be interpreted as a "communication device," which receives private input messages from many agents and sends private output messages to many agents. We could rule out such "communication devices" and consider a more restricted model of *pairwise communication*, in which only private messages between two agents are allowed. A verification version of such pairwise communication is considered by Marschak and Reichelstein (1998), who find that a certain number of agents must then become "coordinators": in addition to observing their own prices (as they must under DBERP), they also get involved in relaying prices between other agents.

Thus, the restriction to pairwise communication creates some "communication overhead."

Note that with pairwise communication it may sometimes make sense to employ agents who possess no private information themselves, but can serve as "communication devices" by aggregating and/or disaggregating messages. While this could only increase the aggregate communication cost, it would now be spread among more agents, possibly reducing individual communication costs. For a survey of the literature on organizations with an endogenous number of agents, see van Zandt (1998).

An even more restricted model is that of *network* communication, which allows only pairwise communication between agents who share an edge in a fixed network. For example, the network could be given by existing Internet links or organizational structure. Marschak and Reichelstein (1998, Section 4) and Feigenbaum et al. (2003) consider a special case in which the communication network is a tree.[31] A simple lower bound on communication along a given edge in a tree can be obtained by letting each agent sharing the edge have all the information on his "side" of the tree (i.e., the subtree obtained by cutting the edge). Feigenbaum et al. (2003) use this approach to show that implementation of some budget-balanced incentive-compatible allocation rules in trees requires the communication cost of a large number of agents to grow proportionately to the total number of agents. For modern internet multicast transmissions involving millions of users, such communication would certainly be impractical.

5.3   Evaluation Costs

Even when the communication cost measured in bits or real numbers is low, it may be costly for agents to evaluate their preferences to send the required messages. The costs of preference evaluation was noted in the computer science literature (Parkes 2000), and was modeled in economics as a cost of "information acquisition."[32] While these costs have recently gained attention in the mechanism design literature (see Bergemann and Valimaki 2005), here we focus on identifying the evaluation costs of a given choice rule under the maintained assumption that agents are sincere.

Just as with the communication cost, we can bound below the evaluation cost of finding an optimal alternative by that of verifying that a given alternative is optimal, and obtain the latter by using minimally informative verifying messages.

---

[31] The restriction to communication on trees may be justified by a large "fixed cost" of communication links. This argument was used by Arrow (1974) to explain the prevalence of hierarchies in firms.

[32] Note that such "evaluation costs" depend not just on how many bits are sent, but on which information agents are asked to report with these bits. E.g., in the example in Section 2, it may be easier for an agent to answer the question "Is your valuation above or below 1.5?" than "Is your valuation an even or odd number?" even though each answer would require 1 bit.

Intuitively, the less informative a message is, the lower is each agent's cost of confirming that his preferences are consistent with the message. Thus, BERP and our characterization of minimally informative budget equilibria again prove useful.

For an illustration, consider the many-to-one matching problem described in Subsection 4.4. Suppose that each agent has a cost of "evaluating" a potential matching partner; without incurring costs, he does not know his preferences regarding matchings with this partner. According to Proposition 4, minimally informative messages verifying a stable matching are equivalent to match-partitional equilibria. To verify such an equilibrium, each potential match has to be evaluated by at least one of the partners, hence verification of stability requires at least FW evaluations. (Note that this this cost must be expended in any state, and not just in the worst case.)

We could also allow different agents to have different evaluation costs. To take a simple example, suppose now it is costly for firms to evaluate workers, while workers do not have any evaluation costs. To verify stability with minimal evaluation costs for firms, we need to use a match-partitional equilibrium in which firms' budget sets are minimal. In fact, when firms have substitutable preferences, all the firms' budget sets can be minimized at once, by choosing the stable match that is Pareto worst for the firms (which exists by Roth and Sotomayor (1990, Theorem 6.8)), and letting each firm's budget set include only the workers who strictly prefer it to their current employer, along with the firm's current workers.

This verification procedure gives a lower bound on the firms' evaluation costs, but this lower bound is in fact achieved by the Gale-Shapley deferred acceptance algorithm in which workers propose (Roth and Sotomayor 1990, Theorem 6.8).[33] In this algorithm, each firm evaluates the minimal number of workers needed to find a stable match. This achieves a tangible evaluation savings over full revelation: e.g., in the one-to-one matching problem in which firms' and workers' preferences are uniformly and independently drawn, it can be calculated that in the worker-proposing deferred acceptance algorithm, a firm in expectation evaluates $1/3$ of all workers. It follows from our verification-based lower bound that this is the minimal expected number of evaluations by each firm that is needed to find a stable match.

5.4   Privacy

One reason to avoid full revelation is to prevent agents from learning about each other's private information – a goal known as *privacy*. In the economic literature, privacy is often needed to prevent self-interested agents from deviating in ways that exploit the revealed information (see, e.g., Myerson (1991, Section 6)). The computer science literature studies privacy as a goal in itself.

---

[33] If we wanted to minimize *workers'* evaluation costs, we would achieve this with the deferred acceptance algorithm in which firms make proposals.

Observe that privacy would be maximized if agents could reveal their information privately to a trusted "mediator" ("communication device") who would then announce an optimal outcome. Then agents would learn nothing about other agents' private information beyond the implemented outcome – a situation known as *full privacy*. In reality, however, trusted mediators may not be available, and the question is how much privacy could still be maintained.

Without a trusted mediator, privacy could be enhanced using private pairwise communication between agents. In fact, with sufficiently many agents, private pairwise communication can usually achieve full privacy. This fact has been exploited in a number of papers that implement correlated equilibrium and communication equilibrium without a trusted mediator, by designing a communication protocol that reveals to each agent only his own prescribed action but nothing else, to prevent him from deviating (e.g., Forges 1990).

Suppose now that all communication is public. (Equivalently, we may assume that each agent is concerned that the other $N - 1$ agents would collude to share all their observed private messages to infer information about the agent's type.) Privacy that can be achieved in in such setting is known as "unconditional privacy."[34]

To bound below unconditional privacy, we can again consider verification with minimally informative messages. To have an example, consider the many-to-one matching model described in Subsection 4.4, and suppose that we want to minimize revelation of information about firms' preferences over workers. This is done using a match-partitional budget equilibrium in which the firms' budget sets are minimal. Recall from Subsection 5.3 that when firms have substitutable preferences, all of their budget sets can be minimized at once using the Gale-Shapley deferred acceptance algorithm in which workers propose. The algorithm reveals nothing about firms' preferences except their minimal budget sets, and so it maximizes the firms' privacy. More generally, our results imply that public communication usually cannot achieve "full privacy" since it must reveal supporting budget sets in addition to the outcome to be implemented.[35]

---

[34] We assume that agents are not computationally constrained. If they are, then privacy can be achieved even with public communication using "public-key cryptography." The idea is that a publicly communicated key from agent 1 to agent 2 can be used by agent 2 to encrypt information with a one-to-one function that is simple to compute but very hard to invert without a matching key for inversion, which only agent 1 has. This is the method currently used to implement secure Internet transactions.

[35] Brandt and Sandholm (2005) show that with public communication and unrestricted preference domains, full privacy is not achievable for a large class of choice functions. However, with a restricted preference domain, full privacy may be achievable. For example, a Pareto efficient allocation x in a smooth convex economy can be verified by announcing a supporting Walrasian equilibrium. The supporting prices only reveal other agents' marginal rates of substitution at x, which each agent would have learned from the allocation x itself by calculating his own marginal rates of substitution at x. Another question is whether "full privacy" is a relevant goal when we are implementing a choice rule that is a correspondence rather than a function. In this setting, the revelation of information depends on *which* alternative x is implemented as a function of the state, and not just on what is revealed in addition to x.

6 FURTHER ISSUES

6.1   Communication versus Verification

We have used the verification cost as a lower bound on the communication cost. This raises the following questions:

- *How tight is the verification bound?*

There are cases in which the gap between the communication cost and the verification cost of an allocation problem measured in bits can be exponential – an example is given in Segal (2005, Example 3). (The gap is never more than exponential, because starting with a b-bit verification protocol, which has at most 2^b messages, we can check all the messages sequentially until one is found that is accepted by all agents, which would take at most $N \cdot 2^b$ bits.)

- *In which cases is the verification bound fairly tight?*

The bound is trivially tight when even verification proves almost as hard as full revelation (e.g., in the combinatorial allocation problem considered in Subsection 4.2). More interestingly, there are some well-known social choice problems in which the gap between verification and communication proves to be small and both are much easier than that of full revelation. For example, in the many-to-one matching problem considered in Subsection 4.4, in which firms have strict substitutable preferences, the Gale-Shapley deferred acceptance algorithm converges quickly to a "match-partitional" equilibrium, which verifies stability using only slightly more bits than that needed for verification, and exponentially less than that needed for full revelation of preferences. Similarly, in a convex economy with the "gross substitute" property, Walrasian tatonnement converges quickly to a Walrasian equilibrium, which verifies Pareto efficiency (Mas-Colell et al. (1995, Section 17.H)). Similar "tatonnement" mechanisms have been proposed for combinatorial auction problems with indivisible goods in which the objects are "substitutes" (e.g., Gul and Stachetti 2000, Nisan and Segal 2004). In all these mechanisms, at each step, the designer offers budget sets for the agents, and the agents report their optimal choices from their respective budget sets. If the choices are inconsistent, the designer adjusts the budget sets to be "closer" to being an equilibrium. A "substitutability" condition on the agents' preferences allows us to construct an adjustment process that is monotonic, and therefore converges quickly (enormously faster than full revelation).

- *What is the role of price queries in communication?*

Many practical mechanisms, such as the ones mentioned in the above paragraph, are "demand-query protocols": they quote to the agents a price list for the allocations (with prices sometimes allowed to be nonlinear and personalized) and ask them to submit demands given the prices, adjusting the prices according to some prespecified rules. Can we always restrict attention to such demand-query protocols without increasing the communication cost substantially? Nisan and Segal (2005) show that the answer is "no," by constructing an allocation problem for which the restriction to demand-query protocols brings about an exponential blowup in the communication cost of finding an efficient allocation. Namely, for this class, an efficient mechanism exists that uses a number of bits that is linear to the number of items, but any demand query mechanism that achieves efficiency (or even any improvement upon the "dictatorial" allocation of all the items to one agent) must use an exponential number of demand queries. Contrast this to the verification problem, in which, according to Proposition 2, we can restrict attention to a demand-query mechanism (valuation equilibrium) without any increase in the communication cost.

To summarize, in several well-known cases the verification lower bound on communication is fairly tight, and efficient communication can be achieved with a demand-query mechanism. However, there are some problems in which these properties fail. It would be interesting to characterize social choice problems that satisfy both properties.

6.2   Incentives

So far we have ignored agents' incentives to follow the strategies prescribed by the protocol. If the agents behave in their self-interest, the designer faces additional "incentive-compatibility" constraints requiring that no agent has an incentive to deviate from his prescribed strategy – i.e., the strategies constitute an equilibrium of the communication game. The number of bits by which these constraints increase the communication cost may be called the "communication cost of selfishness," and it is examined in Fadel and Segal (2005, henceforth FS).

Note that the fact that the protocol must reveal supporting prices (by the Budget Equilibrium Revelation Property) does not ensure that it is incentive-compatible: agents may have the ability to manipulate the prices they face to their advantage. For example, take the setting of Section 2, in which one object is to be allocated between two agents, and consider Protocol 2, in which agent 1 announces his valuation v_1, and agent 2 then announces an efficient allocation x. The protocol reveals a supporting price $p = v_1$. However, if agent 1 is charged this price for winning the object, then he will have an incentive to understate his valuation. In fact, as shown in FS, the protocol does not reveal enough information to compute a price that would motivate agent 1 to be truthful regardless of his beliefs about agent 2's valuation v_2. (Intuitively, when both agents' valuations are in [0,1], agent 1 can only be motivated to be truthful if he is charged price v_2, as in the Vickrey auction, but this price is not revealed by the protocol.)

An agent's incentive to deviate in a protocol depends on his information about the other agents. FS consider two implementation concepts: Bayesian-Nash Incentive Compatibility (BIC), which requires that each agent has no incentive to deviate given his beliefs about other agents' types, and Ex Post

Incentive Compatibility (EPIC), which requires that each agent has no incentive to deviate *regardless* of his beliefs about others' types. Both implementation concepts satisfy the Revelation Principle: If an allocation rule is implementable in *some* protocol, it is implementable in a *direct revelation* protocol, in which agents simultaneously announce their private information (but which may have a high communication cost). Thus, FS consider the communication cost of selfishness for those allocation rules that are implementable in a direct revelation protocol.

In general, agents' incentives in a protocol can be manipulated using two instruments: (1) monetary transfers (the agents' utilities are assumed to be quasilinear in such transfers, as in Subsection 4.2), and (2) information sets that hide information from the agents. For EPIC implementation, the protocol need not hide any information from the agents, and the communication cost of selfishness is entirely due to the need of computing motivating transfers in addition to the nonmonetary allocation. In contrast, for BIC implementation, the cost of selfishness is due to the need to hide information from the agents to restrict their contingent deviations (while computation of transfers does not entail any additional cost).

For both the EPIC and BIC case, FS provide an upper bound on the communication cost of selfishness:

$$\text{Incentive-Compatible Communication Complexity} \leq 2^{\text{Communication Complexity}}.$$

Since this bound is very weak, FS proceed to ask whether it is ever achieved or approached.[36]

For BIC implementation, FS do show that the bound is tight by providing an example in which the communication cost of selfishness is exponential. The example has two agents: An "expert" with private knowledge and a private utility function, and a "manager" with a privately known goal that determines how the expert's knowledge should be used. The expert will reveal his knowledge truthfully if he does not know the manager's goal, but this revelation will take exponential communication in the number of outcomes. Communication could be reduced exponentially by having the manager first announce his goal and then letting the expert say how to achieve it, but this communication is not incentive-compatible – knowing the manager's goal, the expert can manipulate her report to achieve her preferred outcome. FS show that any communication that satisfies the expert's BIC constraints must be almost as long as full revelation of the expert's knowledge.

For the EPIC case, it is not known whether the exponential upper bound is ever achieved or approached. In many studied cases, the communication cost of selfishness for EPIC proves to be low. For example, this is the case if we want to

---

[36] If the communication cost is measured as the *average-case* number of bits sent, as defined in footnote 3, FS show that the communication cost of selfishness can be unbounded, both for EPIC and for BIC.

implement an efficient (surplus-maximizing) allocation.[37] Indeed, suppose that we have a communication protocol that finds an efficient allocation. After running the protocol, ask each agent to report his payoff $\pi_i = u_i(k)$ at the resulting allocation k, and pay each agent i a transfer $t_i = \sum_{j \neq i} \pi_j$.[38] Under this transfer scheme (first proposed by Reichelstein (1984)), each agent's total payoff equals the total surplus, and so the communication game becomes one of common interest (in the terminology of Marschak and Radner (1972), the agents become a "team"). Since the protocol is efficient, the resulting mechanism is EPIC: no deviation by an agent can increase the total surplus.[39]

Another literature on incentive-compatible communication studies a "dual" question: instead of asking how much communication is needed to achieve a given goal, it asks how to maximize a given objective function subject to a fixed communication constraint. Typically the objective is to maximize the profits of one of the agents subject to other agents' participation constraints. See, e.g., Green and Laffont (1987), Melumad et al. (1992), and a recent survey by Mookherjee (2006).

6.3   Average-Case Goals: Prices versus Authority and Coercion

We have examined the problem of achieving a given social goal with certainty. However, given a probability distribution over states, we could allow probabilistic goals – e.g., require approximating the *probability* of finding an efficient outcome, or *expected* surplus.[40] Is it still necessary or desirable to find supporting prices to achieve such approximation? We show that the answer is "no," by giving two examples in which (a) an efficient outcome can be found with a high probability with little or no communication, while (b) verifying efficiency of the outcome by describing supporting prices would require enormously more com-

---

[37] This argument extends to allocation rules that maximize nonnegative affine combinatons of agents' utilities, since they can be interpreted as efficient rules upon rescaling the agents' utilities and adding a fictitious agent. Lavi et al. (2003) show that in some important settings, any dominant-strategy implementable allocation rule must take this form.

[38] Technically, this requires agents to communicate real numbers. If agents can only communicate bits but have real-valued utilities, they can report their rounded-off utilities, in which case the proposed transfer scheme would make the protocol approximately incentive-compatible.

[39] Even if the protocol is not exactly efficient but maximizes expected surplus given some common-knowledge subject to a constraint on communication costs, the proposed strategy profile will satisfy BIC, since no agent would be able to increase expected surplus by deviating. Furthermore, if agents are also made to internalize the communication costs through ex post transfers, then they need not be given any protocol at all – the protocol that maximizes the expected surplus net of communication costs will emerge as a Bayesian-Nash equilibrium of the "free-form" game in which agents can send any messages and implement an allocation. To be sure, this argument relies heavily on the agents' rationality – both individual (being able to calculate an optimal protocol) and collective (having a common prior and being able to coordinate on a protocol). But if agents are not fully rational, it is not clear how to model their incentives in the first place.

[40] In contrast, for example, to approximating the maximum surplus within ε across all states, which was considered in Subsection 4.3.

munication.[41] In one example, the low-communication approximately efficient mechanism can be interpreted as coercion, and in the other, as authority.

Example 5 (Coercion): We need to decide whether to provide an indivisible public good to N agents whose valuations u_i for the good are drawn i.i.d. from $\{0, 1\}$, with $\Pr\{u_i = 1\} = \rho \in (0, 1)$. Let the cost of provision be between $k - 1$ and k, hence efficiency requires providing the good if and only if $\sum_i u_i \geq k$. Observe that when N is large and $k/N < \rho - \alpha$ for some fixed $\alpha > 0$, by the Law of Large Numbers, providing the good without any communication is efficient with a high probability. On the other hand, to *verify* that provision is efficient, by Proposition 2 we need to describe a supporting valuation ("Lindahl") equilibrium, i.e., describe k agents willing to pay price 1 for the good. The probability that any such valuation equilibrium is indeed an equilibrium is ρ^k. Therefore, to find supporting prices with probability $\varepsilon > 0$ we need to use at least ε/ρ^k different equilibria, which requires sending at least $\log_2\left(\varepsilon/\rho^k\right) = k \log_2 \rho^{-1} + \log_2 \varepsilon$. Thus, as $N, k \to \infty$ so that $k/N < \rho - \alpha$, finding a supporting price equilibrium to verify efficiency with any fixed probability ε requires unbounded communication, while providing the good without any communication is efficient with probability approaching 1.

Example 6 (Authority): Two agents have utilities in $\{0, 1\}$ for allocations from set K. The probability distribution is as follows: Each agent for each allocation draws utility 1 with probability ρ_K and 0 with probability $1 - \rho_K$, and the draws are independent across allocations and between the agents. Assume that as $K \to \infty$, (i) $\rho_K K \to \infty$, and (ii) $\rho_K^2 K \to 0$. By (i), the asymptotic probability that there is no surplus-1 allocation for an agent is $\left(1 - \rho_K\right)^K \sim e^{-\rho_K K} \to 0$. By (ii), the asymptotic probability that there is no surplus-2 allocation is $\left(1 - \rho_K^2\right)^K \sim e^{-\rho_K^2 K} \to 1$. Thus, the "authority protocol" in which one agent names the best allocation for him achieves efficiency with probability approaching 1, communicating only $\log_2 K$ bits. On the other hand, to *verify* that there is no allocation with a higher surplus by Proposition 2, we need to announce a supporting valuation equilibrium. The probability that a given valuation equilibrium is an equilibrium conditional on the random state having maximal surplus 1 (which asymptotically occurs with probability 1) can be bounded above by $\left(1 - \rho_K\right)^K \sim e^{-\rho_K K}$.[42] Thus, any protocol announcing a supporting

---

[41] While for simplicity we show this for worst-case number of bits, the same results extend to the *expected* number of bits using Shannon's (1948) entropy lower bound.

[42] To see this, recall first that in the binary-utility setting we could use the valuation equilibria (p_1, p_2, k) with prices $p_1, p_2 \in \{0, 1\}^K$, normalized so that $p_1, p_2 \neq (1, \ldots, 1)$, and $p_1(k') + p_2(k') = 1$ for all $k' \in K$. For such (p_1, p_2, k) to be an equilibrium, the agents' equilibrium utilities $u_i(k) - p_i(k)$ must be nonnegative, and therefore, in a surplus-1 state, both agents' equilibrium utilities must be zero. This can only be an equilibrium in states (u_1, u_2) in which for all k' with $p_1(k') = 0$, $u_1(k') = 0$, and for all other k', $u_2(k') = p_2(k') = 0$. This implies the upper bound.

price equilibrium with a fixed probability $\varepsilon > 0$ must asymptotically use at least $\varepsilon e^{\rho_K K}$ distinct messages, and so communicate $\log_2 \left(\varepsilon e^{\rho_K K} \right) \sim \rho_K K \log_2 e$ bits. This communication cost could be exponentially higher than the $\log_2 K$ bits used by authority (e.g., when $\rho_K = K^{-\alpha}$ with $\alpha \in (1/2, 1)$, which satisfies (i),(ii)).[43]

Example 5 may be interpreted as justifying government provision of public goods when the provision is likely to be efficient, but the communication cost of using Lindahl markets with a large number of agents would be prohibitive. Example 6 may be interpreted as formalizing the view of Coase (1937) and Simon (1951) of firms as "islands of conscious power" in which the price mechanism is superseded by decision-making by authority. In the example, as suggested by Coase, the cost of "discovering what the relevant prices are" proves to be prohibitively high, while the benefit is vanishingly small.

The recent work on understanding the allocation of authority in firms (e.g., Aghion and Tirole 1997, Dessein 2002) has arbitrarily restricted attention mechanisms that allocate formal authority, accompanied by more extensive informal communication. If incentives were the only concern, then it would be optimal to use an extensive formal mechanism. Example 6 offers a potential explanation for the use of formal authority: If the costs of formal communication are higher than that of informal, it could be optimal to use only extremely simple formal communication such as authority, supplemented with extensive informal communication.

6.4   Interdependent Values

We have assumed that each agent knows his own preferences, which are not affected by other agents' private information except through the implemented allocation. A more general formulation would allow *interdependent values*, i.e., direct dependence of one agent's preferences on other agents' private information. One example is when other agents have private information about the quality of the goods allocated to the agent. Another example is when an agent is acquiring assets for future resale, and other agents have relevant private information for predicting the future resale price of the assets.

---

[43] In the same setting, Nisan and Segal (forth., Proposition 14) show that there exists a probability distribution over the two agents' binary utilities for which a surplus-2 allocation is guaranteed to exist, but finding it requires exponential communication in K, and so authority is optimal among subexponential mechanisms. Nisan and Segal (forth.) apply this result to showing the uselessness of practical combinatorial auctions, where "authority" allocation is achievable by giving all the objects to one agent. A shortcoming of this example is that the probability distribution over utilities needed for it to hold may not be a "natural" one. Segal (1995) obtained the same result for the probability distribution over utilities described as in the example, but under the restriction that communication cannot use a common "language" (labeling of allocations).

The performance of price mechanisms in such interdependent-value settings has been extensively studied. The most widely used price equilibrium concept for such settings is *Rational Expectations Equilibrium* (REE), in which agents infer information through the announced prices, and make choices from their budget sets to maximize their expected utilities given the inferred information (see, e.g., Mas-Colell et al. 1995 Section 19.H, Radner 1979, Grossman 1981). Can we offer a normative foundation for rational expectations price equilibria in the interdependent-value setting akin to the Budget Equilibrium Revelation Property for the private-value setting?

Note that in the interdependent-value setting, social goals such as Pareto efficiency may be achieved without revealing supporting REE prices. The simplest example is allocating an object among agents who have a "pure common value" for it, which depends on the agents' private signals. In this example, any allocation would be efficient and could be achieved without any communication, but the REE would typically depend on private information.

One may argue that a statistically efficient aggregation of private information may be desirable for reasons other than allocational efficiency (e.g., to guide investment decisions). Thus, many papers have examined the validity of the (strong form) of the "Efficient Market Hypothesis," which says that REE prices form a sufficient statistic for the value of a security given all the private information. Contrary to the hypothesis, there exist cases in which an REE reveals *no* information about the value of a security, even though pooling agents' private information would reveal the value fully:

- **Example 7 (Feigenbaum et al. (2005)):** There are two risk-neutral agents, each of whom privately observes a fair coin toss. The agent can trade a security whose value is 1 if the two agents' coins fall on the same side and 0 otherwise.[44] There exists an REE with price $1/2$ that does not depend on the agents' private information. Since the price is uninformative, each agent continues to believe the security has value 1 with probability 1/2, and so is willing to trade any amount at price 1/2. On the other hand, pooling both agents' information would reveal the exact value of the security.

One might argue that when agents' type spaces are finite, a continuous price would "generically" be fully revealing. However, when agents' type spaces are continuous, "generically," prices cannot be a sufficient statistic for private signals if the total dimension of the signals exceeds the dimension of the price space (which is realistic when agents observe complex signals or when the number of

---

[44] This construction is known in game theory as a "jointly controlled lottery." For an economic example, let agent 1 be the marketing manager of an auto company, who knows which car body will be in high demand next year, and let agent 2 be the company's manufacturing manager, who knows which car body will be cheap to produce next year. The security is contingent on the company's profits.

agents is large). Formally, we are facing a communication (verification) problem, whose solution may require a larger message space than the available price space (a formal point along these lines is made by Jordan (1983)).

These arguments bring into question the recent popularity of "prediction markets" as means of aggregating dispersed private information to forecast various events, from sales at Hewlett Packard to election outcomes to terrorist attacks (see, e.g., Wolfers and Zitzewitz 2004). While some special communication problems may be solved efficiently with a prediction market, the general applicability of price mechanisms for aggregating common-value information is unclear. In particular, the recent proposals to use prediction markets to replace the managerial task of information aggregation and decision making[45] do not have a theoretical foundation.

7 CONCLUSION

In the past 30 years, economists have focused on the issue of incentives.[46] However, consider a thought experiment in which everybody is honest, and ask whether the fundamental economic institutions, such as markets and firms, would still be recognizable in this hypothetical world. It is our conjecture that the answer is "yes." The primary function of these institutions is to process information and make decisions, and their fundamental features are explained by this function (even though incentives may be important for understanding many of their aspects).

This chapter has focused on one kind of economic institutions – price-based mechanisms. We have shown that, contrary to widespread belief, prices are needed not in order to incentivize the agents, but in order to aggregate distributed information about their preferences into a socially desirable decision. Thus, we have provided a justification for and characterized the scope of the price-based "market design" approach (as opposed to more general mechanism design), and characterized the form of "prices" that must be discovered to solve a given social choice problem.

Some of our extensions also offer promising avenues for understanding non-price allocation mechanisms such as firms and governments. For example, as noted by Coase (1937) and Simon (1951), communication in firms differs fundamentally from that in markets: Decisions in firms are usually made by the authority of managers, without "discovering what the relevant prices are." We indeed find an example where authority may emerge as an optimal communication mechanism (Example 6 in Subsection 6.3): it finds an efficient allocation with a high probability, while the communication cost of verifying

---

[45] E.g., "With employees in the trading pits betting on the future, who needs the manager in the corner office?" *Times Magazine* (2004).

[46] For example, consider the statements "Most of economics can be summarized in four words: 'People respond to incentives.' The rest is commentary" (Landsburg 1993) and "Economics is, at root, the study of incentives" (Levitt and Dubner 2005).

this efficiency by describing prices for all possible allocations is exponentially higher. Another notable aspect of communication in firms is that much of it is done by professional managers who specialize in aggregating information and making decisions. In Subsection 5.2 we noted how hiring such managers may economize on individual communication costs. Thus, while "theories of the firm" based on incentives or incomplete contracts take managerial tasks as given, a theory based on communication may explain what it is that managers actually do.[47]

References

[1] Abelson, H. (1980): "Lower Bounds on Information Transfer in Distributed Computations." *Journal of the Association for Computer Machinery*, 27, 384–392.

[2] Aghion, P., and J. Tirole (1997): "Formal and Real Authority in Organizations," *Journal of Political Economy*, 105, 1–29.

[3] Athey, S., and I. Segal (2005): "Efficient Dynamic Mechanisms," working paper, Stanford University.

[4] Babaioff, M., and L. Blumrosen (2004): "Computationally Feasible Truthful Auctions for Convex Bundles." *Proceedings of the 8th. International Workshop on Approximation Algorithms for Combinatorial Optimization Problems*, Lecture Notes in Computer Science, Springer-Verlag.

[5] Bergemann, D., and J. Välimäki (2005): "Information Acquisition in Mechanism Design." *Advances in Economic Theory: 9th World Congress*, forthcoming.

[6] Bikhchandani, S., and J. Mamer (1997): "Competitive Equilibrium in an Exchange Economy with Indivisibilities," *Journal of Economic Theory*, 74, 385–413.

[7] Bikhchandani, S., and J. Ostroy (2002): "The Package Assignment Model," *Journal of Economic Theory*, 107, 377–406.

[8] Brandt, F., and T. Sandholm (2005): "Unconditional Privacy in Social Choice," In Ron van der Meyden, ed., *Proceedings of Theoretical Aspects of Rationality and Knowledge X*, National University of Singapore, 207–218.

[9] Calsamiglia, X. (1977): "Decentralized Resource Allocation and Increasing Returns," *Journal of Economic Theory*, 14, 262–283.

[10] Calsamiglia, X. (1987): "Informational Requirements of Parametric Resource Allocation Processes." In Theodore Groves, Roy Radner, and Stanley Reiter, eds., *Information, Incentives, and Economic Mechanisms*, Minneapolis: University of Minnesota Press.

[11] Coase, R. (1937): "The Nature of the Firm," *Economica*, 4, 386–405.

[12] Conitzer, V., and T. Sandholm (2005). "Communication Complexity of Common Voting Rules." In *Proceedings of the ACM Conference on Electronic Commerce 2005*.

[13] Cramton, P., Y. Shoham, and R. Steinberg (eds.) (2006): *Combinatorial Auctions*, MIT Press.

[14] Debreu, G. (1952): "A Social Equilibrium Existence Theorem," *Proceedings of the National Academy of Sciences*, 38(10), 886–893.

---

[47] Such a theory may complement existing models in which managers are hired to perform computations, such as addition of numbers – see, e.g., van Zandt (1998).

[15] Debreu, G. (1983): "Neighboring Economic Agents," in *Mathematical Economics: Twenty Papers of Gerard Debreu*, New York: Cambridge University Press, 173–178.

[16] Dessein, W. (2002): "Authority and Communication in Organizations." *Review of Economic Studies*, 69(4), 811–38.

[17] Dobzinski, S., N. Nisan, and M. Schapira (2005). "Approximation Algorithms for Combinatorial Auctions with Complement-free Bidders." *Symposium on Theory of Computing* 2005.

[18] Echenique, F. (2005): "Counting Combinatorial Choice Rules," *Games and Economic Behavior*, forthcoming.

[19] Edgar, G.E. (1990): *Measure, Topology, and Fractal Geometry*. New York: Springer-Verlag.

[20] Fadel, R., and I. Segal (2005a): "Communication Cost of Selfishness: Ex Post Implementation," In Ron van der Meyden, ed., *Proceedings of Theoretical Aspects of Rationality and Knowledge X*, National University of Singapore, 165–176.

[21] Fadel, R., and I. Segal (2005b): "Communication Cost of Selfishness," working paper, Stanford University

[22] Feigenbaum, J., L. Fortnow, D. Pennock, and R. Sami (2005): "Computation in a Distributed Information Market," *Theoretical Computer Science*, 343, 114–132.

[23] Feigenbaum, J., A. Krishnamurthy, R. Sami, and S. Shenker (2003): "Hardness Results for Multicast Cost Sharing," *Theoretical Computer Science*, 304, 215–236.

[24] Forges, F. (1990), "Universal Mechanisms," *Econometrica*, 58, 1341–1364.

[25] Green, J., and Laffont J.-J. (1987): "Limited Communication and Incentive Compatibility," *Information, Incentives, and Economic Mechanisms: Essays in Honor of Leonid Hurwicz*, T. Groves, Radner, R. and Reiter, S. (ed.), Minneapolis: University of Minnesota Press.

[26] Greenberg, J. (1990): *The Theory of Social Situations: An Alternative Game-Theoretic Approach.* Cambridge: Cambridge University Press.

[27] Grossman, S. (1981): "An Introduction to the Theory of Rational Expectations under Asymmetric Information." *Review of Economic Studies*, 48, 541–559.

[28] Gusfield, D., and R.W. Irving (1989): *The Stable Marriage Problem: Structure and Algorithms.* Cambridge: MIT Press.

[29] Hammond, P. (1997): "Game Forms versus Social Choice Rules as Models of Rights," in K.J. Arrow, A.K. Sen, and K. Suzumura (eds.) *Social Choice Reexamined*, Vol. II (IEA Conference Volume No. 117), ch. 11, 82–95, London: Macmillan.

[30] Hatfield, J.F., and P.R. Milgrom (2005): "Matching with Contracts," *American Economic Review*, 95, 913–935.

[31] Hayek, F.A. (1945): "The Use of Knowledge in Society," *American Economic Review*, 35, 519–30.

[32] Hurwicz, L. (1977): "On the Dimensional Requirements of Informationally Decentralized Pareto-Satisfactory Processes," in K.J. Arrow and L. Hurwicz, eds., *Studies in Resource Allocation Processes*, 413–424, New York: Cambridge University Press.

[33] Hurwicz, L., and T. Marschak (2003a): "Finite Allocation Mechanisms: Approximate Walrasian versus Approximate Direct Revelation," *Economic Theory*, 21, 545–572.

[34] Hurwicz, L., and T. Marschak (2003b): "Comparing Finite Mechanisms," *Economic Theory*, 21 (2003), 783–841.

[35] Hurwicz, L., and S. Reiter (2006): *Designing Economic Mechanisms*, Cambridge University Press.

[36] Ishikida, T., and T. Marschak (1996): "Mechanisms That Efficiently Verify the Optimality of a Proposed Action," *Economic Design*, 2(1), 33–68.

[37] Jordan, J.S. (1982): "The Competitive Allocation Process Is Informationally Efficient Uniquely," *Journal of Economic Theory*, 28(1), 1–18.

[38] Jordan, J.S. (1983): "On the Efficient Market Hypothesis," *Journal of Economic Theory*, 51(5), 1325–1343.

[39] Ju, B.-G. (2001): "Nash Implementation and Opportunity Equilibrium," working paper, University of Kansas.

[40] Karloff, H. (1991): *Linear Programming*. Basel: Birkhäuser Verlag.

[41] Kelso, A.S. Jr., and V.P. Crawford (1982): "Job Matching, Coalition Formation, and Gross Substitutes." *Econometrica*, 50, 1483–1504.

[42] Kushilevitz, E., and N. Nisan (1997): *Communication Complexity*. Cambridge University Press.

[43] Landsburg, S.E. (1993): *The Armchair Economist: Economics and Everyday Life.* New York: The Free Press.

[44] Levitt, S., and S. Dubner (2005): "Freakonomics: A Rogue Economist Explores the Hidden Side of Everything," New York: Harper Collins.

[45] Lipton, R. J., E. Markakis, E. Mossel, and A. Saberi (2004): "On Approximately Fair Allocations of Indivisible Goods," *Proceedings of the 5th ACM Conference on Electronic Commerce*, 125–131.

[46] Luo, Z.-Q., and J.N. Tsitsiklis (1991): "Communication Complexity of Algebraic Computation," *Proceedings of the 31st IEEE Symposium on Foundations of Computer Science*, 758–765.

[47] Marschak, T., and S. Reichelstein (1998): "Network Mechanisms, Informational Efficiency, and Hierarchies," *Journal of Economic Theory*, 79, 106–141.

[48] Mas-Colell, A. (1980): "Efficiency and Decentralization in the Pure Theory of Public Goods," *Quarterly Journal of Economics*, 94, 625–641.

[49] Mas-Colell, A., M.D. Whinston, and J. Green (1995): *Microeconomic Theory.* New York: Oxford University Press.

[50] Maskin, E. (1999): "Nash Equilibrium and Welfare Optimality," *Review of Economic Studies*, 66, 23–38.

[51] Melumad, N., D. Mookherjee, and S. Reichelstein (1992): "A Theory of Responsibility Centers," *Journal of Accounting and Economics*, 15, 445–484.

[52] Milleron, J.-C. (1972): "Theory of Value with Public Goods: A Survey Article," *Journal of Economic Theory*, 5, 419–477.

[53] Miyagawa, E. (2002): "Reduced-Form Implementation," Columbia University Working Paper.

[54] Mookherjee, D. (2006): "Decentralization, Hierarchies and Incentives: A Mechanism Design Perspective," *Journal of Economic Literature*, forthcoming.

[55] Mount, K., and S. Reiter (1974): "The Information Size of Message Spaces," *Journal of Economic Theory*, 28, 1–18.

[56] Myerson, R.B. (1991): *Game Theory: Analysis of Conflict.* Cambridge: Harvard University Press.

[57] Nisan, N., and I. Segal (2004): "The Communication Requirements of Efficient Allocations and Supporting Prices," forthcoming, *Journal of Economic Theory*.

[58] Nisan, N., and I. Segal (2005): "Exponential Communication Inefficiency of Demand Queries," In Ron van der Meyden, ed., *Proceedings of Theoretical Aspects of Rationality and Knowledge X*, National University of Singapore, 158–164.

[59] Parkes, D.C. (2000): "Optimal Auction Design for Agents with Hard Valuation Problems," *Agent Mediated Electronic Commerce* (IJCAI Workshop).

[60] Parkes, D.C. (2002): "Price-Based Information Certificates for Minimal-Revelation Combinatorial Auctions," in *Agent-Mediated Electronic Commerce IV*, Padget et al. (eds), LNAI 2531, 103–122, Springer-Verlag.

[61] Radner, R. (1979): "Rational Expectations Equilibrium: Generic Existence and the Information Revealed by Prices." *Econometrica*, 47, 655–678.

[62] Reichelstein, S. (1984): "Incentive Compatibility and Informational Requirements," *Journal of Economic Theory*, 34, 32–51.

[63] Reichelstein, S., and S. Reiter (1988): "Game Forms with Minimal Message Spaces," *Econometrica*, 56(3), 661–692.

[64] Roth, A.E., and M.A.O. Sotomayor (1990): *Two-Sided Matching: A Study in Game-Theoretic Modeling and Analysis*. Cambridge: Cambridge University Press.

[65] Salanie, B. (1997): *The Economics of Contracts: A Primer.* Cambridge: MIT Press.

[66] Sato, F. (1981). "On the Informational Size of Message Spaces for Resource Allocation Processes in Economies With Public Goods," *Journal of Economic Theory*, 24, 48–69.

[67] Segal, I. (1995): "Communication Complexity and Communication by Authority," working paper mimeo, University of California, Berkeley.

[68] Segal, I. (2005): "Communication Requirements of Social Choice Rules and Supporting Budget Sets," working paper, Stanford University.

[69] Sen, A.K. (1970): "The Impossibility of a Paretian Liberal," *Journal of Political Economy*, 78, 152–157.

[70] Serrano, R., and O. Volij (2000): "Walrasian Allocations without Price-Taking Behavior," *Journal of Economic Theory*, 95, 79–106.

[71] Simon, H. (1951): "A Formal Theory of the Employment Relationship," *Econometrica*, 19, 293–305.

[72] Kiviat, B. (2004): "The End of Management?" *Times Magazine*, July 6.

[73] van Zandt, T. (1998): "Organizations that Process Information with an Endogenous Number of Agents," in Mukul Majumdar, ed., *Organizations with Incomplete Information*, Cambridge: Cambridge University Press. Chapter 7, 239–305.

[74] Wolfers, J., and E. Zitzewitz (2004): "Prediction Markets," *Journal of Economic Perspectives*, 18, 107–126.

[75] Walker, M. (1977): On the Informational Size of Message Spaces," *Journal of Economic Theory*, 15, 366–375.

[76] Williams, S.R. (1986): "Realization and Nash Implementation: Two Aspects of Mechanism Design," *Econometrica*, 54, 139–152.

Advances in Dynamic Optimal Taxation
Narayana R. Kocherlakota[1]

1 INTRODUCTION

This paper is about a now classic question in macroeconomics and public finance. A government needs to finance an exogenously given stochastic process of purchases. How do the optimal taxes behave over dates and states?

There is a large literature on this question that uses what I will term the Ramsey approach. Under this approach, the government is restricted to use *linear* taxes on *current* variables like capital and labor income. The government's main goal is then to minimize the social distortions associated with linearity.

The main weakness in the Ramsey approach is obvious: there is no explicit motivation for the restrictions that drive the analysis. Why should the government be restricted to using linear taxes? Virtually all real-world labor income tax codes display nontrivial amounts of nonlinearity. Why should the government be restricted to using functions of current variables? At least in the United States, federal taxes depend in complicated ways on the full history of assetholdings (through the use of basis calculations) and federal (social security) transfers depend in complicated ways on the history of labor incomes.

This weakness in the Ramsey approach has led to a new literature about the optimal taxation question. Under the new approach, instead of specifying an arbitrary set of tax instruments, the investigator first specifies the informational and/or enforcement frictions that limit the government's ability to extract revenue. Then, the investigator designs a tax system that implements a constrained Pareto optimal allocation given these frictions.

A key step in using this approach is knowing what frictions constrain the government. At least so far, the new literature is basically a dynamic extension of Mirrlees' (1971) basic framework, which centers on two key insights. The

[1] The initial draft of this essay was completed while I was a professor at Stanford University. I thank Ellen McGrattan and Torsten Persson for their comments. I acknowledge the support of NSF SES-0350833. The views expressed herein are mine and not necessarily those of the Federal Reserve Bank of Minneapolis or the Federal Reserve System.

first is that a (if not the) major risk in life is skill *risk*. Some people are born with the ability to produce large amounts of output with relatively little effort. Others are not. Over time, some people lose their ability to generate output (because of back pain or mental illness). Others do not.

It is straightforward to design a tax system that fully insures people against skill shocks: tax everyone at 100% and split the proceeds evenly across people, regardless of what they produced. Such a tax system works well, as long as skills and effort are fully observable. With this kind of information in hand, the government can simply order the highly skilled people to work hard.

Mirrlees' second insight explains why this kind of system will not work well: skills and effort are often private information. In terms of the natal risks that Mirrlees himself stresses, people with high IQs can readily mimic people with low IQs. In terms of post-natal skill risks, it is easy to fake back pain or mental illness – there are few non-manipulable physical signs of these ailments.

The equal-split tax scheme by the government can still be used if skills and effort are private information. However, it is no longer desirable. If people are being taxed at 100%, all of the high-skilled people will work as if they are low-skilled. Because it can no longer directly command the high-skilled to work, the government now has to use the tax system to achieve two conflicting goals. As before, the tax system must insure people against skill shocks. But it must also provide *incentives* to motivate the skilled to produce more income than the low-skilled.

It is important to emphasize that the economic forces in this new Mirrlees literature are fundamentally different from the forces in the old Ramsey literature. Under the Ramsey approach, the government is banned from using lump-sum taxes. Its objective is to minimize the social costs associated with using linear taxes. Under the Mirrlees approach, the government is allowed to use lump-sum taxes, but chooses not to. Its objective is to find the optimal trade-off between incentives and insurance.

My goal in this essay is to provide a partial survey of the lessons of the recent dynamic Mirrlees literature. (As we shall see, "recent" really means "recent" – the first published paper in this area appeared in 2003.) The essay is divided into three sections. In the first and larger part of the essay, I focus on wealth taxation. I assume that agents are affected by idiosyncratic shocks to their skills, and that skills and effort are both private information. I impose no restriction on the time series behavior of skills or government purchases. However, I assume (as I do throughout the essay) that preferences are additively separable over time and between consumption and labor.

The main result in this first part of the paper is that it is possible to design an optimal tax system that is *linear* in *current* wealth. This tax system has two surprising features. First, the tax on wealth brought into a given period must depend on the labor income realized in that period. The optimal taxes are *regressive*, so that those who earn surprisingly high labor incomes pay a lower wealth tax. Those who earn surprisingly low labor incomes pay a high wealth tax. As I explain later, this regressive feature helps the tax system provide better incentives. Second, the average tax rate on wealth across individuals is always zero, regardless of the realization of government purchases. Optimal wealth taxes redistribute resources from the surprisingly low-skilled to the surprisingly high-skilled.

In the latter portion of the essay, I consider three other types of taxes. The first is estate taxes. (I turn to them next not because of their importance, but rather because they are closely linked to wealth taxes.) I discuss recent work by Farhi and Werning (2005) on this subject. They show that it is optimal for estate taxes to be negative – estates should be subsidized, not taxed. They also show that the estates of the poor should be subsidized at a higher rate than those of the rich.

I then consider inflation taxes. Here, the key source is a paper by da Costa and Werning (2005). They consider a world in which agents have fixed skills and preferences over consumption, real balances, and labor. They provide conditions on these preferences such that the Friedman Rule (zero nominal interest rates) is optimal. These conditions are sufficiently weak to nest the two most popular models of money demand: cash-in-advance and shopping-time. They also show that the welfare losses from suboptimal monetary policy – that is, positive nominal interest rates – can be considerably higher in a world in which agents have heretogeneous skills.

Inflation taxes, estate taxes, and wealth taxes are all really forms of taxation of different kinds of consumption. This focus on consumption may seem surprising: After all, the heart of the Mirrlees model is the informational friction concerning an individual's willingness/ability to *supply* labor. Mirrlees' (1971) original analysis was designed to understand how an income tax schedule should be designed to resolve the tension between efficiency and equity generated by this friction. Extending his analysis to dynamic settings has proven challenging. I use the work of Battaglini and Coate (2005) to discuss the properties of optimal labor income taxes in a particular setting, in which skills follow a Markov chain with a two-point support and agents are risk-neutral over consumption. The main result of their paper is that under an optimal tax system, labor income taxes are zero for anyone who has ever experienced a high-skill shock in the past.

2 WEALTH TAXES

In this section, I discuss the structure of optimal wealth taxes in a wide class of economic environments. The discussion in the first five subsections closely follows Kocherlakota's (2005) construction of an optimal tax system that is linear in wealth. The sixth subsection discusses other forms of optimal wealth taxes.

2.1   Economic Environment

In this subsection, I describe the environment. The economy lasts for T periods, where T may be infinite and has a unit measure of agents. The economy is initially endowed with K_1^* units of the single capital good. There is a single consumption good that can be produced by capital and labor. The agents have identical preferences. A given agent has von Neumann–Morgenstern preferences and ranks deterministic sequences according to the function:

$$\sum_{t=1}^{T} \beta^{t-1}\{u(c_t) - v(l_t)\}, 1 > \beta > 0 \tag{1}$$

where $c_t \in R_+$ is the agent's consumption in period t, and $l_t \in R_+$ is the agent's labor in period t. I assume that u', $-u''$, v', and v'' all exist and are positive. I also assume that the momentary utility functions u and v are bounded from above and below.

There are two kinds of shocks in the economy: public aggregate shocks and private idiosyncratic shocks. The first kind of shocks works as follows. Let Z be a finite set,[2] and let μ_Z be a probability measure over the power set of Z^T that assigns positive probability to all subsets of Z^T. At the beginning of period 1, an element z^T of Z^T is drawn according to μ_Z. The random vector z^T is the sequence of public aggregate shocks; z_t is the realization of the shock in period t.

The idiosyncratic shocks work as follows. Let Θ be a Borel set in R_+, and let μ_Θ be a probability measure over the Borel subsets of Θ^T. At the beginning of period 1, an element of θ^T is drawn for each agent according to the measure μ_Θ. Conditional on z^T, the draws are independent across agents. I assume that a law of large numbers applies: conditional on any z^T, the measure of agents in the population with type θ^T in Borel set B is given by $\mu_\Theta(B)$.

Both μ_Θ and μ_Z are common knowledge.[3] Any given agent learns the realization of the public shock z_t and his own idiosyncratic shock θ_t at the beginning of period t and not before. Thus, at the beginning of period t, the agent knows his own private history $\theta^t = (\theta_1, \ldots, \theta_t)$ and the history of public shocks $z^t = (z_1, \ldots, z_t)$. This implies that his choices in period t can only be a function of this history.

What is the economic impact of these shocks? First, the shocks determine skills. In period t, an agent produces *effective labor* y_t according to the function:

$$y_t(\theta^T, z^T) = \phi_t(\theta^T, z^T)l_t(\theta^T, z^T)$$

where $\phi_t : \Theta^T \times Z^T \to (0, \infty)$ and is (θ^t, z^t)-measurable. I assume that an agent's effective labor is observable at time t, but his labor input l_t is known only to him. I refer to ϕ_t as an agent's skill in history (θ^t, z^t). The idea here is that everyone shows up for eight hours per day, and their output at the end of

---

[2] I believe that the analysis could be extended to allow Z to be an infinite set, but I have not done so.

[3] Following Wilson (1987), Bergemann and Morris (2005) are rightly critical of making these kinds of strong common knowledge assumptions in mechanism design. They urge the use of what they call *robust* mechanism design, which allows agents to hold differing and unknown beliefs. It would be useful to use robust mechanism design to analyze optimal taxes.

the day is observable. However, it is hard to monitor how hard they are working and what kinds of shocks they face during the day.

The public aggregate shocks influence the aggregate production function in the following way. I define an allocation in this society to be (c, y, K) where:

$$K : Z^T \to R_+^{T+1} \tag{2}$$

$$c : \Theta^T \times Z^T \to R_+^T \tag{3}$$

$$y : \Theta^T \times Z^T \to R_+^T \tag{4}$$

$$K_{t+1} \text{ is } z^t\text{-measurable} \tag{5}$$

$$(c_t, y_t) \text{ is } (\theta^t, z^t)\text{-measurable} \tag{6}$$

Here, $y_t(\theta^T, z^T)$ $(c_t(\theta^T, z^T))$ is the amount of effective labor (consumption) assigned in period t to an agent with type θ^T given that the public aggregate shock sequence is z^T. K_{t+1} is the per-capita amount of capital carried over from period t into period $(t + 1)$.

As mentioned above, I assume that the initial endowment of capital is K_1^*. I assume that the government has exogenous per-capita purchasing needs $G_t : Z^T \to R_+$ in period t, where G_t is z^t-measurable. I define an allocation (c, y, K) to be *feasible* if for all t, z^T:

$$C_t(z^T) + K_{t+1}(z^T) + G_t(z^T) \le F_t(K_t, Y_t, z^T) + (1 - \delta)K_t(z^T) \tag{7}$$

$$C_t(z^T) = \int_{\theta^T \in \Theta^T} c_t(\theta^T, z^T)d\mu_\Theta \tag{8}$$

$$Y_t(z^T) = \int_{\theta^T \in \Theta^T} y_t(\theta^T, z^T)d\mu_\Theta \tag{9}$$

$$K_1 \le K_1^* \tag{10}$$

Here, C_t and Y_t represent per-capita consumption and per-capita effective labor. (Note that (C_t, Y_t) are z^t-measurable.) The aggregate production function $F_t : R_+^2 \times Z^T \to R_+$ is assumed to be strictly increasing, weakly concave, homogeneous of degree one, continuously differentiable with respect to its first two arguments, and z^t-measurable with respect to its last argument.

The idiosyncratic shock θ_t is privately observable. This means that not all physically feasible allocations are actually achievable in this society. For example, consider a physically feasible allocation in which all agents always consume the same amount, but agents with high skills are required to produce a larger amount of effective labor. This allocation is inconsistent with the restriction that skills are privately observable because agents with high skills will always mimic the low-skilled agents and will not generate a large amount of effective labor.

To find the set of achievable allocations, we exploit the Revelation Principle. Under the Revelation Principle, we can restrict attention to *direct* mechanisms in which agents make reports that lie in Θ to a central authority at each date. The

Revelation Principle says that any allocation that is achievable in this setting with private information is an equilibrium allocation of some direct mechanism in which agents find it optimal to tell the truth. Note that the Revelation Principle does not say that different types of agents are necessarily treated differently.

Formally, we proceed as follows. A *reporting strategy* $\sigma : \Theta^T \times Z^T \to \Theta^T \times Z^T$, where σ_t is (θ^t, z^t)-measurable and $\sigma(\theta^T, z^T) = (\theta^{T'}, z^T)$ for some $\theta^{T'}$ (thus, the agent is required to report truthfully about the publicly observable variables). Let Σ be the set of all possible reporting strategies, and define:

$$W(\cdot; c, y) : \Sigma \to R \tag{11}$$

$$W(\sigma; c, y) = \sum_{t=1}^{T} \beta^{t-1} \int_{Z^T} \int_{\Theta^T} \{u(c_t(\sigma)) \\ -v(y_t(\sigma)/\phi_t)\} d\mu_\Theta d\mu_Z \tag{12}$$

to be the expected utility from reporting strategy σ, given an allocation (c, y). (Note that the integral over Z could also be written as a sum.) Let σ_{TT} be the truth-telling strategy $\sigma_{TT}(\theta^T, z^T) = (\theta^T, z^T)$ for all θ^T, z^T. Then, an allocation (c, y, K) is *incentive-compatible* if:

$$W(\sigma_{TT}; c, y) \geq W(\sigma; c, y) \quad \text{for all } \sigma \text{ in } \Sigma \tag{13}$$

An allocation which is incentive-compatible and feasible is said to be incentive-feasible.

An *optimal* allocation is an allocation (c, y, K) that solves the problem of maximizing:

$$\sum_{t=1}^{T} \beta^{t-1} \int_{Z^T} \int_{\Theta^T} \{u(c_t) - v(y_t/\phi_t)\} d\mu_\Theta d\mu_Z \tag{14}$$

subject to (c, y, K) being incentive-feasible. Under this notion of optimality, all agents are treated symmetrically from an ex ante perspective.[4]

2.2   Aspects of the Economic Environment

The class of economic environments described above is large in the sense that skills ϕ_t may be governed by any data generation process. This is desirable because there continues to be an ongoing empirical debate about the time series properties of wages. In particular, the class of environments is sufficiently general that it allows ϕ_t to exhibit persistence of any kind. More subtly, $Var(\phi_t|z^t)$ can be countercyclical. This kind of countercyclical variation in wage inequality has been documented by many authors (including Storesletten, Telmer, and Yaron (2003)), and plays an important role in understanding the behavior of the market price of risk.

---

[4] The notion of social optimality (ex ante symmetric Pareto optima) may seem restrictive. However, the results about wealth taxes are readily generalized to other notions of optimality: ex ante asymmetric Pareto optima, or interim Pareto optima (conditional on period 1 realizations of θ).

The environment is unusually general in at least two respects. It is common when analyzing models with private information to impose restrictions sufficient to guarantee that some form of Spence-Mirrlees single-crossing holds. I have not done so. The relevant results about wealth taxes are valid without single-crossing.[5] Similarly, it is common in dynamic macroeconomics to impose sufficient structure to guarantee recursivity with respect to a small number of state variables. Here, I have not imposed such structure. Recursivity plays no useful role in the characterization of optimal wealth taxes; it is easier to understand the relevant results through the lens of the sequence formulation.

The class of economic environments is special in that preferences are restricted to be additively separable between consumption and labor. With additive separability, any agent's intertemporal marginal rate of substitution for consumption is observable to the planner. Without additive separability, the intertemporal marginal rate of substitution is private information to the agent (because it depends on the agent's level of effort). This kind of private information greatly complicates the nature of optimal wealth taxes. In particular, if utility is nonseparable between consumption and labor, and the support Θ of the idiosyncratic shocks is finite, there is no optimal tax system in which taxes are differentiable in wealth (Kocherlakota (2004)).

2.3 An Intertemporal Characterization of Socially Optimal Allocations

In this subsection, I restate Proposition 1 from Kocherlakota (2005). This proposition establishes that any optimal allocation must satisfy a particular first order condition (similar to that derived in Theorem 1 of Golosov, Kocherlakota, and Tsyvinski (2003) and in Rogerson (1985)).

Proposition 1 *Suppose (c^*, y^*, K^*) is an optimal allocation and that there exists $t < T$ and scalars M^+, M_+ such that $M^+ \geq c_t^*, c_{t+1}^*, K_{t+1}^* \geq M_+ > 0$ almost everywhere. Then there exists $\lambda_{t+1}^* : Z^T \to R_+$ such that:*

$$\lambda_{t+1}^* \text{ is } z^{t+1}\text{-measurable} \tag{15}$$

$$\lambda_{t+1}^* = \beta[E\{u'(c_{t+1}^*)^{-1}|\theta^t, z^{t+1}\}]^{-1}/u'(c_t^*) \text{ a.e.} \tag{16}$$

$$E\{\lambda_{t+1}^*(1 - \delta + F_{K,t+1}^*)|z^t\} = 1 \text{ a.e.} \tag{17}$$

where $F_{K,t+1}^*(z^T) = F_{K,t+1}(K_{t+1}^*(z^T), Y_{t+1}^*(z^T), z^T)$ for all z^T.

Proof. See Kocherlakota (2005).

In this proposition, λ^*_{t+1} is the shadow price of consumption in public history z^{t+1} relative to consumption in public history z^t. (If one wrote out the full planner's problem, λ^*_{t+1} would be the ratio of the multiplier on the resource constraint in z^{t+1} to the multiplier on the resource constraint in z^t.) This shadow price does not depend on idiosyncratic shocks.

Hence, the content of this proposition is twofold. First, it establishes that:

$$\beta\{E(u'(c^*_{t+1})^{-1}|\theta^t, z^{t+1})\}^{-1}/u'(c^*_t)$$

is independent of θ^t. This result is obviously true without private information because in that case, the optimal c^*_t is independent of θ^t. In the presence of private information, it is generally optimal to allow c^*_t to depend on θ^t in order to require high-skilled agents to produce more effective labor. Proposition 1 establishes that even in that case, the *harmonic* mean of $\beta u'(c^*_{t+1})/u'(c^*_t)$, conditional on θ^t and z^{t+1}, is independent of θ^t. The second part of the proposition is more obvious – it simply states that the shadow price λ^*_{t+1} can be used to determine the optimal level of capital accumulation between period t and period $(t+1)$.

A complete proof of this proposition appears in Kocherlakota (2005). Here is a sketch of the proof for the case in which Θ is a finite set. Suppose (c^*, y^*, K^*) is an interior optimum, and fix a positive probability history $(\overline{\theta}^t, \overline{z}^{t+1})$. Consider a perturbation similar to that used by Rogerson (1985), and define a new consumption allocation c' to be the same as c^* except that:

$$u(c'_t(\overline{\theta}^t, \overline{z}^t)) = u(c^*_t(\overline{\theta}^t, \overline{z}^t)) - \varepsilon$$

$$u(c'_{t+1}(\overline{\theta}^t, \theta, \overline{z}^{t+1})) = u(c^*_{t+1}(\overline{\theta}^t, \theta, \overline{z}^{t+1})) + \beta^{-1}\varepsilon \quad \text{for all } \theta \text{ in } \Theta$$

where ε is small and positive. For the agents with skill history $\overline{\theta}^t$, this change is designed to reduce momentary utility in period t by ε, and increase momentary utility in period $(t+1)$ (given any continuation skill history) by $\beta^{-1}\varepsilon$.

The key to the proof is that, by construction, any sequence of reports generates the same (ex ante) utility under (c', y^*) as under (c^*, y^*). Hence, the ranking of reporting strategies must be the same under (c', y^*) as under (c^*, y^*). It follows that if (c^*, y^*) is incentive-compatible, the new plan (c', y^*) must also be incentive-compatible.

Similarly, the new consumption plan (c', y^*) does not change the planner's objective. It follows that the new timing of consumption payments cannot result in extra resources for the planner or (c^*, y^*, K^*) is not optimal. There are $\mu(\overline{\theta}^t)$ agents who have shock history $\overline{\theta}^t$. Hence, for small ε, the new plan frees up $\mu(\overline{\theta}^t)\varepsilon/u'(c^*_t(\overline{\theta}^t, \overline{z}^t))$ units of consumption in period t. Similarly, it costs $\beta^{-1}\varepsilon \sum_{\theta \in \Theta} \mu(\overline{\theta}^t, \theta)/u'(c^*_{t+1}(\overline{\theta}^t, \theta, \overline{z}^{t+1}))$ in period $(t+1)$. By saving the extra period t consumption into period $(t+1)$, the planner has extra resources after paying the costs unless:

$$\mu(\overline{\theta}^t)/u'(c_t^*(\overline{\theta}^t, \overline{z}^t)) \le$$
$$\beta^{-1}\lambda_{t+1}(\overline{z}^{t+1}) \sum_{\theta \in \Theta} \mu(\overline{\theta}^t, \theta)/u'(c_{t+1}^*(\overline{\theta}^t, \theta, \overline{z}^{t+1})) \quad (18)$$

where, as in Proposition 1, $\lambda_{t+1}(\overline{z}^{t+1})$ is the shadow price of consumption in history $\overline{z}^{t+1}$ relative to consumption in history $\overline{z}^t$. Making the same argument with ε small and negative implies the reverse inequality. In other words, at an optimum, the two sides of (18) are equated, which implies Proposition 1.

It is important to note that even if θ^T is public information (so that there is no incentive problem), Proposition 1 is still valid. In this case, full insurance is possible and $u'(c_t^*)$ is deterministic for all t. Proposition 1 immediately implies the standard first order condition:

$$u'(c_t^*) = \beta E\{(1 - \delta + F_{K,t+1}^*)u'(c_{t+1}^*)|z^t\}.$$

Thus, the incentive problem does not create the restriction in Proposition 1. Rather, the incentive problem determines the variance of the marginal utility process that gets plugged into the formula in Proposition 1.

Proposition 1 immediately implies the following corollary.

Corollary 1 *Suppose* $\Pr(Var(u'(c_{t+1}^*)|z^{t+1}, \theta^t) > 0) > 0$. *Then:*

$$\beta E\{u'(c_{t+1}^*)(1 - \delta + F_{K,t+1})|z^t, \theta^t\} > u'(c_t^*) \quad (19)$$

Proof. Jensen's inequality.

The hypothesis in this corollary is that the incentive problem is such that it is optimal for $u'(c_{t+1}^*)$ to be a nondegenerate function of θ_{t+1}. It will not be satisfied, for example, if, conditional on θ^t, ϕ_{t+s} is independent of θ_{t+1} for all $s \ge 1$. In this case, the agent knows his future path of skills with certainty and the inequality in Corollary 1 becomes an equality. More generally though, it is optimal to have a wedge between the intertemporal marginal rate of substitution and the intertemporal marginal rate of transformation: an individual's marginal expected utility from selling capital tomorrow exceeds his marginal disutility from buying capital today.

2.4 The Distinction between Wedges and Taxes

Agents decide how much capital to bring into period $(t + 1)$ using information available up through period t. Hence, it seems logical that the period $(t + 1)$ capital tax itself should be a function only of information up through period t. Under this assumption, the optimal capital tax would be positive. To see this, note that if agents can buy and sell capital in a competitive market subject to a tax, they face the following first order condition:

$$\beta E\{u'(c_{t+1})(1 - \delta + F_{K,t+1})(1 - \tau^k_{t+1})|\theta^t, z^t\} = u'(c_t), \qquad (20)$$

where τ^k_{t+1} is the marginal tax rate on capital. If τ^k_{t+1} is (θ^t, z^t)-measurable, then it must be larger than 0 if the equilibrium allocation is to be optimal.

I show in this subsection that, at least for tax systems that are differentiable in wealth, the above natural logic starts from a wrong premise: Even though the capital accumulation decision is made in period t, the tax on capital accumulation must depend on period $(t + 1)$ information. To see this, consider the following example (which is similar to ones described in Albanesi and Sleet (2005), Golosov and Tsyvinski (2005), and Kocherlakota (2005)). The example has two periods, with no shocks in period 1, and two equally likely possible realizations of skills in period 2.

Specifically, let $u(c) = \ln(c)$, $v(l) = l^2/2$, and $\beta = 1$. Suppose too that $T = 2, \Theta = \{0, 1\}, Z = \{1\}$ (so that there are not aggregate shocks), $F(K, Y) = rK + wY$, and $\delta = 1$. As well, suppose $\phi_1(\theta) = 1$, $\phi_2(\theta, z) = \theta$, $v(l) = l^2/2$, and $\Pr(\theta_2 = 1) = 1/2$. Set $G = 0$. Let (c_{2i}, y_{2i}) denote consumption and effective labor when $\theta = i$. Then, we can re-write the planner's problem as:

$$\max_{c_1, c_{2h}, c_{2l}, y_1, y_{2h}, K_2} \ln(c_1) - y_1^2/2 + \ln(c_{21})/2 + \ln(c_{20})/2 - y_{20}^2/4$$

$$s.t. \; c_1 + K_2 = rK_1 + wy_1$$

$$c_{21}/2 + c_{20}/2 = rK_2 + wy_{21}/2$$

$$\ln(c_{21}) - y_{21}^2/2 \geq \ln(c_{20})$$

$$c_{21}, c_{20}, y_{21}, K_2, y_1 \geq 0$$

(In this statement of the problem, I have set $y_{20} = 0$, as would be true in a social optimum.) The solution to this problem must satisfy the following first order conditions:

$$c_1^* + K_2^* = rK_1 + wy_1^*$$

$$c_{21}^*/2 + c_{20}^*/2 = rK_2^* + wy_{21}^*/2$$

$$\ln(c_{21}^*) - y_{21}^{*2}/2 = \ln(c_{20}^*)$$

$$1/c_1^* = r/[0.5c_{21}^* + 0.5c_{20}^*]$$

$$w/c_{21}^* = y_{21}^*$$

$$y_1^* = w/c_1^*$$

Note that in the social optimum, the highly skilled agent is indifferent between acting high-skilled and acting low-skilled.

Now consider a tax system τ such that if an agent has capital holdings k_2 at the beginning of period 2, and effective labor y_2 in period 2, then in period 2 he pays taxes $\tau^k(k_2) + \tau^y(y_2)$, where τ^k is differentiable with respect to k_2. The additive separability guarantees that the marginal tax rate on capital is known at the time the agent invests. Given this tax system, an equilibrium in this economy is a specification of $(\widehat{c}_1, \widehat{c}_{21}, \widehat{c}_{20}, y_1, \widehat{y}_{21}, \widehat{k}_2)$ such that it solves:

$$\max_{c_1, y_1, c_{2h}, c_{2l}, y_{2h}, k_2} \ln(c_1) - y_1^2/2 + \ln(c_{21})/2 + \ln(c_{20})/2 - y_{21}^2/4$$

$$s.t.\ c_1 + k_2 = rk_1 + wy_1$$

$$c_{21} = rk_2 + wy_{21} - \tau^k(k_2) - \tau^y(y_{21})$$

$$c_{20} = rk_2 - \tau^k(k_2) - \tau^y(0)$$

$$k_2, c_{21}, c_{20}, y_{21}, y_1 \geq 0$$

and markets clear:

$$\widehat{c}_1 + \widehat{k}_2 = rk_1 + wy_1$$

$$\widehat{c}_{21}/2 + \widehat{c}_{20}/2 = r\widehat{k}_2 + w\widehat{y}_{21}/2$$

Note that in equilibrium, $\tau^k(\widehat{k}_2) + 0.5\tau^y(\widehat{y}_{21}) + 0.5\tau^y(0) = 0$, which is the government's budget constraint.

Consider a socially optimal allocation in which $y_{21}^* > 0$. I claim that there is no tax system such that this socially optimal allocation is an equilibrium. Suppose the claim is false. In the socially optimal allocation, a high-skilled agent is indifferent between working y_{21}^* and working 0. Hence, in equilibrium, the agent is indifferent between setting $(y_{21}, k_2) = (y_{21}^*, K_2^*)$ and setting $(y_{21}, k_2) = (0, K_2^*)$. Now suppose the agent chooses $k_2 = K_2^* + \varepsilon$ and sets $y_{21}^* = 0$. His utility from this budget-feasible plan is:

$$\ln(c_1^* - \varepsilon) + \ln(c_{2l}^* + r\varepsilon - \tau^k(K_2^* + \varepsilon))$$

To be in equilibrium, the socially optimal allocation must satisfy the agent's intertemporal first order condition:

$$1/c_1^* = r(1 - \tau^{k\prime}(K_2^*))[0.5/c_{21}^* + 0.5/c_{20}^*]$$

which implies that:

$$1/c_1^* < r(1 - \tau^{k\prime}(K_2^*))/c_{20}^*$$

which means that:

$$\ln(c_1^* - \varepsilon) + \ln(c_{20}^* + r\varepsilon - \tau^k(K_2^* + \varepsilon))$$
$$> \ln(c_1^*) + \ln(c_{20}^*)$$
$$= \ln(c_1^*) + 0.5\ln(c_{21}^*) + 0.5\ln(c_{20}^*) - y_{21}^{*2}/2$$

Given this tax system, the agent can improve upon the socially optimal allocation by saving a little more and then not working.

Intuitively, we have set the capital tax rate to guarantee that the agent does not save too much or too little – assuming that he tells the truth about his type.

The optimal allocation pushes the agent to be indifferent between telling the truth or lying. If he saves a little bit more, and wealth effects are nonzero, then he will prefer to pretend to be disabled when he is actually abled. The *joint* or *double* deviation of saving too much and then shirking beats saving the right amount and telling the truth about one's type.

What this means is that the wedge derived in the previous subsection does not immediately translate into a conclusion about taxes. We have to find a different way to make a connection between the wedge and tax rates.

2.5   A General Optimal Linear Tax System on Wealth

In this subsection, I describe how to design an optimal tax system that is linear in current wealth. I assume throughout that agents hold a positive amount of capital so that they are interior in their capital holdings. I begin by reconsidering the two-period example and designing an optimal system in that context. I then discuss how to design a similar system for the general model described earlier.

2.5.1   Optimal System: Two-Period Example

Recall the two-period example discussed in the prior subsection. Let $(c_1^*, c_{21}^*, c_{20}^*, K_2^*, y_{21}^*)$ be a socially optimal allocation. Define a period 2 tax code by:

$$\tau(k_2, y_2) = \tau_1 k_2 + \alpha_1 \quad \text{if } y_2 > 0$$
$$= \tau_0 k_2 + \alpha_0 \quad \text{if } y_2 = 0$$

where α_i and τ_i are set so as to satisfy:

$$\beta(1 - \tau_i)u'(c_{2i}^*)r = u'(c_1^*) \quad \text{for } i = 0, 1$$
$$w y_{2i} + k_2^*(1 - \tau_i)r - \alpha_i = c_{2i}^* \quad \text{for } i = 0, 1$$

Given this tax system, the individual's choice problem is:

$$\max_{c_1, y_1, c_{2h}, c_{2l}, y_{2h}, k_2} \ln(c_1) - y_1^2/2 + \ln(c_{2h})/2 + \ln(c_{2l})/2 - y_{2h}^2/4$$

$$s.t. \ c_1 + k_2 = rk_1 + wy_1$$

$$c_{21} = r(1 - \tau_1)k_2 + wy_{21} - \alpha_1 \quad \text{if } y_{21} > 0$$

$$c_{21} = r(1 - \tau_0)k_2 - \alpha_0 \quad \text{if } y_{21} = 0$$

$$c_{20} = r(1 - \tau_0)k_2 - \alpha_0$$

$$k_2, c_{20}, c_{21}, y_{21}, y_1 \geq 0$$

I claim that the socially optimal allocation solves this choice problem.

Why is this true? Suppose that the agent works $y_{21} > 0$ in period 2 when abled. Then, his solution for his other choice variables is characterized by:

$$1/c_1 = r[0.5(1 - \tau_1)/c_{21} + 0.5(1 - \tau_0)/c_{20}]$$

$$w/c_1 = y_1$$

$$c_1 + k_2 = rk_1 + wy_1$$

$$c_{21} = r(1 - \tau_1)k_2 + wy_{21} - \alpha_1$$

$$c_{20} = r(1 - \tau_0)k_2 - \alpha_0$$

The starred allocation satisfies these first order conditions.

What if the agent works 0 in period 2 when abled? Then, his first order conditions become:

$$1/c_1 = r(1 - \tau_{k0})/c_{20}$$

$$w/c_1 = y_1$$

$$c_1 + k_2 = rk_1 + wy_1$$

$$c_{21} = r(1 - \tau_0)k_2 - \alpha_0$$

$$c_{20} = r(1 - \tau_0)k_2 - \alpha_0$$

Setting $(c_1, y_1, k_2, c_{21}, c_{20})$ equal to $(c_1^*, y_1^*, k_2^*, c_{20}^*, c_{20}^*)$ satisfies these first order conditions. Hence, the agent is indifferent between working y_{21}^* in period 2 (when able) and not working in period 2.

Thus, we can implement the optimal allocation using a tax schedule that is linear in capital income and nonlinear in labor income. In this implementation, even though agents make their decisions about capital holdings before period 2, the tax rate on capital must depend on the amount of labor income earned in period 2. The tax rate on capital brought into period 2 is necessarily stochastic from the point of view of period 1.

2.5.2 Optimal System: The General Case

The key to the optimal tax system in the two-period example is that wealth tax rates were set so as to equate agents' ex post after-tax marginal rates of substitution with the societal marginal rate of transformation. The general optimal tax system works in the same way. Let (c^*, y^*, K^*) be a socially optimal allocation and let $\lambda_{t+1}^*(z^T)$ be the shadow price of consumption in public history z^{t+1} relative to consumption in public history z^t. Define the tax *rate* τ_{t+1} on wealth brought into period $(t + 1)$ by:

$$(1 - \tau_{t+1}(\theta^T, z^T)) = \frac{\beta^{-1} u'(c_t^*(\theta^T, z^T)) \lambda_{t+1}^*(z^T)}{u'(c_{t+1}^*(\theta^T, z^T))} \tag{21}$$

This tax rate equates the agent's after-tax ex post marginal rate of substitution with the societal marginal rate of transformation (that is, λ).

Kocherlakota (2005) formally proves that, in conjunction with a well-designed labor income tax code, this tax system implements (c^*, y^*, K^*) as an equilibrium. The basic intuition for the proof is as follows. The agent's choice problem is to choose how much to work and how much to save. It is easy to design the labor taxes so that no agent ever chooses an effective labor sequence that is not associated with some type under the socially optimal allocation. (For example, such a choice could result in high fines.) Hence, the agent's problem is basically the same as jointly choosing whether to mimic some other type of person and which capital accumulation strategy to use.

Suppose that the agent chooses his effective labor as if his true type is $\theta^{T'}$. He receives a consumption sequence $c^*(\theta^{T'}, z^T)$ and generates an effective labor sequence $y^*(\theta^{T'}, z^T)$. The agent has the ability to change this consumption stream by buying more or less capital at any date t. But the tax system deters him from doing so; his first order condition for savings is given by:

$$u'(c_t^*(\theta^{T'}, z^T)) - \beta E\{(1 - \tau_{t+1}(\theta^{T'}, z^T)) u'(c_{t+1}^*(\theta^{T'}, z^T))$$
$$\times (1 - \delta + F_{K,t+1}^*) | z^t, \theta^T = \theta^{T'}\}$$
$$= u'(c_t^*(\theta^{T'}, z^T)) - u'(c_t^*(\theta^{T'}, z^T)) E\{\lambda_{t+1}^*(1 - \delta + F_{K,t+1}^*) | z^t\}$$
$$= 0$$

This is the key step in the proof: regardless of what type the agent pretends to be, he has no incentive to alter the resultant consumption profile by buying or selling capital. In other words, adding the ability to buy and sell capital, subject to the tax rate τ, does not change the agent's reporting problem. Since (c^*, y^*) is incentive-compatible, the agent finds it optimal not to mimic anyone else.

It is important to underscore the role of wealth taxes in this setting. It does not matter who owns the capital stock in this economy. Hence, the ability on the part of agents to trade capital is not socially useful; it only serves to undercut the ability of government to achieve desirable outcomes in this setting. Thus, one optimal tax system is for the government to take over the capital stock, and then tax any capital holdings by private agents at 100%. The tax system described above is much less draconian. Private citizens are allowed to hold capital. Instead of banning trade in capital, the linear tax system is carefully designed so that the agents choose not to deviate from their appropriate consumption profiles.

2.5.3   Properties of the Optimal System

What is the expected wealth tax rate in period $(t + 1)$, conditional on (θ^t, z^{t+1})? To answer this question, we compute:

$$E\{(1 - \tau^*_{t+1}(\theta^T, z^T))|\theta^t, z^{t+1}\}$$
$$= E\{\beta^{-1}\lambda^*_{t+1}u'(c^*_{t+1})^{-1}u'(c^*_t)|\theta^t, z^{t+1}\}$$
$$= \beta^{-1}\lambda^*_{t+1}u'(c^*_t)E\{u'(c^*_{t+1})^{-1}|\theta^t, z^{t+1}\}\text{by }(\theta^t, z^{t+1})\text{-measurability of }\lambda^*_{t+1}u'(c^*_t)$$
$$= 1$$

where the last step follows from Proposition 1. Thus, the expected wealth tax rate is zero.

This result has a second, slightly more subtle, implication: wealth taxes are purely redistributional because the government raises no net revenue from them in any public history z^{t+1}. Suppose k^* is an equilibrium process of capital-holdings given that wealth taxes as a function of (θ^T, z^T) equal τ^{**}. Then, we can calculate the total revenue from wealth taxes in each public history:

$$\int_{\theta^T \in \Theta^T} \tau^*_{t+1}(\theta^T, z^T)k^*_{t+1}(\theta^T, z^T)(1 - \delta + MPK^*_{t+1}(z^T))d\mu_{\Theta}$$
$$= (1 - \delta + MPK^*_{t+1}(z^T))E(\tau^{**}_{t+1}k^*_{t+1}|z^{t+1})$$
$$= (1 - \delta + MPK^*_{t+1}(z^T))E(E(\tau^{**}_{t+1}|\theta^t, z^{t+1})k^*_{t+1}|z^{t+1})$$
$$= 0$$

The key step in this calculation is the penultimate one, in which I exploit the Law of Iterated Expectations and the fact that k^*_{t+1} is (θ^t, z^t)-measurable.

Who pays the higher tax? This is also easy to see. Conditional on (θ^t, z^{t+1}), the variance in the wealth tax rate derives from the dependence of $u'(c^*_{t+1})^{-1}$ on θ_{t+1}. The after-tax rate $(1 - \tau^{**}_{t+1})$ is surprisingly high for agents with a surprisingly high $1/u'(c^*_{t+1})$ – that is, a high c^*_{t+1}. Intuitively, the high wealth tax rate on the unskilled is needed to deter agents from doing a joint deviation of saving too much and then working too little when skilled in the following period. In this way, the "regressive" nature of the optimal system – surprisingly poor agents face high wealth taxes – enables the government to provide better social insurance.

The expected optimal tax rate is zero. Nonetheless, for the tax to be optimal, there must be a wedge between the individuals' intertemporal marginal rates of substitution and the social marginal rate of transformation. The optimal tax system generates this wedge in a subtle fashion. The wealth tax rate is high exactly when agents have low consumption. This negative correlation between wealth tax rates and consumption means that the after-tax rate of return on capital is riskier because of taxes. This extra risk is what creates the wedge.

2.6   Other Forms of Optimal Wealth Taxes

It is well known (Chari and Kehoe (1999)) that even if taxes are restricted to
be linear, there may be many optimal tax systems. This indeterminacy is even
more true if taxes are not restricted to be linear, but may be any function of
current and past actions. In this section, I discuss some other types of optimal
wealth taxes.

2.6.1   Non-Zero Expected Wealth Taxes

Albanesi and Sleet (2005) consider an economy in which there are no aggregate shocks and idiosyncratic skill shocks are independently and identically
distributed over time. In this setting, they prove that it is possible to construct
an optimal tax system in which taxes are restricted to be a function only of
current wealth and of current labor income. They show that this optimal tax
system is not necessarily linear in wealth, and the expected marginal tax rate
on wealth need not be zero.

Albanesi and Sleet's tax system is shaped by two key forces. The first is
that when skill shocks are i.i.d over time, the socially optimal allocation has
a simple intertemporal structure. In period t, each agent announces his skill
realization. The planner responds to this realization by giving the agent some
current consumption and promising the agent a certain amount of continuation utility. Then, in period $(t + 1)$, agents are given consumption and future
promised utility as a function only of their current skill shock and their promised
utility from period t. In this way, because of the i.i.d. shock structure, the socially optimal allocation only depends on an agent's past reports through that
agent's continuation utility (as originally described in Green (1987)).

This Markov structure is crucial to Albanesi and Sleet's implementation.
In a market economy, there is typically a one-to-one mapping between wealth
and continuation utility. Since optimal allocations depend on the past only
through continuation utility, optimal tax systems need only condition on current
wealth and current income, rather than conditioning on the full history of skill
shocks.

There is a second, more subtle, feature to Albanesi and Sleet's (2005) analysis. In a centralized allocation, agents are simply given future promised utility
and current consumption as a function of their reports. They cannot re-adjust
these after the planner's allocation. In contrast, in a market economy agents
have the ability to trade between current consumption and future wealth (that
is, promised utility). Albanesi and Sleet (2005) show that, at least when preferences are additively separable between consumption and labor, the optimal
allocation is structured so that agents do not want to deviate in such intertemporal trades.

Why are optimal expected marginal taxes non-zero in Albanesi and Sleet's
(2005) system? In the linear tax system described earlier, the government keeps
track of the entire history of agents' skills. The government gets no information

about the past from wealth, so taxing wealth is only necessary to guard against socially suboptimal deviations. In Albanesi and Sleet's system, the government keeps track of the past through wealth. This mnemonic function played by wealth implies that expected marginal tax rates are no longer necessarily zero.

Albanesi and Sleet restrict their attention to situations in which skill shocks are i.i.d. over time. If skill shocks are not i.i.d., optimal allocations are no longer Markov in promised utility. Hence, it will no longer be possible to construct an optimal tax system in which taxes depend only on current income and current wealth. In this sense, their analysis is pretty special.

However, there is an important general lesson to be learned from their paper. An agent's financial position provides information about his past skill shock realizations.[6] Albanesi and Sleet's work teaches us that the properties of optimal wealth tax rates will depend crucially on how the tax system uses this information about the past encoded in wealth.

2.6.2   Asset Testing

Golosov and Tsyvinski (2004) suggest an alternative solution to the optimal tax problem, which centers on *asset-testing*. To understand their solution, again consider the two-period example described in section 2.4, in which $T = 2$, $u(c) = \ln(c)$, $v(l) = l^2/2$, and $\beta = 1$. Suppose too that $\Theta = \{0, 1\}$, $Z = \{1\}$ (so that there are no aggregate shocks), $F(K, Y) = rK + wY$, and $\delta = 1$. As well, suppose $\phi_1(\theta) = 1$, $\phi_2(\theta, z) = \theta$, $v(l) = l^2/2$, and $\Pr(\theta_2 = 1) = 1/2$. Set $G = 0$. Let (c_{2i}, y_{2i}) denote consumption and effective labor when $\theta = i$.

Suppose $(c_1^*, k_2^*, c_{2i}^*, y_{2i}^*)_{i=1,2}$ is a socially optimal allocation. Consider a tax system τ such that if an agent has capital holdings k_2 at the beginning of period 2 and generates effective labor y_2 in period 2, then he pays period 2 taxes $\tau(k_2, y_2)$, where:

$$\tau(k_2, y_2) = \alpha_0 \quad \text{if } y_2 = 0 \text{ AND } k_2 \leq k_2^*$$
$$= \alpha_1 \text{ otherwise}$$

where:

$$\alpha_i = wy_{2i}^* + k_2^* r - c_{2i}^* \quad \text{for } i = 0, 1$$

Under this tax system, the agent receives a disability insurance payment from the government only if his assets are sufficiently low. In this sense, the disability insurance system exhibits asset-testing.

---

[6] Kapicka (2005) studies a dynamic Mirrlees tax system in which the government can only condition taxes on current incomes. This restriction seems unduly severe given the potential mnemonic role of financial wealth.

Under this tax system, the agent's decision problem is:

$$\max_{c_1,y_1,c_{21},c_{20},y_{21},k_2} \ln(c_1) - y_1^2/2 + \ln(c_{21})/2 + \ln(c_{20})/2 - y_{21}^2/4$$

$$s.t.\ c_1 + k_2 = rk_1 + wy_1$$

$$c_{21} = rk_2 + wy_{21} - \tau(k, y_{21})$$

$$c_{20} = rk_2 - \tau(k, 0)$$

$$k_2, c_{21}, c_{20}, y_{21}, y_1 \geq 0$$

The tax on labor income is lump-sum if $y_{21} > 0$; hence, the agent finds it optimal to set y_{21} equal to y_{21}^* or 0. If the agent chooses $k_2 = k_2^* - \Delta$, $\Delta > 0$, and sets $y_{21} = y_{21}^*$, then the agent's marginal benefit from saving more is:

$$0.5\beta r/(c_{21}^* - r\Delta) + 0.5\beta r/(c_{20}^* - r\Delta) - 1/(c_1^* + \Delta)$$

which is positive from Corollary 1. So the agent wants to save more. This argument applies even more strongly if $y_{21} = 0$, because the agent's second-period consumption is even lower in that case.

Hence, the agent chooses $k_2 \geq k_2^*$. Suppose then that the agent chooses $(c_1', y_1', k_2', (c_{2i}', y_{2i}')_{i=1,2})$, where $k_2' > k_2^*$. Under this choice, the agent makes a positive tax payment to the government regardless of his skill realization in period 2. It follows that the primed allocation is incentive-feasible and uses fewer resources than the original allocation; it must provide less utility to the agent.

Thus, this tax system with asset-testing implements the socially optimal allocation. Golosov and Tsyvinski (2004) show how a similar system can be used in multi-period settings, given that skill shocks follow a two-state Markov chain in which the low realization is an absorbing state. In their system, the asset cutoffs are a function of age only. My own guess is that asset-testing can be used much more generally, as long as the asset cutoffs are allowed to depend on the full history of past income realizations.

2.6.3   Non-Differentiable Taxes

In all of the systems described so far, taxes are nonseparable in wealth and income. But this nonseparability is not an essential feature of tax systems if one allows the tax system to have kinks as a function of wealth. To see this, return to the two-period example described in the subsection 2.4. In this setting, suppose $(c_1^*, k_2^*, c_{2i}^*, y_{2i}^*)_{i=1,2}$ is a socially optimal allocation. Consider a tax system τ such that if an agent has capital holdings k_2 at the beginning of period 2, and effective labor y_2 in period 2, then in period 2, he pays taxes $\tau^k(k_2) + \tau^y(y_2)$. Define wealth taxes by:

$$\tau^k(k) = rk \quad \text{if } k > k_2^*$$

$$= rk_2^* \quad \text{if } k \leq k_2^*$$

and define labor taxes by:

$$\tau^y(y) = \alpha_1 \quad \text{if } y > 0$$

$$= \alpha_0 \quad \text{if } y = 0$$

where:

$$\alpha_i = wy_{2i} - c_{2i}^* \quad \text{for } i = 0, 1$$

I claim that given this tax system, agents find it individually optimal to choose the socially optimal allocation. Given this tax system, a typical agent solves the decision problem:

$$\max_{c_1, y_1, c_{21}, c_{20}, y_{21}, k_2} \ln(c_1) - y_1^2/2 + \ln(c_{21})/2 + \ln(c_{20})/2 - y_{21}^2/4$$

$$s.t. \ c_1 + k_2 = rk_1 + wy_1$$

$$c_{21} = rk_2 + wy_{21} - \tau^k(k_2) - \tau^y(y_{21})$$

$$c_{20} = rk_2 - \tau^k(k_2) - \tau^y(0)$$

$$k_2, c_{21}, c_{20}, y_{21}, y_1 \geq 0$$

Clearly, agents choose $k_2 \leq k_2^*$; choosing to save more than that is tantamount to discarding wealth. Suppose an agent chooses $k_2 = k_2^* - \Delta$, where $\Delta > 0$. The agent's marginal benefit from saving more is:

$$\beta r[0.5/(c_{21}^* - r\Delta) + 0.5/(c_{20}^* - r\Delta)] - 1/(c_1^* + \Delta)$$

$$> \beta r[0.5/c_{21}^* + 0.5/c_{20}^*] - 1/c_1^*$$

$$> 0$$

Hence, the agent finds it optimal to choose $k_2 = k_2^*$. Given this choice of capital, it is easy to prove that the agent's incentive constraint implies that it is optimal to choose $y_{21} = y_{21}^*$.

Thus, this tax system, which is non-differentiable in wealth, implements the optimal allocation. Unlike the linear tax system described earlier or Albanesi and Sleet's (2005) optimal system, the tax system is separable between wealth and labor. While the above analysis takes place in a two-period context, the result is much more general: If taxes are allowed to be non-differentiable, then the tax rate on wealth need not depend on the ex post realization of labor income.

2.6.4   General Lessons?

There are many forms of optimal wealth taxes. This finding is, as I indicated earlier, nothing new in optimal tax theory. Even under the Ramsey approach, in which taxes are restricted to be linear, there is a great deal of indeterminacy. The situation is similar to that in portfolio theory. There, if some assets have perfectly correlated payoffs, then the optimal portfolio is indeterminate. Similarly, if the government has a lot of flexibility in terms of tax instruments, there are many ways to achieve the socially optimal outcome. Indeed, in some ways, we have greatly reduced the potential for indeterminacy by assuming that the government is solely responsible for social insurance. This indeterminacy only becomes more pronounced once one takes into account the possibility that the private sector might also provide social insurance.

I do believe that there are some reasons why the linear tax system is preferable to other forms of taxation. The asset cutoff system or the kinks system are not robust to small errors in the taxation authority's ability to measure a household's wealth. (The Albanesi-Sleet (2005) system does not have this problem because taxes are differentiable with respect to wealth. However, it is very much tailored to the unrealistic case in which skill shocks are i.i.d. over time.) The linear system that I described relies on careful measurement of labor incomes, but is more robust to problems in the measurement of wealth.

It would be desirable to provide necessary conditions that all optimal tax systems must satisfy. However, the above discussion indicates that this task is not an easy one. The necessary conditions end up depending precisely on auxiliary functional form restrictions. For example, if one restricts attention to systems that are differentiable in wealth, then the discussion in section 2.4 shows that the marginal tax rate on wealth must depend on realized income in an optimal system. The discussion in the previous section shows that this implication disappears once one allows the tax system to be non-differentiable.

This kind of indeterminacy is taken by some economists to mean that optimal tax theory has no useful implications. This is not true. For example, at a minimum, any optimal tax system must be consistent with the Euler equation described in Proposition 1. In ongoing research, Luigi Pistaferri and I are examining to what extent this Euler equation holds in United States household consumption data and using our results to suggest ways in which the current wealth tax system might be improved.

3   THE MIRRLEES APPROACH AND OTHER TAXES

I now turn to the results of using the Mirrlees approach to study three other types of taxes: estate taxes, inflation, and labor income taxes.

3.1   Optimal Estate Taxation

In a recent paper, Farhi and Werning (2005) consider the problem of optimal estate taxation. They study a multi-period setting with i.i.d. skill shocks. However, it is easier to understand the economics of their analysis in a simpler model. Suppose there are two periods, and a unit measure of families. Each family consists of a parent and a child. The parent is born at the beginning of period 1 and dies at the end of that period; the child is born at the beginning of period 2 and dies at the end of that period. The parent has utility function given by:

$$u(c_1) - v(l_1) + \beta V_2, \beta > 0$$

where $V_2 = u(c_2) - v(l_2)$ is the utility of the child. Here, $c_t(l_t)$ is the consumption (labor) of the family member alive in period t. I assume that $u', v', -u'', v'' > 0$.

Skills are private information and a child's skill is the same as that of its parent. In this world, the parent and the child share the same ranking over consumption/labor profiles. Hence, we can write the incentive-compatibility constraint of the high-skilled as:

$$u(c_{1H}) - v(y_{1H}/\theta_H) + \beta u(c_{2H}) - \beta v(y_{2H}/\theta_H)$$
$$\geq u(c_{1L}) - v(y_{1L}/\theta_H) + \beta u(c_{2L}) - \beta v(y_{2L}/\theta_H)$$

Here as before, y represents effective labor. (I have dropped the incentive-compatibility constraint of the low-skilled households because it will not bind.) I assume that there are no aggregate shocks (Z is a singleton) and that $F(K, Y) = rK + wY$.

Suppose there is a planner who puts weight 1 on all parents and puts weight β' on their children. Then, we can write the planner's ex ante objective as:

$$\mu_H[u(c_{1H}) - v(y_{1H}/\theta_H) + (\beta + \beta')\{u(c_{2H}) - v(y_{2H}/\theta_H)\}]$$
$$+ \mu_L[u(c_{1L}) - v(y_{1L}/\theta_L) + (\beta + \beta')\{u(c_{2L}) - v(y_{2L}/\theta_L)\}]$$

The key element of this objective is that as long as $\beta' > 0$, the planner puts more weight on children than do their parents.

3.1.1 Characterizing the Optimal Allocation

Using methods akin to those in Kocherlakota (2005), it can be shown that if (c^*, y^*) is socially optimal, then:

$$r\left[\beta + \beta'\frac{u'(c_{1i}^*)}{\mu_H u'(c_{1H}^*) + \mu_L u'(c_{1L}^*)}\right]\frac{u'(c_{2i}^*)}{u'(c_{1i}^*)} = 1, \quad i = h, l \qquad (22)$$

The restriction (22) has two important implications. The first is that:

$$r\beta\frac{u'(c_{2i}^*)}{u'(c_{1i}^*)} < 1 \qquad (23)$$

In this setting, with a dynastic transition from period 1 to period 2, it is socially optimal for the social rate of return to be lower than the parents' rate of time preference. The reason for this result is simple. Society puts more weight on children than parents do. Hence, parents need to be subsidized to provide a socially optimal amount of consumption to their children.

The second implication is more subtle. Suppose first that there is no private information. Then, it is efficient to insure households against their skill shocks by equating c_{1H}^* and c_{1L}^*. The optimality condition (22) implies that:

$$r[\beta + \beta']\frac{u'(c_{2i}^*)}{u'(c_{1i}^*)} = 1 \quad \text{for } i = h, l \tag{24}$$

Without private information, it is socially optimal for the planner to equate his version of the family's intertemporal marginal rate of substitution – namely, $[\beta + \beta']\frac{u'(c_{2i}^*)}{u'(c_{1i}^*)}$ – to the marginal rate of transformation $1/r$. With private information, (22) implies that:

$$r[\beta + \beta']\frac{u'(c_{2H}^*)}{u'(c_{1H}^*)} > 1 > r[\beta + \beta']\frac{u'(c_{2L}^*)}{u'(c_{1L}^*)} \tag{25}$$

The planner's version of the high-skilled (low-skilled) family's intertemporal marginal rate of substitution is larger (smaller) than the marginal rate of transformation.

The surprising feature of this optimal allocation is that the high-skilled family is distorted relative to the full information case. This result violates the general rule in private information problems that in an optimal allocation there is no distortion at the top; the low-skilled family's incentive constraint does not bind, so the high-skilled's allocation should not be distorted. There is a simple argument for why this rule breaks down here. Suppose that:

$$r[\beta + \beta']\frac{u'(c_{2H}^*)}{u'(c_{1H}^*)} = 1 \tag{26}$$

The planner contemplates the following perturbation: increase c_{1H}^* by ε and decrease c_{2H}^* by $r\varepsilon$. This perturbation lowers the planner's objective. However, it makes the high-skilled household better off, which frees up the incentive constraint. The planner can then do a second perturbation (transferring from the high-skilled household to the low-skilled household) that reduces ex ante risk. The loss to the planner from the first perturbation is only second-order because the planner is at a tangency. The gain to the planner from the second perturbation is first-order because the incentive constraint was binding.[7]

3.1.2   Taxes

As we have seen, we need to be cautious in drawing conclusions about taxes from these kinds of characterizations of the socially optimal allocations. Nonetheless, any optimal system that is differentiable with respect to bequests must have two attributes.

---

[7] More generally, as long as the planner's objective deviates from those of the individual decision-maker (because of externalities), then the no-distortion-at-the-top principle will break down. See Amador, Angeletos, and Werning (2005).

First, all households should receive marginal estate subsidies. The planner puts more weight on children than the child's parents do. Hence, the tax system needs to encourage the parent to transfer more to its child.

Second, the size of this marginal subsidy should vary across households. In particular, the estate of a parent who is highly skilled should be subsidized at a lower marginal rate than that of a parent who is low-skilled. This prescription may sound egalitarian. However, it emerges purely from incentive constraints. In particular, if the planner for some reason put *less* weight on children than parents did, then the result would be exactly reversed: The optimal subsidy system would subsidize high-skilled parents at a higher rate than low-skilled parents.

Like Farhi and Werning (2005), I have couched the above discussion in terms of estate taxes. In fact, these tax results apply to *all* transfers from parents to children. Thus, the results provide indirect support for subsidies to child education and other kinds of inter-vivo transfers. Again, the marginal subsidy rate should be larger for low-skilled parents than high-skilled parents.[8]

3.2   Inflation

In a recent working paper, da Costa and Werning (2005) study the behavior of optimal inflation in an economy in which agents receive utility from consumption, leisure, and real balances. They assume that agents have fixed skills that are private information and that the planner maximizes a utilitarian objective. They also assume that the planner cannot observe an agent's holdings of any assets including money.

In this setting, a positive nominal interest rate is a way to tax real balances relative to other forms of consumption. Da Costa and Werning assume that the agents' utility function is such that high-skilled agents demand no more real balances than does a low-skilled agent (given that both types of agent have the same allocation of effective labor and consumption). Under this assumption, a positive nominal interest rate is a tax on a good that the low-skilled likes better than the high-skilled. Such a tax tightens the incentive constraint by making it more attractive for the high-skilled to mimic the low-skilled, given a certain level of reservation utility for the low-skilled. Positive nominal interest rates are suboptimal. In other words, it is optimal for the government to follow the Friedman Rule.

Putting real balances in the utility function is a reduced-form way to capture money demand. Da Costa and Werning consider two deeper models of money demand. One is a cash-credit model in which agents are required to buy some

---

[8] Farhi and Werning (2005) focus on a multi-period environment in which skill shocks are i.i.d. over time. I have described how their estate taxes work in a two-period setting with fixed skills. However, it is possible to show that these restrictions are not essential: analogs of the results can be derived for any skill shock process and for any horizon length. Then, the optimal policy is one of subsidizing all estates with a greater subsidy for low-wealth parents.

consumption goods with cash. The other is a shopping-time model in which agents can economize on the time spent on shopping using real balances. They show that in both models, the high-skilled demand no more real balances than the low-skilled. Thus, in both models, the Friedman Rule is optimal.

There is a large literature describing optimal monetary policy using a Ramsey approach (see Chari and Kehoe (1999) for a discussion). The Friedman Rule also emerges as a prime policy recommendation from this literature. What do we learn from the Mirrlees approach over the Ramsey approach? Researchers using the Ramsey approach have emphasized that the Friedman Rule may be suboptimal if the income elasticity of money demand is sufficiently large. This elasticity, which is somewhat delicate to estimate precisely, is irrelevant under the Mirrlees approach.

The second lesson is probably more important. Da Costa and Werning (2005) assess the welfare losses associated with using a suboptimal monetary policy. They show that these losses are considerably higher in a Mirrleesian economy, in which agents are heterogeneous in skills, rather than in a representative agent economy with the same aggregate money demand function. Positive nominal interest rates make it more costly for the government to provide incentives to the high-skilled. The representative agent economy ignores this effect completely.

3.3   Labor Income Taxes

As of this writing, Battaglini and Coate (2005) have written the only paper that attempts to address the question of the dynamic behavior of optimal labor income taxes when skill shocks are only imperfectly persistent. They consider a setting in which agents are risk-neutral over consumption and face skill shocks that follow a positively autocorrelated Markov chain with two possible realizations. This environment is highly specialized. However, it has the benefit that Battaglini and Coate can solve explicitly for optimal allocations.

Up until now, we have focused on ex ante Pareto optima. These allocations are not of interest to Battaglini and Coate. With risk-neutral consumers, there is no trade-off between insurance and incentives. Hence, the ex ante Pareto optimal tax systems would be lump-sum.

Instead, Battaglini and Coate study allocations that are Pareto optimal, conditional on the realization of period 1 skills. Of course, one of these allocations corresponds to the ex ante Pareto optimum and is again uninteresting to Battaglini and Coate. Battaglini and Coate focus on the set of interim Pareto optima such that the planner puts sufficiently high weight on the initially low-skilled agents that the incentive constraint of the initially highly skilled agents binds.

In this world, if skills are fixed over time, then the labor supply of the highly skilled is not distorted (no-distortion-at-the-top principle) and the labor supply of the low-skilled is distorted downwards. Battaglini and Coate's main result is for the case in which skills are persistent but not perfectly so. Let the support of the skill shocks be $\{\theta_H, \theta_L\}$ where $\theta_H > \theta_L$ and the agents' disutility of labor be given by the function v. Consider an agent who has skill history $\overline{\theta}^t$ such that $\overline{\theta}_s = \theta_H$ for some $s \leq t$. Then in any optimal allocation (c, y):

$$v'(y_t(\overline{\theta}^t)/\overline{\theta}_t) = \overline{\theta}_t \tag{27}$$

After an agent is highly skilled it is never optimal to distort his labor supply, even if he later becomes low-skilled.

The basic idea of the proof of this result is simple. Assume that only high-skilled agents can misrepresent themselves. (Battaglini and Coate prove that the incentive constraints of the low-skilled never bind, so this assumption is without loss of generality.) Suppose:

$$v'(y_t(\overline{\theta}^t)/\overline{\theta}_t) < \overline{\theta}_t \tag{28}$$

so that the agent's labor supply is distorted downwards at time t. Let $s = \max\{r|\overline{\theta}_r = \theta_H\}$. Then, consider a perturbation to the allocation (c, y) in which we simultaneously increase $y_t(\overline{\theta}^t)$ and increase $c_s(\overline{\theta}^s)$ so as to keep the agent's lifetime utility unchanged in history θ^s. Because the agent's labor supply was distorted downward, this perturbation provides more resources for the planner. After period s, the perturbation increases the loss from pretending to be low-skilled. In period s and earlier periods, because the shocks are Markov, the incentive to mis-report has been left unchanged Hence, this perturbation is incentive-compatible and provides the same welfare to agents in the economy at lower cost.

The crux of this perturbation is that we have to roll the gains of increasing labor supply backwards in time to a high type. If we cannot do that, the perturbation will not work. Hence, in general, the labor supply of any agent who has always been low-skilled is distorted downwards. (Battaglini and Coate prove that the size of this distortion is declining to zero over time.)

Battaglini and Coate show that their sharp characterization of the Pareto optimal allocations does not survive if preferences are allowed to exhibit risk aversion. (Fortunately, at least for finite horizons, the optimal allocations are continuous with respect to risk aversion. Thus, for sufficiently low levels of risk aversion, the distortions are small for agents who have ever been highly skilled.) The structure of optimal labor income taxes in a setting with persistent skill shocks and risk aversion remains an important open question.[9]

4   WHERE DO WE GO FROM HERE?

In this last section, I discuss some possible future directions for the new dynamic optimal taxation literature.

---

[9] Zhang (2005) provides a preliminary analysis using a novel continuous-time solution method.

4.1   Hidden Asset Income

In Section 2, we discussed a number of optimal tax systems. All of these tax systems assume that the government is responsible for social insurance. However, Golosov and Tsyvinski (2005) point out that it is possible to implement Pareto optimal allocations without any government intervention at all (except through the enforcement of long-term contracts). In these implementations, a large number of private insurers compete before period 1 to sign up agents to contracts that last for the duration of the economy. These contracts specify consumption and labor supply for all agents as a function of reports that they send to their insurer over their lifetimes.

Golosov and Tsyvinski then change the environment by positing that the agents are able to engage in secret trades of a risk-free asset without being detected by the taxation authority or other insurers. These secret trades allow agents to engage in wealth tax arbitrages, so all agents must face uniform wealth taxes. (The taxes need not be zero; agents are able to secretly borrow and lend with one another, but not secretly accumulate capital.)

Golosov and Tsyvinski show that it is generally optimal for these wealth taxes to be non-zero. They also show that if skills are i.i.d. over time, then the wealth taxes are optimally positive. Intuitively, in the i.i.d. case, agents want to deviate from socially optimal allocations by saving secretly and then shirking. By taxing the return on wealth, this deviation becomes less attractive. Golosov and Tsyvinski argue that only a government has the ability to affect equilibrium prices in this fashion. They conclude that hidden intertemporal side-trades provide a novel rationalization for government intervention in social insurance.

An important difficulty with Golosov and Tsyvinski's analysis is that borrowing and lending require *enforcement*: somebody must compel the borrower to repay their obligation. What kinds of courts can enforce the *secret* intertemporal side-trades in Golosov and Tsyvinski's setup? Golosov and Tsyvinski make reference to informal enforcement mechanisms, such as those that exist within families. However, it is unnatural to model such informal side-contracts through anonymous trades of a risk-free asset. Side-trades within families or other informal coalitions are generally neither anonymous nor non-contingent. It is important for future work to verify whether Golosov and Tsyinvski's conclusions about government intervention and wealth taxes survive a more careful modeling of how exactly secret intertemporal side-trades are being enforced.

As I have done above, Golosov and Tsyvinski assume that capital holdings are fully observable. It would be useful to understand the structure of optimal taxes given weaker assumptions about capital holdings. For example, it may be necessary for the government to pay an auditing cost to ascertain an individual's holdings of physical capital. Similarly, it may be costly for the government to distinguish whether a given flow of income is derived from physical capital or labor.

4.2   Limited Commitment

In deriving the optimal tax systems in sections 2 and 3, we implicitly assumed that the government could fully commit to a tax system at date 0. In the real world, this kind of commitment is difficult to achieve. What happens to the optimal tax systems when the government is allowed to renege on its past promises?

The nature of the time-consistency problem in the Mirrleesian setting is quite different from the usual time inconsistencies that occur in a world with linear taxes. With linear taxes, the government is always tempted to tax current period capital income at a high rate because such a tax is virtually lump-sum. In the Mirrleesian setup, lump-sum taxes are already available to the government. This temptation does not exist.

Instead, the relevant temptation is that the government may want to exploit information that it has learned about agents in earlier periods. The simplest example of this phenomenon is when skills can take on two possible values and are fixed over time. In this case, the optimal tax system with commitment is constant over time and involves distortion of the labor supply of the low-skilled. However, at the beginning of period 2, the government knows who is low-skilled. The government then wants to change the future tax code so that it becomes lump-sum.

There have been several attempts to analyze the optimal (equilibrium?) choices of taxes once the government is no longer able to commit (see Berliant and Ledyard (2004), Sleet and Yeltekin (2005), and Roberts (1984)). However, these analyses have focused on rather simple examples (with either i.i.d. shocks or two periods). Much more needs to be done.

Bisin and Rampini's (2005) recent article is especially provocative. In Golosov and Tsyvinski (2005), and the prior related literature, hidden side-trades are a nuisance that prevent the government and society from achieving desirable outcomes. Bisin and Rampini (2005) consider a series of examples in which the government is not able to commit. They show that in these settings it may be *optimal* for society to allow agents to engage in hidden side-trades. The hidden side-trades prevent the government from fully exploiting its ex post informational advantage.

This line of argument needs to be explored much more fully. Our standard rationalization for markets is the First Welfare Theorem. But it merely says that markets are just as good as benevolent governments. Bisin and Rampini provide a novel rationalization for markets: They are in fact necessary in order to discipline the ex post opportunism of benevolent governments.

4.3   What Are the Right Frictions?

I have often heard the criticism that the Mirrleesian approach is inferior to the Ramsey approach because the optimal Mirrleesian tax systems do not resemble those used in the real world as well as the optimal Ramsey systes do. In particular, it is often said that the Mirrlees approach leads to tax systems that are overly complicated relative to those used in practice, while the Ramsey approach does not.

This criticism strikes me as misguided in two respects. The first problem with it is that the optimal tax systems that emerge from a Mirrleesian analysis are not at all complicated compared to the hundreds of pages necessary to describe actual tax codes. Both the Mirrleesian and Ramsey tax systems are unrealistically simple once one takes this perspective.

But there is a second more fundamental problem with this criticism. Regardless of which approach one uses, optimal taxation is a normative, not a positive, exercise. One does not judge a normative analysis by its prescriptions. The whole point of such analyses is that the government is using a flawed policy and the analyst is attempting to discover better policies. These better policies may differ greatly from conventional practice. Thus, many economists have argued for many years in favor of rarely seen policies like setting farm subsidies or trade barriers to zero.

This does not mean that normative analyses are conducted independently of empirical considerations. One judges a normative analysis by the realism of its assumptions. In this regard, an attractive feature of the Mirrlees approach is that it is more disciplined than the Ramsey approach. Under the Ramsey approach, the set of tax instruments is entirely at the disposal of the modeler. Under the Mirrlees approach, the optimal tax instruments are an endogenous response to exogenously specified private information frictions.

Of course, if this discipline is to be useful, we need to have a way to figure out which frictions are really operational in the world. Right now, the literature has been proceeding by individual researchers thinking up new frictions (or really old ones!) and plugging them into the existing framework. We need to have a much more systematic way to proceed.

In principle, this is not an impossible task. Informational frictions are a specification of a particular type of technology. For example, when we say "effort is hidden," we are really saying that it is infinitely costly for society to monitor effort. The desired approach would be to devise optimal tax systems for different specifications of the costs of monitoring different activities and/or individual attributes.

To be able to implement this approach, we need to accomplish two goals. One is to extend our modes of technical analysis to allow for costs of monitoring other than zero or infinity. The other is to figure out empirical methods of measuring these costs. Neither of these goals will be easy to achieve. But both are essential if the dynamic Mirrlees approach is to survive as more than a collection of theoretical results.

References

[1] ALBANESI, S., and SLEET, C. (2005): "Dynamic Optimal Taxation with Private Information," forthcoming, *Review of Economic Studies*.
[2] AMADOR, M., ANGELETOS, G.-M., and WERNING, I. (2005): "Commitment versus Flexibility," forthcoming, *Econometrica*.

[3] BATTAGLINI, M., and COATE, S. (2005): "Pareto Efficient Income Taxation with Stochastic Abilities," Princeton University working paper.

[4] BERGEMANN, D., and MORRIS, S. (2005): "Robust Mechanism Design," *Econometrica* 73, 1771–1813.

[5] BERLIANT, M., and LEDYARD, J. (2004): "Dynamic Optimal Nonlinear Income Taxation with No Commitment," Washington University working paper.

[6] BISIN, A., and RAMPINI, A. (2005): "Markets as Beneficial Constraints on Governments," forthcoming, *Journal of Public Economics.*

[7] CHARI, V. V., and KEHOE, P. (1999): "Optimal Fiscal and Monetary Policy," in *Handbook of Macroeconomics,* ed. Taylor, J., and Woodford, M. (New York, NY: Elsevier).

[8] DA COSTA, C., and WERNING, I. (2005): "On the Optimality of the Friedman Rule with Heterogeneous Agents and Nonlinear Income Taxation," MIT working paper.

[9] FARHI, E., and WERNING, I. (2005): "Inequality, Social Discounting, and Estate Taxation," MIT working paper.

[10] GOLOSOV, M., KOCHERLAKOTA, N., and TSYVINSKI, A. (2003): "Optimal Indirect and Capital Taxation," *Review of Economic Studies* 70, 569–587.

[11] GOLOSOV, M., and TSYVINSKI, A. (2004): "Designing Optimal Disability Insurance," MIT working paper.

[12] GOLOSOV, M., and TSYVINSKI, A. (2005): "Optimal Taxation with Endogenous Insurance Markets," MIT working paper.

[13] GREEN, E. (1987): "Lending and the Smoothing of Uninsurable Income," in *Contractual Arrangements in Intertemporal Trade,* ed. E. Prescott and N. Wallace, Minneapolis, MN: University of Minnesota Press.

[14] KAPICKA, M. (2005): "Optimal Taxation with Hidden Human Capital Accumulation," University of California–Santa Barbara working paper.

[15] KOCHERLAKOTA, N. (2004): "Wedges and Taxes," *American Economic Review* 94, 109–113.

[16] KOCHERLAKOTA, N. (2005): "Zero Expected Wealth Taxes: A Mirrlees Approach to Dynamic Optimal Taxation," *Econometrica* 73, 1587–1621.

[17] MIRRLEES, J. (1971): "An Exploration in the Theory of Optimum Income Taxation," *Review of Economic Studies* 38, 175–208.

[18] ROBERTS, K. (1984): "The Theoretical Limits of Redistribution," *Review of Economic Studies* 51, 177–95.

[19] ROGERSON, W. (1985): "Repeated Moral Hazard," *Econometrica* 53, 69–76.

[20] SLEET, C., and YELTEKIN, S. (2004): "Credible Social Insurance," Carnegie-Mellon working paper.

[21] WILSON, R. (1987): "Game-Theoretic Analyses of Trading Processes," in *Advances in Economic Theory: Fifth World Congress,* ed. T. Bewley, Cambridge, UK: Cambridge University Press, Chap. 2, 33–70.

[22] ZHANG, Y. (2005): "Dynamic Contracts, Persistent Shocks, and Optimal Taxation," Federal Reserve Bank of Minneapolis working paper.

CHAPTER 8

Quantitative Macroeconomic Models with Heterogeneous Agents

Per Krusell* and Anthony A. Smith, Jr.*

1 INTRODUCTION

The present paper reviews recent research aimed at constructing a theoretical model of the macroeconomy with five key elements: (i) it is based on rational decision-making by consumers and firms using standard microeconomic theory beginning with assumptions on preferences and technology; (ii) it is dynamic, so that savings and investment decisions are determined by intertemporal decisions; (iii) it has stochastic aggregate shocks, which lead to macroeconomic upswings and downswings; (iv) it considers general equilibrium, so that factor prices and interest rates are endogenous; and (v) it has a heterogeneous population structure where consumers differ in wealth and face idiosyncratic income shocks against which they cannot fully insure. As argued by Lucas (1976), the four first elements seem necessary in any model that aims to evaluate the effects and desirability of economic policy, and they are by now standard and rather broadly accepted as very important if not indispensable. What is new in the present work is the fifth element: heterogeneity.

The incorporation of a cross-section of consumers, with an accompanying nontrivial determination of the wealth distribution and of individual wealth transitions, is important for at least two reasons. First, it constitutes a robustness check on representative-agent macroeconomic models. Wealth is very unevenly distributed in actual economies. Moreover, a wide range of applied microeconomic studies suggests that, because of the incompleteness of insurance markets, wealth aggregation – equal propensities to save, hedge against risk, and work – fails.[1] Indeed, an important goal of the work discussed here is to establish a solid connection with the applied microeconomic literature studying consumption and labor supply decisions. So, put differently, the first reason to worry about inequality is that it may influence the macroeconomy.

* We would like to thank Torsten Persson for valuable comments and the National Science Foundation for financial support.
[1] For surveys, see Attanasio (2005) Blundell and Stoker (2003), and Browning, Hansen, and Heckman (2005).

Second, there is widespread interest in the determination of inequality per se, and in the possibility that macroeconomic forces influence inequality. Specifically, business cycles may affect the rich and the poor differently, and macroeconomic policy may also have important distributional implications. If so, they ought to be taken into account in the welfare evaluation of policy.

The purpose of the present paper is not, however, to answer the two questions above: We will not provide a detailed assessment of the extent to which inequality influences the macroeconomy, and neither will we explore in any generality how inequality is determined. We will, instead, focus on the methodological aspect of these questions. The task of solving macroeconomic models with nontrivial heterogeneity appears daunting. In short, the determination of the equilibrium dynamics of the cross-section of wealth requires both solving dynamic optimization problems with large-dimensional state variables and finding fixed points in large-dimensional function spaces. Because of the so-called "curse of dimensionality," computer speed alone cannot suffice as a remedy to the problem of high dimensionality. Recent progress, however, now permits such analysis to take place. Thus, we will review in detail how and why the new methods work. In so doing, we will also provide some illustrative results touching on the two motivating questions.

The illustrations we use allow the reader to obtain insights into how to make this kind of theory operational. They also constitute examples of two important points. First, for some issues, the incorporation of inequality does not seem essential. The aggregate behavior of a model where the only friction – indeed the only reason why exact aggregation would not apply – is the absence of insurance markets for idiosyncratic risk is almost identical to that of a representative-agent model. Thus, for purely aggregate issues where this model is deemed appropriate, one could simply analyze a representative-agent economy: the representative-agent model is robust.

Second, for other issues and other setups, the representative-agent model is not robust. Though we do not claim generality, we suspect that the addition of other frictions is key here. As an illustration we add a certain form of credit-market constraints to the setup with missing insurance markets. We show here that for asset pricing – in particular, the determination of the risk-free interest rate – it can make a big difference whether one uses a representative-agent model or not.

The key insight to solving the model with consumer heterogeneity using numerical methods is "approximate aggregation" in wealth. Exact aggregation in wealth means that all aggregates, such as prices and aggregate capital, depend only on average capital (or, more generally, wealth) in the economy. Thus, under aggregation, propensities to undertake different activities (such as saving, portfolio allocations, and working) are equalized among consumers of all wealth levels, so that redistribution of capital among agents does not influence totals. *Approximate* aggregation means that aggregates *almost* do not depend on anything but average capital. The implication of approximate aggregation therefore is that individual decision makers make very small mistakes by ignoring how higher-than-first moments of the wealth distribution influence future prices.

If, in contrast, aggregation fails, such moments by definition do influence savings, portfolio decisions, and so on, thus affecting not only the future distribution of wealth, but also average resources available in the future, and hence also future prices relevant to the agent's current decisions. Thus, approximate aggregation allows one to solve the problems of forward-looking agents with a very small set of state variables – aggregate capital only – and attain nonetheless a very high degree of accuracy. This is the key insight. The specific numerical procedure we outline here is the natural one, given this insight, but it does not constitute the only method that could be used to exploit this insight.

The computational algorithm has two key features. First, it is based on *bounded rationality* in the sense that we endow agents with boundedly rational perceptions of how the aggregate state evolves: They think that no other moments than the first moment of the wealth distribution matters. Second, we use *solution by simulation*, which works as follows: (i) given the boundedly rational perceptions, we solve the individuals' problems using standard dynamic-programming methods; (ii) we draw individual and aggregate shocks over time for a large population of individuals; (iii) we evaluate the decision rules for an initial wealth distribution and the simulated shocks and, using a method for clearing markets in every time period along the simulation, we generate a time series for all aggregates; and finally (iv) we compare the perceptions about the aggregates to those in the actual simulations, and these perceptions are then updated. We think that this approach – bounded rationality and solution by simulation – can be productive also for other applications, and we therefore devote space to a careful description of it.[2]

The present paper consists of two parts. In the first part we outline and show how to solve the "big model" – the infinite-horizon, stochastic general-equilibrium model with idiosyncratic risk and incomplete insurance. For ease of exposition, we focus in this part on idiosyncratic employment risk. We point out that the baseline model without heterogeneity in anything but wealth and employment status generates much less wealth inequality than that seen in the data. Based on this insight, we discuss what kinds of (richer) model frameworks might generate more wealth dispersion. Moreover, we argue that it is important to analyze this issue further because the evaluation of policy aimed at improving the allocation of risk likely critically depends on what determines the wealth dispersion.

The second part of the paper contains a two-period version of the big model. The two-period model is useful because it is a convenient laboratory for illustrating, and testing the robustness of, approximate aggregation. In particular, in the two-period model, one can solve for an equilibrium with arbitrary precision:

---

[2] We note that it has been employed in a variety of other contexts, e.g., Cooley, Marimon, and Quadrini (2004), Cooley and Quadrini (2006), Khan and Thomas (2003, 2005), and Zhang (2005).

Because the wealth distribution in the first period is exogenous we can vary it to trace out how aggregates move.

In contrast, in the infinite-horizon model the wealth distribution evolves in a fundamentally endogenous manner, and equilibria are constructed in a guess-and-verify manner: Assuming that individuals perceive only one moment of the wealth distribution to matter, one proceeds to find a(n almost) fixed point. In this model, it is not clear if this is the only (approximate) equilibrium or, perhaps more fundamentally, whether the approximate equilibrium is actually close to an exact equilibrium.

In the two-period model, we can examine such doubts. We find, for the two-period model, that the equilibrium with approximate aggregation, constructed as for the corresponding infinite-horizon economy, is indeed very close to the exact (and unique) equilibrium. To our knowledge, this kind of two-period model has not been analyzed before, and we think it is a very valuable tool to use for "pilot studies" of more complex economies. We also use the two-period model to illustrate how aggregate policy can have differing effects on the welfare of different kinds of consumers. Finally, we look at a version of the two-period model where there is another friction – entrepreneurs have to fund their investment projects out of own funds or borrowed money and cannot sell equity – and demonstrate that the determination of the risk-free rate is quite different in this model than in its representative-agent counterpart.

The organization of the paper may look a little backward. It starts with two sections on the big model: Section 2 discusses the representative-agent model and Section 3 discusses the model with partially insurable idiosyncratic risk. Section 4 then discusses the two-period model. A reverse order – thus starting with the simple setup and adding complication later – might for some purposes be appropriate, and indeed it is possible to read the paper in such an order. We begin with the big model for two reasons. First, we find it useful to state the goal of the work at the outset, which is to analyze the infinite-horizon problem with all its features. In doing this, we also motivate the work in the sense of explaining the problem that needs to be overcome – the dynamic determination of a large-dimensional object. Second, the specific computational method we use in the infinite-horizon model – one based on boundedly rational perceptions – can be applied in the two-period model. Though the two-period model does not require this method – it can be solved exactly – using the method in this context illustrates how our infinite-horizon method works, while at the same time showing that it works well also in the two-period model. What is less unusual is that our concluding section, Section 5, comes last.

2 THE REPRESENTATIVE-AGENT ECONOMY

We describe our main framework in this section and in Section 3. It is, in essence, a typical "real business-cycle" model – aggregate fluctuations have their origin in technology shocks and there is no money – with consumer heterogeneity and incomplete insurance against idiosyncratic unemployment risk.[3] In this section we lay out the representative-agent model – in which consumers can insure fully against idiosyncratic risk – and then in Section 3 we lay out the heterogeneous-agent model in which consumers cannot.

The representative-agent economy, our baseline setup, has preferences given by

$$E\left[\sum_{t=0}^{\infty} \beta^t u(c_t, 1 - n_t)\right],$$

where consumption, c_t, has to be non-negative and labor, n_t, has to be in $[0, 1]$. The resource constraint is

$$c_t + k_{t+1} = F(z_t, k_t, n_t) + (1 - \delta)k_t + a,$$

where k_t also has to be non-negative. Standard assumptions on primitives, which we will adopt here, are that β and δ are in $[0, 1]$, that u is strictly concave, increasing in each argument, and twice continuously differentiable, and that F is strictly increasing in all arguments, homogenous of degree in one and concave in the second two arguments, and twice continuously differentiable. Assumptions are also needed on the stochastic process for z_t, but we defer description of this process until later. The non-negative constant a is a form of endowment, perhaps interpreted as an exogenous amount of home production.

2.1   Sequential Competitive Equilibrium

A decentralized equilibrium for this economy can be described as follows. Consumers solve

$$\max_{\{c_t, k_{t+1}, n_t, b_{t+1}\}_{t=0}^{\infty}} E\left[\sum_{t=0}^{\infty} \beta^t u(c_t, 1 - n_t)\right] \text{ s.t.}$$

$$c_t + q_t b_{t+1} + k_{t+1} = b_t + (1 + r_t - \delta)k_t + w_t n_t + a \quad \forall t;$$

here, we use b_t to be the units of riskless bonds held, q_t the time-t price of a bond that pays one unit at time $t + 1$ in all states of nature, and r_t and w_t the rental rates of capital and labor, respectively. The consumer takes prices as given when solving this problem. We suppress the dependence of all variables – prices as well as choice variables – on the uncertainty: in effect, we are dealing with stochastic processes. Finally, the maximization problem above presumes another condition, namely a constraint that prevents running Ponzi schemes.

Similarly, firms maximize profits at each date and state, implying that $r_t = F_k(z_t, k_t, n_t)$ and $w_t = F_n(z_t, k_t, n_t)$. A sequential competitive equilibrium is a

---

[3] The reliance on a real model and on technology shocks is mainly chosen for convenience. We suspect that the key findings are robust to the exact mechanism driving business cycles, though such a robustness check has not been performed.

set of stochastic sequences for all quantities and prices such that (i) the quantities solve the consumer problem; (ii) quantities and prices satisfy the firm's first-order conditions stated above; (iii) the resource constraint is satisfied; and (iv) the bond market clears, i.e., b_t equals zero for all t (it is assumed that $b_0 = 0$).

Note that this economy can be interpreted as one with a continuum of agents with identical preferences and identical initial wealth where, in equilibrium, since each consumer's maximization problem has a unique solution, all consumers choose the same savings, portfolio allocation, and hours worked.

2.2   Recursive Competitive Equilibrium

To solve dynamic equilibrium models numerically, it is useful to use recursive methods; in our economy with idiosyncratic risk, these methods are especially helpful if not indispensable. Using recursive language involves, first and foremost, expressing behavior and prices as a function of individual and aggregate *state variables*. The aggregate state variable here is $(\bar{k}, z)$, where by $\bar{k}$ we now mean aggregate (mean, or total) capital: this is what is predetermined in any given period, and relevant, because it is what determines prices and therefore any behavior.

A recursive competitive equilibrium for the representative-agent model is defined as functions V, h^k, h^n, h^b, H^k, H^n, R, W, and Q such that

1. $V(\omega, \bar{k}, z)$ solves

$$V(\omega, \bar{k}, z) = \max_{k', n, b'} u(\omega + h + nW(\bar{k}, z) - k' - Q(\bar{k}, z)b')$$
$$+ E[V(b' + k'(1 - \delta + R(H^k(\bar{k}, z), z')), H^k(\bar{k}, z), z')|z]$$

   for all $(\omega, \bar{k}, z)$.
2. $(h^k(\omega, \bar{k}, z), h^n(\omega, \bar{k}, z), h^b(\omega, \bar{k}, z))$ attains the maximum, for all $(\omega, \bar{k}, z)$, in the above maximization problem.
3. The input pricing functions satisfy, for all $(\bar{k}, z)$,

$$R(\bar{k}, z) = F_k(z, \bar{k}, H^n(\bar{k}, z)) \quad \text{and} \quad W(\bar{k}, z) = F_n(z, \bar{k}, H^n(\bar{k}, z)).$$

4. Consistency: for all $(\bar{k}, z)$,

$$H^k(\bar{k}, z) = h^k(\bar{k}(1 - \delta + R(\bar{k}, z)), \bar{k}, z),$$
$$H^n(\bar{k}, z) = h^n(\bar{k}(1 - \delta + R(\bar{k}, z)), \bar{k}, z),$$

   and

$$0 = h^b(\bar{k}(1 - \delta + R(\bar{k}, z)), \bar{k}, z).$$

Thus, we use ω to denote individual asset wealth in the beginning of any period, a variable which in equilibrium must equal $\bar{k}(1 - \delta + R(\bar{k}, z))$, since bonds are in zero net supply. The consistency conditions simply require that, at the equilibrium value for ω, the individual behaves as the aggregate behaves, with h representing the individual and H the aggregate.

Notice that $(\bar{k}, z)$ in the consumer's problem are not directly influencing the consumer; if consumers knew current prices and perceived a distribution for future prices, $(\bar{k}, z)$ would be superfluous. However, $(\bar{k}, z)$ determines current prices directly, and by determining the representative agent's behavior, it determines the distribution of future prices as well.

Our market structure assumes that there are two assets: capital and bonds. If the domain for z' has only two values given any current z, then two assets suffice for completing markets. What if the domain for uncertainty is larger? A complete-markets structure would then require more assets, and it is often convenient to introduce, in addition to capital and bonds, "Arrow securities" or "contingent claims," which pay 1 unit of consumption in one of the states next period and 0 otherwise. But it is not necessary to introduce these assets in a representative-agent economy. Because consumers are identical in this model, each consumer's holdings of each of the added contingent claims have to be zero in equilibrium, just as holdings of bonds have to be zero. Thus, the market structure does not matter in a representative-agent economy, and for this reason we do not need to include the additional assets in the equilibrium definition. For the same reason, bonds do not have to be included either. We include bonds here because doing so offers a convenient parallel with the model in the next section, where bonds are present and play a nontrivial role.

2.3   Aggregation

Suppose now that we were to permit differences in individual wealth. It is well known that if u is in a certain class (e.g., if it equals $\alpha \log c + (1 - \alpha)$ $\log(1 - n)$), then there is aggregation in wealth, presuming that the market structure is complete (for the purpose of this discussion, suppose that capital and bonds complete the asset markets).[4] Aggregation in wealth means, in terms of the recursive equilibrium definition, that $h^k(\omega, \bar{k}, z)$ is linear in ω (and similarly for h^n and h^b), i.e., that it can be written $h^k(\omega, \bar{k}, z) = \mu(\bar{k}, z) + \lambda(\bar{k}, z)\omega$. The key point is that μ and λ are functions that depend only on $\bar{k}$ and z, so that the function h^k is linear in individual wealth, i.e., consumers with different wealth levels have equal marginal propensities to save out of individual wealth. In this case, with heterogeneity in the distribution of ωs across people, total capital savings and total hours worked do not depend on anything but the mean of the distribution of ωs, i.e., on $\bar{k}(1 - \delta)R(\bar{k}, z))$.

In the economy with idiosyncratic, imperfectly insurable risk decision rules will not be linear in individual wealth. However, as we shall see, decision rules will be *almost* linear in wealth.

---

[4] Here, we have to presume interior solutions for leisure. For a description of the class of preferences that delivers aggregation, see Altug and Labadie (1994).

2.4   Computation

How is a recursive competitive equilibrium of the representative-agent economy computed numerically? There are two ways to proceed. One is to solve the planning problem for allocations directly, since the equilibrium is Pareto optimal in the absence of frictions. Given the allocations, one would then simply construct R and W using the marginal-product expressions. For Q, one would just use the first-order condition for bonds from the equilibrium definition, evaluated using the allocation obtained in the previous step.

The other approach is to only use conditions from the equilibrium definition. If one is interested in aggregate allocations and prices only (and not in value functions and individual decision rules), one can also compute the equilibrium easily, without the need to find either value functions or individual decision rules. This is achieved by first deriving first-order conditions using the consumer's dynamic-programming problem and using the envelope condition to eliminate the value-function derivative from these first-order conditions. In those first-order conditions – one for savings and one for leisure – one then replaces all individual choice variables with the equilibrium functions, and one replaces the pricing functions R and W with their marginal-product versions. Thus, one arrives at two functional first-order conditions: The two equations have to hold for all $\bar{k}$ and z. The unknowns in the two functional equations are the two functions $H^k(\bar{k}, z)$ and $H^n(\bar{k}, z)$. Since the equilibrium, again, is Pareto optimal, these functional first-order conditions are identical to those implied by the planning problem. However, the approach of solving the functional first-order conditions of the representative agent for the equilibrium decision rules works also in the case where there are taxes or other reasons why the equilibrium is not optimal (e.g., in the presence of monopolistic competition), in which case the equilibrium cannot be found just by solving a planning problem.

A variety of numerical methods can be employed for solving the dynamic-programming problem, either in its value-function version or its first-order-condition version. We will not discuss these methods here, since there is ample literature on this topic.

3   THE ECONOMY WITH IDIOSYNCRATIC UNEMPLOYMENT RISK

In this section, we incorporate imperfectly insurable unemployment risk into the baseline model described in Section 2.

3.1   Preliminaries: A Steady State Without Aggregate Shocks

We first study the model without aggregate shocks. The classic references here are Bewley (undated) and Aiyagari (1994); Huggett (1997) studies steady states and transitional dynamics.[5]

---

[5] For further characterization and comparative statics, see Miao (2002).

Suppose that $\epsilon \in \{\epsilon_\ell, \epsilon_h\}$ denotes the employment status of a particular consumer, with ϵ_h and ϵ_ℓ denoting the number of "employed" and "unemployed" labor input units, respectively (we will mostly assume $(\epsilon_\ell, \epsilon_h) = (0, 1)$). ϵ is random and statistically independent across consumers.[6] Let the transitions between employment states for an individual be governed by a two-state Markov chain whose probability transition matrix has typical element $\pi_{\epsilon|\epsilon}$. We assume that ϵ satisfies a law of large numbers: at any point in time, the total fraction of consumers with $\epsilon = 1$ is known with certainty.

Suppose moreover that there are no other assets in the economy than those mentioned above, i.e., bonds and capital. Finally, suppose that there are constraints on the agents ability to borrow, such as separate lower bounds on capital and bonds or a lower bound on net next-period asset wealth.[7] Then the consumer's budget constraint in period t can be written as

$$c_t + q_t b_{t+1} + k_{t+1} = b_t + r_t k_t + \epsilon_t w_t n_t + a,$$

with $b_{t+1} \geq \underline{b}$ and $k_{t+1} \geq \underline{k}$.[8]

These individual-level assumptions are the key assumptions on which the model with idiosyncratic risk rests. The equilibrium is otherwise defined as in the previous sections, apart from the special attention that needs to be paid to exactly how the distribution of wealth evolves over time.

To this end, let Γ denote the current measure over wealth and employment status. We need to define a *joint* measure, since these two variables will be related in equilibrium: employment outcomes will influence wealth. So $\Gamma(B, \epsilon)$ reports how many consumers have $\omega \in B$ and this value for ϵ, for any interval B and ϵ.

The idea now is that, though for any initial distribution Γ_0 there will be a nontrivial transition path for the distribution of wealth, one can imagine a stationary equilibrium, or steady state, where Γ has settled down to a time-invariant function. In such a case, individuals continue to experience shocks over time, but for every interval B and value for ϵ, $\Gamma(B, \epsilon)$ is constant: people move around within the distribution, but the number of employed with less than

---

[6] A common alternative assumption is that ϵ is individual-specific productivity, which can take on many more values than two: there is wage risk. We adopt our simpler setup here for ease of exposition.

[7] The assumption of exogenously incomplete asset markets of this sort, along with restrictions on borrowing, is made in order to mimic real-world arrangements. Clearly, it would be preferable to make assumptions on a more primitive level so that the market structure would (i) be derived endogenously and (ii) maintain the key realistic features. Fully satisfactory such setups do not, to our knowledge, yet exist, but Allen (1985) and Cole and Kocherlakota (2001) are promising attempts. For an "in-between" approach, where some institutional features are given exogenously but others derived, see Chatterjee et al. (2002).

[8] The constraint could also be imposed in other ways, such as in terms of a lower bound on total savings. What is key is that one insures that the agent can pay back – while maintaining non-negative consumption – no matter what shocks are realized. The loosest possible borrowing constraint, thus, is that which just ensures solvency; see Aiyagari (1994) for a detailed discussion.

a given amount of wealth is the same in every period. In a steady state, total assets are constant, so that the interest rate and the wage rate are constant. In a steady state, moreover, and indeed also during any transition, the return on capital must equal the return on the riskless bond, so the two assets are identical from the consumer's perspective, and we can ignore bonds. So the consumer solves

$$V(\omega, \epsilon) = \max_{k' \geq \underline{k}, n \in [0,1]} u(\omega + a + n\epsilon w - k', 1 - n)$$
$$+ \beta E[V(k'(1 - \delta + r), \epsilon')|\epsilon]$$

for all (ω, ϵ). This leads to decision rules $h^k(\omega, \epsilon)$ and $h^n(\omega, \epsilon)$.

Thus, as in Aiyagari (1994) and Huggett (1993), we can define a stationary equilibrium by prices r and w, decision rules h^k and h^n, and a stationary distribution Γ such that

1. $h^k(\omega, \epsilon)$ and $h^n(\omega, \epsilon)$ attain the maximum in the consumer's problem for all (ω, ϵ).
2. $r = F_k(\bar{k}, \bar{n})$ and $w = F_2(\bar{k}, \bar{n})$, where $\bar{k} \equiv (\sum_\epsilon \int_\omega \omega \Gamma(d\omega, \epsilon))/(1 - \delta + r)$ and $\bar{n} \equiv \int_\omega h^n(\omega, 1)\Gamma(d\omega, 1)$.
3. $\Gamma(B, \epsilon) = \sum_{\tilde{\epsilon}} \pi_{\epsilon|\tilde{\epsilon}} \int_{\omega:h^k(\omega,\tilde{\epsilon}) \in B} \Gamma(d\omega, \tilde{\epsilon})$.

The last condition is new: Given the decision rule for saving, it is a fixed-point problem determining the function Γ. The condition counts up, on the right-hand side and over wealth and employment statuses, all the consumers who save so that their next-period-wealth belongs to the interval B, which is a deterministic event. It then multiplies by the probability of ending up in state ϵ, thus using the law of large numbers to obtain the actual size of the group of agents ending up with this value for ϵ, and wealth in B.

It is straightforward to compute a stationary distribution. Given that F has constant returns, one can guess on r, which implies a value for the capital-labor ratio and therefore for w, and then the consumer's problem can be solved using standard dynamic-programming techniques: In this dynamic-programming problem there is one endogenous state variable, ω, and one exogenous variable, ϵ, with two states. The obtained decision rules can then be used to find the implied fixed point for Γ. The fixed point can be computed either by iterating on the fixed-point condition giving a starting value for Γ, or by simulating a single individual's decisions over time. For the latter procedure, one simulates a very long time series for the shock ϵ and then, given an initial condition for wealth ω, uses the decision rule h^k to generate a simulated time series for wealth. Using ergodicity (the state (ω, ϵ) follows a stationary process now), it must be the case that the average value for ω in the long time series equals the average value in the stationary cross-section: i.e., it equals $\bar{k}(1 - \delta + r)$. Similarly, the average number of hours worked in the time series equals $\bar{n}$. Given these aggregates, one can check condition 2 of the stationary equilibrium: One can check whether the implied interest rate is equal to the initially conjectured interest rate. If it is, a stationary equilibrium is obtained; if it is not, r can be adjusted and the procedure can be repeated, until the initial guess is close enough to the implied value.[9]

3.2   Assumptions on z and ϵ

We now introduce an aggregate shock, z, which is assumed to take on one of two values, z_g (good times) or $z = z_b$ (bad times), with typical transition probability $\pi_{z'|z}$, i.e., with a first-order Markov structure given by (with slight abuse of notation)

$$\begin{pmatrix} \pi_{g|g} & \pi_{g|b} \\ \pi_{b|g} & \pi_{b|b} \end{pmatrix}.$$

As in the model without aggregate shocks, the individual employment shock, ϵ, is identically distributed across consumers but is serially correlated. Moreover, it satisfies a law of large numbers: Conditional on knowing the aggregate shock, the total fraction of consumers with $\epsilon = 1$ is known with certainty. More precisely, if $z = z_g$, then the number of unemployed always equals u_g, and if $z = z_b$, a fraction u_b of the consumers are unemployed, with $u_g < u_b$. That is, individual and aggregate shocks are correlated, but controlling for z, individual shocks are independently distributed.

We implement these assumptions in the easiest possible way – we employ a Markov structure on (z, ϵ):

$$\Pi' = \begin{pmatrix} \pi_{g1|g1} & \pi_{g1|b1} & \pi_{g1|g0} & \pi_{g1|b0} \\ \pi_{b1|g1} & \pi_{b1|b1} & \pi_{b1|g0} & \pi_{b1|b0} \\ \pi_{g0|g1} & \pi_{g0|b1} & \pi_{g0|g0} & \pi_{g0|b0} \\ \pi_{b0|g1} & \pi_{b0|b1} & \pi_{b0|g0} & \pi_{b0|b0} \end{pmatrix}.$$

For example, this means that the probability that an unemployed consumer will be employed tomorrow will depend not just on his own status but on the current aggregate state as well: It is $\pi_{g1|j0} + \pi_{b1|j0}$, where j is the current aggregate state.

3.3   Recursive Competitive Equilibrium

In the presence of aggregate shocks, the measure Γ evolves over time stochastically: given a Γ_0 we can, in principle, compute all agents' asset accumulation decisions, and therefore determine how much wealth each consumer starts with tomorrow. Does this mean that Γ_1 is known? No, because we know only the *marginal* wealth distribution tomorrow. We know how many of those employed in period 0 will be in different wealth groups, but we do not know how many

---

[9] A specific algorithm for a similar problem was described in Huggett (1993) and, for something closer to the present model, in Aiyagari (1994).

of those consumers will be employed: This depends on the total number of employed tomorrow, which in turn depends on the realization of the random variable z_1.

The difficulty in the model with aggregate shocks is precisely to determine the stochastic evolution of Γ. To analyze this model, we need to employ recursive methods. Thus, we need to specify the aggregate and individual state variables. The aggregate state variable, unlike in the representative-agent economy, now contains more than just the total capital stock and the current value for the productivity shock: Since different consumers have different amounts of wealth and their propensities to save are not equal, the distribution of a given amount of total capital will influence total savings. Thus, the distribution of wealth is a state variable. That is, the relevant aggregate state is (Γ, z).

The individual state, relevant in the individual's maximization problem, is then $(\omega, \epsilon; \Gamma, z)$; ω and ϵ are directly budget-relevant, and Γ and z are relevant for determining prices. Here, thus, for the individual to know $\bar{k}'$, it is not sufficient to know $\bar{k}$: It is necessary to know Γ. As in the representative-agent economy, the individual predicts $\bar{k}'$ with a law of motion, but here the consumer needs to predict the entire Γ' too in order to predict $\bar{k}$ in periods beyond the next one. We let H denote the equilibrium transition function for Γ:

$$\Gamma' = H(\Gamma, z, z').$$

The transition function contains z' because Γ also describes how many agents are unemployed (for each set of wealth levels), and it is not possible to know that for tomorrow until z', and thus u', is known.

A recursive competitive equilibrium for the model with idiosyncratic shocks is now defined as functions V, h^k, h^n, h^b, H, H^n, R, W, and Q such that

1. $V(\omega, \epsilon, \Gamma, z)$ solves

$$V(\omega, \epsilon, \Gamma, z) = \max_{k',n,b'} u(\omega + a + n\epsilon W(\Gamma, z) - k' - Q(\Gamma, z)b')$$
$$+ E[V(b' + k'(1 - \delta + R(H(\Gamma, z, z'), z')), \epsilon',$$
$$H(\Gamma, z, z'), z')|z]$$

   for all $(\omega, \epsilon, \Gamma, z)$.
2. $(h^k(\omega, \epsilon, \Gamma, z), h^n(\omega, \epsilon, \Gamma, z), h^b(\omega, \epsilon, \Gamma, z))$ attains the maximum, for all $(\omega, \epsilon, \Gamma, z)$, in the above maximization problem.
3. The input pricing functions satisfy, for all (Γ, z),

   $$R(\Gamma, z) = F_k(z, \bar{k}, \bar{n}) \text{ and } W(\Gamma, z) = F_n(z, \bar{k}, \bar{n}),$$

   where now $\bar{k} = (\sum_\epsilon \int \omega \Gamma(d\omega))/(1 - \delta + R(\Gamma, z))$ and $\bar{n} = H^n(\Gamma, z)$.

4. Consistency: for all (Γ, z) and (when applicable) (B, ϵ) and z',

$$H(\Gamma, z, z')(B, \epsilon)$$
$$= \sum_{\tilde{\epsilon}} \pi_{z', \epsilon | z, \tilde{\epsilon}} \int_{\omega: h^k(\omega, \tilde{\epsilon}, \Gamma, z)(1-\delta+R(H(\Gamma, z, z'), z'))+h^b(\omega, \tilde{\epsilon}, \Gamma, z) \in B} \Gamma(d\omega, \tilde{\epsilon}).$$

$$H^n(\Gamma, z) = \int_\omega h^n(\omega, 1, \Gamma, z) \Gamma(d\omega, 1)$$

and

$$0 = \sum_\epsilon \int_\omega h^b(\omega, \epsilon, \Gamma, z) \Gamma(d\omega, \epsilon).$$

Though the notation is more intense, this definition is a straightforward generalization of the equilibrium definition in the representative-agent case.

The main difficulty in finding an equilibrium for this economy is readily noted by inspecting the consumer's dynamic optimization problem: The state variable contains Γ, a variable of, in principle, infinite dimension (it is a function!). This is not only more difficult to handle than having the one-dimensional state variable $\bar{k}$: For a general solution to this problem, this state variable is simply too large, no matter how fast one's computer. Thus, to the extent that there really is nontrivial dependence of consumer decisions on the entire function Γ, there is little hope for finding accurate solutions even to the consumer's problem. Furthermore, the consistency conditions need to be met for every (Γ, z), a very large set of equations. In sum, how could one ever hope to numerically compute this equilibrium?

The answer lies not in computational methods, but in properties of the economy just described. It turns out that the dependence of consumer decisions on Γ is *almost* degenerate when this economy is calibrated: consumers' decisions depend on Γ only in a very, very limited way. One indication of this fact could be obtained from studying the steady state, because by solving for a steady state (i.e., an equilibrium without aggregate uncertainty, as outlined above) for a calibrated economy, one can inspect the obtained decision rules. They are *almost linear* in individual wealth. Thus, redistribution of capital among consumers, subject to a given total, almost would not change aggregate savings or aggregate hours worked. So at least if in an economy with aggregate shocks the fluctuations in Γ – subject to a given total – are not too large, it would seem plausible that the finding from the steady-state economy would carry over. That is, one would (almost) need to know no more than $\bar{k}$ in order to know aggregate decisions.

We will now explore this line of thinking in detail. In particular, we will employ a computational algorithm that makes heavy use of the idea that only the first moment of Γ matters for aggregates.[10]

---

[10] As we describe in more detail below, should the approach based on first moments fail to produce sufficiently accurate results, one could keep track of additional information about the distribution Γ, such as second-order moments, in the hope of increasing accuracy. The

3.4   Algorithm I: Trivial Price Determination Within the Period

In order to describe the algorithm and the basic finding that there is approximation aggregation in this economy, it is convenient to focus on a special case of the model where (i) leisure is not valued and (ii) bonds are not traded. In this case, price determination is significantly easier: As for (i), wages and interest rates are given immediately from knowing $\bar{k}$, since hours worked are exogenous, and as for (ii), there is no bond-price determination. The resulting model has the feature that current prices are pinned down from knowing just the aggregate capital stock and the aggregate productivity shock. This would not be true for wages and rental rates if hours were endogenous, since then the distribution of wealth would influence total hours: In the absence of aggregation consumers with different amounts of wealth have different marginal propensities to work.[11] Similarly, the bond price would depend on the distribution of wealth to the extent that marginal propensities to take on risk differ across people. The fact that the level of savings does not change any current prices in this version of the model also reflects the perfect substitutability between consumption and investment; if inputs were costly to move across these two activities, or if production technologies were different for these two goods (either of which would mean less than perfect substitutability), then the relative price of investment would be endogenous and depend on the total amount of saving: It would depend on the demand for investment.

The algorithm we use specifies individual perceptions of how Γ evolves that are *boundedly rational*: individuals perceive a very simple law of motion for it (even though in actuality the law of motion is very complex). Then optimal individual behavior implied by these perceptions is derived. Based on the obtained decision rules and an initial wealth distribution Γ_0, aggregate and individual shocks are then drawn and the resulting behavior is *simulated* for an economy with a large number of agents. This means that in period zero, shocks are drawn for the aggregate and for many agents, savings levels across the population are computed and, based on draws of shocks in the next period, the distribution Γ_1 is obtained. Based on the value for k_1 implied by Γ_1 and the new shocks, new savings decisions are computed across the population, date-2 shocks are drawn, and Γ_2 is obtained. Thus, a very long sequence for Γ_t is simulated, and it can be used for assessing the accuracy of individuals' perceptions. Finally, perceptions are updated, and the process is repeated until the perceptions are good enough in a sense to be made precise, at which point the algorithm has reached its end. The finding, as we will see, is that if $\bar{k}_{t+1}$ is believed to depend only on $\bar{k}_t$ (aside from its dependence on the aggregate shocks), this belief is almost exactly confirmed in the simulation.

computational algorithms that we describe in Sections 3.4 and 3.5 generalize easily to setups in which consumers keep track of more features of the distribution. For a survey and a discussion of different algorithms, see Ríos-Rull (2001).

[11] In a version of the model where there are no wealth effects in labor supply, propensities to work out of more wealth would also be equalized (at zero) among agents.

We call this kind of algorithm *solution by simulation* since Γ is updated from period to period using simulation of a large number of agents, rather than using integration according to the equilibrium definition of how the updating of Γ occurs.[12] An advantage with simulation is that no functional form for Γ needs to be known or approximated. In addition, when there is nontrivial determination of within-period prices there are other advantages from solution by simulation. Simulation has been used in other contexts (see, e.g., Den Haan and Marcet (1990) on parameterized expectations) but then in a context of solving a decision problem; here, simulation is not used for solving the decision problems, but rather for solving for the equilibrium, since the key unknown is the equilibrium law of motion.[13]

An example serves to illustrate the workings of the algorithm. Suppose that perceptions are given by

$$z = z_g : \bar{k}' = a_{0g} + a_{1g}\bar{k}$$
$$z = z_b : \bar{k}' = a_{0b} + a_{1b}\bar{k}. \tag{1}$$

Then the agent solves the following problem:

$$V(\omega, \epsilon, \bar{k}, z) = \max_{k' \geq \underline{k}} u(\omega + F_2(\bar{k}, u_z, z)\epsilon + h - k')$$
$$+ \beta E[V(k'(1 - \delta + F_1(\bar{k}', u_{z'}, z')), \epsilon', \bar{k}', z')|z, \epsilon]$$

subject to

$$\bar{k}' = a_{0g} + a_{1g}\bar{k} \quad \text{if } z = z_g$$
$$\bar{k}' = a_{0b} + a_{1b}\bar{k} \quad \text{if } z = z_b.$$

This implies an optimal decision rule $k' = h^k(\omega, \epsilon, \bar{k}, z)$, and this rule is then used to simulate the economy with a sample of N agents (with N large). Then the "stationary region" of the simulated data is used to estimate – using least-squares regression – the parameters of the linear law of motion for $\bar{k}$. Using these estimates, the law of motion is updated, and the procedure is repeated until a fixed point in these parameters is found. Thus, the chief computational task is to find the fixed point $(a_0^*, a_1^*, b_0^*, b_1^*)$: Individual perceptions have to be consistent with the aggregate economy's simulated evolution, where these parameters represent the best goodness-of-fit to the simulated data. At this stage, the maximal goodness-of-fit represents a measure of how close approximate aggregation is to exact. Krusell and Smith (1998) discuss different goodness-of-fit measures, but the simplest one is R^2. Thus, if the R^2 is very close to 1, we say that we have approximate aggregation.[14]

---

[12] Den Haan (1997) develops a related method that does not involve simulation.

[13] In a very similar context to that here, Obiols-Homs (2003) uses parameterized expectations for solving the consumer's problem and solution by simulation in order to determine the law of motion for aggregate capital.

[14] It is conceivable that a poor goodness-of-fit is obtained not due to a lack of approximate aggregation but because the mapping from $\bar{k}$ (and shocks) to $\bar{k}'$ is nonlinear. Then, one could parameterize such a nonlinear relationship and another goodness-of-fit could be used. This has not turned out to be a problem in any existing applications, however.

Using a calibration of the model which is standard in the macroeconomic literature – based on the parameterizations $u(c) = \frac{c^{1-\gamma}-1}{1-\gamma}$ and $F(z, k, n) = zk^{\alpha}n^{1-\alpha}$ – and using a log-linear law of motion for aggregate capital, one obtains R^2 measures in each of the two equations (i.e., for good times as well as for bad times) of around 0.999998. Thus, the fit is not perfect, but close to perfect. As for the "not perfect" part, one can show that a significantly (in a statistical sense) better fit can be obtained using higher moments of Γ in explaining the simulated series of aggregate capital stocks, but the improved fit has negligible impact on the role of $\bar{k}$ in predicting $\bar{k}'$, and the improvements in price forecasts are negligible as well.

The algorithm leaves open whether the finding of approximate aggregation is a case of a "self-fulfilling prophecy": Given that agents believe in a certain simplified law of motion, this simplified law of motion is (almost) confirmed. Does the model with boundedly rational agents have multiple equilibria? There are several ways of addressing this question.

First, the present algorithm naturally lends itself to a generalization which is to include more moments in agents' perceptions. The question then is whether including more moments alters the computed equilibrium in a quantitatively significant way. Such an algorithm proceeds, first, by postulating that agents only think future prices depend on a finite set of current moments of Γ (in addition to the dependence on the aggregate shocks): $m \equiv (m_1, m_2, \ldots, m_M)$, where this dependence is expressed using a function H_M: $m' = H_M(m, z, z')$. Second, one derives the aggregate behavior implied by these perceptions and assesses the extent to which the agents' perceptions differ from how the economy behaves. Thus, one (i) selects M; (ii) guesses on H_M in the form of some given parameterized functional form, and guesses on parameter values; (iii) solves the consumer's problem given H_M and obtains the implied decision rules f_M; (iv) uses these decision rules to simulate the behavior of an economy with many agents; and (v) evaluates the fit and updates until the best possible fit within this class. If the fit is satisfactory, stop. If it is not satisfactory, increase M, or, as a less ambitious step, try a different functional form for H_M. For the calibrated economies studied, the addition of more moments does not alter the initial, simpler law of motion based on one moment in any economically significant way.

Second, one can try to isolate and investigate those properties of decision rules and movements in Γ – and their determinants – that seem to underlie approximate aggregation. This analysis points to important economic mechanisms about which we elaborate below. But one relevant observation has already been made: Decision rules are almost linear in the steady-state equilibrium of this kind of economy (when reasonably calibrated), and this near-linearity thus makes it difficult for higher moments to influence aggregates. Steady-state equilibria can be solved with arbitrary accuracy, and they therefore offer reliable information about the shapes of decision rules when the aggregate shocks are not too large.

Third, and this is a route we will explore below, one can obtain important insights from studying a two-period model with otherwise the same assumptions on preference, technology, and market structure. In particular, in a two-period model the initial wealth distribution is exogenous and can therefore be altered in order to examine the effects of its higher moments on aggregates. Because the two-period model can be solved to any degree of accuracy, one can directly verify whether approximate aggregation, to the extent that it holds, is due to a self-fulfilling prophecy.

3.5   Algorithm II: Nontrivial Price Determination
Within the Period

Consider now the model with nontrivial determination of prices within the period, because the bond is reintroduced and because leisure is valued. A straightforward extension of the algorithm above would postulate, alongside the law of motion for $\bar{k}$, a pricing function for bonds, Q, and a function for aggregate hours worked, H^n, both with $\bar{k}$ as argument (and no higher moments of Γ), and these functions would then be used in the consumer's dynamic programming problem to derive behavioral rules for savings, hours worked, and bond demand. These rules could then, as in the previous algorithm, be simulated. However, in this simulation, how would market clearing for hours worked and for bonds be guaranteed at every point in time? Unless the functions are exactly the right ones – and we know that lack of perfect aggregation implies that these functions need to include Γ as an argument, and not just its first moment – market clearing will never hold exactly. Moreover, in the case of bonds, it turns out, as described in more detail in Krusell and Smith (1997), that an algorithm that does not pay attention explicitly to market clearing yields larger and larger deviations from zero excess demand as the simulation goes on, no matter how Q is chosen

Here, one could accept deviations from market clearing – if they are not large – but a more attractive alternative is to insist on market clearing at each point along a simulation so that the only deviation from full satisfaction of the equilibrium conditions is in the perceptions that agents have about future prices. Thus, as before, we will insist on boundedly rational perceptions as a way of computing equilibria while demanding that all markets clear and that consumers act rationally conditionally on the assumed perceptions.

Implementation of these principles follows a two-stage procedure. Consumers view *future* prices as being given by the aggregate laws Q and H^n (and, of course, H^k, as before, so that w and r can be computed), but they observe directly all current prices while making decisions. That is, current prices are parameters in a consumer's problem, and decision rules for current savings, bonds, and hours worked therefore depend explicitly on these prices. In the simulation then, these prices can be varied to ensure market clearing at all points in time, and the simulated price outcomes can then be compared to those implied by the perceived price functions.

Thus, we derive the decision rules as follows. Extending the example from the previous section, we first specify H^k as in equation (1), but with more compact notation:

$$\bar{k}' = H^k(\bar{k}, z) = a_{0z} + a_{1z}\bar{k}$$

but then add similar perceptions for Q and H^n:

$$q = Q(\bar{k}, z) = b_{0z} + b_{1z}\bar{k}$$
$$\bar{n} = H^n(\bar{k}, z) = c_{0z} + c_{1z}\bar{k}.$$

Then the agent solves the following problem:

$$V(\omega, \epsilon, \bar{k}, z) = \max_{k' \geq \underline{k}, n \in [0,1], b' \geq \underline{b}} u(\omega + F_2(\bar{k}, H^n(\bar{k}, z), z)n\epsilon$$
$$+ a - k' - Q(\bar{k}, z)b', 1 - n)$$
$$+ \beta E[V(k'(1 - \delta + F_1(H^k(\bar{k}, z),$$
$$H^n(H^k(\bar{k}, z), z'), z')), \epsilon', H^k(\bar{k}, z), z')|z, \epsilon].$$

Thus, in this problem, $\bar{k}'$, q, and $\bar{n}$ are all given as their representative functions of aggregate capital and the aggregate shock.

Equipped with the key output of this problem – the value function – we can then specify the problem of an agent at any point in time in a simulation:

$$\max_{k' \geq \underline{k}, n \in [0,1], b' \geq \underline{b}} u(\omega + F_2(\bar{k}, \bar{n}, z)n\epsilon + a - k' - qb', 1 - n)$$
$$+ \beta E[V(k'(1 - \delta + F_1(H^k(\bar{k}, z), H^n(H^k(\bar{k}, z), z'), z')),$$
$$\epsilon', H^k(\bar{k}, z), z')|z, \epsilon],$$

where current q and $\bar{n}$ are now treated as parameters – note that they appear in the current payoffs – but their future values are given by the functions Q and H^n, respectively, as is $\bar{k}'$, which is also replaced by H^k in the agent's assessment of the future. This maximization problem gives rise to decision rules $h^k(\omega, \epsilon, \bar{k}, z; q, \bar{n})$, $h^n(\omega, \epsilon, \bar{k}, z; q, \bar{n})$, and $h^b(\omega, \epsilon, \bar{k}, z; q, \bar{n})$, and it is these rules that are used in the simulations because they now have an explicit dependence on current q and $\bar{n}$, the latter pinning down w and r. Thus, all markets can be made clear at every point in the simulation.

In summary, there are two differences compared to the simpler case in Section 3.4. First, decision rules require a two-state derivation. Second, once these rules are obtained, the simulation requires an additional step at each point in time, which is to vary $(q, \bar{n})$ so as to clear markets for bonds and labor. Notice, therefore, that the use of the simulation offers a way of clearing markets at each date here. Thus, solution by simulation offers a way of dealing with an otherwise nontrivial task.

3.6   Origins of Approximate Aggregation

Why is there approximate aggregation? Inspection of the decision rules, both in the case of the steady-state equilibrium and in the case of aggregate uncertainty, reveal *near linearity in individual wealth*. More precisely, for all agents but the very poorest, marginal propensities are almost all identical. Figure 8.1

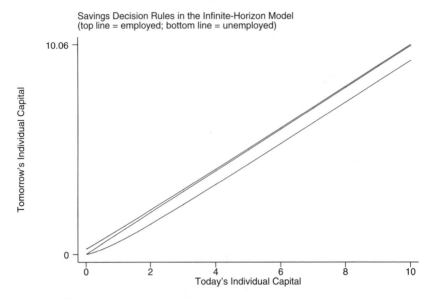

Figure 8.1.

displays typical decision rules. The line above the 45-degree line (i.e., the middle line) is the decision rule of an employed agent (holding fixed the aggregate state variables), and the line below is the decision rule of an unemployed agent.

As the graph shows, for the poorest (and especially the poorest unemployed) agents, there are large differences in slopes of decision rules: The slope of the savings rule is, in fact, zero for those who are borrowing-constrained, but there is also a small region of values for ω where slopes are positive but noticeably lower than for richer agents.

For several reasons, however, these differences in marginal propensities play only a very minor role. First, the region where there are different marginal propensities to save is very small. Second, the distribution of wealth is very thin in the tails and contains few consumers in the region where marginal propensities are different. Third, the consumers in the left tail have, by definition, very little wealth and simply do not matter in the determination of aggregate savings: Those with the bulk of savings have wealth and therefore (almost) have the same marginal savings propensity. Fourth and finally, for deviations from aggregation to be important, one needs large redistributions involving this subsegment of population, and Γ does not seem to vary enough to make such effects quantitatively visible. In conclusion, a number of conditions need to be satisfied to cause significant deviations from aggregation, and none of these conditions are present in an important way.

What causes these features? In the case of the steady-state equilibrium, this near linearity is clearly not due to boundedly rational perceptions (and it will be found to be present in the two-period model below as well, where an equilibrium is also computed with controlled accuracy), and the addition of price uncertainty does not change the finding. In fact, the finding of linearity is remarkably robust to changes in the utility function: Very large amounts of risk aversion are needed to cause precautionary savings motives to make savers differ significantly in marginal propensities. The finding seems related to other observations: the equity premium puzzle (see Mehra and Prescott (1985)) and the low estimates for the welfare costs of business cycles (see Lucas (1987)) both suggest that the utility functions that seem consistent with micro data do not give large costs of bearing moderate risks.

In addition, though the presence of incomplete insurance opportunities makes agents de facto more sensitive to shocks, precautionary savings are allowed here and they seem to be effective in providing (partial) insurance against shocks. When an agent is allowed to save, for given fluctuations in ϵ (labor income), the wealthier an agent is in terms of initial asset wealth, the less important are these fluctuations to the agent. As a result, the marginal propensity to consume ends up being determined by permanent-income considerations: For every additional dollar of asset income, the agent consumes only the interest component and keeps the principal intact, thus making the savings propensity independent of wealth for high enough wealth levels.[15] It simply turns out, then, that very little wealth is needed for this (approximate) constancy to start to hold.

It is also possible to understand why there are few agents in the region with the very lowest asset levels: Agents do suffer from a lack of assets, because marginal utility of consumption is very high there. Thus, with a long enough time horizon, agents save ex ante so as to avoid ending up in this region. Preferences with higher risk aversion make being in this region even more costly, and the distribution of wealth thus moves to the right endogenously. In models with short enough life spans for consumers and no bequests, it is easier to find equilibria with more agents in the left tail of the distribution; see, e.g., Gourinchas (2000) and Storesletten, Telmer, and Yaron (2004a). However, in these cases it is still the case that the small amounts of wealth held by these agents still make their different marginal propensities not matter much for aggregate savings and other aggregates.

The approximate aggregation result has surprising generality for all the above reasons. For studies that investigate the limits of approximate aggregation, see, for example, Young (2004a), and for a discussion of a set of circumstances in which approximate aggregation may fail in the context of overlapping-generations economies, Krueger and Kubler (2004). The preliminary findings suggest that models that violate approximate aggregation need parameterizations that are quite different than those in standard macroeconomic calibrations.

---

[15] See Bewley (1977).

3.7   A Sample of Positive Results

For illustration, we will review some properties of the basic model described above. The purpose here is thus not to discuss the ultimate value of specific models, but rather to make some remarks about quantitative work in this area and about what approximate aggregation does and does not imply.

Aggregates.   The time series for aggregates generated by the model can be compared to those generated by the corresponding representative-agent model. Here, a striking finding is the robustness of the representative-agent setting: The aggregate time series are almost identical in the two models. This fact follows rather directly from approximate aggregation: One can construct a representative agent – with the same preferences as those of all agents and the same kind of budget constraint, though with labor income being the mean labor income of all agents – and endow this agent with the aggregate (mean) capital stock, and this agent will then save (almost exactly) as in the aggregate economy with heterogeneity.

However, as we will discuss in the context of a few examples, further extensions of the model give different time series properties than the basic representative-agent model of Section 2, even when approximate aggregation holds. In particular, in the extended models one cannot identify a(n approximate) representative agent with the representative agent of the model in Section 2.

1. Heterogeneity in discount rates   The easiest way to illustrate this is perhaps the extension in Krusell and Smith (1998), where consumers are assumed to have stochastic discount factors, and where the movements in these discount factors, like employment risk, are not directly insurable. Thus, at any point in time there is a nontrivial distribution of discount factors in the population. This model displays approximate aggregation, for much the same reasons as discussed above, even though there is heterogeneity in attitudes toward saving in the population. The added heterogeneity generates larger differences in the marginal propensities to consume in the population, but now there is in addition an offsetting mechanism: More patient agents accumulate more wealth, and therefore aggregate savings are more concentrated. Since savings come (almost) entirely from this group, the deviations from perfect aggregation are again extremely small. Thus, interest rates are largely pinned down by the marginal rates of substitution of the rich, patient agents.

At the same time, however, poor and impatient agents do command a large fraction of total income, since they work and therefore receive labor income, and this implies that aggregate consumption is influenced more by the poor than are aggregate savings. In particular, the poor look more like hand-to-mouth consumers, since their discount rates tend to be significantly higher than the interest rate: unlike the rich, who display permanent-income-like behavior, poor agents who receive positive income shocks consume most of the added income. Thus, aggregate consumption and aggregate income co-move more strongly than in the model of Section 2: We tend to see more of a traditional "consumption function" here. Since there is approximate aggregation, though, should there not be a representative-agent counterpart of this setup? Perhaps, but the question then is what the preferences of such an agent would look like.[16] Instead, it seems more appropriate to think of a two-agent "shortcut" of this model: a model with rich savers and poor workers, who do not save at all.

2. Individual vs. aggregate labor supply   In an effort to make the above macroeconomic model consistent with the estimates of labor supply in the applied labor literature, Hansen (1985) and Rogerson (1988) assume that labor supply is indivisible: consumers can choose either to work or not to work, so that labor supply is highly inelastic on the individual level. Using a lottery mechanism with complete consumption insurance, they showed that aggregate labor supply in this case would be infinitely elastic, with adjustments of total hours taking place on the extensive margin only. Clearly, though, their assumption of complete insurance markets is questionable (and furthermore leads unemployed workers to have higher utility than employed workers). Chang and Kim (2004, 2006), however, pursue the idea that the interaction of partial insurance and indivisible labor could generate different aggregate implications. Incorporating indivisible labor into the kind of model developed in the present paper, they find that indeed aggregate labor supply is significantly more elastic in the aggregate than one might guess based on the inelastic labor supply of any given individual. Approximate aggregation holds, but at the same time the model produces aggregate time series behavior that is different from that in either a standard representative-agent model with highly inelastic labor supply or in a Hansen-Rogerson economy (which features a representative agent with quasi-linear preferences).[17]

3. Idiosyncratic risk and asset prices   Imperfectly insurable individual risk as an explanation of asset prices has been explored within the same class of models discussed here. One of the first to explore this idea was Mankiw (1986), who studied a two-period model. Constantinides and Duffie (1996), Heaton and Lucas (1996), Krusell and Smith (1997), Storesletten, Telmer, and Yaron (2004b), and others have built infinite-horizon models to examine this possibility. Whereas Constantinides and Duffie explore assumptions under which complete analytical characterization is possible (e.g., only permanent – fully uninsurable – idiosyncratic shocks), the latter two papers explore quantitatively

---

[16] One might think that the answer should be the complete-markets version of the model, but this turns out not to be correct. For simplicity, consider the case with permanent differences in discount factors, which is a model with much the same properties. There, the complete-markets version leads to concentration of wealth over time among the agent with the highest discount factor – all other agents "disappear" from the economy in the long run. In the long run, therefore, the economy would look like a representative-agent economy like the one in Section 2, which we know displays very different behavior.

[17] For another labor-market application, see Gomes, Greenwood, and Rebelo (2001).

restricted settings of the sort described in this paper, and approximate aggregation applies in each case. There are two general findings here: The "market price of risk" increases and the risk-free rate falls. Underlying the higher market price of risk is the assumption that idiosyncratic risk is larger in bad times than in good times. This qualitative point, which was made in Mankiw's early paper, appears in Krusell and Smith's setting in the form of unemployment risk, which is naturally countercyclical, and in Storesletten, Telmer, and Yaron (2004c), who document and explore the implications of countercyclical idiosyncratic wage risk.

To understand why the risk-free rate decreases, it is useful to consider a variant of the steady-state model in Section 3.1 developed by Huggett (1993). Huggett's model is a pure exchange economy without aggregate uncertainty in which the only asset is a risk-free bond in zero net supply.[18] In this model, consider setting the borrowing constraint on bonds to 0: $\underline{b} = 0$. In such a case, the equilibrium is by necessity autarkic: The bond price must adjust so that no consumer wants to hold positive amounts of bonds, i.e., it must be determined by the intertemporal marginal rate of substitution of the agent who is willing to pay the most for the safe asset.[19] If the idiosyncratic shock follows a two-state Markov chain, then it turns out that consumers with the high shock – who face the possibility of an income loss, unlike consumers with the low shock – determine the bond price. Such a consumer's Euler equation can be written

$$q \geq \beta \frac{\pi_{h|h} \epsilon_h^{-\gamma} + (1 - \pi_{h|h}) \epsilon_\ell^{-\gamma}}{\epsilon_h^{-\gamma}},$$

which exceeds β whenever $\epsilon_h > \epsilon_\ell$, $\pi_{h|h} < 1$, and $\gamma > 0$. Intuitively, this consumer would like to accumulate bonds to protect himself against the possible income loss, but he cannot because the borrowing constraint precludes consumers with low shocks from lending to him, so to restore equilibrium in the bond market, the price of the bond must rise relative to value of the discount factor (which equals the bond price under complete markets). Thus the risk-free return falls. The expression above also allows us to show that as ϵ_h/ϵ_ℓ grows large (i.e., as the gap between rich and poor increases), the interest rate declines monotonically from $1/\beta$ – its value in the economy without idiosyncratic risk – to zero. Second, the less persistent the high endowment shock – the more likely the income loss – the lower the risk-free rate. Third and finally, the lower the risk-free rate, the more risk-averse the agent (the higher is γ). Depending on primitives, thus, the gross risk-free return can be anywhere in $(0, 1/\beta)$.[20]

---

[18] Huggett's setup is obtained by setting $F(z, k, n) \equiv n$.

[19] For another paper that uses this kind of modeling in an analysis of foreign exchange risk premia, see Leduc (2002).

[20] In a Huggett-style endowment economy with aggregate shocks, the bond price chiefly depends on the aggregate shock, and not on the higher moments of the asset distribution (recall that its

The effect of consumer heterogeneity on the risk-free rate can also be examined in other contexts, such as the economies with entrepreneurial risks considered by Angeletos (2005), Angeletos and Calvet (2004), and Covas (2005). There, entrepreneurs make investment decisions that due to market incompleteness will be tied with their consumption decisions, and thus any borrowing using state-uncontingent bonds will deliver a risk-free interest rate that is disproportionately influenced by the less wealthy lucky entrepreneurs, who are more worried about risk. We will explore this kind of setup in the context of the two-period model below.

Inequality.   The second main output of this model is time series for inequality, both in terms of wealth and consumption. Here, we only briefly note the main findings for wealth inequality.

One can use the time series for inequality to compute unconditional moments for the Gini coefficient or some other measure of inequality in wealth and in consumption. The variations in Γ are not so large that a model with aggregate shocks is really necessary for the analysis of long-run properties, however: analysis of steady state suffices, along the lines of the discussion in Section 3.1. There is quite a large number of papers in this general vein, and it is broadly recognized that the present model has a difficult time generating wealth dispersion to the extent observed in U.S. (and other) data. As an example, the Gini coefficient for wealth in the model calibrated in Aiyagari (1994) is 0.3, whereas in the data it is 0.8; the fraction of wealth held by the 1% richest is much less than its value in the data of 30% (see Díaz-Giménez et al. (1997) and Rodríguez et al. (2002) for a documentation of facts about inequality in the U.S.), and there are few agents that have very low levels of wealth.

A number of ways of altering the basic framework have been suggested and evaluated. To generate a large mass of agents at the lowest levels of wealth, one can introduce a feature common to many modern economies, namely specific welfare benefits to the very poorest (this idea was considered in Hubbard, Skinner, and Zeldes (1995) and put into an equilibrium model by Huggett (1996)). Thus, poor agents are given disincentives to save. To generate extreme wealth concentration, one can follow Krusell and Smith (1998) who hypothesize discount-rate heterogeneity and show that a small amount of such heterogeneity is sufficient for generating realistic wealth Ginis and a large concentration of wealth among the richest; this mechanism also helps create a class of very poor agents.

As a somewhat related mechanism, one can consider some form credit-market imperfection that implies that the rates of return on savings earned by

---

first moment always has to be zero); in the case with a zero-borrowing constraint, this result holds exactly. For an analysis, see Young (2004b).

wealthy agents is higher than those for poor agents. It remains to be seen whether a fully microfounded setting can be constructed that delivers this result as an equilibrium outcome (models of costly participation in different markets can perhaps be developed, or models where information is asymmetric and costly to acquire); investigations with versions of increasing returns to saving can be found in Quadrini (2000), Campanale (2005), and Cagetti and De Nardi (2004, 2005).[21]

Castañeda et al. (2003b) pursue another approach. They formulate a steady-state model with idiosyncratic wage-rate shocks and find that it is possible to generate large wealth inequality without any other form of heterogeneity (i.e., without preference or rate-of-return heterogeneity). The required wage process has drastically higher dispersion: it features a very small probability of entering a state with enormous wages, while having strong regression to the mean for this group.

Thus, in short, several different stories have been proposed to account for the stark inequality in wealth, and each has shown some success. Does it matter, then, which story is most relevant quantitatively? It does. Models with preference heterogeneity suggest that the poor are poor because they choose to be poor, and thus welfare policy aimed at distribution toward the poor is hard to defend on the grounds of efficiency: It is not that the lack of insurance markets explains poverty, but rather that some consumers choose poverty.[22] In contrast, the model where inequality is due to a wage process with very large variance predicts that the poor are poor because they were unlucky. Based on such a model, hence, it seems easier to argue for redistribution on efficiency grounds.[23] Thus, it is important for future research to sort out and compare these different mechanisms; we are still far from a stage where all the properties, especially in the time-series dimension but also cross-sectionally, have been explored for these models.

Turning now to the cyclical properties of wealth inequality, the baseline model, with or without preference heterogeneity, predicts that measures of wealth inequality are countercyclical. However, whereas the data on income inequality is quite good (for recent studies of U.S. data, based on different sources, see Castañeda et al. (2003a) on short-run fluctuations and Piketty and

---

[21] In principle, different risk attitudes between the rich and the poor can help: If wealth lowers de facto risk aversion, then the rich earn a higher return on average, and thus become even richer. However, it is difficult for such a mechanism to be potent quantitatively unless one departs radically from what is considered to be reasonable specifications for individual risk attitudes: A very high degree of risk aversion is needed to generate a substantial equity premium, even in the presence of wealth heterogeneity and incomplete insurance against idiosyncratic shocks.

[22] It should be noted that for such a stance one must assume that "discounting," or "impatience," is a primitive, and not an outcome of a social or cultural process. This is not a foregone conclusion.

[23] Of course, the extent to which efficiency can be used as an argument in these models is somewhat unclear, since the market incompleteness has not been modeled from first principles. That is, why can the government provide valuable insurance when the markets cannot?

Saez (2003) for a longer-run perspective), there are too few observations on the wealth distribution for a meaningful time-series analysis of it.

3.8   Policy Evaluation

Approximate aggregation does not mean that there is close to full consumption insurance; in fact, the models considered in this paper feature substantial consumption inequality.[24] Furthermore, macroeconomic policies, such as stabilization policy, influence consumption inequality. Because the models considered in this paper allow for macroeconomic variation, they can be used to evaluate the distributional effects of macroeconomic policies. Macroeconomic policy affects prices (such as wages and interest rates) through general equilibrium channels, thereby changing the allocation of risk across consumers with different compositions of financial and human wealth; we will revisit this idea formally in Section 4.1.3 below. So far, there are only a few papers exploring these issues; one example is a set of papers exploring how the elimination of business cycle risk affects the welfare of different groups in the economy (Atkeson and Phelan (1994), İmrohoroğlu (1989), Krebs (2003), Krusell and Smith (1999, 2002), Mukoyama and Şahin (2005), and Storesletten, Telmer, and Yaron (2001); see also Lucas (2003)). Additional examples include Heathcote (2005), who studies the distributional effects of shocks to taxes in an economy of the kind discussed here (where Ricardian equivalence fails to the extent that borrowing constraints bind), and Gomes (2002), who studies the welfare effects of countercyclical unemployment insurance.

3.9   Summing Up: Implications of Approximate Aggregation

Does approximate aggregation mean that macroeconomists might as well limit attention to representative-agent models? For many issues, the answer is "no": Both aggregate quantities and prices behave quite differently in many of the models discussed above than in the standard representative-agent model. We think, moreover, that more radical departures from the representative-agent model will occur when idiosyncratic uninsurable risk is *combined* with other frictions or other elements of heterogeneity. But it is premature to speculate in this direction.[25]

Another point to stress is that there is significant consumption inequality in the model with idiosyncratic risk, even in the baseline version where the wealth distribution has much less variance than in the data. That is, approximate aggregation does not say that inequality in consumption and wealth are eliminated by means of precautionary savings; after all, *all* the consumption and

---

[24] Moreover, Cordóba and Verdier (2005) show that the potential welfare gains from eliminating U.S. consumption inequality, relative to those from eliminating suboptimal growth and business cycles, can be very large.

[25] Carroll (2000) draws a more radical conclusion than we do on this issue and pronounces a "requiem" for the representative-agent model.

wealth inequality in the present model are due to market incompleteness. A generalization of the steady-state models of Bewley, Huggett, and Aiyagari, show that the present model is also stationary: The distribution of wealth is (in all the applications in the literature, at least) unique, so any effects of initial wealth differences among agents disappear over time, and the long-run differences in consumption and wealth among agents are thus due to idiosyncratic shocks and the absence of full insurance.

In addition, this class of models does deliver nontrivial and interesting implications for the evolution of wealth and consumption inequality that are still far from completely understood. The tools are now available to use general-equilibrium models of inequality to tackle the empirical challenges in a serious way.

4   USING TWO-PERIOD MODELS

In this section we develop and analyze a series of two-period models with the aim of (i) illustrating and further analyzing approximate aggregation; (ii) evaluating the method of solution by simulation in a case where alternative methods are feasible; (iii) investigating the robustness of the representative-agent model; and (iv) examining the social insurance role of macroeconomic policy. The first model we describe shares many features with the "big model" above but ends after two periods. The second model introduces entrepreneurs, following Angeletos (2005), Angeletos and Calvet (2004), and Covas (2005), to study approximate aggregation in a slightly different context with additional credit-market frictions. It also serves to illustrate a mechanism for generating a lower risk-free rate.

4.1   1998 Setup, Baby Version

We focus on a version of the model without valued leisure. Preferences are given by $u(c_1) + \beta E(u(c_2))$; we assume that $u(c)$ has constant relative risk aversion. The technology is the standard neoclassical one: Consumption and investment are perfect substitutes in the first period, and an aggregate investment of $\bar{k}_2$ units in period 1 delivers output $\bar{k}_2^\alpha + (1 - \delta)\bar{k}_2$ in period 2. There is no aggregate technology shock in the second period, but there are idiosyncratic wage shocks (i.e., we depart somewhat from the model above in focusing on income uncertainty due to wage, not unemployment, risk). Finally, in the first period the resources are given exogenously; there is no production. In the second period, each consumer is endowed with one unit of time, which he supplies inelastically.

The decentralized economy has individual budgets that read

$$c_1 + k_2 = \omega \quad \text{and} \quad c_2 = (1 + F_2(\bar{k}_2, 1) - \delta)k_2 + F(\bar{k}_2, 1)\epsilon + a.$$

We assume that ϵ is lognormally distributed (with mean normalized to 1), and that shocks are independently and identically distributed across agents so that, in the second period, the distribution of ex post realizations of ϵs is lognormal. Moreover, we assume that the (exogenous) distribution of ωs is lognormal; we denote this distribution Γ_1 in line with the notation in the big model.

For any initial wealth distribution Γ_1, this model can be solved with arbitrary accuracy using a simple guess-and-verify procedure: One guesses on $\bar{k}_2$, which implies a rental rate and a wage rate in the second period. Based on these prices, it is straightforward to solve the consumer's problem, which is strictly concave, by solving a first-order condition with one unknown: the individual's capital holdings. One then sums up, over a large number of agents (or integrates numerically), the savings and then checks whether the obtained number equals $\bar{k}_2$. It is easy to show that there is a unique value for $\bar{k}_2$ that constitutes a fixed point, and a standard Newton-Raphson algorithm converges securely to it, thus generating an equilibrium decision rule $k_2 = h^k(\omega)$. Then one can repeat this for any alternative initial wealth distribution, Γ_1, and thereby obtain $k_2 = h^k(\omega, \Gamma_1)$. This decision rule can now be compared to the dynamic decision rule for savings in Section 3: it has the entire wealth distribution as a state variable, though this distribution is exogenous here. The task, thus, is to vary the wealth distribution Γ_1 and to explore how it impacts on the macroeconomic equilibrium. As above, the lack of insurance markets for idiosyncratic risk makes the answer nontrivial.

4.1.1   Results for the Baseline Setup

We assume that utility has a relative risk aversion coefficient of 3, and the other parameters satisfy: β (discount factor) $= 0.99$, α (exponent on capital in the production function) $= 0.36$, and δ (rate of depreciation) $= 0.025$. Since Γ_1 is lognormal, the key variable of interest for us is σ_ω: the standard deviation of the initial distribution of income. Given a value for mean wealth, does σ_ω matter for equilibrium savings? If it (almost) does not, we have approximate aggregation.

Table 8.1 summarizes the key findings.

The left panel in Table 8.1 tabulates the equilibrium capital stock, $\bar{k}_2$, as a function of the amount of idiosyncratic risk (σ_ϵ), horizontally, and the amount of initial wealth dispersion (σ_ω), vertically, and the right panel tabulates the interest rate as a function of the same variables. We normalize $\bar{k}_2$ so that it is 1 in the case of no idiosyncratic risk (the first column): in this case, since preferences admit exact aggregation, and we indeed see that the dispersion of initial

Table 8.1.

	$\bar{k}_2$	σ_ϵ			$1/q$	σ_ϵ		
		0	0.5	1		0	0.5	1
	0	1.000	1.003	1.012	0	5.41%	5.40%	5.34%
σ_ω	0.5	1.000	1.003	1.012	0.5	5.41%	5.40%	5.34%
	1	1.000	1.003	1.012	1	5.41%	5.40%	5.34%

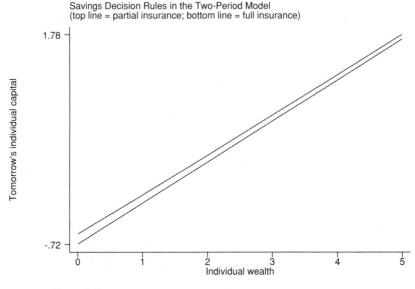

Figure 8.2.

wealth does not influence total savings.[26] In the second column, total savings are higher since there is now idiosyncratic risk: There is some *precautionary savings*. However, looking down rows in the second column, we see identical numbers: The amount of initial wealth dispersion does not seem to influence total savings, even though there are incomplete markets. Here, in fact, it is possible to detect small differences – if one examines more significant digits, but there is, clearly, *approximate aggregation*. In fact, all columns have identical numbers up to 4 significant digits, simply revealing no economically significant aggregate effects of wealth inequality on total savings or, as seen in the right panel, on interest rates.

Table 8.1 also shows that the representative-agent model is rather robust to the introduction of idiosyncratic risk in this case. The top left corners of the two panels show the representative-agent model: the model with no idiosyncratic risk and no wealth dispersion. But in fact all four entries in the first column are identical because preferences admit exact aggregation over initial wealth in the absence of idiosyncratic shocks. In terms of the interest rate, we thus see that the presence of uninsurable risk, and wealth inequality, does not lower the interest rate by more than 7 basis points (i.e., seven-hundredths of one percent).

Under the surface of the aggregates in Table 8.1, there is significant consumption inequality and, in addition, consumption risk. Thus, approximate aggregation does not imply an elimination of fluctuations in consumption: "self-insurance" using capital is not capable of doing this. Nonetheless,

---

[26] We also normalize so that average productivity is constant across experiments.

self-insurance, at least given the preferences considered here and in most of the macroeconomic literature, is very effective in insuring consumers in *utility terms*. That is, the remaining consumption risk just does not hurt consumers enough to change their overall attitudes toward saving much, and hence aggregate savings and interest rates are hardly influenced at all by idiosyncratic risk.

The effectiveness of self-insurance is reflected in consumers' decision rules, as depicted in Figure 8.2. The top line is a typical decision rule with partial insurance. The bottom line provides a point of comparison: It is the decision rule of a consumer who faces the equilibrium prices from the model with partial insurance but has a complete set of assets to insure fully against idiosyncratic risk.

The decision rule under full insurance has a constant marginal propensity to save: For the class of preferences we use, it is *exactly* linear. By contrast, the marginal propensity to save (or slope) of the decision rule under partial insurance increases with wealth. In addition, as wealth increases, the decision rule becomes more and more like the full-insurance decision rule for total savings: Not only marginal savings propensities but average propensities become identical. In other words, with wealth sufficiently large, idiosyncratic risk plays a negligible role in the decision-making of consumers; these statements are proved in detail in the Appendix. However, what is important here is quantitative: The variations in the slope are very small and are concentrated among poor consumers. This is the key finding underlying approximate aggregation in this model.

Given that there is consumption inequality due to uninsurable shocks, one can investigate how macroeconomic policy – i.e., aggregate policy – influences the distribution of consumption and, possibly, may improve the market's imperfect ability to insure agents. We will examine this issue in Section 4.1.3 below.

We will also demonstrate more clearly that the approximate aggregation is not exact, i.e., that there is no "theorem" here, even though Table 8.1, with its 4 significant digits, does not reveal *any* effects of wealth inequality on the equilibrium. So we will consider two changes: we will impose strict borrowing constraints – consumers cannot borrow at all – and we will consider much larger changes in wealth inequality than those in the above tables, which were based on empirically plausible changes in inequality. The results are contained in Table 8.2.

Table 8.2.

| | $\bar{k}_2$ | σ_ϵ | | | $1/q$ | σ_ϵ | | |
		0	0.5	1		0	0.5	1
	0	1.000	1.004	1.014	0	6.05%	6.03%	5.98%
Gini$_\omega$	0.32	1.000	1.004	1.015	0.5	6.05%	6.03%	5.97%
	0.68	1.026	1.032	1.043	1	5.91%	5.88%	5.83%

On the vertical axis, we now display the Gini coefficient of wealth instead, which ranges from 0 to 0.68. Such wide variation in this coefficient is rarely (if ever) observed in U.S. data, especially not in the short run. When the Gini coefficient is 0.32, a little less than one percent of the consumers are borrowing-constrained, whereas when the Gini coefficient is 0.68, roughly 30% of the consumers are constrained. Thus, moving from row 2 to row 3 in Table 8.2 involves huge amounts of redistribution, and this redistribution occurs in large part between a group with zero marginal savings propensity and a group with much higher propensity. The result, indeed, is a more radical departure from aggregation: We now see aggregate capital increase – when doubling the Gini from 0.32 to 0.64 and 30% of the consumers become constrained – an increase in the total capital stock by around 3 percentage points and an intereste-rate decrease of around 15 basis points. Also, note that even the economy without idiosyncratic risk fails to meet aggregation: In column 1 (and 4), rows 2 and 3 differ. This is because some consumers want to borrow here and cannot: Markets, thus, are not complete, and this restriction binds for a group of agents. In sum, this economy clearly does not feature exact aggregation: The previous findings of approximate aggregation is a *quantitative* result.

In the big, quantitative model, the two channels just combined will not operate in any important way. The reason is twofold. First, in the quantitative model, most consumers are not constrained. Of course, there are no direct empirical observations of whether consumers have "binding" borrowing constraints, so it is possible that indeed a large fraction of consumers are constrained; however, though there are disagreements, most empirical researchers would probably set the fraction of households with binding constraints at a number much lower than 30%. Second, in Table 8.2, we exogenously change the wealth distribution from one with a Gini of 0.32 to one of 0.64, thus effectuating a huge redistribution across the population. Such huge redistributions simply do not occur in the data, and they clearly do not occur in the big model either; the model roughly, at least, reproduces the wealth distribution dynamics.

4.1.2   Assessing Solution by Simulation

The results in the previous section are obtained with controlled – and for the numbers we report, very high – accuracy. We now use the knowledge of what the "exact" equilibrium is in order to assess how solution by simulation works in the two-period model. For this purpose, let the mean and variance of the (lognormal) wealth distribution be random variables drawn from known distributions. Consumers are now assumed to be boundedly rational: Their perceptions are given by a view of what $\bar{k}_2$ is that depends only on mean wealth. We thus specify, as in the big model, a mapping from mean wealth today to future wealth that is simple; it is parameterized by θ, and we choose θ so that, given the parametric form, it gives the best fit for consumers. To pin down the parameters θ of this "forecasting rule," solution by simulation is employed: (i) we draw simulated values for the mean and variance of the wealth distribution, thus for each draw obtaining the value of $\bar{k}_2$ implied by the initial guess on θ; (ii) we use the simulated data to estimate a new value for θ; and (iii) we iterate to convergence and assess the fit of the forecasting rule.

Notice that the solution by simulation, by construction, allows the possibility of a self-fulfilling prophecy. That is, agents' behavior is based on certain (boundedly rational) perceptions, and then one could imagine that their implied behavior, due to the imperfect perceptions, somehow, would (almost) confirm these perceptions. Fully rational expectations, at least in models with complete markets, eliminate self-fulfilling equilibria, and we do not expect there to be multiple expectational equilibria in the big model; in the two-period model considered in this section, we can prove that the equilibrium is unique. The point, thus, is that without rational expectations, little is known regarding uniqueness, which is why it is important to examine the issue here, where we know the exact equilibrium and can compare it to the equilibrium we find using boundedly rational perceptions and solution by simulation.

We let the mean and standard deviation of the wealth distribution vary by 10%; the average wealth Gini is 0.51. The results can be summarized in two observations. First, in all cases, the fit of the forecasting rule is nearly perfect: $R^2 \approx 0.99999$, with a residual standard deviation of about 0.04%.[27] Second, the solution by simulation was extremely close to the exact solution: The deviations are on the order of 0.001%!

Thus, we conclude that the solution found by solution by simulation is not produced due to a self-fulfilling prophecy, as expected. The basic reason why our algorithm works really is the fundamental workings of this model: Decision rules are extremely close to linear, and they are linear because very little wealth suffices to insure very well in utility terms.

4.1.3   Illustrating the Social Insurance Role of Macro Policy

One of the interesting aspects of macroeconomic models with heterogeneous consumers is that they allow us to trace effects of policy across different consumer groups. Thus, one can use these models to examine the effects – positive and normative – of government insurance policy, aimed explicitly at improving on market outcomes from the insurance perspective. Perhaps more interestingly, the model also makes clear how purely aggregate policy actually may have nontrivial and interesting effects on inequality. Here we will illustrate the effects of a tax on investment using a simple example from Davila, Hong, Krusell, and Ríos-Rull (2005).

For the sake of the argument, assume that there is no initial wealth inequality in the two-period model: ω is the same for all consumers. Moreover, suppose

---

[27] When we use the extreme changes in wealth inequality, the lowest recorded R^2 was 0.99919.

that ϵ can only take on two values (as in the employed/unemployed case): ϵ_1 occurs with probability π. A competitive equilibrium is now simply a vector $(\bar{k}_2, r, w)$ such that (i) $\bar{k}_2$ solves

$$\max_{k \in [0, y]} u(\omega - k) + \beta \left(\pi u(rk + we_1) + (1 - \pi)u(rk + we_2) \right)$$

and (ii) $r = F_2(\bar{k}_2, \bar{n}_2)$ and $w = F_2(\bar{k}_2, \bar{n}_2)$, with $\bar{n}_2 = \pi e_1 + (1 - \pi)e_2$.

By changing prices (wages and interest rates), a tax or subsidy on initial investment would influence the allocation of risk in this economy, and thus it would influence ex post inequality. Could it in fact improve welfare? We will reproduce the analysis of Davila et al. here and demonstrate that a *tax on investment* is welfare-improving. We will though simply look at how welfare is changed when $\bar{k}_2$ is changed away from the laissez-faire equilibrium by a small amount. The government balances its budget, returning the proceeds of the tax in the form of lump-sum subsidies.

Differentiating the indirect equilibrium utility with respect to aggregates and using the fact that individuals are making an optimal savings decision when the tax is zero, we obtain:

$$dU = \beta \Bigg(\left(\pi u_c(r\bar{k}_2 + we_1) + (1 - \pi)u_c(r\bar{k}_2 + we_2) \right) \bar{k}_2 dr$$
$$+ \left(\pi u_c(r\bar{k}_2 + we_1)e_1 + (1 - \pi)u_c(r\bar{k}_2 + we_2)e_2 \right) dw \Bigg).$$

This expression shows that changes in factor prices are what is key here; these prices influence de facto insurance in this economy with incomplete markets.

How are factor prices affected? We have $dr = F_{11}(\bar{k}_2, \bar{n}_2)d\bar{k}_2$ and $dw = F_{21}(\bar{k}_2, \bar{n}_2)d\bar{k}_2$. A tax on investment decreases aggregate savings (i.e., $d\bar{k}_2 < 0$), so the interest rate falls and the wage rate rises provided that the marginal product of capital is strictly decreasing and that capital and labor are complements. Then using Euler's theorem one can show (see Davila et al. (2005) for all the algebra) that $dU > 0$ if $(u_c(r\bar{k}_2 + we_1) - u_c(r\bar{k}_2 + we_2))F_{11}\bar{k}_2 d\bar{k}_2 > 0$. This inequality follows from the strict concavity of u and F and the fact that the tax on investment decreases aggregate savings. Thus, even though aggregate policy does not redistribute directly, it has an impact on social insurance through its effects on prices. In a complete-markets environment, such an effect would still be present, but it could not be welfare-improving, whereas here it is. We see, from the logic of the proof, specifically, that a lower capital stock alters the prices so as to reduce de facto risk: Lucky consumers are lucky through labor income, and an overall decrease in the wage thus has the effect of lowering wage risk. This is what the investment tax accomplishes: It lowers investment, thus raising the return to capital and lowering the wage rate in the second period.

If one considers a three-period model, one can see that an investment tax need not be appropriate at all times. For in the second period, lucky consumers will save part of their proceeds from having a high wage outcome. This means that a subsidy to investment may be appropriate at that point in time: It will raise w_3 and lower r_3, thus reducing the de facto risk in period-2 wages. Of course, if period-3 wages are also random, a period-2 investment subsidy would increase risk from that perspective, so whether a subsidy or a tax is appropriate is a quantitative matter in a longer-horizon model. Davila et al. indeed show that steady-state capital stocks are too high for some calibrations and too low for others. Quantitatively, they argue, based on a calibration for the wealth distribution based on luck, not discount-factor heterogeneity, that a subsidy looks most appropriate.

Finally, let us comment briefly on a methodological aspect of the kind of welfare analysis undertaken here. In our analysis, markets are incomplete *by assumption*: the restrictions consumers face in being able to insure against the idiosyncratic shocks are not derived from first principles based on explicit frictions, such as asymmetric information or enforcement problems. This means that welfare experiments are hazardous, because one might imagine that a change in policy would also change the market structure: Economic agents would change their behavior in response to the new policy. That is, one could raise a form of "Lucas critique" here.

Indeed, the recent literature on dynamic contracting is in large part motivated by such concerns, see Kocherlakota (2005). One of the goals of that literature is to "endogenously derive" what we perceive as empirically plausible market imperfections, and also to try to explain observed taxation patterns in terms of optimal insurance policy for these dynamic environments (thus building intertemporal versions of the work of Mirrlees (1971)). This work is promising and very interesting from the present perspective, since it delivers implications for inequality. However, because it is still in its infancy, its most successful attempts are not that close to what we perceive as a realistic setting from the perspective of typical households in the data. In contrast, the model we use here seems much more descriptively accurate – it is what empirical microeconomic researchers use, and also seems appealing from the (admittedly limited) perspective of our own lives. Therefore, it does seem reasonable to examine its welfare properties. We also think that the mechanisms emphasized here can be evaluated on their own terms to some extent; for example, the price manipulations a government would undertake according to the results discussed above are intuitive. Hopefully, a more complete analysis will be possible in the future, and it is far from impossible that the mechanisms we discuss here also play an important role in such an analysis.

4.2   The Risk-Free Rate: An Economy with Entrepreneurs

Finally, we consider a model that is a step further from the neoclassical growth model: Production does not take place using a ubiquitous technology. Put differently, factors of production are not costlessly mobile across production sites. We will use this setup to demonstrate that, with otherwise unchanged assumptions – idiosyncratic shocks with no direct insurance available, and initial wealth

Table 8.3.

$\bar{k}_2$	σ_ϵ 0	0.5	1	$1/q$	σ_ϵ 0	0.5	1
0	1.000	1.006	1.020	0	5.41%	4.57%	2.74%
σ_ω 0.5	1.000	1.006	1.020	0.5	5.41%	4.57%	2.74%
1	1.000	1.006	1.020	1	5.41%	4.57%	2.74%

inequality – some new features materialize: The asset-pricing implications are far from those of the neoclassical economy.

We look at a two-period version of Covas (2005), which itself can be viewed as a version of Angeletos (2005) where entrepreneurs cannot hire labor. More precisely, entrepreneurs invest in capital in period 1 and face idiosyncratic productivity risk in the second period: If an entrepreneur invests k, his second-period output is ϵk^α, with ϵ lognormal and i.i.d.[28] As in the previous two-period model, there is then no aggregate risk in the second period. Capital is immobile ex post: Two entrepreneurs with different realizations for their ϵs cannot increase output by letting capital move towards the more productive entrepreneur. Moreover, the production technology makes clear that the amount of labor input is also fixed (at a normalized value of one); this could reflect an assumption that the entrepreneur himself is an unsubstitutable input, or it could reflect an assumption that the labor input takes even longer to reallocate across production sites than does the capital input. The productivity risk cannot be insured against with any direct insurance markets; moreover, there is a "financing friction" in that the only individual capable of investing in an entrepreneur's technology is the entrepreneur himself. That is, equity cannot be traded.

The budget of a typical entrepreneur reads:

$$c_1 + k_2 + q b_2 = \omega \quad \text{and} \quad c_2 = \epsilon k_2^\alpha + b_2 + a.$$

Thus, the entrepreneur can borrow, or lend, at a risk-free interest rate $1/q$.

Table 8.3 summarizes the equilibrium behavior of this model for a range of parameter settings.

Table 8.3 illustrates two points quite clearly: (i) approximate aggregation obtains again; and (ii) the model has very different implications than its representative-agent counterpart. As for the first point, again all the numbers in any given column are the same: Differences appear only if more significant digits are included. As for the effects of entrepreneurial risk on asset prices, we now see very large effects. With higher idiosyncratic risk, interest rates fall drastically – Table 8.3 reveals a fall of over 2.5 percentage points. Even though decision rules for investment/savings are quite linear in wealth here in the relevant range, the demand for bonds is influenced significantly by the poorer

---

[28] Notice that risk in some sense is different here: It is complementary with the investment choice. That is, higher investment increases individual risk. Conversely, zero investment, which is feasible, allows risk to be eliminated entirely.

entrepreneurs who value insurance more. The rich entrepreneurs invest up to an amount that roughly equalizes the expected return from investment with the risk-free rate, whereas the poorer entrepreneurs do not, thus stopping short: For them, the marginal resources otherwise invested are better saved at a safe rate. Thus, they value consumption in the future more on the margin: They are willing to pay more for a bond, everything else equal.

5 CONCLUSIONS AND FINAL REMARKS

We have reviewed what has become a rather active quantitative research area in the intersection of macroeconomics and the applied consumption-savings, labor, and finance/asset-pricing literatures. The overall idea is to use available insights from these applied literatures to construct aggregate models with realistic underpinnings. Besides performing an important "robustness check" on the standard representative-agent macroeconomic model, this research allows an understanding of the equilibrium determination of inequality. Moreover, it opens up an interesting avenue for exploring effects of macroeconomic policy – namely, on the cross-section of consumers, and on their ability to insure risk effectively – that have hitherto been ignored, or abstracted from.

Much of the work reviewed here emphasizes the methodological advances. In particular, we illustrate and explain the finding of *approximate aggregation*, a feature of economies with heterogeneous agents that has greatly expanded the class of models that can feasibly be studied. The boundaries of the applicability of approximate aggregation are far from known; so far, we know of no quantitatively convincing models with large departures from aggregation, but our imagination is admittedly limited, and we foresee important examples of such phenomena to be discovered in future research. Indeed, we think that the exploration of this boundary is an important task for the future work in this area.

Finally, we develop a two-period model in Section 4, which not only is useful for illustration, we think, but also for conducting "pilot studies" within this area. Thus, one likely obtains important insights about whether approximate aggregation will hold, and about what interesting features a model might have, by first investigating a two-period model of the sort we examine here.

Almost by necessity, the work on dynamic macroeconomic equilibrium models requires heavy use of numerical methods, but computers are powerful now and the numerical methods available are becoming standard fare in many graduate programs all over the world. The original model in Krusell and Smith (1998) can now be solved in a matter of minutes using our own code, and that code was not written for the purposes of maximizing speed.

It seems obvious to us that many exciting issues are now open for exploration using the kinds of theoretical structures discussed here. There is ongoing work that attempts to integrate the present model with risk-averse individuals and incomplete asset markets with more explicit models of labor market frictions, along the lines of Mortensen and Pissarides (1994), where wage/employment shocks are endogenous. The work on policy – examining macroeconomic policy from a social insurance perspective, and comparing it with, and looking at how it complements, more explicit social insurance/welfare policy – has also begun. Similarly, there is some work that incorporates firm heterogeneity, credit-market frictions, and immobility of input factors – which appear to be plausible sources of idiosyncratic shocks both to workers and firm owners – but there is much to do. Here, our two-period example economy of Section 4.2 shows that it has not yet been solved in an infinite-horizon version. This illustrates the value of using the two-period model for pilot studies: We have identified a feasible paper to be written, namely the examination of aggregate risk in environments like those studied by Covas (2005) and Angeletos (2005). Approximate aggregation will almost certainly hold there, and the asset-pricing implications of such a model seem quite promising.

In contrast, there is very little work examining further elements of heterogeneity, such as the heterogeneity of consumption goods. Here, one may not expect that distinguishing between different kinds of cereal to be an important step forward for macroeconomics, but it may be important to makes distinctions between broad categories: nondurable consumption, durable consumption, services, and housing consumption. Further, preference heterogeneity seems very important to explore: If preferences for cereal are as different as they are (Tony likes Grape-Nuts and Per Mueslix), then isn't it reasonable to expect differences between consumers also in dimensions that appear to be of greater macroeconomic relevance, such as their attitudes toward risk and saving?

Finally, we expect that work on asymmetric information – different views among consumers and firms regarding future events – to be an important element of future macroeconomic models; after all, it seems that most of real-world asset-market trade and the associated investments are not just explained by risk-sharing or liquidity needs. Another area with which the quantitative literature on consumer heterogeneity has had relatively little overlap so far is monetary economics; recent work by Doepke and Schneider (2004) suggests that monetary policy shocks may have important consequences for inequality.

A very final point is that, with computer speed still growing at a significant rate, we foresee the possibility that the class of models studied here can be estimated structurally. Here as well, methodological work, both in numerical analysis and statistics, is expected to be an important component for the next several years.

APPENDIX: APPROXIMATE LINEARITY
IN THE TWO-PERIOD MODEL

Consider first the case with full insurance; let the price of a state-contingent bond paying 1 in state ϵ and zero otherwise be $qf(\epsilon)$, where $f(\epsilon)$ is the probability density associated to state ϵ (the distribution function is denoted $F(\epsilon)$, with an expected value of $\bar{\epsilon}$); thus, for comparison with the incomplete-markets economy, we assume actuarially fair insurance and that the price of a riskless bond is q. It is straightforward in this case to show that $a(\omega, \epsilon)$, the optimal holding of this state-contingent bond, must satisfy

$$a(\omega, \epsilon) = \frac{\omega - q(\bar{\epsilon} - \epsilon) - \epsilon \left(\frac{q}{\beta}\right)^{\frac{1}{\gamma}}}{q + \left(\frac{q}{\beta}\right)^{\frac{1}{\gamma}}}.$$

Thus, this amount is linear in ω, and therefore so is the total amount of bonds:

$$\int a(\omega, \epsilon) F(d\epsilon) = \frac{\omega - \bar{\epsilon}\left(\frac{q}{\beta}\right)^{\frac{1}{\gamma}}}{q + \left(\frac{q}{\beta}\right)^{\frac{1}{\gamma}}}.$$

Thus, the marginal propensity to buy bonds is $1/(q + (q/\beta)^{1/\gamma})$, and as wealth goes to infinity, this also equals the average propensity (i.e., bond holdings over total initial wealth).

In the economy with only a riskless bond, the first-order condition reads

$$\frac{q}{\beta}(\omega - qa(\omega))^{-\gamma} = \int (\epsilon + a(\omega))^{-\gamma} F(d\epsilon)$$

for all ω. This allows us to see that $a(\omega)$ must be increasing. Take the derivative with respect to ω and obtain

$$\frac{q}{\beta}(\omega - qa(\omega))^{-\gamma-1}(1 - a'(\omega)) = \left(\int (\epsilon + a(\omega))^{-\gamma-1} F(d\epsilon)\right) a'(\omega).$$

These two equations can be rewritten as

$$\frac{q}{\beta} = \int \left(\frac{\omega - qa(\omega)}{\epsilon + a(\omega)}\right)^{\gamma} F(d\epsilon) \tag{2}$$

and

$$\frac{q}{\beta}\frac{1 - a'(\omega)}{a'(\omega)} = \int \left(\frac{\omega - qa(\omega)}{\epsilon + a(\omega)}\right)^{\gamma+1} F(d\epsilon). \tag{3}$$

Let $s(\omega, \epsilon) \equiv \frac{\omega - qa(\omega)}{\epsilon + a(\omega)}$; s is the ratio of current to future consumption. It is positive and decreasing in ϵ. One can show that there exists an ϵ^* such that $s_1(\omega, \epsilon^*) = 0$, $s_1(\omega, \epsilon) > 0$ for all $\epsilon > \epsilon^*$, and $s_1(\omega, \epsilon) < 0$ for all $\epsilon < \epsilon^*$.[29]

---

[29] To see this, first note that the derivative of $\frac{\omega - qa(\omega)}{\epsilon + a(\omega)}$ equals $\frac{(1 - qa'(\omega))(\epsilon + a) - (\omega - qa(\omega))a'(\omega)}{(\epsilon + a)^2} = \frac{1}{\epsilon + a(\omega)}\left(1 - a'(\omega)\frac{q\epsilon + \omega}{\epsilon + a(\omega)}\right) = \frac{1}{\epsilon + a(\omega)}\left(1 - qa'(\omega)\frac{q\epsilon + \omega}{q\epsilon + qa(\omega)}\right)$. This expression cannot be zero for more than one value of ϵ; call that value ϵ^*. Moreover, since $\omega > qa(\omega)$, $\frac{q\epsilon + \omega}{q\epsilon + qa(\omega)}$ is increasing in ϵ and therefore $\frac{1}{\epsilon + a(\omega)}\left(1 - qa'(\omega)\frac{q\epsilon + \omega}{q\epsilon + qa(\omega)}\right) > (<) 0$ for all $\epsilon > (<) \epsilon^*$.

Now we can write equations (2) and (3) as

$$\frac{q}{\beta} = \int s(\omega, \epsilon)^{\gamma} F(d\epsilon) \qquad (4)$$

and

$$\frac{q}{\beta} \frac{1 - qa'(\omega)}{a'(\omega)} = \int s(\omega, \epsilon)^{\gamma+1} F(d\epsilon). \qquad (5)$$

The left-hand side of equation (4) is constant. Therefore, the right-hand side of the equation does not depend on ω either. This means that

$$\int s(\omega, \epsilon)^{\gamma-1} s_1(\omega, \epsilon) F(d\epsilon) = 0. \qquad (6)$$

To find out whether the right-hand side of equation (5) is increasing or decreasing, we need to sign

$$\int s(\omega, \epsilon)^{\gamma} s_1(\omega, \epsilon) F(d\epsilon).$$

The sign of the latter is the same as the sign of

$$s(\omega, \epsilon^*) \left(\int_{-\infty}^{\epsilon^*} s(\omega, \epsilon)^{\gamma-1} s_1(\omega, \epsilon) \frac{s(\omega, \epsilon)}{s(\omega, \epsilon^*)} F(d\epsilon) \right.$$
$$\left. + \int_{\epsilon^*}^{\infty} s(\omega, \epsilon)^{\gamma-1} s_1(\omega, \epsilon) \frac{s(\omega, \epsilon)}{s(\omega, \epsilon^*)} F(d\epsilon) \right).$$

The first of these integrals is negative, and the second one is positive, since $s_1(\omega, \epsilon) > (<) \, 0$ for all $\epsilon > (<) \, \epsilon^*$. So the sign of the overall expression must be negative, since comparing to equation (6) and recalling that $\frac{s(\omega, \epsilon)}{s(\omega, \epsilon^*)} < (>) \, 1$ when $\epsilon > (<) \, \epsilon^*$, the positive integral must become smaller and the negative integral must become larger (in absolute value). Thus, we conclude that the right-hand side of equation (3) is decreasing in ω and, thus, that $(1 - qa'(\omega))/a'(\omega)$ must be decreasing in ω. This implies that $a'(\omega)$ is *increasing*.[30]

Equation (3) also implies that $a'(\omega) \in (0, 1/q)$. So we know that $a'(\omega)$ is increasing and is bounded above. Therefore, it has a limit; let it be denoted a'. Also, let $\bar{a}(\omega) \equiv a(\omega)/\omega$, so that equation (3) can be written

$$\frac{q}{\beta} = \int \left(\frac{1 - q\bar{a}(\omega)}{\frac{\epsilon}{\omega} + \bar{a}(\omega)} \right)^{\gamma} F(d\epsilon).$$

This equation implies that $\bar{a}(\omega)$ must be increasing. Since it is bounded above by $1/q$, it must have a limit, which we denote $\bar{a}$. Thus, taking limits, we have two equations in two unknowns:

$$\frac{q}{\beta} = \left(\frac{1 - q\bar{a}}{\bar{a}} \right)^{\gamma}$$

---

[30] The convexity of the savings function in a long-horizon model is demonstrated in Carroll and Kimball (1996).

and

$$\frac{q}{\beta} \frac{1 - qa'}{a'} = \left(\frac{1 - q\bar{a}}{\bar{a}} \right)^{\gamma+1}.$$

It follows that

$$a' = \bar{a} = \frac{1}{q + \left(\frac{q}{\beta} \right)^{\frac{1}{\gamma}}},$$

i.e., that the marginal and average propensities to save converge to the same value. Moreover, this is the value that obtains with full insurance.

References

Aiyagari, S.R. (1994), "Uninsured Idiosyncratic Risk and Aggregate Saving," *Quarterly Journal of Economics* 109, 659–684.

Allen, F. (1985), "Repeated Principal-Agent Relationships with Borrowing and Lending," *Economics Letters* 17, 27–31.

Altug, S. and P. Labadie (1994), *Dynamic Choice and Asset Markets*, Academic Press.

Angeletos, G.-M. (2005), "Uninsured Idiosyncratic Investment Risk and Aggregate Saving," manuscript.

Angeletos, G.-M. and L. Calvet (2004), "Idiosyncratic Production Risk, Growth and the Business Cycle," manuscript (forthcoming in *Journal of Monetary Economics*).

Atkeson, A. and C. Phelan (1994), "Reconsidering the Costs of Business Cycles with Incomplete Markets," in: S. Fischer and J. Rotemberg, eds., *NBER Macroeconomics Annual 1994*, 187–207.

Attanasio, O. (2005), "Consumption," Chapter 11 in J. Taylor and M. Woodford, eds., *Handbook of Macroeconomics*, North-Holland, 741–812.

Bewley, T. (undated), "Interest Bearing Money and the Equilibrium Stock of Capital," manuscript.

Bewley, T. (1977), "The Permanent Income Hypothesis: A Theoretical Formulation," *Journal of Economic Theory* 16, 252–292.

Blundell, R. and T. Stoker (2003), "Models of Aggregate Economic Relationships that Account for Heterogeneity," manuscript (forthcoming in *Handbook of Econometrics*, Volume 6).

Browning, M., L.P. Hansen, and J. Heckman (2005), "Micro Data and General Equilibrium Models," Chapter 8 in J. Taylor and M. Woodford, eds., *Handbook of Macroeconomics*, North-Holland, 543–633.

Cagetti, M. and M. De Nardi (2004), "Taxes, Entrepreneurship, and Wealth," manuscript.

Cagetti, M. and M. De Nardi (2005), "Entrepreneurship, Frictions, and Wealth," manuscript.

Campanale, C. (2005), "Increasing Return to Savings and Wealth Inequality," manuscript.

Carroll, C. (2000), "Requiem for the Representative Consumer? Aggregate Implications of Microeconomic Consumption Behavior," *American Economic Review, Papers and Proceedings* 90, 110–115.

Carroll, C. and M. Kimball (1996), "On the Concavity of the Consumption Function," *Econometrica* 64, 981–992.

Castañeda, A., J. Díaz-Giménez, and J.-V. Ríos-Rull (2003a), "Exploring the Income Distribution Business Cycle Dynamics," *Journal of Monetary Economics* 42, 93–130.

Castañeda, A., J. Díaz-Giménez, and J.-V. Ríos-Rull (2003b), "Accounting for the U.S. Earnings and Wealth Inequality," *Journal of Political Economy* 111, 814–857.

Chang, Y. and S.-B. Kim (2004), "Heterogeneity and Aggregation in the Labor Market: Implications for Aggregate Preference Shifts," manuscript.

Chang, Y. and S.-B. Kim (2006), "From Individual to Aggregate Labor Supply: A Quantitative Analysis Based on a Heterogeneous-Agent Macroeconomy," manuscript (forthcoming in *International Economic Review*).

Chatterjee, S., D. Corbae, M. Nakajima, and J.-V. Ríos-Rull (2002), "A Quantitative Theory of Unsecured Consumer Credit with Risk of Default," manuscript.

Cole, H. and N. Kocherlakota (2001), "Efficient Allocations with Hidden Income and Hidden Storage," *Review of Economic Studies* 68, 523–542.

Constantinides, G.M. and D. Duffie (1996), "Asset Pricing with Heterogeneous Consumers," *Journal of Political Economy* 104, 219–240.

Cooley, T. and V. Quadrini (2006), "Monetary Policy and the Financial Decisions of Firms," *Economic Theory* 27, 243–270.

Cooley, T., R. Marimon, and V. Quadrini (2004), "Aggregate Consequences of Limited Contract Enforceability," *Journal of Political Economy* 112, 817–847.

Córdoba, J.C. and G. Verdier (2005), "Lucas vs. Lucas: On Inequality and Growth," manuscript.

Covas, F. (2005), "Uninsured Idiosyncratic Production Risk with Borrowing Constraints," manuscript (forthcoming in the *Journal of Economic Dynamics and Control*).

Davila, J., J. Hong, P. Krusell, and J.-V. Ríos-Rull (2005), "Constrained Efficiency in the Neoclassical Growth Model with Uninsurable Idiosyncratic Shocks," manuscript.

Den Haan, W.J. (1997), "Solving Dynamic Models with Aggregate Shocks and Heterogeneous Agents," *Macroeconomic Dynamics* 1, 355–386.

Den Haan, W.J. and A. Marcet (1990), "Solving a Growth Model by Parameterized Expectations," *Journal of Business and Economic Statistics* 8, 31–34.

Díaz-Giménez, J., V. Quadrini, and J.-V. Ríos-Rull (1997), "Dimensions of Inequality: Facts on the U.S. Distributions of Earnings, Income, and Wealth," *Federal Reserve Bank of Minneapolis Quarterly Review* 21, 3–21.

Doepke, M. and M. Schneider (2004), "Real Effects of Inflation through the Redistribution of Nominal Wealth," manuscript.

Gomes, J. (2002), "The Right Stimulus: Extended Unemployment Insurance Benefits or Tax Cuts?" manuscript.

Gomes, J., J. Greenwood, and S. Rebelo (2001), "Equilibrium Unemployment," *Journal of Monetary Economics* 48, 109–152.

Gourinchas, P.-O. (2000), "Precautionary Saving, LifeCycle, and Macroeconomics," manuscript.

Hansen, G.D. (1985), "Indivisible Labor and the Business Cycle," *Journal of Monetary Economics* 16, 309–27.

Heathcote, J. (2005), "Fiscal Policy with Heterogeneous Agents and Incomplete Markets," *Review of Economic Studies* 72, 161–188.

Heaton, J. and D.J. Lucas (1996), "Evaluating the Effects of Incomplete Markets on Risk Sharing and Asset Pricing," *Journal of Political Economy* 104, 443–487.

Hubbard, R.G., J. Skinner, and S.P. Zeldes (1995), "Precautionary Saving and Social Insurance," *Journal of Political Economy* 103, 360–399.

Huggett, M. (1993), "The Risk-Free Rate in Heterogeneous-Agents, Incomplete Markets Economies," *Journal of Economic Dynamics and Control* 17, 953–969.

Huggett, M. (1996), "Wealth Distribution in Life-Cycle Economies," *Journal of Monetary Economics* 38, 469–494.

Huggett, M. (1997), "The One-Sector Growth Model with Idiosyncratic Shocks: Steady States and Dynamics," *Journal of Monetary Economics* 39, 385–403.

İmrohoroğlu, A. (1989), "The Cost of Business Cycles with Indivisibilities and Liquidity Constraints," *Journal of Political Economy* 97, 1364–1383.

Khan, A. and J. Thomas (2003), "Nonconvex Factor Adjustments in Equilibrium Business Cycle Models: Do Nonlinearities Matter?" *Journal of Monetary Economics* 50, 331–360.

Khan, A. and J. Thomas (2005), "Inventories and the Business Cycle: An Equilibrium Analysis of (S,s) Policies," manuscript.

Kocherlakota, N. (2005), "Advances in Dynamic Optimal Taxation," manuscript.

Krebs, T. (2003), "Growth and Welfare Effects of Business Cycles in Economies with Idiosyncratic Human Capital Risk," *Review of Economic Dynamics* 6, 846–868.

Krueger, D. and F. Kubler (2004), "Computing Equilibrium in OLG Models with Stochastic Production," *Journal of Economic Dynamics and Control* 28, 1411–1436.

Krusell, P. and A.A. Smith, Jr. (1997), "Income and Wealth Heterogeneity, Portfolio Selection, and Equilibrium Asset Returns," *Macroeconomic Dynamics* 1, 387–422.

Krusell, P. and A.A. Smith, Jr. (1998), "Income and Wealth Heterogeneity in the Macroeconomy," *Journal of Political Economy* 106, 867–896.

Krusell, P. and A.A. Smith, Jr. (1999), "On the Welfare Effects of Eliminating Business Cycles," *Review of Economic Dynamics* 2, 245–272.

Krusell, P. and A.A. Smith, Jr. (2002), "Revisiting the Welfare Effects of Eliminating Business Cycles," manuscript.

Leduc, S. (2002), "Incomplete Markets, Borrowing Constraints, and the Foreign Exchange Risk Premium," *Journal of International Money and Finance* 21, 957–980.

Lucas, Jr., R.E. (1976), "Econometric Policy Evaluation: A Critique," in: A. Meltzer and K. Brunner, eds., *The Phillips Curve and Labor Markets* (Vol. 1 of Carnegie-Rochester Conference Series on Public Policy), 19–46.

Lucas, Jr., R.E. (1987), *Models of Business Cycles* (Basil Blackwell).

Lucas, Jr., R.E. (2003), "Macroeconomic Priorities," *American Economic Review* 93, 1–14.

Mankiw, N.G. (1986), "The Equity Premium and the Concentration of Aggregate Shocks," *Journal of Financial Economics* 17, 211–219.

Mehra, R. and E.C. Prescott (1985), "The Equity Premium: A Puzzle," *Journal of Monetary Economics* 15, 145–161.

Miao, J. (2002), "Stationary Equilibria of Economies with a Continuum of Heterogeneous Consumers," manuscript.

Mirrlees, J. (1971), "An Exploration in the Theory of Optimum Income Taxation," *Review of Economic Studies* 38, 175–208.

Mortensen, D. and C.A. Pissarides (1994), "Job Creation and Job Destruction in the Theory of Unemployment," *Review of Economic Studies* 61, 397–415.

Mukoyama, T. and A. Şahin (2005), "Costs of Business Cycles for Unskilled Workers," manuscript (forthcoming in *Journal of Monetary Economics*).

Obiols-Homs, F. (2003), "Incomplete Unemployment Insurance and Aggregate Fluctuations," *Review of Economic Dynamics* 6, 602–636.

Quadrini, V. (2000), "Entrepreneurship, Saving, and Social Mobility," *Review of Economic Dynamics* 45, 1–40.

Piketty, T. and E. Saez (2003), "Income Inequality in the United States: 1913-1998," *Quarterly Journal of Economics* 118, 1–39.

Ríos-Rull, J.-V. (2001), "Computation of Equilibria in Heterogeneous Agent Models," in Marimon, R. and A. Scott, eds., *Computational Methods for the Study of Dynamic Economies: An Introduction*, Oxford University Press, 238–280.

Rodríguez, S.B., J. Díaz-Giménez, V. Quadrini, and J.-V. Ríos-Rull (2002), "Updated Facts on the U.S. Distributions of Earnings, Income, and Wealth," *Federal Reserve Bank of Minneapolis Quarterly Review* 26, 2–35.

Rogerson, R. (1988), "Indivisible Labor, Lotteries and Equilibrium," *Journal of Monetary Economics* 21, 3–16.

Storesletten, K., C. Telmer, and A. Yaron (2001), "The Welfare Costs of Business Cycles Revisited: Finite Lives and Cyclical Variation in Idiosyncratic Risk," *European Economic Review* 45, 1311–1339.

Storesletten, K., C. Telmer, and A. Yaron (2004a), "Consumption and Risk Sharing over the Life Cycle," *Journal of Monetary Economics* 51, 609–633.

Storesletten, K., C. Telmer, and A. Yaron (2004b), "Asset Pricing with Idiosyncratic Risk and Overlapping Generations," manuscript.

Storesletten, K., C. Telmer, and A. Yaron (2004c), "Cyclical Dynamics in Idiosyncratic Labor-Market Risk," *Journal of Political Economy* 112, 695–717.

Young, E. (2004a), "Approximate Aggregation: An Obstacle Course for the Krusell-Smith Algorithm," manuscript.

Young, E. (2004b), "Solving the Heterogeneous-Agent Stochastic Growth Model with Finite Forecasting Restrictions," manuscript.

Zhang, L. (2005), "The Value Premium," *Journal of Finance* 60, 67–103.

CHAPTER 9

Modeling Inefficient Institutions*
Daron Acemoglu

1 INTRODUCTION

Many economists and social scientists have recently emphasized the importance of government policies, economic, political and legal institutions, and more broadly, the organization of society.[1] There is also mounting evidence that various institutional features are indeed important for economic growth.[2] Nevertheless, despite important theoretical advances, we still lack an organizational framework to analyze the determinants of institutions.[3] In particular, if institutions matter (so much) for economic performance, why do societies choose or end up with institutions that do not maximize economic growth or aggregate economic welfare? This paper discusses potential answers to this question.

The main focus is on modeling the emergence and persistence of inefficient institutions, meaning institutions that do not maximize the growth potential of a society.[4] The purpose of the paper is not to provide a survey but to construct a relatively simple unified model that illustrates both various issues already raised in the existing literature and a number of new mechanisms that appear to be important in understanding inefficient institutions.

* I thank Alexandre Debs for suggestions and excellent research assistance and Timothy Besley, Gerard Padro-i-Miquel, Torsten Persson, James Robinson and Pierre Yared for comments.
[1] For general discussions, see North and Thomas (1973), Jones (1981), North (1981), Olson (1982), North and Weingast (1989), Eggertsson (2005), Dixit (2004), and Acemoglu et al. (2005).
[2] See, among others, the empirical evidence in Knack and Keefer (1995), Mauro (1995), Barro (1999), Hall and Jones (1999), Acemoglu et al. (2001, 2002) or Persson (2005).
[3] Austen-Smith and Banks (1999) and Persson and Tabellini (2000) are excellent introductions to recent advances in political economy.
[4] A potentially weaker definition of "inefficiency" would be Pareto inefficiency, whereby a set of institutions would be Pareto inefficient if a different set of institutions would make everybody better off. This definition, though important for certain theoretical analyses, is too weak in the context of political economy discussions, since one set of institutions may enrich a particular narrow social group, while causing stagnation or low growth for the society at large, and we may wish to refer to this set of institutions as "inefficient."

To understand why inefficient institutions emerge and persist, we first need to understand: (i) what type of equilibrium policies and allocations emerge within different institutional frameworks; (ii) the preferences of different individuals and groups over these policies and allocations. This will enable us to derive *induced preferences* over institutions. Inefficient institutions will emerge and persist, in turn, when groups that prefer the inefficient (non-growth enhancing) policies that these institutions generate are sufficiently powerful, and when other social arrangements that compensate these powerful groups, while reaching more efficient allocations, cannot be found.

In this paper, I provide one example of such an approach. I start with a simple baseline model, which is then enriched to discuss a number of mechanisms that lead to the emergence and persistence of inefficient policies and institutions. The model includes three groups: workers, elite producers and non-elite (middle-class) producers. The latter two groups have access to investment opportunities with varying degrees of productivity. The key policies in the model are taxes imposed on producers.[5] There are two different institutional dimensions. The first is political institutions, which govern the allocation of *de jure* power in society.[6] This power determines, for example, which groups (or individuals) have control over fiscal policies. To start with, I suppose that the elite have de jure political power.[7] Economic institutions, on the other hand, relate to the constraints and rules governing economic interactions. They include, among other things, enforcement of property rights, entry barriers, regulation of technology, and the set of contracts that can be enforced.[8] In the model, restrictions on expropriation, taxation and redistribution, or the ability to regulate technology, correspond to economic institutions.

The model is first used to highlight various sources of inefficiencies in policies:

1. *Revenue extraction:* the group in power – the elite – will set high taxes on middle-class producers in order to extract resources from them. These taxes

---

[5] This should be interpreted as an example standing for many other forms of distortionary ways of transferring resources from one group to another. These include simple violations of property rights (as, for example, when land tenure is removed or assets are expropriated from certain groups), entry barriers (used to indirectly transfer resources from more efficient to less efficient producers or to manipulate factor prices as we will see below), or other distortionary policies, for example, the use of marketing boards in order to depress the prices paid for certain agricultural products (e.g., see Bates (1981), a classic analysis of the use of marketing boards in Ghana and Zambia).

[6] See Acemoglu and Robinson (2006a) and Acemoglu et al. (2005) for the distinction between de jure and de facto political power.

[7] Throughout I retain the assumption that political and economic groups coincide, thus all members of "the elite" will have the same preferences over economic policies and will somehow be able to coordinate their policy actions. In practice who "the elite" are is a key question, on which I am remaining agnostic in this paper (though the model will illustrate that the productivity of the elite has an important effect on the efficiency of equilibria).

[8] Naturally, the distinction between economic and political institutions is somewhat arbitrary. For example, restrictions on taxes and expropriation are interpreted as "economic institutions" here, though they clearly require limits on the political power of certain groups.

are distortionary. This source of inefficiency results from the absence of non-distortionary taxes, which implies that the distribution of resources cannot be decoupled from efficient production.[9]

2. *Factor price manipulation:* the group in power may want to tax middle-class producers in order to reduce the prices of the factors they use in production. This inefficiency arises because the elite and middle-class producers compete for factors (here labor). By taxing middle-class producers, the elite ensure lower factor prices and thus higher profits for themselves.[10]

3. *Political consolidation:* to the extent that the political power of the middle class depends on their economic resources, greater middle-class profits reduce the elite's political power and endanger their future rents. The elite will then want to tax the middle class in order to impoverish them and consolidate their political power.[11]

Although all three inefficiencies in policies arise because of the desire of the elite to extract rents from the rest of the society, the analysis reveals that of the three sources of inefficiency, the revenue extraction is typically the least harmful, since, in order to extract revenues, the elite need to ensure that the middle class undertakes efficient investments. In contrast, the factor price manipulation and political consolidation mechanisms encourage the elite to directly impoverish the middle class. An interesting comparative static result is that greater state capacity shifts the balance towards the revenue extraction mechanism, and thus, by allowing the elite to extract resources more efficiently from other groups, may improve the allocation of resources.

Additional inefficiencies arise when there are "commitment problems" on the part of the elites, in the sense that they may renege on policy promises once key investments are made. Following the literature on organizational economics, I refer to this as a *holdup problem*. With holdup, taxes are typically higher and more distortionary. Holdup problems, in turn, are likely to be important, for

---

[9] Many models in the literature emphasize the revenue extraction mechanism. See, among others, Grossman (1991), Grossman and Kim (1995), McGuire and Olson (1996). The costs of redistributive taxation in models of democracy are also related (e.g., Romer (1975), Roberts (1977), Meltzer and Richard (1981)). See also Besley and Coate (1998) for a discussion of inefficient redistribution because of limits on fiscal instruments.

[10] This mechanism is most closely related to Acemoglu (2003a), where incumbents may impose entry barriers in order to affect factor prices. It is also related to models in which there is a conflict between agricultural and capitalist producers, or between users of old and new technologies, for example, Krusell and Rios-Rull (1996), Parente and Prescott (1999), Bourguignon and Verdier (2000), Nugent and Robinson (2002), Galor et al. (2003), and Sonin (2003). The discussion of the taxation policies and migration and occupational controls towards blacks in South Africa in Feinstein (2005) provide a clear example of the factor price manipulation mechanism.

[11] The mechanism of political consolidation is most closely related to Acemoglu and Robinson (2000a, 2006b), where a ruler may block technological change in order to increase the probability of staying in power. In that model, the reason why technological change may threaten the ruler is that it erodes its incumbency advantage. See also Robinson (2001), Rajan and Zingales (2000) and Bueno de Mesquita et al. (2003). Empirical evidence related to the political consolidation mechanism from various historical contexts is discussed in Acemoglu and Robinson (2000a).

example, when the relevant investment decisions are long term, so that a range of policies will be decided after these investments are undertaken.

The inefficiencies in policies translate into inefficient institutions. Institutions determine the framework for policy determination, and economic institutions determine both the limits of various redistributive policies and other rules and regulations that affect the economic transactions and productivity of producers. In the context of the simple model here, I associate economic institutions with two features: limits on taxation and redistribution, and regulation on the technology used by middle-class producers.[12] The same forces that lead to inefficient policies imply that there will be reasons for the elite to choose inefficient economic institutions. In particular, they may not want to guarantee enforcement of property rights for middle-class producers or they may prefer to block technology adoption by middle-class producers. Holdup problems, which imply equilibrium taxes even higher than those preferred by the elite, create a possible exception, and may encourage the elite to use economic institutions to place credible limits on their own future policies (taxes). This suggests that economic institutions that restrict future policies may be more likely to arise in economies in which there are more longer-term investments and thus more room for holdup.

The model also sheds light on the conditions under which economic institutions discourage or block technology adoption. If the source of inefficiencies in policies is revenue extraction, the elite always wish to encourage the adoption of the most productive technologies by the middle class. However, when the source of inefficiencies in policies is factor price manipulation or political consolidation, the elite may want to *block* the adoption of more efficient technologies, or at the very least, they would choose not to invest in activities that would increase the productivity of middle-class producers. This again reiterates that when the factor price manipulation and political consolidation mechanisms are at work, significantly more inefficient outcomes can emerge.[13]

While economic institutions regulate fiscal policies and technology choices, political institutions govern the process of collective decision-making in society. In the baseline model, the elite have *de jure political power*, which means that they have the formal right to make policy choices and influence economic decisions. To understand the inefficiencies in the institutional framework, we need to investigate *the induced preferences* of different groups over institutions. In the context of political institutions, this means asking whether the elite wish to change the institutional structure towards a more equal distribution of political power. The same forces that make the elite choose inefficient policies also imply that the answer to this question is no. Consequently, despite the inefficiencies that follow, the institutional structure with elite control tends to persist.

---

[12] More generally, these correspond to various rules and arrangements that put constraints on fiscal and regulatory policies of governments, and shape the set of contracts and technology choices available to firms.

[13] The framework in this paper is applied to the inefficiency of institutions in an open economy setting in Segura-Cayuela (2006).

The framework also enables me to discuss issues of appropriate and inappropriate institutions. Concentrating political power in the hands of the elite may have limited costs (may even be "efficient"), if the elite are sufficiently productive (more productive than the middle class). However, a change in the productivity of the elite relative to the middle class could make a different distribution of political power more beneficial. In this case, existing institutions, which may have previously functioned relatively well, become inappropriate to the new economic environment.[14] Yet there is no guarantee that there will be a change in institutions in response to the change in environment.

Finally, I present a framework for analyzing changes in political institutions.[15] Political institutions regulate the allocation of de jure political power, as in the example of constitutions or elections determining the party in government. There is more to political power than this type of de jure power, however. Certain groups may be able to disrupt the existing system, for example, by solving their collective action problem and undertaking demonstrations, unrest, protests, revolutions or military action. Each group may therefore possess *de facto political power* even when excluded from de jure political power. In this context, middle-class producers, even though they have no formal say in a dictatorship or an oligarchic society, may sometimes have sufficient de facto political power to change the system or at least to demand some concessions from the elite. Under these circumstances, changes in political institutions may emerge as an equilibrium outcome. They are useful as a way of committing to future allocations because, by affecting the distribution of de jure political power in the future, they shape future policies and economic allocations. Such a commitment may be necessary when the current elite need to make concessions in response to a shift in the distribution of de facto political power and when their ability to make concessions within a given political system is limited. Consequently, changes in political institutions take place when the elite are forced to respond to temporary changes in de facto political power by changing the political system (and thus the distribution of de jure political power in the future). The analysis also shows that changes in political institutions are less likely when *political stakes* are higher because, in this case, the elite will fight and use repression to defend the existing regime. Rents from the natural resources or land tend to increase political stakes and thus contribute to institutional persistence. Interestingly, state capacity, which makes redistribution more efficient, also increases political stakes and may create dynamic costs by increasing the longevity of the dictatorship of the elite.

The rest of the paper is organized as follows. Section 2 presents the basic economic model and characterizes the equilibrium for a given sequence of policies.

---

[14] How a given set of institutions may first increase but then retard economic growth is also discussed in Acemoglu (2003a) and Acemoglu et al. (2003).

[15] This framework builds on my previous work with James Robinson, but applies these ideas to the environment considered here which contains richer economic interactions. See in particular Acemoglu and Robinson (2000b, 2001, 2006a).

The rest of the paper investigates how these policies are determined. Section 3 analyzes the revenue extraction, factor price manipulation and political consolidation mechanisms, and also discusses holdup problems and distortions in the process of technology adoption. Section 4 analyzes the emergence of inefficient economic institutions, while Section 5 discusses emergence and persistence of inefficient political institutions. Section 6 presents a model of endogenous institutional change and institutional persistence. Section 7 concludes.

2   BASELINE MODEL

2.1   Environment

Consider an infinite horizon economy populated by a continuum $1 + \theta_e + \theta_m$ of risk neutral agents, each with a discount factor equal to $\beta < 1$. There is a unique non-storable final good denoted by y. The expected utility of agent j at time 0 is given by:

$$U_0^j = \mathbb{E}_0 \sum_{t=0}^{\infty} \beta^t c_t^j, \tag{1}$$

where $c_t^j \in \mathbb{R}$ denotes the consumption of agent j at time t and $\mathbb{E}_t$ is the expectations operator conditional on information available at time t.

Agents are in three groups. The first are workers, whose only action in the model is to supply their labor inelastically. There is a total mass 1 of workers. The second is the elite, denoted by e, who initially hold political power in this society. There is a total of θ^e elites. Finally, there are θ^m "middle-class" agents, denoted by m. The sets of elite and middle-class producers are denoted by S^e and S^m respectively. With a slight abuse of notation, I will use j to denote either individual or group.

Each member of the elite and middle class has access to production opportunities, represented by the production function

$$y_t^j = \frac{1}{1-\alpha}(A_t^j)^\alpha (k_t^j)^{1-\alpha}(l_t^j)^\alpha, \tag{2}$$

where k denotes capital and l labor. Capital is assumed to depreciate fully after use. The Cobb-Douglas form is adopted for simplicity.

The key difference between the two groups is in their productivity. To start with, let us assume that the productivity of each elite agent is A^e in each period, and that of each middle-class agent is A^m. Productivity of the two groups differs, for example, because they are engaged in different economic activities (e.g., agriculture versus manufacturing, old versus new industries, etc.), or because they have different human capital or talent.

On the policy side, there are activity-specific tax rates on production, τ^e and τ^m, which are constrained to be nonnegative, i.e., $\tau^e \geq 0$ and $\tau^m \geq 0$. There are no other fiscal instruments (in particular, no lump-sum non-distortionary taxes). In addition there is a total income (rent) of R from natural resources. The proceeds of taxes and revenues from natural resources can be redistributed as nonnegative lump-sum transfers targeted towards each group, $T^w \geq 0$, $T^m \geq 0$ and $T^e \geq 0$.[16]

Let us also introduce a parameter $\phi \in [0, 1]$, which measures how much of the tax revenue can be redistributed. This parameter, therefore, measures "state capacity," i.e., the ability of the states to penetrate and regulate the production relations in society (though it does so in a highly "reduced-form" way). When $\phi = 0$, state capacity is limited and all tax revenue gets lost, whereas when $\phi = 1$ we can think of a society with substantial state capacity that is able to raise taxes and redistribute the proceeds as transfers. The government budget constraint is

$$T_t^w + \theta^m T_t^m + \theta^e T_t^e \leq \phi \int_{j \in S^e \cup S^m} \tau_t^j y_t^j dj + R. \tag{3}$$

Let us also assume that there is a maximum scale for each firm, so that $l_t^j \leq \lambda$ for all j and t. This prevents the most productive agents in the economy from employing the entire labor force. Since only workers can be employed, the labor market clearing condition is

$$\int_{j \in S^e \cup S^m} l_t^j dj \leq 1, \tag{4}$$

with equality corresponding to full employment. Since $l_t^j \leq \lambda$, (4) implies that if

$$\theta^e + \theta^m \leq \frac{1}{\lambda}, \tag{ES}$$

there can never be full employment. Consequently, depending on whether Condition (ES) holds, there will be excess demand or excess supply of labor in this economy. Throughout, I assume that

$$\theta^e \leq \frac{1}{\lambda} \text{ and } \theta^m \leq \frac{1}{\lambda}, \tag{A1}$$

which ensures that neither of the two groups will create excess demand for labor by itself. Assumption (A1) is adopted only for convenience and simplifies the notation (by reducing the number of cases that need to be studied).

---

[16] The assumption that taxes and transfers are nonnegative is standard in the literature (which, naturally, does not make them innocuous). The non-negativity of transfers will play an important role in the analysis by forcing redistributive policies to be distortionary. Although this structure of fiscal instruments can be motivated as restrictions imposed by "economic institutions," the most compelling reason for assuming this structure is that it is a tractable reduced-form formulation, which captures potential inefficiencies that will arise because of informational problems in richer settings (e.g., Mirrlees (1971)).

2.2   Economic Equilibrium

I first characterize the economic equilibrium for a given sequence of taxes, $\{\tau_t^e, \tau_t^m\}_{t=0,1,\ldots,\infty}$ (the transfers do not affect the economic equilibrium). An *economic equilibrium* is defined as a sequence of wages $\{w_t\}_{t=0,1,\ldots,\infty}$, and investment and employment levels for all producers, $\left\{\left[k_t^j, l_t^j\right]_{j \in S^e \cup S^m}\right\}_{t=0,1,\ldots,\infty}$ such that given $\{\tau_t^e, \tau_t^m\}_{t=0,1,\ldots,\infty}$ and $\{w_t\}_{t=0,1,\ldots,\infty}$, all producers choose their investment and employment optimally and the labor market clears.

Each producer (firm) takes wages, denoted by w_t, as given. Finally, given the absence of adjustment costs and full depreciation of capital, firms simply maximize current net profits. Consequently, the optimization problem of each firm can be written as

$$\max_{k_t^j, l_t^j} \frac{1 - \tau_t^j}{1 - \alpha} (A^j)^\alpha (k_t^j)^{1-\alpha} \left(l_t^j\right)^\alpha - w_t l_t^j - k_t^j,$$

where $j \in S^e \cup S^m$. This maximization yields

$$k_t^j = (1 - \tau_t^j)^{1/\alpha} A^j l_t^j, \text{ and} \tag{5}$$

$$l_t^j \begin{cases} = 0 & \text{if } w_t > \frac{\alpha}{1-\alpha}(1 - \tau_t^j)^{1/\alpha} A^j \\ \in [0, \lambda] & \text{if } w_t = \frac{\alpha}{1-\alpha}(1 - \tau_t^j)^{1/\alpha} A^j \\ = \lambda & \text{if } w_t < \frac{\alpha}{1-\alpha}(1 - \tau_t^j)^{1/\alpha} A^j \end{cases} \tag{6}$$

A number of points are worth noting. First, in equation (6), the expression $\alpha(1 - \tau_t^j)^{1/\alpha} A^j / (1 - \alpha)$ is the net marginal product of a worker employed by a producer of group j. If the wage is above this amount, this producer would not employ any workers, and if it is below, he or she would prefer to hire as many workers as possible (i.e., up to the maximum, λ). Second, equation (5) highlights the source of potential inefficiency in this economy. Producers invest in physical capital but only receive a fraction $(1 - \tau_t^j)$ of the revenues. Therefore, taxes discourage investments, creating potential inefficiencies.

Combining (6) with (4), equilibrium wages are obtained as follows:

   (i) If Condition (ES) holds, there is excess supply of labor and $w_t = 0$.
   (ii) If Condition (ES) does not hold, then there is "excess demand" for labor and the equilibrium wage is

$$w_t = \min\left\langle \frac{\alpha}{1 - \alpha}(1 - \tau_t^e)^{1/\alpha} A^e, \frac{\alpha}{1 - \alpha}(1 - \tau_t^m)^{1/\alpha} A^m \right\rangle. \tag{7}$$

The form of the equilibrium wage is intuitive. Labor demand comes from two groups, the elite and middle-class producers, and when condition (ES) does not hold, their total labor demand exceeds available labor supply, so the market clearing wage will be the minimum of their net marginal product.

One interesting feature, which will be used below, is that when Condition (ES) does not hold, the equilibrium wage is equal to the net productivity of one of the two groups of producers, so either the elite or the middle class will make zero profits in equilibrium.

Finally, equilibrium level of aggregate output is

$$
Y_t = \frac{1}{1 - \alpha} (1 - \tau_t^e)^{(1-\alpha)/\alpha} A^e \int_{j \in S^e} l_t^j dj
$$
$$
+ \frac{1}{1 - \alpha} (1 - \tau_t^m)^{(1-\alpha)/\alpha} A^m \int_{j \in S^m} l_t^j dj + R. \tag{8}
$$

The equilibrium is summarized in the following proposition (proof in the text):

Proposition 1 Suppose Assumption (A1) holds. Then for a given sequence of taxes $\left\{ \tau_t^e, \tau_t^m \right\}_{t=0,1,\ldots,\infty}$, the equilibrium takes the following form: if Condition (ES) holds, then $w_t = 0$, and if Condition (ES) does not hold, then w_t is given by (7). Given the wage sequence, factor demands are given by (5) and (6), and aggregate output is given by (8).

3 INEFFICIENT POLICIES

Now I use the above economic environment to illustrate a number of distinct sources of inefficient policies. In this section, political institutions correspond to "the dictatorship of the elite" in the sense that they allow the elite to decide the policies, so the focus will be on the elite's desired policies. The main (potentially inefficient) policy will be a tax on middle-class producers, though more generally, this could correspond to expropriation, corruption, or entry barriers. As discussed in the introduction, there will be three mechanisms leading to inefficient policies: (1) Resource Extraction; (2) Factor Price Manipulation; and (3) Political Consolidation.

To illustrate each mechanism in the simplest possible way, I will focus on a subset of the parameter space and abstract from other interactions. Throughout, I assume that there is an upper bound on taxation, so that $\tau_t^m \leq \bar{\tau}$ and $\tau_t^e \leq \bar{\tau}$, where $\bar{\tau} \leq 1$. This limit can be institutional, or may arise because of the ability of producers to hide their output or shift into informal production.

The timing of events within each period is as follows: *first*, taxes are set; *then*, investments are made. This removes an additional source of inefficiency related to the holdup problem, whereby groups in power may seize all of the output of other agents in the economy once it has been produced. Holdup will be discussed below.

To start with, I focus on Markov Perfect Equilibria (MPE) of this economy, where strategies are only dependent on payoff-relevant variables. In this context, this means that strategies are independent of past taxes and investments (since there is full depreciation). In the dictatorship of the elite, policies will be chosen to maximize the elite's utility. Hence, a *political equilibrium* is given by a sequence of policies $\left\{ \tau_t^e, \tau_t^m, T_t^w, T_t^m, T_t^e \right\}_{t=0,1,\ldots,\infty}$ (satisfying (3)), which maximizes the elite's utility, taking the economic equilibrium as a function of the sequence of policies as given.

More specifically, substituting (5) into (2), we obtain elite consumption as

$$c_t^e = \left[\frac{\alpha}{1-\alpha}(1-\tau_t^e)^{1/\alpha} A^e - w_t \right] l_t^e + T_t^e, \tag{9}$$

with w_t given by (7). This expression follows immediately by recalling that the first term in square brackets is the after-tax profits per worker, while the second term is the equilibrium wage. Total per elite consumption is given by their profits plus the lump sum transfer they receive. Then the political equilibrium, starting at time $t = 0$, is simply given by a sequence of $\left\{ \tau_t^e, \tau_t^m, T_t^w, T_t^m, T_t^e \right\}_{t=0,1,\dots,\infty}$ that satisfies (3) and maximizes the discounted utility of the elite, $\sum_{t=0}^{\infty} \beta^t c_t^e$.

The determination of the political equilibrium is simplified further by the fact that in the MPE with full capital depreciation, this problem is simply equivalent to maximizing (9). We now characterize this political equilibrium under a number of different scenarios.

3.1   Revenue Extraction

To highlight this mechanism, suppose that Condition (ES) holds, so wages are constant at zero. This removes any effect of taxation on factor prices. In this case, from (6), we also have $l_t^j = \lambda$ for all producers. Also assume that $\phi > 0$ (for example, $\phi = 1$).

It is straightforward to see that the elite will never tax themselves, so $\tau_t^e = 0$, and will redistribute all of the government revenues to themselves, so $T_t^w = T_t^m = 0$. Consequently taxes will be set in order to maximize tax revenue, given by

$$\text{Revenue}_t = \frac{\phi}{1-\alpha} \tau_t^m (1-\tau_t^m)^{(1-\alpha)/\alpha} A^m \lambda \theta^m + R \tag{10}$$

at time t, facedown where the first term is obtained by substituting for $l_t^m = \lambda$ and for (5) into (2) and multiplying it by τ_t^m, and taking into account that there are θ^m middle-class producers and a fraction ϕ of tax revenues can be redistributed. The second term is simply the revenues from natural resources. It is clear that tax revenues are maximized by $\tau_t^m = \alpha$. In other words, this is the tax rate that puts the elite at the peak of their Laffer curve. In contrast, output maximization would require $\tau_t^m = 0$. However, the output-maximizing tax rate is not an equilibrium because, despite the distortions, the elite would prefer a higher tax rate to increase their own consumption.

At the root of this inefficiency is a limit on the tax instruments available to the elite.[17] If they could impose lump-sum taxes that would not distort investment,

---

[17] See the discussion in footnote 16 and the further analysis and discussion in Besley and Coate (1998).

these would be preferable. Inefficient policies here result from the redistributive desires of the elite coupled with the absence of lump-sum taxes.

It is also interesting to note that as α increases, the extent of distortions are reduced, since there are greater diminishing returns to capital and investment will not decline much in response to taxes.[18]

Even though $\tau_t^m = \alpha$ is the most preferred tax for the elite, the exogenous limit on taxation may become binding, so the equilibrium tax is

$$\tau_t^m = \tau^{RE} \equiv \min\{\alpha, \bar{\tau}\} \tag{11}$$

for all t. In this case, equilibrium taxes depend only on the production technology (in particular, how distortionary taxes are) and on the exogenous limit on taxation. For example, as α decreases and the production function becomes more linear in capital, equilibrium taxes decline.

This discussion is summarized in the following proposition (proof in the text):

Proposition 2 Suppose Assumption (A1) and Condition (ES) hold and $\phi > 0$, then the unique political equilibrium features $\tau_t^m = \tau^{RE} \equiv \min\{\alpha, \bar{\tau}\}$ for all t.

3.2   Factor Price Manipulation

I now investigate how inefficient policies can arise in order to manipulate factor prices. To highlight this mechanism in the simplest possible way, let us first assume that $\phi = 0$ so that there are no direct benefits from taxation for the elite. There are indirect benefits, however, because of the effect of taxes on factor prices, which will be present as long as the equilibrium wage is positive. For this reason, I now suppose that Condition (ES) does not hold, so that equilibrium wage is given by (7).

Inspection of (7) and (9) then immediately reveals that the elite prefer high taxes in order to reduce the labor demand from the middle class, and thus wages, as much as possible. The desired tax rate for the elite is thus $\tau_t^m = 1$. Given constraints on taxation, the equilibrium tax is $\tau_t^m = \tau^{FPM} \equiv \bar{\tau}$ for all t. We therefore have (proof in the text):

Proposition 3 Suppose Assumption (A1) holds, Condition (ES) does not hold, and $\phi = 0$, then the unique political equilibrium features $\tau_t^m = \tau^{FPM} \equiv \bar{\tau}$ for all t.

This result suggests that the factor price manipulation mechanism generally leads to higher taxes than the pure revenue extraction mechanism. This is because, with the factor price manipulation mechanism, the objective of the elite is to reduce the profitability of the middle class as much as possible, whereas for

---

[18] More explicitly, (5) implies that $\partial^2 \ln k_t^j / \partial \tau_t^j \partial \alpha = 1/\left(\alpha^2 \left(1 - \tau_t^j\right)\right) > 0$.

revenue extraction, the elite would like the middle class to invest and generate revenues. It is also worth noting that, differently from the pure revenue extraction case, the tax policy of the elite is not only extracting resources from the middle class, but it is also doing so indirectly from the workers, whose wages are being reduced because of the tax policy.

The role of $\phi = 0$ also needs to be emphasized. Taxing the middle class at the highest rate is clearly inefficient. Why is there not a more efficient way of transferring resources to the elite? The answer relates to the limited fiscal instruments available to the elite (recall the discussion in footnote 16). In particular, $\phi = 0$ implies that they cannot use taxes at all to extract revenues from the middle class, so they are forced to use inefficient means of increasing their consumption, by directly impoverishing the middle class. In the next subsection, I discuss how the factor price manipulation mechanism works in the presence of an instrument that can directly raise revenue from the middle class. This will illustrate that the absence of any means of transferring resources from the middle class to the elite is not essential for the factor price manipulation mechanism (though the absence of non-distortionary lump-sum taxes is naturally important).

3.3   Revenue Extraction and Factor Price Manipulation Combined

I now combine the two effects isolated in the previous two subsections. By itself the factor price manipulation effect led to the extreme result that the tax on the middle class should be as high as possible. Revenue extraction, though typically another motive for imposing taxes on the middle class, will serve to reduce the power of the factor price manipulation effect. The reason is that high taxes also reduce the revenues extracted by the elite (moving the economy *beyond the peak* of the Laffer curve), and are costly to the elite.

To characterize the equilibrium in this case again necessitates the maximization of (9). This is simply the same as maximizing transfers minus wage bill for each elite producer. As before, transfers are obtained from (10), while wages are given by (7). When Condition (ES) holds and there is excess supply of labor, wages are equal to zero, and we obtain the same results as in the case of pure resource extraction.

The interesting case is the one where (ES) does not hold, so that wages are not equal to zero, and are given by the minimum of the two expressions in (7). Incorporating the fact that the elite will not tax themselves and will redistribute all the revenues to themselves, the maximization problem can be written as

$$\max_{\tau_t^m} \left[\frac{\alpha}{1-\alpha} A^e - w_t \right] l_t^e$$
$$+ \frac{1}{\theta^e} \left[\frac{\phi}{1-\alpha} \tau_t^m (1 - \tau_t^m)^{(1-\alpha)/\alpha} A^m l_t^m \theta^m + R \right], \tag{12}$$

subject to (7) and

$$\theta^e l_t^e + \theta^m l_t^m = 1, \text{ and} \tag{13}$$

$$l_t^m = \lambda \text{ if } (1 - \tau_t^m)^{1/\alpha} A^m \geq A^e. \tag{14}$$

The first term in (12) is the elite's net revenues and the second term is the transfer they receive. Equation (13) is the market clearing constraint, while (14) ensures that middle-class producers employ as much labor as they wish, provided that their net productivity is greater than those of elite producers.

The solution to this problem can take two different forms depending on whether (14) holds in the solution. If it does, then $w = \alpha A^e / (1 - \alpha)$, and elite producers make zero profits and their only income is derived from transfers. Intuitively, this corresponds to the case where the elite prefer to let the middle-class producers undertake all of the profitable activities and maximize tax revenues. If, on the other hand, (14) does not hold, then the elite generate revenues both from their own production and from taxing the middle-class producers. In this case $w = \alpha(1 - \tau^m)^{1/\alpha} A^m / (1 - \alpha)$. Rather than provide a full taxonomy, I impose the following assumption:

$$A^e \geq \phi(1 - \alpha)^{(1-\alpha)/\alpha} A^m \frac{\theta^m}{\theta^e}, \tag{A2}$$

which ensures that the solution will always take the latter form (i.e., (14) does not hold). Intuitively, this condition makes sure that the productivity gap between the middle class and elite producers is not so large as to make it attractive for the elite to make zero profits themselves (recall that $\phi(1 - \alpha)^{(1-\alpha)/\alpha} < 1$, so if $\theta^e = \theta^m$ and $A^e = A^m$, this condition is always satisfied).[19]

Consequently, when (A2) holds, we have $w_t = \alpha(1 - \tau_t^m)^{1/\alpha} A^m \tau_t^m / (1 - \alpha)$, and the elite's problem simply boils down to choosing τ_t^m to maximize

$$\frac{1}{\theta^e} \left[\frac{\phi}{1 - \alpha} \tau_t^m (1 - \tau_t^m)^{(1-\alpha)/\alpha} A^m l^m \theta^m + R \right] - \frac{\alpha}{1 - \alpha} (1 - \tau_t^m)^{1/\alpha} A^m \lambda, \tag{15}$$

where I have used the fact that all elite producers will employ λ employees, and from (13), $l_m = (1 - \lambda \theta^e) / \theta^m$.

---

[19] To see why this condition is sufficient for (14) not to hold, first use (13) (and drop the R term, which plays no role here) to write the objective of an elite agent as $(\alpha A^e / (1 - \alpha) - w) l^e + \phi \tau^m (1 - \tau^m)^{(1-\alpha)/\alpha} A^m (1 - l^e) / (1 - \alpha) \theta^e$. The maximum of this expression when (14) holds is $U^1 = \phi \alpha (1 - \alpha)^{(1-\alpha)/\alpha} A^m \theta^m \lambda / (1 - \alpha) \theta^e$. When it does not hold, let the value be $\max_{\tau^m} U^2 (\tau^m)$. Note that when $\tau^m = 1$, we have $w = 0$ and $U^2 (\tau^m = 1) = \alpha A^e \lambda / (1 - \alpha)$, so when Assumption (A2) holds,

$$\max_{\tau^m} U^2 (\tau^m) > U^2 (\tau^m = 1) = \alpha A^e \lambda / (1 - \alpha) \geq U^1,$$

establishing that (A2) is sufficient for the elite to prefer a tax policy that yields positive profits for them.

The maximization of (15) gives

$$\frac{\tau_t^m}{1 - \tau_t^m} = \kappa\left(\lambda, \theta^e, \alpha, \phi\right) \equiv \frac{\alpha}{1 - \alpha}\left(1 + \frac{\lambda\theta^e}{(1 - \lambda\theta^e)\phi}\right).$$

The first interesting feature is that $\kappa\left(\lambda, \theta^e, \alpha, \phi\right)$ is always less than ∞. This implies that τ_t^m is always less than 1, which is the desired tax rate in the case of pure factor price manipulation. Moreover, $\kappa\left(\lambda, \theta^e, \alpha, \phi\right)$ is strictly greater than $\alpha/(1 - \alpha)$, so that τ_t^m is always greater than α, the desired tax rate with pure resource extraction. Therefore, the factor price manipulation motive always increases taxes above the pure revenue-maximizing level (beyond the peak of the Laffer curve), while the revenue-maximization motive reduces taxes relative to the pure factor price manipulation case. Naturally, if this level of tax is greater than $\bar{\tau}$, the equilibrium tax will be $\bar{\tau}$, i.e.,

$$\tau_t^m = \tau^{COM} \equiv \min\left\{\frac{\kappa\left(\lambda, \theta^e, \alpha, \phi\right)}{1 + \kappa\left(\lambda, \theta^e, \alpha, \phi\right)}, \bar{\tau}\right\}. \tag{16}$$

It is also interesting to look at the comparative statics of this tax rate. First, as ϕ increases, taxation becomes more beneficial (generates greater revenues), but τ^{COM} declines. This might at first appear paradoxical, since one may have expected that as taxation becomes less costly, taxes should increase. Intuition for this result follows from the observation that an increase in ϕ raises the importance of revenue extraction, and as commented above, in this case, revenue extraction is a force towards lower taxes (it makes it more costly for the elite to move beyond the peak of the Laffer curve). Since the parameter ϕ is related, among other things, to state capacity, this comparative static result suggests that higher state capacity will translate into lower taxes because greater state capacity enables the elite to extract revenues from the middle class through taxation, without directly impoverishing them. In other words, greater state capacity enables more efficient forms of resource extraction by the groups holding political power.[20]

Second, as θ^e increases and the number of elite producers increases, taxes also increase. The reason for this effect is again the interplay between the revenue extraction and factor price manipulation mechanisms. When there are more elite producers, reducing factor prices becomes more important relative to gathering tax revenue. One interesting implication of this discussion is that when the factor price manipulation effect is more important, there will typically be greater inefficiencies. Finally, an increase in α raises taxes for exactly the same reason as above; taxes create fewer distortions and this increases the revenue-maximizing tax rate.

Once again summarizing the analysis (proof in the text):

Proposition 4 Suppose Assumptions (A1) and (A2) hold, Condition (ES) does not hold, and $\phi > 0$. Then the unique political equilibrium features $\tau_t^m = \tau^{COM}$

---

[20] This is a very different argument for why greater state capacity may be better for economic outcomes than the standard view espoused, for example, in Evans (1995).

as given by (16) for all t. Equilibrium taxes are increasing in θ^e and α and decreasing in ϕ.

3.4   Political Consolidation

I now discuss another reason for inefficient taxation, the desire of the elite to preserve their political power. This mechanism has been absent so far, since the elite were assumed to always remain in power. To illustrate it, the model needs to be modified to allow for endogenous switches of power. Institutional change will be discussed in greater detail later. For now, let us assume that there is a probability p_t in period t that political power permanently shifts from the elite to the middle class. Once they come to power, the middle class will pursue a policy that maximizes their own utility. When this probability is exogenous, the previous analysis still applies. Interesting economic interactions arise when this probability is endogenous. Here I will use a simple (reduced-form) model to illustrate the trade-offs and assume that this probability is a function of the income level of the middle-class agents, in particular

$$p_t = p\left(\theta^m c_t^m\right) \in [0, 1], \tag{17}$$

where I have used the fact that income is equal to consumption.[21] Let us assume that p is continuous and differentiable with $p' > 0$, which captures the fact that when the middle-class producers are richer, they have greater de facto political power. This reduced-form formulation might capture a variety of mechanisms. For example, when the middle class are richer, they may be more successful in solving their collective action problems or they may increase their military power.

This modification implies that the fiscal policy that maximizes current consumption may no longer be optimal. To investigate this issue we now write the utility of elite agents recursively and denote it by $V^e(E)$ when they are in power and by $V^e(M)$ when the middle class is in power. Naturally, we have

$$V^e(E) = \max_{\tau_t^m} \left\{ \begin{array}{l} \left[\frac{\alpha}{1-\alpha} A^e - w_t\right] l_t^e + \frac{1}{\theta^e}\left[\frac{\phi}{1-\alpha}\tau_t^m(1-\tau_t^m)^{(1-\alpha)/\alpha} A^m l_t^m \theta^m + R\right] \\ \quad +\beta\left[(1-p_t)V^e(E) + p_t V^e(M)\right] \end{array} \right\}$$

subject to (7), (13), (14) and (17), with $p_t = p\left(\frac{\alpha}{1-\alpha}(1-\tau_t^m)^{1/\alpha} A^m l_t^m \theta^m - w_t l_t^m \theta^m\right)$. I wrote $V^e(E)$ and $V^e(M)$ not as functions of time, since the structure of the problem makes it clear that these values will be constant in equilibrium.

The first observation is that if the solution to the static problem involves $c_t^m = 0$, then the same fiscal policy is optimal despite the risk of losing power. This implies that, as long as Condition (ES) does not hold and (A2) holds, the political consolidation mechanism does not add an additional motive for inefficient taxation.

---

[21] Alternatively, one can assume, with qualitatively identical results, that it is the income of the middle class relative to that of the elite that matters for political power.

To see the role of the political consolidation mechanism, suppose instead that Condition (ES) holds. In this case, $w_t = 0$ and the optimal static policy is $\tau_t^m = \tau^{RE} \equiv \min\{\alpha, \bar{\tau}\}$ as discussed above and implies positive profits and consumption for middle-class agents. The dynamic maximization problem then becomes

$$V^e(E) = \max_{\tau_t^m}$$
$$\left\{ \begin{array}{l} \frac{\alpha}{1-\alpha} A^e \lambda + \frac{1}{\theta^e} \left[\frac{\phi}{1-\alpha} \tau_t^m (1 - \tau_t^m)^{(1-\alpha)/\alpha} A^m \lambda \theta^m + R \right] \\ + \beta \left[V^e(E) - p \left(\frac{\alpha}{1-\alpha} (1 - \tau_t^m)^{1/\alpha} A^m \theta^m \lambda \right) (V^e(E) - V^e(M)) \right] \end{array} \right\}.$$
(18)

The first-order condition for an interior solution can be expressed as

$$\phi - \phi \frac{1-\alpha}{\alpha} \frac{\tau_t^m}{1 - \tau_t^m} + \beta \theta^e p' \left(\frac{\alpha}{1-\alpha} (1 - \tau_t^m)^{1/\alpha} A^m \theta^m \lambda \right)$$
$$\left(V^e(E) - V^e(M) \right) = 0.$$

It is clear that when $p'(\cdot) = 0$, we obtain $\tau_t^m = \tau^{RE} \equiv \min\{\alpha, \bar{\tau}\}$ as above. However, when $p'(\cdot) > 0$, $\tau_t^m = \tau^{PC} > \tau^{RE} \equiv \min\{\alpha, \bar{\tau}\}$ as long as $V^e(E) - V^e(M) > 0$. That $V^e(E) - V^e(M) > 0$ is the case is immediate since when the middle class are in power, they get to tax the elite and receive all of the transfers.[22]

Intuitively, as with the factor price manipulation mechanism, the elite tax *beyond the peak* of the Laffer curve, yet now not to increase their revenues *but to consolidate their political power*. These high taxes reduce the income of the middle class and their political power. Consequently, there is a higher probability that the elite remain in power in the future, enjoying the benefits of controlling the fiscal policy.[23]

An interesting comparative static is that as R increases, the gap between $V^e(E)$ and $V^e(M)$ increases, and the tax that the elite sets increases as well. Intuitively, the party in power receives the revenues from natural resources, R. When R increases, the elite become more willing to sacrifice tax revenue (by overtaxing the middle class) in order to increase the probability of remaining in power because remaining in power has now become more valuable. This contrasts with the results so far where R had no effect on taxes. More interestingly, a higher ϕ, i.e., greater state capacity, also increases the gap between $V^e(E)$ and $V^e(M)$ (because this enables the group in power to raise more tax revenues) and thus implies a higher tax rate on the middle class. Intuitively, when there is no political competition, greater state capacity, by allowing more efficient forms of transfers, improves the allocation of resources. But in the

---

[22] More specifically, $V^e(E)$ is given as the solution to (18), while the expression for $V^e(M)$ is given by equation (24) in Section 6.

[23] This result is similar to that in Acemoglu and Robinson (2006b) where a ruling elite may want to block beneficial technological change in order to increase the probability of political survival.

presence of political competition, by increasing the *political stakes*, it leads to greater conflict and more distortionary policies.

Summarizing this discussion (proof in the text):

Proposition 5   Consider the economy with political replacement. Suppose also that Assumption (A1) and Condition (ES) hold and $\phi > 0$, then the political equilibrium features $\tau_t^m = \tau^{PC} > \tau^{RE}$ for all t. This tax rate is increasing in R and ϕ.

3.5   Subgame Perfect Versus Markov Perfect Equilibria

I have so far focused on Markov perfect equilibria (MPE). In general, such a focus can be restrictive. In this case, however, it can be proved that subgame perfect equilibria (SPE) coincide with the MPE. This will not be true in the next subsection, so it is useful to briefly discuss why it is the case here.

MPE are a subset of the SPE. Loosely speaking, SPEs that are not Markovian will be supported by some type of "history-dependent punishment strategies." If there is no room for such history dependence, SPEs will coincide with the MPEs.

In the models analyzed so far, such punishment strategies are not possible even in the SPE. Intuitively, each individual is infinitesimal and makes its economic decisions to maximize profits. Therefore, (5) and (6) determine the factor demands uniquely in any equilibrium. Given the factor demands, the payoffs from various policy sequences are also uniquely pinned down. This means that the returns to various strategies for the elite are *independent of history*. Consequently, there cannot be any SPEs other than the MPE characterized above. Therefore, we have:[24]

Proposition 6   The MPEs characterized in Propositions 2–5 are the unique SPEs.

3.6   Lack of Commitment – Holdup

The models discussed so far featured full commitment to taxes by the elites. Using a term from organizational economics, this corresponds to the situation without any "*holdup*." Holdup (lack of commitment to taxes or policies) changes the qualitative implications of the model; if expropriation (or taxation) happens after investments, revenues generated by investments can be *ex post* captured by others. These types of holdup problems are likely to arise when the key

---

[24] A formal proof of this proposition requires additional notation, so I only provide a sketch in this footnote. *A history* is defined as the complete list of actions up to a certain point in the game. Let $\mathcal{H}^{t-1}$ denote the set of all possible histories of play up to $t-1$, and denote a particular history by $h^{t-1} \in \mathcal{H}^{t-1}$. The essence of the proof is that, since each producer is infinitesimal, they will always choose their factor commands according to (5) and (6) at the time t for all $h^{t-1} \in \mathcal{H}^{t-1}$. This implies that the maximization problem of the elite is independent of history and establishes the result.

investments are long term, so that various policies will be determined and implemented after these investments are made (and sunk).

The problem with holdup is that the elite will be unable to commit to a particular tax rate before middle-class producers undertake their investments (taxes will be set after investments). This lack of commitment will generally increase the amount of taxation and inefficiency. To illustrate this possibility, I consider the same model as above but change the timing of events such that first individual producers undertake their investments and then the elite set taxes. The economic equilibrium is unchanged, and in particular, (5) and (6) still determine factor demands, with the only difference that τ^m and τ^e now refer to "expected" taxes. Naturally, in equilibrium expected and actual taxes coincide.

What is different is the calculus of the elite in setting taxes. Previously, they took into account that higher taxes would discourage investment. Since, now, taxes are set after investment decisions, this effect is absent. As a result, in the MPE, the elite will always want to tax at the maximum rate, so in all cases, there is a unique MPE where $\tau_t^m = \tau^{HP} \equiv \bar{\tau}$ for all t. This establishes (proof in the text):

Proposition 7   With holdup, there is a unique political equilibrium with $\tau_t^m = \tau^{HP} \equiv \bar{\tau}$ for all t.

It is clear that this holdup equilibrium is more inefficient than the equilibria characterized above. For example, imagine a situation in which Condition (ES) holds so that with the original timing of events (without holdup), the equilibrium tax rate is $\tau_t^m = \alpha$. Consider the extreme case where $\bar{\tau} = 1$. Now without holdup, $\tau_t^m = \alpha$ and there is positive economic activity by the middle-class producers. In contrast, with holdup, the equilibrium tax is $\tau_t^m = 1$ and the middle class stop producing. This is naturally very costly for the elite as well since they lose all their tax revenues.

In this model, it is no longer true that the MPE is the only SPE, since there is room for an implicit agreement between different groups whereby the elite (credibly) promise a different tax rate than $\bar{\tau}$. To illustrate this, consider the example where Condition (ES) holds and $\bar{\tau} = 1$. Recall that the history of the game is the complete set of actions taken up to that point (recall footnote 24). In the MPE, the elite raise no tax revenue from the middle-class producers. Instead, consider the following trigger-strategy combination: The elite always set $\tau^m = \alpha$ and the middle-class producers invest according to (5) with $\tau^m = \alpha$ as long as the history consists of $\tau^m = \alpha$ and investments have been consistent with (5). If there is any other action in the history, the elite set $\tau^m = 1$ and the middle-class producers invest zero.[25] With this strategy profile, the elite raise

---

[25] More formally, let history $\hat{h}^{t-1}$ be such that $\tau_s^m = \alpha$ for all $s \leq t-1$ and $k_s^j = (1-\alpha)^{1/\alpha} A^m$ for all $j \in S^m$ and all $s \leq t-1$. Then, the trigger strategy profile in question is as follows: if $h^{t-1} = \hat{h}^{t-1}$ $\tau_t^m = \alpha$ and $k_t^j = (1-\alpha)^{1/\alpha} A^m$, and if $h^{t-1} \neq \hat{h}^{t-1}$, then $\tau_t^m = 1$ and $k_t^j = 0$.

a tax revenue of $\phi\alpha(1 - \alpha)^{(1-\alpha)/\alpha} A^m \lambda\theta^m / (1 - \alpha)$ in every period, and receive transfers worth

$$\frac{\phi}{(1 - \beta)(1 - \alpha)}\alpha(1 - \alpha)^{(1-\alpha)/\alpha} A^m \lambda\theta^m. \tag{19}$$

If, in contrast, they deviate at any point, the most profitable deviation for them is to set $\tau^m = 1$, and they will raise

$$\frac{\phi}{1 - \alpha}(1 - \alpha)^{(1-\alpha)/\alpha} A^m \lambda\theta^m. \tag{20}$$

The trigger-strategy profile will be an equilibrium as long as (19) is greater than or equal to (20), which requires $\beta \geq 1 - \alpha$. Therefore we have (proof in the text):[26]

Proposition 8 Consider the holdup game, and suppose that Assumption (A1) and Condition (ES) hold and $\bar{\tau} = 1$. Then for $\beta \geq 1 - \alpha$, there exists a subgame perfect equilibrium where $\tau_t^m = \alpha$ for all t.

An important implication of this result is that in societies where there are greater holdup problems, for example, because typical investments involve longer horizons, there is room for coordinating on a subgame perfect equilibrium supported by an implicit agreement (trigger-strategy profile) between the elite and the rest of the society.

3.7   Technology Adoption and Holdup

Suppose now that taxes are set before investments, so the source of holdup in the previous subsection is absent. Instead, suppose that at time $t = 0$ before any economic decisions or policy choices are made, middle-class agents can invest to increase their productivity. In particular, suppose that there is a cost $\Gamma(A^m)$ of investing in productivity A^m. The function Γ is non-negative, continuously differentiable and convex. This investment is made once and the resulting productivity A^m applies forever after.[27]

Once investments in technology are made, the game proceeds as before. Since investments in technology are sunk after date $t = 0$, the equilibrium allocations are the same as in Propositions 2–5 above. Another interesting

---

[26] Some authors, for example Greif (1994), also view differences between the MPE and the SPE as corresponding to "institutional differences," since different equilibria create different incentives for individual agents (and are supported by different "beliefs"). I find it more transparent to reserve the term "institutions" for arrangements that determine the economic or political rules of the game (i.e., limits on fiscal policies or distribution of political power) rather than using this term also for the equilibria that arise for a given set of rules.

[27] The fact that technology choices are made once, or at any rate, more infrequently, partly distinguishes them from the investments in k, which are made in every period.

question is whether, if they could, the elite would prefer to commit to a tax rate sequence at time $t = 0$.

The analysis of this case follows closely that of the baseline model, and I simply state the results (without proofs to save space):

Proposition 9 Consider the game with technology adoption and suppose that Assumption (A1) holds, Condition (ES) does not hold, and $\phi = 0$, then the unique political equilibrium features $\tau_t^m = \tau^{FPM} \equiv \bar{\tau}$ for all t. Moreover, if the elite could commit to a tax sequence at time $t = 0$, then they would still choose $\tau_t^m = \tau^{FPM} \equiv \bar{\tau}$.

That this is the unique MPE is quite straightforward. It is also intuitive that it is the unique SPE. In fact, the elite would choose exactly this tax rate even if they could commit at time $t = 0$. The reason is as follows: In the case of pure factor price manipulation, the only objective of the elite is to reduce the middle class' labor demand, so they have no interest in increasing the productivity of middle-class producers.

For contrast, let us next consider the pure revenue extraction case with Condition (ES) satisfied. Once again, the MPE is identical to before. As a result, the first-order condition for an interior solution to the middle-class producers' technology choice is:

$$\Gamma'\left(A^m\right) = \frac{1}{1 - \beta} \frac{\alpha}{1 - \alpha} (1 - \tau^m)^{1/\alpha} \tag{21}$$

where τ^m is the constant tax rate that they will face in all future periods. In the pure revenue extraction case, recall that the equilibrium is $\tau^m = \tau^{RE} \equiv \min\{\alpha, \bar{\tau}\}$. With the same arguments as before, this is also the unique SPE. Once the middle-class producers have made their technology decisions, there is no history-dependent action left, and it is impossible to create history-dependent punishment strategies to support a tax rate different than the static optimum for the elite.[28] Nevertheless, this is not necessarily the allocation that the elite prefer. If the elite could commit to a tax rate sequence at time $t = 0$, they would choose lower taxes. To illustrate this, suppose that they can commit to a constant tax rate (it is straightforward to show that they will in fact choose a constant tax rate even without this restriction, but this restriction saves on notation). Therefore, the optimization problem of the elite is to maximize tax revenues taking the relationship between taxes and technology as in (21) as given. In other words, they will solve: $\max \phi \tau^m (1 - \tau^m)^{(1-\alpha)/\alpha} A^m \lambda \theta^m / (1 - \alpha)$ subject to (21). The constraint (21) incorporates the fact that (expected) taxes affect technology choice.

---

[28] The fact that each middle-class producer is infinitesimal is important here. Otherwise, it would be possible to create a strategy profile where middle-class producers would collectively deviate from (5).

The first-order condition for an interior solution can be expressed as

$$A^m - \frac{1-\alpha}{\alpha} \frac{\tau^m}{1-\tau^m} A^m + \tau^m \frac{dA^m}{d\tau^m} = 0$$

where $dA^m/d\tau^m$ takes into account the effect of future taxes on technology choice at time $t = 0$. This expression can be obtained from (21) as:

$$\frac{dA^m}{d\tau^m} = -\frac{1}{1-\beta} \frac{1}{1-\alpha} \frac{(1-\tau^m)^{(1-\alpha)/\alpha}}{\Gamma''(A^m)} < 0.$$

This implies that the solution to this maximization problem satisfies $\tau^m = \tau^{TA} < \tau^{RE} \equiv \min\{\alpha, \bar{\tau}\}$. If they could, the elite would like to commit to a lower tax rate in the future in order to encourage the middle-class producers to undertake technological improvements. Their inability to commit to such a tax policy leads to greater inefficiency than in the case without technology adoption. Summarizing this discussion (proof in the text):

Proposition 10   Consider the game with technology adoption, and suppose that Assumption (A1) and Condition (ES) hold and $\phi > 0$, then the unique political equilibrium features $\tau_t^m = \tau^{RE} \equiv \min\{\alpha, \bar{\tau}\}$ for all t. If the elite could commit to a tax policy at time $t = 0$, they would prefer to commit to $\tau^{TA} < \tau^{RE}$.

An important feature is that in contrast to the pure holdup problem where SPE could prevent the additional inefficiency (when $\beta \geq 1 - \alpha$, recall Proposition 8), with the technology adoption game, the inefficiency survives the SPE. The reason is that, since middle-class producers invest only once at the beginning, there is no possibility of using history-dependent punishment strategies. This illustrates the limits of implicit agreements to keep tax rates low. Such agreements not only require a high discount factor ($\beta \geq 1 - \alpha$) but also frequent investments by the middle class, so that there is a credible threat against the elite if they deviate from the promised policies. When such implicit agreements fail to prevent the most inefficient policies, there is greater need for economic institutions to play the role of placing limits on future policies.

4   INEFFICIENT ECONOMIC INSTITUTIONS

The previous analysis shows how inefficient policies emerge out of the desire of the elite, who possess political power, to redistribute resources towards themselves. I now discuss the implications of these mechanisms for inefficient institutions. Since the elite prefer to implement inefficient policies to transfer resources from the rest of the society (the middle class and the workers) to themselves, they will also prefer inefficient economic institutions that enable and support these inefficient policies.

To illustrate the main economic interactions, I consider two prototypical economic institutions: (1) *Security of property rights.* There may be constitutional or other limits on the extent of redistributive taxation and/or other policies that reduce profitability of producers' investments. In terms of the model above, we can think of this as determining the level of $\bar{\tau}$.[29] (2) *Regulation of technology*, which concerns direct or indirect factors affecting the productivity of producers, in particular middle-class producers.

As pointed out in the introduction, the main role of institutions is to provide the framework for the determination of policies, and consequently, preferences over institutions are derived from preferences over policies and economic allocations. Bearing this in mind, let us now discuss the determination of economic institutions in the model presented here. To simplify the discussion, for the rest of the analysis, and in particular, throughout this section, I focus on MPE.

4.1   Security of Property Rights

The environment is the same as in the previous section, with the only difference that at time $t = 0$, before any decisions are taken, the elite can reduce $\bar{\tau}$, say from $\bar{\tau}^H$ to some level in the interval $[0, \bar{\tau}^H]$, thus creating an upper bound on taxes and providing greater security of property rights to the middle class. The key question is whether the elite would like to do so, i.e., whether they prefer $\bar{\tau} = \bar{\tau}^H$ or $\bar{\tau} < \bar{\tau}^H$.

The next three propositions answer this question:

Proposition 11   Without holdup and technology adoption, the elite prefer $\bar{\tau} = \bar{\tau}^H$.

The proof of this result is immediate, since without holdup or technology adoption, putting further restrictions on the taxes can only reduce the elite's utility. This proposition implies that if economic institutions are decided by the elite (which is the natural benchmark since they are the group with political power), they will in general choose not to provide additional security of property rights to other producers. Therefore, the underlying economic institutions will support the inefficient policies discussed above.

The results are different when there are holdup concerns. To illustrate this, suppose that the timing of taxation decision is after the investment decisions (so that there is the holdup problem), and consider the case with revenue extraction and factor price manipulation combined. In this case, the elite would like to commit to a lower tax rate than $\bar{\tau}^H$ in order to encourage the middle class to undertake greater investments, creating a useful role for economic institutions (to limit future taxes):

Proposition 12   Consider the game with holdup and suppose Assumptions (A1) and (A2) hold, Condition (ES) does not hold, and $\phi > 0$, then as long as τ^{COM} given by (16) is less than $\bar{\tau}^H$, the elite prefer $\bar{\tau} = \tau^{COM}$.

---

[29] A difficult question, which is being sidestepped here, is how such upper bounds on taxes or security of property rights are enforced while the distribution of political power remains unchanged. For this reason, as noted above, limits on taxes may be considered to be related to political institutions as much as to economic institutions.

The proof is again immediate. While τ^{COM} maximizes the elite's utility, in the presence of holdup the MPE involves $\tau = \bar{\tau}^H$, and the elite can benefit by using economic institutions to manipulate equilibrium taxes.

This result shows that the elite may provide additional property rights protection to producers in the presence of holdup problems. The reason is that because of holdup, equilibrium taxes are too high even relative to those that the elite would prefer. By manipulating economic institutions, the elite may approach their desired policy (in fact, it can exactly commit to the tax rate that maximizes their utility).

Finally, for similar reasons, in the economy with technology adoption discussed above, the elite will again prefer to change economic institutions to restrict future taxes:

Proposition 13 Consider the game with holdup and technology adoption, and suppose that Assumption (A1) and Condition (ES) hold and $\phi > 0$, then as long as $\tau^{TA} < \bar{\tau}^H$, the elite prefer $\bar{\tau} = \tau^{TA}$.

As before, when we look at SPE, with pure holdup, there may not be a need for changing economic institutions, since credible implicit promises might play the same role (as long as $\beta \geq 1 - \alpha$ as shown in Proposition 8). However, parallel to the results above, in the technology adoption game, SPE and MPE coincide, so a change in economic institutions is necessary for a credible commitment to a low tax rate (here τ^{TA}).

4.2   Regulation of Technology

Economic institutions may also affect the environment for technology adoption or more directly the technology choices of producers. For example, by providing infrastructure or protection of intellectual property rights, a society may improve the technology available to its producers. Conversely, the elite may want to *block*, i.e., take active actions against, the technological improvements of the middle class.[30] Therefore the question is: Do the elite have an interest in increasing the productivity of the middle class as much as possible?

Consider the baseline model. Suppose that there exists a government policy $g \in \{0, 1\}$, which influences only the productivity of middle-class producers, i.e., $A^m = A^m(g)$, with $A^m(1) > A^m(0)$. Assume that the choice of g is made at $t = 0$ before any other decisions, and has no other influence on payoffs (and in particular, it imposes no costs on the elite). Will the elite always choose $g = 1$, increasing the middle-class producers' productivity, or will they try to block technology adoption by the middle class?

---

[30] The decision to "block" technology adoption may also be considered a "policy" rather than an "economic institution." The reason why it may be closer to economic institutions is that it influences the set of options available to economic agents and is plausibly slower to change than certain fiscal policies, such as taxes or government spending. See Acemoglu and Robinson (2006b) for a more detailed discussion of the elite's incentives to block technology.

When the only mechanism at work is revenue extraction, the answer is that the elite would like the middle class to have the best technology:

Proposition 14   Suppose Assumption (A1) and Condition (ES) hold and $\phi >$ 0, then $w = 0$ and the elite always choose $g = 1$.

The proof follows immediately since $g = 1$ increases the tax revenues and has no other effect on the elite's consumption. Consequently, in this case, the elite would like the producers to be as productive as possible so that they generate greater tax revenues. Intuitively, there is no competition between the elite and the middle class (either in factor markets or in the political arena), and when the middle class is more productive, the elite generate greater tax revenues.

The situation is different when the elite wish to manipulate factor prices:

Proposition 15   Suppose Assumption (A1) holds, Condition (ES) does not hold, $\phi = 0$, and $\bar{\tau} < 1$, then the elite choose $g = 0$.

Once again the proof of this proposition is straightforward. With $\bar{\tau} < 1$, labor demand from the middle class is high enough to generate positive equilibrium wages. Since $\phi = 0$, taxes raise no revenues for the elite, and their only objective is to reduce the labor demand from the middle class and wages as much as possible. This makes $g = 0$ the preferred policy for the elite. Consequently, the factor price manipulation mechanism suggests that, when it is within their power, the elite will choose economic institutions so as to reduce the productivity of competing (middle-class) producers.

The next proposition shows that a similar effect is in operation when the political power of the elite is in contention (proof omitted).

Proposition 16   Consider the economy with political replacement. Suppose also that Assumption (A1) and Condition (ES) hold and $\phi = 0$, then the elite prefer $g = 0$.

In this case, the elite cannot raise any taxes from the middle class because $\phi = 0$. But differently from the previous proposition, there are no labor market interactions, since there is excess labor supply and wages are equal to zero. Nevertheless, the elite would like the profits from middle-class producers to be as low as possible so as to consolidate their political power. They achieve this by creating an environment that reduces the productivity of middle-class producers.

Overall, this section has demonstrated how the elite's preferences over policies, and in particular their desire to set inefficient policies, translate into preferences over inefficient – non-growth enhancing – economic institutions. When there are no holdup problems, introducing economic institutions that limit taxation or put other constraints on policies provides no benefits to the elite.

However, when the elite are unable to commit to future taxes (because of holdup problems), equilibrium taxes may be too high even from the viewpoint of the elite, and in this case, using economic institutions to manipulate future taxes may be beneficial. Similarly, the analysis reveals that the elite may want to use economic institutions to discourage productivity improvements by the middle class. Interestingly, this never happens when the main mechanism leading to inefficient policies is revenue extraction. Instead, when factor price manipulation and political consolidation effects are present, the elite may want to discourage or block technological improvements by the middle class.

5   INEFFICIENT POLITICAL INSTITUTIONS

The above analysis characterized the equilibrium under "the dictatorship of the elite," a set of political institutions that gave all political power to the elite producers. An alternative is to have "the dictatorship of the middle class," i.e., a system in which the middle class makes the key policy decisions (this could also be a democratic regime with the middle class as the decisive voters). Finally, another possibility is democracy in which there is voting over different policy combinations. If $\theta^e + \theta^m < 1$, then the majority are the workers, and they will pursue policies to maximize their own income.[31]

I now briefly discuss the possibility of a switch from the dictatorship of the elite to one of these two alternative regimes. It is clear that whether the dictatorship of the elite or that of middle class is more efficient depends on the relative numbers and productivities of the two groups and whether elite control or democracy is more efficient depends on policies in democracy. Hence, this section will first characterize the equilibrium under these alternative political institutions. Moreover, for part of the analysis in this subsection, I simplify the discussion by assuming that

$$\theta^m = \theta^e < \frac{1}{2}, \tag{A3}$$

so that the number of middle-class and elite producers is the same, and they are in the minority relative to workers.[32]

5.1   Dictatorship of the Middle Class

With the dictatorship of the middle class, the political equilibrium is identical to the dictatorship of the elite, with the roles reversed. To avoid repetition, I will not provide a full analysis. Instead, let me focus on the case, combining

---

[31] More generally, we could consider various different political institutions as represented by social welfare functions giving different weights to the elite, the middle class and the workers (see, for example, the Appendix to Chapter 4 in Acemoglu and Robinson (2006a)).

[32] Otherwise, there is no median voter and the analysis of political equilibrium requires further assumptions about parties and political procedures.

revenue extraction and factor price manipulation. The analog of Assumption (A2) is:

$$A^m \geq \phi(1 - \alpha)^{(1-\alpha)/\alpha} A^e \frac{\theta^e}{\theta^m}. \tag{A4}$$

Given this assumption, a similar proposition to that above immediately follows; the middle class will tax the elite and will redistribute the proceeds to themselves, i.e., $T_t^w = T_t^e = 0$, and moreover, the same analysis as above gives their most preferred tax rate as

$$\tau_t^e = \tilde{\tau}^{COM} \equiv \min \left\{ \frac{\kappa\,(\lambda, \theta^m, \alpha, \phi)}{1 + \kappa\,(\lambda, \theta^m, \alpha, \phi)}, \bar{\tau} \right\}. \tag{22}$$

Proposition 17 Suppose Assumptions (A1) and (A3) hold, Condition (ES) does not hold, and $\phi > 0$, then the unique political equilibrium with middle-class control features $\tau_t^e = \tilde{\tau}^{COM}$ as given by (22) for all t.

Comparing this equilibrium to the equilibrium under the dictatorship of the elite, it is apparent that the elite equilibrium will be more efficient when A^e and θ^e are large relative to A^m and θ^m, and the middle-class equilibrium will be more efficient when the opposite is the case.

Proposition 18 Suppose Assumptions (A1)–(A4) hold, then aggregate output is higher with the dictatorship of the elite than the dictatorship of the middle class if $A^e > A^m$ and it is higher under the dictatorship of the middle class if $A^m > A^e$.

Intuitively, the group in power imposes taxes on the other group (and since $\theta^m = \theta^e$, these taxes are equal) and not on themselves, so aggregate output is higher when the group with greater productivity is in power and is spared from distortionary taxation.

5.2   Democracy

Under Assumption (A4), workers are in the majority in democracy, and have the power to tax the elite and the middle class to redistribute to themselves. More specifically, each worker's consumption is $c_t^w = w_t + T_t^w$, with w_t given by (7), so that workers care about equilibrium wages and transfers. Workers will then choose the sequence of policies $\{\tau_t^e, \tau_t^m, T_t^w, T_t^m, T_t^e\}_{t=0,1,\dots,\infty}$ that satisfy (3) to maximize $\sum_{t=0}^{\infty} \beta^t c_t^w$.

It is straightforward to see that the workers will always set $T_t^m = T_t^e = 0$. Substituting for the transfers from (3), we obtain that democracy will solve the following maximization problem to determine policies:

$$\max_{\tau_t^e, \tau_t^m} w_t + \frac{\phi}{1 - \alpha} \left[\tau_t^m (1 - \tau_t^m)^{(1-\alpha)/\alpha} A^m l^m \theta^m \right.$$
$$\left. + \tau_t^e (1 - \tau_t^e)^{(1-\alpha)/\alpha} A^e l^e \theta^e \right] + R$$

with w_t given by (7).

As before, when Condition (ES) holds, taxes have no effect on wages, so the workers will tax at the revenue-maximizing rate, similar to the case of revenue extraction for the elite above. This result is stated in the next proposition (proof omitted):

Proposition 19 Suppose Assumption (A1) and Condition (ES) hold and $\phi > 0$, then the unique political equilibrium with democracy features $\tau_t^m = \tau_t^e = \tau^{RE} \equiv \min\{\alpha, \bar{\tau}\}$.

Therefore, in this case democracy is more inefficient than both middle-class and elite control, since it imposes taxes on both groups.[33] The same is not the case, however, when Condition (ES) does not hold and wages are positive. In this case, workers realize that by taxing the marginal group they are reducing their own wages. In fact, taxes always reduce wages more than the revenue they generate because of their distortionary effects.[34] As a result, workers will only tax the group with the higher marginal productivity. More specifically, for example, if $A^m > A^e$, we will have $\tau_t^e = 0$, and τ_t^m will be such that $(1 - \tau_t^m)^{1/\alpha} A^m = A^e$ or $\tau_t^m = \alpha$ and $(1 - \alpha)^{1/\alpha} A^m \geq A^e$. Therefore, we have:

Proposition 20 Suppose Assumption (A1) and (A4) hold and Condition (ES) does not hold. Then in the unique political equilibrium with democracy, if $A^m > A^e$, we will have $\tau_t^e = 0$, and $\tau_t^m = \tau^{Dm}$ will be such that $(1 - \tau^{Dm})^{1/\alpha} A^m = A^e$ or $\tau^{Dm} = \alpha$ and $(1 - \alpha)^{1/\alpha} A^m \geq A^e$. If $A^m < A^e$, we will have $\tau_t^m = 0$, and $\tau_t^e = \tau^{De}$ will be such that $(1 - \tau^{De})^{1/\alpha} A^e = A^m$ or $\tau^{De} = \alpha$ and $(1 - \alpha)^{1/\alpha} A^e \geq A^e$.

Most of the proof of this proposition follows directly from the analysis so far. The only part that is not obvious is that workers prefer to set zero taxes on the less productive group, and this is proved in Appendix A (included in the working paper version). The intuition for this is that wages are determined by the marginal productivity of the less productive of the two entrepreneurial groups, and positive taxes on this group will reduce wages by more than the gain in tax revenues (by a similar argument as in footnote 34).

The most interesting implication of this proposition comes from the comparison of the case with and without excess supply. While in the presence of excess

---

[33] Naturally, in this case we may expect workers to ultimately become entrepreneurs, and this extreme inefficiency to be ameliorated. See Acemoglu (2003a).

[34] To see this, suppose there is only one group with productivity A. With a tax rate of τ, the wage is $\alpha (1 - \tau)^{1/\alpha} A / (1 - \alpha)$, and in addition there is per worker transfer equal to $\phi\tau (1 - \tau)^{(1-\alpha)/\alpha} A / (1 - \alpha) + R$, so the total consumption of a worker is $\tilde{c}_t^w = (1 - \tau)^{(1-\alpha)/\alpha} A [\alpha (1 - \tau) + \phi\tau] / (1 - \alpha) + R$. The derivative of this expression with respect to τ is

$$-\frac{1}{1 - \alpha} (1 - \tau)^{(1-2\alpha)/\alpha} A \left[\frac{\phi - \alpha}{\alpha} \tau - (1 - \phi) \right],$$

which is always negative, implying that $\tilde{c}_t^w$ is maximized at $\tau = 0$, establishing the claim.

labor supply, democracy taxes both groups of producers and consequently generates more inefficiency than the dictatorship of the elite or the middle class; when there is no excess supply, it is in general less distortionary than the dictatorship of the middle class or the elite. The intuition is that when Condition (ES) does not hold, workers understand that high taxes will depress wages and are therefore less willing to use distortionary taxes.[35]

5.3   Inefficiency of Political Institutions and Inappropriate Institutions

Consider a society where Assumption (A4) is satisfied and $A^e < A^m$ so that middle-class control is more productive (i.e., generates greater output). Despite this, the elite will have no incentive, without some type of compensation, to relinquish their power to the middle class. In this case, political institutions that lead to more inefficient policies will persist even though alternative political institutions leading to better outcomes exist.

One possibility is a Coasian deal between the elite and the middle class. For example, perhaps the elite can relinquish political power and get compensated in return. However, such deals are in general not possible. To discuss why (and why not), let us distinguish between two alternative approaches.

First, the elite may relinquish power in return for a promise of future transfers. This type of solution will run into two difficulties: (i) such promises will not be credible, and once they have political power, the middle class will have no incentive to keep on making such transfers;[36] (ii) since there are no other, less distortionary fiscal instruments, to compensate the elite, the middle class will have to impose similar taxes on itself, so that the alternative political institutions will not be as efficient in the first place.[37]

Second, the elite may relinquish power in return for a lump-sum transfer from the middle class. Such a solution is also not possible in general, since the net present value of the benefit of holding political power often exceeds any transfer that can be made. Consequently, the desire of the elite to implement inefficient policies also implies that they support political institutions that enable them to pursue these policies. Thus, in the same way as preferences over inefficient policies translate into preferences over inefficient economic institutions, they also lead to preferences towards inefficient political institutions. I will discuss how political institutions can change from the "ground-up" in Section 6 below.

---

[35] This is similar to the reasons why workers (democracy) are less in favor of entry barriers than oligarchic societies (see Acemoglu (2003a)). Another reason for democracy to be more efficient, emphasized in Acemoglu (2003a), is that policies that differentially affect the productivity of different groups will lead to a misallocation of talent.

[36] See Acemoglu (2003b).

[37] The exception is when there are holdup problems and manipulating economic institutions was not sufficient to deal with them. In this case, there can be significant gains from changing political institutions.

Another interesting question is whether a given set of economic institutions might be "appropriate" for a while but then become "inappropriate" and costly for economic activity later. This question might be motivated, for example, by the contrast of the Northeastern United States and the Caribbean colonies between the 17th and 19th centuries. The Caribbean colonies were clear examples of societies controlled by a narrow elite, with political power in the monopoly of plantation owners, and few rights for the slaves that made up the majority of the population.[38] In contrast, Northeastern United States developed as a settler colony, approximating a democratic society with significant political power in the hands of smallholders and a broader set of producers.[39] While in both the 17th and 18th centuries, the Caribbean societies were among the richest places in the world, and almost certainly richer and more productive than the Northeastern United States,[40] starting in the late 18th century they lagged behind the United States and many other more democratic societies, which took advantage of new investment opportunities, particularly in industry and commerce.[41] This raises the question as to whether the same political and economic institutions that encouraged the planters to invest and generate high output in the 17th and early 18th centuries then became a barrier to further growth.

The baseline model used above suggests a simple explanation along these lines. Imagine an economy in which the elite are in power, Condition (ES) does not hold, ϕ is small, A^e is relatively high and A^m is relatively small to start with. The above analysis shows that the elite will choose a high tax rate on the middle class. Nevertheless, output will be relatively high, because the elite will undertake the right investments themselves, and the distortion on the middle class will be relatively small since A^m is small.

Consequently, the dictatorship of the elite may generate greater income per capita than an alternative society under the dictatorship of the middle class. This is reminiscent of the planter elite controlling the economy in the Caribbean.

However, if at some point the environment changes so that A^m increases substantially relative to A^e, the situation changes radically. The elite, still in power, will continue to impose high taxes on the middle class, but now these policies have become very costly because they distort the investments of the more productive group. Another society where the middle class have political power will now generate significantly greater output.

This simple example illustrates how institutions that were initially "appropriate" (i.e., that did not generate much distortion or may have even encouraged growth) later caused the society to fall substantially behind other economies.

---

[38] See, for example, Beckford (1972) and Dunn (1972).

[39] See, for example, Keyssar (2000).

[40] Although the wealth of the Caribbean undoubtedly owed much to the world value of its main product, sugar, Caribbean societies were nonetheless able to achieve these levels of productivity because the planters had good incentive to invest in the production, processing and export of sugar. See Eltis (1995) and Engerman and Sokoloff (1997).

[41] See, for example, Acemoglu et al. (2002) or Engerman and Sokoloff (1997).

6 INSTITUTIONAL CHANGE AND PERSISTENCE

To develop a better understanding for why inefficient institutions emerge and persist, we need an equilibrium model of institutional change. I now briefly discuss such a model.[42]

It is first useful to draw a distinction between de jure and de facto political power. De jure political power is determined by political institutions. In the baseline model, de jure political power is in the hands of the elite, since the political institutions give them the right to set taxes and determine the economic institutions. De facto political power, which comes from other sources, did not feature so far in the model (except in the discussion of political consolidation). The simplest example of de facto political power is when a group manages to organize itself and poses a military challenge to an existing regime or threatens it with a revolution. I will conceptualize institutional change as resulting from the interplay of de jure and de facto political power.

Imagine a society described by the baseline model above where de jure political power is initially in the hands of the elite. In each period, with probability q the middle class solves the collective action problem among its members and gather sufficient de facto political power to overthrow the existing regime and to monopolize political power (establish a dictatorship of the middle class). However, violently overthrowing the existing regime is still costly, and in particular, each middle-class agent incurs a cost of ψ in the process. Moreover, in the process, the elite are harmed substantially. In particular, I assume that following a violent overthrow, the elite receive zero utility.

Let us assume that the dictatorship of the middle class, if established, is an absorbing state and once the middle class comes to power, there will never be any further institutional change. With probability $1 - q$, the middle class has no de facto political power. Also denote the state at time t by the tuple (P_t, s_t), where $P_t \in \{E, M\}$ denotes whether the elite or the middle class is in control, and $s_t \in \{H, L\}$ denotes the level of threat (high or low) against the regime controlled by the elite.

When the middle class amasses de facto political power, the elite need to respond in some way, since letting the middle class overthrow the existing regime is excessively costly for them. The elite can respond in three different ways: (i) they can make temporary concessions, such as reducing taxes on the middle class, etc.; (ii) they can give up power; (iii) they can use repression, which is costly, but manages to prevent the regime from falling to the middle class. I assume that repression costs μ for the elite as a whole.

Throughout this section, I focus on MPE. In an MPE, strategies are only a function of the state s_t, so when $s_t = L$, the elite will set the policies that maximize their utility, which were characterized above. So the interesting actions take place in the state $s_t = H$. Moreover, to simplify the discussion, I

---

[42] The model here heavily builds on my previous work with James Robinson. See in particular Acemoglu and Robinson (2000b, 2001, 2006a).

assume throughout that Condition (ES) is satisfied, so that the main motive for inefficient policy is revenue extraction.

Let us first calculate the value of a middle-class agent when the middle class is in power. Since Condition (ES) is satisfied, the above analysis shows that they will not tax themselves, set a tax of $\tau^e = \tau^{RE}$ on the elite in every period, and redistribute all the revenue to themselves. To write the resulting value function, let us introduce the following notation: $T^j(\tau) \equiv \phi\tau(1-\tau)^{(1-\alpha)/\alpha}A^j\theta^j\lambda/(1-\alpha)$ as the tax revenue raised from group j at the tax rate τ, and $\pi^j(\tau) \equiv \alpha(1-\tau)^{1/\alpha}A^j\lambda/(1-\alpha)$ as the profit of a producer in group j facing the tax rate τ. Then, using M to indicate a value function under the dictatorship of the middle class, we have

$$V^m(M) = \frac{\pi^m(0) + \left(T^e\left(\tau^{RE}\right) + R\right)/\theta^m}{1-\beta}, \tag{23}$$

where τ^{RE} is given by (11). The first term in the numerator is their own revenues, $\alpha A^m\lambda/(1-\alpha)$, and the second is the distribution from the revenue obtained by taxing the elite and from natural resources. The term $1-\beta$ provides the net present discounted value of this stream of revenues. Similarly, the value of an elite producer in this case is

$$V^e(M) = \frac{\pi^e\left(\tau^{RE}\right)}{1-\beta}. \tag{24}$$

What about the dictatorship of the elite? Let us write this value recursively starting in the no threat state:

$$V^m(E, L) = \pi^m\left(\tau^{RE}\right) + \beta(1-q)V^m(E, L)$$
$$+ \beta q V^m(E, H). \tag{25}$$

This expression incorporates the fact that, in the MPE, during periods of low threat, the elite will follow their most preferred policy, $\tau^m = \tau^{RE}$ and $T^m = 0$. The low threat state recurs with probability $1-q$. What happens when $s_t = H$? As noted above, there are three possibilities. Let us first start by investigating whether the elite can prevent a switch of political power by making concessions in the high threat state. For this purpose, let us denote the highest possible value to the middle class under the dictatorship of the elite by $\bar{V}^m(E, H)$. Then, the condition for concessions within the given political regime to prevent action by the middle class is simply

$$\bar{V}^m(E, H) \geq V^m(M) - \psi, \tag{26}$$

where recall that ψ is the cost of regime change for the middle class. When this constraint holds, the elite could make sufficient concessions to keep the middle class happy within the existing regime.

Therefore, to determine whether concessions within the dictatorship of the elite will be sufficient to satisfy the middle class, we simply need to calculate $\bar{V}^m(E, H)$. Note that the best concession that the elite can make is to adopt a policy that is most favorable for the middle class, i.e., $\tau^m = 0$, $\tau^e = \tau^{RE}$, and $T^m = \left(T^e \left(\tau^{RE} \right) + R \right) / \theta^m$. Therefore,

$$
\begin{aligned}
\bar{V}^m (E, H) = \pi^m (0) &+ \left(T^e \left(\tau^{RE} \right) + R \right) / \theta^m \\
&+ \beta (1 - q) \, \bar{V}^m (E, L) + \beta q \, \bar{V}^m (E, H)
\end{aligned}
\tag{27}
$$

where $\bar{V}^m (E, L)$ is given by expression (25), with $\bar{V}^m (E, H)$ replacing $V^m (E, H)$ on the right-hand side. Combining (27) and (25), we obtain:

$$
\begin{aligned}
&\bar{V}^m (E, H) \\
&= \frac{\beta (1 - q) \pi^m \left(\tau^{RE} \right) + (1 - \beta (1 - q)) \left[\pi^m (0) + \left(T^e \left(\tau^{RE} \right) + R \right) / \theta^m \right]}{(1 - \beta)}.
\end{aligned}
\tag{28}
$$

This is the maximum credible utility that the elite can promise the middle class within the existing regime. The reason why they cannot give them greater utility is because of commitment problems. As (28) makes clear, the elite transfer resources to the middle class only in the state $s_t = H$. Even if they promise to make further transfers or not tax them in the state $s_t = L$, these promises will not be credible (they cannot commit to them), and in the MPE, when the state $s_t = L$ arrives, the elite will choose their most preferred policy of taxing the middle class and transferring the resources to themselves.[43]

If given this expression, (26) is satisfied, then the elite can prevent a violent overthrow by making concessions within the existing regime. Nevertheless, the elite may not necessarily prefer such concessions. To investigate this issue, we first need to determine the exact concessions that the elite will make. They will clearly not follow the most preferable policy for the middle class, since this will give more than sufficient utility to prevent an overthrow. Instead, the elite will choose a policy combination $\left(\hat{\tau}^m, \hat{\tau}^e, \hat{T}^m, \hat{T}^e \right)$ such that $V^m (E, H) = V^m (M) - \psi$, i.e., they will make the middle class just indifferent between overthrowing the regime or accepting the concessions. The value of such concessions to the elite is, by similar arguments, given by:

$$
\begin{aligned}
&\hat{V}^e (E, H) \\
&= \frac{\beta (1-q) \left(\pi^e (0) + \left(T^m \left(\tau^{RE} \right) + R \right) / \theta^e \right) + (1 - \beta (1-q)) \left[\pi^e (\hat{\tau}^e) + \hat{T}^e \right]}{(1-\beta)}.
\end{aligned}
\tag{29}
$$

Whether the elite will make these concessions or not then depends on the values of other options available to them. Another alternative is the use of repression whenever there is a threat from the middle class. Such repression is

---

[43] If instead of the MPE, we consider the SPE, the elite can promise a greater value to the middle class, but again there will be limits to this; once the state $s_t = L$ arrives, the elite will have an incentive to renege on their promises. See Acemoglu and Robinson (2006a) for an analysis of the SPE in a related game.

always effective, so the only cost of this strategy for the elite is the cost they incur in the use of repression, μ. Denote by $V^e(O, s_t)$ the value function to the elite it uses repression and the state is s_t. By standard arguments, we can obtain this value by writing the following standard recursive formulae: $V^e(O, H) = \pi^e(0) + \left(T^m\left(\tau^{RE}\right) + R\right)/\theta^m - \mu + \beta(1-q)V^e(O, L) + \beta q V^e(O, H)$ and $V^e(O, L) = \pi^e(0) + \left(T^m\left(\tau^{RE}\right) + R\right)/\theta^m + \beta(1-q)V^e(O, L) + \beta q V^e$ (O, H). These two expressions incorporate the fact that, when using the repression strategy, the elite will always choose their most preferred policy combination, and will use repression when $s_t = H$ to defend their regime. Combining these two equations, we obtain:

$$V^e(O, H) = \frac{\pi^e(0) + \left(T^m\left(\tau^{RE}\right) + R\right)/\theta^m - (1 - \beta(1-q))\mu}{1 - \beta}. \tag{30}$$

Consequently, for the elite to prefer concessions, it needs to be the case that $\hat{V}^e(E, H) \geq V^e(O, H)$.

Finally, the third alternative for the elite is to allow regime change, and obtain $V^e(M)$ as given by (24).[44] Evidently, $V^e(M)$ is less than $\hat{V}^e(E, H)$, since in the latter case they only make concessions (in fact limited concessions) with probability q. Therefore, regime change will only happen when (26) does not hold. In addition, for similar reasons, for regime change to take place, we need $V^e(M) \geq V^e(O, H)$. Note that all of the values here are simple functions of parameters, so comparing these values essentially amounts to comparing nonlinear functions of the underlying parameters.

Putting all these pieces together and assuming for convenience that when indifferent the elite opt against repression, we obtain the following proposition:

Proposition 21 Consider the above environment with potential regime change and suppose that Condition (ES) holds. Then there are three different types of political equilibria:

1. If (26) holds and $\hat{V}^e(E, H) \geq V^e(O, H)$, in the unique equilibrium the regime always remains the dictatorship of the elite. When $s_t = L$, the elite set their most preferred policy of $\tau^m = \tau^{RE}$, $\tau^e = 0$ and $T^m = 0$, and when $s_t = H$, the elite make concessions sufficient to ensure $\hat{V}^m(E, H) = V^m(M) - \psi$, i.e., they adopt the policy $\left(\hat{\tau}^m, \hat{\tau}^e, \hat{T}^m, \hat{T}^e\right)$.

2. If (26) holds but $\hat{V}^e(E, H) < V^e(O, H)$, or if (26) does not hold and $V^e(M) < V^e(O, H)$, then the regime always remains the dictatorship of the elite. The elite always set their most preferred policy of $\tau^m = \tau^{RE}$, $\tau^e = 0$ and $T^m = 0$, and when $s_t = H$, they use repression against the middle class.

3. If (26) does not hold and $V^e(M) \geq V^e(O, H)$, then there is equilibrium institutional change. When $s_t = L$, the elite set their most preferred policy of

---

[44] By construction, this is always better for the middle class than a violent overthrow, since they do not have to incur the cost ψ.

$\tau^m = \tau^{RE}$, $\tau^e = 0$ and $T^m = 0$, and when $s_t = H$, the elite voluntarily pass political control to the middle class.

This proposition illustrates how various different institutional equilibria can arise. The most interesting case is 3, where there is equilibrium institutional change as a result of the elite voluntarily relinquishing political control. Why would the elite give up their dictatorship? The reason is the de facto political power of the middle class, which threatens the elite with a violent overthrow – an outcome worse than the dictatorship of the middle class. The elite then prevent such a violent overthrow by changing political institutions to transfer de jure political power to the middle class. This transfer exploits the role of political institutions as a commitment device (a commitment to a different distribution of de jure political power), and acts as a credible promise of future policies that favor the middle class (the promise is credible, since institutional change gives de jure political power and thus the right to set fiscal policy in the future to the middle class).

This discussion highlights that institutional change has two requirements: (i) that concessions within the existing regime are not sufficient to appease the middle class; (ii) that repression is sufficiently costly for the elites to accept regime change.

The comparative statics of regime change are also interesting. First, when repression is more costly, i.e., μ is higher, institutional change is more likely. Moreover:

$$
\begin{aligned}
&V^e\left(O, H\right) - V^e\left(M\right) \\
&= \frac{\pi^e\left(0\right) - \pi^e\left(\tau^{RE}\right) + \left(T^m\left(\tau^{RE}\right) + R\right)/\theta^m - \left(1 - \beta\left(1 - q\right)\right)\mu}{1 - \beta}
\end{aligned}
$$

is increasing in R and ϕ. This implies that when R is high, so that there are greater rents from natural resources, $V^e\left(M\right) \geq V^e\left(O, H\right)$ becomes less likely, and the elite now prefer to use repression rather than allowing institutional change. Similarly, greater ϕ, which corresponds to greater state capacity, has the same impact on institutional equilibrium, since greater state capacity enables greater tax revenues in the future. This implies that, as already suggested by the results in subsection 3.4, greater state capacity, which typically leads to less distortionary policies, also increases political stakes and makes the use of repression by the elite the more likely. Nevertheless, increases in R or ϕ do not make institutional change unambiguously less likely, since they also make (26) more likely to be violated, making it more difficult for the elite to use concessions to appease the middle class.[45] Therefore, when the trade-off for

---

[45] In particular, (26) can be written as:

$$
\begin{aligned}
&\bar{V}^m\left(E, H\right) - V^m\left(M\right) + \psi \\
&= \beta\left(1 - q\right)\left[\pi^m\left(\tau^{RE}\right) - \left(\pi^m\left(0\right) + \left(T^e\left(\tau^{RE}\right) + R\right)/\theta^m\right)\right]/\left(1 - \beta\right) + \psi \geq 0
\end{aligned}
$$

and increases in R and ϕ make this constraint less likely to hold.

the elite is between repression and institutional change, greater R and ϕ make repression more likely, whereas when the trade-off is between concessions and institutional change, they may encourage institutional change.[46]

This analysis also illustrates the conditions for institutional persistence. Persistence is the natural course of things and something unusual, the success of the middle class in solving their collective action problem and amassing de facto political power, creates the platform for institutional change. However, even the possibility of collective action by the middle class is not sufficient, since the elite can use costly methods to defend the existing regime. Therefore, institutions will be more persistent when the elite are unwilling to give up the right to determine policies in the future, which will in turn be the case when there is significant distributional conflict between the elite and the middle class, for example because tax revenues are important (i.e., high ϕ) or because rents from natural resources, R, are high. Therefore, a set of political institutions will persist when political stakes are high, i.e., when alternative institutional arrangements are costly for those who currently hold political power and have the means to use force to maintain the existing political institutions.

The model also suggests the possibility of interesting interactions between economic forces and institutional equilibria. The first is an interaction between economic and political institutions. Suppose that economic institutions impose a low $\bar{\tau}$. This implies that control of fiscal policy will generate only limited gains, reducing political stakes, and the elite will have less reason to use repression in order to defend the existing regime. Consequently, institutional persistence might be more of an issue in societies where economic institutions enable those with political power to capture greater rents.[47]

When the ability of the middle class to solve their collective action problem is endogenous (as in the model used above to illustrate the political consolidation effect), there will be a further interaction between economics and politics. In particular, suppose that the probability q that the middle class will be able to pose an effective threat to the regime is endogenous and depends on the profits of the middle class. In this case, the elite realize that the richer are the middle class, the greater the threat from them in the future. When political power is very valuable, for example because tax revenues or rents from natural resources are high, the elite will wish to "overtax" the middle class to impoverish them and to reduce their political power. These higher taxes will, in turn, increase institutional persistence by making it more difficult for the middle class to solve their collective action problem and mount challenges against the dictatorship of the elite. This suggests another interesting interaction, this time between inefficient policies and institutional persistence.

---

[46] This is similar to the non-monotonic effect of inequality on democratization in Acemoglu and Robinson (2006a).

[47] This is related to the result in Acemoglu and Robinson (2006a) that democracy is less likely to emerge, and to consolidate when it emerges, in agricultural societies where the political stakes are high for the elite.

7 CONCLUDING REMARKS

This paper developed a simple framework to investigate why inefficient – non-growth-enhancing – institutions emerge and persist. Political institutions shape the allocation of political power. Economic institutions, in turn, determine the framework for policy-making and place constraints on policies. Groups with political power – the elite – choose policies in order to transfer resources from the rest of the society to themselves. Consequently, they have *induced preferences* over institutions, depending on how institutions map into policies and economic outcomes. This methodological approach therefore necessitates a baseline model in which preferences over policies can be studied.

The bulk of the paper analyzed such a baseline model. Though relatively simple, this model is rich enough to encompass various distinct sources of inefficient policies. These include revenue extraction, factor price manipulation and political consolidation. According to the revenue extraction mechanism, the elite pursue inefficient policies to extract revenue from other groups. The factor price manipulation mechanism implies that the elite seek to reduce the demand for factors from other groups in order to indirectly benefit from changes in factor prices. Finally, political consolidation implies that to increase their political power, the elite may wish to impoverish other groups that are competing for political power. The elite's preferences over inefficient policies translate into inefficient economic institutions. Consequently, institutions that can restrict inefficient policies will typically fail to emerge. Instead, the elite may choose to manipulate economic institutions to further increase their income or facilitate their rent extraction. The exception is when there is a holdup problem (e.g., because there are investments that involve long horizons), so that equilibrium taxes and regulations are worse than the elite would like from an ex ante point of view. In this case, economic institutions that place limits on future policies and provide additional security of property rights to other groups can be useful.

The paper also provided a framework for the analysis of institutional change and institutional persistence. The key mechanism for institutional change is challenges from groups without de jure political power. The model shows how the elite may be forced to change political institutions in order to make concessions in response to these challenges. The important result from this analysis is that, when political stakes are high, for example, because of large rents from natural resources or the importance of tax revenues, the elite will be unwilling to make such concessions and may prefer to use repression in order to deal with outside challenges. In this case, existing (potentially inefficient) political and economic institutions are more likely to persist. There is also an interesting interaction between economic and political institutions: If economic institutions limit policies and thus reduce political stakes, change in political institutions may be easier.

The paper also highlights a number of important areas for future research:

1. While the model featured three distinct groups, it sidestepped issues of political coalitions. One major area for the theory of political economy is the analysis of coalitions between different social groups.

2. Relatedly, as noted in the Introduction, to map a model like this to reality, one needs to know who "the elite" are. However, the concept of the elite is both abstract and a shorthand for a variety of groups that are able to capture political power. The identity of the elite often changes in practice, and a dynamic model is necessary for understanding how such changes may occur in practice.

3. The discussion of inappropriate institutions also raised questions related to institutional flexibility. While the discussion here focused on inefficient institutions, another important dimension is whether a given set of institutions are flexible, i.e., capable of changing rapidly in the face of changes in the environment. Which features makes institutions flexible and whether institutional flexibility matters for economic performance are also interesting areas for future research.

4. The model presented here features only limited intertemporal interactions. Introducing capital accumulation (without full depreciation) is one important area of investigation. This will enable both an analysis of dynamic taxation and also of questions related to how inefficiencies change as the economy becomes richer.

5. The class of models used for political economy also needs to be enriched by considering more realistic policies. Although taxes here stand for various different distortionary redistributive policies, explicitly allowing for these policies is likely to lead to new and richer results. Most importantly, such a generalization will allow a discussion of the "optimal" and equilibrium mix of policies in the context of political economic interactions.

6. In the model, government policy is purely redistributive. Another important area of investigation is the interaction of the rent-seeking and efficiency-enhancing roles of governments.[48]

7. Last, but not least, there is much more that needs to be done on institutional persistence. In practice, there is a mixture of frequent changes in certain dimensions of institutions (e.g., switches from dictatorship to democracy), associated with relative persistence in other dimensions (such as the political power of different groups or the inefficiency of various economic institutions). Constructing dynamic models that can shed light on these issues is a major area for future research.

References

ACEMOGLU, D. (2003a): "The Form of Property Rights: Oligarchic Versus Democratic Societies," NBER Working Paper No. 10037.

——— (2003b): "Why Not a Political Coase Theorem? Social Conflict, Commitment, and Politics," *Journal of Comparative Economics*, 31, 620–652.

——— (2005): "Politics and Economics in Weak and Strong States," *Journal of Monetary Economics*, 52, 1199–1226.

ACEMOGLU, D., P. AGHION, AND F. ZILIBOTTI (2003): "Distance to Frontier, Selection, and Economic Growth," *Journal of the European Economic Association*, forthcoming.

---

[48] See Acemoglu (2005) for an attempt in this direction.

ACEMOGLU, D., S. JOHNSON, AND J. A. ROBINSON (2001): "The Colonial Origins of Comparative Development: An Empirical Investigation," *American Economic Review*, 91, 1369–1401.

—— (2002): "Reversal of Fortune: Geography and Institutions in the Making of the Modern World Income Distribution," *Quarterly Journal of Economics*, 117, 1231–1294.

—— (2005): "Institutions as the Fundamental Cause of Long-Run Economic Growth," in *Handbook of Economic Growth*, ed. by P. Aghion and S. Durlauf, Amsterdam: Elsevier.

ACEMOGLU, D. AND J. A. ROBINSON (2000a): "Political Losers as a Barrier to Economic Development," *American Economic Review*, 90, 126–130.

—— (2000b): "Why Did the West Extend the Franchise? Democracy, Inequality, and Growth in Historical Perspective," *Quarterly Journal of Economics*, 115, 1167–1199.

—— (2001): "A Theory of Political Transitions," *American Economic Review*, 91, 938–963.

—— (2006a): *Economic Origins of Dictatorship and Democracy*, New York: Cambridge University Press.

—— (2006b): "Economic Backwardness in Political Perspective," *American Political Science Review,* 100, 115–131.

AUSTEN-SMITH, D. AND J. S. BANKS (1999): *Positive Political Theory I: Collective Preference*, Ann Arbor: University of Michigan Press.

BARRO, R. J. (1999): *Determinants of Economic Growth: A Cross-Country Empirical Study*, 2nd edition, Cambridge, MA: MIT Press.

BATES, R. H. (1981): *Markets and States in Tropical Africa: The Political Basis of Agricultural Policies*, Berkeley: University of California Press.

BECKFORD, G. L. (1972): *Persistent Poverty: Underdevelopment in Plantation Economics of the Third World*, New York: Oxford University Press.

BESLEY, T. AND S. COATE (1998): "Sources of Inefficiency in a Representative Democracy: A Dynamic Analysis," *American Economic Review*, 88, 139–156.

BOURGUIGNON, F. AND T. VERDIER (2000): "Oligarchy, Democracy, Inequality and Growth," *Journal of Development Economics*, 62, 285–313.

BUENO DE MESQUITA, B., A. SMITH, R. SIVERSON, AND J. MORROW (2003): *The Logic of Political Survival*, Cambridge, MA: MIT Press.

DIXIT, A. K. (2004): *Lawlessness and Economics: Alternative Modes of Governance*, Princeton: Princeton University Press.

DUNN, R. S. (1972): *Sugar and Slaves: The Rise of the Planter Class in the English West Indies, 1624–1713*, Chapel Hill: University of North Carolina Press.

EGGERTSSON, T. (2005): *Imperfect Institutions: Possibilities and Limits of Reform*, Ann Arbor: University of Michigan Press.

ELTIS, D. (1995): "The Total Product of Barbados, 1664–1701," *Journal of Economic History*, 55, 321–338.

ENGERMAN, S. L. AND K. L. SOKOLOFF (1997): "Factor Endowments, Institutions, and Differential Paths of Growth Among New World Economies: A View from Economic Historians of the United States," in *How Latin America Fell Behind: Essays in the Economic Histories of Brazil and Mexico, 1800–1914*, ed. by S. Haber, Stanford: Stanford University Press, 260–304.

EVANS, P. (1995): *Embedded Autonomy: States and Industrial Transformation*, Princeton: Princeton University Press.

FEINSTEIN, C. H. (2005): *An Economic History of South Africa: Conquest, Discrimination and Development*, London, UK: Cambridge University Press.

GALOR, O., O. MOAV, AND D. VOLLRATH (2003): "Land Inequality and the Origin of Divergence and Overtaking in the Growth Process: Theory and Evidence," Brown University Mimeo.

GREIF, A. (1994): "Cultural Beliefs and the Organization of Society: A Historical and Theoretical Reflection on Collectivist and Individualist Societies," *Journal of Political Economy*, 102, 912–950.

GROSSMAN, H. I. (1991): "A General Equilibrium Model of Insurrections," *American Economic Review*, 81, 912–921.

GROSSMAN, H. I. AND M. S. KIM (1995): "Swords or Plowshares? A Theory of the Security of Claims to Property," *Journal of Political Economy*, 103, 1275–1288.

HALL, R. E. AND C. I. JONES (1999): "Why Do Some Countries Produce So Much More Output Per Worker Than Others?" *Quarterly Journal of Economics*, 114, 83–116.

JONES, E. L. (1981): *The European Miracle: Environments, Economies, and Geopolitics in the History of Europe and Asia*, New York: Cambridge University Press.

KEYSSAR, A. (2000): *The Right to Vote: The Contested History of Democracy in the United States*, New York: Basic Books.

KNACK, S. AND P. KEEFER (1995): "Institutions and Economic Performance: Cross-Country Tests Using Alternative Institutional Measures," *Economic and Politics*, 7, 207–227.

KRUSELL, P. AND J. V. RIOS-RULL (1996): "Vested Interests in a Positive Theory of Stagnation and Growth," *Review of Economic Studies*, 63, 301–329.

MAURO, P. (1995): "Corruption and Growth," *Quarterly Journal of Economics*, 110, 681–712.

MCGUIRE, M. C. AND M. OLSON (1996): "The Economics of Autocracy and Majority Rule: The Invisible Hand and the Use of Force," *Journal of Economic Literature*, 34, 72–96.

MELTZER, A. H. AND S. F. RICHARD (1981): "A Rational Theory of the Size of Government," *Journal of Political Economy*, 89, 914–927.

MIRRLEES, J. A. (1971): "An Exploration in the Theory of Optimal Income Taxation," *Review of Economic Studies*, 38, 175–208.

NORTH, D. C. (1981): *Structure and Change in Economic History*, New York: W.W. Norton & Co.

NORTH, D. C. AND R. P. THOMAS (1973): *The Rise of the Western World: A New Economic History*, Cambridge, UK: Cambridge University Press.

NORTH, D. C. AND B. R. WEINGAST (1989): "Constitutions and Commitment: The Evolution of Institutions Governing Public Choice in Seventeenth-Century England," *Journal of Economic History*, 49, 803–832.

NUGENT, J. B. AND J. A. ROBINSON (2002): "Are Endowments Fate?" CEPR Discussion Paper 3206.

OLSON, M. (1982): *The Rise and Decline of Nations: Economic Growth, Stagflation, and Social Rigidities*, New Haven: Yale University Press.

PARENTE, S. L. AND E. PRESCOTT (1999): "Monopoly Rights: A Barrier to Riches," *American Economic Review*, 89, 1216–1233.

PERSSON, T. (2005): "Forms of Democracy, Policy and Economic Development," Mimeo, Stockholm University.

PERSSON, T. AND G. TABELLINI (2000): *Political Economics: Explaining Economic Policy*, Cambridge, MA: MIT Press.

RAJAN, R. G. AND L. ZINGALES (2000): "The Tyranny of Inequality," *Journal of Public Economics*, 76, 521–558.

ROBERTS, K. W. S. (1977): "Voting Over Income Tax Schedules," *Journal of Public Economics*, 8, 329–340.

ROBINSON, J. A. (2001): "When Is a State Predatory?" Harvard University Mimeo.

ROMER, T. (1975): "Individual Welfare, Majority Voting, and the Properties of a Linear Income Tax," *Journal of Public Economics*, 4, 163–185.

SEGURA-CAYUELA, R. (2006): "Inefficient Policies, Inefficient Institutions and Trade," MIT Mimeo.

SONIN, K. (2003): "Why the Rich May Favor Poor Protection of Property Rights," *Journal of Comparative Economics*, 31, 715–731.

CHAPTER 10

Whither Political Economy? Theories, Facts and Issues

Antonio Merlo[1]

1 INTRODUCTION

Political Economy has undergone a process of dramatic change over the years. This process, which spans over more than two centuries, has helped to define the boundaries of the field's domain, organize its subject matter and establish an identity for modern political economy.

At the risk of trivializing, it might be useful to summarize some of the steps along the process that has characterized the evolution of the meaning of the term political economy. Starting from the late 1700s, when the work of Adam Smith and David Ricardo played a fundamental role in establishing economics as an autonomous discipline, political economy and economics were for a long time synonymous.[2]

Economics started to organize itself into fields at the beginning of the 20th century. However, while political economy clearly did not fit all of the subject matter of some of the fields, it did not define a separate field. In fact, it was not until the 1950s that the term political economy started to have a different, more precise meaning, separate from the generic notion that politics and government policy are intimately interrelated. The change of emphasis emerges quite clearly from Buchanan and Tullock (1962) and Downs (1957). At the same time, Arrow (1951) marked the birth of social choice theory, which provided vital impetus for the development of analytical tools to study the (economic and political) outcomes of political processes.[3]

[1] Financial support from National Science Foundation grant SES-0213755 is gratefully acknowledged. I thank Arianna Degan and Andrea Mattozzi for their help at various stages of this project, George Mailath, Andy Postlewaite and Ken Wolpin for useful conversations, and Tim Besley, Steve Coate, Gilat Levy and Torsten Persson for helpful comments and suggestions. Claire Lim provided excellent assistance.
[2] An indication of the long-lasting lack of separation between political economy and economics is that when in 1892, following the inception of the *Quarterly Journal of Economics* in 1886 and the *Economic Journal* in 1891, the University of Chicago Press also started to publish a general interest journal in economics, it was entitled the *Journal of Political Economy*.
[3] Another important contribution was Black (1958).

During the last twenty-five years, the systematic study of the interactions between political and economic factors has grown considerably within many fields in economics. At the same time, the increased interest in applications has been paralleled by a surge in theoretical research aimed at developing a common, rigorous language and a coherent class of models to analyze political institutions and outcomes as endogenous, equilibrium phenomena. It is the combination of the outcomes of these efforts that now defines political economy as a field.

As we progress into the 21st century, it seems legitimate at this juncture to try to assess some of the more recent developments in political economy and place them in perspective, with the hope of enhancing our understanding of the directions in which research in the field is moving. Rather than embarking on the impossible task of producing a comprehensive (or even partial) survey of the literature, however, I focus here on a small number of specific issues and attempt to summarize the state of knowledge of these issues, both from a theoretical and an empirical point of view, as well as present my own take on the subjects.

One of the fundamental premises of political economy is that the actions of governments can be understood only as consequences of the political forces that enable governments to acquire and maintain power. Hence, a large fraction of the existing literature has focused on the role of different political institutions in shaping economic policy and their effects on the economy. This literature, which by and large characterizes the macroeconomic side of political economy, is well documented and surveyed in two recent textbooks by Drazen (2000) and Persson and Tabellini (2000), and I do not touch upon it here.[4]

Another defining feature of current research in political economy is the attempt to fully integrate political actors and institutions with private decision-makers in a "general equilibrium theory" of the political economy. Much of the recent literature on the microeconomic side of political economy has been devoted to developing models where the set of individuals, their preferences and the set of available technologies (which include all the technologies that pertain to the political process) are the only primitives, while voters, politicians, political parties, legislatures, interest groups, governments and, ultimately, policies and constitutions are equilibrium outcomes.[5] While no general theory exists to date where all the variables of interest are simultaneously determined in equilibrium, substantial progress has been made to develop classes of models where each of these variables is treated as endogenous.

In this article, I focus on four of the topics addressed by this literature, which correspond to four of the basic building blocks of political economy. In Section 2, I analyze the behavior of voters. In Section 3, I address the issue of endogenous politicians. I discuss the role of political parties in Section 4.

---

[4] See also the recent monographs by Acemoglu and Robinson (2005) and Persson and Tabellini (2005).

[5] Austen-Smith and Banks (1999, 2005) provide systematic accounts of the social-choice and game-theoretic foundations of this literature, respectively.

In Section 5, I analyze the formation and dissolution of coalition governments. For each of these topics, I identify and discuss some of the salient questions that have been posed and addressed in the literature, present some stylized models and examples and summarize the main theoretical findings. Furthermore, I describe the available data, review the relevant empirical evidence and discuss some of the challenges for empirical research in political economy. Concluding remarks are contained in Section 6.[6]

2 VOTERS

Voting is a cornerstone of democracy and citizen participation and voting decisions in elections and referenda are fundamental inputs in the political process that shape the policies adopted by democratic societies. Hence, understanding observed patterns of turnout and voting represents a fundamental step in the understanding of democratic institutions. Also, from a theoretical standpoint, voters are the most fundamental component of political economy models. Different assumptions about their behavior are bound to have important consequences on the implications of these models and, more generally, on the equilibrium interpretation of the behavior of politicians, parties and governments they may induce.

These considerations raise the following two fundamental questions: (i) Why do citizens vote (or abstain from voting)? (ii) How do voters vote? In the remainder of this section, I address each of these two questions in turn.

2.1   Turnout

As pointed out in the Introduction, much of what is new in political economy is the application of modern methods of economic theory to problems that have been addressed for a long time. The issue of understanding citizen participation in elections is one of these problems.[7] There is considerable cross-section and time-series variation in turnout both within and across countries, as well as within and across types of elections (e.g., Blais (2000)). By and large, the fractions of eligible voters who participate or abstain in any election at any time in any modern democracy are both significant.[8] Also, participation and abstention rates are in general not uniform in the population of eligible voters, but appear to be correlated with several demographic characteristics, such as,

---

[6] For an extended version of the survey, which also incudes an expanded list of references, see Merlo (2005). For a recent monograph that analyzes the role of special interest groups, a topic I do not cover here, see Grossman and Helpman (2001).

[7] Henceforth, I use the word election to refer to any situation where eligible voters are asked to express their opinion through voting. This also includes referenda.

[8] In general, while various penalties for failing to vote exist in some countries, they tend to be rather minimal, and abstention is a noticeable phenomenon even where voting is compulsory (see, e.g., Blais (2000)).

for example, age, education, gender and race (e.g., Wolfinger and Rosenstone (1980)). Moreover, participation rates tend to increase with the importance of the election.[9] These are some of the most salient observations that emerge from the data.[10]

Can political economy explain these observations? The starting point of theoretical research on voter turnout is represented by the "calculus of voting" framework, originally formulated by Downs (1957) and later developed by Tullock (1967) and Riker and Ordeshook (1968). According to this framework, given a citizenry of size N facing an election e where there are two alternatives (e.g., two candidates or two policy proposals), citizen $i \in N$ votes in the election if $p_i^e B_i^e + D_i^e \geq C_i^e$ and abstains otherwise. Here, p_i^e is the probability that citizen i's vote decides the election (i.e., her vote is pivotal), B_i^e is the indirect benefit to citizen i associated with inducing her desired electoral outcome, D_i^e is the direct benefit from voting in election e, which includes any benefit citizen i may derive from fulfilling her civic duty of voting, and C_i^e is citizen i's cost of voting in election e. The terms $p_i^e B_i^e$ and D_i^e are often referred to as capturing the instrumental (or investment) and expressive (or consumption) value of voting, respectively.

In the original formulation of the model, B_i^e, D_i^e and C_i^e are specified as fundamental components of a citizen's preferences and are therefore treated as primitives. Also, as long as the size of the electorate N is large, p_i^e is typically thought of as being virtually equal to zero, thus making the term $p_i^e B_i^e$ negligible. Hence, to the extent that the unobservable D_i^e and C_i^e are heterogeneous in the citizenry and correlated with observable demographic characteristics, and their distributions (possibly conditional on location and election specific characteristics) differ across citizenries and elections, the model can potentially account for the patterns observed in the data. At the same time, however, since differences in behavior are mechanically induced by differences in preferences (which are both exogenous and unobservable), the model fails to provide a theory that can explain the evidence.

In light of this failure, most of the recent theoretical research on voter turnout has been focused on developing models where p_i^e, D_i^e and C_i^e are endogenous variables, derived in equilibrium from more fundamental primitives. It is useful to divide these models in three groups, depending on whether their main objective is to endogenize p_i^e, D_i^e or C_i^e, respectively. Pivotal-voter models (e.g., Borgers (2004), Ledyard (1984) and Palfrey and Rosenthal (1983, 1985)) endogenize the probability that a citizen's vote is decisive. Ethical-voter models (e.g., Coate and Conlin (2004), Feddersen and Sandroni (2002) and Harsanyi (1980)) endogenize the concept of civic-duty. Uncertain-voter models (e.g.,

[9] For example, turnout is generally higher in national than in local elections and referenda, and in presidential elections than elections for other public offices (see, e.g., Blais (2000)).

[10] Official records of voter participation in elections are available at the aggregate level for most countries. Survey data at the individual level are also available for a limited number of countries, including Australia, Canada, the U.K. and the U.S.

Degan and Merlo (2004), Feddersen and Pesendorfer (1996, 1999) and Matsusaka (1995)) endogenize a component of the cost of voting. For each class of models I present a simple example that illustrates the main intuition, and I discuss their general implications for interpreting the empirical evidence.[11]

Pivotal-voter models: Consider the following example based on Borgers (2004) and Palfrey and Rosenthal (1985). A society has to decide between two alternatives, a and b, in an election e. There are N citizens, where N is large but finite, indexed by $i \in \{1, \ldots, N\}$. The citizenry is divided between supporters of a and supporters of b, where each citizen knows the alternative she supports. Each citizen is either a supporter of a or b with equal probability. This is known by all citizens. However, citizens do not know the number of supporters of each alternative. If alternative $j \in \{a, b\}$ is implemented, each supporter of j receives a utility benefit equal to 1, while each supporter of the other alternative incurs a utility loss equal to -1. Citizens decide whether to vote or abstain. If they choose to vote, they vote in favor of the alternative they support. Voting is costly and citizens do not derive any direct benefit from voting (i.e., $D_i^e = 0$ for all $i \in \{1, \ldots, N\}$). Voting costs are distributed in the citizenry according to a uniform distribution on the support [0, 1]. Each citizen i only knows her own voting cost C_i^e and the distribution of voting costs in the population.

Since the probability p_i^e that citizen i's vote decides the election depends on the endogenous composition of the electorate, this situation describes a game of incomplete information, where the choice of participating is a strategic decision. Given the number of citizens who participate in the election, the alternative $j \in \{a, b\}$ that receives a majority of the votes is implemented. In the event of a tie, each alternative is implemented with probability $1/2$.

In the environment described here, the only motivation for voting is the possibility of affecting the electoral outcome. Since many citizens share the same preferences for one alternative over the other, and the electoral outcome is a public good, individuals may have an incentive to free-ride and abstain. On the other hand, there is an element of competition due to the fact that different groups of citizens prefer different alternatives. The existence of such conflict provides an incentive for people to participate in the election. The combination of these two opposing forces determines the equilibrium turnout and electoral outcome.

Following the literature, we look for a symmetric Bayesian-Nash Equilibrium of the game, in which all citizens use the same cutoff strategy (i.e., each citizen votes only if her voting cost is below some critical level). Let C^* denote the equilibrium cutoff level. To characterize C^*, consider the decision of a generic citizen i and let v be the ex ante probability, before learning C_i^e, with which any individual votes given the equilibrium strategy. Suppose the remaining $N - 1$ citizens are playing according to the equilibrium strategy, and let σ denote the number of individuals other than i who choose to vote.

---

[11] For recent surveys see, e.g., Aldrich (1993), Dhillon and Peralta (2002) and Feddersen (2004).

Note that the distribution of the random variable σ is binomial with parameters $N - 1$ and v, and since in equilibrium $v = \Pr\left\{C_i^e \leq C^*\right\} = C^*$, when the other $N - 1$ citizens are playing according to the equilibrium strategy, for any $s \in \{0, \ldots, 1 - N\}, \Pr\{\sigma = s\} = \binom{N-1}{s}(C^*)^s (1 - C^*)^{N-1-s}$.

Let $p_i^e(C^*)$ be the probability that citizen i's vote is pivotal. Since alternative $j \in \{a, b\}$ is implemented for sure if a majority of the voters supports it and is implemented with probability $1/2$ in the event of a tie, citizen i's vote is pivotal only if either her preferred alternative is behind by one vote or the number of votes for each alternative is equal. In either case, citizen i's vote increases her expected utility by 1. In no other circumstance, will her vote affect the electoral outcome and, consequently, her expected utility. Hence, $p_i^e(C^*)$ is the probability that the number of votes for i's preferred alternative minus the number of votes for the other alternative is either -1 or 0, and i's expected benefit of voting is $p_i^e(C^*) B_i^e = p_i^e(C^*)$. Since citizen i will want to vote only if $p_i^e B_i^e$ exceeds her cost of voting C_i^e, we have that in equilibrium $p_i^e(C^*) = C^*$.

To compute the equilibrium we need to know the function $p_i^e(C^*)$, where we know that $p_i^e(0) = 1$ and $p_i^e(1) = 0$. Let $\pi_i^e(s)$ denote the probability that voter i is pivotal conditional on the number of other voters being s. Note that $\pi_i^e(0) = 1$ and $\pi_i^e(1) = 1/2$. In general, if $s \geq 1$ and s is odd, then citizen i's vote is pivotal only if the number of other votes for her preferred alternative is $(s - 1)/2$ and the number of votes for the other alternative is $(s + 1)/2$. This event occurs with probability $\pi_i^e(s) = \binom{s}{(s-1)/2}(1/2)^s$, which is non-increasing in s. Since $p_i^e(C^*) = \sum_{s=0}^{N-1} \Pr\{\sigma = s\}\pi_i^e(s)$, it follows that $p_i^e(C^*)$ is strictly decreasing in C^*. Hence, there exists a unique $C^* \in (0, 1)$ such that $p_i^e(C^*) = C^*$.

While a closed form expression for C^* as a function of N cannot be derived, C^* can easily be computed numerically for different values of N. For example, for N equal to 100, 500 and 5000, these calculations yield values of C^* equal to $0.18, 0.11$ and 0.05, respectively, and as $N \to \infty$, $C^* \to 0$. Hence, positive turnout occurs in equilibrium. However, as the size of the electorate becomes large, turnout decreases and in the limit everybody abstains.

While these results were obtained in the context of a very specific example, they extend to more general environments and are typical of pivotal-voter models. Hence, pivotal-voter models can in principle explain positive levels of participation in elections, but only when the number of eligible voters is relatively small. For large electorates, on the other hand, extending the calculus of voting framework by making p_i^e endogenous in a game-theoretic environment fails to provide a theory that can explain the empirical observations.

Empirical research has attempted to establish whether, holding everything else constant, voter turnout increases with the expected closeness of an election, which relates to the probability of being pivotal.[12] By and large, evidence based on individual-level data shows that this is not the case in large elections (e.g., Ferejohn and Fiorina (1975), Kirchgaessner and Schulz (2005) and Matsusaka

---

[12] See, e.g., Matsusaka and Palda (1999) for a survey.

and Palda (1993)). Regardless of whether or not one believes that this is a robust empirical finding, however, this is hardly a "test" of pivotal-voter models. Coate, Conlin and Moro (2004), on the other hand, directly address the question of whether this class of models can explain voter participation in small-scale elections. Their analysis, which is based on the structural estimation of a pivotal-voter model using data on local referenda in Texas, shows that while the model is capable of predicting observed levels of turnout quite well, at the same time it predicts closer electoral outcomes than they are in the data. In other words, the only way the theory behind pivotal-voter models can explain actual turnout, is if elections are very close, which makes their outcome very uncertain and hence individual votes more likely to be pivotal. These circumstances, however, are not consistent with what is observed in reality, thus leading to a rejection of this class of models as useful tools to interpret the evidence.

Ethical-voter models: Consider the following example based on Coate and Conlin (2004). For consistency of exposition, I use a formulation similar to that of the previous example. A society has to decide between two alternatives, a and b, in an election e. There is a continuum of citizens of measure one, where i denotes a generic citizen. The citizenry is divided between supporters of a and supporters of b, where each citizen knows the alternative she supports but does not know the actual fraction of supporters of each alternative in the population. From the point of view of a generic citizen i, the fraction of citizens who support alternative a is the realization of a random variable μ, which has a uniform distribution on the support $[0, 1]$. Hence, the expected fraction of citizens supporting each alternative is equal to $1/2$. If alternative $j \in \{a, b\}$ is implemented, each supporter of j receives a utility benefit equal to 1, while each supporter of the other alternative incurs a utility loss equal to -1.

Citizens have to decide whether to vote or abstain. If they choose to vote, they vote in favor of the alternative they support. Voting is costly and voting costs are distributed in the citizenry according to a uniform distribution on the support $[0, 1]$. Each citizen i only knows her own voting cost C_i^e and the distribution of voting costs in the population. The electoral outcome is determined by majority rule, where alternative a is implemented if the fraction of votes in favor of a exceeds the fraction of votes in favor of b.[13]

Citizens are ethical, in the sense that they are "group rule-utilitarians," where a group is defined by which alternative a citizen prefers. More precisely, individuals follow the voting rule that, if followed by everybody else in their group, would maximize their group's aggregate utility. Hence, each group's optimal voting rule specifies a critical voting cost, such that all individuals in the group whose voting cost is below the critical level should vote.

Let C_a and C_b denote the critical voting costs for the supporters of a and b, respectively. If citizen i is a supporter of alternative $j \in \{a, b\}$, she votes if $C_i^e < C_j$ and abstains otherwise. Hence, the ex ante probability, before learning

---

[13] Since there is a continuum of voters, ties are a measure zero event and can therefore be ignored.

C_i^e, that a generic supporter of alternative j votes is $\Pr\left\{C_i^e < C_j\right\} = C_j$ and her expected voting cost is equal to $C_j^2/2$. Alternative a is therefore implemented if $\mu C_a > (1 - \mu) C_b$, or equivalently $\mu > C_b/(C_a + C_b)$.

In the environment described here, since there is a continuum of voters, no single vote can ever be pivotal (i.e., $p_i^e B_i^e = 0$ for all i). Hence, the only motivation for voting is to fulfill one's civic duty to "do the right thing." The contribution of ethical-voter models is to make this notion precise and characterize equilibrium voter turnout in game-theoretic environments where citizens are rule-utilitarians.[14] In particular, the key innovation of this class of models is to assume that each citizen has an action (i.e., either to participate or to abstain) that is optimal for her to take on ethical grounds, and receives an additional payoff from taking this action. Moreover, what is the ethical thing to do for each citizen is not predetermined, but is instead endogenously derived as an equilibrium outcome of a game.

In the context of the example, an equilibrium is given by a pair of critical costs, C_a^* and C_b^* such that, for each $j, j' = a, b$, $j' \neq j$, C_j^* maximizes the aggregate expected utility of the group of supporters of alternative j given $C_{j'}^*$. To characterize the equilibrium, note that the aggregate expected utility of the group of citizens who support alternative a is given by $U_a(C_a, C_b) = 1/2 - [C_b/(C_a + C_b)]^2 - C_a^2/4$. Similarly, the aggregate expected utility of the group of citizens who support alternative b is given by $U_b(C_a, C_b) = 2C_b/(C_a + C_b) - 1/2 - [C_b/(C_a + C_b)]^2 - C_b^2/4$. It follows that there exists a unique pair of interior equilibrium levels of voting costs $C_a^* = C_b^* = C^* = \sqrt{2}/2 = 0.71$, such that each citizen votes if her voting cost is below C^* and abstains otherwise. Hence, while a significant fraction of the population of eligible voters abstains in equilibrium, voter turnout may be substantial.

The main logic illustrated in the simple example also holds in more general environments, where different specifications of the benefits citizens derive from various alternatives, the distribution of the fraction of citizens who support them and the distribution of voting costs in the population generate interesting additional predictions. For instance, if in the example we replace the assumption that the fraction μ of citizens who support alternative a has a uniform distribution, with the alternative assumption that the density function of μ is equal to 2μ (which implies that the expected fraction of citizens supporting alternative a is equal to 2/3 instead of 1/2), we obtain that the equilibrium critical costs are $C_a^* = 0.68$ and $C_b^* = 0.85$. Hence, equilibrium turnout is higher among the "minority" (i.e., the group with the smaller expected number of supporters).

These considerations suggest that ethical-voter models provide a promising framework to confront the empirical evidence. Not only do they provide a theory that can explain observed patterns of voter turnout, but they also place additional restrictions on the data that make the theory falsifiable (from a Popperian

---

[14] For a general discussion of rule-utilitarianism, see Feddersen and Sandroni (2002) and Harsanyi (1980).

perspective). An excellent example of using this theory as a way to impose discipline on an empirical investigation of voter turnout in local referenda is the article by Coate and Conlin (2004), who specify a group rule-utilitarian model and structurally estimate it using data on local liquor referenda in Texas. Their analysis shows that the estimated model is capable of reproducing all of the important features of the data well and generates interesting implications for the interpretation of the evidence.

Uncertain-voter models: Consider the following example based on Degan and Merlo (2004). As in the two previous examples, a society has to decide between two alternatives, a and b, in an election e. To simplify exposition, it is convenient to formulate this example in a spatial context, where alternatives correspond to positions on a unidimensional ideological space (e.g., the liberal-conservative ideological spectrum), $[-1, 1]$. In particular, alternatives a and b are a pair of random variables that take values $(y_a, y_b) \in Y = Y_a \times Y_b$, where $Y_a = \{-1/2, -1/4, 0\}$ and $Y_b = \{0, 1/4, 1/2\}$. The joint distribution of (a, b), $P = \{p(y_a, y_b)\}_{(y_a, y_b) \in Y}$, is such that $p(0, 0) = 0$ and $p(y_a, y_b) = 1/8$ for all $(y_a, y_b) \neq (0, 0)$.

There is a continuum of citizens of measure one, where i denotes a generic citizen. Each citizen has a preferred ideology, or ideal point, $y_i \in [-1, 1]$, and evaluates alternative ideologies $y \in [-1, 1]$ according to the payoff function $u_i(y) = -(y_i - y)^2$. The distribution of preferred ideologies in the citizenry is uniform on the support $[-1, 1]$.

Citizens have to decide whether to vote or abstain, and if they vote, which alternative to support. Each citizen i derives a direct benefit from voting by fulfilling her civic duty, D_i^e. These benefits are distributed in the citizenry according to a uniform distribution on the support $[0, 1]$. Citizens do not know the realization (y_a, y_b) of the pair of alternatives (a, b), but only know the distribution P. Clearly, because citizens are uncertain about the alternatives in the election, they may make "voting mistakes" or, equivalently, vote for the "wrong alternative." This is what makes voting potentially costly in this framework.

Let $C_i(a) = \sum_{(y_a, y_b) \in Y} 1\{u_i(y_a) < u_i(y_b)\}[(u_i(y_b) - u_i(y_a))p(y_a, y_b)]$ be the (expected) cost for citizen i of voting for alternative a, where $1\{\cdot\}$ is an indicator function that takes the value one if the expression within braces is true and zero otherwise. This cost corresponds to the expected utility loss for citizen i if she were to vote for candidate a in states of the world where the realizations (y_a, y_b) are such that she should instead vote for b. Analogously, $C_i(b)$ is the (expected) cost for citizen i of voting for alternative b.

Like in the previous example, since in the environment described here there is a continuum of voters, no single vote can ever be pivotal (i.e., $p_i^e B_i^e = 0$ for all i).[15] Hence, the only trade-off that is relevant in a citizen's decision to participate in an election is the comparison of the costs and benefits of voting. In

---

[15] In other uncertain-voter models, e.g., Feddersen and Pesendorfer (1996, 1999), voters may be pivotal. However, my primary objective here is to isolate the distinctive characteristic of each class of models.

uncertain-voter models, the emphasis is on deriving the cost of voting endogenously. In particular, voting may be costly because of citizens' uncertainty (or lack of information) about the alternatives they are facing in an election, which may lead them to make mistakes they may regret. The extent to which voting is costly for different citizens, and hence their propensity to participate in elections, will in general depend on their ideological preferences relative to the distribution of the possible alternatives they may be facing, as well as the their degree of uncertainty.

Following Degan and Merlo (2004), the decision problem of each citizen can be formulated as a two-stage optimization problem, where in the first stage the citizen decides whether or not to participate in the election and, in the second stage, she decides who to vote for (conditional on voting). To solve this problem we work backwards, starting from the last stage. In the second stage, citizen i's optimal voting rule is $v_i^*(y_i) = a$ if $C_i(b) > C_i(a)$, $v_i^*(y_i) = b$ if $C_i(b) < C_i(a)$, and in the event that $C_i(b) = C_i(a)$ citizen i randomizes between the two alternatives with equal probability. Here, $v_i^*(\cdot) = j$ indicates that if citizen i were to vote, she would vote for alternative $j \in \{a, b\}$. Using the expressions for $C_i(a)$ and $C_i(b)$, and the definition of Y and P, we obtain that $C_i(b) - C_i(a) = -9y_i/8$, which implies that $C_i(b) < C_i(a)$ if and only if $y_i > 0$. Hence, $v_i^*(y_i) = a$ if $y_i < 0$, $v_i^*(y_i) = b$ if $y_i > 0$, and citizens with ideal points equal to zero randomize.

This voting rule implies a cost for citizen i of participating in election e, $C_i^e(y_i) = C_i\left(v_i^*(y_i)\right)$. Hence, in the first stage, citizen i's optimal participation rule is such that she participates if $C_i^e(\cdot) < D_i^e$ and abstains otherwise. To calculate the voting costs, note that for each possible realization (y_a, y_b) of (a, b), given the optimal voting rules of all citizens, we can determine if a citizen would be making a mistake or not if she were to vote, and calculate the cost associated with the mistake. If $(y_a, y_b) = (-1/2, 0)$, the cost is positive only for citizens with $-1/4 < y_i < 0$, and is equal to $1/4 + y_i$; if $(y_a, y_b) = (-1/2, 1/4)$, it is positive only for citizens with $-1/8 < y_i < 0$, and is equal to $3/16 + (3/2)y_i$; if $(y_a, y_b) = (-1/4, 0)$, it is positive only for citizens with $-1/8 < y_i < 0$, and is equal to $1/16 + y_i/2$. In all these cases, some citizens would vote for a but should instead vote for b. The cost calculations for the remaining four possible realizations of (a, b) are the same except that they apply to citizens with positive ideal points (who could sometimes be making mistakes by voting for b when they should instead vote for a). Hence, we obtain that if $y_i \in [-1, -1/4] \cup [1/4, 1]$, $C_i^e(y_i) = 0$; if $y_i \in (-1/4, -1/8) \cup (1/8, 1/4)$, $C_i^e(y_i) = (1 - 4|y_i|)/32$; and if $y_i \in [-1/8, 1/8]$, $C_i^e(y_i) = (1 - 6|y_i|)/16$. Since citizens participate in the election if $C_i^e(\cdot) < D_i^e$ and abstain otherwise, we have that while citizens with relatively extreme ideal points always participate, all other groups of citizens abstain to various degrees. In particular, the more "moderate" a citizen, the higher the probability she will abstain.

Once again the results derived in this simple example generalize to more complicated environments, and uncertain-voter models offer a valid alternative to ethical-voter models as useful tools for interpreting the empirical evidence. In fact, the class of uncertain-voter models provides theoretical explanations for much of the evidence on voter turnout, relates it to fundamentals, such as information and ideology, and places additional restrictions on the data that can be used to validate the models. Degan and Merlo (2004), for example, propose an uncertain-voter model to explain observed patterns of turnout and voting in U.S. presidential and congressional elections. They structurally estimate the model using individual-level data for the 2000 elections and use the estimated model to evaluate the effects of counterfactual experiments on electoral outcomes. Their analysis implies a relationship between information and turnout (since uninformed citizens are more likely to make "voting mistakes" and hence have larger expected costs of voting, they abstain more than informed citizens), which can be quantified and related to demographic characteristics. It also provides an explanation for the fact that, in every presidential election year, we always observe more abstention in congressional elections than in the presidential election. Their estimates imply that the average cost of voting in the presidential election is always smaller than in a congressional election, due to the fact that, in general, there is more information, and hence less uncertainty, about presidential candidates than congressional candidates.

2.2   Voting

The second fundamental issue I address in this section has to do with the way voters vote. In particular, I am interested in the way the political economy literature has addressed the question of whether citizens vote "sincerely" or "strategically." In order to even understand this question, we have to start by defining what sincere and strategic behavior mean in the context of voting. Consider a situation where a society of size N is facing an election e where there are $M \geq 2$ alternatives and each citizen $i = 1, \ldots, N$ has a strict preference ranking of these alternatives. Putting aside the issue of abstention (e.g., think of a situation where $D_i^e > C_i^e$ for all $i \in \{1, \ldots, N\}$), citizens vote sincerely if they cast their vote in favor of the alternative they most prefer, independently of what other citizens do. They vote strategically if their voting decision is a best-response to what other citizens do.

Clearly, the notion of strategic voting is intimately related to the endogenous probability that a vote is decisive, and the characterization of the equilibria of a voting game depends on the voting rule that is used to determine the outcome of the election and on the equilibrium concept that is chosen to solve the game. Both of these aspects have been extensively addressed in the literature, and I will not discuss them here.[16] Instead, I will briefly discuss the restrictions that sincere and strategic voting place on the data and their implications for interpreting the empirical evidence.

---

[16] See, e.g., Austen-Smith and Banks (2005) and the references therein.

In the context of the situation described above, if we consider a single, isolated election where there are only two alternatives, sincere and strategic voting are equivalent, since voting sincerely is the unique undominated decision for each citizen. In other words, since sincere and strategic voting induce the same voting profiles, and hence the same outcomes, they are observationally equivalent. This implies that there are no restrictions coming from the theory that allow a researcher to use only data on how voters vote in a single election where there are only two alternatives to discriminate among alternative models. In such context, identification must rely on additional data. Also, the issue of model validation should not be addressed solely on the basis of within-sample fit, but should also rely on the comparison of the relative out-of-sample performance of alternative models.

The equivalence between sincere and strategic voting, however, breaks down as soon as there are more than two alternatives. In fact, this is in general true even when we consider elections with only two alternatives but where either the same election is repeated through time (e.g., presidential elections in the U.S.), or there are multiple simultaneous elections that are interrelated (e.g., presidential and congressional elections in the U.S.). In all of these situations, strategic considerations are likely to induce voters to vote differently than what would be predicted by sincere behavior, and may lead to different electoral outcomes. In principle, different theories may therefore impose different restrictions on the data, which can then be used to provide discipline in assessing the empirical relevance of various models.

By and large, however, strategic-voting models have multiple equilibria, and their predictions often differ (sometimes dramatically) across equilibria. In fact, the set of Nash equilibria of a voting game may include virtually all possible voting profiles and electoral outcomes. The multiplicity is more severe the larger the size of the electorate and is a common feature of large voting games regardless of the solution concept that is used. Moreover, as already pointed out with respect to the issue of abstention, the probability that a voter is pivotal becomes minuscule in large electorates, thus making strategic calculations less relevant. These considerations impose serious challenges on the use of strategic-voting models to explain the empirical evidence and severely limit the possibility of taking them to the data. Sincere-voting models, on the other hand, are typically very tractable and tend to generate sharp predictions that can be compared with the data. In order to evaluate the limitations of sincere-voting models, it seems therefore useful to try to assess the extent to which sincere-voting models may fail to explain certain aspects of the data.

To address this issue, I present here a simple calculation, related to the work by Degan and Merlo (2006), aimed at empirically assessing the extent to which sincere voting can account for observed patterns of voting in an environment where strategic voting is typically thought of as being necessary to explain the evidence. Consider the situation faced by U.S. voters in a presidential election year, where presidential and congressional elections occur simultaneously. A prominent feature that emerges from the data is that often people vote a "split ticket" (i.e., they vote for candidates of different parties for President and for

Congress). In particular, in the eight presidential election years between 1972 and 2000, the percentage of voters who split their ticket varies between 16% in 2000 and 27% in 1980.[17]

The sizeable presence of split-ticket voting in the data has been interpreted by many as direct evidence of strategic voting, and has lead to the development of strategic-voting models that can explain some of the aggregate stylized facts (e.g., Alesina and Rosenthal (1995, 1996) and Chari, Jones and Marimon (1997)). However, before embracing the notion that in order to explain split-ticket voting one needs to resort to strategic voting, it is useful to ask whether this observed phenomenon can also be explained as the natural outcome of the aggregation of individual decisions of citizens with heterogeneous ideological preferences. In other words, to what extent can sincere voting account for split-ticket voting? To answer this question, note that while the presidential election is nationwide (i.e., all citizens face the same set of candidates regardless of where they reside), congressional elections are held at the district level (i.e., citizens residing in different congressional districts face different sets of candidates).[18] Suppose that the positions of all candidates can be represented as points in the unidimensional ideological space $[-1, 1]$, and that citizens have single-peaked (Euclidean) preferences over this space, with the peaks representing their ideal points. Hence, it is, in principle, possible that candidates' positions are such that some voters in some districts have ideal points that are closer to the candidate representing one party in one election and at the same time to the candidate representing the other party in the other election. Some citizens may therefore sincerely vote for the Republican candidate for President and the Democratic candidate for Congress or vice versa.

This argument is illustrated in Figure 10.1 for arbitrary candidates' positions in two hypothetical districts, where D_H (R_H) and D_P (R_P) are the positions of the Democratic (Republican) candidate running for a House seat and the Presidency, respectively, and DD, DR, RD and RR are the possible voting profiles (where the first element refers to the vote in the presidential election and the second to the vote in the congressional election). Note that for any configuration of candidates' positions in a district, sincere voting is consistent with only three of the four possible voting profiles (except for a measure zero event where the voters are indifferent between two profiles). Hence, sincere voting can fail to account for some (and possibly all) of the instances of split-ticket voting observed in the data.

To perform this calculation I use two sources of data: the American National Election Studies (NES) and the Poole and Rosenthal NOMINATE Common Space Scores. For each presidential election year, in addition to the individual

---

[17] The data comes from the American National Election Studies, which contain individual-level information on how people vote in presidential and congressional elections for a representative (cross-section) sample of the American voting-age population.

[18] Consistent with the existing literature on split-ticket voting, I restrict attention to House elections, which are held every election year for every district. Hence, each citizen faces both a presidential election as well as a House election. Senate elections, on the other hand, are staggered and only about a third of all states have a Senate election in any given election year.

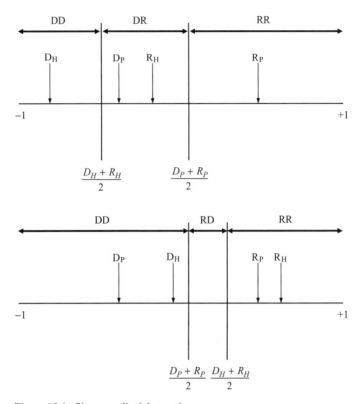

Figure 10.1. Sincere split-ticket voting

voting decisions in presidential and congressional elections of a representative sample of the voting age population, the NES contains information on the congressional district where each individual resides, the identity of the Democratic and the Republican candidate competing for election in his or her congressional district and whether any of the candidates is an incumbent in that district. Using data on roll call voting by each member of Congress and support of roll call votes by each President, Poole and Rosenthal (1997) developed a methodology to estimate the positions of all politicians who ever served either as Presidents or members of Congress on the liberal-conservative ideological space $[-1, 1]$. These estimates, called NOMINATE scores, are comparable across politicians and across time.

Given the two data sets, I match each voter in the NES sample for each presidential election year with the positions of the candidates running in his or her congressional district that year. If one of the two candidates is an incumbent, I assume that his position is known and given by his NOMINATE score. For challengers, on the other hand, I assume that their positions are not known, but are drawn from populations of potential candidates whose distributions are known and given by the empirical distributions of the NOMINATE scores for

Democratic and Republican members of Congress. I allow these distributions to differ across U.S. regions. In addition, in each presidential election all voters face the same set of candidates, and I assume that their positions are known and given by their NOMINATE scores. For each presidential election year between 1972 and 2000, I then calculate whether the observed voting profile of each voter is consistent with sincere voting. Since straight-ticket voting is always consistent with sincere voting, I only need to calculate the fraction of split-ticket voting that can be explained by sincere voting.

The results of this calculation indicate that sincere voting can explain nearly all of the individual-level observations. In particular, in six of the eight presidential election years considered, sincere voting can account for over 95% of split-ticket voting. Its worst "failures" are the inability of accounting for 2% and 3% of the observations (i.e., 9% of the 27% and 20% of the 17% of voters who split their ticket), in 1980 and 1996, respectively. As "errors" of this magnitude are within the margin of tolerance when one allows for sampling (or measurement) error, I conclude that a compelling case cannot be made on empirical grounds to dismiss a sincere-voting interpretation of split-ticket voting in favor of more complicated explanations that rely on strategic voting.

More generally, I believe that strategic-voting models provide a coherent analytical framework to understand the potential effects of strategic interactions among citizens in a political economy, and their importance should not be evaluated solely on the basis of their empirical performance. On the other hand, sincere-voting models, while perhaps less sophisticated, often provide a useful theoretical guide to analyze the data and interpret the evidence, and their empirical performance should be assessed first, before resorting to more sophisticated, but often less tractable, models.

3 POLITICIANS

The very existence and functioning of representative democracy, where citizens delegate policy-making to elected representatives, hinges on the presence of politicians. In his famous 1918 lecture entitled *Politics as a Vocation*, Max Weber writes:

> Politics, just as economic pursuits, may be a man's avocation or his vocation. [...] There are two ways of making politics one's vocation: Either one lives 'for' politics or one lives 'off' politics. [...] He who lives 'for' politics makes politics his life, in an internal sense. Either he enjoys the naked possession of the power he exerts, or he nourishes his inner balance and self-feeling by the consciousness that his life has meaning in the service of a 'cause.' [...] He who strives to make politics a permanent source of income lives 'off' politics as a vocation. [from Gerth and Mills (1946, pp. 83–84)]

The view expressed by Weber is indicative of the way in which early research in political economy approached the study of politicians. By taking the existence of politicians as given (i.e., by treating them as a primitive), the main objective of this literature has been for a long time that of addressing the following question: What are the motivations of politicians?

Starting with Downs (1957), a long tradition in political economy builds on the assumption that the main objective of politicians is to win an election. Within this framework, known as the "downsian" paradigm, (office-concerned) opportunistic candidates shape their policy platforms to please the (policy-concerned) electorate, so as to maximize their probability of winning and collect the rents of public office. Several authors have challenged this view by proposing alternative theories where politicians are assumed to be policy-motivated (e.g., Alesina (1988), Hibbs (1977) and Wittman (1977, 1983)). Within this framework, known as the "partisan" paradigm, candidates choose their policy platforms by trading-off their policy preferences with their desire to win the election in order to affect policy outcomes.[19]

A major turning point in the literature occurred when researchers started to challenge the basic assumption that the set of political candidates competing for public office is exogenous. This challenge defines most of the current political economy research on this topic and has generated an alternative approach to the study of politicians known as the "citizen-candidate" paradigm (e.g., Besley and Coate (1997) and Osborne and Slivinski (1996)). This framework removes the artificial distinction between citizens and politicians prevalent in the other approaches by recognizing that elected officials are selected by the citizenry from those citizens who choose to become politicians and run for election in the first place. By doing so, this approach makes the question of what are the motivations of politicians moot. Since politicians are citizens, their preferences can no longer be specified in an ad hoc fashion separately from the specification of the preferences of voters. In other words, the preferences of elected politicians must be represented in the citizenry. At the same time, the citizen-candidate framework poses two new important questions: (i) Who chooses to become a politician? (ii) What are the returns to an individual from becoming a politician?

In light of these considerations, in the remainder of this section I first illustrate the logic of the citizen-candidate approach by presenting a simple example and discussing the implications of different assumptions about voters' behavior. I then address the empirical question of what are the returns to an individual from being a politician.[20]

3.1   The Citizen-Candidate Framework

Consider the following example based on Besley and Coate (1997) and Osborne and Slivinski (1996). A society has to elect a representative to implement a policy y in the unidimensional policy space $Y = [-1, 1]$. There is a large, finite

---

[19] For a description of the two paradigms see, e.g., chapters 3 and 5 in Persson and Tabellini (2000).

[20] Another important line of research, which is not considered here, concerns the behavior of elected politicians and the extent to which voters can discipline them. See, e.g., Besley (2005) for a survey.

number of citizens indexed by $i \in \{1, \ldots, N\}$, which, for expositional convenience, can be approximated by a continuum of measure one.[21] Citizens evaluate
alternative policies $y \in [-1, 1]$ and monetary payoffs $z \in \mathbb{R}$ according to the
indirect utility function $U_i(y, z) = u_i(y) + z$, where $u_i(y) = -(y_i - y)^2$ and
$y_i \in [-1, 1]$ denotes citizen i's most preferred policy. The distribution of ideal
points in the citizenry, which is common knowledge, is uniform on the support
$[-1, 1]$.

Citizens decide whether to become candidates in the election. Running for
public office entails a cost $C \in (0, 1/6]$. After all citizens have made their
entry decision, the ideal point of each candidate is observed by all citizens.
Since candidates cannot commit in advance to a policy, a candidate's ideal
point represents the policy he would implement if elected. Given the set of
candidates, all citizens vote for one of them. The candidate who wins a plurality
of the votes is elected and implements his most preferred policy. In addition,
the elected politician receives a payoff $B \in [2C/3, 2C)$, which represents the
rents from holding public office. In the event of a tie, a random draw among
the tying candidates selects the winner. If nobody runs as a candidate, every
citizen gets a utility of -1. If a generic citizen i chooses to run for election,
his payoff is equal to $B - C$ if he is elected and $-(y_i - y_j)^2 - C$ if another
citizen j is elected. If, on the other hand, he chooses not to run, his payoff is
equal to $-(y_i - y_j)^2$ if a citizen j is elected, or -1 in the event that no citizen
runs for election.

I distinguish between two cases that correspond to two alternative assumptions about the behavior of voters. In the first case, citizens are assumed to
vote sincerely (i.e., each citizen votes for his most preferred candidate, and if
there are k candidates all with the same ideal point y, each of these candidates
receives a fraction $1/k$ of the votes of all citizens whose ideal points are closer
to y than to the ideal points of any other candidate). In the second case, citizens
vote strategically (i.e., each citizen's voting strategy is a best-response to the
voting strategies of all other citizens, and no citizen uses weakly dominated
voting strategies).[22]

While the model admits equilibria with different number of candidates, I
focus on equilibria where only two citizens run for election.[23] Before considering the characterization of two-candidate equilibria in each of the two cases,
recall that sincere and strategic voting are equivalent when there are only two
alternatives. This implies that in all equilibria with two candidates, each citizen
votes for his most preferred candidate (regardless of whether out of equilibrium
voters vote sincerely or strategically). Since running for election is costly, it is

---

[21] In particular, the probability that each vote is pivotal is not zero, although potentially very small.

[22] The first case is considered by Osborne and Slivinski (1996), the second by Besley and Coate
(1997).

[23] In this example, there are also equilibria where only one candidate runs unopposed. Equilibria
with more than two candidates do not exist here, although they are possible in more general
formulations.

also true that in any equilibrium no citizen ever runs unless either he has a
positive probability of winning, or he affects the electoral outcome by running
(regardless of the number of equilibrium candidates). The combination of these
two results implies that in all two-candidate equilibria, each candidate must
win with equal probability and, therefore, the ideal points of the citizens who
run as candidates must be symmetric around the median of the distribution of
ideal points in the citizenry, 0. It follows that, in all two-candidate equilibria,
the ideal points of candidates, and hence the two possible policy outcomes, are
described by a vector $(-y^*, y^*)$. Also, any difference in the properties of two-
candidate equilibria between the model with sincere voting and the one with
strategic voting arises from differences in the out-of-equilibrium behavior of
voters. In particular, in order to characterize two-candidate equilibria we must
consider the deviation where a third citizen may decide to run as candidate, and
the voters' response to this deviation is different in the two cases.

Sincere voting: The set of two-candidate equilibria is such that $y^* \in$
$[\sqrt{(2C - B/4)}, 2/3)$. To see that this is the case, note that the lower bound
on y^* is given by the fact that each candidate must find it optimal to run and win
with probability $1/2$, rather than let their opponent run uncontested and win for
sure. Since running is costly, for a citizen to run it must be that the ideal point
of the other citizen running is far enough from his own ideal point. Otherwise,
he may prefer to delegate the policy choice to his opponent. If a citizen with
ideal point y^* runs against a citizen with ideal point $-y^*$, his payoff is equal to
$-2y^{*2} + B/2 - C$, while if he does not run and lets his opponent win, his payoff
is equal to $-4y^{*2}$. Hence, in equilibrium, it must be that $y^* \geq \sqrt{(2C - B)/4}$.

The upper bound on y^* derives from the fact that in all two-candidate equilibria each candidate must win with positive probability (in fact, with probability
$1/2$). This requires that the ideal points of the two candidates cannot be too far
apart from each other. Otherwise, a citizen with the median ideal point would
find it profitable to run and win the election for sure. In fact, if a citizen with
ideal point equal to 0 enters and wins, his payoff is equal to $B - C$. If, on the
other hand, he does not run against the pair of candidates with ideal points
$(-y^*, y^*)$, his payoff is equal to $-y^{*2}$. Hence, since $y^* \geq \sqrt{(2C - B)/4}$, and
$B \in [2C/3, 2C)$, it is always true that $-y^{*2} \leq B - C$, which implies that the
citizen with median ideal point would always want to run if he could be sure of
victory. However, if he were a sure loser, it would never be profitable for him
to run (since he would not affect the policy outcome and would have to pay the
cost of running).[24]

Hence, the upper bound on y^* is derived by finding the value $\bar{y}$ such that a
candidate with ideal point equal to 0 would receive $1/3$ of the votes if he were
to run against a pair of candidates with ideal points $(-\bar{y}, \bar{y})$. Since the density

[24] Note that it is also true that no other citizen with ideal point between $-y^*$ and y^* would want
to run as a sure loser. In fact, if his ideal point is closer to y^* $(-y^*)$, his decision to run would
induce the policy outcome $-y^*$ (y^*), which is always worse for him than the lottery between $-y^*$
and y^*.

of ideal points in the citizenry is uniform on the support $[-1, 1]$, this condition implies that $\overline{y} = 2/3$. Finally, note that if a citizen with ideal point equal to 0 were to run against a pair of candidates with ideal points $(-2/3, 2/3)$, the outcome of the election would be a three-way tie. Since the citizen would find it profitable to run, it follows that $y^* < 2/3$.[25]

Strategic voting: The set of two-candidate equilibria is such that $y^* \in [\sqrt{(2C - B)/4}, 1]$. The lower bound on y^* is obtained from the same argument that was used above, which does not depend on how citizens vote. In order to explain why, if citizens vote strategically, it is also an equilibrium for two citizens with ideal points $(-y^*, y^*)$ such that $y^* \in [\overline{y}, 1]$ to run, consider the following argument. Suppose that $y^* = \overline{y}$, and consider the possible deviation where a citizen with ideal point equal to 0 decides to run as a candidate. Would enough citizens strategically vote for the new candidate to make it profitable for him to run? Not necessarily. In fact, recall that with only two candidates the voting population splits their vote 50/50 between the two candidates with ideal points $(-\overline{y}, \overline{y})$, and each voter votes for the candidate he most prefers. Then, if no citizen uses weakly dominated voting strategies, it is a Nash equilibrium for the voters to continue to split their vote 50/50 between the two candidates with ideal points $(-\overline{y}, \overline{y})$. In this equilibrium, the candidate with ideal point 0 does not receive any vote and hence chooses not to run, thus supporting the two-candidate equilibrium where $y^* = \overline{y}$. To see that this is the case, note that it is a weakly dominated strategy for any citizen whose ideal point is closer to 0 than to either $-\overline{y}$ or $\overline{y}$ to switch his vote and vote for the candidate with ideal point 0 instead (which is what sincere voting would prescribe). By doing so, since the ideal point of such voter switching must be between $-\overline{y}$ and $\overline{y}$, the voter would change the electoral outcome against the candidate he was supporting before the switch, and would therefore be worse off.[26] Clearly, no citizen with ideal point outside the interval $(-\overline{y}, \overline{y})$ would want to switch his vote either. Similar arguments also apply for all $y^* \in [\overline{y}, 1]$.

While citizens with relatively extreme ideal points cannot be elected (and therefore never run), if citizens vote sincerely, a situation where two candidates whose policy preferences are at the opposite ends of the spectrum compete for election may be an equilibrium if citizens vote strategically. The set of two-candidate equilibria under sincere and strategic voting, however, also share some common features. In particular, to the extent that running for office is costly, no two candidates will share the same ideal point, and the higher the cost relative to the benefit the larger the minimum distance between the two candidates.

The simple parametric example considered here illustrates some of the appealing features of the citizen-candidate framework. By treating electoral

---

[25] Note that the payoff from running is equal to $B/3 - C - 8/27$, which, for all $C \in (0, 1/6]$ and $B \in [2C/3, 2C)$, is always larger than the payoff from staying out, $-4/9$.

[26] The "weak" qualifier derives from the fact that all citizens with ideal point equal to 0 are indifferent between $-\overline{y}$ and $\overline{y}$ and would therefore remain indifferent after breaking the tie.

candidates as endogenous equilibrium objects, citizen-candidate models provide useful theoretical foundations for addressing the question of who becomes a politician. In particular, the "type" of citizens who choose to run for public office in equilibrium, and hence the characteristics of elected representatives, are a function of the relative costs and benefits of becoming a politician, as well as the preferences of the citizenry. While in the original specification proposed by Besley and Coate (1997) and Osborne and Slivinski (1996) citizens only differ with respect to their policy preferences, the basic structure can also be extended to richer environments that encompass additional dimensions of heterogeneity (e.g., Caselli and Morelli (2004) and Messner and Polborn (2004)). More generally, the citizen-candidate framework represents a useful analytical tool that is both flexible and tractable and can be generalized to address a number of interesting issues in political economy.[27]

3.2   Private Returns to Political Experience

The previous discussion highlighted the importance of the relative costs and benefits of electoral success to analyze the incentives of politicians. The benefits of public office include both instantaneous payoffs, which are realized upon electoral success, as well as future payoffs, which accrue over time and depend on current and future decisions. Also, these payoffs have a monetary, observable component (e.g., the salary while in office or future wages in other occupations), and a non-pecuniary, unobservable component (e.g., the benefit from participating in the policy-making process and possibly affecting policy outcomes).

In order to focus attention on the dynamic aspects of the career decisions of politicians, consider the situation faced by an elected representative in his first term in office. At the risk of oversimplifying, consider a simple example where the horizon of the dynamic decision problem is two periods. In the first period, the politician has to decide whether to run for reelection. In the second and last period, if he is still in office, in addition to rerunning for his office the politician has also the opportunity of running for a higher office. If the politician leaves politics (either voluntarily or via electoral defeat), he works in the private sector.

The political office currently occupied by the politician pays a per-period salary S and generates a per-period benefit B. Moreover, if the politician is successful in implementing his most preferred policy, he receives an additional benefit P. Similarly, the payoffs in the higher office are $S' > S$, $B' > B$ and $P' > P$. The cost of running for election, C, is normalized to zero. Private sector wages increase with political experience. Let $e \in \{1, 2\}$ denote an individual's political experience (i.e., the number of periods he

---

[27] These issues include lobbying (e.g., Besley and Coate (2001) and Felli and Merlo (2004)), parties (e.g., Levy (2004) and Morelli (2004)), coalition governments (e.g., Bandyopadhyay and Oak (2004)) and inefficient public policy (e.g., Besley and Coate (1998)).

has served in a political office), and W_e his per-period wage in the private sector, where $S < B + S < W_1 < B' + S' < W_2 < B + S + P < B' + S' + P' = 2(B + S + P)$, and $(W_2 - W_1) > (W_1 - (B + S))$. Suppose there is no discounting.

Politicians differ with respect to their electoral skills, which affect their probability of winning an election. Let $j \in \{b, g\}$ denote the individual's electoral type, π_j his probability of being reelected, and π'_j his probability of winning an electoral bid for higher office, where $0 = \pi'_b < \pi_b = 1/2 = \pi'_g < \pi_g = 1$. Politicians also differ with respect to their policy skills, which affect their probability of successfully implementing their most preferred policy. Let $k \in \{l, h\}$ denote the individual's policy type and p_k the per-period probability of implementing his most preferred policy while in office, where $0 = p_l < p_h = 1$. Hence, there are four possible types of politicians denoted by $\tau = (j, k) \in \{(b, l), (b, h), (g, l), (g, h)\}$.

To analyze the politician's dynamic optimization problem, consider first the decision he faces in the last period (i.e., $t = 2$). If the politician decides to run for reelection, his expected payoff is equal to $\pi_j (S + B + p_k P) + (1 - \pi_j) W_2$, while if he runs for higher office it is equal to $\pi'_j (S' + B' + p_k P') + (1 - \pi'_j) W_2$, and to W_2 if he decides to voluntarily leave office. Clearly, the politician's optimal decision depends on his type τ. If $\tau = (g, h)$ the politician runs for higher office, if $\tau = (b, h)$ he runs for reelection, and if $\tau = (b, l)$ or $\tau = (g, l)$ he exits politics. Let $V_2(\tau)$ denote the expected continuation payoff of an individual of type τ given his optimal period 2 decision. We have that $V_2(g, h) = (S' + B' + P')/2 + W_2/2$, $V_2(b, h) = (S + B + P)/2 + W_2/2$, and $V_2(b, l) = V_2(g, l) = W_2$. Consider now the decision problem of the politician when $t = 1$. His expected payoff is equal to $\pi_j (S + B + p_k P + V_2(\tau)) + (1 - \pi_j) 2W_1$ if he runs for reelection, and $2W_1$ if he exits. Hence, the politician always runs for reelection, independently of his type. Let $V_1(\tau)$ denote the expected payoff of an individual of type τ at the time of his election to public office given his optimal period 1 decision. We have that $V_1(g, h) = (S + B + P) + (S' + B' + P')/2 + W_2/2$, $V_1(b, h) = 3(S + B + P)/4 + W_2/4 + W_1$, $V_1(b, l) = (S + B + W_2)/2 + W_1$ and $V_1(g, l) = S + B + W_2$. It may therefore be optimal for a politician to remain in a particular office for a while and then either attempt to get elected to a higher office or leave politics altogether. As illustrated in this example, current and future benefits from public office are likely to affect the behavior of politicians. The effects will in general depend on the relative magnitudes of the various components of the returns to an individual from a career in politics. Also, different components are likely to affect different politicians in different ways, depending on their (observable and unobservable) characteristics. These considerations suggest that in order to improve our understanding of the career decisions of politicians it is important to quantify the private returns to political experience.

This empirical question is the focus of the work by Diermeier, Keane and Merlo (2005), who specify a dynamic model of career decisions of a member of the U.S. Congress, and estimate this model using a newly collected data set that contains detailed information on all members of Congress in the post-war period. A novel feature of the data is that it incorporates information about post-congressional employment and earnings when members exit Congress, which allows them to estimate the returns to congressional experience in post-congressional employment. The framework they propose also allows estimation of the relative importance of the utility politicians derive from being in office and the monetary returns to a career in Congress. Using data on important legislative achievements by members of Congress, they relate part of the non-pecuniary rewards from serving in Congress to the desire for policy accomplishments. Using the estimated model, they also investigate the extent to which politicians' career choices respond to wage incentives.

As in the simple example above, the model of Diermeier, Keane and Merlo (2005) takes into account that the decision of a member of Congress to seek reelection is likely to depend not only on current payoffs, which in turn depend on the probability of winning today, but also on the option value of holding the seat. This option value may depend, among other things, on the probability of being named to a committee, as well as the probability of winning a bid for higher office in the future (e.g., a member of the House may run for a seat in the Senate). Their empirical framework also incorporates politicians' unobserved heterogeneity (both with respect to their electoral ability and policy effectiveness), and observed characteristics (e.g., their age, education and family background, party affiliation and prior political experience), into the analysis of their career choices.

For the purpose of the discussion here, there are two main empirical findings of Diermeier, Keane and Merlo (2005). First, congressional experience significantly increases post-congressional wages in the private sector. In particular, holding everything else constant, winning reelection in the House (Senate) for the first time increases post-congressional wages in the private sector by 4.4% (16.7%). However, the marginal effect of congressional experience on post-congressional wages diminishes quite rapidly with additional experience, and the average effect of an additional term in the House (Senate) is equal to 2.4% (5.2%). Second, the non-pecuniary rewards from being in Congress are rather large (especially in the Senate). General non-pecuniary rewards amount to over $200,000 per year for a senator and about $30,000 per year for a representative (in 1995 dollars).[28] In addition, non-pecuniary rewards from an important legislative accomplishment are comparable for representatives and senators, and quite large (i.e., about $350,000 and $400,000, respectively). These findings suggest that policy motivations and benefits of office play important roles in the career decisions of politicians. In particular, monetary returns alone (i.e., wages in Congress and post-congressional payoffs), cannot explain the observed

---

[28] The average annual salary of a member of Congress in 1995 dollars over the period 1947–1994 is $120,378.

behavior of politicians, and the effect of the congressional salary on their behavior is quite modest.

4   PARTIES

Political parties represent another fundamental institution of representative democracy, and have long been recognized as key players by the political economy literature (see, e.g., Downs (1957)). However, the question "what is a party?" in political economy is as difficult and elusive as the question "what is a firm?" in industrial organization. The boundaries between political parties and interest groups or other citizens' organizations are rather blurry, and it is conceptually difficult to discriminate among alternative definitions of parties. It should therefore not be surprising that not much progress has been made to date to provide a compelling answer to this important question. In fact, as compared to the other topics discussed here, the study of political parties as endogenous equilibrium institutions is still in its infancy.

Most of the recent political economy literature on parties has tried to "unbundle" these institutions by focusing on specific purposes parties serve, thus providing alternative (complementary) rationales for their existence. Among all the possible purposes of parties that have been considered in the literature, I focus here on two that are closely related to the topics of the previous sections. These are the choice of policy platforms (e.g., Levy (2004), Morelli (2004) and Testa (2004)), and the selection of politicians and the choice of electoral candidates (e.g., Caillaud and Tirole (2002), Carrillo and Mariotti (2001), Mattozzi and Merlo (2005a, 2005b) and Snyder and Ting (2002)).[29] For each of these issues, I present a simple example based on a model drawn from the literature to illustrate possible ways of modeling the role of parties. Since it is not clear what kind of empirical evidence is most relevant to study political parties, I do not attempt here to relate theoretical and empirical research on this topic, or to emphasize specific features of the data.[30]

4.1   Choice of Policy Platforms

At a basic level, parties are groups of politicians. While members of the same party are more likely to share similar views than members of different parties,

---

[29] Other functions performed by parties include the mobilization of voters (e.g., Shachar and Nalebuff (1999)), the organization and coordination of electoral campaigns (e.g., Osborne and Tourky (2004)), the formation of bargaining coalitions in the legislature (e.g., Jackson and Moselle (2002)) and disciplining the behavior of elected representatives (e.g., Harrington (1992)).

[30] Most of the empirical literature on parties has tried to assess whether parties affect the roll call voting behavior of senators and representatives in the U.S. Congress (see, e.g., Cox and McCubbins (1993) and Poole and Rosenthal (1997)). Stylized facts about political parties concern for the most part their relative number across different political systems (see, e.g., Lijphart (1999)). There is also a large theoretical literature on the equilibrium number of parties, which I do not consider here. See, e.g., Cox (1997) for an overview.

these groups are by no means homogeneous. Hence, a legitimate question is whether parties matter, in the ex ante sense of imposing some discipline on the policy platforms of their representatives, or their existence can simply be rationalized as an ex post agglomeration of like-minded politicians.

In order to explore this issue, consider the following example taken from Levy (2004). A society has to elect a representative to implement a policy $y = (y_1, y_2)$ in the two-dimensional policy space $Y = Y_1 \times Y_2$, $Y_1 = Y_2 = [-1, 1]$. There is a continuum of citizens of mass one divided into three separate groups of equal size, where $j \in \{a, b, c\}$ denotes a generic group of citizens. All citizens within the same group have the same preferences, and citizens in group $j \in \{a, b, c\}$ evaluate alternative policies according to the indirect utility function $u_j(y) = -(y_1^j - y_1)^2 - (y_2^j - y_2)^2$, where $y^j = (y_1^j, y_2^j) \in Y$ denotes group j's most preferred policy, or ideal point, and $y^a = (-1, -1)$ $y^b = (1, 1)$and $y^c = (-1, 1)$. One citizen in each group is a politician, and let $j \in \{a, b, c\}$ also denote the politician from group j. The three politicians are organized into parties, and the five possible party configurations are: $(\{a\}, \{b\}, \{c\})$ (which denotes that each politician is in a separate party), $(\{a, b\}, \{c\})$ (which denotes that politicians a and b are in the same party, while politician c is in a separate party), $(\{a\}, \{b, c\})$, $(\{a, c\}, \{b\})$ and $(\{a, b, c\})$.

Parties choose whether or not to compete in the election and, if so, which policy platform to propose. Decisions within each party are made by unanimity rule. If all the members of a party are indifferent between running and not running, the party does not run. If a party competes in the election, a partisan politician runs as its representative. Since there are no direct benefits from holding office and, if elected, a politician implements his party's platform, the choice of the party's representative is inconsequential.

The set of policy platforms a party can propose is represented by its Pareto set (i.e., the set of feasible policies that are efficient from the point of view of the party). Hence, the role of parties here is to expand the set of policies politicians can offer when they run for office. Recall that in the citizen-candidate framework, politicians cannot commit to implement any policy other than their ideal point. In this environment, on the other hand, parties can commit to implement any policy, as long as it is efficient for its members (and hence enforceable after the election). Let $k \in \{\{a\}, \{b\}, \{c\}, \{a, b\}, \{a, c\}, \{b, c\}, \{a, b, c\}\}$ denote a generic party and P^k its Pareto set. We have that $P^{\{a\}} = (-1, -1)$, $P^{\{b\}} = (1, 1)$, $P^{\{c\}} = (-1, 1)$, $P^{\{a,b\}} = \{(y_1, y_2) : y_1 = y_2 \in [-1, 1]\}$, $P^{\{a,c\}} = \{(-1, y_2) : y_2 \in [-1, 1]\}$, $P^{\{b,c\}} = \{(y_1, 1) : y_1 \in [-1, 1]\}$ and $P^{\{a,b,c\}} = \{(y_1, y_2) : y_1, y_2 \in [-1, 1], y_1 \geq y_2\}$. Given the set of parties running for election and their policy platforms, citizens vote sincerely (i.e., they vote for the platform they most prefer, and if they are indifferent they vote for the party of their politician). The platform that receives the largest number of votes is then implemented.

Following Levy (2004), the equilibrium characterization proceeds in two steps: (i) for any given party configuration, solve for the pure-strategy Nash equilibria of the platform game and determine which policy platforms are implemented; (ii) derive the set of equilibrium party configurations, where a party configuration is an equilibrium if it is stable (i.e., it is such that no politician, or group of politicians wants to quit its party and form a smaller one, thus inducing a different equilibrium policy outcome).

Equilibrium platforms: Consider party configuration $(\{a\}, \{b\}, \{c\})$. If party $\{j\}$, $j \in \{a, b, c\}$, runs, its policy platform is y^j. The citizens in group a strictly prefer y^c to y^b, and similarly, the citizens in group b strictly prefer y^c to y^b. In equilibrium, the politician in party $\{c\}$ runs unopposed and the policy platform $(-1, 1)$ is implemented. Next, consider party configuration $(\{a, b\}, \{c\})$. If party $\{a, b\}$ runs it can offer policy platforms in the set $\{(y_1, y_2) : y_1 = y_2 \in [-1, 1]\}$, while if party $\{c\}$ runs its policy platform is $(-1, 1)$. If party $\{a, b\}$ offers a policy platform (y, y) such that $y \in [-1, \sqrt{2} - 1)$, the citizens in group a strictly prefer such policy to $(-1, 1)$, and if it offers a policy platform (y, y) such that $y \in (1 - \sqrt{2}, 1]$, the citizens in group b strictly prefer such policy to $(-1, 1)$. In equilibrium, one of the two politicians in party $\{a, b\}$ runs unopposed and offers a policy platform $y \in (1 - \sqrt{2}, \sqrt{2} - 1)$, which is implemented. Suppose now that the party configuration is $(\{a, c\}, \{b\})$. If party $\{a, c\}$ offers any policy platform in its Pareto set $\{(-1, y_2) : y_2 \in [-1, 1]\}$, the citizens in groups a and c strictly prefer such policy to $(1, 1)$ (the preference is weak for citizens in groups c if $y_2 = -1$). In equilibrium, one of the two politicians in party $\{a, c\}$ runs unopposed and offers a policy platform $(-1, y_2)$, where $y_2 \in [-1, 1]$, which is implemented. Similarly, if the party configuration is $(\{b, c\}, \{a\})$, in equilibrium one of the two politicians in party $\{b, c\}$ runs unopposed and offers a policy platform $(y_1, 1)$, where $y_1 \in [-1, 1]$, which is implemented. Finally, if the only party is $\{a, b, c\}$, then any policy platform in $P^{\{a,b,c\}}$ can be offered and implemented in equilibrium.

Equilibrium party configurations: Party configuration $(\{a\}, \{b\}, \{c\})$ is stable by definition. Party configuration $(\{a, b\}, \{c\})$ is stable, since neither politician a nor politician b can gain by leaving party $\{a, b\}$ and forming their own parties; the break-up of the party would in fact lead to the policy outcome $(-1, 1)$. Party configurations $(\{a, c\}, \{b\})$ and $(\{b, c\}, \{a\})$ are stable only if the platform that is offered is $(-1, 1)$; otherwise, in either case politician c would find it profitable to leave his party and form his own party, thus inducing the policy outcome $(-1, 1)$. Finally, party configuration $\{a, b, c\}$ is stable only if the platform that is offered is $(0, 0)$, which is the only platform that prevents either politicians a and b to form a party together or c to form his own party (note that $(0, 0)$ is the platform in the set of equilibrium policies of party $\{a, b\}$ that maximizes the utility of politician c).

The main conclusion we draw from this insightful example (which extends to the general environment considered by Levy (2004)), is that parties may matter. By imposing discipline on the policy platforms that are offered by their politicians in an election, parties may affect equilibrium policy outcomes. In particular, the partisan policy platforms that are implemented may differ from any of the ideal points of the politicians, which are the only possible policy outcomes in the absence of parties.

4.2   Selection of Politicians

Another important function played by political parties is the selection of candidates for a variety of public offices. This function interacts in interesting ways with the voters' desire to have the best possible politicians in office, and with the career ambitions of individuals who want to become politicians. There are several important aspects of this interaction. One aspect is that since parties may have several opportunities to interact with individuals with political aspirations before they run for office, they may have more information about the political skills of potential politicians than voters, who can only observe the political skills of politicians after they are in office. A second aspect is that since politicians are typically "under the spotlight," receiving the attention of the media and a variety of citizens' organizations, they may have relatively better chances to display their sector-specific skills than people working in other sectors. Finally, to the extent that political skills may also be valuable outside the political sector (either directly, or because they are correlated with other skills), politicians may eventually decide to leave politics to work in another sector.

In order to investigate these issues, consider the following example based on Mattozzi and Merlo (2005a). A political economy has two sectors: a market sector and a political sector. In every period $t = 0, 1, \ldots$, a large, finite number of citizens is born, which, for convenience of exposition, can be approximated by a continuum of measure one. Individuals live for two periods, and are heterogeneous with respect to their market ability m and their political skills p. Let $m \in \{l, h\}$, where $m = l$ ($m = h$) denotes an individual with low (high) market ability. Three-fourths of the population have high market ability with probability $1/4$ and have no political skills, that is $p = 0$. The remaining one-fourth of the population is heterogeneous with respect to their political skills $p \in [0, 1]$, which are distributed according to a uniform distribution. The probability of being high market ability is positively correlated with political skills and is equal to $\pi(p) = 1/4 + p/2$. Each individual only knows his own political skills, and does not know his market ability. Also, $\pi(p)$ and the distribution of political skills in the citizenry are common knowledge.

In the first period of life, an individual can either work in the market sector or be a politician. If an individual becomes a politician, his political skills become publicly observable. Politicians may also remain in the political sector during their second period of life, or work in the market sector. If an individual works in the market sector, during his first period of employment his market ability is revealed with probability $1/2$. Individuals make their career decisions to maximize their earnings.

The market sector is perfectly competitive, and $W_l = 0$ and $W_h = 1$ denote the competitive market wage rates associated with each ability level. The political sector is characterized by a single political office that pays a politician a per-period salary $S \in (1/5, 1/4)$. While in office, a politician with political skills p performs a public service that generates a public benefit $B(p) = p$.

Hence, politicians with higher political skills generate higher benefits, and are thus more desirable from the point of view of the voters. If in a period the political office remains vacant, then no benefit is generated that period.

There is an infinitely lived political party that in each period when the political office is vacant can nominate a candidate. The political mechanism that determines the appointment and possible re-appointment of a politician is as follows. If no politician is in office, then at the beginning of the period all individuals born in that period decide whether or not to apply to become a partisan politician. The party then observes the political skills of a randomly drawn individual from the pool of applicants and decides whether to nominate him for the political office, or reject him and forgo the opportunity of nominating somebody in that period. A party's nominee is either approved or not approved by the voters according to majority rule. Only individuals in their second period of life vote. If a party's nominee is approved by a majority of the voters, he is then in office for that period, while all other individuals work in the market sector. If, on the other hand, the party's nominee does not receive the approval of a majority of the voters, or the party does not propose a nomination, then all individuals in their first period of life decide whether or not to run for the political office as independents. A random draw then determines who will be in office for that period. If nobody runs, the political office remains vacant for a period.

If a politician is in office, at the beginning of the period the voters decide by majority rule whether or not to confirm the incumbent for a second term. If the incumbent is not confirmed, all individuals born in that period decide whether or not to run for the political office as independents. If instead the incumbent is confirmed by the voters, he decides whether to remain in the political office for a second term, or leave politics and work in the market sector. If he chooses to remain in office, all other individuals work in the market sector. If he chooses to work in the market sector, the political office becomes vacant and the party can then propose a new nominee for the political office in that period.

In his second term in office, a politician with political skills p generates private benefits denoted by $z(p) = \sqrt{p}/2$. If the incumbent is a partisan, these benefits are shared between the party and the politician in office. The politician's share τ is equal to the minimum between his potential wage in the market sector net of the political salary and the entire benefit, while the party appropriates the rent $z(p) - \tau$. If instead the incumbent politician is an independent, his earnings in his second term in office are equal to $S + z(p)$. Let $\delta \geq 1/2$ be the party's discount factor, and normalize the individuals' discount factor to 1.

Following Mattozzi and Merlo (2005a), under a weak-monotonicity restriction on the out-of-equilibrium beliefs of voters, the model has a unique Markov Perfect Equilibrium. In equilibrium, there exist two levels of political skills, $p^* = 11/8 - 4S$ and $p'' = 2S + \sqrt{2S - 1/4}$, $0 < p^* < (1 + p^*)/2 < p'' < 1$, such that only individuals with political skills $p \in [(1 + p^*)/2, 1]$ apply to become partisan politicians, and the party always nominates an applicant for the political office. If given an opportunity, all individuals with political skills

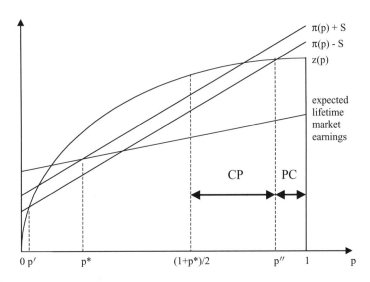

Figure 10.2. Selection and careers of politicians

$p \geq p^*$ would run for office as independents. Partisan nominees are always approved by the voters to a first term in office and confirmed to a second term. All partisan politicians with political skills $p \in [(1 + p^*), p'']$ spend their entire life working in the political sector (i.e., they are career politicians), while if $p \in (p'', 1]$ they eventually leave politics to work in the market sector (i.e., they have political careers). An illustration of the equilibrium is depicted in Figure 10.2, where CP denotes career politicians and PC political careers.

To see that this is an equilibrium, first note that if an individual works in the market sector his first-period wage is based on the expected market ability in the population, since neither his market ability nor his political skills are observable. In the second period of employment, on the other hand, an individual's expected wage depends on his expected market ability, since his market ability, which is correlated with his (privately known) political skills, is revealed with some probability. If, instead, an individual is a politician in his first period of life, his potential second-period wage in the market sector depends on his expected market ability conditional on his political skills (which, because of his experience in the political sector, become publicly known). This potential market wage also determines a politician's second-period earnings if he remains in office for a second term.

It follows that the cost for an individual of becoming a politician is equal to the difference between the first-period market wage that is forgone by not working in the market sector and the political salary, $5/16 - S$. The return is equal to the (possibly) higher earnings in the second period after political skills are revealed (regardless of whether the higher earnings are realized by staying in politics or working in the market sector), $p/4 - 1/32$. While the cost does not depend on an individual's political skills, the return is increasing in his political skills. Hence, for individuals with relatively low political skills (i.e., $p < p^* = 11/8 - 4S$), the cost of becoming a politician is higher than the return, so that they prefer to work in the market sector. On the other hand, individuals with higher political skills would want to become politicians. Furthermore, an incumbent politician with political skills p would be willing to remain in office for a second term rather than leave politics and work in the market sector only if $S + \sqrt{p}/2 \geq 1/4 + p/2$, which implies that $p \in [p', p'']$, where $p' = 2S - \sqrt{2S - 1/4}$, $p'' = 2S + \sqrt{2s - 1/4}$ and $0 < p' < p^* < p'' < 1$. Individuals with political skills between p' and p'' are also the only ones who could potentially generate rents for the party if they were to become partisan politicians and be confirmed in office.

Since p^* represents the lower bound on the political skills of individuals who would want to become politicians, it pins down the "outside option" available to the voters if they choose not to approve a partisan nominee and appoint an independent politician instead. In particular, it implies that the voters never confirm an incumbent with political skills below $(1 + p^*)/2$ to a second term in office. Since politicians are valuable to the party only if they are approved and confirmed by the voters, it follows that the party is only willing to nominate individuals with political skills $p \geq (1 + p^*)/2$. Partisan nominees with political skills $p \in [(1 + p^*), p'']$ are valuable to the party because in their second term in office they generate rents for the party. If their political skills are above p'', in spite of the fact that they do not generate any rents for the party, they are valuable because they allow the party to maintain control of the political office. Hence, individuals with relatively high political skills use the party to reveal them and obtain high market wages. At the same time, the party is willing to nominate them since they enhance the party's reputation with the voters.

Note that as S increases, politics becomes relatively more attractive an option for all levels of political skills, thus lowering the quality of the worst potential politician, p^*. At the same time, the party can retain relatively better politicians since the amount it has to pay to keep them in office for each level of political skills is lower. This increases the quality of the best career politician, p'', and decreases the proportion of politicians who have political careers. Hence, an increase in the political salary decreases the average quality of politicians but increases the average quality of career politicians and decreases turnover in office.

This example highlights several interesting insights that also extend to the more general environments considered by Mattozzi and Merlo (2005a). In equilibrium, not everybody who would want to become a politician does so. In particular, the party prevents individuals with low political skills from becoming politicians. Also, not everybody who becomes a politician remains in politics throughout his working life. Politicians with relatively better political skills may eventually leave politics to work in the market sector, although career politicians are still better than average. Finally, monetary incentives and other features of the political-economic environment affect the quality of politicians and their careers.

The mechanism behind these results is the equilibrium interaction between the voters, the party, and the political aspirations of individuals. Voters want the best politicians in office. The party wants politicians who generate rents. In equilibrium, the party and the voters compromise. The party discards individuals with low political skills who would want to become politicians and could generate rents for the party, and supports the nomination of politicians with high political skills who do not generate any rents. In exchange, the voters always approve the party's nominees and confirm in office incumbent politicians who, although relatively mediocre, generate rents for the party. By preventing individuals with low political skills from becoming politicians, the party fulfills a screening function that is valuable to the voters. Hence, the voters are willing to trust the party in selecting politicians.

Since politicians with better political skills have better employment prospects in the market sector, they are relatively expensive for the party to keep in the political sector. The fact that relatively better politicians may leave politics to work in the market sector is not a concern for the voters, since they at least get high quality politicians in office for some time. Although these politicians do not generate rents, the fact that they leave politics is also not an issue for the party, since they too serve a valuable purpose for maintaining its reputation. When they voluntarily leave politics, given the party's track record, the voters are willing to replace them with other partisan nominees, thus allowing the party to maintain control of the public office, which generates expected rents in the future. This provides a rationale for the existence of political parties and their survival through time.

5 GOVERNMENTS

The last topic I consider concerns the executive, or government, which is ultimately responsible for implementing policy. Like each of the previous topics, the government represents a fundamental institution of democracy and has always been at the forefront of research in political economy. Also, like with the analyses of politicians and parties, the major turning point that characterizes the current approach to the analysis of government in the political economy literature was defined by addressing the issue of its endogeneity.

In presidential democracy, the executive (i.e., the President) is directly elected by the citizens. Hence, the analysis of the government as an endogenous equilibrium institution is derivative of the analyses of voters, politicians and parties. In parliamentary democracy, on the other hand, the executive (i.e., the cabinet) derives its mandate from and is responsible to the legislature. This implies that who forms the government is not determined by an election alone, but is the outcome of a negotiation among the elected members of the legislature. Furthermore, it implies that the government may terminate at any time before the end of a parliamentary term if it loses the confidence of the legislature.

Given these considerations, most of the modern political economy literature on the endogenous formation and dissolution of governments focuses on parliamentary democracy, and views governments as equilibrium outcomes of a multilateral bargaining game among the parties represented in parliament.[31] Some of the models only focus on government formation (e.g., Austen-Smith and Banks (1988), Bandyopadhyay and Oak (2004), Baron (1991, 1993), Baron and Diermeier (2001), Baron and Ferejohn (1989), Eraslan (2002) and Persson, Roland and Tabellini (2003)). Others consider environments where the composition and the stability of coalition governments are both determined in equilibrium (e.g., Baron (1998), Diermeier, Eraslan and Merlo (2002, 2003), Diermeier and Feddersen (1998), Diermeier and Merlo (2000), Laver and Shepsle (1996), Lupia and Strom (1995) and Merlo (1997)).[32]

Multiparty parliamentary democracy is the predominant regime in Western Europe, and a number of interesting observations emerge from data on governments in West European countries in the post-war period (e.g., Diermeier, Eraslan and Merlo (2003), Laver and Schofield (1990), Muller and Strom (2000) and Woldendorp, Keman and Budge (2000)). Since several parties typically compete and win seats in parliamentary elections, single-party majority governments (where one party controls the majority of parliament and hence forms the government), are extremely rare. Coalition governments are instead the norm, and minority (i.e., coalitions that control less than 50% of the parliamentary seats), minimum-winning (i.e., coalitions that control at least 50% of parliament and are such that each party in the coalition is essential to retain majority status), and surplus governments (i.e., coalitions that control more than 50% of parliament and are such that there is at least one party in the coalition which is not necessary to have majority status), are all prevalent in the data. Governments frequently terminate before the end of the legislature, and reshuffles (i.e., a situation where a government is replaced by an identical coalition, but with a different allocation of cabinet positions), are a common phenomenon. Moreover, minority governments are, on average, less stable than either minimum-winning or surplus governments.

These general features are common across West European parliamentary democracies. Countries differ, however, with respect to the specific rules in their constitutions that prescribe how their governments form and terminate. They also differ systematically with respect to the observed duration of their government formation processes, the type (i.e., minority, minimum-winning, or surplus) and size of the government coalitions that result from these processes, and the relative durability of their governments. For example, in some countries like Denmark, minority governments are virtually the norm, while in Germany they are a rare occurrence. Also, surplus governments are rather frequent in Finland, while they never occur in Sweden. Similarly, governments in Italy

---

[31] For an early attempt to formalize this idea, see Riker (1962).

[32] In Austen-Smith and Banks (1988), Bandyopadhyay and Oak (2004), Baron and Diermeier (2001) and Persson, Roland and Tabellini (2003), voters are the only primitive, while representatives, parties and governments are all equilibrium outcomes. All other models treat parties as primitives.

are notoriously unstable, while Dutch governments frequently last the entire legislative period

These observations raise the following important questions: (i) Can political economy explain the evidence? (ii) What determines the composition and stability of coalition governments? (iii) Can institutional differences account for observed differences in government outcomes? In order to answer these questions, recent developments in political economy have relied on a structural approach. This approach consists of specifying bargaining models of government formation and dissolution, structurally estimating these models, assessing their ability to account for key features of the data and then simulating the estimated models to conduct counterfactual experiments of comparative constitutional design (e.g., Diermeier, Eraslan and Merlo (2002, 2003) and Merlo (1997)). This approach allows us to interpret important features of the data as equilibrium phenomena and to quantify the equilibrium responses of government outcomes to changes in the institutional environment.[33]

To illustrate some of the key features and implications of the class of models that have been proposed in the literature, consider a simple example based on Diermeier and Merlo (2000). A parliament has to form a government to implement a policy $y = (y_1, y_2)$ in the two-dimensional policy space $\mathbb{R}^2$. There are three parties, $N = \{a, b, c\}$, and two periods, $t = 1, 2$. Each party $i \in N$ evaluates alternative policies $y \in \mathbb{R}^2$ and distributive benefits $z \in \mathbb{R}$ according to the (per-period) payoff function $U_i(y, z) = u_i(y) + z$, where $u_i(y) = -\left(y_1^i - y_1\right)^2 - \left(y_2^i - y_2\right)^2$ and $y^i = \left(y_1^i, y_2^i\right) \in \mathbb{R}^2$ denotes party i's most preferred policy, or ideal point, where $y^a = (0, 0)$, $y^b = (1, 0)$ and $y^c = (1/2, \sqrt{3}/2)$. Distributive benefits can either be government posts other than cabinet ministries that can be allocated to all parties, or ministerial positions that can only be allocated to government parties. Aggregate transfers are normalized to 0 in each period (i.e., $z_a + z_b + z_c = 0$), and parties discount future payoffs with a common discount factor $\delta \in [0, 1]$. Each party $i \in \{a, b, c\}$ controls a fraction π_i of parliamentary seats, where $\pi_a = 5/11$, $\pi_b = \pi_c = 3/11$.

In period $t = 1$ there is a default policy $q \in \{y^a, y^b, y^c\}$, which is implemented if no government forms in that period. If $q = y^i$, i is the party favored by the the default policy. At the beginning of the period, party a is the "formateur" (i.e., the party in charge of conducting negotiations to form the government).[34] The formateur chooses the proto-coalition $D \in \Delta_a = \{\{a\}, \{a, b\}, \{a, c\}, \{a, b, c\}\}$, where D represents the set of parties that agree to talk to each other about forming a government together. Then D selects a set of non-negative transfers to parties outside the proto-coalition, $T(D, q) = (T_j(D, q))_{j \in N \setminus D} \in \mathbb{R}_+^{|N \setminus D|}$, which are payments to non-coalition parties that may be necessary to sustain the proposed government coalition.

---

[33] See Diermeier, Eraslan and Merlo (2006) for an overview.
[34] For an empirical investigation of formateur selection see, e.g., Diermeier and Merlo (2004).

Given D and T, the parliament votes to approve the formateur's proposal under majority rule. If the proposal is defeated, the default policy is implemented and each party $i \in N$ receives a period 1 payoff of $U_i(q, 0)$. If the formateur's proposal is accepted, the members of D bargain over a policy $y(D, q) \in \mathbb{R}^2$ and benefits to coalition members $B(D, q) = (B_j(D, q))_{j \in D} \in \mathbb{R}^{|D|}$. The bargaining procedure takes no real time and is such that for as long as no agreement is reached, each party in D is independently selected to make a proposal with probability $1/|D|$. An agreement entails unanimous approval of the proto-coalition members. If the members of D do not reach an agreement on a common policy and vector of transfers, then the government formation attempt fails and each party $i \in N$ receives a period 1 payoff of $U_i(q, 0)$. If instead an agreement is reached, then D forms the government and each party $i \in D$ receives a period 1 payoff of $U_i(y(D, q), B_i(D, q))$, while each party $j \notin D$ receives a period 1 payoff of $U_j(y(D, q), T_j(D, q))$.

At the beginning of period $t = 2$ a new default policy $q' \in \{y^a, y^b, y^c\}$ is realized with probabilities $(1/3, 1/3, 1/3)$. If a government formed in period 1, then after observing q' the incumbent government can renegotiate its agreement. Renegotiation is similar to government formation, except for the fact that the coalition is fixed and given by the incumbent government D. Hence, first the government may choose a set of period 2 transfers to the parties outside the government coalition, $T'(D, q') = (T'_j(D, q'))_{j \in N \setminus D} \in \mathbb{R}_+^{|N \setminus D|}$. Given $T'(D, q')$, a vote is then taken to determine whether the incumbent government retains the confidence of a parliamentary majority to continue its mandate. If the government retains the confidence of the parliament, it then bargains over a policy $y'(D, q')$ and benefits to its members $B(D, q') = (B'_j(D, q'))_{j \in D} \in \mathbb{R}^{|D|}$ for period 2. If an agreement is reached, then D continues as a government and period 2 payoffs to the parties are determined as a function of $y'(D, q')$, $B'(D, q')$ and $T'(D, q')$. If D fails to reach an agreement or loses the confidence of the parliament, then D terminates. If the incumbent government terminates or no government formed in period 1, then a new government formation process begins in period 2 with the selection of a formateur $k \in \{a, b, c\}$, where the probability each party i is chosen to be the formateur is equal to π_i. Like in period 1, the outcome of the government formation process determines the period 2 payoffs to the parties. In particular, if a government $D' \in \Delta_k$ forms, then each party $i \in D'$ receives a period 2 payoff of $U_i(y'(D', q'), B'_i(D', q'))$ while each party $j \notin D'$ receives a period 2 payoff of $U_j(y'(D', q'), T'_j(D', q'))$. If instead no government forms, then each party $i \in N$ receives a period 2 payoff of $U_i(q', 0)$.

Following Diermeier and Merlo (2000), we characterize the unique subgame perfect equilibrium of the game using backward induction. Suppose first that a new government formation process begins in period $t = 2$ and D' is chosen as the proto-coalition. Then D' forms the government, which implements policy $y'(D', q') = \sum_{i \in D'} y^i / |D'|$, and equilibrium benefits and transfers are equal to $B'_i(D', q') = -\sum_{j \in D', j \neq i} u_j(q') / |D'| + (|D'| - 1)u_i(q') / |D'|$, $i \in D'$ and $T'_j(D', q') = 0$, $j \in N \setminus D'$. To see that this is the case, note that if D' contains either 2 or 3 parties (i.e., it is a majority), it does not need any support from outside the coalition to be approved by parliament. Hence, $T'_j(D', q') = 0$. If instead D' contains only one party (i.e., it is a minority), it may need the support of another party to be approved by parliament. But in this case the formateur party would want to implement its most preferred policy, and since the locations of the three parties' ideal points are symmetric, and the payoff function u_i (y) has circular indifference curves, there will always be at least a party other than the formateur who is indifferent between the default policy q' and the policy most preferred by the formateur, and hence will be willing to support a minority government for free. It follows that $T'_j(D', q') = 0$ for all D' and q'.

Next, note that efficient bargaining within the proto-coalition implies that the policy chosen is the one that maximizes the sum of the payoffs of the parties in the coalition. Given the quadratic specification of u_i (y) this policy is given by the average of the ideal points of the parties in the coalition, independent of the default policy q'. Since in the event of disagreement, the policy outcome is q', however, the default policy affects the allocation of benefits. In particular, the "cake" that is available for distribution to the proto-coalition is equal to the sum of the differences in the payoffs of the parties within the coalition evaluated at $y'(D', q')$ and q', $C(D', q') = \sum_{i \in D'}[u_i(y'(D', q')) - u_i(q')]$. This represents the total increment in the payoffs of the coalition partners from implementing the optimal policy $y'(D', q')$ rather than q'. Given the structure of the bargaining game, the parties within the proto-coalition unanimously agree to a split of the cake where each party receives a fraction $1/|D'|$. Hence, each party $i \in D'$ receives a payoff equal to $u_i(q') + C(D', q')/|D'|$, or equivalently, $u_i(y'(D', q')) + B'_i(D', q')$, where $y'(D', q')$ and $B'_i(D', q')$ are given in the expressions above. It follows that for all $q' \in \{y^a, y^b, y^c\}$, $y'(\{a\}, q') = (0, 0)$, $y'(\{b\}, q') = (1, 0)$, $y'(\{c\}, q') = (1/2, \sqrt{3}/2)$, $y'(\{a, b\}, q') = (1/2, 0)$, $y'(\{a, c\}, q') = (1/4, \sqrt{3}/4)$, $y'(\{b, c\}, q') = (3/4, \sqrt{3}/4)$ and $y'(\{a, b, c\}, q') = (1/2, \sqrt{3}/6)$. Moreover, for $q' = y^i$ and $i, j, l \in \{a, b, c\}, i \neq j \neq l, C(\{i\}, y^i) = 0, C(\{j\}, y^i) = C(\{l\}, y^i) = 1$, $C(\{i, j\}, y^i) = C(\{i, l\}, y^i) = 1/2$, $C(\{j, l\}, y^i) = 3/2$ and $C(\{a, b, c\}, y^i) = 1$.

The formateur party k then chooses the proto-coalition that maximizes its payoff. Since each party $i \in D'$ receives a payoff equal to $u_i(q') + C(D', q')/|D'|$ and $u_i(y^i) = 0$ and $u_i(y^j) = -1$, for all $i, j \in \{a, b, c\}, i \neq j$, it follows that if $q' = y^k$, then k chooses $D' = \{a, b, c\}$, while if $q' \neq y^k$, then k chooses $D' = \{k\}$. This implies that the payoff to the formateur party k is equal to $1/3$ if $q' = y^k$ and 0 if $q' \neq y^k$ while the payoff to a party i that is not the formateur is equal to -1 if $q' \neq y^k$ and $-2/3$ if $q' = y^k$. Let V_i (q') denote party i's expected continuation payoff if a new government needs to be formed in period 2 when the default policy is q'. Note that, for all $i, j \in \{a, b, c\}$, $i \neq j, V_i$ $(y^i) = 4\pi_i/3 - 1$ and V_i $(y^j) = \pi_i + \pi_j/3 - 1$. This implies that if $q' = y^a, V_a$ $(y^a) = -13/33$ and V_b $(y^a) = V_c$ $(y^a) = -19/33$, while if $q' \neq y^a$, V_a $(q') = -5/11$ and V_b $(q') = V_c$ $(q') = -7/11$.

Consider now the renegotiation problem faced by an incumbent government D after the realization of q'. Recall that since party a is the formateur in period 1, it must be the case that $D \in \Delta_a = \{\{a\}, \{a, b\}, \{a, c\}, \{a, b, c\}\}$. Since renegotiation is similar to proto-coalition bargaining, except that failure to reach agreement leads to an expected payoff of $V_i(q')$ instead of $u_i(q')$, it follows that if the incumbent government D is a majority (i.e., $D \neq \{a\}$), then D remains in power in period 2 and implements policy $y'(D, q')$ equal to the average of the ideal points of the parties in the government coalition. The expression for the benefits to the coalition partners is also similar to the one derived above, but where $V_i(q')$ replaces $u_i(q')$, and transfers to parties outside the government coalition are equal to zero. If instead $D = \{a\}$ (i.e., it is a minority government), then if $q' = y^a$ the government terminates; while if $q' \neq y^a$ the minority government remains in power with the external support of one of the other parties, implements policy y^a and makes a transfer equal to $4/11$ with equal probability either to party b or to party c (and no transfer to the other party). The result follows immediately from the fact that if $q' = y^a$, the payoff gain to party a from staying in power is equal to $13/33$ and either one of the other parties would need a transfer of $14/33$ to support the government; while if $q' \neq y^a$ the payoff gain to party a from staying in power is equal to $5/11$ and either one of the other parties would only need a transfer of $4/11$ to support the government. Let $V_i'(D)$ be party i's expected continuation payoff at the beginning of period 2, prior to the realization of q', if government D is in power. Since each realization of q' is equally likely, we have that for party a, $V_a'(\{a\}) = -37/99$, $V_a'(\{a, b\}) = V_a'(\{a, c\}) = -7/44$ and $V_a'(\{a, b, c\}) = -7/33$. Similarly, for parties $i, j \in \{b, c\}$, $i \neq j$, $V_i'(\{a\}) = -73/99$, $V_i'(\{a, i\}) = -15/44$, $V_i'(\{a, j\}) = -3/4$ and $V_i'(\{a, b, c\}) = -13/33$.

The last step of the equilibrium characterization involves solving for D. Since proto-coalition bargaining in period $t = 1$ is similar to the bargaining problems analyzed before, if D is chosen as the proto-coalition it forms the government. If D is a majority (i.e., $D \neq \{a\}$), then again it implements policy $y(D, q)$ equal to the average of the ideal points of the parties in the proto-coalition. The expression for the benefits to the coalition partners is also the same as the one derived above, except that $u_i(q)$ replaces $u_i(q')$, and transfers to parties outside the government coalition are equal to zero. If, on the other hand, $D = \{a\}$ (i.e., it is a minority), then it implements policy y^a, and makes a transfer equal to $\delta(4/33)$ to the party that is not favored by the default policy q (or, if neither party is favored, to either party with equal probability), in order to obtain its external support. This result follows from the fact that if both parties were to vote against $D = \{a\}$, then q would be implemented in period 1, and a new government negotiation would follow in period 2, yielding the party that is not favored by the default policy q an expected payoff equal to $-1 - 61\delta/99$, as opposed to $-1 - 73\delta/99$. These calculations imply that if $q = y^a$, the payoffs to the formateur party a from choosing each possible proto-coalition D, $W_a(D; q = y^a)$, are equal to $W_a(\{a\}; q = y^a) = -49\delta/99$, $W_a(\{a, b\}; q = y^a) = W_a(\{a, c\}; q = y^a) = 1/4 - 7\delta/44$ and $W_a(\{a, b, c\}; q = y^a) = 1/3 - 7\delta/33$. Similarly, if $q = y^i$, $i, j \in \{a, b\}$, $i \neq j$, these payoffs are equal to $W_a(\{a\}; q = y^i) = -49\delta/99$, $W_a(\{a, i\}; q = y^i) = -3/4 - 7\delta/44$, $W_a(\{a, j\}; q = y^i) = -1/4 - 7\delta/44$ and $W_a(\{a, b, c\}; q = y^i) = -2/3 - 7\delta/33$.

Given the default policy q, the formateur party a chooses the government that maximizes its payoff. Hence, if $q = y^a$, the government that forms in period 1 is the surplus coalition $\{a, b, c\}$, which remains in power for two periods. If, on the other hand $q \neq y^a$, then if $\delta < 3/4$, the minority government $\{a\}$ forms in period 1 and terminates in period 2 with probability $1/3$; while if $\delta > 3/4$ the government that forms in period 1 is the minimum-winning coalition between party a and the other party that is not favored by q. If it forms, the minimum-winning government lasts until the end of the second period. Regardless of whether the surplus or the minimum-winning government forms in period 1, in period 2 majority coalitions reshuffle the allocation of distributive benefits to their members with probability $1/3$ (i.e., when $q' \neq q$), but do not change their policy.

Several interesting implications emerge from this example. Minority, minimum-winning and surplus governments can all form in equilibrium. Furthermore, the stability and the relative occurrence of different types of governments are closely related. When choosing a government coalition, a formateur faces a fundamental trade-off between "control" and "durability." On the one hand, relatively larger coalitions may be associated with longer expected durations and hence relatively larger cakes. On the other hand, because of proto-coalition bargaining, by including additional parties in its coalition the formateur party would receive a smaller share of the pie, and share the power to choose policy. The equilibrium coalition choice, and hence the stability of government, depend on the terms of this trade-off, which in general will depend on characteristics of the environment where government negotiations take place. Since the choice of the government coalition is endogenous, changes in the institutional environment are likely to induce an "equilibrium replacement effect," where governments that are optimally chosen in equilibrium in a particular environment may be replaced by different coalitions in response to changes in the underlying environment. These implications also extend to the more general (and more realistic) models estimated by Diermeier, Eraslan and Merlo (2002, 2003) using data from nine West European countries over the period 1947–1999. Their empirical analysis accounts for all the empirical regularities summarized above and interprets them in the context of an equilibrium framework that fits the data well. Moreover, it assesses the propensity of different political systems to generate government coalitions of different types, sizes and durations and quantifies the effects of constitutional features on government outcomes.

6 CONCLUSIONS

In this article, I have focused on some of the recent developments that have characterized research in political economy from a microeconomic perspective over the last twenty years. In spite of the obvious differences due to the specific nature of each topic, there is a key element of commonality in this research, which has contributed to define modern political economy as a field. It is the use of a common language (a consistent set of analytical tools) and a coherent class of models that allow us to analyze political institutions and outcomes as endogenous, equilibrium phenomena.

The path traced by the work of a large number of economists and political scientists over more than two centuries started from a situation where political institutions could not fit in the precise definition of an economy. Since voters, politicians, parties, bureaucrats, interest groups and governments were not considered as part of the primitives that describe an economy, these scholars made them primitives of a political economy. Much of the research in this area over the last fifty years has been devoted to taking the analysis of political institutions to a deeper, more fundamental level. This path has led to a more precise notion of what the primitives of a political economy are, and how to model political institutions as endogenous objects, which depend on such primitives.

This does not mean that the field of political economy has reached maturity or the status of "normal science." In fact, much effort is currently being devoted to confront the difficult challenges that arise from the notion that constitutions and the rules of democracy are themselves equilibrium phenomena. But the set of tools developed in the recent past for the specific purpose of analyzing political institutions can only help to push the discipline further in this exciting direction.

The fundamental notion that political institutions are endogenous also raises an important challenge for empirical research in economics. Empirical work in several fields of economics constantly relies on differences in institutions to provide a fundamental source of exogenous variation to address many different questions with important policy implications. Recognizing that political institutions are equilibrium outcomes may severely limit the usefulness of several common approaches to empirical research. However, theoretical developments in political economy provide a better understanding of the equilibrium relationships between primitives and institutions and offer important insights for analyzing the data and interpreting what we observe. These developments will hopefully prove beneficial to further empirical research on these important topics.

References

ACEMOGLU, D., AND J. A. ROBINSON (2005): *Economic Origins of Dictatorship and Democracy*. New York: Cambridge University Press.

ALDRICH, J. H. (1993): "Rational Choice and Turnout," *American Journal of Political Science*, 37, 246–278.

ALESINA, A. (1988): "Credibility and Policy Convergence in a Two-Party System with Rational Voters," *American Economic Review*, 78, 796–806.

ALESINA, A., AND H. ROSENTHAL (1995): *Partisan Politics, Divided Government, and the Economy*. Cambridge: Cambridge University Press.

—— (1996): "A Theory of Divided Government," *Econometrica*, 64, 1311–1341.

ARROW, K. J. (1951): *Social Choice and Individual Values*. New Haven: Yale University Press.

AUSTEN-SMITH, D., AND J. S. BANKS (1988): "Elections, Coalitions, and Legislative Outcomes," *American Political Science Review*, 82, 405–422.

—— (1999): *Positive Political Theory I: Collective Preferences*. Ann Arbor: University of Michigan Press.

—— (2005): *Positive Political Theory II: Strategy and Structure*. Ann Arbor: University of Michigan Press.

BANDYOPADHYAY, S., AND M. OAK (2004): "Party Formation and Coalition Bargaining in a Model of Proportional Representation," Unpublished Manuscript, University of Birmingham.

BARON, D. P. (1991): "A Spatial Bargaining Theory of Government Formation in Parliamentary Systems," *American Political Science Review*, 85, 137–164.

—— (1993): "Government Formation and Endogenous Parties," *American Political Science Review*, 87, 34–47.

—— (1998): "Comparative Dynamics of Parliamentary Governments," *American Political Science Review*, 92, 593–609.

BARON, D. P., AND D. DIERMEIER (2001): "Elections, Governments, and Parliaments in Proportional Representation Systems," *Quarterly Journal of Economics*, 116, 933–967.

BARON, D. P., AND J. A. FEREJOHN (1989): "Bargaining in Legislatures," *American Political Science Review*, 83, 1181–1206.

BESLEY, T. (2005): "Political Selection," *Journal of Economic Perspectives*, 19, 43–60.

BESLEY, T., AND S. COATE (1997): "An Economic Model of Representative Democracy," *Quarterly Journal of Economics*, 112, 85–114.

—— (1998): "Sources of Inefficiency in a Representative Democracy: A Dynamic Analysis," *American Economic Review*, 88, 139–156.

—— (2001): "Lobbying and Welfare in a Representative Democracy," *Review of Economic Studies*, 68, 67–82.

BLACK, D. (1958): *The Theory of Committees and Elections*. Cambridge: Cambridge University Press.

BLAIS, A. (2000): *To Vote or Not to Vote: The Merits and Limits of Rational Choice Theory*. Pittsburgh: University of Pittsburgh Press.

BORGERS, T. (2004): "Costly Voting," *American Economic Review*, 94, 57–66.

BUCHANAN, J. M., AND G. TULLOCK (1962): *The Calculus of Consent: Logical Foundations of Constitutional Democracy*. Ann Arbor: University of Michigan Press.

CAILLAUD, B., AND J. TIROLE (2002): "Parties as Political Intermediaries," *Quarterly Journal of Economics*, 117, 1453–1489.

CARRILLO, J. D., AND T. MARIOTTI (2001): "Electoral Competition and Political Turnover," *European Economic Review*, 45, 1–25.

CASELLI, F., AND M. MORELLI (2004): "Bad Politicians," *Journal of Public Economics*, 88, 759–782.

CHARI, V. V., L. E. JONES AND R. MARIMON (1997): "The Economics of Split-Ticket Voting in Representative Democracies." *American Economic Review*, 87, 957–976.

COATE, S., AND M. CONLIN (2004): "A Group Rule-Utilitarian Approach to Voter Turnout: Theory and Evidence," *American Economic Review*, 94, 1476–1504.

COATE, S., M. CONLIN, AND A. MORO (2004): "The Performance of the Pivotal-Voter Model in Small-Scale Elections: Evidence from Texas Liquor Referenda," Unpublished Manuscript, Cornell University.

COX, G. W. (1997): *Making Votes Count: Strategic Coordination in the World's Electoral Systems.* New York: Cambridge University Press.

COX, G. W., AND M. D. McCUBBINS (1993): *Legislative Leviathan: Party Government in the House.* Berkeley: University of California Press.

DEGAN, A., AND A. MERLO (2004): "A Structural Model of Turnout and Voting in Multiple Elections," Unpublished Manuscript, University of Pennsylvania.

DEGAN, A., AND A. MERLO (2006): "Do Voters Vote Sincerely?" Unpublished Manuscript, University of Pennsylvania.

DHILLON, A., AND S. PERALTA (2002): "Economic Theories of Voter Turnout," *Economic Journal*, 112, F332–F352.

DIERMEIER, D., ERASLAN, H. AND A. MERLO (2002): "Bicameralism and Government Formation," PIER WP 02–10, University of Pennsylvania.

—— (2003): "A Structural Model of Government Formation," *Econometrica*, 71, 27–70.

—— (2006): "The Effects of Constitutions on Coalition Governments in Parliamentary Democracies," in *Democratic Constitutional Design and Public Policy: Analysis and Evidence*, ed. by R. D. Congleton and B. Swedenborg. Cambridge: MIT Press.

DIERMEIER, D. AND T. J. FEDDERSEN (1998): "Cohesion in Legislatures and the Vote of Confidence Procedure," *American Political Science Review*, 92, 611–621.

DIERMEIER, D., M. KEANE AND A. MERLO (2005): "A Political Economy Model of Congressional Careers," *American Economic Review*, 95, 347–373.

DIERMEIER, D., AND A. MERLO (2000): "Government Turnover in Parliamentary Democracies," *Journal of Economic Theory*, 94, 46–79.

—— (2004): "An Empirical Investigation of Coalitional Bargaining Procedures," *Journal of Public Economics*, 88, 783–797.

DOWNS, A. (1957): *An Economic Theory of Democracy.* New York: Harper Collins.

DRAZEN, A. (2000): *Political Economy in Macroeconomics.* Princeton: Princeton University Press.

ERASLAN, H. (2002): "Uniqueness of Stationary Equilibrium Payoffs in the Baron-Ferejohn Model," *Journal of Economic Theory*, 103, 11–30.

FEDDERSEN, T. J. (2004): "Rational Choice Theory and the Paradox of Not Voting," *Journal of Economic Perspectives*, 18, 99–112.

FEDDERSEN, T. J., AND W. PESENDORFER (1996): "The Swing Voter's Curse," *American Economic Review*, 86, 408–424.

—— (1999): "Abstention in Elections with Asymmetric Information and Diverse Preferences," *American Political Science Review*, 93, 381–398.

FEDDERSEN, T. J., AND A. SANDRONI (2002): "A Theory of Participation in Elections," *American Economic Review*, forthcoming.

FELLI, L., AND A. MERLO (2004): "Endogenous Lobbying," *Journal of the European Economic Association*, forthcoming.

FEREJOHN, J. A., AND M. P. FIORINA (1975): "Closeness Counts Only in Horseshoes and Dancing," *American Political Science Review,* 69, 920–925.

GERTH, H. H., AND C. W. MILLS (1946): *From Max Weber: Essays in Sociology.* New York: Oxford University Press.

GROSSMAN, G. M., AND E. HELPMAN (2001): *Special Interest Politics.* Cambridge: MIT Press.

HARRINGTON, J. E. JR. (1992): "The Role of Party Reputation in the Formation of Policy," *Journal of Public Economics*, 49, 107–121.

HARSANYI, J. C. (1980): "Rule Utilitarianism, Rights, Obligations and the Theory of Rational Behavior," *Theory and Decision*, 12, 115–133.

HIBBS, D. (1977): "Political Parties and Macroeconomic Policy," *American Political Science Review*, 71, 1467–1487.

JACKSON, M. O., AND B. MOSELLE (2002): "Coalition and Party Formation in a Legislative Voting Game," *Journal of Economic Theory*, 103, 49–87.

KIRCHGAESSNER, G., AND T. SCHULZ (2005): "Expected Closeness or Mobilization: Why Do Voters Go to the Polls? Empirical Results for Switzerland, 1991–1999," CESifo WP 1387, Munich.

LAVER, M., AND N. SCHOFIELD (1990): *Multiparty Government: The Politics of Coalition in Europe*. Oxford: Oxford University Press.

LAVER, M., AND K. A. SHEPSLE (1996): *Making and Breaking Governments: Cabinets and Legislatures in Parliamentary Democracies*. Cambridge: Cambridge University Press.

LEDYARD, J. O. (1984): "The Pure Theory of Large Two-Candidate Elections," *Public Choice*, 44, 7–41.

LEVY, G. (2004): "A Model of Political Parties," *Journal of Economic Theory*, 115, 250–277.

LIJPHART, A. (1999): *Patterns of Democracy: Government Forms and Performance in Thirty-Six Countries*. New Haven: Yale University Press.

LUPIA, A., AND K. STROM (1995): "Coalition Termination and the Strategic Timing of Parliamentary Elections," *American Political Science Review*, 89, 648–665.

MATSUSAKA, J. G. (1995): "Explaining Voter Turnout Patterns: An Information Theory," *Public Choice*, 84, 91–117.

MATSUSAKA, J. G., AND F. PALDA (1993): "The Downsian Voter Meets the Ecological Fallacy," *Public Choice*, 77, 855–878.

—— (1999): "Voter Turnout: How Much Can We Explain?" *Public Choice*, 98, 431–446.

MATTOZZI, A., AND A. MERLO (2005a): "Political Careers or Career Politicians?" PIER WP 05–32, University of Pennsylvania.

—— (2005b): "Mediocracy," Unpublished Manuscript, University of Pennsylvania.

MERLO, A. (1997): "Bargaining over Governments in a Stochastic Environment," *Journal of Political Economy*, 105, 101–131.

—— (2005): "Whither Political Economy? Theories, Facts and Issues," PIER WP 05–33, University of Pennsylvania.

MESSNER, M., AND M. POLBORN (2004): "Paying Politicians," *Journal of Public Economics*, 88, 2423–2445.

MORELLI, M. (2004): "Party Formation and Policy Outcomes under Different Electoral Systems," *Review of Economic Studies*, 71, 829–853.

MULLER, W. C., AND K. STROM, EDS. (2000): *Coalition Governments in Western Europe*. Oxford: Oxford University Press.

OSBORNE, M. J., AND A. SLIVINSKI (1996): "A Model of Political Competition with Citizen-Candidates," *Quarterly Journal of Economics*, 111, 65–96.

OSBORNE, M. J., AND R. TOURKY (2004): "Party Formation in Single-Issue Politics," Unpublished Manuscript, University of Toronto.

PALFREY, T. R., AND H. ROSENTHAL (1983): "A Strategic Calculus of Voting," *Public Choice*, 41, 7–53.

—— (1985): "Voters Participation and Strategic Uncertainty," *American Political Science Review,* 79, 62–78.

PERSSON, T., G. ROLAND AND G. TABELLINI (2003): "How Do Electoral Rules Shape Party Structures, Government Coalitions, and Economic Policies?" Unpublished Manuscript, Stockholm University.

PERSSON, T., AND G. TABELLINI (2000): *Political Economics: Explaining Economic Policy.* Cambridge: MIT Press.

—— (2005): *The Economic Effects of Constitutions.* Cambridge: MIT Press.

POOLE, K. T., AND H. ROSENTHAL (1997): *Congress: A Political-Economic History of Roll Call Voting.* New York: Oxford University Press.

RIKER, W. H. (1962): *The Theory of Political Coalitions.* New Haven: Yale University Press.

RIKER, W. H., AND P. C. ORDESHOOK (1968): "A Theory of the Calculus of Voting," *American Political Science Review,* 62, 25–42.

SHACHAR, R., AND B. NALEBUFF (1999): "Follow the Leader: Theory and Evidence on Political Participation," *American Economic Review*, 89, 525–547.

SNYDER, J. M. JR., AND M. M. TING (2002): "An Informational Rationale for Political Parties," *American Journal of Political Science*, 46, 90–110.

TESTA, C. (2004): "Party Polarization and Electoral Accountability," Unpublished Manuscript, Royal Holloway University of London.

TULLOCK, G. (1967): *Toward a Mathematics of Politics.* Ann Arbor: University of Michigan Press.

WITTMAN, D. (1977): "Candidates with Policy Preferences: A Dynamic Model," *Journal of Economic Theory*, 14, 180–189.

—— (1983): "Candidate Motivation: A Synthesis of Alternative Theories," *American Political Science Review*, 77, 142–157.

WOLDENDORP, J., H. KEMAN AND I. BUDGE (2000): *Party Government in 48 Democracies (1945–1998).* Dordrecht: Kluwer Academic Publishers.

WOLFINGER, R. E., AND S. J. ROSENSTONE (1980): *Who Votes?* New Haven: Yale University Press.

CHAPTER 11

Comments on Acemoglu and Merlo
Timothy Besley

It is a pleasure to discuss two such rich and interesting papers. The scope of the two papers is really rather different and they complement each other well.

Antonio Merlo's paper is largely driven by inspecting the tools that we are accumulating to study issues at the intersection of politics and economics. He highlights four main areas where real progress has been made. The first is the study of voting where he discusses both the decision to vote (the determinants of turnout) and the way in which people vote (particularly whether voting is strategic). Next, he looks at politicians as a unit of analysis. He then pursues the (correct in my view) path towards studying parties as collections of citizens. Finally, he looks at legislative policy making. For the most part, he looks at theoretical issues. As we would expect in this kind of *Econometric Society* address, he gets into some of the modeling details.

Daron Acemoglu's paper is more focused on issues. In fact, he does not get much into the richness of political processes since he is trying to get at broader systemic questions about how politics and economics interact. A feature of his paper is the use of a unified dynamic modeling framework that can be used to illustrate a wide range of phenomena. One of the main ambitions of the paper is to look at different institutional arrangements and their implications for economic resource allocation. He also gets into the question of how to model endogenous institutional change – one of the central challenges of modern political economy.

I will organize my discussion of these papers in three parts. I will begin with a few general comments on things that occurred to me while reading both papers. I will then present some specific comments on each of the papers. These will be selective and specific. Finally, I will return to some themes that were missing in both papers, which I will flag for interest's sake and to focus on topics for further work.

Those who have worked in the field of political economy have a variety of ambitions. But broadly, the field as it has emerged in the past ten to fifteen years is aiming to increase the competence of economists in analyzing policy issues where some understanding of political decision making is necessary. High on the list of relevant issues is the need to be able to evaluate differences between political institutions. These can be the kinds of grand differences that are studied in Acemoglu's paper – democracy versus autocracy. However, more typically, there is a need for advice on specific constitutional reforms – such as whether to introduce some element of direct democracy or to change the term lengths of representatives. For any of these issues, we need a flexible kit-bag of tools that are adaptable and tractable. This is what Merlo reviews. Conducting a comparative institutional analysis of the best form of constitution requires a precise normative framework.

One of the crowning achievements of welfare economics has been to develop a normative approach based on equity and efficiency. This stands in contrast to the literature in political science, which tends to use less precise normative categories, such as how representative or accountable are political systems. While these are useful and important ideas, which are often salient in discussions about politics, their normative status is not clear. Does an increase in representativeness map easily into a higher level of social welfare? If so, in what terms? This is where the economic approach offers the most useful basic tools for studying issues of constitution design.

The need for a normative framework is important when asking whether the positive economics of policy choice yields systematic divergences from normative ideals. Indeed, many discussions about political processes by economists are motivated in terms of trying to understand why some policies that are not ideal (such as trade protection) are implemented. Terms like *political failure* or *government failure* are often used rather loosely in such debates.

In any debates about institutions, the term efficiency has to be used carefully and consistently.[1] In applications to markets, Pareto efficiency has been for nearly fifty years the most intellectually satisfactory construct for a rigorous notion of market failure. However, in applied welfare economics, notions of market surplus have had more play. Yet, as is well known, unless compensations are paid by gainers to losers, the latter is essentially different from Pareto efficiency with an implicit distributional assumption about the relative merits of gainers and losers. The benchmark of social surplus does have the attraction that it seeks solutions that make the pie as large as possible. However, this is a social judgment that is not entirely self-evident to those who might lose out in the process. For similar reasons, it is even less clear that selecting policies that increase economic growth is normatively justifiable. Again this depends on the possibilities for compensation if there are some who lose out in that process.

The social surplus criterion is best thought of as a specific social welfare function. But to call failure to achieve a criterion that trades off the utility of gainers and losers an *efficiency* criterion, does require some kind of defense. In this respect, I would have preferred that Acemoglu used a more qualified notion of good institutions and government inefficiencies than the one that he uses for

---

[1] See Besley (2006, chapter 2) for a general discussion of the idea of government failure.

most of his paper. For the most part, he studies cases where the inefficiency comes in the form of output being "too low" rather true economic inefficiencies. This is an important criterion, but I would prefer to give it a different name rather than using the term "inefficiency" to describe it.

Political economy as presently constituted is a young field. This makes it all the more exciting for those who are working in it. There is less need to play by any ground rules and even preliminary steps can seem like giant leaps forward. But this makes the job of the reviewer and synthesizer much harder. One of the lasting contributions of these papers could be to help to set the ground rules and to set the agenda. This means making clear that certain things should be viewed with great suspicion. For example, there are cases where assuming that voting is sincere in multi-candidate settings yields absurd conclusions – for example, when one citizen can switch their vote and get an outcome that they prefer to what is currently on offer. The literature seems also to have been remarkably cavalier in positive models of policy choice when making assumptions about credibility. This has long been discredited in normative models since the discovery of time consistency problems for benevolent governments. Thus, there are areas where elements of good theoretical practice still need to be discussed.

A good test of success probably comes from showing that the models we are developing also have explanatory power empirically. Being able to make claims of this sort for the field of political economy at present is probably premature, and this may explain why these papers do not enter that terrain too much.[2] Nonetheless, I do predict that the papers will have some kind of agenda setting power.

I now turn to some specific observations on each paper beginning with Daron Acemoglu's.

Acemoglu's paper covers a lot of territory. There are some quite specific features of Acemoglu's model for studying interaction between government and the economy. In Acemoglu's model, all government activity is redistributive – there is no role for government in funding public goods or providing social insurance, as would happen with redistribution in a stochastic economy. Benabou (2003) shows that such policies can be growth enhancing. Even in Acemoglu's framework, there is no guarantee that reducing taxation leads to *Pareto* improvements even if it does increase income per capita. Thus to describe low growth as an *inefficiency* is somewhat misleading.

The paper focuses initially on three kinds of policy distortion in a model where a particular group holds political office. These are problems of: (i) resource extraction – when tax rates are set to reduce incentives to produce, (ii) factor price manipulation – when changing factor prices serves to transfer rents and (iii) political consolidation – when distorting policies are manipulated to allow the incumbent to remain in office.

---

[2] Books like Persson and Tabellini (2003) are pointing the way forward in studying the empirical consequences of political institutions.

The first two of these are really classic problems in dynamic optimal taxation. In fact the revenue extraction argument is a dynamic Ramsey tax problem with limited commitment. The second is an interesting example of a case where there are insufficient instruments for the classic Diamond and Mirrlees production efficiency theorem to hold. Here the outcome would be Pareto dominated if the government had sufficient instruments.

The political consolidation arguments are much more central to the concerns of the political economy literature. Again, however, a more careful treatment of the efficiency issues is probably warranted. Besley and Coate (1998) show that there are even concerns about political survival that lead to policy distortions; this does not imply that the outcome is Pareto inefficient even though that may sometimes be true.

The most exciting area in Acemoglu's paper is the discussion of efficient institutions and endogenous institutional change. This an important and novel area of investigation, and this paper is helping to lead the way. However, it should be acknowledged that this is also an old tradition, going back to some of the early public choice research, even though the modern tools are making progress. For example, Buchanan (1967) anticipates this line of enquiry when he says:

> Theoretical welfare economics enables us to define the necessary marginal conditions that must be satisfied for an allocation of economic resources to be efficient. Straightforward extension of this analysis to 'theoretical institutional economics' should enable us to define a similar set of conditions that would have to be met if an institutional arrangement or rule is to be classified as 'efficient.' It now seems quite possible that future developments will in fact allow for general statements of such conditions. http://www.econlib.org/library/Buchanan/buchCv4Contents.html, 4.19.36.

As Acemoglu points out, what we need in the first instance is a clean mapping from policy into institutions and thence the form of induced preferences over political institutions. Having found this, there are both positive and normative issues. On the positive side, there is an issue of the right way to model institutional choice. This could itself be a political process – with a constitutional change where individuals vote for the institutions that they prefer. However, it could also be a less internally driven process as when a colonial power endows a country with a constitution or, as in the U.S., where a small group of founding fathers got together to draft a constitution. It could also involve a more abrupt change due to a revolution or coup.

The normative issues concern the right way to evaluate constitutional choices. The standard economic criteria of equity and efficiency are fine here. This leaves open the possibility of Pareto dominated institutions being adopted. In fact the issues exactly parallel those considered when studying Pareto inefficient policies. In particular, if a new constitution favors a particular group, and no ex post compensations can be paid, then a Pareto inefficient set of institutional rules may continue.

In Acemoglu's model, democracy is modeled as the dictatorship of the most numerous group. While there are a variety of simple voting models that back this up, it is a quite simplistic view. Political scientists have rightly seen democracy as, in many instances, a vehicle for elites to gain influence. There is a host of contributions that stress that multi-dimensional and single-issue politics are very different.[3] There are also interesting issues of political recruitment – political institutions (such as parties) may be set up to limit the extent to which certain groups gain effective political representation. There is also evidence that the form of democracy matters.[4]

Promoting democracy on the basis that it is good for economic performance – either measured in terms of aggregate output or any other criterion – is not too plausible from a theoretical point of view. There are many good reasons to be democratic, but the case for growth enhancing democracy is far from clear even on the most simplistic accounts of the difference between democracies and autocracies.

In earlier work and in this paper, Acemoglu has emphasized the need to understand the failure of the Coase theorem in order to understand the process of institutional change.[5] The key intellectual issue is to understand the source of second best outcomes in institution design.[6] In particular, we need to understand whether the lack of instruments for redistribution, limitations on credibility of future policies or failures of incentive compatibility due to imperfect information are at the heart of the particular inefficiency being studied. Only then can we make constructive recommendations for institutional change. This has much wider applicability than just studying the design of political institutions – it applies to any scenario where competing "rules of the game" are being debated.

It is also important to understand the process of institutional change. Acemoglu's work with Jim Robinson is seminal here (see Acemoglu and Robinson (2006)). They study discrete shifts between democracy and dictatorship. But we also need models of more continuous change in institutions. Some polities experience large abrupt changes in their regime, while others are on slower more incremental paths. Similarly, we need models that allow for varieties of democracy and dictatorships. There are some dictatorships that have effectively fostered long-run growth or increases in life-expectancy, while others have the opposite consequences. Equally there are democracies that have the formal institutions of elections but with repression of the media and the opposition.

The need to bring a more pluralistic approach to studying institutions, while challenging, fits in well with the main theme of Antonio Merlo's paper, which is about the heterogeneity of modeling approaches in a broadly democratic setting.

---

[3] See, for example, Roemer (1998).

[4] See Persson (2005).

[5] See Acemoglu (2003).

[6] See Besley (2006, Chapter 2) for further discussion.

Merlo's paper has an interesting discussion of the history of the term political economy. A small note on this since he does not mention the work of John Neville Keynes (father of John Maynard Keynes) in his discussion of the history of political economy. Keynes (1891) identifies three branches of economics: positive science (what is), normative or regulative science (what ought to be) and the art of political economy. He characterizes the latter as the branch of economics by which practical maxims are formulated. He notes that

> when we pass . . . to problems of taxation, or problems that concern the relations of the State with trade and industry, or to the general discussion of communistic and socialistic schemes – it is far from being the case that economic considerations hold the field exclusively. Account must be taken of the ethical, social, and political considerations. . . . (Keynes (1891, page 55)).

This bears note since Keynes seems to be using the term political economy in its contemporary connotation – to describe the interaction between the economy and politics.

The first topic in Merlo's paper is the study of voters and voting decisions. This is an area where, prima facie, I am sympathetic to "behavioral" models. That said, there is good (at least circumstantial) evidence that people are somewhat strategic. However, there is a long tradition of political scientists working with models where voter loyalty towards parties is a key idea.[7] Just how to understand the form that these loyalties take and whether they have an underlying rationale (in terms of economic interests) is an important issue. At one extreme, such loyalties could simply be like loyalties to football teams that defy an easy "rational" explanation. It is clear, that if there are important behavioral elements in voting, this has implications for how we model political competition. It may blunt the ability of electoral competition to discipline politicians on policies and corruption. But I do agree with the thrust of Merlo's discussion that we need to push rationality as far as we can first before introducing behavioral elements. However, I remain less sanguine about the progress that we have made here using standard economic tools than he is.

One missing theme in Merlo's discussion of voting, concerns how votes aggregate. One key question is how votes translate into seats – since the latter determine political control. The pattern of districting is key here. The seats–votes relationship can be rather different depending on the pattern of voter concentration across districts. This seems to be important empirically, given that proportional representation systems have rather different economic policies compared to majoritarian systems. Indeed, Persson and Tabellini (2003) argue persuasively that there are substantial differences between majoritarian electoral systems and proportional electoral systems in terms of policy outcomes.

I very much welcome Merlo's emphasis on politicians as a group. His recent work on understanding careers of politicians is an important and long overdue

---

[7] See, for example, Green et al. (2004) for a useful review on this topic.

agenda. More generally, the topic of political selection has not received the attention that it deserves, perhaps because economists are more comfortable with the study of incentives. Political selection can be important as a means of establishing credibility to the extent that some policy positions are supported by "sincere preferences." Selection may also be important because the political class is more honest and competent in some places compared to others. It is important then to see how institutions shape the selection process. One reason for the downfall of hereditary systems of government was surely that bloodline is a poor basis for political selection. However, different democratic institutions may work better as filters.

Merlo's paper also discusses models of political parties. Currently, one of the big challenges in the field is to have better models for the internal workings of parties. I was a bit surprised, however, to see that, after the discussion of voting in an earlier section, the model of voter mobilization that Merlo studies is largely behavioral. So there is a bit of a disconnect between this approach and his earlier discussion. It was also not too clear to me how mobilization really differs from a model of campaign spending financed by a special interest. This in turn raises some important issues about the way in which parties coordinate campaign finance and the interplay between party campaigning and special interest influence. This discussion could also usefully be tied to some of the emerging literature on the effectiveness of "get out the vote" experiments. This is a fruitful area where much remains to be done, but it is still evolving. The emphasis placed on this in Merlo's paper is an important pointer to future research.

The issue of political credibility is central to understanding policy formation. This is an area where the role of parties and institutions play a large role. Alesina and Spear's (1988) model of overlapping generations of politicians has surprisingly not spawned much subsequent interest in these issues. But surely a key role of parties is to act as long-lived players that protect reputations even when politicians themselves are ephemeral.

Parties also play a central role in political recruitment. Just what incentives parties use to recruit for particular political offices must affect the kinds of people who enter political life. Some parties appear (superficially) to be more open and democratic, while others are more hierarchical and controlled by narrow elites. The scope for creating a genuine internal organization theory for parties and their role both in selection and incentives is a major challenge. Here, contracting issues seem central in understanding how well parties are able to regulate behavior of their members who hold political office. There is a need for an integration of political agency models with models of party behavior.

To sum up, Merlo shows how we are developing models that give us an understanding of a wide array of phenomena. But there are also so many new and exciting avenues to pursue. In each case, the challenge of bringing theory and data together is immense. But it is a distinctive piece of the challenge that the new political economy literature is meeting.

Finally, I turn to some of the missing themes in both papers. It is interesting that neither author spends much time on the role of special interests in policy making. This is not a problem, except to note that a lot of time and effort is spent in political economy on this aspect of politics and its consequences for economics (see, for example, Grossman and Helpman (2001)). A more complete discussion of recent progress in political economy would probably have put more weight on such models.

Both papers focus on how political institutions work on their own merits. However, good government flourishes in the context of a wide range of institutions, some of them beneficial and others malign. Examples include the role of the media in monitoring government and providing information, the role of think-tanks in scrutinizing policy proposals, the role of social organizations, such as religious groups. Also important in many countries is the role of the army in either supporting or hindering the task of government. It may even be that it is the strength of these institutions, rather than of purely political institutions that matters most to effective government. The next generation of work will increasingly study the interaction between these social and economic forces in shaping policy processes. As a result, our understanding of how government works will be further enhanced. It will also ideally create a better appreciation of comparative institutional solutions.

I mentioned at the outset that the aim of modern political economy is to enhance the competence of economists in studying policy problems. Both of these papers show how the tools of economics can be used this way. But they also demonstrate that the task is not yet complete. But by taking stock of progress, I have no doubt that these papers will inspire further contributions.

References

[1] Acemoglu, D. [2003], "Why Not a Political Coase Theorem?" *Journal of Comparative Economics*, 31, 620–52.

[2] Acemoglu, D. and J. Robinson [2006], *Economic Origins of Dictatorship and Democracy*, Cambridge University Press.

[3] Alesina, A. [1988], "Credibility and Policy Convergence in a Two-Party System with Rational Voters," *American Economic Review*, 78(4), 796–806.

[4] Alesina, A. and S. Spear [1988] "An Overlapping Generations Model of Electoral Competition," *Journal of Public Economics* 37(3), 359–379.

[5] Benabou, R. [2002], "Tax and Education Policy in a Heterogeneous Economy: What Levels of Redistribution Maximize Growth and Efficiency," *Econometrica*, 70(2), 481–518.

[6] Besley, T. [2006], *Principled Agents? The Political Economy of Good Government*, Oxford: Oxford University Press.

[7] Buchanan, J. [1967], *Public Finance in Democratic Process,* Chapel Hill: University of North Carolina Press, also at http://www.econlib.org/library/Buchanan/

[8] Green, D., B. Palmquist and E. Schickler [2004], *Partisan Hearts and Minds: Political Parties and the Social Identities of Voters*, New Haven, CT: Yale University Press.

[9] Grossman, G. and E. Helpman [2001], *Special Interest Politics*, Cambridge, MA: MIT Press.

[10] Keynes, J. N. [1891], *The Scope and Method of Political Economy*, London: Macmillan.

[11] Persson, T. [2005], "Forms of Democracy, Policy and Economic Development," working paper.

[12] Persson, T. and G. Tabellini [2003], *The Economic Effects of Constitutions*, Cambridge, MA: MIT Press.

[13] Roemer, J. E. [1998]. "Why the Poor Do Not Expropriate the Rich: An Old Argument in New Garb," *Journal of Public Economics*, 70(3), 399–424.

Name Index

Abelson, H., 251
Abreu, D., 143, 150, 151, 175, 177, 179
Acemoglu, D., 382, 426
Adamic, L. A., 8
Aghion, P., 262
Ahn, I., 140
Aiyagari, S. R., 305–308, 321, 324
Akerlof, G., 102, 125
Albanesi, S., 278, 284
Albert, R., 9, 11, 17
Aldrich, J. H., 385
Alesina, A., 393, 396, 428
Allen, F., 38, 306
Altug, S., 304
Amador, M., 290
Anant, T., 92
Anderson, R. M., 39
Andreoni, J., 171, 173
Angeletos, G.-M., 290, 321, 324, 332, 334
Ansell, C. K., 3
Armstrong, M., 115
Arrow, K. J., 254, 381
Asheim, G., 175
Athey, S., 131, 154
Atkeson, A., 323
Attanasio, O., 298
Attar, A., 65
Aumann, R., 22, 143
Auriol, E., 124
Austen-Smith, D., 382, 391, 411
Ausubel, L., 124

Babaioff, M., 245
Bagwell, K., 116, 146, 154
Bailey, N. T. J., 39
Baker, G., 137, 171
Bala, V., 38
Baliga, S., 86, 87, 89, 175
Ballester, A., 35, 44
Bandyopadhyay, S., 400, 411
Banks, J. S., 382, 391, 411
Barabási, A., 2, 9, 11, 17
Baron, D., 60, 83, 90
Baron, D. P., 411
Battaglini, M., 271, 292
Bearman, P., 11
Benabou, R., 424
Benoit, J., 175
Bergemann, D., 73, 125, 127, 254, 272
Berliant, M., 295
Bernheim, D., 62, 70, 73, 175
Besanko, D., 90
Besley, T., 396, 397, 400, 423, 425, 426
Bewley, T., 305, 317, 324
Biais, B., 66, 77
Biglaiser, G., 77, 86
Bikhchandani, S., 235, 244
Bisin, A., 295
Black, D., 381
Blais, A., 383, 384
Bloch, F., 2, 25, 31, 44, 46
Blumrosen, L., 245
Blundell, R., 298
Bollobás, B., 1, 8, 12, 14
Bond, E., 77, 85
Boorman, S., 21, 46

Other titles in the series *(continued from page iii)*